THE RAVES ARE IN!
SWANSON ON SWANSON
IS A HIT!

"LIVELY . . . REVEALING . . . WHEN MOV-IES WERE MOVIES AND STARS LEGENDARY GODS AND GODDESSES."

—*Chicago Tribune*

"THE MOST SIGNIFICANT BOOK ON HOLLY-WOOD'S HEYDAY YET PUBLISHED . . . THE MOST REVEALING EVER WRITTEN BY AN AUTHENTIC MOVIE QUEEN."

—*John Barkham Reviews*

"JUICY, LURID, FUNNY, MEMORABLE . . . THE LOWDOWN ON LOVEMAKING, MOVIE-MAKING [BY] A TOUGH, INDEPENDENT WOMAN AHEAD OF HER TIME . . . THE BOOK'S *PIECE DE RESISTANCE* IS, OF COURSE, HER AFFAIR WITH JOSEPH P. KEN-NEDY."

—*Vogue*

"THE QUEEN OF THE SILENTS TELLS AN EYE-POPPING ALL . . . ART AND FINANCE AND FINAGLING IN THE MOVIES' SALAD DAYS . . . THE HIGHS AND LOWS OF SIX MARRIAGES . . . AFFAIRS WITH BIG NAMES . . . THIS IS IRRESISTIBLE!"

—*Kirkus Reviews*

Swanson on Swanson

An Autobiography

PUBLISHED BY POCKET BOOKS NEW YORK

Cover photograph © by Ellen Graham

POCKET BOOKS, a Simon & Schuster division of
GULF & WESTERN CORPORATION
1230 Avenue of the Americas, New York, N.Y. 10020

Copyright © 1980 by Gloria's Way, Inc.

Published by arrangement with Random House, Inc.
Library of Congress Catalog Card Number: 80-5270

ISBN: 0-671-43354-7

First Pocket Books printing December, 1981

10 9 8 7 6 5 4 3 2 1

POCKET and colophon are trademarks of Simon & Schuster.

Printed in the U.S.A.

ACKNOWLEDGMENTS

Grateful acknowledgment is made to the following for permission to reprint previously published material: Arno Press Inc.: Excerpts from "Acting for the Screen: The Six Great Essentials," from *Opportunities in the Motion Picture Industry,* are reprinted courtesy Arno Press Inc., 1970. Associated Press: Excerpt from the March 25, 1951, issue of the Louisville *Courier-Journal* was provided by Associated Press. Reprinted by permission of Associated Press. Alfred A. Knopf, Inc.: Excerpt reprinted from *The Prophet,* by Kahlil Gibran, by permission of Alfred A. Knopf, Inc. Copyright 1923 by Kahlil Gibran and renewed 1951 by Administrators C.T.A. of Kahlil Gibran Estate, and Mary G. Gibran. *New York Post:* Excerpt by Eugenia Sheppard from the February 22, 1980, issue of the *New York Post.* Reprinted by permission of the *New York Post.* © 1980, New York Post Corporation. Random House, Inc.: Excerpt from *Life Is a Banquet,* by Rosalind Russell and Chris Chase. Copyright © 1977 by Frederick Brisson, as an individual, and Frederick Brisson, Executor of the Estate of Rosalind Russell. Reprinted by permission of Random House, Inc. Time Inc.: "Oscars for José and Judy," *Life* © 1951 by Time Inc. Reprinted with permission.

Foreword

Writing the story of your own life, I now know, is an agonizing experience, a bit like drilling your own teeth. At least fifty times in the past fifteen months I have wanted to throw these pages—or myself—out the window. But now that the book is finally finished, I realize that the experience was rewarding as well as painful, for it made me use muscles in my mind that I had never used before, and that is always thrilling. Forced to look intensely at the eighty years behind me, I have been amazed again and again to see patterns emerge and issues crystallize and relationships yield their significance in ways that were never quite clear while the events of those years were occurring. For that I'm grateful.

Wherever possible, I have avoided the usual Hollywood gossip and stuck as closely as I could to my own personal story. Even so, with eighty years' worth of files and scrapbooks and photographs and films and letters and documents to sort through and choose from—I never throw anything away—the job of selection was a formidable one, and the book is longer than I ever intended it to be.

In going through thousands of clippings and news releases, I have been consistently appalled at how inaccurate reports in the press often are. No two ever seem to agree even on the spelling of people's names, let alone on the facts. Nevertheless, since so much of my life has been public, I have deliberately seasoned this book with journalists' accounts of my actions, and I have quoted them without corrections or comments. For your enjoyment, I recommend that you read them carefully.

As for the manuscript itself, I have relied greatly on the help of three people: Brian Degas, who conceived of the dramatic structure for the book, helped me see things that I was unwilling to see and was the lifeblood through all the stages of getting it published in its present form; Wayne Lawson, who took all the drafts and corrections and revisions and helped me weld them into the final version; and my husband, William Dufty, who tirelessly helped me research and prepare all the early material.

My children and their families deserve special thanks for helping me recall our past life together and for not disowning me when I called to ask them the same question for the second or third time, just to make sure I had the facts straight in a form that would not displease them.

I am also indebted to all my friends and colleagues, past and present, here and abroad, who have made my life what it has been. So many of them have helped me clear up facts and remember situations that I cannot name them all. They know I love them. As for the many people in the book who were no longer alive to advise me, I hope I've dealt fairly and feelingly with them all.

My greatest debt will always be to the moviegoing public of yesterday and today, without whose love and devotion I would have had no story to tell.

GLORIA SWANSON
July 1980

Part One

CHAPTER 1

DATELINE: Paris, Universal Service, January 28, 1925
BY-LINE: Basil Woon

GLORIA, FILM BEAUTY,
BRIDE OF MARQUIS

Gloria Swanson, thousand-dollar-a-day film actress is
now Marquise de la Falaise. She was married today in
the almost romantic secrecy of the Passy Town Hall.
Only nine persons were there. They, including your
correspondent, did not know what was afoot until an
hour before the ceremony.

I'm going to start with the moment in my life when I thought
I had never been happier, because until that moment, I
hadn't ever assessed the events that had come before it, and
once it was over, I could never view my life or my career in
the same way again.

That blissful morning in Passy in 1925 when I married my
gorgeous marquis lifted me to the very pinnacle of joy, but at
the same time it led me to the edge of the most terrifying
abyss that I had ever known. One moment I had everything I
had ever wanted, the next I was more wretched than I had
ever been before; and in the days that followed, the more I

blamed my misery on the fame and success I had achieved in
pictures, the more famous and successful I seemed destined
to become.

I was then twenty-five and the most popular female celebrity in the world, with the possible exception of my friend
Mary Pickford. Headlines in North and South America and
Europe usually referred to me by my first name only. I had
starred in more than thirty successful films, six in a row
directed by Cecil B. De Mille, and my leading men had
included all the great heartthrobs from Wallace Reid to
Rudolph Valentino. Not only was I the first American star to
have filmed a major picture abroad, but I was also the first
celebrity in pictures to be marrying a titled European. All
over the world, fans were rejoicing because Cinderella had
married the prince.

My salary at Paramount—$7,000 a week—was common
knowledge, and columnists were already betting that when
my contract was up in a year, Jesse Lasky would have to offer
me at least a million a year to keep me. Moreover, Doug
Fairbanks had unofficially invited me to join United Artists as
an independent producer as soon as my contract terminated,
promising that I could make much more with UA than I could
ever make with Paramount or any other studio on a salaried
contract. Oh, I was the golden girl, and everyone said so.

What the press and fans didn't know that January morning
was that I was pregnant. Not even my dear, sweet Henri knew
that, and I didn't have the heart to tell him, for well
connected though he was, he had no money, and I couldn't let
him take the responsibility for a decision I would have to
make alone. What I knew was that if I had Henri's child in
seven months, my career would be finished. The industry and
the public would both reject me as a morally unsound
character, unfit to represent them. In 1925, the Hays Office
with its rigid censorship ruled Hollywood with an iron fist.
Therefore, I took a single close friend into my confidence and
with his help arranged to have a secret abortion the day after
my marriage. The very idea horrified me, but I was convinced
that I had no choice. I consoled myself with the fact that
Henri and I were young and could therefore have other
children. I already had two, a girl of my own and an adopted
boy. Surely, I told myself—peremptorily so that I wouldn't
argue back—I could have more. With that I stifled my fears
and doubts and kept the dreaded appointment.

If the operation had gone as smoothly as I was assured it

would, I would have continued my life as usual later that same day and gone on living normally for years to come, with twinges of guilt, of course, but probably never with any full realization of my proper feelings about what I had done. However, the doctor bungled the simple operation, and the next day I was unconscious with fever. Then for weeks I lay between life and death in a Paris hospital, having nightmares about the child I had killed, wishing I were dead myself.

Ironically, all the while I was struggling with my soul in anguish, too weak to talk, my public was growing more ardent. Day after day the newspapers published my temperature, and millions of fans held their breath. They didn't know the cause of my illness, only that I was mortally ill; and when I recovered, they loved me more than ever—more even, for the moment, than they loved Mary Pickford. Suddenly I was not only Cinderella who had married the prince, but also Lazarus who had risen from the dead.

Through me Paramount was receiving millions of dollars' worth of free publicity. In a steady stream of cablegrams Mr. Lasky and Mr. Zukor begged me to speed up my convalescence and sail with my marquis to America in time for the New York premiere of *Madame Sans-Gêne,* the film I had just made in Paris. Then, they said, they would transport us across the country for the Hollywood premiere, and then back again to New York, where I would start my next picture as soon as I felt up to it.

I wanted to refuse them. I wanted to hold them responsible for my misery and blame them for controlling lives like mine that didn't really belong to them, and for making me destroy my baby. But I am a very pragmatic person. I could not, after all, back up and undo what I had done, so I cabled Mr. Lasky that I would attend both premieres. I sent my children on ahead with their governess and a few trusted friends, and Henri and I sailed on the *Paris* the third week in March.

From the moment we got off the boat in New York, adoring crowds nearly smothered us wherever we went. On the pier and again in the lobby of the Ritz Hotel, reporters and photographers trapped us for interviews while fans behind barricades cheered in the street. When we entered our suite, which was banked with flowers, both phones were ringing, and they never stopped. The Ritz switchboard was so swamped with incoming calls asking us to go here, go there, be photographed, be interviewed, that it was several hours before I could get through to my house in Croton-on-Hudson and speak to my daughter, little Gloria, and my baby Joseph. Valets, butlers, and maids were in and out of the suite every minute. They carried a constant stream of reports to the newspaper people down the hall: what food we ordered, what color Henri's pajamas were, what I was going to wear to the banquet in our honor the following night at the new Park Lane Hotel and to the Broadway premiere of *Madame Sans-Gêne*.

Our second day in the city, Mr. Lasky had arranged a special parade to Astoria, Long Island, to the studio where I'd been making all my pictures since 1923, when I'd escaped from Hollywood. The streets of Astoria were decked with signs and banners of welcome. Children in costume strewed flowers. Jesse Lasky and Adolph Zukor were both on hand, and there were speeches and ceremonies to welcome me back to my dressing room.

The night of the premiere of *Madame Sans-Gêne* at the Rivoli Theatre, the police had to route all traffic around the block. Crowds filled the street in front of the theater, and from a block away, as we crawled closer in our limousine, we could see my name, in gigantic letters ten feet high spelled out with hundreds of light bulbs, over the entire façade of the building. We couldn't get anywhere near the curb. A flying wedge of policemen got to the car and stood guard as Henri got out. The crowd surged when they saw me, so the police made a circle around us and slowly walked us to the lobby. There they advised us to leave early by a side door, which we did, minutes after the picture started. After that we stayed in the hotel suite most of the time, and friends had to come there to see us.

I couldn't wait for the peace and quiet of the private car we had been promised on the train to California. When we got to the station, however, I was told that Paramount had rented the whole train. The rest of the cars were full of studio executives, exhibitors, and theater owners. My maid was the only other woman aboard.

I was worn out and edgy. The doctors in France had told me to take it easy, but I had not relaxed in New York for a minute of the six days we had been there, so Henri guarded the door to our car like a lion. He let in only very special pals, like Allan Dwan the director, Dick Halliday from the public relations department at Paramount, and René Hubert, my costumer. The instant the train moved, I went into my drawing room to rest. All I wanted was a massage that would last until Pittsburgh and then a long sleep free of telephones from Pittsburgh to Chicago.

Henri wakened me gently an hour later. When I opened my eyes, the conductor and the whole hierarchy of Paramount top executives were before me, begging me to stick my head out the rear platform door. Hundreds of people were waiting to see me.

I said I was covered with mineral oil and this wasn't a regular stop. "Yes, Miss Swanson, we know, but all these children have been let out of school to come down and see you, and if they don't, they'll be very disappointed." I was furious that schoolchildren had got involved in this carnival, but it was too late now. I yanked on a robe and stuck my head out of the window. Hundreds of children were lined up along the tracks, shouting my name. I waved to them and told them they should be in school.

"We wanna see your haircut," they were screeching. When I was ill with fever in Paris, the nurses had cut off most of my hair. It was still sheared off in back like a man's. When the reporters had written about it, many of them mistakenly thought it was the latest Paris style. Naturally, therefore, the children wanted to see it. So I showed them the back of my head, told them how it had happened, and begged them to leave their own beautiful hair alone. They couldn't hear me.

"We wanna see the prince," they were chanting.

I threw on a coat and took Henri by the hand. We walked out on the rear platform and tried to smile while they screamed happily and jumped up and down. Then the whistle blew and the train began moving away from the sea of tiny faces.

"Is it going to be like this from here to California?" Henri asked.

Allan Dwan nodded his answer. "If Gloria were thirty-five instead of twenty-five, she could run for President," he said. "There's no one else like her."

I felt like the half-dead whale that P. T. Barnum had once shipped from Canada to New York on a flatcar, which people had lined the tracks to see.

"Once we get past Chicago and into the Great Plains, you'll have a chance to rest up," the conductor promised. Until then there would be whistle-stops all along the way. According to advance news reports, crowds were gathering all the way to Albuquerque. Sometimes these included official delegations; other times they were just mobs of curious fans. Henri astonished them all, whether they were mayors, cowboys, or Indians, with his dignity, friendliness, and charm. France had never had a better ambassador.

In the forward cars of the train, studio executives and exhibitors were busy playing poker and trying to figure out how to exploit the Swanson gold mine to the fullest. Theater owners called me the mortgage lifter because for the past five years, in a run of twenty pictures beginning with *Male and Female,* all they had had to do was put my name on the marquee and watch the money roll in. It didn't matter very much whether the pictures I played in were good, bad, or so-so. People went to all of them. They thought of me as part of their families. They liked to visit me regularly; see if I had changed since the last picture. Nobody knew how long it would last, but while it did, I was worth millions of dollars a year to the studio and the exhibitors, and all the men on that train, therefore, wanted my signature on a new Paramount contract as soon as my present one ran out. All this hoopla and publicity and private train were their way of wooing me.

Henri and I were on the back platform as the train slipped slowly into the Los Angeles station. Two bands were playing, and we could see troops of policemen on horseback, Sid Grauman's theater usherettes on white ponies, a red carpet ten yards wide, and a huge platform decorated with flowers and bunting and signs of welcome. The faces on that platform were like the Last Judgment—everyone I'd worked with or known in Hollywood. Mary Pickford, Douglas Fairbanks, Charlie Chaplin, Joe Schenck, Norma Talmadge, and D. W. Griffith were there in a very conspicuous bloc. They were after me to join them in their company, United Artists, and they wanted the Famous Players-Lasky-Paramount contingent to get the message. If Paramount wanted to keep me in the family, UA was saying, a million dollars a year would not be enough to ensure it. Paramount had most certainly got the message and had rounded up its most famous faces too and brought them down for the welcome—most notably, Mr. De Mille and Rudy Valentino.

In addition to these two competing delegations were the mayor, the city officials, and all the rest of filmdom, it seemed: Mickey Neilan, Lightning Hopper, Clarence Badger, Al Parker, Frank Borzage, Sam Wood, Jack Conway, Francis X. Bushman, Elliott Dexter, Lew Cody, Tommy Meighan, Jack Holt, Bebe Daniels, Lila Lee, Monte Blue, William S.

Hart, Hoot Gibson, Sally Eilers, Milton Sills, Richard and
Maude Wayne, Teddy Sampson, Ford Sterling, Chester
Conklin, Charley Chase, Mack Sennett, Ricardo Cortez, Rod
La Rocque, Lilyan Tashman, Ben Lyon—everybody. Every-
body but Wallace Reid, who was dead of drug addiction, and
Wallace Beery, my first husband, who had once told me he
prayed I would be a failure so I would come back to him.

I hadn't set foot in California since 1923. To all of Hollywood gathered at the station that day, I was, in addition to
being Cinderella married to the prince and Lazarus risen, the
prodigal returned in triumph. They waved and called their
approval.

We were carried to the platform. I was terrified I would
have to say something because I knew I would burst into
tears. Poor Henri was so bewildered that he later told me he
was absolutely numb. We had never kissed so many people in
our lives. Sid Grauman, the mastermind of Hollywood bally-
hoo, had choreographed everything. After the speeches,
rows upon rows of people lining the endless red carpet tossed
flowers as we made the long walk to the open white Rolls-
Royce waiting for us in front of the station.

A platoon of motorcycle cops cleared traffic for the parade
of limousines. The streets were festooned with banners.
When we got to Hollywood, we slowed down at the corner of
Sunset and Vine under the biggest banner of all: WELCOME
GLORIA. Famous Players-Lasky-Paramount had shut down for
the morning, and hundreds of studio employees were in the
street throwing flowers into the car. The parade halted while
we got out and shook hands with everyone from the secretaries to the hairdressers, especially Hattie, the little black
woman who had ironed my hair the first morning I went to
work for Mr. De Mille.

The parade continued up Sunset Boulevard to my house in
Beverly Hills. Inside, there was hardly time to show Henri
where to hang his hat before the rush began to unpack, bathe,
and get dressed for the West Coast premiere of *Madame
Sans-Gêne* at Sid Grauman's Million Dollar Theatre in down-
town Los Angeles.

It had opened its doors in 1919 with the world premiere of
Male and Female. Then its entire audience had gasped when I
walked out of the Santa Cruz surf in a shipwreck scene with
my shredded satin evening dress soaked and clinging to my
skin. Now they were gathering to gasp at me again tonight.

I was twenty pounds thinner than I had been in 1919, and I was wearing a gown of clinging silver lamé. Henri looked elegant in his white tie and tails. I made him wear his Croix de Guerre ribbon across his chest and his other decoration in his lapel. Even my mother had given in to the present storm of excitement. She arrived at the house all dressed up, willing to break her rule and go along to the first premiere she'd ever attended in her life.

We caused a tremendous traffic jam near the tunnel on Third Street. The motorcycle cops told us the streets were filled with people for ten blocks in every direction. There was no way around them. They would have to ease us inch by inch through the mob, which was cheering in unison like a football crowd. The car couldn't budge. Finally the police cleared a path and I got out of the car. The police went ahead of me, and Mother and Henri followed behind. The din was unbelievable.

There were barricades in front of the theater, and the lobby was completely empty, except for a troop of ushers, who were obviously waiting for me.

"Has the picture started?" I asked.

"Yes, Miss Swanson. Right this way, please."

"Just a minute," I said, and turned to wait for Mother and Henri.

More ushers with flashlights hurried the three of us through the dark inner lobby to the main aisle door. As they held it open and we entered, the blackened theater burst into a blaze of light. The orchestra struck up "Home, Sweet Home," I could hear the gasp of a thousand people catching their breath, and then the audience gave out a tremendous roar. Amazed and bewildered, I grabbed Henri's hand.

People were standing and yelling like Indians. Women were throwing orchids in the aisle. I couldn't move. Then ushers escorted us to our seats down in front. As soon as we came into view of the people in the balcony, they too began pelting me with orchids and gardenias. Everyone was singing "Home, Sweet Home." Among all the familiar faces I picked out the English actor Ernest Torrence, noticeable in a wheelchair; Mickey Neilan, my wild Irish love; and Mary Pickford and Doug Fairbanks. I turned around and threw kisses. They seated Henri between Mrs. De Mille and my mother. I was seated between Cecil B. De Mille and Mack Sennett, who was drying his eyes. The audience continued to whoop and roar until I got up again and threw more kisses. Mr. Lasky came out on the stage and tried to make a speech, but they wouldn't stop cheering and yelling until the lights dimmed and the picture came on.

A few minutes later the head usher came down the aisle and knelt at our feet to tell me the police couldn't handle the crowd anymore. They were bringing our car around to the alley and wanted us to leave immediately through the orchestra pit and backstage. Mr. De Mille said, "They're right. Hollywood has paid you a tribute tonight, young fellow, that has never been equaled. Every star, every director, every president of every film company in town is here. Everybody wants you to survive. Young fellow, it's time for you to go home to bed."

So Henri and Mother and I sneaked out in the darkness to the alley, where the car was waiting, and the police escorted us on our slow drive home.

It was our first quiet moment in days, the first time I could really think.

Mother finally said, "Glory, you're so quiet. This should be the happiest night of your life."

My mother and I could always look out the same window without ever seeing the same thing.

I shook my head. "No, Mother," I said, "it's the saddest. I'm just twenty-six. Where do I go from here?"

I suddenly felt empty and sick and bitter and exhausted and desolate. Henri took my hand. I'm sure he knew what I was thinking.

I was thinking that every victory is also a defeat. Nobody gets anything for nothing.

I was thinking of the price I had paid two months ago to be able to walk down that orchid-strewn aisle tonight. I was wondering what all those glamorous and important people would have thought if I had stood up and shushed them and spelled out that price for them; if I had told them that in order not to break my contract or create a scandal, I had had to sneak to a French surgeon like a criminal and sacrifice a child I was carrying.

Would they have forgiven me, all those glamorous people? Would they have thought I had paid sufficiently by nearly dying of blood poisoning in a Paris hospital? I honestly didn't care. I knew only too well that most of them had sad and awful secrets of their own, so their hypothetical forgiveness meant nothing to me. The only thing that mattered was whether I would ever be able to forgive myself.

Even if Sid Grauman built me an Arch of Triumph in California as colossal as the one in Paris, it would always have a tomb under it, the tomb of an unborn baby who had picked Henri and me for parents and who was now dead.

CHAPTER 2

I feel sure that unborn babies pick their parents. They may spend a whole lifetime trying to figure out the reasons for their choice, but nothing in any human story is accidental.

This time, for instance, I obviously wanted a long, exciting life. Millions of boys and girls made love in the summer of 1898, but I waited for the right moment between a young man named Joe Swanson and his wife, Addie, before I willed my way from infinity to the second floor of 341 Grace Street in Chicago. I decided to be a girl.

I was born on March 27, 1899, under the sign of Aries. My maternal grandmother, who was in attendance, leaned down to my pale, exhausted mother and said, "She's beautiful." Then she turned to the doctor, and lowering her voice so that her daughter wouldn't hear, asked, "But aren't her ears awfully large?"

March 27 was a Monday and the first day of Holy Week, so my father decided to call me Glory. Eventually I was christened Gloria May Josephine Swanson. May was my maternal grandmother's maiden name, and Josephine was for my father, Joseph.

I had picked a good time and place to be born. The automobile was not much older than I was, so there weren't many of them. Trolleys and wagons were pulled by horses, and none of them went too fast. It was a safe, clean time. When you were thirsty in the summer, your mother made a pitcher of lemonade. And everyone did the family wash on Monday and hung it out in the fresh air to dry.

I was absolutely mad for dolls. I learned to walk by pushing a toy carriage with a baby doll in it. Later, my greatest pleasure was pushing a doll buggy through Lincoln Park and noisily playing Mommy. I wouldn't even speak to other little girls if they didn't have babies of their own. When people asked me who my baby's daddy was, I would reply without hesitation, "Happy Hooligan." I considered this hero of the funny papers handsome, marvelous, and mine and mine alone. I hated kindergarten from the first day for the simple reason that girls couldn't take their babies to school.

The size of my ears, which had alarmed my grandmother Bertha Lew the day I was born, continued to worry my mother in the years to come. My big blue eyes were one thing; my big ears were something else. So for years, while all the other girls my age were wearing teeny tiny hair ribbons, my mother made giant silk bows and poufs for me to hide my ears.

Her worries increased when I lost my baby teeth and the first new one came in. She rushed me to the dentist and demanded to know why this tooth was the size of two. All other girls had little mouse teeth. Why didn't Glory? The dentist said, "As soon as her face changes to match her teeth, she'll be all right." But I'm sure that didn't satisfy Mother.

Determined to have a beautiful little girl she could boast about in spite of these physical drawbacks, she began to dress me in fancy and unusual clothes. She loved sewing pretty things for me, as well as matching outfits for my dolls. She was as particular about the seams and linings as she was about the outside. No matter what other children were wearing, my mother always wanted me to look different, unique. Grandma Lew told her she ought to dress me like other girls if she didn't want a problem on her hands, but she never did. And strangely enough, I was shy about everything except my clothes. I enjoyed them and took it for granted that I was on display. I was the only girl in school who wore short socks and Buster Brown collars and a Buster Brown bob. When other girls said, "My mama wants to know where your mama got that hat," I'd always say I didn't know. I knew Mother wouldn't want me to tell, and besides, I didn't really want anyone to have a hat like mine. Most girls wore shiny patent-leather Mary Janes with everything, but my mother detested black patent leather, so my good shoes were always white kid or suede the color of my dress. In school I wore oxfords so that I would have a nice instep and good arches. My ready-made coats, tailored with little brass buttons, came from the boys' department. I was always one of a kind.

One of my first teachers in grade school complained to my mother that I didn't pay attention. She said she frequently found me drawing pictures when I was supposed to be copying out arithmetic problems. "Well, in that case she's obviously artistic," Mother said, and the next thing I knew she had enrolled me in a drawing class at the Art Institute. This museum in Grant Park was the most beautiful building I had ever seen. Built in 1893 for the World's Columbian Exposition, it looked to me like a palace. My mother took me there every Saturday. The first week I drew several rabbits with charcoal. The second week I drew a big duck. One day I peeked into another classroom at the museum and saw grownups drawing a live man with hardly any clothes on, like the statues out in the big hall. I thought to myself, Now, those are *real* artists, and I wanted to be a grownup as soon as possible so that I could be a real artist too.

From then on I dreamed steadily of being grown-up. I hated being a child and I hated school. And in those days there was no such thing as a teenager in between. I couldn't wait to wear long skirts and put my hair up on top of my head and wear a wedding ring and be Mrs. Somebody with twelve children—six on each side of the dining-room table.

Because I was so shy, I didn't make friends easily. I had no brothers or sisters, so I slowly had to get used to being alone; and like every only child, I seemed to spend more time with my parents than most children did. Even in my prayers at night, there were just the three of us. I used to kneel and say my prayers out loud. They were the same every night. "Now I lay me down to sleep. I pray the Lord my soul to keep. If I should die before I wake, I pray the Lord my soul to take. God bless Daddy and God bless Mommy and make me a good girl." After I climbed into bed, I always added a silent prayer that God would somehow find a way for me to get out of going to school without being sick.

When I was eight, I thought my prayers were answered. Daddy came home from his office with exciting news from the War Department in Washington. He was going to be put in charge of transportation for the United States Army somewhere; maybe in the Philippines, where Admiral Dewey had licked the Spanish navy the year before I was born, maybe in

Puerto Rico, maybe even in Panama, where our engineers were building the great canal.

We would be moving! Traveling! I was tickled to death. No more school, I thought. No more classes. I didn't need classes, anyway. Daddy could teach me; he knew more than an encyclopedia. Every night I would have questions when he came home, and I would make him sit with me for hours until he taught me everything he knew. And he would be in a uniform and look handsome and we would all learn a new language. Far away from Chicago! All the maps I looked at told me I would be taking a great voyage on a huge ship.

Things did not turn out quite that way. Daddy was sent not to the Philippines or Puerto Rico or Panama, but to Key West, a tiny island in the ocean off the tip of Florida. The language there was just plain English. Daddy would not wear a uniform either. He explained that he would wear one only in case of another war. He would have the rank of captain. Many jobs in the army, he said, were held by people who did not wear a uniform. Even the Secretary of War did not wear a uniform. Also, Key West would not mean the end of school for me. There would be a regular grade school there for me to go to. It would not mean the end of Chicago either. Mother and I would spend the summers in Chicago with our relatives. That's what families of army personnel usually did.

When Mother said "our relatives," she meant *her* relatives. Her grandparents on her mother's side were Alsatian. They spoke German most of the time, but they also knew French. They said everybody had to know both in Alsace. My Great-grandfather May used to give me marzipan when we went to visit them. He said it came from Baden-Baden, where his family came from. As a young man he had also lived in Switzerland, Holland, and Germany, where he had been a chef in the royal household. In 1852, at the age of twenty-six, he had come to America. He had a huge white beard, and he loved to talk about the Great Chicago Fire of 1871. Their house on La Salle Street had burned to the ground. They had saved their children and the clothes on their backs, that was all, he said.

My mother's mother, my Grandmother Bertha, was the oldest of their thirteen children. She was independent and strong-willed. When she was very young, she married Grandfather Klanowski, a Pole. They had three children, the first of whom, Adelaide, was my mother. Then Grandmother Bertha divorced Grandfather Klanowski and married Grandfather Lew.

Grandpa Klanowski had a black beard and mustache, and people said he was a skinflint. He drove a two-wheeled carriage and lived in an apartment near the entrance to Lincoln Park. In the same building was a dry goods store in which his other daughter, my Aunt Clara, worked. He owned property, but nobody knew how much, and he became a woman hater, people said, after Grandmother Bertha divorced him. He even had a man cook and clean for him. Perhaps he worried over the fact that he was known as a skinflint. One time he started to give me a dime, but then, after studying the expression on my face most carefully, gave me a quarter instead.

My father's parents, Johanna and Jons Swanson, were Swedish Lutherans. They took their children—thirteen in all—to church every Sunday and would not allow drinking or dancing or card playing in their home. People always said later that that was why several of their sons, including my father, turned out to be heavy drinkers when they grew up.

Their oldest son, my Uncle Charlie, was an adventurer who claimed he had visions. He was in the Klondike prospecting for gold when I was born. He later told everyone how he had seen a strange light one night in March and had dreamed that Joe had a baby girl. In fact, he even wrote it down in his diary, and sure enough his dream had occurred on my birthday. He later became a landscape artist. Daddy's youngest brother, Jonathan, was a sculptor. He entered a competition and won a scholarship to study at the Art Institute. The Swansons were all very proud of him. My favorite relative on my father's side was Aunt May, who loved children so much that when she found out she couldn't have any, adopted one. Daddy worked for a congressman in Chicago for a number of years, and because his moral Swedish family didn't think much of politics as an honest profession, they all joked that Joe would have made a good lawyer or a great crook.

Daddy went first to Florida. Mother and I stayed in Chicago long enough to pack our clothes and ship the few pieces of furniture Mother wanted to keep. Then we boarded the train and started the long journey I had been dreaming of. It lasted three days and two nights, and the further south we went, the hotter it got in our car. If we opened the windows, we got covered with little specks of soot. When we finally got to Tampa, my hair was really and truly dirty, for the first time in my life. But at least, I thought, I wasn't in school in Chicago.

Tampa seemed like another world, with palm trees and the smell of oranges and tangerines in the air. At the beautiful Tampa Bay Hotel, where we stayed, there were fans on the ceiling and nets that they lowered over our beds at night to keep the mosquitoes out. I soaked in a big tub for hours, and we had dinner in the enormous dining room.

Daddy arrived from Key West on the boat in the morning and said that we had a few hours to sightsee before the boat went back. He took us to a big aquarium full of tropical fish, where I fell in love with the baby alligators. Daddy bought me one, and I carried it to the boat in a cardboard box with holes in it. As soon as we arrived at our house in Key West, however, I had to give it up before I had even had it for a full day, because the black girl Daddy had hired to help Mother said she wouldn't stay if there was going to be an alligator in the house.

The house we lived in was on the Key West Army Base. Right in front of it was the dock where they kept the army launch and little dinghies for fishing. The house stood on pillars, to protect it in the event of flooding, and it had a veranda that gave out on beautiful views in every direction.

Key West for me was a tropical island paradise. Daddy took me grunt fishing, and in the afternoons I watched the soldiers play baseball beside the barracks. I learned to tell time by the different bugle calls and I loved to visit the commissary, where they always gave me lemon drops. Even school in Key West was not so bad. I went to a small private school in town. Every morning a soldier drove four or five of us army brats, as we came to be known, there in a buckboard. On warm days the teacher would take us outside and we would recite our lessons under the palm trees.

I also started going to Sunday school in Key West because I liked the singing. One Sunday the teacher asked me if I would care to prepare a solo, and I told her all right, but it would have to be something I already knew. "Listen to the Mockingbird" was my favorite song, I said, but the teacher said she thought it should be something serious. The only serious song I knew was "The Rosary," which was awfully Catholic for a

Protestant Sunday school, the teacher said, but she thought it over and decided it would be all right.

The next Sunday I took the music and managed to get through it somehow. I had heard my mother sing it often enough not to be nervous. I just sang it the way she did. Afterward a pretty lady who was visiting the class told me I had a very nice voice and asked me whom I studied with. I told her I'd never had lessons, but that my mother had, and that I'd learned it all from her. The woman's name was Venice Hayes. She was an actress from New York, she said, and she was spending the winter in Key West with her father on account of his health. A week later she called Mother up and invited us over. Her father wanted to hear me sing, she said. Mother and Daddy liked the Hayeses very much. Miss Hayes's father, Frank Hayes, was also in the theater. He dressed elegantly, but he seemed terribly thin to me and he smelled funny. Mother explained to me that he had TB, but that he was not contagious if we kept the windows open and didn't get too close to him. Mr. Hayes was helping the local people to put on a show, and after he heard me sing he asked Mother if I could be in it. Venice would play the lead. Mother was pleased and agreed. She suggested that I sing "As the World Rolls On," and Mr. Hayes said that would be perfect.

Mother coached me and made me a new dress. It was white dimity, and I wore a white ribbon with big black polka dots in my hair and white socks with a border of black polka dots.

The night of the show, Mother was backstage and Daddy was in the audience with some people from the base. I was not the least bit nervous. As we watched Venice play her love scene I was enthralled. I'd never heard people talk about being in love in a big, open, romantic way. In fact, I got so caught up in it that I didn't realize the man in the scene with her had forgotten what to say. The next thing I knew, Mr. Hayes was shoving me onstage and whispering, "Sing your song, Glory. Now." There was no one at the piano to give me my note, so I looked back to make sure there wasn't some mistake. Mr. Hayes and my mother were both nodding violently, meaning, Yes, yes, now. So I opened my mouth and sang "As the World Rolls On." Everyone clapped when I finished, and Mother hugged me as I came offstage. Mr. Hayes was beaming. I couldn't imagine why. I hadn't even had the piano accompanying me, and during the whole second chorus I hadn't been able to think of a single thing except that I'd forgotten to go to the bathroom before I put on my dress. How could they possibly have thought that that was the best I could do? I decided I should stick to drawing.

Mother worried from the start about hurricanes in the Florida Keys, but Daddy said that hurricanes always occurred during the summer, when families of army personnel were on vacation. He also said our house, which was the newest one on the post, had been built to "ride out" hurricanes.

In March of our very first year in Key West, however, which was not the season for hurricanes, the sky looked so threatening one morning when the buckboard came to take me to school that Mother said she didn't want me to go and sent the driver away. Within an hour the gusting wind built to a roar. Outside, the trees were bending and we could see things flying through the air. Then we could hear the ocean washing under the house, and floating logs smashed against the floor with a frightening thud. I screamed for Daddy, even though I knew he was on the base. Mother grabbed me and I clung to her. She held her hands over my ears so I wouldn't hear the awful sounds outside. Water was coming through the floorboards and the roof. We held each other tightly and prayed that the house wouldn't float away. Suddenly Mother said she heard Daddy's voice. Then I could hear him too. We saw him holding on to the banister at the top of the stairs, soaked to the skin. The three of us huddled together and waited, as the kitchen chimney came down with a crash. Daddy said we had to stay away from the windows, because roof slates were flying around like feathers. It was afternoon before the wind finally died down and Daddy dared to say he thought the storm was over. Only then did I realize how brave he had been to fight his way to us. He had also been right about our house; it had ridden out the hurricane. We all smiled at each other. We even laughed, and I realized what a joy it is to live through danger and come out safely on the other side.

That freak March hurricane was the worst anyone could remember. Church steeples were down, stores were full of sopping merchandise, and the public market was washed completely away. The only thing that kept us alive, Daddy said, was a cement causeway that had been built by the Florida East Coast Railroad to connect the Florida Keys. It had prevented tidal waves from sweeping over the land.

School was suspended and all women and children had to be evacuated. The army was still clearing away the mess days later when the boat arrived to take Mother and me to New York. From there we went by train to Chicago, where we had to repeat the story of the hurricane over and over. Finally I got so I enjoyed telling it, with all the grisly details. I also found that I liked to tell how different our life on an army base was from life in Chicago, and I pretended to know all about everything military. I would quote things I had heard Daddy say. "Would you rather be a colonel with an eagle on your shoulder," I would ask one of our baffled relatives, "or a private with a chicken on your knee?" In addition, some of the formality that clings to an army base had rubbed off on me. One day that summer Grandmother Lew's stepbrother dropped in to see her, and I remarked afterward that I was very surprised that he wasn't wearing a coat in her parlor and that he had put his feet up on the table. I guess I had become an army brat, and I suspect our relatives sighed with relief when Daddy wrote that the hurricane repairs would be completed by September, in plenty of time for me to return to school in Key West.

The year I was eleven, we moved to San Juan, Puerto Rico. If Key West had seemed like exotic territory to me, San Juan really was. At the tip of the old part of the city stood El Morro, a huge Spanish fort four hundred years old. At the other end of the city was Fort San Cristóbal, and even that was a hundred and fifty years old. In between was Artillery Park, where we lived along with one other American family, Major and Mrs. Stewart and their son, Peter. Colonel Howes, the base commander, and his wife and two children, Bobby and Harriet, lived in the governor's Pink Palace nearby. So did the Shantons, who had one daughter, Margaret. Mr. Shanton was the chief of police. Most of the other Americans, including my friend Beena Fields, whose father was a captain, lived in quarters on the grounds of Morro Castle.

The rest of the people around us spoke Spanish and had darker skin than ours and their cooking tasted strange to us. We were really foreigners in Puerto Rico, which had been under American control only since the Spanish-American War, a mere twelve years. We were aware from the day we arrived that we were privileged, special, and as a girl who had not yet reached the age of twelve herself, I loved the feeling.

I soaked up the new smells and sounds of this beautiful city in the Caribbean where everyone but us was Catholic—the smells of tamarinds and mangoes and papayas in the open markets, and of a thousand new kinds of fabulous flowers everywhere, and of kerosene on the tile floors to drive away insects, and of garlic and beans, and of ashes and incense and funeral wreaths; and the sounds of church bells and priests chanting Latin, of funerals and weddings and street carnivals, of guitars. I also loved the way the people moved. I started carrying my books home from school on my head, the way I saw local women carry wood and water pots. That's how I learned to walk properly.

Even the stars were different from the stars up north. On balmy evenings the Southern Cross and the other constellations hung so low over our roof garden you felt you could touch them. I wanted to know the name and distance and size of every one. Nothing in school was half as worthwhile learning about as what was going on out there in the great night sky. Daddy knew all of them and taught me their names and tried to suggest to me the enormous mystery that included them all: infinity.

My first boyfriend, Peter Stewart, was for a long time simply my favorite playmate. A roof connected Major Stewart's apartment with ours, so Peter and I played together there and eventually became inseparable. He was a year younger than me, but we got along together perfectly. For a while we owned a goat jointly and a wagon for the goat to pull us around on. When we outgrew that, we explored together and built a tent on the roof with a partition separating his half of the space from my half. Soon other separations followed. Peter loved the beach, for example, but I had a terrible fear of the water and refused to learn to swim and dive. The sport I enjoyed was horseback riding, but I always rode with Margaret Shanton and the girls who lived in the garrison, and Peter refused to be included in all-girl parties. Next he and I started to be aware of our age and our bodies, and a natural embarrassment turned our friendship into something more formal and reserved.

Peter and I went to private school, but all the girls I knew went to public school. Harriet Howes begged me to switch because their school was going to put on a musical show called *The American Girl* and everyone thought I would be wonderful in it. My mother agreed, and I changed to public school. We rehearsed the play for weeks. It was set in a girls' school, and Harriet played the principal because she was the tallest girl in the class and looked the oldest. I played the lead—a willful girl who left school and had to be tricked by her friends into going back. Colonel Howes somehow managed to commandeer the beautiful old rococo opera house in San Juan for the two performances.

On opening night I found a gold star on my mirror and my name painted under it—not Glory, which everyone usually called me, but the grown-up version I'd been christened with and had started signing on my papers at school: Gloria. It was obviously the work of my father. Next a messenger delivered a box of flowers with a card in a tiny white envelope that said: "Good luck from Peter." Then I went onstage and sang my first number, with a whole chorus of girls behind me, and everyone applauded. And suddenly I knew I was no longer shy little Glory. I was the lead and I was good.

I decided that night in the San Juan opera house that I would be an opera singer. I had never been to an opera in my life. I didn't even know what an opera was. Venice Hayes had once shown me pictures of Emma Eames and Louise Homer all decked out in velvet gowns and jewels, but they hadn't meant much to me in Key West. Now I felt that an opera singer had to be the most exciting thing a woman could hope to be, and I determined that I would be one.

I had just turned thirteen, and I was discovering new things about myself every day. Some of them my mother reluctantly and sketchily explained to me. Other things remained mysterious. For instance, I realized that I stood out from the crowd. People stared at me when they passed on the street, especially men. I knew it wasn't my ears they were staring at, or my clothes. I was light-skinned, but so were my friends, and when I asked them if people stared at them, they said of course not. "It's your blue eyes, Glory," they said. "You look like a Cuban princess with your dark hair and your big blue eyes."

That year I received my first letter from a man, and I was afraid to show it to my parents. It wasn't from Peter Stewart. Since the play he and I had gone back to being just friends. Probably my new sense of self-importance put him off, although I doubt if playmates ever honestly grow up to feel romantic about each other. They know each other too well. My "love letter" came from someone I hardly knew at all, a handsome blond man of about twenty-one, who had visited San Juan the previous winter. His name was Horace Swiggett, and his father was the local haberdasher. Horace lived in New York. His letter to me was not offensive or even passionate. It was just that he sent it to *me*, and that he said he would like to see *me* when Mother and I passed through New York the following summer. I was embarrassed but pleased, and when I mentioned the letter in passing to my parents, they both said they thought it was very sweet of Horace to think to write to me. I knew there was more to the letter than they imagined, but I didn't know specifically what it could be.

The only person I dared to communicate with on the subject was my newest friend, Medora Grimes, who was from Staten Island. She and her parents were on a cruise, and it was part of my father's duties to show such visitors around. Medora was a year older than me. We liked each other from the start, but as soon as we got acquainted they had to leave. Nevertheless, we exchanged pictures and discussed my letter from Horace Swiggett with many gasps and sighs. Medora said I must visit her soon on Staten Island, and then the Grimeses sailed away.

The only other person I ever discussed the fascinating subject of maturity and men with was Beena Fields. Beena was intrigued, but she just wasn't knowledgeable, although she pretended to be. Beena and I always rode our horses together, and one day at the stable we discovered a darling newborn colt. It was beige naturally, Beena said.

"Naturally?" I asked. "What do you mean, naturally?"

"Don't you know?" Beena asked. "It takes after its father, the beige stallion."

"Its father? Horses don't get married."

"Glory, you know what I mean."

I didn't, but I felt I should, so I pressed Beena for an explanation. It turned out, however, that her mother hadn't been any more helpful than mine had. Medora Grimes knew as much as Beena, but even she admitted to being confused about the *real* relations of men and women. She yearned for understanding in the matter. We all did. But we sensed with acute discomfort that we were still far from the truth of things.

CHAPTER 3

By the time I was fifteen, my mother had turned me into a real clotheshorse. She loved to dress me up and I loved to show off the outfits she made for me. June of 1914 gave her the greatest challenge so far along those lines. Medora Grimes had been after me for two years to visit her, and now I was finally going. Once Mother and I got back to Chicago, that summer after my first year of high school in Puerto Rico, we started buying patterns and having fittings every day so that I would not look like somebody's poor relation when I entered the swanky world of the Grimeses for a month. For weeks my plump little mother stitched frantically.

Daddy was temporarily stationed on Governors Island, a dot in the water between Manhattan Island and Staten Island, so there was a double purpose to my trip. I could see him on his days off. Our future was not quite certain. He might be sent back to Puerto Rico after his tour of duty on Governors Island or he might be transferred to some other army base. In any case, he and I would be spending whole days together while I was in New York, so I couldn't wait to board the train. I would be traveling by myself for the first time.

One morning Aunt Inga, my mother's brother's sister-in-law, dropped by Grandmother Lew's house to see if I would go with her to a place where they made motion pictures on Argyle Street on the North Side. The owner, Mr. Spoor, had invited her to come out someday when she was free, and she didn't want to go alone. Aunt Inga knew all sorts of interesting people. As a trained nurse for wealthy families she made a good living, and she also loved a good time. She was the only woman I knew who smoked.

She asked us if we had ever seen any motion pictures in Puerto Rico. We said yes, and they were terrible. Most of them were made in Sweden or Denmark. They flashed them on a white sheet in the hot little movie house that used to be a store. First you saw a picture of a polar bear on a globe. Then you could see people moving around waving their arms, and then some words printed in Swedish, and then more people making faces. In ten minutes it was all over. Once you'd seen how it worked, you never needed to waste another nickel to see it again.

"Well, you haven't seen *Quo Vadis?,* then," Aunt Inga said, grandly exhaling a thin stream of smoke.

"What's that?" my mother asked through a mouthful of pins.

It was a new Italian motion picture, Aunt Inga said, and she had positively loved it. They were showing it in the opera house and it cost a dollar to get in. The music alone was worth the price of admission. A live symphony orchestra played all through the picture. There were chariot races and slave galleys and an arena full of lions and you felt as if you were right there. She said *Quo Vadis?* had proved to her that motion pictures could be very educational. That's why she was ready to take George Spoor up on his invitation and see if Americans were doing anything nearly as good as the Italians. Mr. Spoor had one studio in Chicago and another in California.

Mother showed no interest whatsoever, but I loved to tag along anywhere with Aunt Inga, so I told her to wait ten minutes while I put on one of the new Staten Island outfits I was dying to wear. It was a black-and-white checkered skirt with a slit in the front from an Irene Castle pattern and a black cutaway jacket with a green waistcoat. I wore a perky little Knox felt hat with it.

Mr. Spoor's studio was called the Essanay Company, which stood for S and A, *S* for Mr. Spoor and *A* for Mr. G. M. Anderson, who made cowboy pictures at their studio in California under the name of Broncho Billy. From the outside it looked like a factory. Mr. Spoor was out of town on business, but his brother came out to meet us and wouldn't let us leave until we had had a look around. He found a nice young man to be our guide, and the young man led us downstairs.

At one end of a cavernous cement basement room made close by the heat of many lamps on stands and the smell of perspiration was a pile of screaming, thrashing bodies. A man with a pistol in his belt and a whistle around his neck was sitting on an upturned barrel yelling, "Kick him! Fall on his face! That's right, sit on his head!" There must have been a dozen people piled up, but all we could make out were arms and bodies and legs and feet with roller skates on them. Occasionally you could distinguish faces. Some were boys, some girls.

"Funny! Good!" the man screamed. "Now do it all over again!"

I looked at Aunt Inga and she looked at me. I certainly didn't think it was funny, especially when the skaters scrambled to their feet and dusted off their clothes and we could see that they had all been sitting on a great big woman who was lying in the middle of the floor.

"That's our comedy director, Lightning Hopper, the Nebraska Cyclone," our guide explained. "Some pep he's got. Yells himself hoarse every day." Mr. Hopper was rehearsing the skaters now, waving his arms and screaming.

"That bird over there in women's clothes they were all lying on is Wallace Beery. He went on for Raymond Hitchcock one night in *Yankee Consul* on Broadway and was famous overnight. He's Sweedie the maid in our slapstick comedy series. Some guy. We do two a week. Can't give the people enough of it. They cry like babies for it all the time."

The man in women's clothes looked to us as if he were injured. "Naw," our guide said. "That's where he fell in the last scene. He's got to stay there until the camera picks him up in the next."

We hadn't even noticed the camera or the quiet little man fussing over it.

The director was still yelling. "He's keeping them keyed up," our guide explained, "on their toes." One girl was skating in a circle. Most of the other skaters were sitting on benches, exhausted. Two of the men skaters were trying to prop up the man in women's clothes. As soon as they had him standing he fell, and the two men fell on top of him. They did this three times and then the director screamed, "Let's go," and fired his cap pistol into the air with a loud crack.

The quiet little man started grinding the camera, the director started screaming louder than ever, and they did it all over again. "Kick him! Sit on his head! Fall on his face! Now everybody—Whoa! Spoiled. Got to do it over." Somebody had knocked Mr. Beery's wig off and a fat man was sitting on it.

I didn't know about Aunt Inga, but I didn't want to see any more. I thought it was vulgar, disgusting, and stupid.

"Everyone loves slapstick," our guide said. "Mr. Hopper says it doesn't matter how refined your audiences are, they want to see comedy actors get all banged up—fall down, get hit over the head, fall in the water, break dishes, throw custard pies. He says you gotta give people a chance to laugh at something they'd cry about at home."

The director blew his whistle and a bunch of policemen with painted faces rushed in. Sweedie tripped them and they all fell down. The director blew the whistle again and they scrambled to their feet and saluted the chief policeman, who was cross-eyed. He screamed at the skaters. Then they yelled at him, and after the whistle blew again, Sweedie started talking nonsense in a stupid Swedish accent and kicking the policemen. They all fell down and Sweedie escaped. Aunt Inga was laughing because of Sweedie's Swedish accent, but except for the cross-eyed policeman, I didn't think any of it was funny.

Meanwhile our guide was telling us about all the famous stage people who worked at the studio, like Francis X. Bushman, Beverly Bayne, Ruth Stonehouse, and Gerda Holmes. He said some of them might be filming that day and asked if we would like to see them. We said yes and he led us upstairs, where a director and technicians were filming a wedding scene.

"Oh, how wonderful," I said to Aunt Inga. "Isn't it beautiful?"

"That's Gerda Holmes," our guide said, indicating the bride, "and the man is Richard Travers."

While I was watching, enthralled, a man walked over and introduced himself as Mr. Babile, the casting director for Essanay. He said he wondered if I would give him my address and telephone number. I looked at Aunt Inga and she said, "Go ahead." Mr. Babile said their directors were looking for interesting new types all the time and he was in charge of finding them. He wrote my name, address, and phone number on a little card and then he excused himself.

"What do you think of that?" Aunt Inga asked.

"I'm sure it's this suit," I said. "It's an Irene Castle pattern."

The very next morning Mr. Babile telephoned to ask me to come in at one o'clock and be in a picture. I told him I'd have to ask my mother, and when Mother said she didn't see anything wrong with it as long as Mr. Spoor was a friend of Aunt Inga's and I was on vacation, I told him yes and asked him what I should wear. He told me to wear the same outfit he had noticed me in the day before. I knew it, I thought to myself. I said I would not wish to roller-skate in that dress, and he assured me I wouldn't have to.

Then, for the second day in a row, I took the noisy trolley to Essanay. Mr. Babile led me upstairs, where about twenty people were being coached for a continuation of the same wedding scene I had watched the day before. Gerda Holmes was expected at any moment. The leading man, Richard Travers, was already there. When the director looked at me, he asked his assistant to get me a bouquet of flowers. Then he showed me how he wanted me to hand it to the bride.

After Miss Holmes arrived, we rehearsed the scene for about five minutes. The director seemed happy with it and hollered, "All right, let's go!" When my turn came, I rushed in with the flowers and Miss Holmes gave me a big smile when she took them from me and then she smiled at Mr. Travers. It was all over in a few minutes. The director said, "That's it for this one." Then someone shouted "Strike!" and a gang of men came in and started taking down the scenery. Nearby another gang of men were putting up an entirely different set.

An assistant told a group of us to stop at the office downstairs for our pay on our way out, and there a girl gave me a little brown envelope with my name on it. Walking to the trolley, I stopped at a delicatessen for a dill pickle. In those days you bought a dill pickle the way kids today buy a Coke or a candy bar. I casually opened the envelope to pay for the dill pickle and found three dollar bills and a quarter in it. An absolute fortune! For an hour! For doing nothing! I thought they must have made a mistake. If it wasn't a mistake, it was no wonder those boys and girls in the basement were willing to fall in a heap on roller skates over and over again. And how much, I asked myself, did *they* get for *that?*

When I got home I telephoned Aunt Inga and told her what had happened. She was thrilled, and we made a date to go shopping the next day at Marshall Field's. We started off early and spent all day in the big stores. When we got home, Mother was terribly annoyed. Those people from the Essanay

Company had phoned all morning. They had wanted me back there in my Irene Castle outfit for a scene outside the church. Mother had finally told them to stop bothering her and had slammed down the receiver.

Three days later they called again. They wanted me in an hour, and I decided I could always use another $3.25 for my trip to New York. I asked them what they wanted me to wear. They said it was going to be a dinner scene in a fancy café, so I put on another pretty new dress I was saving for New York, pinned up my hair, and ran for the trolley.

All day I had to sit at a little table behind the one where the leading actors played their scene. Nobody told me what to do. They just kept puttering with lights and moving other people around. I felt I was just part of the scenery. It got very tiresome, so I started studying the other girls in the scene. Most of them had lots of white powder on their faces, and every time the lights were turned off, they would take out little mirrors and dust their faces with more. If I used any of that stuff, I thought, I would look as if I had a skin disease. I was olive-complexioned to begin with and still tanned from Puerto Rico. My face was shiny and brown like the people's in San Juan. I certainly didn't look like anyone else at Essanay that day, and I supposed that was the reason they wanted me in party scenes. I tried to avoid smiling, knowing that if anyone saw my big teeth, I would certainly never get another call.

When I went to the office that night to pick up my money, the girl said Mr. Webster, one of their best directors, had noticed me in the café scene and wanted to use me in the picture he was starting.

"I probably can't," I said. "I'm leaving for New York next week."

The next time the studio called, I had Mother tell them I was busy. I had made up my mind I wasn't going to be part of the scenery anymore. When they called two days later, I answered the phone myself and told them so. But Mr. Babile got on the line and said it was a glamorous party scene, so I said I'd do it. I took a beautiful white jacket Mother had made me, although I was in mortal terror of getting it soiled. However, I thought, it might be worth it if I ran into Mr. Webster.

The assistant director paired me off with an older man. All I had to do was walk in on his arm, shake hands with the host and hostess, and then disappear. We waited and waited for our signal. When we finally got it, we walked in. From the darkness behind the camera a swarthy man in a business suit emerged, roaring with rage. He came up and shook his fist in my face, cursing and claiming I had cost the studio hundreds of dollars by not showing up for the portrait scene. He said he had had an artist working all night painting a portrait of me and a seamstress making a skirt to match the one in the portrait.

I tried to say I was sorry; there must be some mistake. I knew nothing about any portrait; he must have me confused with someone else. He only roared more loudly, until I began to cry. I was so embarrassed I wanted to die, being yelled at in front of all those people. But he wouldn't stop. When I turned and ran out, he followed me down the stairs, shouting and swearing.

By the time I got to the office, *I* was the angry one. "Give me my envelope," I said to the girl at the window, and pointing at the man who was still behind me, I said, "and tell that crazy man to leave me alone!"

"Why that's Mr. Webster," she said.

I was so upset that I couldn't turn around until she told me he was gone. Then I dried my eyes and left the studio. Munching on a dill pickle a few minutes later, I decided that if that was one of the best motion picture directors, then I had had enough of motion pictures. They were boring and vulgar, anyway. I had made $9.75 in them; that was plenty. I was leaving in two days for New York. We would be moving away from Chicago altogether as soon as Daddy was transferred from Governors Island. And besides, I wanted to be an opera singer.

Daddy met me at Grand Central Station and took me on a tour of New York. Then we took the ferry to Staten Island. From the deck we could see the Statue of Liberty and Governors Island. Then he delivered me to the Grimeses, who lived in an enormous stone house near Grymes Hill, which was named after Medora's ancestors. The house was surrounded by sprawling lawns, a huge flower garden, and a tennis court.

Medora said I could have my own room if I wanted, but she had planned for us to share hers because it would be more fun and because we had so much to catch up on and only a month to do it in. I said that was fine.

The room took my breath away. To begin with, it was as big as the living rooms my family usually had, but more than that, it was a whole personal world. Medora had picked the draperies and the bedspread and the carpets herself. She had huge closets and a big dresser and a vanity all to herself, as well as her own bathroom with curtains and rugs to match. From her window the view to the bay stretched for miles. I tried to imagine what it would be like having your own room in your own house near a landmark named after you and living there all your life. I had lived out of suitcases most of my life. I'd already been to many different schools, and I couldn't count the number of apartments and houses we'd lived in. We had never had one of our own. Even when we called it our house, it really wasn't; it belonged to the army or Aunt Clara or Grandmother Lew or Great-grandma May. The only new house we'd ever lived in was the one that had been hit by the hurricane. Much of my life I had slept under somebody else's blankets, on somebody else's mattress. I'd never even had a dresser of my own. I'd had beautiful clothes all my life—my mother always saw to that—but I'd never had a room of my own to fix up the way I wanted it, with carpets and draperies and a place for my pictures. That's what I wanted—a room of my own; not a separate room in the Grimes house for a month, but a room of my own.

"Why, Medora Grimes!" I said when she came out of the bathroom puffing on a cigarette. "Do you smoke?"

"Not really," Medora said. "It's just that some boy might dare you to smoke, so you'd better be ready."

That made sense to me, so I took a puff. As soon as I did, I realized I could never be good at it in time for the party Medora's parents had planned for the following week. They had invited lots of young people, most of them Medora's friends who had heard about the Cuban Princess and wanted to meet me. It would be right in their own garden, with a real orchestra. It was called a tea dance, the latest thing in New York. They would cover the tennis court and turn it into a dance floor.

My first Saturday night on Staten Island the Grimeses took me to dinner at the country club. I took pains dressing because Medora said we might run into some of the boys she knew who wanted to meet me, but we didn't. She said that was because most boys our age hated the idea of getting dressed up just to have dinner with their parents, even if they liked to dance with girls. They showed up mainly at special parties, where they could get away from the adults. The club was so beautiful, with inlaid floors and carved ceilings and urns of flowers and acres of stiff white linen, that I couldn't believe anyone who had the right wouldn't want to be there every night, every week. But who could tell about boys?

The first man I met on Staten Island was old enough to be my father. Mr. Grimes introduced us at the country club, and I was so nervous that he would ask me to dance that I forgot myself and said *"Buenas noches, señor"* instead of "Good evening" and held out my hand. At that the man bowed stiffly from the waist and kissed my hand. I felt a bit ridiculous, but I liked it. Before dinner was over, however, several people came to our table and asked me if I was the Cuban Princess. Medora choked with laughter while I steamed with embarrassment. "I live in Puerto Rico," I said each time, "not Cuba." But that just tickled Medora and her parents more than ever. No matter what I did, I couldn't live it down. On Staten Island I was the Puerto Rican Princess, or the Spanish Princess, or the Cuban Princess.

I'd never been to a tea dance or even heard of one before my visit, so I had no idea what to wear. The night before the dance, we went through all my dresses to see which one would be right. Medora wound up her phonograph and taught me all the steps she knew. She had all the latest records, including a tango, but she didn't know how to dance that. Most of their friends still considered the tango too wicked for Staten Island, she said, although maybe her parents would let the orchestra play one at the dance, as long as it was being held outside. My favorite record was "Too Much Mustard."

Then Medora said it was no good looking at clothes on the bed; I'd have to try them on to see how they fit around the bosom.

"Medora!"

"There's no use trying to hide them, Glory," she said. "First of all, I'm not going to have you moping around at a party in your honor with your arms crossed in front of you like you lost your lemonade; and second of all, if you dance with a boy and he's holding you close, he's going to *know*. Anyway, they always *want* to know if you're old enough to have them. If you wear the right dress, they can tell by just looking."

Medora had to see every dress on me before she could give her opinion. We settled on my mother's prize creation, a brown taffeta dress with a fitted bust, and I promised Medora I would not fold my arms once.

The afternoon of the party turned into the loveliest summer evening imaginable. As I stood in front of Medora's mirror for a final primping, I heard the sound of pebbles striking the bedroom window. How romantic! Some boy was signaling Medora that the orchestra was about to play. I looked out to tell him she was already downstairs but he darted away as soon as he saw I wasn't Medora. The garden below looked magical in the gathering twilight. Japanese lanterns glowed in all the trees, and maids and butlers in black uniforms scurried between linen-covered tables with huge silver dishes and platters of food and trays of glasses. The arriving guests looked terribly swank. The boys were mostly in white flannels and blue blazers, and as I studied the dresses on the girls, I knew that Medora had chosen correctly. My dress was just right and not at all like anyone else's at the party.

When I heard the band playing "Too Much Mustard," I went downstairs. Medora was with her parents greeting the guests, but she ran over as soon as she saw me and introduced me to a few people. "I can't start dancing until more of the guests arrive," she said, "but don't let that stop you."

I told her about the pebbles at the window. "Oh, really?" she said. "Well, he's mine. Go find your own. By the way, they *are* going to play a tango. Don't dance it, though, Glory. We don't know how."

Then she left me, and I walked slowly around the terrace, aware that people were staring at me because I was Medora's friend. I made an effort not to appear shy and cover up my bosom. In a little while a boy wearing an orange tie with his blue blazer and white pants came up and asked me to dance. He seemed fatally handsome in the fading light.

"It's not a tango, is it?"

"No," he said. "They never play tangos on Staten Island."

He took me by the hand and led me to the tennis court. When we stepped onto the floor, he took my other hand. Medora was right. He was trying to hold me terribly close. He said his name was Livingston Parmalee, Jr. He already knew mine, as well as the nickname I'd acquired. He danced very well and he smelled wonderful. It was exciting to be held that close and a little bewildering. I felt a kind of dizziness on the turns, and that was not like me at all. I also felt out of breath when the music stopped. I excused myself and headed for the house. The boy walked me to the foot of the stairs, where he leaned over, with his buttons scraping the front of my dress, and kissed me on the mouth. I was trembling so that I thought I would faint before he stopped. Then he was talking to me, but my mind was so far away I couldn't make out the words. I needed to be all by myself for a second to see what was happening to me. I excused myself again and rushed upstairs. Minutes later I was fine, but the earth had shaken under me and I felt I would never be the same.

As soon as Medora and I were alone that night, I told her I thought I was going to have a baby. I explained how I had suddenly felt weak after the kiss and how I had noticed a strange feeling in my body.

"Where?" she asked.

"*There*, Medora," I said.

"Oh," she said, nervous but intrigued. "But I've kissed lots of boys at parties, Glory. Why wouldn't *I* have had a baby?"

"All I know, Medora, is that something powerful happened. I'm sure you don't have a baby *every* time you kiss someone. I think it's only when you kiss a certain person a certain way at a certain time of the month. Anyway, I'm sure something happened tonight. And I don't care. If it means marrying Livingston, I will."

That convinced Medora. She went and woke her mother, and soon Mrs. Grimes came in and sat on the foot of the bed with us. She gently explained to us that I was mistaken. Girls didn't get babies by kissing boys. "Just don't make a habit of it, though, either of you," she said. "Your mother will tell you what you need to know when you need to know it, Glory. For now, just go to sleep."

I liked her very much and she was trying to be helpful, but I knew what had happened because it had happened to me. How could she possibly know what I had felt? And although she advised me to forget what had taken place, I knew I never would. It had been the most mysterious thing that had ever happened to me, and I would remember it to the day I died. This simply meant that I would not marry Livingston Parmalee, Jr. Mrs. Grimes explained that his family would consider him much too young to marry. In fact, I might never even see him again. Nevertheless, he would always be very important to me, for in addition to kissing me until I mistakenly thought I was going to have a baby, he had also whispered what I had always wanted to hear. He had said I was beautiful. And I had no reason to doubt him. After all, why would a handsome, rich boy want to kiss someone who wasn't?

Two or three nights later I had more exciting news to share with Medora when we were alone.

"Not another baby," she said and giggled.

"Medora Grimes, stop that! Here, read this."

I gave her a typewritten letter that Mother had forwarded from Chicago. It was from the manager of the Essanay Company, who was offering me a position as a guaranteed stock extra in motion pictures. At $13.25 a week, whether I worked one day or four. If I worked a whole week, including Saturday, the weekly pay would be almost $20. There it was, in black and white. A way out of school. And although Mother had read it, she hadn't torn it up. That must mean that she didn't think it was out of the question. I could always go back to high school if I didn't like it. I had already changed schools so many times that one more slowdown wouldn't matter. On the other hand, with my own money I could take classes at the Art Institute and take singing lessons with a good teacher. All I had dreamed of for years was being a grownup. Here was my chance.

Medora couldn't understand why I was so excited. "But, Glory, you said that place in Chicago was terrible. Isn't that where the man chased you out screaming and all the girls wore make-up? Your father will never let you quit high school to work in a place like that."

"Medora, do you realize how much money they're offering me?"

"Thirteen dollars isn't all that much."

"Not to you, Medora. But to us it is. My mother couldn't make that. I doubt if my Aunt Inga makes that. I know army captains don't make very much, because I've heard my parents argue over money for years."

"But still, the people in that studio sound awful."

"They are. I know it. Look, I don't want to spend my whole life making stupid motion pictures. I want to take lessons and be an opera singer. With this much money I could."

"I'm sure your father won't let you."

"We'll see. Don't say a word about it to him or to your parents. Promise, Medora."

"I promise, Glory."

During my last week on Staten Island, Mrs. Grimes invited Daddy to dinner. Almost as soon as he arrived at the house, I knew Medora and I would have no trouble keeping my secret. He and Mr. Grimes spent the whole evening talking about the war that had broken out in Europe. Austria had just declared war on Serbia, and it looked as if other nations—Germany and Russia especially—would take sides. America was not involved, but all our army bases were on permanent alert, Daddy said.

He didn't expect to be stationed on Governors Island much longer. But it was very uncertain now where his next assignment would be. There were rumors it might be Manila. We would just have to wait and see.

That settled things in my mind. No matter what school I went to in Chicago that fall, I would have to withdraw as soon as Daddy sent for us. So I told Medora I would try to persuade Mother to let me take the job at Essanay.

Daddy took me to the train. I'd had a wonderful vacation, but I was actually looking forward now to going back to Chicago. Daddy seemed a little sad, maybe on account of what he knew about the war, maybe just because we were saying good-bye. He had a way of seeing around corners, but at that point I couldn't read his mind. In the few minutes before train time, I told him I wasn't looking forward to school at all, that I hated it, but he didn't pick up on the subject. I said I'd much rather study privately and I hinted that I might even make money as a singer. Mr. Hayes and Venice had thought so.

"Take your time, Glory," Daddy said. "Remember, life is ninety-five percent anticipation and only five percent realization." With that he kissed me and I boarded the train.

Everything worked out as I had hoped. Because of the war and the uncertainty of our future, Mother said I could leave school and work in pictures as long as we stayed in Chicago. She said that once I had a regular schedule, we would also arrange for voice lessons. In the meantime, we moved from Grandma Lew's house, where we had lived for the past five summers, to our own apartment.

I reported to the studio and was assigned to a little cubicle of a dressing room with a girl named Virginia Bowker. The next day we were told that we both were playing society ladies in one of the Sweedie comedies starring Wallace Beery. Lightning Hopper, the director, had asked for us after going through all the pictures at the casting grille, the tiny cage or office where they kept the casting records. We were supposed to act stuck-up and look snooty, so I penciled on dramatic new eyebrows and we wore our best clothes.

Mr. Beery wore a crazy wig and a maid's uniform with a white apron and cap. He was a tall, good-looking, rugged man, so he looked absolutely ridiculous playing the dumb Swedish maid. These silly two-reel comedies were very successful, and Mr. Beery knew just how to get every laugh. He told Virginia and me to act as if we were completely fooled by his disguise. We should be so snooty that we took the maid for granted and never looked at Sweedie above the wrists when she was serving us tea. Then the audience would feel they were smarter than us and sympathize totally with Sweedie. "Remember," he said, "it's the maids just off the boat who go to pictures. Society folks don't."

Mr. Beery had a beautiful singing voice. He had appeared in New York in musicals and operettas. He probably hated the Sweedie pictures as much as Virginia and I did. We obviously all wanted to be in dramatic pictures.

Promptly at six o'clock the studio closed for the night. One evening Mr. Beery asked if he could drive me home. I said that would be very nice and went to change clothes. Virginia was delighted when I told her. She said every girl in the studio, including her, had been dying to ride in Mr. Beery's Stutz Bearcat, which he parked every day next to Francis X. Bushman's lavender sedan. They considered him a great catch, and he wasn't married or keeping company with anyone in particular.

I wasn't interested in him that way in the least. He was probably old enough to be my father. But I thought it would be fun to ride through the streets of Chicago in an open roadster, and it was, even though he turned out to be a terrible show-off. He had been a racing driver and he wanted everyone to know it. He had run away from home as a youngster and joined a circus, and he drove as though he were still in it. But he really did know how to handle a motorcar. It was a thrill to ride with him.

I let him drive me home several times, until one day he went out of the way and stopped on a side street.

"I just thought I'd show you where I hang my hat," he said.

I knew he was daring me to go into his apartment. That sort of thing just wasn't done. Mother had told me as much and I knew she was right. But I didn't want him to think I was scared or insecure.

"I'll look but I can't stay," I said. "You can leave the motor running."

The apartment, as I had expected, was just another furnished apartment. Once we were inside I felt his hand on my hip. I wasn't startled in the least; I guess I had expected that too. I turned calmly and walked out the door. Outside I waited for him to open the car door for me, and then he drove me home.

We were in one more picture together at Essanay, which was not a Sweedie picture. Although we were friendly, I always managed to be busy at six o'clock. I stuck close to Virginia, who was also in the picture, and avoided any chance for invitations to be driven home. I even had a family friend who owned a Stanley Steamer pick me up several evenings at closing time. Everyone at the studio loved to gossip, but if they ever gossiped about me it was in connection with the man who owned the Stanley Steamer, not in connection with Wallace Beery.

Mr. Beery was soon involved in serious gossip. Some girl's parents had complained to Mr. Spoor about him. They had threatened to go to the authorities because their daughter was a minor, and the studio couldn't afford such a scandal. Mr. Beery quietly disappeared, and we were told that he had gone out west to work at the other Essanay studio in California.

Within a week the payroll department demanded birth records on all the girls who worked at the studio, and men's and women's dressing rooms were strictly separated. But word of the scandal must have leaked out, because Virginia's father marched onto the set one morning and demanded to see his daughter. Virginia was floating in the air suspended on a harness, playing an angel in a white robe and wings, but her father shouted so loudly and angrily that the director stopped the filming and had the crew unhook her. Her father dragged her out of the studio, hollering that no daughter of his would work in that place anymore. I thought Mother would probably do the same if she thought anything bad was going on.

That night I looked at myself carefully in the mirror Virginia and I had shared. I saw the beaded lashes, the Psyche-knot hairdo, the heavy eyebrows, and the society clothes of the thirty-year-old woman I was playing, but I realized that underneath the gloves and veils and parasol I was still a minor myself, not even sixteen. I was as much a female impersonator as Mr. Beery was. I decided that those girls at the studio who were excited by the so-called glamour, who loved to gossip and whisper about Mr. Beery and the other big actors, and who were tempted to throw their reputation away on the chance of being seen with a studio executive were just plain stupid, and I would not have any more to do with them.

As if to confirm these new feelings, the one true, wonderful, lovable, and talented friend I made in Chicago that winter could not get into pictures. The studio sent me to a photographer in the Loop one Saturday afternoon for new photographs. Movie people were talking a great deal at that time about something they called "personality," and this photographer was supposed to be able to bring it out. I wasn't at all sure what it was or if I had it. But at the photographer's I met a girl who did. She was bubbly and funny and outgoing—the very opposite of me. Her name was June Walker. When I asked her about her parents, she startled me by saying she didn't have any. She had a grandmother way out on the poor South Side and she stayed with her when she couldn't pick up a job and support herself. I invited her home for supper and she stayed with us on and off for several months.

She could play absolutely anything on the piano by ear. She played and I sang. She was also a perfectly fabulous dancer and she knew all the new dance steps. How I envied her. She was exactly my size, so Mother let me give her a dress. She had hated school as much as I had and wanted to be a grownup as badly as I did. Mother adored her, and June loved Mother's cooking. We were a perfect little family. June was fascinated by my work, and I thought with all her talent she would be a natural in motion pictures. I tried and tried to get her a job at the studio, but it never worked out. Everybody at Essanay liked her, and everyone admitted that she definitely had "personality," but they said it didn't come through on the screen.

I began to thank heaven I had sane, lovable June at home because working at the studio got to be like going to school. The hours seemed endless if a scene was boring or if a director didn't know what he wanted, and we often worked six days a week if there was a rush to finish a picture. Sundays

I had to spend keeping my wardrobe up to snuff. I soon gave up the idea of taking painting classes or singing lessons. There just wasn't time. Medora Grimes had been right. I could make money in pictures, but I really didn't enjoy the work.

Some of the girls were very ambitious. They worried and fretted about the parts they were given to play. I didn't bother. In fact, I couldn't tell the good parts from the bad ones. Every picture started out new and different and ended up just like the last one. Most of the stories were written by people who worked in the story department. But one day they told me at the casting grille that I'd been picked to play in a special picture. The studio had bought a fable by the famous author George Ade. This was the first of his stories to be made into a picture.

I was to play Gerda Holmes's daughter. They told me I'd be in the picture from beginning to end, so I'd need plenty of changes of clothing. I was really looking forward to something refined and important, but when the director told us the drift of the story, I realized it was the same old thing. My father strikes it rich. My mother takes me to Europe. We come back home with highfalutin ideas and wear gloves and eat with finger bowls and manage to break into high society. The story was so exaggerated and so obvious that it was ridiculous. The girl I played was called Farina. Her mother, Elvira, had found the name in a cookbook. The picture was called *Elvira, Farina, and the Meal Ticket*. The meal ticket was the father, who provided all the money for the mother and the daughter to get so stuck-up. I thought the whole idea was absolutely stupid and once more I wished I had listened to Medora when she advised me not to go into motion pictures because they were vulgar. I was very disappointed in Mr. George Ade, too, although I had never read a word by him.

Then two news items arrived to convince me that my boring career in pictures would soon be over. Daddy wrote to say he was being transferred to Manila in the Philippines and that he would send for us as soon as possible. Then out of the blue I received a postcard from California signed Wally.

"Who's Wally?" Mother asked.

"Wallace Beery. He's a well-known actor. He used to drive me home occasionally when he worked at Essanay before he went to make pictures for them in California."

The California studio was in Niles Canyon, near San

Francisco. That's where Broncho Billy, Mr. Spoor's partner, made all his westerns. On the postcard Wally asked why I didn't come out and make a few pictures in California.

In my final months at the Essanay Company I met a number of the famous people who worked there, but none of the encounters could be called very successful. I worked for one whole morning with an English comedian who had just arrived from California. His name was Charlie Chaplin, and he was the highest-paid actor on the payroll. The rumor was that he was on contract for $1,200 a week. He had made some pictures in California, and everyone said he was very funny with his little mustache and seedy clothes. When he came to Essanay, the management let him try out anyone he might like for a comic partner. He picked me and spent one morning trying to get me to work up routines with him. These all involved kicking each other in the pants, running into things, and falling over each other. He kept laughing and making his eyes twinkle and talking in a light, gentle voice and encouraging me to let myself go and be silly. He reminded me of a pixie from some other world altogether, and for the life of me I couldn't get the feel of his frisky little skits.

All morning I felt like a cow trying to dance with a toy poodle. Moreover, I knew after one hour that I didn't want to spend the next month or so trying to be cute and elfish, so I made very little effort and finally told him I just didn't see the humor in many of the things he was asking me to do. We were both perfectly pleasant and polite after that, but I could see that he was hurt and annoyed. The next day they told me at the casting grille that Mr. Chaplin had felt that I didn't have a strong enough comic sense to be in his picture. He had asked them to find someone else. I was absolutely delighted and considered his rejection a real compliment. I would have been mortified if anybody I knew had ever seen me get kicked in the pants or hit with a revolving plank by an odd sprite in a hobo outfit.

After that they assigned me to serious pictures. The director asked if I thought I'd need any help in producing tears, and I said I was sure I wouldn't. I was right. I just thought of my scene with Mr. Webster the summer before and all the terrible things he'd said to me and how humiliated I'd been, and when the moment came I wailed and carried on until I became almost hysterical. The director and all the other actors were stunned. When the scene was over, I

started primly for my dressing room. As I passed Helen
Dunbar, the grand, elderly character actress with the beautiful white hair and the regal deportment, she said, "You
know, young lady, one day you'll be a good actress." Still
sniffling from the scene, almost unconscious of what I was
saying, I replied, "Thank you, ma'am. Yes, I know. I'm going
to be very famous." When I realized what I'd said, I couldn't
believe it. I hurried to the dressing room crimson-faced. I was
too mortified even to apologize to Helen Dunbar, who always
watched me with a circumspect eye for the rest of my days at
Essanay.

One of the top Essanay writers, along with Louella Parsons
and several others, was very attentive to me in a different
way. Edmund Lowe had very good manners and called me
Miss Swanson, which I liked. When he suddenly invited me to
a theater party, I said I would let him know. He said we'd be
going with Ruth Stonehouse and her husband. I had been in
one picture with Miss Stonehouse. She was one of the studio's
big stars and old enough to be considered a chaperone, but
that would mean nothing to Mother, whose only strict rule
was that I never be out after midnight.

When Mr. Lowe called for me, Mother explained the
midnight rule and he said he understood perfectly. Then our
theater party drove off in a chauffeured car. The play was
Seven Keys to Baldpate, the huge success by George M.
Cohan, and I loved it. I had never worked so hard at playing
grown-up as I did that night. People stared at Miss Stonehouse, and I felt very important at her side.

"Do you like Sophie Tucker?" she asked me during the
intermission.

"Very much," I said, assuming Sophie Tucker was someone in the play.

"Then that settles it. She's singing at the College Inn. Let's
all run over there after the play."

I'd put my foot in it, and there was no turning back.

It was one-thirty when Edmund Lowe delivered me at our
door. I would have eloped with him if he'd asked me, rather
than face my mother. I dreaded what she might say. Actually
she said only a few words. "I thought I had your promise, Mr.
Lowe. Good night."

That was enough to keep Edmund Lowe at a goodly
distance ever after.

My last encounter was with the great god of Essanay
himself—Francis X. Bushman.

The dressing room I shared first with Virginia Bowker and later with Agnes Ayres and two other girls had wall partitions that did not extend all the way to the ceiling. Next door Beverly Bayne had a star dressing room all to herself. Male performers were not supposed to come anywhere near the women's dressing rooms, but Francis X. Bushman, the biggest star in motion pictures, was of course a law unto himself. Whenever we heard whispering in Miss Bayne's dressing room, we always knew Mr. Bushman was breaking the rules. We would climb on our dressing tables and try to hear what was going on. Beverly Bayne and Francis X. Bushman always starred together, and naturally the gossips said they were madly in love.

Mr. Bushman wore a large violet amethyst ring on his finger and he had a spotlight inside his lavender car that illuminated his famous profile when he drove after dark. Everybody at Essanay knew he was married and had five children, but to the public that was a deep dark secret. Studios felt that if word got out that stars were married and had children like ordinary people, it might destroy their image as romantic lovers.

One afternoon I was sitting on the wardrobe counter waiting for the wardrobe mistress to find a strip of elastic for my costume. Mr. Bushman came out of the men's costume department and walked over and stood beside me. Without saying a word, he confidently, casually, put his hand on my right knee. With no more conscious thought than I had been aware of the day I told Helen Dunbar I was going to be famous, I heard my hand colliding with his face. We didn't exchange a word.

Mother announced early in 1915 that we would stop for a while in California on our way to Manila. Grandpa Klanowski, the skinflint, had recently died and left the bulk of his estate to Mother and her sister, so Mother told me that we could afford to take a proper vacation for once in our lives. I thought it was strange that she wasn't anxious to get to Manila as soon as possible, but I didn't question her. Instead, I said I would write and ask Wallace Beery if he knew where we could stay in Los Angeles when we arrived. Mother thought that was a good idea. In addition, Mr. Babile said he was sorry to see me leave Essanay and asked how long I would be staying in California and where. I said we would be the whole time in Los Angeles, but I didn't know how long that would be. In that case, he said, I should look up a man he knew there named Mr. Sennett, and he gave me a letter of introduction to him. "It might be useful to know someone who knows you've been in pictures," he said.

Just before we left Chicago, Mother took me to a famous singing teacher. "My daughter will never be able to study with you because we're leaving the city," she said. "But I'm prepared to pay you for an honest opinion. I want to know if her voice is good enough to invest in lessons."

The professor accompanied me and I sang "The Rosary." When I had finished, he beamed and spoke to my mother as if I were not there. "But yes, she must study. She has a very lovely voice, and she deserves the best teachers."

His words must have thrilled the musician in Mother and persuaded her to return to the original plan for my life. I would be a singer.

Mother had never understood the value of movies. She had never even been tempted to see *Quo Vadis?* I hadn't either, really, in spite of Aunt Inga's enthusiasm. I had played an extra in numerous pictures in the past six months and had had featured roles in four others, but I still found motion pictures crude and silly. I had never seen a single one of the films I had been in from beginning to end. They had even changed my name on the posters for one film; they had called me Gloria Mae because they thought it sounded much better than Gloria Swanson. Finally, motion pictures didn't have any sound, so they were hardly the proper place for a girl whose fortune was supposed to be in her singing voice.

When we boarded the train for California, we kept looking frantically for June. She had promised to see us off. Just as the train was pulling out, we spotted her emerging from the station onto the platform at full gallop, one arm gesturing pedestrians out of her way, the other clutching a big bouquet of flowers. She didn't manage to catch up with our car before she reached the end of the platform, but she certainly did have personality.

CHAPTER 4

Since I could remember, I had wanted to be grown-up, and for the past year, since I was fifteen, I had actually been paid by Essanay to play sophisticated thirty-year-old women because they felt I did it so convincingly. Suddenly, on the long train ride to California, I learned that in real life I was not sophisticated at all. Moreover, I did not even understand the two grown-ups I had spent my whole life with.

While I was writing a letter to Medora Grimes I asked Mother if she would please try to be specific about when we were sailing for Manila so I could tell my friend.

"We might not go to Manila," Mother said.

"What do you mean?"

"What I said. Glory, I've been putting this off for some time, but we have to have a talk. A serious one. Woman to woman. I don't know if I can go on living with your father."

She told me then the story of their unsuccessful marriage. Many things she told me I seemed to know before she said them. I knew, for instance, that Daddy drank, and could even remember hearing them argue about it, but I didn't know how much or how often, and I didn't know that he gambled, too, and ran up gambling debts. I also didn't know they had not been, in Mother's word, "close" for the last five years, or that the past year and more of separation had given rise on Mother's part to the idea of a permanent separation.

She made it very clear that she had loved Daddy once and that she expected me to go on loving him forever because he was in many ways a wonderful person. But the life he had given her had been so disappointing for so long that she didn't

46

love him anymore, and furthermore, she was afraid she might never be able to care for him again.

She viewed the trip to California as a test. She wanted to think things out calmly far away from Grandma Lew and Daddy's relatives and everyone else who was always too quick to advise her. If she decided, after all, that no other life was possible for her, we might both go to Manila. In his letters over the past year, Daddy had begged her, she said, to give him another chance. On the other hand, she had to feel free to say no if she decided not to try again. With her small inheritance, she didn't have to be dependent on Daddy or anyone else while she made up her mind.

When she finished, I was too shocked even to cry. "Don't you really love him?" I asked.

"Not just now, and I haven't for some time. I could change, but I doubt it. He's not an easy man to live with. And we have nothing in common any longer, Glory, except you."

Although my mother and I were nothing alike, I realized that I was her girl more than I had ever been my father's. She had made me stand out from other girls, had dressed me, had taught me to sing, had let me quit school. And now she was encouraging me to grow up, to discuss problems. Daddy had never even hinted at any problems the previous summer in New York. Much as I loved him, I saw that I hardly knew him at all.

"Your father's biggest problem," Mother explained, "is that he can't face problems."

Wallace Beery, tanned and handsome, was at the station to meet us. He was spiffily dressed and on his best behavior. He couldn't have been more charming, and I could see that Mother liked him from the start. He said he had driven down from Niles Canyon the night before and had found a little place for us to stay in which he hoped would be all right.

"How far is Niles Canyon from here?" I asked.

"An eight-hour drive, but it's beautiful country."

"Eight hours! I would never have written if I'd known it was that far away, Mr. Beery."

"Wally," he corrected me. "Wally to both of you. You got that? It was nothing. I have a brother living here, and besides, I use any excuse to get away from Niles. That's like the Klondike up there."

He had a new, open motorcar, with large carriage lamps on

the sides and a heavy leather belt over the hood, in which he
drove us around for a look at Los Angeles. There was not
much to see. The city seemed to be composed entirely of
factories, empty lots, gas stations, telephone wires, drug-
stores, open markets, and barns. Here and there cows ate
weeds beside rickety houses. Wally said most of the beautiful
homes were off the main drag or up in the hills. When we
started seeing signs that read FOR RENT: DOGS AND ACTORS NOT
WANTED, Wally laughed and said, "This is it. This is Hollywood. Look at some of these freaks. No wonder homeowners
won't put them up. They'll do anything to attract attention to
themselves and get into movies."

The men, women, children, and animals all looked absurd.
I had never seen such weird costumes—loud suits, ruffled
dresses, fur jackets, cowboy boots, and crazy hats. On every
finger and ear, it seemed, jewelry flashed in the afternoon
sun. "Fake, all of it," Wally said with affection. "They're
desperate. Everyone wants to get into pictures. They don't
realize it's all in the faces and the physiques. The stars don't
dress like gypsies. These birds won't either, once they get
jobs. My brother Noah is an actor here in Hollywood, and he
doesn't dress up like some crazy pirate. He loves the place.
When I finish this series of pictures I'm making in Niles, I'm
coming down here too. It's *the* place; no question. Noah and I
are looking for a house here so we can move our folks out
from Kansas City."

The apartment he'd found for us was on Cahuenga Boulevard, a tree-lined street right in Hollywood, in a two-story
house painted a hideous green. The apartment itself was fine,
two nice rooms on the second floor, with furniture that wasn't
too bad and a cute little balcony. Wally hauled in our bags
and waited while we scrubbed off the train dirt.

Later, in a restaurant, he kept us in hysterics all evening
with his stories about making films in Niles and with his
imitation of Broncho Billy. He said it was the boondocks up
there—no bathrooms, squeaky iron beds, bare light bulbs
instead of lamps. He couldn't wait to come down and get
started in Hollywood once his contract with Essanay ran out.
If people in Hollywood still felt he was too ugly to play
anything but villains in pictures, he would go back to New
York and work on the stage.

"Who says you're ugly?" I asked.

"Do you really want to know?" he said, and laughed as he
counted off every producer and director in Hollywood,

starting with D. W. Griffith and ending up with Mack Sennett.

"Do you know Mack Sennett?"

"I've met him long enough to hear him say no, and I do a wonderful impersonation of him. Why?"

I told him Mr. Babile at Essanay in Chicago had written me a letter to Mr. Sennett, but I hadn't really planned on going to see him because Mother and I didn't know when we'd be leaving for Manila.

He said he couldn't believe his ears. He was appalled that I didn't know that Keystone was *the* studio or that Mack Sennett was a genius. "You act as if you don't care anything at all about pictures."

"I don't."

"Addie," he said to my mother, "Babile is no fool." Then he said to me, "Look, Gloria, do yourself a favor. Take your little letter in your little purse and get out to Mack Sennett as fast as your little legs will carry you. You can always go to Manila."

I could see that this was a new Wallace Beery. He wasn't such a playboy anymore, or such a show-off. He had clearly learned his lesson. Maybe the scandal in Chicago had done him good in the end. He seemed serious and ambitious, and he looked marvelous with his California tan. I was being perfectly honest when I said I'd love to see him on his next trip down. And he was being as firm as a father when he said, "You go out and see Sennett, you hear?"

The following Monday I got on a streetcar and took the long ride to the Keystone studio in Edendale. Remembering what Wally had said about the desperate gypsies of Hollywood, I wore the most dignified, elegant outfit I owned, and I had spent a full hour on my hair and face. The building was a large, sprawling shed with slanting glass roofs, topped by a big printed sign that said MACK SENNETT STUDIOS. When I entered the tiny office, which stood beside the shed, it was absolutely mobbed with people trying to see producers. There was no place to sit or stand. I tried to explain to several people that I had a letter of introduction, but they looked at me as if I were crazy. I was on the verge of leaving when someone called out my name.

"Gloria Swanson, what are you doing in California?" The speaker was a pale, thin man, and I couldn't place him or think of his name until he laughed and started singing "As the World Rolls On" in a tiny falsetto voice. It was Frank Hayes from Key West, who after seven years still remembered my song, my face, and my name. He and Venice had moved out west for the climate and he was working at Keystone. I told him why Mother and I were in Los Angeles and what I'd done since I'd seen him in Florida. We exchanged addresses and I invited him over to Cahuenga Boulevard to see us.

"Hampton!" he called to a strange-looking man hurrying past. "This young lady has a letter to Mr. Sennett."

The other man sized me up and said, "She doesn't need a letter. What a crazy day." Then he said to me, "I'm Hampton Del Ruth. Come with me." He grabbed me by the hand and dragged me down a corridor to an office with Mr. Sennett's name on it. Mr. Sennett was not there. So Mr. Del Ruth dragged me outside to a back lot. "Wait right here," he said, "I see him." A few minutes later he came back with a man of about thirty in shirt sleeves and suspenders. "What about her?" he asked the man.

I smiled sweetly, but Mr. Sennett didn't say a word. He raised the brim of his hat an inch, chewed on his cigar, spat out the juice on the ground, and studied me as though I were a pony at a county fair. "The clothes are terrible," he said. Then he came up close and said, "And that make-up is a joke." I was absolutely furious and at the same time stung with embarrassment. As he walked away, he called back over his shoulder to Mr. Del Ruth, "Have her call on Thursday."

"You hear that?" Mr. Del Ruth said.

"I heard it," I said.

"So call Thursday."

"Thank you," I said icily.

When I got home I told Mother that the Hayeses were in California and that Frank would call us sometime soon. I also told her I had seen Mr. Sennett—I could hardly say I'd met him—and that he had been terribly rude.

"Well, then, that's that," she said, her bad faith in movie people firmly restored.

I decided not to call on Thursday. Instead Mother and I washed our hair and sat on the balcony to dry it.

On Friday morning a man in a chauffeur's uniform rang our bell. "Miss Swanson, please."

"I'm Miss Swanson."

"Mr. Sennett has sent his car for you."

I said there must be some mistake.

"Are you Gloria Swanson from Chicago?"

"Yes."

"Then there's no mistake. Hurry, please, they're waiting for you."

I was totally bewildered. No one had ever been ruder to me than Mack Sennett, but nobody had ever sent a car for me before, either. I took a look at myself in the mirror. My hair was a mess, but after what he'd said the other day, I thought, what difference did it make? My eyes didn't look too bad.

"I'm sure I'll be right back, Mother. Shall I invite the Hayeses to dinner if I see Frank?"

"Yes. How about Sunday?" she called.

The chauffeur drove me to a bungalow across the street from the Keystone offices. Before he could open the door for me, a man ran out to shake my hand and introduced himself as Charley Parrott. He took me inside, where a group of men began to clap and cheer as soon as they saw me. A cute young boy ran up to shake hands with me. He said he was Bobby Vernon. He was a little runt of a thing, just my size. He pulled me into the middle of the room and stood there with me while everyone stared at us and nodded. Then Bobby introduced me to the director, Clarence Badger. Everyone in the room was talking excitedly. Bobby was terribly nice. He explained to me how Mr. Sennett had signed him the week before to be the lead in a new light romantic comedy company. Once Bobby was set for it, everyone had started looking for the right girl. Because Bobby was so tiny, it had to be someone very short. Hundreds of girls had shown up who were either too tall or too old for Bobby. Then on Monday Mr. Sennett had told Mr. Badger he had found the perfect girl; there was no need to look any further. When I didn't show up on Thursday, Mr. Sennett had had a fit. He almost fired everyone in the office because no one had my address. No one even knew my name. There was such a commotion that Frank Hayes finally heard about it and told Mr. Sennett who I was: Gloria Swanson from Chicago. Then Mr. Sennett's chauffeur had had to drive Frank to his house for my address. It had been a day of hysterics, which was why they were all so pleased to see me.

I told Bobby Mr. Sennett had caused all the commotion himself by being so rude.

"He isn't rude. He's just shy," Bobby said. "Besides once he was sure what you would be like without a lot of make-up, what was there to say?"

"What was wrong with my make-up?"

"It made you look thirty, Mr. Sennett said. We're both supposed to look and act like lovable fifteen in this comedy. How old are you, really?"

"Sixteen."

"Well, act fifteen," Bobby Vernon said, "and so will I."

So that was it. At Essanay, with my hair up and smoking endless cigarettes, I'd been playing grown-up, well-dressed society ladies, and I had thought that that was what acting in pictures was all about. Now here was Mr. Sennett saying there were plenty of thirty-year-olds around to do that. He was demanding what for me was probably the hardest thing in the world: that I throw away the fancy clothes and wipe off the make-up and *act my age*. Bobby was the cute little boy next door, and Mr. Sennett had looked through all the eye liner and veiling and picked me to be his cute little girl. The earth had shifted under my feet again.

The Sennett system of making pictures, strange though it was after Essanay, was actually fun. For the first time, I enjoyed making movies. The California system was nothing but surprises. You never knew what the person next to you was going to do. Stunt men and gagmen and comics were all jabbering constantly and struggling to get their ideas accepted. As soon as someone thought of something he would jump to his feet and act it out. "Look," he'd say, "what if Bobby starts to dance close and Gloria backs off?" Then someone else would say, "Wait! What if *Gloria* starts to dance close and *Bobby* backs off?" Then, without fail, everyone would start roaring a different version, and the set would turn into a shouting match with the director as the referee. "Let's try it again So-and-so's way," he would say. Then Bobby would grab me and we'd act out the version the director had liked best.

I felt funny at first, being the only girl, but Bobby was a wonderful actor and treated me just as if we were going steady. He would ask me to dance and I would accept and we would do a few steps without any music. Then everyone would clap in unison and Bobby would spring a few ridiculous steps on me. I would begin to loosen up and follow him no matter how silly what he was doing was. Eventually I even forgot I was tongue-tied and suggested some ideas of my own. Mr. Badger said they were fine and left them in. When a gagman suggested something else, Mr. Badger said, "No, I like it Gloria's way." I was suddenly part of a family.

At Essanay we had spent most of our time changing clothes

and waiting in the basement until our turn came. Then the director would tell us exactly where to walk and what to do; only he ever saw the script and knew what the scene you were doing had to do with anything else. But at Mr. Sennett's we made up our own stories as we went along. We got to know each other and to know how everyone in the company would react in a given situation. After a few hours of trying out different ideas and settling on the ones we liked, we would pile in a car and drive off to the location. There the cameraman would watch our rehearsal and then, when the light was right, would shoot the scene.

I never had time to worry about make-up or costumes. Every time I tried to look at myself in the mirror, all the men would kid me and tell me I looked perfect just as I was. They didn't care at Keystone if every hair was in place or whether the lights would ruin my mascara. Rather, as soon as the sun came out, it was like a four-alarm fire to race to the location and shoot. Then, as soon as it clouded over, back we would race to the bungalow to work out more routines. It was a wonderful way to earn a living.

When the picture was finished, Mr. Sennett screened it and had Mr. Badger call us all together so that he could pronounce his verdict. Mack Sennett, everyone knew, was not an easy man to please and he never gushed, so we were all very nervous when he entered the room. He said he hadn't liked all of the picture, that in fact some of it would have to be done over, but—and he paused—that if audiences didn't find it fresh and funny, they were crazy. He complimented Clarence Badger and said all he mainly wanted to do was to guarantee our group that we would go right on making pictures for Keystone.

We were ecstatic. Mr. Badger took me aside and told me Mack Sennett had thought I was terrific—the perfect match for Bobby. The studio was preparing a contract for me, and Mr. Badger said I should let him know if it was not satisfactory. In the meantime, my salary would be $100 a week. I could hardly believe my huge ears. That was $86.75 more a week than Essanay had paid me to start. Maybe pictures weren't so bad, after all.

Away from the studio, there was no one to share my newfound enthusiasm with. Mother was impressed by the salary and said I could stay in movies if I really liked them, but I knew that for her pictures on a strip of film were no closer to the singing stage now than they had been in that stifling little movie house in San Juan. I couldn't be so stupid as not to see that what Mother was really encouraging me to do was to grow up and free her at least partially of the responsibility of having a child. If I was old enough to leave school and command a large salary, then I was old enough to stay home alone nights and give her a chance to have some life of her own.

Quickly and noticeably, she was becoming a different person in California. For the first time in years she was having fun, and it showed in her pretty, plump face. If I had to be at the studio all day every day, she didn't; and if I didn't have any time to meet new people outside the studio, she did. She was clearly meeting lots of new people through the Hayeses. She was receiving invitations and gadding about. Through Frank Hayes, she also found a new apartment, larger than the one we were in, so that she could entertain some of her new friends. She was making more clothes for herself now and fewer for me, and she went to several parties with someone she said was very nice whose name was Matthew Burns.

I knew what her next decision would be before she made it, or at least before she told me she'd made it. "Glory, your father and I are getting a divorce." Daddy was an impulsive person like me, but Mother was slow and methodical. She had obviously thought about this for a long time, and her mind was made up. Anyway, divorce was nothing new in her family, what with her mother having divorced Grandpa Klanowski to marry Grandpa Lew when Mother was just a girl. That, I thought, must be Mother's reason too.

"Are you going to marry someone else?" I asked her.

"Good heavens, it's much too soon to think about that. In California you get an interlocutory decree, which doesn't become final for a year."

I assumed, of course, that she must be thinking about it, and that the man must be Matthew Burns. She stammered and blushed whenever his name came up, and eventually I began to tease her about him. This seemed to make her terribly happy, as if I were giving her my blessing, and I so enjoyed seeing her have fun that I kidded her more and more as I grew more and more curious to see the person who was the cause of the change in her.

When at last I met Mr. Burns, I could hardly believe my eyes. He was a small man with ginger hair and a ginger mustache. He had a funny voice and smelled of cough drops. How could my mother, I wondered, who had been married for almost twenty years to a man as handsome and dapper and strong as Daddy, possibly care for a man like Mr. Burns? He and I sat and talked politely in the living room while Mother finished getting ready. My natural shyness probably concealed the fact that I could not think of a thing to say to him, mainly because inside my head, wheels were spinning over the topics of love and marriage and the reasons for attraction between men and women. I could see no reason in the world why my mother should blush at the mention of this man's name. I couldn't wait for them to leave on their date because I loved my mother and I didn't want her to read any of my confusion on my face.

Once they had left and I was alone, I decided that I could never accept Mr. Burns as a replacement for Daddy. I might accept him as Mother's new husband, but I knew I was too old to adjust to living with them in the event that they married. I was happy for my mother, because I sensed that she was happy, but I could see less and less place in her life for me.

There was, of course, no place at all for me in my father's military world. Now that I knew some of the truth about him, I even had trouble writing letters to him for fear I would slip and say something that might hurt him. I couldn't tell him I agreed or disagreed with the reasons for the divorce. I couldn't tell him that Mother was looking ten years younger and having the time of her life. I couldn't even tell him—much as I would have done anything to please him—my salary, for how could he possibly be anything but ashamed to hear that at sixteen I was probably making as much money as he was, for acting silly with Bobby Vernon? In the end I wound up writing him as few letters as possible, about nothing that mattered.

More and more, I found that the only person I could talk to about everything in my life that did matter was Wallace Beery.

When I wrote to say I had taken his advice and gone to Keystone and been hired practically on the spot, he wrote back that he would drive down the following weekend to celebrate. Mother said she had made other plans for the day, so Wally told me to get in the car and we would drive to the San Bernardino Mountains. It was a glorious afternoon. At Big Bear Lake he rented a boat and we went troll fishing. The last time I had been fishing was in Key West with Daddy. Wally was a wonderful teacher. While we floated on the lake I asked him a million questions about acting in movies and he told me how to deal with such and such an actor, how to play such and such a scene. On the way back we stopped for some supper at a little roadside tavern. They had a piano and I asked him if he played.

"What do you want to hear?" he asked.

"How about 'Whispering'?"

He played it and sang it, too. He had a marvelous voice. Like June Walker, he could play anything by ear. In between he told jokes, and within minutes half of the customers were crowded around him, asking him to sing this, play that. "Wait a minute. She has to be in on this, too," Wally said, pointing at me, so they made room for me beside him. He must have sung and played steadily for over an hour. I'd never seen an audience love a performer so much. Driving back to Los Angeles, I told him he was crazy to work in movies when he could sing like that. "Oh, really?" he said. "But you're in pictures, aren't you?"

When we got home, he walked me to the door, held both my hands for a minute, and then leaned over and kissed me on the forehead. "I got to start driving back to Niles tonight," he said, "but I'll come down again soon, O.K.?"

"O.K. Sure," I said. In a way I was disappointed that he didn't even try to put his arms around me. I wouldn't have minded because this was not at all the man I had been wary of in Chicago. This was one of the most lovable people in the world.

He drove to Los Angeles about once a month after that, and we always saw each other when he did. He was on his best behavior with me, and I felt comfortable and relaxed with him. Early in March he wrote to say he would pick me up at the studio after work on Saturday and take me to dinner. When his car pulled up, an actress named Teddy Sampson got out. "Thanks," she said with a flirtatious laugh as Wally waved and yelled, "Hey! Gloria!" He was wearing a sporty new jacket and was tanned as an Indian from driving all day in the sun.

He knew everyone. He joshed familiarly with Maude Wayne and threw his arm around Clarence Badger and told him what he would do to him if he didn't do right by his little girl, meaning me. Then he picked up Bobby by the seat of his pants and snapped his suspenders. Next he put his arm around me and began giving orders to everyone while he spat and held an imaginary cigar. We all laughed, because he had

Mack Sennett down to a tee. Wherever he went, he was the life of the party. Because of my stiffness and shyness, I often made people uncomfortable and I could tell it. But Wally put everyone at ease.

We stopped at the office for my paycheck, and when I realized that the new contract they wanted me to sign was also in the envelope, I asked Wally if he would look it over. He said sure, and immediately I felt confident that if he said it was all right, it was all right.

At the restaurant he looked over the contract and said it seemed fine. Then he asked me if I had missed him. I treated it as a joke, because everyone knew he had lots of girls. "Come on," I said, "if you hadn't found me at the studio, Teddy Sampson would be sitting where I am and I'd be at home reading my contract."

"You just happen to be dead wrong," he said. "I think about you all the time." He reached across the table and grabbed my hands. "Don't go to Manila with your mother, Gloria."

"Nobody's going to Manila, Wally," I said. "That's been off for months. My mother is getting a divorce." I told him the whole story, including Mr. Burns.

When I finished he said, "Then marry me."

I couldn't believe my ears. I had imagined getting all kinds of proposals from Wallace Beery, but never a serious proposal of marriage. He didn't ask if I had any other boyfriend. He didn't say he loved me or ask me if I loved him. He was probably afraid to. After all, he had to be almost twice my age. If he had asked and had pressed me for an answer, I would certainly have had to say no.

"Well, don't just look through me. Say something, Gloria."

"Let me think it over."

"Good! Fine! Just don't say no."

He told me in the car that he and Noah planned to move their parents to California the following month. It would be a simple matter to find a house big enough for two couples instead of one, and his mother loved cooking and housekeeping.

"Will you let me know next week?" he asked.

"Yes," I said and watched him drive off waving.

Could I ever love him? I asked myself. And then I asked myself the bigger question: What is love? Was it young, handsome Livingston Parmalee, Jr., of Staten Island kissing

me in the twilight? Surely I'd come a long way from believing
that. All I could think of was what Mother had said on the
train coming out from Chicago. She said she and Daddy had
nothing in common any longer. Wally and I, on the other
hand, had everything in common except age. If that was a real
basis for love, perhaps I loved him already.

When he pulled up in front of the house the next week, I
was waiting for him. I got into the car, and without speaking
we headed for Griffith Park. He could tell what my answer
would be before he stopped the car. He got out first and lifted
me down with a great big bear hug.

"It's yes?"

"Yes."

"When?"

"In two weeks. I'll be seventeen then. And, Wally? I've
decided I want to elope."

"Elope! Are you sure? You'll have to lie about your age if
we elope."

"I don't care. Oh, Wally, please."

"All right. Anything you say."

Everything was different now, the touch of his hands, the
feel of his body, the sound of his voice. I had no reason to be
uncomfortable with him because I knew what his intentions
were. He wanted to take care of me and help me in my career
and make me happy. What more could I ask? That night he'd
have to leave again, and as soon as he came back we'd elope.
Only for this one day in Griffith Park would we be engaged.

"How do you want to spend it?" Wally asked.

"Teach me to drive. You said you would."

"All right, let's go," he said, clapping his hands once.

First he helped me to memorize all the buttons. Then he
blindfolded me so I could find them in the dark. He explained
the pedals, the choke, and the ignition, and let me get the feel
of the wheel. Then he cranked up the car, the motor caught,
and I pushed my foot down. The car moved, and I started
steering it down the long dirt road. I'd never had such a thrill.
Nothing existed in the whole world but the power of that car.
The tiniest turn of the wheel and the whole thing responded. I
had the feeling I could go anywhere and nothing could stop
me.

Suddenly I realized Wally was not in the car. He had not
jumped in as he was supposed to. I could hear him running
behind me, shouting. My mind was a blank. I had forgotten
everything he'd told me. Finally my foot slipped off the pedal

and I knew I'd done the right thing by accident. I just hung on to the wheel until Wally, panting and laughing, caught up with me. He jumped in and pushed in the brake.

There was roaring in my ears. My hands were wet. I was more exhausted than he was. But I loved the feeling of all that power, frightening though it was. No wonder Wally was happy-go-lucky. He'd found the secret of how to escape. And now he was sharing it with me. I had lots more to learn before I could drive by myself, but I would always remember that first thrilling Sunday. It was almost as exciting as being engaged.

On the twenty-first Mother asked me if I had made any plans for my birthday or if I wanted her to. I said I didn't need anything and I was too old for a birthday cake. I told her I was expecting to hear from Wally. If he could get an extra day off, I might take one too. He wanted to show me Santa Barbara. I felt guilty telling her these half-truths, as I had felt guilty not telling Daddy I hoped to quit school when he saw me off at the train station in New York, but I wanted to make this decision all by myself.

I sent Wally a wire so that he would let me know what day to ask for. When I didn't hear the next day, I began to think I'd made the whole thing up. His answer came the following day: TAKE SATURDAY ARRIVING EARLY LOVE WALLY.

Mr. Badger said that of course I should take Saturday off if I wanted to; I deserved it. Besides, he said, we were about to introduce a dog into the comedy series, and Bobby could use a full day to get accustomed to the pup. It was all so easy, I thought. When I left the studio Friday night I wondered if anyone would miss me when one day I would leave for good to live happily ever after in New York with my husband, Wallace Beery, the famous Broadway entertainer.

I was awake at dawn, waiting for the sound of Wally's car. I had a small bag packed and had warned Mother that I'd be leaving before she was up. He arrived just after eight, and although he had been driving most of the night, he looked ready to explode with pleasure and excitement.

In those days the two-hour drive from Los Angeles to Santa Barbara was one long stretch of unspoiled beauty. Traveling thirty miles an hour in an open roadster on that clear spring morning, I felt I was either in paradise or heading there. We stopped several times beside the road to soak in the heavenly view of mountains sweeping in a straight line down to the Pacific. When we got to Santa Barbara I saw it was everything

Wally had promised—the perfect honeymoon retreat. Spanish-style houses and landscaped resort hotels spread out in a line parallel to the sandy beach.

The municipal building sat on an expansive green lawn, and its bright, echoing halls were cool in spite of the warm air outside. Wally was charm itself with the thin, spinsterish woman in the license bureau. She gave us a long form to fill out and a few instructions and then stood casually by tapping her pencil while we answered the questions and supplied the necessary information. When we had both signed the form, Wally took out his billfold.

"How much will that be?" he asked.

"Just one moment, please," the woman said; "I'll be right back." She picked up the form and went through a door at the rear of the office. A few minutes later she came back and asked me for proof of age.

"I wrote it down," I said. "I'm nineteen."

"Yes . . . well," the woman said, "you're also required to show a birth certificate or a baptismal certificate."

"But she didn't know that," Wally said. "And we've driven all the way from Los Angeles. You'll be closed tomorrow."

"I'm sorry," the woman said sweetly and turned to me. "If you don't have either of those certificates, you must have proof of parental consent."

Wally acted outraged and tried to argue, but the woman said that was the law. I knew I must be beet-red with humiliation and I couldn't wait to get away from the woman's calm, impassive face.

Once on the street, Wally slammed his fist on the car fender. "Son of a—"

"Wally, please!"

"—bitch! Why didn't you put down twenty-three? Nineteen sounds like a lie."

"It is a lie!" I snapped back.

"Look, I'm sorry, Gloria. It's not your fault. It's that old maid's in there."

"No, it isn't. It's ours. I should have told Mother in the first place. Now we'll have to tell her. Can we go and get her and bring her back?"

"There's not time. Wait a minute. Are you sure she's home?"

"Pretty sure."

"O.K., let me think. How about Pasadena?"

"What do you mean?"

"We don't want to spend our honeymoon in L.A., do we? And we can't get back to Santa Barbara. So-o-o-o," he said, stringing out the syllable until he got me laughing, "how about Pasadena?"

By then Wally had been driving almost steadily for ten hours, but he threw himself into the contest ahead with the extra energy we seem to get when we want something desperately and race the clock to get it, that energy that Mack Sennett understood so well and delighted American audiences with month after month. We tore back down that road to Los Angeles with the wind screaming past us and the sun in our eyes, scarcely noticing the magnificent scenery I had oohed and aahed over all the way up.

It was a little after one when we pulled up in front of the house.

"Do you want me to come in?" Wally asked.

"No. Let me do it."

"Well, hurry. No, wait," he said, as I started into the house. "Turn around."

"What *is* it, Wally?" I said, with the mock impatience mixed with laughter that girls affect with big strong men they trust.

"You're driving me crazy, that's all. Every time I look at you. Now hurry up."

The minute I saw my mother, I knew she would say yes. She herself was preoccupied with romance at the time, and I must have been a walking advertisement for it that afternoon, flushed with the wind and sun after four hours in the car and childishly animated in the expression of my feelings for Wally and the urgency of getting to the license bureau. She didn't have to ask me if I was sure, as mothers are supposed to do; our world was very tiny, so she could see I was sure. I only regretted I had not told her the truth from the start. In fact, during the time she called Wally in and hugged him and ran to the next room for her best hat, I kept wondering why I hadn't told her.

At half past two, with Mother and me both squinched into the right-hand barrel seat of the car, we set off on the last lap of my race into marriage. Every time Wally speeded up, Mother got nervous and pleaded with him to slow down. Every time he slowed down, I got impatient and pleaded with him to speed up. Mother clutched me close to her for fear I would fall out of the open car, and each time the wind picked up, I would clamp one hand on her head and one on my own to hold our wedding hats on. We laughed excitedly at the thought of the clock ticking away and simply entrusted Wally with getting us there in time.

Pasadena was not as pretty as Santa Barbara, but it was pretty, and everyone at the city hall there helped to race us on our way. With Mother in the company, there couldn't be any legal hitch. The judges, it turned out, were all gone for the day, but the man at the desk rattled off a list of ministers who lived nearby. We picked the nearest one and found him sitting down to supper with his wife. They postponed their meal, and he ushered us into his study. This was the first wedding I'd ever attended, but the words were so familiar they were like a song I'd been hearing all my life. When Wally put the ring on my finger, I remembered my first real ring, which Daddy had given me when I was seven. As a child I had turned the tiny pearl around into the palm of my hand and pretended I was married.

Mother kissed us both and burst into tears, at which point we all burst out laughing and Wally said it was time to celebrate a little. I knew that he must be exhausted from all the driving he had done that day, and furthermore, he had to get up early the next morning to drive the eight hours back to Niles Canyon, but he insisted that we owed Mother a wonderful dinner. Mother said no, we should have a few hours to ourselves. She asked us instead to drive her to the station so that she could go back to Los Angeles. After half an hour of trying to persuade her to stay and have dinner with us, we finally gave in and drove her to the little station in Pasadena, only to find that the last train to Los Angeles had departed. So we drove frantically around the fancy streets until we found a hotel that suited us, and there we booked two honeymoon rooms instead of one, side by side. Seated in the dining room an hour later, Wally said that Broncho Billy would not believe that he had spent his wedding night with two women in adjoining rooms. Mother and I shrieked with laughter, while Wally drank most of the bottle of fancy wine we had got to celebrate. We all decided at once it was getting late. Signing the bill, Wally leaned over to me and whispered, "You're driving me crazy."

Mother kissed us both good night and went upstairs. I told Wally to give me fifteen minutes to get ready, and he kissed me and said all right, he would have one quick drink in the bar.

I was brushing my hair when he came into the room. He

gave me a look that made me turn away, but he didn't say anything. Then he turned out the light and in the darkness pulled me to him. I gave a coquettish little command to stop that I thought would make him laugh. Still he said nothing. He turned me and pushed me backward until I fell on the bed. He fell beside me, and there was nothing romantic about the way he began to repeat that I was driving him crazy. He was raking his hands over me and pulling at my nightie until I heard it rip. I pleaded with him to stop, to wait, to turn on the light. His beard was scraping my skin and his breath smelled. He kept repeating obscene things and making advances with his hand and tongue while he turned his body this way and that and awkwardly undid his buttons and squirmed out of his clothes. Then he forced my body into position and began hurting me, hurting me terribly. I couldn't stand it. I begged him to stop, to listen to me, and finally, when I couldn't stand it any longer, I screamed. He told me to be quiet, not to wake the whole hotel, and he said it in a voice of quiet, filthy conspiracy. The pain became so great that I thought I must be dying. I couldn't move for the pain. When he finally rolled away, I could feel blood everywhere.

I lay there absolutely terrified and repulsed until I heard him snoring. I turned on a light and gasped at all the blood. I crawled to the bathroom, afraid to look at myself for fear my insides were dropping out. First I wrapped myself in cold towels, and when that didn't stop the pain, I tried hot towels. Most of the night I sat in a state of bewilderment and regret. I was a silly, stupid minor, I thought; underage, just the kind he liked, I thought; and I hated him. I also hated everyone— Mother, Mrs. Grimes, Livingston Parmalee, the minister, everyone—who had ever led me to think for a minute that love was moonlight and ballads. I had spent a whole day racing around California, even lying, to get a marriage license as if it were a ticket to heaven, and I had only managed to be brutalized in pitch-blackness by a man who whispered filth in my ear while he ripped me almost in two. I finally walked back to the bed as dawn was breaking and lay down. Even then, hours later, the pain was excruciating. Slowly I covered myself with a blanket and turned my back to the man who had just raped me.

He woke me up with a little kiss and said he loved me as sweetly as if it were still the day before. Then he shaved and dressed and came over to kiss me again while I pretended the whole time to be half asleep. Only when I heard him go out and got up and locked the door after him could I close my eyes and rest.

Mother and I sat on the train back to Los Angeles in an unspoken pact of silence. It was Sunday, and the two of us must have appeared as if we were meditating or saying our prayers. What was there to say? It was too late for me to ask her anything. It was too soon for her to offer me advice. She could hardly welcome me to the world of married women after her confession a year before to me on the train from Chicago that she had found only disillusionment there herself. Moreover, she was dreaming every day now, I knew, about reentering that world under happier circumstances, so I could hardly utter just then the only word that was on my mind: *divorce*. Curiously, the only thing I was dying to ask her was whether she had heard me scream during the night, but I knew I could not be so cruel. We sat as if we were the two most serene creatures on the earth that day, quietly looking out of the window. I chose not to speak, I guess, because I suddenly realized then and there that although my mother and I were looking out of the same window, we were not seeing the same things on the other side, and we never would.

"Where will you live?" she asked sweetly and matter-of-factly as we pulled into Los Angeles.

"With you until Wally and Noah find their parents and us a house," I said. "O.K.?"

"Fine," my mother said.

CHAPTER 5

I was now a member of the great conspiracy of silence. I had joined it the moment I stifled my screams after Wally said to be quiet or I would wake up the whole hotel. I started paying in dues during the first weeks of my marriage by talking with my mother about anything except how unhappy I was. I recognized how many other members belonged as I sadly began to study the faces of women around me at work, in stores, on the street. And I realized to my dismay that no one could warn off Medora Grimes or Beena Fields or Gloria Swanson or any of the other starry-eyed girls who couldn't wait to be initiated. The world of 1916 was a man's world, in America as well as in Europe, where by now almost all of the men were in uniform. In America it was business as usual, which I now understood to mean business run entirely by men.

Wally drove down from Niles on weekends, and I submitted reluctantly, and as infrequently as possible, to his demands. Although my mother and her mother before her had divorced their husbands, I knew they would have plugged up their ears if I had suggested a divorce after one night of marriage. They would have patted my hand and said I hadn't tried. So for the next month I tried, but though I might teach myself to submit to Wally for brief periods, I could never bring myself to trust him again.

Between his visits I began to throw myself into work at the studio. If I had once seen Wally as my means of escape from a life in the movies, movies now became my means of escape from Wally. I tried harder every day, and I could feel myself becoming better. In the story sessions I was still shy, and I was never very good in rehearsals. But once the cameras were grinding, I found I could let myself go. I learned how to turn on switches in myself and respond fully at the precise moment. Once I started to see how much the quality of my acting depended on the director and technicians, I became fascinated by all the mechanics of lenses and cameras and the new technical devices that cropped up every day. The motion picture business was booming, and the whole process of technology at the service of the actor and vice versa intrigued me. If I was going to be in movies, I decided, I was going to be good in movies. I studied my craft minutely, and from then on I grew a little in each of the short romantic comedies Bobby Vernon and I made together.

I did not tell Mr. Sennett or Clarence Badger or Charley Parrott or even Bobby that I was married. It wasn't that I thought my awful mistake would go away if I remained silent about it. It was just that at the moment I was their darling golden girl, and I wanted to stay that way, at least until I had adjusted to my new existence. I was so mortified at the thought of what I had done with my life, which for the first time I was beginning to see as one with a promising future, that I could not bring myself to tell them for fear of what the expression on their faces would be. I didn't lie; after Santa Barbara I hoped I was through lying forever. I just postponed telling the truth because the truth shamed and saddened me.

Wally told them. One night in April several weeks after my wedding, Clarence Badger and I were the last people to finish up on the lot, along with a few of the technicians. It was the middle of the week, so the last person I expected to see was Wally. He pulled up in his car, jumped out, and ran over and kissed me loudly and jubilantly. "Hi, Clarence," he said to Mr. Badger. Then he put his arms around me and lifted me off the ground and spun around several times. I could tell he was putting on a show—Wally Beery never stopped putting on a show—but I could also see that he was truly happy.

"What do you think?" he said. "I start at Sennett-Keystone on Monday! Mack Sennett knows about us, and he says we might even make some pictures together. Isn't that great, sweetheart? Hey, I'm not spilling secrets, am I? Clarence knows about us, doesn't he?"

"No," I said. Then I heard myself go directly into a performance I must have been rehearsing subconsciously since Pasadena. "We've been so busy I haven't got around to it. Mr. Badger? Wally and I were married on my birthday."

"I don't believe it! You're too young to get married. Both of you," he added, laughing. "Gloria, darling, best wishes," he said, taking me in his arms and kissing me warmly on both cheeks. "You too, Wally. Well! Can I help you celebrate?"

"How about a rain check, Clarence?" Wally said. "Gloria's been staying at her mother's until now, but I have a little surprise for her. My brother and I have been getting a house ready for my folks and Gloria and me. The folks got here from Kansas City a few days ago, and I'm anxious to have Gloria meet them."

Clarence Badger must have been as bewildered by this strange state of affairs as I was, but he said, "How nice! Where is it?"

"Alvarado Street. You'll have to come over soon."

Then he pulled me into the car and we drove off.

"Is it true that your parents are here?" I asked.

"What do you mean, is it true? Of course it's true."

"And you told Mack Sennett about us?"

"Yes, of course I did."

"When?"

"Two weeks ago."

"Wally, we have to have a talk. This whole marriage was a mistake, I think."

"Now, Gloria, I want you to listen to me." He parked the car and spoke calmly and tenderly for about fifteen minutes. We were married, he said, because we both had wanted to be married. He hadn't shoved me. I had begged to elope. Lots of girls were frightened and uncertain after the wedding night; sometimes the adjustment took weeks to make. I was not being fair. What would my mother say if she could hear me, after I had dragged her to Pasadena with us? What would Clarence Badger say after what I had just told him on the lot? He said we couldn't talk about separating until we had seriously tried living together. I simply had to give him a chance, he said, to prove he loved me.

He was right, of course. Although I didn't believe him, everything he said was true. I had willfully rushed into marriage with someone I barely knew, and now I was stuck. For all I knew at seventeen, maybe all marriages were disappointing or worse. In any case, I was far too unsure of myself to take any kind of stubborn stand against him.

"Will you?" he coaxed, teasing, beseeching, turning on every ounce of his charm.

"All right," I said.

"That's my girl," he said and gave me a big kiss and a hug. "We're going to have a great life together. You just have to trust me."

Once I moved into Wally's world, it took me no time at all to understand who this man I had married was. Under all the joking and clowning and backslapping and flirting, he was a desperate gypsy, not very different from the ones on the streets of Hollywood he kidded about. At thirty he was a bachelor who had never quite succeeded anywhere at anything. Everybody knew him because he was such a show-off and liked him because he was wild and fun to have around, but when all was said and done they always wound up casting him lately in small parts, usually as the villain. He lived from one paycheck to the next, spending money foolishly when he had it on cars, fancy clothes, and cute girls, borrowing or making deals when he didn't have it. He was like a child. If he did something wrong, he would scramble awkwardly, frantically, like a St. Bernard pup on a slippery floor, to make up for it. But if he saw something he wanted, he would grab it and run, without ever considering how he would pay for it or take care of it.

The house on Alvarado Street was not a two-family house at all. It was a dinky little place in which we had one room on the first floor, a room that was hardly large enough to hold all of Wally's things, let alone mine. Wally's solution was to kick half of his things out of sight—under the bed, out in the hall—in order to make room for my things, but I still had to leave most of my clothes in Mother's apartment. Wally's parents were past middle age. They paid almost no attention to me and were as silent as Wally was talkative. They sat for hours in the kitchen, especially, it seemed, whenever I was in the house. The meals we ate together were unendurable, and my mother-in-law's cooking often consisted of things I particularly disliked, boiled cabbage, for instance. We were a sorry combination of people, and I was happy to spend as much time away from the house as possible.

Clarence Badger cast us both in a two-reeler called *A Dash of Courage* right after Wally started at Keystone. It amounted to only a few days' shooting, but Wally poured himself into it and impressed everybody favorably. Mr. Badger said another picture was coming up soon which would feature Keystone Teddy, the big brown dog we had incorporated into the company just before Wally and I eloped, and that he planned to use both of us in it. In the meantime, however, we had roles in different pictures, and I preferred that. I didn't want Wally to talk us up as some sort of inseparable team.

When I went to collect my paycheck that week, the girl in the office told me Wally had picked it up for me earlier in the day. That infuriated me because I had been at the studio longer than he had and knew I made more than he did. I expected that we would share what we made, but I resented having him collect my money without asking me. I walked back to Alvarado Street and found him in our room waiting for me. I asked him where my salary check was, and he said he had had to use some of it to catch up a back payment on the car. If he hadn't, we'd have lost it.

"You mean you don't own the car?"

"On an actor's wages? No actor can afford to own anything outright, Gloria, unless he's Bushman or Chaplin. People won't even rent actors apartments in Hollywood if they know they're actors. The only reason I got the car in the first place was because in Niles I worked part-time as the studio manager so I could be in the electricians' union. My card says electrician, not actor. Look, sweetheart, I'll pay you back."

"Wally—"

"In fact, I'll start right now. Here."

He reached for a hatbox on the floor behind him and handed it to me. He was beaming. Inside was a stunning hat, dark-brown felt, the only gift Wally had ever bought me, and I was touched even though I knew he had gotten it with part of my salary to keep me from being angry about his having spent the rest.

"So now it's your car too, right? Come on, let's go out for dinner. I've still got a few bucks left."

The St. Bernard was scrambling on the slippery floor, but at such times he could usually make people smile and forgive him.

Sometimes he let me drive when he was in the car, and each time he did I felt the old power urge I had felt the day we became engaged in Griffith Park. Driving a car was exciting for me the way riding horseback had been when I was twelve in San Juan. One morning when I was driving to work I found myself answering some command from deep inside me and started putting on speed until I had Wally screaming in the seat beside me. I tore past the Keystone gates and almost missed the turn into our lot across the street. I roared up to the bungalow, jumped on the brake, and stopped on a dime.

When the dust settled, half a dozen people ran out of the building. They couldn't believe it was Baby Gloria behind the wheel. They hadn't had such a shock since they first saw me smoke a cigarette. As soon as Charley Parrott said, "What a great gag that would be to start off a picture," they were all off and running. Within a week they had rented a racing car and hired a stunt man named LeRoy to give me lessons. They also had a rough script for the picture and a title: *The Danger Girl*.

I turned out to be a natural. I couldn't wait for LeRoy to pick me up in the morning. Each day he set up a new obstacle course, and I quickly learned to wheel around in tight circles, go into instant reverse, and take bumps and curves. He told me I had good reflexes and a good eye for measuring distances. I also had plenty of confidence and a fair amount of courage.

My costume for the car sequence was a man's evening dress suit with a top hat and white vest, exactly like Bobby's. In order to be a racing driver, the girl I was playing had to impersonate a playboy. Everyone laughed at rehearsals when I put on the costume and started to build my character—a bit of Daddy here, a bit of Wally there, a gesture from Hampton Del Ruth, a silly thing I'd noticed Francis X. Bushman do with his hands. By the last rehearsal I had thrown all the bits away and become my own man. I had always been a good mimic, but now I was a step beyond mimicry. I was getting at least a sniff of what it must be like to be a man.

We filmed the car sequences in the garden behind the Beverly Hills Hotel, a quiet, secluded hotel a long way out of town, frequented mostly by old, wealthy clients. It had plenty of curved cement driveways and just the right look for the picture. The sun was not quite down when we finished, so we walked into the hotel in our costumes. Elderly couples with their timid nieces stared at us as if we were giant goldfish in a bowl.

LeRoy dared me to give them a show, so I put on the top hat, picked up the cane, lit a cigarette, and strolled away from my friends toward the area where the thickest carpets were. Glancing ever so discreetly to the left and right, I could tell that I was passing, that I had entered, as if on tiptoe, the world of men.

I had noticed a beautiful house across the street from the hotel earlier in the day, and I could see it again now through an open doorway from where I was standing. "Excuse me, please," I said to a fashionably dressed matron of about sixty, "but do you have any idea who lives in that house?"

"You must be from out of town, young man," she said. "That's the house King Gillette built for his two sisters. Isn't it marvelous?"

"Yes, it certainly is," I said, stringing her along because I knew that from a distance LeRoy and Bobby and the others must be enjoying this. "Any idea what it's worth?"

"Plenty. Why?"

"Because I intend to buy it."

"You *what?*"

"You heard me," I said and winked at her.

By the way she swished away, I could tell I had fooled her. For a minute, in fact, I had almost fooled myself, into feeling what it was like to be a man, admiring another man who had become a millionaire by inventing the safety razor, which millions of men in America used at least once a day. Why, oh why, I thought, coming back to myself, did I decide to be a girl?

By the time we finished shooting *The Danger Girl,* I was pretty sure I was pregnant. Ever since I had pushed toy prams and claimed I was Happy Hooligan's wife, I had dreamed of having babies—lots of them; and in spite of my doubts about Wally and my misgivings about our marriage, I was thrilled. The greatest compensation a woman could have for not being a man was being able to have babies. Perhaps if I had to stop work for a while and Wally had to assume full responsibility for me and a baby, it would make all the difference in our life together.

I waited a few more days to be certain. Then one evening early in May I left the studio planning to sit down with Wally and talk about the future. For one thing, I couldn't go on making action films like *The Danger Girl* for long if I was going to have a baby. For another, it was time to find a place of our own.

Wally was late getting home and obviously had something

on his mind that was bothering him, so I decided to wait until we were alone that night to talk. He sat in the living room and read the newspaper until it was time to eat, and at the table during supper he and his parents outdid each other in being silent. He avoided any conversation with me, and after the meal he said he had to go out and see a friend. I went to bed and fell asleep before he returned.

The next morning he was silent and morose again. He dropped me at the lot and said he had to go and pick up something in town. I said I'd see him at the house that night, that I had something to tell him, but before I could say any more he had driven off.

Studio gossips and tactful friends work at approximately the same rate of speed in the movie business. Within an hour I had had several of both quietly inform me that Wally had been fired the previous afternoon. No one seemed sure why, but they all knew it was Mack Sennett himself who had done the firing, and that Sennett had been furious when he called Wally in. Judging from my informants' rolling eyes, and knowing Wally, I assumed that probably meant girls, liquor, or borrowed money, or a combination of the three, and one month earlier I would certainly have used the situation to get rid of Wally myself, but no longer. Instead, I threw myself into saving the father of my baby.

I went straight to Clarence Badger and asked him if he knew why Mr. Sennett had fired Wally. He said he didn't. All he knew was that Wally had phoned Universal and several other studios the previous day asking for work, but that was *after* Sennett had fired him; it wasn't the *reason* Sennett had fired him.

"He's ashamed," I said.

I walked across the street to the main office after lunch and told Lola, Mr. Sennett's secretary, that I had to see him. She said a few words into her phone and sent me right in. Mr. Sennett stood up and smiled, two things he rarely did for anyone, so I decided to go straight to the point.

"I understand you have discharged Wallace Beery," I said. "Is that correct?"

He nodded and said, "I'm sorry, Gloria. I had to."

"Mr. Sennett, if you can't give him his position back," I said, "I'll have to leave too."

Mack Sennett looked startled for a minute, as if he had just seen me eat a nail or grow six inches. He stared at me long and hard the way he had stared at me the first day I met him, as if I were a pony at a county fair. He took his time before he smiled again.

"All right, Gloria, if it'll make you happy. I'll send Beery a wire right now."

"Thank you, Mr. Sennett. Thank you," I said and turned and walked out the door.

I couldn't go back to work. I was too pleased with myself and excited. I had put my career on the line in front of Mack Sennett and had saved my husband and my baby. That was enough work for one day. It was a beautiful afternoon and I felt like walking. I cut through the clover field next to the studio and headed for the main road. When I was about a hundred feet from the road, I saw Wally drive past in the roadster, with a girl who looked like me in the seat beside him. By the time I got my bearings, the car was already lost in a cloud of dust, but the image of it was stamped on my brain. I hadn't been seeing things. There had been a girl beside him in the front seat, and she had . . . yes . . . *been wearing my hat,* the brown hat Wally had bought me with my paycheck. I slowly reached up and took off the hat I was wearing. Then I had the second half of the revelation: *I was wearing the same hat.*

Rage and sadness struggled for supremacy while I began to cry. What could it mean? Was it a coincidence? Had the other girl bought the same hat? Was that what had made him notice her? Or had he bought two, so that people we knew would think he was out with me if they saw him? That he was a joker, a gypsy, and a womanizer I knew, but was he also a cad, an operator, a monster? Was he trying to protect me at the studio while he fooled around? Was he so depressed about being in debt or about being fired that he had to bolster himself by having a woman on each of the Hollywood Hills—all dressed alike? Or was he just stupid? Had Mack Sennett seen him with a girl in my hat or heard about it and fired him because of it?

The more questions I asked, I realized, the more I wished to remain ignorant of the truth. It all came down to one thing; I had a baby inside me and I cared about it. He had put that baby there, which was the reason I had just risked everything to have Mack Sennett spare him. Therefore, I would lay down the law to Mr. Wallace Beery once and for all that night, and if he was willing to turn over a new leaf, fine. If not, fine too.

It was late again when he showed up at the house. He

pulled me sweetly to our room and held me tightly against him. I had never known him to be so loving. He told me everything was going to be different. He was glad the whole mess had happened, because he had learned his lesson. Mr. Sennett had sent him a telegram and he had gone to see him and they had talked man to man, pulling no punches, for over an hour. Mr. Sennett had told him how I had gone to bat for him. Nobody had ever gone to bat for him like that before. He would never forget it. He was ready to do things my way. He was going to straighten out. Mr. Sennett had told him he had big plans for me, and that the two of us would get a chance to work together again. He'd told Sennett he had an idea he wanted to kick around with Clarence Badger. If it went through, he would soon be making a big salary even for Hollywood.

"Do you know that?" he said, finishing as he often did with a great big optimistic question.

"You're sure?" I asked with firmness. I had the hat sitting conspicuously on the bureau, a sort of silent witness for the prosecution, and I had planned to confront him with it. If he saw it, he didn't register anything, and when he had finished speaking about Sennett and Clarence Badger and his big plans I thought, Oh well, what's the use in having a fight? He was where I had hoped to bring him with scenes and threats. Why not tell myself I had won the victory without having to fight the battle, and let it go at that?

"I'm sure. I'll never let you down again," he promised, and I really believed he meant it. We could fight another day. In the meantime, Wally was Wally, and perhaps I had no right to ask pears of the elm.

"Because I'm going to have a baby, Wally," I said.

He stopped for a second, perplexed, then said, "You *are?* Wonderful!"

"I was only certain a few days ago."

"That's wonderful," he repeated. "How do you feel?"

"Not too good in the morning. Otherwise fine."

"Come on. Let's go out and have dinner and celebrate," he said. In the restaurant he persuaded me it would be good for me to go on working as long as I felt all right or until I showed.

Four days later I awoke before daylight. I had severe cramps and I felt nauseated. Wally was sound asleep, so I moved quietly in the still-dark room. I tried going to the bathroom, and when that didn't help, I tried sitting up and walking around. Nothing helped much. As soon as it got light, I shook Wally awake and told him I had terrible pains. He dressed and said he would go and try to find a doctor or a druggist. I heard him whispering in the hall with his mother and then I heard him close the front door. I waited weak and aching from the time I heard the car start until I heard it return and screech to a stop outside.

Wally came into the room and put a bottle of medicine on the table beside the bed. He said he had been lucky to find a drugstore nearby that opened early. If this stuff didn't make me feel better in a couple of hours, he would get a doctor to come and see me. Then he went and got some water from the kitchen.

"How many shall I take?"

"Four or five capsules, the druggist said. Take five."

I saw Wally's mother standing in the doorway watching me take the medicine. Then she disappeared. I began to feel very sick after that. My stomach ached and I started gagging. The pain was awful. All of a sudden I felt too weak to stand up, and I could feel myself start to topple.

When I came to, everything smelled different. A nurse was wiping my forehead and wrists and telling me I was doing fine. "You're strong as an ox," she said, "just like your husband. He said he'll pick you up sometime after six."

I tried to ask her where I was, but the words came out wrong. My voice sounded funny. I could move, but I was weak all over. I had never been in a hospital in my life. I wanted to know what time it was. The nurse was trying to be nice but she wasn't answering any of my questions. She was trying to cheer me up. I wanted to know where my clothes were. I was crying but I couldn't explain why. She handed me a handkerchief.

"There's nothing to be down in the mouth about, honey," she said. "You're young. You're pretty. You've got all the time in the world to have another baby."

Oh, no, oh, no, I thought sobbing. Wally brought me here. He stood right there and told me to take that poison, and when I was unconscious he brought me here so they could finish the job.

I told the nurse I didn't want to see any visitors, so she put a sign on the door: DO NOT DISTURB. I asked her when I could leave, and she said my husband had said he would come for me. I asked if I could leave earlier, and she said of course, whenever I felt strong enough. After I'd cried for an hour, I tried walking around. It was no more painful than lying down. About two-thirty I asked the nurse to bring me my clothes. I dressed myself and said I was ready to leave.

"So soon? Are you sure?" the nurse asked.

"Yes!" I said.

She brought me a paper to sign before they could release me. I didn't read it. I just signed "Mrs. W. Beery" and realized I had never written it that way before. I never would again either, unless it was on a request for divorce.

Outside, the sun was still shining. I had to change trolleys twice to get to Alvarado Street. Wally's car was gone. When I opened the door, his mother looked at me silently from the kitchen. I was exhausted, but I was afraid that if I lay down for even a minute, I wouldn't be able to get up. As I opened my suitcase on the bed and started to throw things in it, I saw that the medicine bottle was still there. I screwed on the top and looked at the label. The address of the druggist on it couldn't be far away. I put it in my purse. I filled up the suitcase and closed it, only to find I was too weak to carry it, so I left it. I walked out the door without a word and headed for the drugstore. It was quite close by, but I was so weak that it seemed miles before I got there.

The place was empty. An overhead bell rang when I opened the door. A tall man in a white coat came out from behind a glass counter and asked if he could help me. I took the bottle out of my purse and put it on the counter. He picked it up and read the label but he didn't say anything.

"I'd like a refill of this, please."

He looked sad and embarrassed. "Do you know what this is?"

"A friend of mine told me it's very good for indigestion and stomach pains and morning sickness."

He looked me straight in the eye. "Anyone who told you that couldn't be much of a friend, miss, if you'll excuse my saying so."

I was trembling and fighting back tears when I asked, "What do you recommend?"

"Well," he said, "what I usually recommend when folks come in here and ask for this stuff is that they think it over. If I were you, I wouldn't take a chance on killing myself. I'd just go ahead and have the baby."

"Thanks. I *will* think about it," I said. I turned to leave and got as far as the soda fountain before I had to sit down. He asked if I was all right. "Yes," I said, "I'm fine."

I walked outside, got on a trolley, and went to my mother's apartment.

I was only seventeen and my whole marriage had lasted just under two months.

When I went back to the studio on Monday, Clarence Badger proudly told me the next picture for Bobby and me would be one he'd been planning since Wally started at Keystone, *Teddy at the Throttle*. He said it had a juicy villain's part for Wally and the best role so far for Keystone Teddy, our featured dog. Obviously Mr. Badger thought I'd be delighted. He said Wally had been thrilled when he told him.

I usually made a point of not talking about my private life with people at the studio. I enjoyed working with them, but I never socialized with them after studio hours. In this case, however, I simply had to be honest with Clarence Badger, at least to the extent of saying that Wally and I were no longer living together.

"I'm glad" was all he said. "Shall we shelve *Teddy at the Throttle* for now and come back to it? Or get another villain?"

I could hear the disappointment in his voice. "You think it's good, don't you?" I asked.

"I think it could be the best film we've all done together."

"Then let's do it," I said.

I avoided Wally as much as possible during the shooting, which annoyed him, because he had been dying to set us up as a married team at Keystone and here I was, ignoring him, pricking his balloon, in front of the whole company. I couldn't help it. I gave him professional courtesy, but that was all. His jokes no longer made me laugh. His terrible temper no longer frightened me.

At the end of the picture the villain ties the sweet young heroine to the railroad tracks, but before the train can run over her, her boyfriend's marvelous dog, Teddy, alerts the engineer and saves the day. Mr. Badger said we would shoot the train scenes on location in San Bernardino.

For these scenes I wore a flimsy white dress. Mr. Badger said I should step out of a small tent the crew had set up beside the tracks and look from side to side. Then Wally would grab me and carry me struggling to the tracks, where he would tie me up. We rehearsed the scene as little as possible because Clarence Badger could see I had a real aversion to having Wally touch me. This made Wally furious, of course, and although he held his anger back, I could feel a tremendous nervous tension building up between us.

The day we filmed the final scenes, I stepped out of the tent and Wally, in full villain's make-up, let out a roar and grabbed me, but much too hard, it seemed. I panicked and he got carried away. It was extraordinary. He leered at me, I started hammering on his chest, and he raced with me to the tracks. He threw me down and tied me to the tracks with a length of chain. The more I pounded him with my fists, the more he laughed. Then he tied my hands together, much too tightly. I tried to kick him but I couldn't move my legs. The chain was cutting me. Suddenly Mr. Badger yelled, "Cut! That's it! Wonderful!" He came over himself to untie my hands, and as he did so, he could see the red marks on my wrists and feel me shaking like a leaf.

"Are you all right?" he asked in a worried voice.

"Of course. I panicked because I couldn't see the camera, that's all."

He knew that wasn't the reason, but he said, "Fine. Well! That's it for you today." Then he shouted to the crew to get the stunt man into the white dress for the cowcatcher shot.

The heroine was supposed to dig enough dirt away to make a hole and huddle in it just before the cowcatcher passed over her. By then Teddy would have stopped the train, just in time. The idea of being in a hole under a huge, hissing train engine had frightened me up to then, so we had always planned to use a stunt man for the shot.

I heard men call down the line to find the stunt man, and I watched two assistants run and motion to the engineer to get ready. As I stood beside the track and listened to Clarence Badger instruct the cameraman and the technicians, all the actors and extras moved in to watch the filming of the last sequence. They stood in a large circle around the area of the tracks where I had been tied and where the hole was. Then the stunt man ran up and entered the circle. He was wiry and muscular and looked a trifle absurd in a white scarf and dress just like the ones I was wearing. He came over and stood by me, and when one of the men noticed us standing side by side, he started to laugh. Then all of the men forming the ring around us started to laugh, Wallace Beery, as usual, louder than all the rest.

"Ready?" Clarence Badger called through his megaphone.

"Wait a minute," I yelled. "Let me try it."

Clarence tried to dissuade me, but I insisted. They tied me up on the track again, but this time the chain was loose so that I could slide easily into the hole. All of the men in the circle stood transfixed.

I asked the cameraman to get right up close so that I could hear the camera grinding and to be sure to start shooting before they moved the train. If a stunt man can do it, I told myself, I can do it.

On the signal I heard the camera start to grind. Then I heard the train whistle and the terrifying rumble of the engine as it began to move down the track. I slipped easily out of the chain and slid into the hole. Moments later the sky over me was blacked out, and then I heard the screech of engine wheels stopping. When they got me out of the hole and I stood up in my little fluttering white dress, all the men applauded. Clarence Badger rushed over and kissed me. I felt wonderful.

I knew that Wally must be looking at me, but I didn't look back. I had just said good-bye to him forever.

Because everyone raved about what a great success *Teddy at the Throttle* was, I was completely mystified when Mack Sennett up and sold the Keystone name to the Triangle Company in Culver City. Talk flew around the studio. People said Sennett was in financial difficulties, but for the life of me I couldn't understand how you could make a product that everyone loved and paid money to see, and that could be used over and over again, and lose money on it. The world of business was simply beyond my comprehension.

Bobby and the whole light-comedy company were sold, along with the name Keystone. I was the only company member Mr. Sennett kept, and soon articles started to appear in the newspapers saying that I was slated to be a Sennett star. I knew what that meant. It meant a very big increase in salary, but it also meant that instead of making sweet, homespun comedies with Bobby Vernon and Charley Parrott, I would be playing a dumb little cutie serving as a foil to the broadest slapstick comedians in the world, Sennett's stock-in-trade, men like Chester Conklin and Mack Swain. The female stars who made such pictures, like Mable Normand and Teddy Sampson, spent all of their time having their skirts lifted and dodging flying bricks.

I tried to see Mr. Sennett and register my doubts about

such stardom, but he was in New York on business. His assistants told me he had left instructions that I was to begin work immediately on a picture called *A Pullman Bride*. My heart sank when they told me that both Mack Swain and Chester Conklin were to star in it.

I reported to wardrobe the following morning and they outfitted me in a perfectly hateful bathing suit and a beach hat topped by a loud checkered bow. I told them I couldn't swim and had a deadly fear of the ocean, but they said there was no swimming in the picture, or even any beach scenes. The swimming costumes were for publicity pictures. That afternoon they drove me, along with the famous Sennett Bathing Girls, to a nearby beach where we spent hours posing for ridiculous cheesecake publicity pictures. In some we had to romp and scamper along the beach in twos and threes. In others I had to sit on a rock being cuddled by Mack Swain, who was wearing a striped bathing suit stretched over his bulging stomach and a silly hat perched on top of his clown face. I was absolutely miserable every minute I had to pretend I was having the time of my life.

I continued to be miserable throughout the shooting of *A Pullman Bride*. I had plenty of personal reasons for being unhappy; moreover, I missed Charley Parrott and Bobby and all the others I had made ten pictures with in the course of the past year. But what really bothered me was that I knew the world of slapstick was not for me. I felt about it the way my mother felt about motion pictures in general—it was somehow not respectable. I could never feel the tempo of it and I hated the vulgarity that was just under the surface of it every minute. It was a world of falling planks and banana peels and wet paint and sticky wads of gum, of funny-looking fat men with painted mustaches blowing the foam off beer at each other, of stern battle-axes wielding rolling pins and wearing curlers in their hair, and of cute giggly hoydens getting teased, tickled, and chased. Becoming a Sennett star meant becoming one of those hyperactive giggly girls.

As soon as we finished the picture I made an appointment to see Mack Sennett. He must have thought I wanted to discuss money because he had my contract in front of him on the desk.

"What can I do for you, Gloria?" he asked, smiling, almost playful.

I told him I didn't want to make any more pictures like *A Pullman Bride*.

"Why not?"

"Because they make me uncomfortable. I don't like pictures where people throw pies and spill soup."

"Nobody's thrown any pies at you, have they?"

"No."

"That's right," he said. "I wouldn't allow it. It's not funny with a pretty girl."

"It's not funny with anybody," I said.

"I'll be the judge of that," the King of Comedy said. He looked at me in a sternly appraising way. "Look, Gloria, I've got big plans for you in Sennett comedies. We've already spent a lot of money on publicity for you. I think I can even make another Mabel Normand out of you."

That was exactly what I didn't want to hear.

"I'm sorry, Mr. Sennett," I said, "but I don't want to be another anybody."

He put down his cigar, picked up my contract, and held it with both hands in a position to tear it. Then he paused, with a faint threatening smile on his face. If he was angry, he didn't show it. He was simply saying that it was my move. I owed him everything, really, and we both knew it. He had put me in the first pictures that people could remember me in. He had put my name in the newspapers. He had let me use him for a personal favor when I asked him. By making sure I was cast properly, he had even made me learn how to act. But now I had to say I would act a whole new way for him or not act for him at all.

A silent clock counted ten for both of us. I waited until he tore the contract in two. Then I left.

CHAPTER 6

Aries, born 1899: Between divine law and your will, you should go far. . . . You are not your mother, not your father, not your teacher, clergyman, or boss. Resilience and positivism elevate your mind, guide you toward a wide range of possibilities. You educate yourself, travel, develop your own set of beliefs. The world's big, and you will see it all. You're an arrow as it travels between the bow and the target.

—MICHAEL LUTIN
Saturn Signs

On March 1, 1917, when Americans learned that Arthur Zimmermann, the German foreign minister, had sent a secret telegram to Germany's minister in Mexico suggesting an alliance of Germany, Mexico, and Japan against the United States, they began to demand action from their leaders by means of demonstrations all over the country. Up to then President Wilson had kept America out of the war, but on April 6 he and the Congress said they had no choice but to declare war on Germany and call for half a million troops. For my eighteenth birthday, which fell between these two historic dates, my father wrote from Manila saying that he hoped America would stay neutral but doubted that it could, and that he wished me happiness and success and was sure any decisions I was making about my marriage and my career were the right ones. He had never seemed so vague, so timid, so far away.

I would have had to scour this great country in order to find any eighteen-year-old girl willing to swap her existence for mine on that March 27 when I reached adulthood. I had left Wally but I would not be free of him for at least a year, as I discovered when I contacted him through a lawyer Mother knew and he said he would not give me a divorce. I had also quit the only work I had ever known, and prospects for a divorced woman with a ninth-grade education were bleak. Moreover, I was almost out of money and would soon be a dead weight on my mother, who was within a few months of obtaining her own divorce and who was trying to keep steady company with Matthew Burns, difficult as that was with me around. It was hard to believe I was the same girl who, two and a half years before, had thought she was pregnant after a boy in a blazer touched her lips with his tongue when he kissed her. What, I asked myself, would Medora and Mr. and Mrs. Grimes think of their Cuban Princess now?

A few days after the President's declaration of war, however, I woke up for the first time in over three months determined instead of depressed. I decided I couldn't sit moping forever; I had to do something. If I wanted my life to change, then I had better get a move on, because no one else was going to change it for me. I picked up the phone and called Clarence Badger at the Triangle Company.

Mr. Badger was delighted to hear from me. He said he and Bobby and the other members of the old company were making one picture after another over at Triangle. He was shocked that I hadn't worked since I left Mack Sennett and sorry that I hadn't called him sooner. He told me to come out the next day and he would sign me up for a little one-reeler they were starting in a day or two. He said he was sure there would be more work after that, although no one could tell what the war would do to pictures. He didn't know what the pay would be, but he said he would see what he could do.

That afternoon I put every cent I had in my purse and went shopping in the new Los Angeles department stores. It felt grand to be out and acting extravagant. I bought one or two small things to make myself feel good, and I was about to call it a day when I saw a bottle-green suit with a squirrel collar that made me bite my tongue. The saleslady could see I was mad for it and urged me to try it on. It fit perfectly and seemed in a minute to wipe out the last six months of my life.

When the saleslady told me it was $300, I gulped at the enormous amount and started for the dressing room. But I knew I didn't want to take it off, and seeing me hesitate, the saleslady said they had a layaway plan if I wished to make a deposit. I said no, that wouldn't be necessary, and counted out all the money I had in the world except for about four singles. "Wrap it up," I said, and now it was her turn to gulp.

It was the most beautiful thing I had ever owned by far, and I wore it the next day to Triangle when I went to see Clarence Badger. I had to make three trolley changes to get to the studio, so I allowed myself more than enough time and arrived almost an hour early.

Culver City was miles out of town. The year before, a rich real estate man named Harry H. Culver had given twelve acres of land to Thomas H. Ince, the movie director, to build a studio on, hoping that people working in the motion picture business would then buy land around the studio and establish a colony, but so far nobody had chosen to live way out there. Near Ince's studio was Triangle. It was enormous, ten times as big as Keystone. It had an imposing front gate and a series of large glass-enclosed buildings for shooting inside in natural light. When I told the uniformed gateman that I had an appointment with Mr. Badger, he told me it was too far for me to walk and telephoned a driver to come and pick me up. A touring car soon arrived, and a chauffeur opened the door of the spacious backseat for me. He drove me through the beautiful grounds, past one shiny new building after another, to the main offices. I still had time to spare; Clarence Badger was nowhere to be seen, so I told the driver I would sit in the car and wait. He nodded, and the two of us sat silent as statues.

After a time I became aware of being scrutinized and looked up to see that a nice-looking man, probably in his thirties, was connected to the footsteps I was hearing go by me for the third time. He was wearing a light tweed suit and had a camel's-hair polo coat over his shoulders. Our eyes met and I looked away. I could hear the footsteps stop for a considerable count and then retreat into the main-office building. If that was D. W. Griffith, I should know it, I said to myself, but before I could ask the driver, another man scurried out of the office and came right up to me.

"Excuse me," he said, "but were you in a picture called *The Danger Girl* for Mack Sennett?"

"Yes," I said.

"Good. We were sure it was you. Would you mind coming in to Mr. Conway's office for a minute?"

"Who's Mr. Conway?"

"Jack Conway, the director."

I told the driver to tell Mr. Badger when he arrived that I would be right back and followed the man to an office inside the building. On the way he grabbed a large pliable booklet, and when he had seated me on a comfortable couch in the roomy light office, he handed the booklet to me. "Mr. Conway will be right with you. Here's a script. Maybe you'd like to look it over," he said. Then he disappeared and Mr. Conway's secretary came in to take down my address and phone number.

Alone again, I turned the script over in my hands. It was the first script I'd ever had a chance to hold and read. At Essanay there had been only one copy of a script and it had always been under the director's arm. At Keystone, scripts didn't exist; the company made them up as they went along. This one was called *Smoke*, and the title page said it was based on a *Saturday Evening Post* story. I got just far enough to know that it was about a girl who creates a scandal by flirting with a married man when the door opened and the man I had seen with the polo coat over his shoulders entered.

He said he was Jack Conway and that he knew who I was. He was tall and lean, with blue eyes and wavy hair and a marvelous smile. He offered me a cigarette out of a box on the table, took one himself, and lit them with a gold lighter he pulled out of his jacket pocket. Tossing his coat over the arm of a chair by the door, he sat down opposite me and quietly admired me for a minute. He seemed to possess everything I thought of as refined and stylish behavior. He was like that man women in fashion magazines always had by the arm, the kind of man who automatically had a manicure when he had a haircut. He smelled faintly of cologne.

"You know, it's the damnedest thing," he began, as if we had known each other for years, "but when I first read that script, I thought of you. I'd seen you in a picture called *The Danger Girl*, where you drove hell out of a car, I even had my secretary call Sennett, but they said you'd left months ago. So for three days I've been interviewing Triangle actresses. Then suddenly just now here you are, parked at the front door as if God had delivered you. I believe in fate, don't you?"

"Yes," I said, remarking to myself that he even swore in a refined way, as if swearing were the sophisticated person's shortcut to saying things so that they would be believed.

"Then let's not fight it. Let's agree right now that you'll play the lead in this picture. I know you're right for it."

"How do you know that?"

"Because the girl's got to be a hellion on a horse or in a car, and I've seen you be that already in *Danger Girl*. But more than that, she's got to have style, or class, or whatever you want to call it. And you've got it."

"Are you sure?"

"Never surer. Your hair, your face, the way you sit, the way you smoke a cigarette, that fantastic green suit you're wearing . . . even your name is stylish. You're exactly what I want."

"When would I start?"

"Tomorrow if you're free."

"I don't know. I'll have to talk with Clarence Badger. You see, I actually came out here today to see him about a one-reeler he's starting tomorrow or the next day."

"Tell him no. Or I'll tell him. Look, I don't want to make promises I can't keep, but I swear that a film like *Smoke* could make you a star."

He asked how much I'd been making at Sennett and said he would try to get Roy Aitken, one of the two brothers who headed the studio, to match it or better. In the meantime I should read over the script and decide what I wanted for costumes. He would leave the choice of clothes entirely up to me. Anything I didn't have, he said, I could tell the wardrobe department to get for me. With a wicked twinkle in his eye, he added that in my biggest scene I would wear nothing but a teddy bare, a snug, sleeveless undergarment also called an "envelope chemise." That was the scene in which Patricia, the heroine, jumps into the ocean to rescue her crippled lover. Then he called in his secretary and told her to have his driver take me home and pick me up at nine in the morning. He said if I had any questions, I could reach him at the Hollywood Athletic Club.

This shifting of the poles of my life had taken only about fifteen minutes. As Mr. Conway's chauffeur was leading me out the front door to the car, Clarence Badger arrived for our appointment. I told him what had happened and asked if he could find someone else for the one-reeler. If not, I would do it. He said of course he could find someone else; at the most it was a half-hour's shooting. He had offered it only because he wanted to cheer me up and get me back in pictures.

"What's it about?" I asked.

"Oh, it's just a little sight gag about two hats. One of the young writers sold me on it. Bobby's married in the skit and buys a hat for his wife that she raves so much about that he buys the same hat for his cute secretary. Then he drives the secretary home and they pass his wife on the street and both girls are wearing the same hat. Tears. A fight. A box of candy. They make up. It's nothing—just cute, you know, just a sight gag. I wanted you to play the wife."

"So Bobby's married now in the movies?" I asked in order to change the subject before I burst into tears, as I had done the day I appeared in the story in real life.

"That's right. We're all growing up, Gloria," Clarence said. He told me to call him for lunch as soon as I was settled in at Triangle, and I waved to him as the chauffeur pulled out of the driveway.

After that, how could I not believe in fate?

Making a film with Jack Conway was like going to an elegant party every day. *Smoke* was about well-off, well-dressed people moving in the upper circles of society, and Jack Conway knew how to give it the authentic touch. He always had wonderful bits to add, even in scenes where I was racing a car or riding a horse, and in my close-ups he stood right beside the camera and played the scene with me. When he read a title to me, he was better than any actor I'd ever worked with. His timing was so perfect that I found myself reacting naturally, without effort. It was like dancing with a perfect partner.

He understood acting technique so well because he'd been in pictures for years before he started directing them, and before that he'd been a stage actor. He'd played the lead in the first motion picture ever made in California. He laughed about it at lunch one day. He'd got the part purely and simply because he could ride a horse, which was not much of a feat for, he said to my amazement, a Minnesota farm boy.

He taught me a million things about acting, and he also had such an eye for my make-up and my hair that I hardly needed a mirror. He was the first person to explain to me where stage actors frequently went wrong in motion pictures. They were trained to express emotion through dialogue, and therefore some of their best work wound up on the cutting-room floor, replaced by a printed title. In silent pictures you had to convey everything in the first few words of a line and still have something left for the end. You had to know where the titles were going to be. Listening and reacting had to be delayed, controlled. What seemed unnatural on the set became natural on the screen. Once you'd learned that, though, he said, you had to forget it. In fact, if you didn't, the camera would catch you thinking.

I had never met anyone like him. He was refined, sensitive, intelligent, and generous, and he was amusing and unaffected and attractive besides. I began to develop a serious crush on him and went out of my way to learn everything I could about him, from the titles of all of his pictures to the name of the cologne he always used. The gossips were quick to let me know that he was married, albeit separated, and a devoted father. If there were women in his life, he was very discreet about it. He certainly never fooled around with anyone working at the studio, they said. I could have told them, to my regret, that he was certainly the very soul of discretion with me. If I did something that pleased him in a scene, he would come over and squeeze my upper arms, but he never ventured so much as a hug.

As the time approached to shoot the big scene where I would have to peel down to an undergarment and jump into the ocean, he jokingly said he hoped I knew how to swim. I said I hadn't swum for years; I didn't say eighteen years, because I was so determined to please him in everything that I decided I would take swimming lessons on the sly. However, my one visit to a Y was such a fiasco that I barely learned to float, and I never went back. But still I didn't tell him that I couldn't swim a stroke.

I actually felt faint when the technicians told me one morning late in the shooting that we would film the suicide and rescue sequence that night on the Wilmington docks, in the busiest part of the port of Los Angeles. Jack Conway told me to be sure to wear a teddy bare under my white evening dress and said he would pick me up. I timidly said I hoped he didn't expect me to be an expert night swimmer, and he said no, the sequence would require just one dive. Dive! I thought. At night! I thought, but still I held my peace. Obviously he was planning to have a crew there to haul me out as soon as I touched the water, and probably the whole sequence could be shot without any real swimming or diving at all.

When he opened the car door for me that night, I was surprised to find another girl sitting in the front seat beside the chauffeur. He introduced us by name and we said hello. After driving for a few minutes in silence, I asked the girl if she was an actress.

"No," she said, "I'm a swimming instructor."

I wanted to hug her, until Jack Conway said, "Just in case. You know."

"I know," I said. Then I said to the girl, "But you're not wearing a white evening dress."

"I've got it in my bag," she said. "Just in case."

When we got to the docks, a large crowd of stevedors were gathered around and the crew were testing magnesium flares to light the sequence. The flares lit up the sky and the dock for a few minutes and then died away. We went over to the dock, and Jack Conway led the actor playing my lover and me through the scene. The actor would come hobbling in on his crutches. He would stop at the edge of the dock for a minute and then plunge into the water. Then I would see him from my car, jump out, pull off my evening dress, and dive in and rescue him. The whole scene would come out under ninety seconds.

"Are you sure you want to do the dive?" Jack Conway asked me.

"How deep is the water?" I asked.

"Sixty feet, and the dock is fifteen feet above the water. O.K.?"

I walked to the edge of the dock and looked around. A freighter fifty feet to one side. Black whirlpools below. A tiny boat near the pilings with men with hurricane lamps in it. No stars. Darkness. The edge of the world. A chilly breeze was lifting.

The leading man was waiting there with his crutches. The crew were preparing the flares. I saw the men with the cameras. I saw Jack Conway.

"All right," I said. "I'm ready." Suddenly I was like a horse at the starting gate, prancing, wanting to get on with it. Jack yelled "Action!" and the flares lit up the sky. The leading man hobbled to the dock's edge, threw down his crutches, and plunged over the side. Someone counted to five and then called my character's name: "Patricia!" I raced onto the dock as though I had been shot out of a cannon. I ripped my evening dress getting it off and stood in the light of the flares in a pink teddy bare. Then I put my hands over my head and shot through the air into the water. I struggled underwater for what seemed an eternity before I came to the surface. Then I paddled somehow to the waiting boat, all by instinct, and people pulled me up and wrapped me in a blanket. My leading man, also wrapped in a blanket, was in the boat beside me.

In the dying light of the flares I could see Jack Conway on the dock.

"Do you want me to do it again?" I shouted.

I could hear him laughing. "No," he shouted back. "But we'll shoot it once again just in case with the double."

They gave me towels and dry clothes and led me back to the car, where Jack joined me.

"I thought you were faking," he said.

"I was. I can't swim a stroke."

"Well, I'll be damned," he said and put his arms around me and kissed me feelingly on the lips. "I've got to talk to you," he said. "Let's have dinner at the Alexandria Hotel on Friday."

The Alexandria Hotel was the most luxurious hotel in Los Angeles, all crystal chandeliers, marble columns, potted palms, and Oriental rugs. It was where the snobs dined and had their fancy parties. Jack Conway picked me up in a chauffeured studio car at half past eight and we arrived at the Alexandria at nine. In the car we began to call each other Jack and Gloria for the first time. We were in the smartest evening clothes, and as the waiter led us to a corner table in the opulent dining room, a dozen heads turned. Jack ordered wine, and when the waiter poured it, we touched glasses and drank to each other. Then Jack gave me a beautiful beaded bag as a memento of our first film together and ordered a number of things for us to eat that I had never heard of. A little orchestra was playing at one end of the room, and I suddenly felt very glamorous and worldly. I hung the bag on my arm and with the other hand reached across the table and squeezed Jack's hand.

"Thank you," I said.

"I'm glad you like it. My daughter helped me pick it out."

I realized he was sending me a signal and slowly moved my

hand away from him. "How many children do you have?" I asked.

"Just one. One little daughter. I wouldn't give her up for the world. Now let's talk about you. Gloria, I told you the first day I met you, you have style."

"You were wrong."

"No, I wasn't. *You're* wrong. A person is born with style. You were. I've just helped you bring it out. Remember, I started out as a Minnesota farm boy myself. I shouldn't say this before we finish the picture, but you're also going to be famous, Gloria. That's one of the reasons you can't get involved with me, much as I would love it. My wife is a jealous, vindictive woman. She checks up on me like a detective. And I don't want anything to mess up your career. That's why we have the driver tonight. This is an official studio evening."

My eyes bulged as he outlined my future. He told me Mr. Aitken had seen the rushes of our film and was excited. They were changing the billing and the title to read: Gloria Swanson in *You Can't Believe Everything*. They had decided to make me a Triangle star as big as Alma Rubens and the Gish sisters. They would not release the picture until later in the year. In the meantime they wanted to co-star me in a couple of pictures with some well-known leading men, namely William Desmond and J. Barney Sherry. That would give them time to build me up to the public. After that they would release *You Can't Believe Everything* with lots of publicity and promotion.

"Does this mean we'll work together again?" I asked.

"You bet your life. Aitken wants your next two pictures in a hurry. While I'm editing this one, Frank Borzage will direct you in another. They're already looking for scripts. I'll do the one after that. You're going to be a busy girl. But from now on, you can ask for just about anything you want, within reason. What do you want?"

"Seriously?"

"Seriously. Ask. Aitken says it's all right."

I told him I wanted a better apartment, with enough space for my mother. He said he'd try to get me into Court Corinne, where many women in pictures lived. It would be a good, respectable publicity move. Then I told him I wanted a car. He asked me what kind and I said a Kissel coupe, although I hardly knew one make from another. He said he'd have his secretary order one the next day.

"Anything else?"

"One more thing. I want a divorce. Did you know I was married to Wallace Beery?"

"The actor? Good God, no."

"Only for two months. We worked together at Keystone. I left him but he won't give me a divorce."

"How old is he?"

"Thirty-one."

"He's probably waiting for the new draft registration. All men between eighteen and forty-five will have to register, and married men will automatically be deferred. Once he's deferred, I'm sure my lawyer will be able to handle it for you."

"What an evening," I said. "By the way, whose dive did you use, mine or the double's?"

"Yours, of course. Did you doubt it? Incidentally, Mr. Aitken is going to call you in and tell you most of this all over again tomorrow, so act surprised."

We did not dance a single dance. He kissed me good night in the car and then walked me ceremoniously to the door of Mother's apartment. As Daddy had said, life is ninety-five percent anticipation. But I still had hopes.

Within a week, while we were shooting the final scenes of *You Can't Believe Everything,* I got the Kissel coupe, and Mother and I moved up in the world from St. Francis Court to Court Corinne, which was a double row of modest bungalows in a good location near the studios, full, as Jack had said, of single actresses. I had never lived around lots of women before, and it didn't take me long to realize I would not have made a good nun or sorority sister. Teddy Sampson and Maude Wayne, with whom I worked at Keystone, both lived there, and so did a friend of theirs named Alice Lake. Theda Bara had once lived there but didn't any longer, they told us, and an unknown young actress had recently died in one of the apartments from an abortion, paid for by D. W. Griffith. The social life of the place consisted mostly of movie gossip and parties and sunbathing. Anything that happened in the world of movies on a given day was common knowledge in Court Corinne by sundown. Probably for that reason, the two women I liked most there were Sylvia Joslin, a quiet divorcée who was an artist, and an unsuccessful actress named Beatrice La Plante from Toronto. She had played in two white-slavery pictures with Sessue Hayakawa and had not worked since.

Bea La Plante lived with her sister, also an unsuccessful actress, but she spent more time in our bungalow than in theirs. She became another June Walker for me, and Mother doted on her as she had doted on June. Bea was a perfectly marvelous human being; she was amusing, intelligent, and feisty, the kind of person you feel good having around. I determined that as long as the sun was shining on me at Triangle, I would try to get Bea work there. I took her to the studio with me for a whole day, posing her here and there so people would notice her and introducing her to all the directors I knew, but nobody made the slightest move to hire her, not even Jack Conway for my sake. Jack did, however, like her as a person and see in her the perfect opportunity for chances for him and me to be together. He invited both of us to go duck hunting on the flats around Ventura with him and a friend the following Sunday. The friend's name was John Gilbert, who Jack told me was almost as unsuccessful as Bea. He had played bit parts and wanted to be a director. Jack said he would like to use him as his assistant and teach him directing before he got depressed and left pictures altogether. Bea thought John Gilbert was terribly attractive, but he didn't seem the least bit interested in her, except in a friendly way. Compared with Jack Conway, I found him totally boring, but if Bea liked him, I thought, a day of duck hunting might not be too bad, particularly if it gave me a chance to see Jack for once in real life, relaxed, away from the studio.

The only time I had ever been hunting was with Wally, and I remembered it as a grisly experience. We had driven out to a field at sunset and waited for it to get dark. Then Wally took out his gun and switched on his headlights. Rabbits on the ground sat perfectly still, stunned by the glare, while he shot them. It was horrible. But flying targets had a chance, so I wasn't repelled. In fact, Jack kept at me, teasing and coaxing, until I actually took aim and shot a duck, and to my surprise was quite proud of having done so. Everywhere Jack was the perfect teacher and for the moment, to me, all other men seemed vulgar or dull beside him.

Frank Borzage, for example, who directed my second picture at Triangle, was a charming and gifted man. He had been a stage actor and a leading man in pictures just like Jack, but his presence behind the camera was totally different. He didn't have the magic or the zip that Jack had. He shot the entire picture in the studio, avoiding location scenes altogether. The story itself was silly and old-fashioned, about a

mannequin who tries to crash London society, not knowing
she has noble blood all along. William Desmond, the leading
man, was a star, and it was obvious that the studio was using
his name in this picture to promote me. Mr. Borzage had
orders to shoot endless close-ups of me in couturier dresses,
so if Mr. Desmond felt neglected and resentful and showed it,
I couldn't blame him. He was twice my age, with a reputation
and a following. I must have seemed to him a complete
nobody, yet I wound up wearing more clothes than all the rest
of the cast put together, including Lillian West and Lillian
Langdon, two regulars in the Triangle stable. The studio
called the picture *Society for Sale* and released it immediately. I sensed that it was poor stuff, and I couldn't wait for it
to be over so that I could begin working again with Jack
Conway.

The new picture was called *Her Decision*, and the studio
demanded a rush job so that audiences could see me in two
pictures simultaneously with well-known actors. In this case
the leading man was J. Barney Sherry, who claimed to be the
first stage actor to desert the legitimate theater for work in
pictures. I played a private secretary who marries her boss for
his money and then falls in love with him. The story was so
weak that even Jack couldn't do much to save it. He
concentrated mostly on making me stand out, and this
solution didn't appeal to J. Barney Sherry any more than it
had appealed to William Desmond. I could tell that Jack had
no faith in this film and that he resented being pressured into
finishing it in a hurry. Each day he seemed more frustrated
and unhappy than the day before. For the whole last week he
had been smoldering, but he never exploded or even showed
his anger in front of the actors.

"I'm leaving Triangle," he said to me the day we finished
shooting. "I'll edit *Her Decision* for your sake, but then they
can find another boy."

"But why? Just tell me why."

He said that the Aitkens and the rest of the studio
executives had gone back on their word to him. They had told
him he would have full say in how his pictures were released,
and now they were refusing to let him touch publicity at all.
For the duration of the war they had decided to appeal in
their advertising to the American dream, to the American
family. They were going to spend a fortune to promote a
single slogan: Clean Pictures for Clean People.

"The stupid asses," Jack sputtered. "They think they're

selling soap. Don't they know pictures are stars? They've rushed me and badgered me through these last two pictures, and after all our work they're going to serve them up in one big pot along with all the other Triangle garbage. They'll get lost in the shuffle."

"Wait a minute! Where will you go?"

"I don't know yet. I need a vacation to think things out. My wife is also on the rampage again."

"Why?"

"Because I asked her for a divorce. She'll try to smear any actress I'm working with now. That's another reason I'm leaving. I want you to make it big. And you can. No matter how they advertise your pictures. No matter how many jealous wives there are in the world."

He looked at me admiringly, as if I were a picture he had just finished painting, and I started to cry. He put his arms around me and sighed sadly. "You know what our problem is, Gloria? It's that nobody around here except you and me has any class."

At the start of 1918, having finished three pictures in rapid succession, I had a break before I had to go back to work on my next picture. Now that Jack Conway was gone from Triangle, I waited without much enthusiasm to hear what that picture would be, and without any enthusiasm at all to hear who would be directing it.

"Miss Swanson, please."

"This is Miss Swanson."

"Good morning, Miss Swanson. I'm Oscar Goodstadt, the casting director at Famous Players-Lasky and I'm calling on behalf of Cecil B. De Mille. Mr. De Mille would like to see you at your earliest convenience. Could you come in at three today? Miss Swanson?"

"Oh! Yes. Yes, I can."

Mr. Goodstadt started to tell me how to get to the studio, but I said I knew where it was. Everybody knew where it was. It took up a whole block at Sunset and Vine. It was where Mary Pickford worked. And Douglas Fairbanks. And Almighty God himself, Cecil B. De Mille.

Any notions I may have had of style or elegance evaporated the moment I was ushered into Mr. De Mille's paneled office. It was vast and somber, with tall stained-glass windows and deep polar-bear rugs. Light from the windows shone on ancient firearms and other weapons on the walls, and the elevated desk and chair resembled nothing so much as a throne. I felt like a peanut poised on teetering high heels.

When he stood up behind the desk, he seemed to tower. Not yet forty, he seemed ageless, magisterial. He wore his baldness like an expensive hat, as if it were out of the question for him to have hair like other men. A sprig of laurel maybe, but not ordinary hair. He was wearing gleaming boots and riding breeches that fit him like a glove. He came over and took my hand, led me to a large sofa and sat down beside me, and proceeded to look clear through me. He said that he had seen me in a little Sennett picture and had never forgotten me, and that at the moment he was preparing a picture in which he wanted to use me. He asked me what kind of contract I had at Triangle.

"I have no contract at all."

"Well, then, who represents you?"

"No one."

"You mean your parents handle your business affairs?"

"Oh, no, Mr. De Mille. I'm over eighteen. I'll be nineteen the twenty-seventh of March."

"Ah, Aries, of course," he said and smiled. "If you have no contract with Triangle, then nothing prevents you from working with me. You're sure about that?"

"Absolutely," I said. "They talked about a contract after I made my first picture with Mr. Conway, but nothing came of it. They gave me a fifteen-dollar raise, that's all."

"And you're not shooting a picture for them now?"

"No."

"Good!" He got to his feet, an unmistakable sign that the interview was over. At the door he said, "One thing more—do you think you would *like* to work in my new photoplay?"

"Oh, yes, Mr. De Mille," I said.

"Good!" he said, putting his hand on my shoulder by way of bidding me good-bye.

Two days later I got a call from the general director of Triangle telling me to report for a new picture. It was my big moment and I was ready. "I'm sorry," I said, "I won't be able to. I'm going to work for Cecil B. De Mille."

The general director paused and hung up. Thirty minutes later Mr. De Mille's secretary called and asked me to come in right away. When I got there, Mr. De Mille sat me down again.

"Everything you told me turned out to be true," he said.

"However, lawyers have a way of complicating things. Triangle's legal department has raised the possibility that even though you did not sign a contract with the studio, you *did* accept a raise in salary. They are contending that when you accepted the raise, you in effect agreed to a verbal contract. So it may be possible you still belong to them. Were you over eighteen when you accepted the raise?"

I nodded, trying to hold back the tears. Mr. De Mille put his arm around me. "These things happen," he said. "That's why we have a motion picture association. The Triangle attorneys will present their case to an impartial arbitrator selected by the association. His decision will be binding. We won't go to court about it. There isn't time. We'll just hope everything turns out all right. Whatever happens, thank you for coming over, Miss Swanson."

The arbitrator didn't waste any time. Within forty-eight hours Mr. De Mille's secretary called to say the decision had gone against Famous Players-Lasky. Mr. De Mille was terribly sorry, but I belonged to Triangle. When I hung up, I felt shattered, numb, betrayed. The greatest opportunity of my life had been snatched away unjustly.

But I knew that if I ever wanted to work in pictures again, there was nothing I could do about it. Bitter and deflated as I was, I forced myself the next afternoon to get in my car and drive to Culver City, where I signed the hateful contract without so much as reading a word of it.

Almost immediately Triangle began to publicize my pictures in all the papers. Teddy Sampson ran over from her bungalow to show me the first notice that appeared. It was on the society page. It said: "Gloria Swanson will have the starring role in her next film, *You Can't Believe Everything,* with Jack Richardson and Darrell Foss." Just one line. No mention of Jack Conway. I was disgusted.

All the girls at Court Corinne began to watch me with new eyes. They must have thought if lightning could strike a little shrimp with a turned-up nose and horse teeth and a mole on her chin, it could strike anywhere. I instantly became for them someone they should know. Four or five a day, on the average, they came over to show me clippings or invite me to parties. Only Bea La Plante had any idea that the very mention of Triangle was enough to drive me up the wall.

I didn't know what to do until, as if by magic, Mother up

and married Matthew Burns one weekend without a word of warning and moved to a big house on Kinsley Avenue, and Bea's sister gave up for good on Hollywood and moved back to Toronto. I told Bea that since I now had a contract and nothing but money, I was moving out of Court Corinne and taking her with me. "You can be my secretary, my dependent, anything you want. Just call a real estate agent and get us out of here," I said. A beautiful house turned up on Harper Avenue that belonged to the distinguished stage actor Tyrone Power, Sr. It was expensive, but it was beautifully furnished, with wonderful grounds all around, so I said to Bea, "Let's take it. Why not? If I run myself into debt, maybe they'll fire me. Get a maid."

We had wonderful times in the place. It was like a big dollhouse—a ridiculous toy. It was perfect for parties, and we opened it up several times during the war to soldiers and sailors stationed in Los Angeles. Bea took charge of the place, as well as looking after all my personal affairs.

In the meantime in Culver City, I was on the Triangle treadmill, serving my sentence. I didn't disguise the fact that I felt myself trapped there or that I thought the pictures the company made were getting worse by the minute. More often than not they were foolish melodramas related to the war. I treated my first new director, Gilbert Hamilton, as a mortal enemy just because he wasn't Jack Conway, until I found out that he was serving his sentence just like me. He didn't like the script of *Everywoman's Husband* any more than I did and told me so. After that we got through it somehow and even managed to be friends. The company was grinding out bad pictures at such a rate, however, that we didn't have time to become good friends.

My next director was a rather eccentric Englishman named Albert Parker. We made two pictures together, and there was no way on earth I could dislike him. He was too much fun. He was also an excellent director, with very fine taste.

"Do I cry a lot in this one?" I asked him about the first picture before we started filming.

"Indeed you do," he said. "The writer is making the villain a Teuton."

"What's that?"

"That's what certain people here are calling Germans. Teutons or Huns. They're the same people who call sauerkraut 'liberty cabbage' and consider Beethoven's music seditious. There seem to be quite a few of them in the studio. And these awful patriotic scripts! Aren't they putrid? In this one the villain tries to blackmail you into being a spy for the kaiser."

He sent me flowers and took me to dinner several times and flirted shamelessly until one of the actresses working on the picture told me with raised eyebrows that he was married. I told him I was shocked and annoyed.

"But why? My wife's awful."

"So's my husband, but my divorce isn't final and I don't want him to have any grounds for prolonging it."

"I suppose you're right. My wife could certainly do the same. But can't we meet somewhere and discuss it privately? Perhaps I could persuade you. Please?"

"No, Albert."

"Look, we can't discuss it in the studio. Please?"

I felt that the easiest way to end the silly situation without hurting Albert, whom I liked very much in a nonromantic fashion, was to yield and let him talk. I told him to leave the studio right after me that evening and follow me to a quiet spot I remembered near the Beverly Hills Hotel. When I got there, Albert drove up in front of me and parked; then he walked over and stood beside my car.

"I don't want to be ridiculous and difficult," he said. "It's just that you're damn attractive."

"So are you, Albert, but not to me, not that way. We're friends. That's enough, isn't it?"

"No!" he exclaimed, and I started to laugh and then so did he.

At that moment I saw another car pull up on the deserted road and park on the other side. The next thing I knew, Wallace Beery got out of it and came storming toward us. He was in a fury. Before I could say a word, he charged up and punched Albert Parker in the nose and knocked him on the ground. Then he glowered at me and turned and walked away.

"My God, who was that?" Albert Parker said, picking himself up.

"My husband," I groaned. "You see what you've done? Now he'll report that he found us together."

Albert Parker suddenly became noble and very British. "Don't worry, Gloria," he said grandly. "No one will believe him. You know why? Because I'm going to drive my car into a tree on the way back. That will prove I wasn't here, but somewhere else. It's insured, so it doesn't matter." Then he said in a lecturing tone, "Really, Gloria, he's awful. You must get your divorce immediately."

The dear sweet man did just what he said he'd do. He ran his car into a tree to ensure us of our divorces. A month later we made our second picture together, a spy story at least as bad as the first one, called *Secret Code*, and had a perfectly marvelous time. We were more than just friends now. We were friends with a secret.

Between pictures with Albert Parker I made a picture called *Station Content* with a director named Arthur Hoyt. It was quite poor, but a masterpiece compared with the picture I made after *Secret Code*. The new film was called *Wife or Country*. In it I was not only successfully tricked into spying for the enemy, I also had to pay for my wrongdoing by swallowing a bottle of poison. At my first meeting with the director, E. Mason Hopper, I discovered that he was the former Lightning Hopper, the man who had directed Wally and me in *Sweedie Goes to College* at Essanay, the man Aunt Inga and I had heard scream himself hoarse the first time I ever saw a film being made. I had to grin and bear it for a week and a half of overacted, overdirected, overpatriotic nonsense. Where do I go from here? I thought to myself as I swallowed the bottle of poison and Lightning Hopper screamed "Perfect! Cut!"

The following morning the studio manager called to ask if he could come to the house in an hour and talk to me. I couldn't imagine what that meant, so I told Bea not to leave. When he arrived, it was to announce that Triangle was facing bankruptcy.

"Does that mean you're closing the studio?" I asked.

"The studio has two months more to exercise its option," he explained. "But Mr. Aitken and his brother thought you might want to get out of your contract immediately. That's why I'm here."

"Oh, they did, did they? After what they did to me?"

"The truth of the matter is, Miss Swanson, Mr. De Mille still wants you. He's tried several times to borrow you. His office called again yesterday."

"Why didn't anybody tell me?"

"There was no reason to make you more unhappy than you already were. If you like, I'll call Famous Players for you right now."

I showed him to the telephone. In five minutes he reappeared, saying, "Mr. Goodstadt is waiting to talk to you."

"Good morning, Miss Swanson," Mr. Goodstadt said. "I think you should come right over if you can. By the time you get here, I'll have a chance to talk to Mr. De Mille. I know he's most anxious to replace his leading lady—if you're available, that is. You might bring the gentleman from Triangle along if he has a copy of your contract with him. I'd like to look it over."

The studio manager and I had nothing more to say to each other as he drove me to Sunset and Vine. What a difference, I thought, between Triangle, where they shot an entire picture, with retakes, in ten days, and Mr. De Mille, who could stop in the middle of a costly picture and change leading ladies.

Mr. Goodstadt was waiting for us in his office. "I talked to Mr. De Mille," he said. "He's delighted you're available. You can come in tomorrow morning at seven. Hattie will be waiting for you to do your hair."

CHAPTER 7

"The public, not I, made Gloria Swanson a star."
—CECIL B. DE MILLE

When I drove up to the studio the next morning, one of Mr. De Mille's assistants was waiting to show me to my dressing room. It was spacious and comfortable, with a mirrored wall and dressing table, a soft lounging couch, and several upholstered chairs. Vases of freshly cut flowers stood on almost every flat surface. The assistant next led me to the hairdressing department and turned me over to Hattie, a tiny black woman who was standing at an old-fashioned ironing board ironing a long switch of dark-brown hair. She was wearing a narrow-brimmed black straw hat, beneath which she seemed to have very little hair of her own, and she kept a watchful eye on the ten or fifteen girls who worked under her. "This is your hair I'm ironing," she said with an enormous smile. "Over there are the sketches. See if you like it."

Hattie blended my own hair with the switch and tied the creation with a ribbon band. While she worked I did my make-up and we talked. She told me Mr. De Mille was the most remarkable man she had ever met—a real perfectionist. Everything had to be just so or he sent it back. He never started work until ten in the morning and he never overworked his artists. He had a violinist playing on the set to create a mood and make the actors feel good, and whenever Elsie Ferguson was in one of his pictures, he always escorted her onto the set himself while the musician played one of her favorite songs.

When my hair was in place, two women brought in my costume, a beautiful white day dress, and helped Hattie get it on over my hair. A few minutes later, Pinkerton detectives arrived with three velvet-lined jewel chests. Everything was real, and I was supposed to pick what I wanted to go with the dress. Mr. De Mille always had his actresses pick out the jewelry they wore in his films so that they would act as if they owned it. I chose a delicate necklace and earrings, and an assortment of rings and bracelets. A few minutes before ten I heard a violin start to play nearby, and an assistant director came to lead me to the set.

We stood off to one side as Mr. De Mille entered like Caesar, with a whole retinue of people in his wake. The assistant director beside me pointed out Jeanie Macpherson, an actress who wrote most of Mr. De Mille's screenplays, and Sam Wood, the first assistant director. Everyone stood in rapt silence as Mr. De Mille's eyes swept over the set. Looking at every detail with absolute concentration, he peeled off his field jacket and a Filipino boy behind him caught it as it left his hand. When he was ready to sit down, the Filipino boy deftly shoved a director's chair under him. Mr. De Mille motioned a propman over to him and spoke to him in a low, stern voice. The propman nodded and speedily replaced several tired roses in a vase on the set with perfect specimens he selected out of a tubful of fresh roses over in a corner.

Mr. De Mille beamed when he saw me. He came over, took my hand, and led me toward the set. "This is your home," he explained. "Take all the time you need to get acquainted with it. If anything seems wrong, we'll talk about it."

I thanked him and took a slow, careful walk through the beautiful rooms, fluffing pillows, touching the keys of the grand piano, opening the French doors that led to the garden, sitting on the arm of a chair, falling back onto a sofa, rearranging a vase of lilies.

After Mr. De Mille had huddled with the cameraman, he came over to me. In a voice not much louder than a whisper he said we would begin with a simple scene in which I hurriedly pack a trunk. He pointed to the closet where the trunk would be, and to another closet where he said I should select the things I wanted to pack. Then I should put them in the trunk. That was all. He didn't tell me why I was packing or where I was going. He didn't even tell me the name of the film. He just said they would start shooting as soon as I was ready.

I collected myself, studied the bedroom set, and said I would go out in the hall and enter from there. Mr. De Mille gave orders to the crew in a brusque, military voice, and in a few seconds I could hear the camera grinding. I hurried back into the room, pulled out the trunk and opened it, and then began filling it with things from the other closet. To my horror, I heard people laughing and whistling. Then I heard shouts and screams, but I went right on packing. Men and women roared and cheered as I slammed the trunk shut, but still I refused to be distracted or acknowledge that I had to do anything in the world but grab the heavy bag and hurry out of the room.

Just then Mr. De Mille walked onto the set and took me gently by the arm. He was radiant with joy. "Excuse me, Miss Swanson, forgive me. Wonderful. We are going to stop now for today. Word has just come that an armistice has been declared. The war is over, Miss Swanson."

"What's the date?" somebody asked.

"November fifth," somebody else said.

By then everyone was jumping up and down and shouting and kissing everyone else. I started to cry with happiness because Daddy had been with the American Expeditionary Force in France for some months, and I had worried about his safety. Hattie ran up and hugged me and took me back to my dressing room. On all sides, people were rushing out to celebrate. Hattie helped me off with my costume and took off the switch, and the Pinkerton men carried my jewelry away. When I got into my car to drive home, I saw by the studio clock it was not yet noon.

Of course, it turned out to be a false alarm, which meant that we had another day of celebration a week later. Both times Mr. De Mille was wild with happiness. He was an extremely patriotic man, as Hattie told me, and was an officer in the reserves.

By the time the armistice was really signed, on November 11, I had become accustomed to the procedure under Mr. De Mille. The actors never used a script. Mr. De Mille told us very carefully what the story was about and what each scene meant, but he never gave specific instructions or directions. One day shortly after I started work on the film, a young actor asked Mr. De Mille if he would explain to him how he wanted him to play such and such a scene.

"Certainly not!" Mr. De Mille bellowed. "This is not an acting school. I hired you because I trust you to be professional. *Professional!*" he thundered. "When you do something wrong, *that* is when I will talk to you!"

Each day during the lunch hour he watched the previous day's rushes, and he allowed his actors to watch them too, in order to catch their mistakes, discover any bad habits they saw themselves developing and eliminate them, and fill out the characters they were playing. I looked at them every day and soon learned to watch myself with total objectivity. Up to then, even under Jack Conway, everything in my performances had been spontaneous, intuitive. Under Mr. De Mille I began to see how telling small gestures and expressions could be if an actress knew how to control them, and I started to build up a whole bag of tricks with which I could heighten a moment or save a scene.

It was part of Mr. De Mille's genius to let his actors make up their own characters, just as he let them pick their own jewelry. That way they became real people in the films, not just mannequins moving here and there and saying this or that on cue.

The name of the film was *Don't Change Your Husband.* The screenplay by Jeanie Macpherson told of a woman who leaves her busy, neglectful husband to marry another man, only to discover that the new husband is a drinker, a gambler, and a ladies' man; then the woman divorces him and sets out to win back her first husband, whose true value she finally appreciates. Elliott Dexter played my first husband, and the most moving scene in the whole picture for me was the one in which he realizes I've left him. He looks into the camera stunned, miserable, alone and full of regret. I watched the rushes of the scene over and over, until it finally dawned on me what motion pictures could mean to the audience if they were wonderfully acted and directed. Here was what every woman who had ever left a husband wanted to see—how he looked when he first understood that she was gone. Motion pictures allowed her to be a fly on the wall at the most secret moment of her husband's life. No wonder people sat enthralled in darkened theaters all over the world in the presence of those big close-ups. Their effect was indelible.

Nothing we had ever had before, in books or plays, written or spoken, could begin to match their impact.

Elliott Dexter must have sensed that I was out of my depth when I first arrived at Paramount. I was clearly not used to making pictures with real jewels and real roses any more than I was used to being treated like a duchess by a director who behaved and spoke like a sultan. Elliott, on the other hand, had been a star for years and moved with perfect ease in that land of dreams, and he obligingly made a point of going ahead and clearing a path for me each time a new type of scene came up.

He and his wife, the gorgeous English actress Marie Doro, also took me under their wing socially from time to time. Marie was a true beauty. No one could resist her bright charm. Famous Players-Lasky had brought her over to star in pictures, and here she had met and married Elliott. They were probably the happiest and most popular couple in Hollywood.

One night they took me to the Ship Café, which was then the favorite spot of the movie industry's glamorous set. Fitted out like a real ship, it extended a block and a half into the Pacific and featured a fancy restaurant, a beautiful dance floor, some of the best orchestras and bands in America. Each night some of the well-known actors and actresses who were dining at the Ship would get up and perform spontaneously or sit in with the band and play an instrument. They treated the place as their clubhouse, where they could let their hair down and have fun. Within an hour, half of the people there had stopped by our table to say hello to the Dexters. Having spent three years in pictures in Hollywood, I recognized most of them, but only after Elliott told them I was playing the lead in "the new De Mille" did most of them pretend to recognize me.

As people I didn't know approached, Elliott would whisper a couple of identifying words to me, such as "British director. Terrible phony." By way of describing a handsome young man with black curly hair who came up and kissed Marie late in the evening, all he said was "Pasadena millionaire. Not in pictures." Marie introduced the man to me as Craney Gartz. He smiled and asked me to dance immediately, shaking my hand and raising me up to lead me to the floor almost in the same gesture. His good looks were of a very high order as

women judge men, and he was a wonderful dancer. He held
me tightly and hummed all the tunes in my ear and I didn't
mind in the least. On the contrary, he was the most attractive
man I had met in a long time as long as he remained silent.
But his talk—and he was a volcano full of it—was a combination of boasts, insults, and ugly remarks about this country's
government.

"Emma Goldman certainly wouldn't think much of this
place, would she?" he began.

"I have no idea," I said with a chill in my voice to cover up
the fact that I didn't know who Emma Goldman was. Then I
felt guilty about being deceitful and attempted some serious
conversation myself. "Wasn't it terrible that Vernon Castle
had to die in the war? Poor Irene Castle."

"Well, he didn't exactly die in the war," Craney Gartz said.
"He died on a training flight in Fort Worth."

He had shut me up and cut me off again, so I remained
silent. But he never stopped talking. He said he hoped I
didn't take the sham world of motion pictures seriously; it was
shallow in the extreme, he felt, except for the work of a few
European filmmakers. He said he was too rich to work, which
I thought was a blessing because hating the capitalistic
bourgeois system as he did, he would surely take a bomb with
him in his lunch pail wherever anyone might be stupid enough
to employ him. He said there was nothing worth working for
in America, anyway; that although the capitalists paid lip
service to the old institutions, the war and the revolution in
Russia had proved them rotten and dead. Intelligent people
couldn't be shackled by them any longer. The only exciting
place in the world to be alive just then was Russia, and what,
he asked, were Americans doing for the most hopeful area on
the earth? They were providing troops to defeat the noble
Russian people in order to restore czarist tyranny.

He said the whole war had been a mockery, and Wilson
most of all. He himself had started out to be a conscientious
objector, but on the advice of Jack London he had enlisted
instead in order to convince the rank and file from within. He
supposed, he said, I had dreams of marrying a rich man and
leaving pictures. Why? Marriage was dead as an institution;
Isadora Duncan and Ibsen and Nietzsche had all proved that
in their own ways. He said he would never marry. Marriage
killed the will of both partners. He said I might not know or
care, but he and his mother had spent a small fortune trying
to get lawyers to defend Joe Hill, but that the capitalists had

demanded a human sacrifice out of the IWW, so their pains had been for nothing. He said a few artists and theorists in Europe were destroying the old order, or trying to, but that here in America everyone was twiddling his thumbs and would probably continue to do so until the armies of the workers smashed down every last factory wall.

Exhausted from time to time by his own efforts to provoke me or convince me, he would become silent as a tomb and dance divinely. He was an incredibly dashing and handsome man, and in spite of my desire to tell him he should go fly a kite, I found myself physically content to nestle in his arms. I could also tell that he was attracted to me and took for granted the fact that I was attracted to him. Much of his disconnected talk, I felt, was uttered solely to keep me dancing. We not only danced four dances in a row; we also danced most of the time between numbers, when there was no music.

Suddenly he asked me if I would care to spend the night with him. I told him no and he asked me why not. Because I believed in marriage and work and all the rest of the ridiculous institutions, I said.

"How can you say that?" he asked.

"Because it's the first chance you've given me to say anything."

"Wait a minute."

"No, *you* wait a minute and let me ask you two questions. Have you ever worked a day in your life?"

"No."

"Well, I have, almost every day, since I was fifteen. Have you ever been married?"

"No."

"Well, I have, to the wrong man, but I still believe in the institution."

"What are you saying?"

"I'm saying you don't know what you're talking about."

We returned to the table and sat for another hour with Elliott and Marie. I had used up my emotions in my outburst, so I just sat and tried to be as bright and cheerful as I knew how. Craney Gartz sat stunned. When it was time to leave, he asked if he could drive me home. I said that would be fine if it wasn't out of his way. While he and Elliott were getting the cars, Marie said, "What *is* going on?"

"Why?" I asked.

"Because I know Craney Gartz," she said. "I've seen him run roughshod over a hundred gorgeous women who would do anything for his money, but I've never seen him acting the way he's acting tonight. I'm sure he's in love with you."

"Not, he's not. He's in love with himself, I think."

"Just remember, that marvelous-looking creature is worth over thirty million. His mother is the heiress to Crane bathroom fixtures. He's difficult, I know, but money's something, Gloria."

On the drive home, Craney asked me if he could see me again. He said I might get a kick out of dining at the Pasadena Country Club, to which people in movies were generally not admitted.

"All right," I said, "if you'll tell me who Nietzsche—is that his name?—is."

"You don't know?"

"I've never heard of him."

"My God, no wonder you don't agree with me. Of course I'll tell you."

Patiently, carefully, he lectured me right to my door about the German philosopher who had thrown out conventional morality and dreamed of some sort of state where men were godlike, beyond the reaches of petty society. He told me about Nietzsche's tragic life, his syphilis and his madness, and he outlined his works one by one. I was amazed at his knowledge. Craney Gartz may not have worked but he had studied, and I realized to my horror, as he told me about Nietzsche, how many more great minds there must be that I had never even heard of. In fact, I had never had the time or training to read a single difficult book in my life. I had read books here and there for pleasure. I had never studied a book. I had given an impression of winning an argument on the dance floor, but in fact the real reason Craney Gartz had made me angry in the first place was that he had rattled off a list of names and institutions I had never heard more than a passing mention of: Joe Hill, Isadora Duncan, the IWW, Fabians, Bolsheviks, Karl Marx, Charles Darwin, Sigmund Freud.

"Isn't this a big house for a single woman?" he asked me when we got to Harper Avenue.

"I share it with another single woman."

"May I kiss you?"

"All right, if you hurry, but I have to be at work at seven."

He kissed as well as he danced, or better, and although Bea's light was still on and I knew she was waiting for me, I let him take his time.

The next day while I was at the studio, a delivery man arrived at the house with a big box of books. On top was *The Soul of Man under Socialism* by Oscar Wilde, and under that were works by George Bernard Shaw, Henrik Ibsen, D. H. Lawrence, Karl Marx, Gabriele D'Annunzio, James Joyce, Sigmund Freud, and Friedrich Nietzsche.

Working for Mr. De Mille was like playing house in the world's most expensive department store. Going home at night to your own house and furniture was always a bit of a letdown. I finally said to him one day, "Mr. De Mille, you're giving me terribly expensive tastes." Other people called him Chief and C.B., but I always called him Mr. De Mille.

"There's nothing wrong with wanting the best," he said. "I always do. That's why I want you to be the leading lady again in my next film." Before I could say anything, he laughed and grabbed my hand and patted it.

After we finished *Don't Change Your Husband,* he gave me a contract to look over. I was almost too excited to read a word, for fear the charmed moment would end and he would change his mind. I would have signed anything just to be able to work with him forever. He explained that the $150 a week the studio was paying me would be raised automatically to $200 a week at the end of four months. In two years I would be making $350. That seemed an unbelievable figure, and I was absolutely thrilled. We signed it on December 30, 1918, just Mr. De Mille and I.

Immediately I started to have fittings for the next picture, which was to star Elliott Dexter again, as well as Tom Forman. Preparations went on for weeks. One morning all the girls who worked under Hattie were twittering like birds, so I asked what was going on.

"Haven't you heard?" Hattie exclaimed. "Your picture has been held over for a second week. They got word from New York this morning."

I didn't know what that meant, so Hattie explained. Pictures usually opened on a Sunday and played two or three days, or they opened Thursday and finished Saturday night. A picture had to be wonderful to play an entire week. But two weeks was almost unheard of. Hattie was jubilant. "If the

Chief likes you, that's one thing," she said. "But if people don't like you, it doesn't matter what the Chief thinks. Look at what happened to *Cecilia of the Pink Roses*."

There had been lots of talk about *Cecilia* and innumerable puffs in the Hearst papers because it starred Marion Davies, Hearst's mistress. At the New York premiere the management had framed the screen with thousands of pink roses and wafted perfume out over the audience by means of special fans. But the picture had not been a success. "Who wants to see a picture called *Cecilia of the Pink Roses* when they can see one called *Don't Change Your Husband?*" Hattie said. "C.B. keeps up with the times. And I blame Marion Davies' hairdresser, too. These curly-haired little blond things are all going to be back numbers."

Hattie had been with Mr. De Mille for years. I asked her how the film he had tried to hire me for a year before had turned out.

"Don't ask," she said. "People hated it and everybody around here wants to forget it. Just thank the Lord you wasn't in it. It could have held you back."

Everyone at the studio congratulated me, of course, but that was just the beginning. It seemed that everywhere I went from then on, people recognized me. Women my mother's age came up and asked if they could touch me. Policemen, waitresses, filling-station attendants, and delivery boys began to yell "Hey, Gloria!" or whisper "Good evening, Miss Swanson." High school girls pointed and shrieked while their boyfriends whistled.

One morning when Bea and I walked out the door, a gasoline truck was blocking the driveway. Before we could tell the driver to move, he jumped out of the cab and came over to us. "Gloria, do you remember me?" he asked in deliberate tones, as if much were at stake in my reply.

"Now let me see . . ." I began, stalling.

"The night you ran out of gas on La Brea—remember? I got your car going. A Kissel coupe. Remember?"

"Of course, I remember. There's the coupe," I said, pointing.

"You see?" the man said to Bea. "People think I made up that story." Then he said to me, "How have you been, Gloria?"

"Just fine," I said. He asked for a picture, so I took him inside and gave him one and had the maid make him some coffee. He told me he and his wife had seen *Don't Change*

Your Husband twice. "Nobody believes I met you that time, a year ago. Nobody's going to believe this either," he said, including with one sweep of his huge hand and arm the kitchen, the picture, the coffee, the maid, and me. "You take care of yourself," he said. "I mean it."

A week or so later Mr. De Mille himself came over to me when we finished shooting for the day and said in a playful stage whisper that everyone on the set could hear, "Leave the key under the mat as usual." Sam Wood, his assistant, and the cameraman started laughing, but I said I didn't get the joke.

"Haven't you heard?" Mr. De Mille asked. "You and I are having a torrid love affair. That's what the columnists say."

Now everybody was roaring with laughter, but I was stiff with shock.

"There, there. You'll just have to get used to that sort of thing," Mr. De Mille said. "It's what happens when you become famous in Hollywood. Besides, columnists never bother to print the truth if they can think of something more interesting."

I was still stunned an hour later, when I was alone in my dressing room with Hattie. "Don't feel bad about being famous," Hattie said. "That's what everyone out here wants to be. Why, I'm famous myself on Central Avenue now, just because I work with you."

A few days later I had a note from Mrs. De Mille inviting me to a dinner party. Hattie told me that's what Mrs. De Mille did every time stories appeared about her husband and another woman. She invited the other woman right to her home to quash the story. For years the columnists had gossiped about what they called Mr. De Mille's harem, which included Jeanie Macpherson, Annie Bauchens, and Julia Faye. Now I was part of it, at least in the minds of the columnists, and I would remain so, Hattie said, as long as they could keep readers interested.

No wonder Mr. De Mille made such marvelous pictures about the marital intrigue of high-society people, I thought. He knew what it was all about. I myself was too much in awe of him to fall in love with him, but I could see how it could happen. We dealt every minute in our pictures with love and marriage. I wasn't surprised that people thought of us as creatures who did nothing *but* fall in love, on the screen as well as off, and in fact, they seemed to discourage us from doing anything else. That didn't mean they flirted or took liberties. Not at all. The strangers who said hello to me always said it as if I were their sister or as if they were touching a rabbit's foot. Yet in the tone of their voices I began to sense a sort of psychic pressure on me to be in love, or to fall in love if I wasn't already, to get married to someone else who was famous, to live the romantic dreams they invested in every time they bought a ticket to one of my pictures.

The strangest part of all in the matter of becoming famous was hearing from people I really knew. I got excited letters from June Walker and Medora Grimes and girls I had gone to school with in Puerto Rico, and relatives I had not been close to for years. What they really hoped to discover, of course, was whether I had changed, whether they could say they still knew me; and having gone through so much so quickly, I honestly didn't know, when I stopped and thought about it, whether they still knew me or not.

Mr. De Mille made a practice of inserting into many of his films special episodes which he referred to as his "visions." He included one in the second picture we made together, *For Better, For Worse.* The film was a modern story about the war, but Mr. De Mille added one whole scene in costumes of the twelfth century. Tom Forman wore armor over a tunic of chain mail, and I wore a medieval gown and headdress. We stood for all lovers of all periods taking fond leave before the man goes off to war.

The first day we shot the episode, Craney Gartz showed up at my dressing room during the lunch break to invite me to dinner. He had started calling frequently after our first meeting, and we enjoyed being together, although we fought. I had just been watching the previous day's rushes, and I was chattering enthusiastically about Mr. De Mille. Craney asked me why I was wearing a medieval costume, so I tried to describe to him the "vision" episode, assuming he would be impressed by the poetic content—the meaning—of the scene. It was the very sort of thing he loved to analyze for me out of the writings of the authors he read, and I was happy to be able to show him I was learning to analyze and appreciate things on my own.

"It makes the modern story more significant," I said. "The sequence starts in 1917. Tom and I say good-bye before he goes off to fight in the war. Then the scene fades and you see Tom and me saying good-bye in the clothes of centuries ago as he goes off on the Crusades. That way it becomes more than patriotic or romantic. Mr. De Mille has added a whole beautiful, religious feeling. It's marvelous.''

"Really?" Craney said. "To me it sounds stupid."

"That's because you didn't think of it."

"Come on, Gloria. De Mille doesn't have any real patriotic or religious feelings."

"*Mister* De Mille is *very* patriotic and the whole religious feeling of the scene is absolutely sincere."

"Look, De Mille's pictures are fancy-dress tear-jerkers. They're totally commercial."

"You love to criticize Mr. De Mille because he's a great artist and you're not."

I tried to say this in a cool, detached voice, but I found myself getting angry instead, as I always did with Craney. He knew exactly how to tease me to the boiling point and then say I was beautiful when I was angry while I hotly denied that I was angry. That day he found the perfect way to infuriate me. He started singing the IWW version of "Onward, Christian Soldiers" in a rich, mock-serious tone:

"Onward, Christian soldiers, duty's way is plain;
Slay your Christian neighbors or by them be slain . . ."

"Craney, you're making me angry."

"Ladies in wimples aren't supposed to get angry."

"Get out!"

He kissed me, made the sign of the cross, and turning dramatically as if he were leaving for the Crusades, said, "I'll pick you up at eight."

He was exasperating, and the more he exasperated me, the more I thought I was falling in love with him. Marie Doro was right; he was difficult, but he was marvelous-looking.

The problem with very rich men is that they want what they want when they want it. Craney couldn't understand why I wouldn't give up pictures and run away with him. I told him I wasn't going to live with anybody I wasn't married to. I wasn't even divorced. He said if I had lived with Wally for those two months *without* getting married, I would never have had all the trouble I'd had getting divorced. I told him I also had a contract with Mr. De Mille. He said he was worth $30 million and could buy and sell Cecil B. De Mille any day of the week. I told him he could not touch Mr. De Mille if he were standing on stilts.

One night we arrived at the Alexandria Hotel for dinner. It seemed ages since I had entered that dining room for the first time with Jack Conway in a mixture of wonder and nervousness. Tonight it was Craney's turn to be uncomfortable at the grand old Alexandria. The maître d'hôtel called me by name and said he would see I had the best table in the room. Craney said we already had a table reserved, under the name of Gartz. The maître d' apologized in that tone people use with madmen and said, "Right this way, Miss Swanson."

During the whole dinner one excited person after another came over to speak to me or congratulate me. A number of them said they had met me at parties and dinners I knew I had not attended. They were a mixture of society people and movie people. A few of the society people knew Craney and spoke to him. Most of the movie people had no idea who he was. On a mean impulse I introduced him to the owner of a Los Angeles newspaper as Mr. Blodgett. The man was courteous, even patronizing, and that made Craney so furious that I did it again several times that evening, always with the same result.

In order to turn the stream of table visitors off, Craney dragged me to the dance floor and kept me there for long periods. "Are you enjoying yourself?" he asked sarcastically.

"Of course I am, because I've learned your secret."

"What do you mean?"

"I know what you want."

"Surely I haven't made any secret about *that*."

"I'm not talking about *that*. You want to be famous, Craney. That's what you would like."

"Why would I want fame? It would seem to me you've got enough of that for both of us."

"That's what's so funny. Deep down, I don't care about fame. All I want is a beautiful home and lovely clothes and nice things."

"Come away with me and you'll have them."

"It's not the same if it's your money. I want to make it myself." Then I told him a story I'd almost forgotten. Medora Grimes and I had played a game when I visited her. We'd asked each other, "What did you see today that you want?" One day Medora said, "A house on Murray Hill. What about you?" To her amazement I said, "That factory we saw across the river." "A factory, Glory? Why?" "Because I could be rich if I owned a factory."

"It takes a long time to make a fortune," Craney said. "By

the time you do, you'll look like Hetty Green. Why don't you just help me spend mine?"

"But don't you see, Craney? Then I'd lose what it is *you* want."

"Fame?"

"Yes. And I'd also lose what I want more than money. What you spend all you time laughing at."

"What's that?"

"A family and children."

He tried to dismiss the whole discussion with a joke. "I knew I shouldn't have given you *Ana Karenina* to read," he said.

"Don't worry. I haven't had time to read it yet. Should I?"

"Why ask me? You should probably ask Mr. De Mille."

"Shut up and dance, Blodgett," I said, and for once he obeyed me. Nobody could dance like Craney Gartz.

On the last day of shooting on *For Better, For Worse*, Mr. De Mille took me aside and told me his next picture was going to be a very important one and I was going to be in it. Later he announced to the press that the film would be an adaptation of *The Admirable Crichton* by the renowned Scottish playwright Sir James M. Barrie. He then assembled in his office about forty of the actors, cameramen, set designers, costumers, animal trainers, and engineers who would work on the project and held us spellbound as he told us the story, scene by scene. A titled British family with two spoiled daughters set out on a cruise. Their yacht is shipwrecked on a desert island, and there the social tables are turned. The butler, Crichton, becomes lord and master by virtue of his common sense and native skills in the art of survival, and snobbish, spoiled Lady Mary falls in love with him. When they return to England, however, they revert to the normal social order. Thomas Meighan, a tall, handsome Irishman, was playing Crichton; Theodore Roberts was playing the head of the family; and Lila Lee was playing the scullery maid who secretly adores the butler.

As Lady Mary, I would wear the most exotic array of costumes imaginable. In society I would wear afternoon dresses of the finest Belgian lace, and evening gowns made of satin and moleskin and gold beads. On the desert island I would wear animal skins. I would also have an elaborate bathtub scene wearing nothing at all, and if that weren't enough, Mr. De Mille and Jeanie Macpherson had added a "vision" set in ancient Babylon in which I would wear a dress of pearls and feathers and be tossed into a den of real lions.

Plans called for at least two weeks of location shooting on the uninhabited island of Santa Cruz off the California coast at Santa Barbara. While we were there, we would rough it like the characters in the story.

Fittings went on for days. Clare West made some of my clothes, and a man brought over from Paris did some others. For the scene with the lions, a designer named Mitchell Leisen had an entire crew working on the pearl gown and headdress. Mr. De Mille told Hattie she would have to surpass herself with new hairdos, and I picked out enough jewelry to fill a good-sized vault.

As usual, we did not see the script. Mr. De Mille recounted the story in great detail, and from then on we lived it scene by scene, day by day, starting with the scenes in England which we filmed in the studio.

I could tell from the first day that this film was a major challenge for Mr. De Mille, and all of us gave every ounce of our energy every minute to make it important and special. We could feel a new kind of excitement in our work, and we wondered, each of us, secretly, if we might not be making something way beyond what could be thought of as just another picture. I told Craney, for instance, in no uncertain terms that this film was no tear-jerker. It was a great story by one of the world's major playwrights, and I could sense that it was making Mr. De Mille reach higher and conceive on a grander scale than he had ever done before. The film would be a profound study of society that even someone like Craney would have to take seriously.

As the time for moving to location approached, I told Craney I would not see him for a least a month and forbade him to come anywhere near Santa Cruz. But he drove to the coast to see us film the scenes in which the family embark on their cruise, and there he presented me with a book by Karl Marx to read on location by way of belittling anything by so paltry a writer as Barrie, but by then everyone working on the film was so deeply involved in and devoted to the project that Craney's usual disrespectful barbs could not find a single vulnerable point to enter. He stayed only for a few hours, during which he was almost poignantly left out of everything and ignored by everyone. Then he said he would see me when I returned from Santa Cruz, and drove off in his Packard convertible.

The studio had rented a princely yacht from one of the richest bankers in America for the film. We shot the departure scenes on the shore, and then the crew loaded everything onto the yacht for the trip to the island encampment that had been built for us on Santa Cruz. The strange cargo included crates of chickens, as well as boxes of exotic feathers to stick on the chickens in the scenes where they are supposed to be native birds that Crichton catches to make into a stew. Other crates were full of tropical plants and trees, which would be used to transform the natural landscape of the island. Mr. De Mille had planned everything, down to the tiniest detail, including a lavish picnic lunch on deck for us during the crossing to Santa Cruz.

We were feeling festive and pleased with ourselves after a morning of shooting, and all of us in the cast sat down to lunch in the fancy traveling costumes of the characters in the play. A tremendously strong group feeling had already built up among us, whether we were working or playing, so as soon as Lila or somebody started talking in an English accent, we all joined in, being very la-di-da and ordering tea and scones and saying how much we would miss Ascot this year. Within minutes, it seemed, as we sat joking, the sky became overcast, the sea rose, and a strong wind blew several hats and napkins over the side. Soon the pitch and toss of the boat made it necessary to move the picnic into the yacht's lounge. Lila and I stood at the rail watching the crew and technicians remove everything from the slippery deck. When we started to go below ourselves, we found that we were unable to. I tried to hold on to Lila, and we both sprawled across the wet boards. Tommy Meighan and some crew members grabbed us and helped us to the staircase. By then the sky was nearly black.

Inside the boat everyone was moaning and green. Maids, makeup men, actors, and technicians were all in the same state. The combined smell of uneaten food and vomit turned the strongest stomachs, and when the pitching and rolling continued for hour after hour, the atmosphere of discomfort gave way to one of panic.

Finally the channel was calm enough for us to head into Santa Cruz. When they told us the yacht was secured and we could disembark, we were the saddest, most bedraggled lot that ever climbed out of a hold. Our beautiful clothes were ruined, and those people not too sick to walk had to help the others up onto the deck. To make matters worse, the expert in charge of navigational matters had had the dock built at a place where we couldn't tie up. Facing us in the darkness was a steep cliff with a pathway that would give pause to a goat. With nothing but a few kerosene lamps for light, we had to trudge up the slippery trail, carrying our belongings, and make our way to the encampment of tents and huts where we would live for the next few weeks. Exhausted as we were, Sam Wood insisted on gathering us all together for a head count, at the end of which we realized that one technician was missing, the very man, in fact, who had had the dock built in the wrong place. Sam and a crew member had to crawl back down the steep path and search while the rest of us began worriedly to settle into the camp. Sam soon came back to report that the technician was in one of the cabins on the yacht with his head in a pail and that he had begged Sam to let him stay there until morning. There was hot food for those of us who felt like eating, Sam said, and Mr. De Mille gave orders for all of us to rub dry and dress warmly before we turned in. We could not afford any cases of pneumonia.

Lila and I shared a small hut, and lying in the dark waiting to fall asleep, we discussed what no one in our whole company could be unaware of: the eerie similarities in our experiences so far since embarking and the experiences of the characters in Barrie's play. Throughout the filming up to then we had felt innumerable vibrations that we were engaged in a project of almost mystical import. Now that we were really on the island, we looked forward to the days ahead with brave, excited anticipation.

Like the Almighty himself, Mr. De Mille managed to bring order out of chaos, and he didn't have seven days to do it. By the time we woke up the next morning he had everything in perfect readiness to film the shipwreck. While always considerate of our wishes, he was efficiency itself. He let nothing stand in his way, and soon he had infused us all with his spirit. We did things cheerfully on Santa Cruz that we would flatly have refused to do in any other picture or for any other director.

Tommy Meighan, for example, had a scene where as Crichton he has to go back on board the wrecked vessel to look for a silly trinket left behind by Lady Mary. Tommy wasn't much of a swimmer, and we could all see that he was nervous when the day come to shoot the scene. Mr. De Mille had waited for days for a calm sea, but each morning the water had been rough and choppy; he couldn't delay the shooting any longer. As a company, we were interested by now in every scene. We didn't watch rushes on Santa Cruz; we all watched the real thing. So as the camera started grinding, we were all sitting to one side watching Tommy jump from a rock onto the set of the wrecked yacht. We gasped when he lost his footing and slid down the hull into the churning water. Mr. De Mille jumped in front of the camera and began to shout orders for men to bring ropes. As if knowing there was no time for that, Johnny, our Hawaiian propman, leaped onto the hull and from there into the sea. I was terrified they would both be bashed against the hull or the rocks. Tommy was in deep water, out of sight. I was on the verge of screaming when I suddenly saw two heads bobbing in the water. Everybody cheered as Johnny inched Tommy toward the rocks against the pull of the tide and finally caught hold of a rope the crew threw to him. He had unquestionably saved Tommy's life. Without him we would have had no picture. The incident brought home to everybody there the sense of teamwork that pervaded every moment of the making of *Crichton*. Tommy Meighan, Johnny, the crew member with the rope—all of us were indispensable and strangely inseparable. Only Mr. De Mille loomed over everyone else.

Given this spirit that everyone could feel as if it were a living thing, I plunged into my hazardous scenes with a resolution verging on eagerness. I wasn't asked to swim, but I had to wade out of the surf in a beaded gown and crawl up an incline of slippery rocks. After having watched Tommy's harrowing adventure, I knew I had nothing to complain about. On the contrary, I felt lucky to be crawling on dry, if slippery, land. When I finished the scene my knees were bloody, my hands were scratched, and pieces of crushed beads had dug into my thighs. Mr. De Mille asked me if he should send for a doctor. I said of course not, and had my maid bring me tweezers and help me pick the broken beads out of my flanks. The crew cheered me, and Mr. De Mille began to call me "young fellow," as if I were one of the boys. In the days and weeks that followed, he never called me anything else.

The weeks on the island were harsh and exhausting for people who customarily worked on luxurious sets in designer clothes, but by the second week we were all strangely happy and alert and in touch with one another. We behaved as I had never known a bunch of movie people to behave. We seemed to be in a crucible of excitement and tenderness—all of it Mr. De Mille's doing, we knew.

One evening when I noticed Carl, one of the assistant directors, looking anxiously out to sea, I asked him if anything was wrong. He said he was worried about Johnny, the Hawaiian boy who had saved Tommy Meighan. Johnny had left that morning alone in a small boat to run errands on the mainland, and he was not back.

"Don't worry," I said. "He's all right. He's with people who aren't Hawaiian."

As soon as I said it, I wondered why. So did Carl. "What did you say?" he asked, but his words couldn't stop a flow of images I was experiencing.

"Is he a musician?" I asked. "Because he's sitting at a piano."

"I don't think so," Carl said in a faraway voice. He told me later that I seemed so absorbed he didn't know whether to answer me or not. But I was fully conscious, he said, not at all like a sleepwalker.

A minute later I said, "He's stopped playing. He's eating a bunch of radishes."

"Radishes!" Carl said, in a tone so explosive that it made us both laugh, and the incident was over.

Johnny showed up safe and sound the next day, and a night or two after that I got Carl to go with me and talk to him. As casually as I could, I asked him what he had done the night he was away.

"Visited some Russians I know," he said.

Carl and I looked at each other. I had said he was with people who weren't Hawaiian. "Were you there for dinner?" I asked.

"No. I got there too late."

"So what did you do?" I said, trying not to prompt.

"I just sat and talked."

"Did you happen to be near a musical instrument?" I asked, and for the first time Johnny looked at me strangely, so I said that something had happened to me on the island after he left, and would he please try to remember.

"It's funny. I can't play the piano, but I have always wanted to. My Russian friends have a beautiful piano, and that night I sat down and plunked the keys."

Carl and I looked at each other again.

"You said you didn't have dinner. Did you have anything to eat?" I asked.

At first he said no. Then he remembered something that seemed to embarrass him. "I went into their kitchen late in the evening because I was hungry, and all I could find was a bunch of radishes. I ate them all."

The incident itself was trivial. But the circumstances were unusual, and Carl was a witness that I hadn't faked or prodded. I felt like a baby discovering for the first time that it can move its toes. In exactly the same way, I had discovered that I had some kind of muscles in my mind that I had never used before. I didn't know how I had got them going. I didn't know if I would ever be able to call on them again. Furthermore, I'm sure I would have forgotten the incident altogether if still stranger connections had not been made for me a few days later. When I got back to Los Angeles, Bea told me a cable had arrived from my father while I was in Santa Cruz. He was being shipped back to the States from France and would have a few free days to spend with me when he arrived. But of course! I suddenly exclaimed to myself. Daddy's brother, my Uncle Charlie, claimed to have visions. In fact, he had claimed to dream of my birth the very night I was being born. That I should suddenly have a first visionary experience practically on the eve of Daddy's return, when I had not seen him for five years, made me want to tear through the great sheet of stars overhead once and for all and ask infinity its name.

Bea and I got a room ready, and I told the maid to stock the liquor cabinet with everything imaginable. There was constant talk of prohibition of liquor sales going into effect across the country any day, and I didn't want to be unprepared. I had not seen Daddy since I was fifteen; we had long distances to span back to each other. Therefore I was absolutely determined to make him comfortable while he was with me. If he drank copiously—and I knew he probably would—I decided to create a situation in which I would avoid the least feelings of guilt or suspicion on either of our parts while we were together. I called Mother to tell her he was coming, but she said she didn't wish to see him. It would be awkward for Mr. Burns, she felt. A few months before, Grandmother Lew had moved in with Mother after her own mother, my

Great-grandma May, had died, so we were in touch again frequently, though usually just by phone. My mother still had no interest whatsoever in my movie career, and her life had long been totally separate from mine. Her blunt refusal to see Daddy prompted me more than ever to do everything I could to make him happy. I told Bea that if he arrived while I was at the studio, she should bring him over at once.

Mr. De Mille had saved the most dangerous scenes in *The Admirable Crichton*—the "vision" in Babylon—until the very last. Except for a dozen black slaves in leopard skins who would carry me in on an elaborate litter, the only other characters in the scene were Tommy Meighan, Bebe Daniels, and half a dozen lions. Tommy as the King of Babylon has me brought before his throne. He tells me to renounce my religion and become his bride or face a den of lions on the other side of a golden door situated at the foot of the steps to the throne. I choose the lions, of course, and Mr. De Mille said I should confront them in the manner of a very dignified Christian saint. Only on rare occasions did Mr. De Mille impose specific acting tasks on his performers, and these occasions frequently had to do with his historical visions. He believed in reincarnation and tried to demonstrate it in these pageants, these switches in time, these presentations of people living in different ages simultaneously on the screen. He actually believed that people had to come back to earth and suffer for the sins of their past lives.

The set was tremendous. It consisted of the lions' den and the throne room. The lions' den was an enormous swimming pool, converted into an arena and painted entirely with black lacquer, so that when I entered it in an all-white costume I would look like a frail, virginal, moving target. There were arches all around the edge of the arena and a flight of steps descending into it. At the bottom of the steps was a golden filigree gate. The whole set was enclosed with heavy wire mesh, like a cage in the circus or a zoo. The only people who could be inside the wire mesh with the lions were Tommy, Bebe, Mr. De Mille, the cameraman, the trainers, and I. Mr. De Mille and the trainers, none of whom could be seen by the camera, had whips and guns to control the lions.

The greatest risk for me was the sheer weight of my costume. Two maids had to help me carry it when I was not on the set. The gown was made entirely of pearls and white beads—enough to fill a bushel basket—and the towering headdress was made of white peacock feathers, which were a source of great consternation in the wardrobe department, for many people thought they brought bad luck. Because of the long train, I also had two-inch cork lifts on my shoes, so maneuverability was a serious problem.

There were two sequences to shoot. In the first I had to descend the steps and approach the filigree gate. I was told to remain perfectly calm, for the gate was made of painted wood and therefore easily breakable. If a lion happened to get excited or angry and jumped up against it, he could smash right through it. However, the lions were not expected even to come near the gate, the trainers said. In the second sequence, I had to lie on my stomach and have a lion put his paw on my bare back.

Once I was in costume, Mr. De Mille escorted me into the great enclosed set. When the lights hit me, I walked across the floor of the throne room toward the steps, and at a given moment the trainers cracked their whips and the lions were released. I could see the shapes of the animals beyond the gate. I took a few more steps forward, then froze, petrified, as one lion unexpectedly moved to the side of the gate and bounded up out of the den, landing a few feet away from me. We stared at each other for a split second, and then one of the trainers whisked me off my feet like a bean bag and carried me outside the enclosure while another forced the lion to jump back down into the arena. There were gasps and whispers on all sides, and an assistant director brought me a glass of sherry, but since I could see that Mr. De Mille was perfectly thrilled at the way the scene had gone, I said I didn't need anything, that I was fine.

Then we did it again, and this time everyone on the crew, as well as Mr. De Mille, carried a stick or a chair. As I slowly descended the steps, one of the animals—I couldn't tell if it was the same one—sprang forward and crouched menacingly just on the other side of the wooden gate. I was afraid to turn my back to him. Men behind me were calling instructions, but I stood absolutely still. The lion and I stared at each other, hypnotized, until a trainer stepped in front of me and drove him back with a whip and a chair. Somehow I then managed to pick up the train of that beaded dress as if it were the sheerest nightie and scramble over to another trainer, who helped me off the set. There was pandemonium in the studio. "That's it! Cut! Fine!" Mr. De Mille was shouting.

He rushed over and asked me if I was all right.

"Yes," I said in a small, white voice.

"We didn't know they could leap up to this level," Mr. De Mille said. "But it looked marvelous and we got all of it. Are you sure you're all right, young fellow?"

"Yes, of course."

"Good," he said, and paused. "In fact, I think we'll omit the scene with the lion on your back."

I could tell he was frightened for me, and that was enough to fill me with courage.

"Oh, please, Mr. De Mille," I urged. "You've said right from the start that you wanted the scene of *The Lion's Bride*."

It was true. We had talked about the scene many times. As a child I had been fascinated by a picture with that name hanging in my grandmother's house. There was a story that went with it. A young girl has trained a lion. She steps into her friend's cage on her wedding day, and while her betrothed stands outside, the lion out of jealousy strikes her to the ground with his paw and kills her. Mr. De Mille knew the painting too.

"I'm not frightened," I said. "The trainer and you will be right near me."

"Are you absolutely certain?" Mr. De Mille asked, staring straight through me.

I knew how much he wanted the shot in the film, so I said very calmly, "Of course, Mr. De Mille."

"All right, young fellow," he said, almost bursting with anticipation, "let's go," and with that he took me by the hand and escorted me back onto the set and down the steps to the lions' arena.

This time I had to lie on the floor and remain absolutely still. I would ruin the scene if I couldn't control my breathing. My back was bare to the waist. I could hear a lion's claws scratching the floor as the trainer led him in on a leash. Then I could hear another trainer whisper to Mr. De Mille, who came and knelt beside me.

"I must ask you something for your own safety," he whispered. "You're not menstruating, are you?"

"No," I replied very softly.

He stood up and said to the trainer, "We can proceed. Everything's fine."

Then I could hear the lion breathing near me. They put a piece of canvas on my back to keep the lion's manicured claws from making the slightest scratch. Then they brought the lion up to me and put his paw on the canvas. Ever so slowly they pulled the canvas aside until I could feel his paw on my skin. Every hair on my head was standing on end. I could hear the camera grinding and then the crack of the trainer's whip. Every cell in my body quivered when the animal roared. His hot breath seemed to go up and down my spine.

For an instant I opened my eyes a slit. Without raising my head, I saw lines of people ringing the set, motionless, absolutely silent. Among them, in his uniform, his eyes popping almost out of his head, was Daddy. His mouth hung open with horror at the sight of his one and only child with a man holding a gun beside her and a roaring lion standing over her. It was our first glimpse of each other in five years.

When the scene was over, I could tell that Mr. De Mille was ecstatic. He said we would not reshoot it. He could tell it was perfect. He said if I had any energy left, he would like me to get into the moleskin evening gown so that he could redo one or two close-ups. Then the shooting would be finished.

By then Daddy was beside me and we embraced. Overcome with emotion, I indicated Mr. De Mille and blurted out, "Daddy, I want you to meet my father."

Immediately we all laughed and I cleared up the confusion, but as I did so I realized that what I had said was perfectly true. Mr. De Mille, as soon as he understood who the man in uniform was, couldn't have been more charming. I had told him, of course, that Daddy had served in France. He invited us to spend a few days anytime at Paradise, his ranch-estate. Then I went to my dressing room to change and Daddy followed me.

Suddenly I was pale and trembling. All my strength was gone. I grabbed a coat, told Daddy to wait for me, and went to Mr. De Mille's office.

"Mr. De Mille, I don't think I can do any more today. I—I—"

I was sobbing. The lion, the tension, and Daddy's appearance had been too much.

"How lovely," Mr. De Mille said. "I was beginning to think that you were the perfect machine, that you could do anything. But now I know you're much more than that. You're a real woman." He looked at me with a combination of satisfaction and amusement. "Come over here and sit down."

He sat me on his knee, and from one of his desk drawers he pulled out a velvet tray covered with brooches, rings, necklaces, and a whole array of other beautiful jewelry. He told me he had planned to give me something at the finish of the picture, but that he thought I should have it now. He smiled broadly, patted me on the hand, and said, "Take your choice."

I looked carefully at every piece, but my eyes kept going back to a delicate little gold-mesh purse with a square sapphire in the center. I picked it up and smiled at him with gratitude, and he gave me his handkerchief again to blow my nose.

"Good!" he said. "We'll finish the picture tomorrow instead of today. And I'll tell you a secret. I'm changing the title. When I met with the promotion people, none of them knew how to pronounce 'Crichton' and they all kept saying 'admiral' instead of 'admirable.' I finally said, 'If you damn fools don't know the difference between *admiral* and *admirable*, I'll change the title.' I'm going to call it *Male and Female Created He Them*—from the Bible. Do you like it?"

"Oh, Mr. De Mille, it's beautiful."

In the car Daddy and I began to catch up. He said he would be stationed at Fort MacArthur, outside Los Angeles. He had seen two of my pictures in the Philippines, before he was sent to France, but he said he hadn't admitted to the men on the base that I was his daughter. He said he felt that was none of their business; that he liked to keep his family affairs to himself. I told him Great-grandma May had died and that Grandma Lew had moved in with Mother and Mr. Burns.

"How is she, Glory?" he finally asked, meaning Mother. He never mentioned Matthew Burns.

"She's fine."

"She's well off, I guess."

"Yes," I said, "the man she married has some money."

"That's good," he said. "And you?"

"Oh, fine," I said. "I'm almost divorced myself."

He quickly changed the subject, as if he had no right to talk about things that had happened to me since we had seen each other. I had not imagined how hard it would be to communicate with him. He obviously had no idea who Mr. De Mille was. Or Wallace Beery. Or Jack Conway. If I had told him a brash young snob worth $30 million wanted me to live with him free of the bourgeois constraints of a marriage license, he surely wouldn't have believed me. He couldn't have imagined that anyone in our family, even Aunt Inga, could ever meet somebody with that much money.

After another long pause, he said, with difficulty, "How does she look?"

"Wonderful," I said. "The same. You look the same too."

He didn't, of course, but then neither must I, from his point of view. He looked thin and peaked, and his eyes were red and tired. He seemed ten years older, not five. As soon as we got to the house, he had a large drink and excused himself to get ready for dinner. He stayed in his room for over an hour. At dinner he was polite and attentive, and Bea took up any slack in the conversation with stories about Court Corinne and the rest of my past that she shared with me. He said very early that he thought he would finish the wine and go to bed; the trip had tired him. When he had gone upstairs, I asked Bea if he seemed all right to her. She knew what I meant, of course, because we had discussed my absent father many times, and Bea was also a trained nurse.

"I don't think his drinking is the worst of it," she said.

"What do you mean? You think there's something else?"

She nodded. "What they used to call the army disease," she said.

"What's that?"

"I could be wrong, but judging from the way he acts, I think he's also taking some kind of narcotic. Maybe it's only one of those stimulants they take in the tropics, but it's something."

After that I hardly slept at all. I lay awake trying to think what I should say to him and what I could do for him. I knew nothing at all about drug addiction. I only knew that I would probably break his heart and destroy his self-respect if I ever mentioned it. But he was so young to waste away, I kept thinking, and the more I thought about it, the more helpless I felt.

Once we were past our first few nervous days together, he seemed more relaxed, more like the dear, sweet man I remembered in San Juan. The day after I finished the picture I drove him out to the San Fernando Valley to the local flying field, where there were two planes and a dilapidated barn of a building in the middle of a large field of grass. An aviator with whom I had posed for publicity pictures when he came back from the war had told me he would take me up anytime and I was dying to say I had flown before it ceased to be a novelty. I also liked the idea of being able to tell Craney that I had flown without him; it would throw his nose out of joint a mile. Mr. De Mille was the only civilian I knew besides Craney who flew an airplane. He sometimes carried a passenger with him to Pasadena, but he flatly refused ever to let me fly with him. Hattie said that was a great compliment if Mr. De Mille wouldn't take any chances with my life in an airplane even if he enjoyed risking his own.

The lieutenant who was my friend was at the field and said the weather was perfect. I had called him that morning, so he had the plane out and ready. He wound up the propeller and helped me in. I waved to Daddy and we took off. Never, *never* had anything thrilled me to the extent that flying did that day. It was a hundred times more exciting than driving a car or facing a lion. I couldn't wait to get my hands on the controls. I motioned to the pilot to do somersaults and turns, and he did six or seven fancy ones. I was elated. I felt completely at home in the air. After a few minutes the pilot began to climb. Then he cut off the engine and we sailed quietly down toward the ground. He shouted that what we were doing was called a flying leaf. I was squealing with joy. He made a beautiful landing, and we taxied up to the hangar, where Daddy was waiting.

"Oh, it's so exciting!" I shouted as I ran to him. "I'm going to start taking lessons every Sunday."

I stopped laughing when I saw his face. It was green, and the muscles were twitching. He had been perfectly calm on the ride out, but now, minutes later, his jaw was so rigid he could hardly speak. His words came out at first as irascible, illogical.

"Glory," he said, "don't you ever go up like that again. That damn fool should know better. He somersaulted."

"But, Daddy," I said, "he flew in the war."

"I don't care. You don't know what that just did to me. Planes aren't safe, Glory. They never will be. Promise me, Glory, promise me you'll never do it again. Promise!"

There were tears in his eyes, and he was almost choking on his words. He put his arms around me. "You're my little girl," he said. "You're all I have. Promise."

He was shaking so badly that I slipped my arms out of his embrace and put them tightly around him. I hugged him until he grew calm. Was this the man who had fought his way through a hurricane to be with Mother and me? Was this the man who had patiently named all the stars for me night after night during those years in San Juan? Was this the man who had told me life is ninety-five percent anticipation and only five percent realization?

"Yes, of course I promise," I said.

CHAPTER 8

DATELINE: The Boston *Post*, November 2, 1919
BY-LINE: Carl Wilmore

GLORIA SWANSON DISCUSSES
LOVE, MEN, DIVORCE

Lasky Studios, Hollywood, Cal.—Gloria Swanson—the tempestuous, Swedish, naïve Gloria—says:

"I'm willing to be myself. What's the use of pretending to think this or that when you really think otherwise? You tell my friends *exactly* what I say, and—well, if they're the right kind of friends, they will like me all the better for it!"

Gloria was at work making her new picture, *Why Change Your Wife?*, a sequel to the picture that made her a star—and one of the finest pictures ever created, rated above *Broken Blossoms* by many—*Don't Change Your Husband.*

. . .

"I'm not temperamental," said Gloria. . . . "I have no swelled head. Why should I have? I've done nothing. Mr. De Mille has done everything for me. . . . I had luck—Mr. De Mille noticed me. A thousand more talented girls, more attractive girls, more intelligent girls are passed over. I had the good fortune to be picked . . . Who said [I had a big head]? I bet it was a woman! . . . Women are awful. . . . They're just cats."

131

· · ·

[The maid] approached us with a tray. . . . Here was
Gloria's lunch—read this, you girls who complain of the
cost of securing sufficient food to sustain life:

1 glass chocolate malted milk
2 lamb sandwiches, cut into inch squares

"The inch-square sandwich is my own invention. I'm
going to have it patented," said Gloria. "Trying to bite
into a whole sandwich will ruin my make-up. But I can
put one of these little squares into my mouth without
touching my make-up at all. Clever, isn't it?" and she
munched away at a square.

· · ·

Gloria Swanson—for I had a chance of observing her
closely—is a shining example of the fact that absolute
beauty is not necessary for great screen success—or
"luck," as she calls it.

And yet, who will not admit that Gloria Swanson is
one of the most beautiful women of the screen? Is it her
really fine eyes? Her strangely appealing smile? Her
individuality of manner? Her undoubted talent? Is it all
of them together? It's hard to tell—but you can see the
result for yourself.

· · ·

[Gloria on marriage:] "Marry—I? Merciful heavens. I
was married. . . . I was married when I was 17. I knew
nothing. I was full of romance. Now there's little romance left in me. . . .

"I've passed through more in the last three years than
my dear mother has passed through in her whole life.
And, by the way, I never really showed any great ability
in my work until three years ago. Maybe it was suffering
that brought it out. They say every artist must have
suffered," and Gloria wiggled one of her pretty little
feet.

"Regarding divorce," said I, "in your famous picture,
Don't Change Your Husband, you tried to show that—"

"I showed that you must be sure that it is all over
before you separate," she interrupted. "The wife in that
picture only imagined she was tired of her husband. She
really loved him deep down.

"In this new picture, the sequel, *Why Change Your*

Wife?, I try to show that a man must look beneath the surface to know his wife; also, that she must know how to hold her husband. At the start she dresses indifferently—she's safely married and no longer dresses to please her husband; the result—he looks elsewhere. But she learns the lesson and before the picture ends we find the wife dressing more stunningly than any of the gay creatures that had attracted her husband."

"Women aren't like that in real life," I said.

"No? Oh, yes, they are, lots of them. Half of them lose their husbands because they become indifferent in their personal appearance. Both sides think it's no longer necessary to go on courting."

"How about men?"

"They're just as bad. . . ."

"But I hear you're marrying again, Gloria. . . ."

"Well, the gossiping women will have me married probably. What they haven't said about me! I am supposed to wear a wig and that's not all. . . ."

"No, but really, Gloria, . . . I heard there was a man out in Pasadena who—"

"That's all off," said Gloria.

"How long since?"

"Until he thought he could make me jump when he said so. I told him flatly, 'This can never go on,' and now he's doing the jumping. He still sends me flowers, but I'm through jumping. He was very nice, as men go," said Gloria. "I've got to change," she continued. "See you in my dressing room in a minute—135."

I followed, but slowly, to give her time to change. When I arrived Gloria was all arrayed in a soft robin's egg blue-green gown. Sitting before her mirror, having his hair curled with a hot iron by Hattie, the Lasky hairdresser, was a foreign-looking man in a dress suit. . . .

"This is my Russian lover," said Gloria, and the Russian lover smiled under Hattie's curling iron. "Theodore Kosloff, you know," and I realized that the noted Russian dancer had now entered pictures.

A box of flowers—12 immense yellow chrysanthemums—lay on the dressing table.

"From Pasadena?" I asked.

"Hm—yes," said Gloria. . . .

Theodore is only playing her lover in the picture, but Gloria insists on fooling away from working hours. . . . Thomas Meighan . . . plays the part of Gloria's husband in the picture.

After playing leading roles in three De Mille pictures in a row, I was becoming public property. Newspapers all over the country asked for "exclusive" interviews, so in addition to watching rushes during the lunch period, I often had to talk to reporters, who outdid one another in thinking up trivial things to ask me. They wanted to know whether I liked tall men or short men, how often I ate dessert, what my favorite breed of dog was, if I dyed my hair, what my favorite color was, if I got depressed on rainy days, what my favorite flower was, if I considered myself stuck-up, if I thought So-and-so was a nice dresser, if I ever obeyed silly impulses. By the time I thought I had finally talked to the last columnist in America, the first one was back at the dressing room door with more questions. I quickly learned that the stories they printed about me were almost always exaggerated and almost never accurate, and that no two of them ever agreed. But it was difficult for me to say no to these people because from the studio's point of view each interview I gave sold more and more movie tickets, not only to my movies and Mr. De Mille's movies, but to all movies distributed by Paramount, in fact to movies in general. America, in the years following the Great War, was movie-crazy.

The sudden rush of publicity affected my friends and family as well as me. Bea La Plante, my companion and pal, was soon transformed into a drudge, answering the phone, taking messages, sorting mail, clipping and filing the endless interviews. She never complained, but I felt terribly guilty nevertheless. Craney Gartz became known to readers across the nation as that fellow from Pasadena who couldn't make Gloria Swanson toe the line, and I took a certain pleasure in keeping reporters informed of my on-again off-again romance with him. It infuriated him that he should be no more in the eyes of the bourgeois press than the temperamental suitor about whom I chatted gaily while my fingernail polish dried and Hattie combed my hair. My mother staunchly turned her back to all reporters, but until they finally believed that she would always be uncooperative, they pestered her and Mr. Burns day and night. To make matters worse, the only person who truly enjoyed my success was Grandma Lew. She loved to come to the studio and take part in interviews in my dressing room, and reporters mentioned her frequently, which of course annoyed Mother.

My father, nervous, jittery, and in poor health, was uncomfortable to be the focus of any attention, perhaps because he was afraid he might embarrass me. It was clear that he did not like to visit the studio, so whenever I could, I arranged ways for us to be alone together. However, on his last night in Hollywood I decided he should have one fancy evening out. I told Bea to call the Alexandria Hotel and have them send a car for us at eight, and when we entered the dining room at half past, the maître d' treated us like long-awaited royalty. "Your table is ready, Captain Swanson," he said, and Daddy beamed.

While we were having drinks, several people sent cards to the table. I smiled pleasantly in the direction of each sender after the waiter pointed out the person, but I was determined for Daddy's sake to keep a very low profile and speak to no one. One card, however, was much more tempting than the rest. "Look at this," I said to Bea. "Equity Pictures Corporation. Herbert K. Somborn, President."

"He's from New York, I'll bet," Bea said, looking at the card. "All the really important people in pictures are in New York."

After we had ordered a second drink and I could see that Daddy was perfectly relaxed, I said, "I'm going to let the president of Equity Pictures come over, all right? Bea, he might get you a part in something."

Minutes after the waiter delivered my message, Herbert Somborn appeared at the table. He was medium-tall, about forty, with a high forehead, light-brown wavy hair, blue eyes, and a large arched nose. His clothes were beautifully tailored. He bowed smoothly and said, "Good evening, Miss Swanson. I was just talking to Clara Kimball Young on the telephone, and I told her you were here. She insisted I tell you how much she enjoyed you in *Don't Change Your Husband*."

Even Daddy knew who Clara Kimball Young was. A

leading star in pictures, the regal, sedate beauty was a household name.

"Miss Young told me if I didn't bring you out for dinner at her home one evening soon, she would never speak to me again. I couldn't afford that," Mr. Somborn said, laughing. "That's why I took the liberty of sending over my card."

He was so calm and affable that when he said he was alone, Daddy invited him to join us for a drink. He protested that he would be intruding, but we all assured him he would not be and he sat down. I told him Bea had been in several films with Sessue Hayakawa, and he listened with polite interest.

"When are we going to see you in New York?" he asked me. I told him I wasn't sure. I'd made three pictures in a year for Mr. De Mille. They had promised to send me to New York when I finished the fourth, which was already in production.

"Do you have a studio in New York?" Bea asked.

Mr. Somborn explained that his New York office handled distribution. The studio was in California. That was to say, Equity Pictures distributed Clara Kimball Young productions, just as Paramount Pictures distributed films for Famous Players-Lasky. He had come to California to arrange for the release of Miss Young's new picture, *Eyes of Youth*. He said he and Miss Young were both very excited about the picture. Al Parker had directed it, he said.

"Really?" I said. "I worked with Mr. Parker at Triangle." Bea and I both kept our faces totally impassive, because Albert Parker was the man whom Wally had punched in the nose across from the Beverly Hills Hotel, and who had then nobly wrecked his car for me. "Please say hello to him for me when you see him."

"I certainly shall. There's a young Italian dancer in the picture whose name is Rudolph Valentino." Turning to Bea, he said, "Have you heard of him?"

"No," Bea said.

"Nobody has, it seems," Mr. Somborn said. "But we think he's very good in it. We hope to use him again in a new picture called *Silk Husbands, Calico Wives*. Wonderful title, isn't it? Well, it's been delightful," he said, finishing his drink and standing up. "What shall I tell Clara, Miss Swanson?"

"Tell her I'd be honored," I said. "But Sunday is my only day off as a rule."

"I'm sure that will be fine," he said. "May I call you?"

"Of course," I said.

After dinner I made Daddy dance with Bea, and I sat and watched them. He seemed much smaller than I'd remembered him, and he looked much older than forty-nine. Then it was my turn to dance with him.

"Well, what do you think of the fancy side of Hollywood?" I asked him when we were on the floor.

"It's too fancy for me. Everyone here is looking at you, Glory, do you know that?"

"They're wondering who the officer is I'm dating."

He hugged me and smiled.

"Who was that fellow who came to the table?"

"Herbert Somborn. I've never met him before. Why?"

"Is he important?"

"I guess so. Why?"

"I was just wondering if he lived with Clara Kimball Young, that's all. Do you think so?"

"Why, Captain Swanson! One week out here and you've started gossiping. You'll be believing everything they say about *me* next."

"They don't say anything bad, do they?"

"They say I'm going to marry a millionaire. Would you like that?"

"I don't know. It's hard to imagine that much money. How much was that other fellow worth?"

"Herbert Somborn? I have no idea."

"No, I mean that fellow Addie married. Burns."

"Oh. I have no idea, Daddy."

At the studio on Monday, I received flowers from Herbert Somborn; not a huge box of chrysanthemums like the ones Craney sent the same day, but a delicate little straw basket full of green moss and strange, fragile blossoms like none I had ever seen before. In a note that was attached he thanked me for a lovely evening and proposed the following Sunday to dine at Clara Kimball Young's.

During the week Daddy was with me I refused to see Craney because I was certain that within minutes he would shock or offend my father. Even if he managed to stay off the topics of Bolshevism and free love, his natural snobbishness would surely intimidate Daddy and probably hurt him as well. But two nights after I drove Daddy to Fort MacArthur for reassignment, I found myself across a dinner table from Craney at the Pasadena Country Club, the one place left, it seemed, where more people recognized him than recognized me.

My instant success in the press had been very hard on him. He knew that his money and good looks and a snap of the fingers would no longer turn the trick. As for his mind and my education, I would always be miles behind him as long as I continued to make films, and I still had a long contract with Mr. De Mille ahead of me. Quite apart from romance, Craney had a formidable rival for my devotion in Cecil B. De Mille and he knew it. For the first time in my life, work was art, under the guidance of a great artist, and that spell would have proved a very hard one for anyone to break, but especially Craney.

We had danced long and tenderly. It was late in the evening and Craney was pushing a velvet box across the table to me.

"What is it?"

"Open it and see."

It was a beautiful white-gold bracelet set with diamonds. He helped me put it on and we danced again. He kissed me and I felt myself melting under his teasing, patrician smiles.

"It's late," I said.

"I know. Let's race to my place, and I'll drive you from there to work in the morning."

"No."

"Why not?"

"Craney, for the one thousandth time, my divorce is still not final and won't be for another month. Wally has been a real bastard."

"So what? No one will find out. Not even the thousands of columnists who count your eyelashes every morning."

"That's not the point."

"Then what is? Darling, it's a simple biological fact that if you've been married, you're not a virgin. So why fight a natural attraction?"

"Why do you think?"

We were both getting scratchy, as we always did at this point.

"I don't know," he said. "Why?"

"Because I'm not Isadora Duncan, at least not yet. I don't want to join the free-love cult. I want to be respectably married."

"To whom, for heaven's sake? Cecil B. De Mille?"

"Craney, I warn you . . ."

"I love you; can't you understand that?"

"I love you, too. Why not try waiting a month and asking me to marry you?"

"Would you?"

"I don't know. Would you ask?"

"I don't know. You know I hate the whole idea. Everybody I know is miserable because they're bound into marriage."

"Craney, this argument always breaks down right here. Tonight I'm going to finish it. Do you know what the real problem is?"

"No, what?"

"Deep down, you're afraid I want to marry you for your money. That's really why you're determined to test me without a marriage license. Otherwise you'd never be sure I loved you, isn't that it?"

"No."

"Yes, it is."

"All right, now that we've come this far, what about you? Why won't you live with me without a marriage license? I'll tell you. Because if you have to give up your career, you don't want to do it under any circumstances of scandal or risk, for fear you couldn't get it back if things between us didn't work out. Who's short on trust now?"

"Help me off with this bracelet."

"You can keep it."

"I don't want to keep it. At least not until we can trust each other. You keep it until then."

After that he drove me home in silence. We had finally uttered what we basically feared in each other: immaturity, lack of trust. We kissed good night with intense passion, but warily—almost, for the moment, resentfully.

That Sunday, Herbert Somborn picked me up and drove me to Clara Kimball Young's. The house was one of the most beautiful I'd ever seen, easily as large and elegantly furnished as the fabled mansions of Pasadena. The first thing I noticed about Miss Young was her jewelry. I had worn real jewels and lots of them for Mr. De Mille on the set, but here was a gracious, amusing woman who was positively glowing with diamonds and sapphires at her own candlelit dinner table. There were only four of us that evening, Miss Young, a man called Harry Garson, Herbert Somborn, and I. Harry Garson was the general manager of Miss Young's company, and he and Herbert Somborn were obviously great friends. They all talked about the picture business on a level I'd never even been aware of before. They seemed to know everybody who was anybody, as well as what everybody was up to.

It was amazing for me to hear Miss Young discuss stock issues, mortgages, bylaws, injunctions, and powers of attorney with the same confidence other women might display in reciting a recipe for angel food cake. In what other business in the world, I wondered, could this delightful, elegant creature be completely independent—turning out her own pictures, dealing with men as equals, being able to use her brain as well as her beauty, having total say as to what stories she played in, who designed her clothes, and who her director and leading man would be.

They talked at length about the bankers and stockholders they dealt with in New York, especially somebody called Patrick Powers, who was a major stockholder in Equity Pictures. When Mr. Somborn remarked that Pat Powers had started out as a policeman in Boston, Miss Young asked, "How does a policeman get to be a banker?" Mr. Somborn gave an example. Suppose, he said, the policeman happens to catch a butcher with his hand on the scale while he's weighing meat. He doesn't arrest him. He just doesn't bother paying for meat when he orders it from the butcher after that.

"Ah, yes, I understand," said Miss Young. "He turns his knowledge into power and profit." She patted Herbert Somborn on the arm and said to me, "This is the most wonderful, clever man in the world. I adore him."

Later she asked Mr. Somborn why New York bankers were suddenly so interested in motion pictures. Because, he explained, there was so much money to be made in pictures. For instance, Powers had an interesting idea that motion pictures were a better form of advertising than billboards or newspapers or magazines. Motion pictures were literally advertising in motion for cars, clothes, curling irons—you name it, he said.

"Why didn't someone out here think of that?" Miss Young

said. "He's absolutely right. Don't you think so, Miss Swanson?"

She was very kind and attentive to me all evening, and it turned out that we even had a few things in common. Like me she had been born in Chicago, and we had both been directed by Albert Parker. We had both become well known in pictures about upper-class marriage and divorce. She advised me to greet my public with open arms. Early in her career, she said, her managers had told her to avoid public places and crowds. They had said that if people could come up to her and speak to her and touch her, she would lose her mystery for them and they would stop going to see her films. She said she had ignored all such advice. She smiled at everyone; she talked to everyone; and it hadn't hurt her popularity one bit. "Let your public know you love them, too," she said, and then added, "but I'm sure you do. I can tell."

I explained to Mr. Somborn on the drive home how much I admired her. He told me she was the first motion picture star to have her own company. She had formed it with Lewis Selznick before Mary Pickford or anybody else had even thought of doing it. Now all the big stars were following her, he said. Charles Ray, for instance, had just left the studio to strike out on his own. He said he felt that in no time I would be able to do the same, and he knew that Clara agreed. When I mentioned her fabulous jewelry, Mr. Somborn smiled and said her first partner, Mr. Selznick, had started in the jewelry business in New York.

He invited me to dinner several times and began to insist that I call him Herbert. He arranged for a private screening of *Eyes of Youth* for Bea and me, and he promised to talk to Harry Garson about considering Bea for a part in one of his pictures. He was a restful person to be with. He did everything well. He never raised his voice, but he always seemed to get what he wanted. Once or twice he surprised me at dinner or in the car by reaching over and holding my hand, and I was completely unprepared, after being with him only five or six times, to find a small jewelry box tucked in some flowers he sent me at home. It contained a beautiful jade necklace, and I suddenly realized that this man Clara Kimball Young had said was so marvelous, knew everything, was seriously courting me.

A few days later I had a dinner date with him. Late in the afternoon a little gardenia tree was delivered to the house with a note saying he would be a half-hour late. We had a marvelous dinner and danced several times. He was quiet, serious, not the type to hold you tightly on the dance floor, but a very smooth dancer nonetheless. When we got back to our table, he took my hand in his and looked at me intensely.

"Will you marry me, Gloria?" he asked.

I didn't know what to reply. I hardly knew the man. I finally explained that I'd been married before and that in fact my divorce was not quite final. He knew all that. He knew everything about me, it seemed. All he wanted was my promise. I blushed and said the most I could promise was to dig out my papers and let him know when I would be free.

He kissed me when we got to the house. He kissed well, without any awkwardness or detachment. He seemed to be saying that although he didn't have the time or inclination for even a few hours of flirtatious petting, I could expect him to make love passionately, seriously, and with thorough competence, for many years to come. "I'll call you in a week," he said, in a tone that implied he was much too busy ever to consider placing a second such call. "Please have an answer by then."

One day during the first week of November, 1919, Craney barged into my dressing room with a rolled-up newspaper in his hand that he was brandishing like a club.

"Gloria, you can't do this!" he snapped.

"Do what?" I said, trying to remain calm.

"You know what I mean. Listen to this." The paper he was carrying was the Los Angeles *Times*. It was opened to the society section, and he started reading the following article aloud:

MISS SWANSON TO WED
FAMOUS FILM BEAUTY ADMITS ENGAGEMENT
By Grace Kingsley

Eros is about to claim another beauty from the Rialto. Gloria Swanson, noted for her attractiveness, is engaged to wed. The young woman admitted this yesterday, the happy man being none other than Herbert Sanborn, wealthy Pasadenan.

The bride to be is one of the most talented film stars

and her popularity since she joined the De Mille forces
exceeds even that of many a star appearing with her
company. She has, as a matter of fact, been a sort of fad
with young women all over the country, so far as her
striking little mannerisms and her particular manner of
dressing is concerned, and this is true among the sophisticated fans of the big towns equally with those of the
small—striking tribute to Miss Swanson's fascination. . . .

I couldn't stop him. He read every word with such disgust
that it would have been hard for a stranger to tell which part
upset him most. At the end he barked, *"Now tell me,* is it
true?"

"No. First of all, his name is Sombor , not Sa bor .
Second, he's not from Pasadena; he's from New York. Third,
I told the reporters he had asked me to marry him. I didn't
say I had accepted."

"I know his name is Somborn. Did you accept him or didn't
you?"

"That's none of your business. I've always told you I
wanted to get married. What have you done about it?"

His eyes were flashing like a tiger's. I was sure he was going
to propose then and there. And if he had, no matter how
furious I was with him for all his foot-stamping tantrums, I
would have said yes. But he only went on shouting. "You
can't marry Somborn. I won't let you! You're only doing it to
make me angry."

"You're going to eat those words, Craney," I said. My
dander was up.

"Don't you *know?*" he was screaming. "Is it possible you
don't know? You can't marry Somborn. He's a Jew!"

I wasn't a good enough actress to pretend I knew. I didn't.
It had never occurred to me. Furthermore, I didn't know if I
had any prejudice against Jews or not. There were certainly
plenty of them in the picture business, and it had never
concerned me. But I did know that Craney's anger was at
least as much anti-Semitic snobbery as it was jealousy. I could
just imagine what his rich friends were saying at the Pasadena
Country Club, where Jews, actors, and dogs were usually
lumped together. The crowning irony was that the reporter in
the *Times* had actually confused Herbert Somborn with
Craney. She had assumed that the man I was considering
marrying was obviously the Pasadena millionaire I had been

coy about with all the columnists for the past six months. That must have upset him and all his friends more than anything.

"You're some radical, Craney," I said. "Get out."

"Gloria, I warn you—"

"*Get out!*"

When he left, I thought with a genuine ache of regret that I had seen the last of him. His words and his attitudes troubled me all day. I was still thinking about him when I turned up Harper Avenue and realized that the Packard convertible was parked in front of the house. As I pulled into the driveway, I could see that he was sitting in it. I started toward the house, but the tone of his voice stopped me.

"Gloria, let me talk to you for five minutes. Then I'll go, if you don't want me to stay."

He got out of his car and we met in the center of the front lawn.

Craney said he had spent an hour with his lawyer after he left me. They had worked out a plan to set up a trust fund for me. I could live off the interest from it for the rest of my life. Craney said he wanted me to be financially independent, even of him. He wanted me to be free, free even to walk away the minute I didn't love him anymore. But he wanted to be free too. He said he had also talked with his mother in Chicago, who said there were noisy threats against Red sympathizers all over the East and Midwest. Since her name was prominent on lists of radical sympathizers, her lawyers were advising her to remain very quiet or to travel until the election the following year had decided the political tenor of the years to come. Craney said he wanted to get away—to Mexico, Canada, Europe, possibly even Russia—anywhere, but now. He said if I went with him, he would also put me in his will. If he died, I would inherit millions.

"But it has to be now," I said, "before my divorce is final, right?"

"Oh, don't let's go over all *that* again," he pleaded. "Do you realize what I'm offering you?"

"Yes," I said. "I also realize what you're not offering."

As we faced each other squarely, I knew that neither of us could ever give in. The strongest, perhaps best, part of our relationship had been arguing like spoiled brats about things we believed in. It was possible that neither of us could endure the idea of resolving our arguments once and for all and living maturely together. Nevertheless, until the instant he drove away, I wanted—I almost willed—him to kiss me and drag me off with him.

The following Saturday night Herbert asked me to dinner. As soon as we were seated at our table, he asked me for my answer. I told him I would marry him in December, as soon as I was free to, and he leaned over and kissed me tenderly on the lips. Then he ordered champagne for us, by name and year. He was without doubt the most cultivated man I had ever met. If I felt no strong passion for him, he had given me no cause. But he never put pressure on me either, and after Craney that was a wonderful relief. Still, as we toasted each other, I realized that I hardly knew this Jewish bachelor of forty. I only knew I felt totally safe with him.

Before we had taken a second sip, an animated man with curly sand-colored hair and glasses stepped over and said, "Herbert! How are you?" And before Herbert could introduce us, the man said he would introduce himself on the dance floor and led me away. He danced beautifully and spoke very amusingly. He said he was a numerologist and if he had my birth date and a few other numbers, he could tell me many things about myself. Then he laughed and said he could tell me the most important thing right off, without any numbers at all.

"And what is that?" I asked.

"Oh, just that I'm going to marry you."

"Sorry," I said, "but I've just told my escort I'm marrying him."

"And you've been married once already, I know all that," he said. "So have I. In fact, I still am. But you and I are both probably going to be married a number of times. I just want to get my name on your list. You can go right ahead and marry Herbert first. I'm not free just now, as I said."

Since I was sure he was joking, I just laughed. But he was so irresistible that if an angel had swooped down at that instant and asked me if I could fall in love with such a man and told me I had to be perfectly honest in my reply, I would have said, "Yes, on the spot."

"You seem to know a lot about me. I don't even know your name," I said.

"Oh, don't you? I'm disappointed. I'm Marshall Neilan," he said. "Your future husband." Before any bell rang in my head, we were back at our table and he turned me over to

Herbert. "She's wonderful," he said. "Call me, Herbert."
And he walked smartly away.

When I asked Herbert who Mr. Neilan was, he looked at
me as if I had just said I didn't know what Japan was.
"Marshall Neilan is Mary Pickford's director," he said. "He's
made all her best movies. Every actress in pictures would give
her eyeteeth to have Mickey Neilan direct her just once."

The next day I went to dinner at the Badgers'. I had not seen
Clarence since Triangle days, so I had accepted with pleasure
when his wife had called to invite me. I hadn't seen any of my
Keystone pals in ages, and I assumed they'd all be there. I
went alone, and I felt strange as soon as I arrived. Bobby
Vernon was not there. In fact, there were only six of us all
together, and to my astonishment one of the six, dressed to
kill and on his best behavior, was Wallace Beery. I guessed
immediately that Wally had put the Badgers up to the whole
thing, and I knew that must have taken some doing because
Clarence had always been a bit suspicious of him and
protective of me.

Wally never stopped looking at me all through the meal,
and he smiled seductively whenever our eyes met. Suddenly,
after everyone else had congratulated me on making four
films in a row with Mr. De Mille and told me how happy they
were for me, he spoke. "This may sound funny, but I want
you to know I've always prayed you'd be a failure, Gloria, so
you would come back to me."

Everyone at the table was stunned into total silence. There
was no way I could hide my astonishment or my contempt.
He had played out his little game and stayed married to me
for the duration of the war, and now he was actually trying to
make it sound to my old friends as if I had been an ambitious
starlet who had used him briefly in my scramble to success,
broken his heart, and then dropped him; and worse yet, as if
he had, nevertheless, sadly kept a light burning in the
window. I smiled very sweetly and said, "I wouldn't count on
it, Wally. You see, just last night I agreed to marry Herbert
Somborn, the president of Equity Pictures."

The papers all said Herbert and I would be married sometime
after the first of the year. Almost for that reason—to avoid
endless publicity and interference—Herbert wanted to get

married quickly and quietly before Christmas. He kept getting telegrams from New York from Pat Powers and Joe Schnitzer, his partners, urging him to return east on matters of business, and he wanted us to be married before he left. Since I had the Christmas holiday free before starting my fifth picture for Mr. De Mille, and since I had always objected to large weddings, I told him to make whatever arrangements he wished. He booked a suite at the Alexandria Hotel and asked a friend of his, a judge, to perform the ceremony there. That way we would avoid a mob of photographers and reporters and business associates. I invited no one, not even Bea or my parents. I knew full well that Mother and Daddy would be miserable in each other's presence, and I felt it would be awkward having only Bea. Therefore, the judge and several friends of Herbert's who acted as witnesses were the only other people in the hotel suite. The whole thing was over in five minutes, and I was married again.

The next morning all the newspapers said we were in San Francisco, so we stayed in Los Angeles. We told the hotel we would keep the suite until further notice and hung the DO NOT DISTURB sign on the door. Of course, we couldn't disconnect the telephone, because of Herbert's business calls, but for the next three weeks we saw virtually nobody except hotel personnel. It was heaven. Neither of us had had a real vacation in years. I had never known the luxury of being absolutely idle for days on end. I was never bored for a minute, and Herbert turned out to be the most generous and considerate man in the world. On Christmas morning we sat propped up in bed opening stacks of gifts and sipping champagne. On New Year's Eve we went downstairs at midnight and danced until three.

I could tell that Herbert was worried and irritated by turns, but he waited until the holidays were over to tell me he would have to go back east at the end of the week. He told me Lewis Selznick, in an effort to control distribution, was threatening to sue theater owners if they showed *Eyes of Youth*, and the owners were canceling bookings because they did not want to get involved in a management squabble. Equity Pictures, therefore, was suing Mr. Selznick in return. The legal bills would be enormous before the battle was over. Moreover, Harry Garson was over budget on the latest Clara Kimball Young picture, and Pat Powers had cut off his money. Herbert had to go to New York and Chicago as soon as possible and try to straighten everything out.

I was amazed that anyone could know so much about business and I tried to get him to explain things to me. He was incredibly patient and clear. At one point he asked me what the terms of my own contract were, and I had to admit that I didn't know. He asked to see it, so I had a hotel chauffeur drive me to Harper Avenue and I fished it out of the drawer where I kept it. Back at the hotel, I handed him the envelope and said, "Here, Daddy. Please take over." It was the first time I ever called him Daddy, but from then on I usually called him that.

As Herbert read over my contract, which was in two parts, I could see that he was furious. "We've got to get you out of the hands of these Eastern European Jews," he said. He spat out the names Lasky and Zukor and a few others I had never heard of. When he realized I had no idea what he was talking about, he held my hands in his and began very gently to ask me questions. Had I ever shown these contracts to a lawyer? No, I said, but Mr. De Mille had had his lawyer look them over. Herbert banged his palm on his forehead and said, "Of course." I felt like a complete idiot, but I defended Mr. De Mille by saying I trusted him completely and would have signed anything he asked me to sign.

Mr. De Mille and I had signed the first contract on December 30, 1918. Under its terms my salary started at $150 a week and would be $350 at the end of two years. Three weeks later, on January 21, 1919, I had signed the second paper, which gave me a raise of $50 a week. But Herbert said it was not a real raise at all. Although the studio had given me the $50 a week extra during 1919, the contract stipulated that the studio would deduct the same amount from my salary starting in January 1920. And that wasn't the worst of it; the second contract included an option clause, which allowed the studio to renew my contract for two additional years at a very small increase in salary.

"Do you realize what happened in the three weeks between these two contracts?" Herbert asked.

"Yes," I said. "We finished *Don't Change Your Husband.*"

"Exactly," he said. "They had a new star and they knew it. But something else also happened. There was a critical shift in the business. Zukor and Lasky tried to get control, not just of production but of distribution as well. They wanted to dictate to the exhibitors. So the exhibitors got together and decided to go into production. They all gathered in this very hotel and planned a forty-million-dollar merger. They hoped to sign up every theater owner in the country to a five-year contract. In that case, small companies like mine and Clara Kimball Young's would have been left out in the cold. Theaters could not buy pictures from us. And that's why Mary Pickford and Chaplin and Fairbanks and Griffith got together and formed their own distributing company, United Artists, to fight the trust. While all that was going on, Zukor and Lasky discovered they had a new star in you, so they sent Mr. De Mille to you with this little paper, to tie you up for four years. For no money—no money at all! Your salary is laughable. Do you realize what we pay Clara Kimball Young?"

"No."

"Twenty-five thousand dollars in salary plus a share of the profits. And her pictures are not making anywhere near what your pictures make."

"But they're not my pictures. They're Mr. De Mille's pictures."

"Then why are theater owners all over the country putting your name up on the marquee? Look," he said, grabbing a Los Angeles paper and riffling through it until he found an ad for *Male and Female*. My name was at the top, ahead of Tommy Meighan's, ahead of Mr. De Mille's. "Paramount distribution salesmen are selling all your pictures as Swanson pictures. And all the pictures you made at Triangle before you went to Lasky are being exhibited as Swanson pictures. Don't you see? They have you sewed up for four years for no money at all. And there's no limit on the number of pictures you have to make for them. They're telling you they're doing you a favor letting you be in De Mille pictures, for two hundred dollars a week."

He went on to explain what block booking was. Mr. Zukor, he said, had invented it. If a theater owner wanted four Swanson pictures a year, he had to agree to buy twenty-five or thirty other films whether he wanted them or not, sight unseen.

"In short," Herbert said emphatically, "everybody is cashing in on you, darling. It's about time you did too."

I asked him what I could do, and he said he would like to show the contracts to a good attorney. He thought that the contract was so unfair on the face of it that surely it could be broken.

"In fact," he said, "let's have some fun. Let's have dinner in the dining room tonight, and as soon as I see someone important, I'll ask him for the name of a good lawyer. I'll make it very clear that we're looking for a way to get you out of your contract so that we can make a picture together with Marshall Neilan. I know I could get the money from Pat Powers in a minute. No matter whom I ask, Lasky and Zukor are bound to hear all about it before a single day goes by. That's the only way to deal with these Eastern European Jews. What do you say?"

For years I'd dreamed of having someone I could trust and lean on. "Whatever you say, Daddy," I said.

Sure enough, in the dining room Herbert snagged Harry Cohn and asked him to suggest a lawyer. He mentioned a man named Goldflam. The next day Herbert had lunch with Mr. Goldflam, showed him the contracts, and asked him for a legal opinion in writing. In his letter, dated January 6, 1920, Mr. Goldflam said: "The option agreement is entirely inadequate . . . one-sided in that it binds Miss Swanson and does not bind Lasky. . . . The contract is inequitable. . . . The Lasky Company would never be able to get an injunction against Miss Swanson if she were to leave their employ on January 1, 1921."

Herbert was delighted. "Now let them all stew awhile," he said. I told him the only part I dreaded was leaving Mr. De Mille, but he said, "Wait until you have a chance to work with Marshall Neilan. He's the greatest director in the business. He's directed Blanche Sweet, Mary Pickford—all of the best. And with a combination like Swanson and Neilan, Pat Powers would give us all the money we needed. Meanwhile we've got a whole year to find the perfect property."

When Herbert left for Chicago and the East five days later, he now had one more important reason for going. He would propose his idea to Pat Powers.

After Herbert and I were married, Bea La Plante shut up the house on Harper Avenue and moved to Pasadena to be near friends she had there. Only after she had gone did I realize how much she had taken off my shoulders in the past year and a half. She had answered the phone, made appointments, and sorted and answered my mail for me. Alone in the Alexandria Hotel after Herbert left for New York, I was appalled at the boxes of letters and telegrams of congratulations that the studio forwarded to me every morning. As more and more people learned where I was living, the hotel switchboard was also flooded with calls. There was no way I could hire and train a secretary because I had never thought to ask Bea how she organized things, and I knew besides that Herbert would find me one when he returned. In the meantime I was happy to start filming again a few days after he left and escape the growing stacks of mail.

The new picture was called *Something to Think About*, and it gave me a chance to work with Elliott Dexter again. He had been ill for several months and so had missed out on the leading roles in *Male and Female* and *Why Change Your Wife?* Neither of us thought much of Jeanie Macpherson's scenario, but we enjoyed working together under Mr. De Mille once more.

We talked about Craney Gartz. Elliott said he and Marie had assumed from all the headlines that said I was marrying a millionaire, that I was marrying Craney. I said I probably would have, but that his notions about marriage and everything else had finally proved to be too radical for me. I had opted instead for security and a family and a husband who was interested and enthusiastic about my career. I told Elliott how Craney had tried to pressure me into running away with him by saying he was in political danger. Elliott said Craney may have been right. With the enforcement of Prohibition that month, there had been threats of revolution in many major cities, and thousands of dissidents and Reds were being arrested every day. I asked him with concern if Craney was safe, and he said that he and Marie had not heard from him in weeks. Elliott suspected he had taken his mother's advice and left the country for a bit. That relieved me.

Herbert was away for several weeks, and I sent him two or three telegrams every day, addressed to hotels and in care of train conductors. He finally wired that he would return on the twenty-first. I hoped to be able to meet him, but Mr. De Mille rearranged our location schedule, so I had to change my plans, but I kept him posted almost every hour.

JAN 18 1920—I HOPE YOU ARE NOT AS IMPATIENT AS I AM   TO-NIGHT WILL SEEM SO LONG AND TOMORROW TOO BUT FIVE OCLOCK JUST HAS TO COME   HURRY MY DADDY I CANT WAIT   ALL MY LOVE YOURS
    GLORIA

JAN 19 1920—DO NOT HAVE TO WORK   WILL MEET YOU AT SAN
BERNARDINO   LOVE
    GLORIA

JAN 20 1920—SORRY I HAVE TO WORK TOMORROW BUT WILL BE IN
HOTEL WAITING FOR YOU   MUCH LOVE AND KISSES
    GLORIA

Herbert's return was practically a second honeymoon. I had the suite banked with gorgeous flowers and I told the desk to have chilled champagne ready the minute Mr. Somborn arrived. He brought me a great stack of gifts—a coat, a hat, stockings, hankies, and scarfs—all beautifully wrapped and all from the best New York stores. Then we put on silk dressing robes and ordered dinner sent up. I told him there were bundles of mail for him to go through, and he said he would start first thing in the morning. I asked him what Pat Powers had said to the idea of a Swanson-Neilan picture, and he said he had decided not to ask him until we had settled on a screenplay, but that he was sure everything would be fine. It was wonderful to have him back.

Several weeks later I finished shooting early one afternoon and returned to the hotel to take a nap. Just as I was lying down, the hotel manager phoned to say that our bill was overdue.

"Really?" I said. "That's very surprising. I'm sure it must have slipped my husband's mind."

The manager said he had already mentioned it to Mr. Somborn twice. Furthermore, he said that if we didn't pay the bill by the end of the week, the Alexandria would have to cut off our credit. I asked him how much the bill was, and he cleared his throat and named a figure well over $3,000. I almost fainted, but I calmly maintained there must be some mistake and said I would mention the matter to my husband as soon as he came in.

After that a nap was out of the question. I started to look through the drawers in the desk and found scores of un-opened bills. It seemed our whole glamorous life together had been charged. Even the necklace Herbert gave me before we were married had not been paid for.

By the time Herbert came in that evening, I was in a state. I demanded an explanation. He remained calm, but he admitted that Equity Pictures was in the midst of a temporary crisis. The whole country, in fact, was in an economic panic. There was no question but that the situation would right itself in a matter of weeks, he said, but in the meantime he needed a few thousand dollars to tide him over. The embarrassing part for him was that he could not ask any of the business associates he dealt with every day for a loan because naturally he didn't want them, of all people, to know he was in need of one. Besides, most of them were more than likely in a similar pinch. In the meantime business was going on as usual, but he couldn't put his hands on any sizable amounts of cash.

"Herbert, you're not lying, are you?" I asked.

"Oh, my darling, no, of course not. Please believe me. I understand business and you don't, that's all."

The next day I made him contact a rental agent for a modest apartment, and we selected one at Wilcox and Yucca. The day after that I took all the money I had in the bank and paid the Alexandria Hotel so that we could move out without causing a scandal.

Within a few weeks it was clear that Herbert was not destitute by any means, but nevertheless, for all he was worth on paper, he was certainly not rich, as I had thought. Also, although he could pull in his belt and sit out slack periods as a bachelor, he could not do so with a wife at his side whom everyone rushed to provide with the most sumptuous commodities available every time she turned around. He was an operator, in a business that went up and down and changed rapidly, and he had obviously counted on my bringing at least a large salary into the marriage. He confessed that he had not been able to conceal his amazement or his rage when he had seen my contracts. For the time being he just asked me to trust him.

So we moved to Wilcox and Yucca and I told him then that he had better be prepared for even greater problems ahead, because I was pregnant. I said I would certainly not be able to make another picture between the finish of *Something to Think About* and my confinement. If he had shown the slightest unhappiness at that, I would have left him, but I could tell that he was as overjoyed as I was. He said not to worry about money. All the difficulties were temporary. All that mattered from now on was us and our gorgeous baby.

He kissed me tenderly over and over and asked, "When?"

"Sometime in October," I said, and I added, smiling, "Daddy."

He was proud, he was happy, but he could never for a minute cease being shrewd, either. "You know," he said, "we might even be able to use this gorgeous baby as a lever in dealing with Lasky."

As soon as we finished *Something to Think About* but before I could be assigned to a new picture, I made an appointment to see Mr. Lasky, who was head of Famous Players-Lasky, and told him I was going to have a baby.

Mr. Lasky and I had met often enough, but we had never talked business. He was a nervous man, very correct, very precise, with a smile that seemed to come and go as it was needed. He peered at me through his rimless glasses as if he were trying to read my mind, and then he said, "Don't, Gloria. A year out of pictures just now will ruin your career."

"You don't understand, Mr. Lasky. It's too late. And I wouldn't change anyway. I'm a woman first and an actress second. I want to be a mother more than I've ever wanted a career."

"But you can't do this to the studio. Do you realize what we've invested in you? *Male and Female* is the biggest picture in America. Tell me, how soon can you work again?"

"Not at all. The baby is due sometime in October and my contract is up in January."

He glowered. Then he buzzed his secretary and told her to bring him my contract. I sat perfectly demure and unruffled because Herbert had primed me down to the slightest detail for what was to come. I was ready when Mr. Lasky mentioned the studio's option to hold me for two more years.

"My husband's attorney says that option is not legal, Mr. Lasky, because it gives everything to you and nothing to me. He says it's inequitable."

When I mentioned Herbert, Mr. Lasky got very cross. He read me a section that said if I was unable to work for any reason, my contract could be extended for the amount of time I was unable to work.

"My husband's attorney says that contract can be invalidated in a minute as of January first, Mr. Lasky. And I can't work before then in any case."

He glowered again. Then he said he would like to talk to Mr. Zukor and Mr. De Mille before he decided anything. He would call me as soon as they had a proposal to make. He didn't threaten to take me off salary, but he did say that he hoped I knew I would be decreasing my selling power immeasurably if I stayed off the screen for a year. The public might forget me in a year or find someone they liked better. I knew he was bluffing, and again I was ready for him. I told him I hoped he was wrong because my husband had hopes of producing pictures with me as soon as my contract with Lasky was up.

Now I could tell he was worried. "Gloria, don't do anything until I get back to you," he said. "Promise. You know we consider you family at Famous Players-Lasky. Let me see what I can do."

As troubled as Herbert was over his own affairs, he chuckled with delight when I told him what had happened. "You see, darling?" he said. "I told you so. From now on you can't lose. If they up your salary enormously, fine. If not, they have proved to you your worth and we'll make our own pictures. We've got them scared to death."

For the next month the studio kept sending me my salary checks for no work. Then Mr. Lasky called and asked me for an appointment. When I arrived, he looked at my inflated stomach and said it was very becoming, that I had never looked better. I smiled and thanked him and we both sat down. I was waiting for him to name a figure, effective as of January 1, but he didn't. Instead he said, "Gloria, I have momentous news for you. We've decided to make you a star."

I waited before I spoke because whereas I had been prepared to bargain at this meeting, I was not prepared for such an announcement. Being a star meant having a private bungalow on the set like Mary Pickford's and around-the-clock maids and studio cars and trips to Europe. But it also meant that I would be totally on my own. My pictures would be billed as Gloria Swanson pictures. No other big names would ever be involved that could detract in the slightest from my name. It meant I would never work with Mr. De Mille again because a picture couldn't be a De Mille picture and a Swanson picture at the same time.

Finally I said, "Mr. Lasky, I don't want to be a star. At least not yet."

He took off his glasses and squinted at me as if I were setting in motion some treachery beyond his imaginings or as if I had gone mad. "There isn't anyone in Hollywood who doesn't want to be a star," he said.

I said I wanted to stay with Mr. De Mille. He said surely five pictures in a row with De Mille had been enough. Then I reminded him of what had happened to me at Triangle. After I had made one decent picture, they made me a star. But then they tried to cash in on me by casting me in one cheap silly story after another. It had been the same thing before that with Mack Sennett.

Mr. Lasky cleared his throat with dignity and assured me that nothing like that would happen at Famous Players-Lasky.

"But I love the pictures I make with Mr. De Mille," I said. "And I trust him. He knows what I can do. I'm not ready yet to be a star on my own."

"I can only tell you Mr. De Mille disagrees with you. He thinks you *are* ready. So does Mr. Zukor. In addition, the studio is prepared to offer you a long-term contract with a very generous increase in salary."

I told him I would like to think about it for a few days and discuss it with my husband. He didn't glower or look annoyed. He didn't bother. He was too confident that he had offered me something no sane person could refuse. He simply said we could all agree on terms and figures later, in consultation with as many attorneys as we liked.

"Thank you, Mr. Lasky," I said.

He smiled. "You just tell us what you want and we'll try to accommodate you. Remember, Gloria, from now on it will be our pleasure to make you great."

As soon as I left Mr. Lasky's office, I set off for Mr. De Mille's. The two of them had either spoken on the phone or read my mind because Mr. De Mille was expecting me. He stood up behind his desk and stretched out his arms toward me as if he were presenting me to a crowd.

"Do you realize what you've done, young fellow?" he said, laughing. "Jesse Lasky is in shock."

"I had to talk to you first," I said. "He told me you wanted me to leave you. Why?"

He put his arm around my shoulder. "Because studios can't

afford to have too many eggs in one basket," he explained.
"You're a star and I'm a star."

I told him I didn't really want to be a star.

"It's too late for that," he said in a mock-stern tone.
"The public and the theater owners have already decided
on it. You know it's the audiences who do the deciding.
We only guess. Sometimes we're right, sometimes we're
wrong. But once *they* decide, the studio has to act accord-
ingly. They're prepared to offer you a lot of money, you
know."

"But that won't make the pictures any good. They'll
save the money somewhere else. Either the stories won't
be any good, or they won't hire good actors to play with
me."

"Oh, yes, they will, because they have to protect
their investment. I've agreed to let Sam Wood direct your
first picture. You like Sam and he adores you. He's been
directing Wallace Reid, who's becoming the most popular
actor in the business, so this is a great chance for both of
you. You have to gamble a little in this business, young
fellow."

I could tell from his tone there was no point in arguing. He
jiggled my shoulder playfully and whispered, "Ask them for
the moon, and I will try to see that you get it."

By the time I got back to the apartment Herbert was
already there, ready to celebrate. He had had lunch with Joe
Engels and Jack Warner, he said, and Harry Cohn had
walked over specially and told them that Jesse Lasky was
going to offer me a five-year starring contract at $2,500 a
week. We had done it, he said.

Although the amount he named staggered me, I did
not like the tone of his voice as he said it, particularly after
Mr. Lasky and Mr. De Mille had both been so kind and
generous. I didn't like the idea that he spent his days with
the boys in the Alexandria dining room gossiping about
my business either. It made me very nervous when he
said he would start the very next day to make a list of the
things I should ask for in my contract. He told me not
to worry about a thing. He said he would handle everything.

I kissed him and asked him not to do anything until the
baby was born. I didn't want anything to upset me before
that. I said we had plenty of time before the first of the year.

What I really hoped was that his own business would start to occupy him full-time again before then. I didn't want people to think that Herbert Somborn was my manager. I had seen all too clearly that Mr. Lasky disliked the very mention of Herbert's name. I wanted my husband to have an identity of his own, independent of mine. I wanted my baby's father to be the head of our household.

An earthquake shook Los Angeles when I was in my fourth or fifth month. Herbert and I were dining out, and the floor of the hotel shook and the chandeliers began to tinkle and sway. People yelled and ran for the exits, but I just sat, afraid to move and afraid to stay, not wanting either way to endanger my baby. After that I stayed very close to home. I didn't even go to Matthew Burns's funeral in August. My mother and I agreed that my presence would only attract a thousand reporters, for I looked at seven months as if I were about to explode.

In our apartment building I made friends with a couple by the name of Urson. Mr. Urson was Marshall Neilan's assistant director, and his wife, Peggy, a delightful, brilliant woman, was a Christian Scientist. During the last half of my pregnancy, Peggy was my constant companion. She gave me a Christian Science prayer book, and we read the lessons together every day. Peggy told me the object for me was to block out even the tiniest unpleasant thought and concentrate on the beautiful miracle happening within me.

I never told anybody about losing my first baby, when I was married to Wally, but I always remembered with dread the hospital room where I woke up. I determined that this baby would be born normally, naturally, at home. I refused to consult a doctor, and as the time approached for my delivery, Peggy said she would stay with me, but she also suggested having a Christian Science practitioner present so that the two of us would not be alone if any complications arose. I told her I was sure it would be an easy birth, just as I was sure the baby would be a girl.

Early in the morning on October 6 I had my first labor pains. Herbert got very frightened and begged me to let him call an ambulance, but I flatly refused. I said I had been born at home and I wanted my baby to be born at home. I told

Peggy to call the practitioner, who turned out to be a real amazon. Peggy held my hand, and the practitioner prayed and tried to steady me during my contractions.

I was very brave and serene in the beginning, but after six, eight, ten hours I felt I could not endure the pain. I was almost too weak to scream. I was also frightened because I knew the labor was going on too long and there was no sign of the baby. By nightfall Herbert was a wreck, and Peggy and the practitioner put up no resistance when he phoned for a doctor. The doctor examined me and told me I was doing very well, but he said the time had come for him to give me a little assistance. I begged him not to inject me with needles, and he said he wouldn't. He told me just to breathe naturally, and before I could count to ten, the chloroform had put me to sleep.

The baby was a girl, and when I opened my eyes, they gave her to me. They had a diaper tied around her head, so she looked like a little Polish peasant. She had a beautiful complexion, but there was a tiny scar on her cheek. The doctor assured me it would be gone in a few days. He said it had been a difficult delivery and he had had to use forceps.

I held her in my arms and tried not to squeeze her. She was quiet as a mouse and her eyes were shut tight, but I could hear her breathing. The first thing she did was to reach for my breast, and the ecstasy overwhelmed me.

She had been born at seven o'clock in the morning. I named her Gloria.

Mr. De Mille came to visit me about a week later. He brought the baby a tiny string of real pearls with a diamond clasp, and I thanked him profusely.

"Don't thank me," he said, "until you hear the favor I've come to ask."

"All right," I said. "Ask."

"Your starring contract begins in January," he said. "I was wondering if you would consider, before you start out on your own, making one last picture for me."

"Oh, Mr. De Mille," I said, "you know I'd rather do that than anything."

"Good!" he said with a huge smile. "I'll call you when I'm ready to start."

Herbert was furious when I told him. He said I should have spoken to him before I made any kind of verbal commitment. He said Lasky and Zukor were not going to get another picture out of me for next to nothing; he would see to that. Then I got angry. I told him I would not listen to another word. I said I owed everything to Mr. De Mille, and if he wanted another picture out of me for next to nothing, he was going to have it. I forbade Herbert to interfere. I said that anytime Mr. De Mille was concerned, I would run my own life without any help from anyone. He said I was being totally unreasonable, and perhaps I was, but deep down I wanted to do another picture with Mr. De Mille and I also wanted Herbert to know that I didn't want him to manage my career.

The picture was called *The Affairs of Anatol*. It was based on a play by the Austrian author Arthur Schnitzler. The play dealt with a dandy and his love affairs with a series of women, and it was still considered shocking twenty-five years after its first performance in Europe. Mr. De Mille was changing the script to include a loving wife, who would appear with Anatol between the episodes and to whom he would return at the end of the film. Mr. De Mille said I could have any part I wanted, but I told him he should choose. In that case I would play the wife, he said; that way I would appear through the whole picture. Wallace Reid, the heartthrob of millions of American women, was Anatol. Elliott Dexter, Bebe Daniels, Agnes Ayres, Monte Blue, Wanda Hawley, Theodore Roberts, Julia Faye, Theodore Kosloff, Polly Moran, and Raymond Hatton were also in the large cast. I thought it would be like old home week.

It turned out instead to be torture. First of all, shooting began before I really felt up to it. I was worried that my figure wasn't quite back to normal, but more than that, I had been torn rather badly during the final stages of labor. The doctor said if I didn't take time to rest and heal, I might have trouble later. In fact, he wanted me to go to the hospital without delay for corrective surgery. But I refused. A promise to Mr. De Mille was for me a sacred promise. In addition, I insisted on nursing Gloria, which meant that I had to be up at least by six every morning besides getting up at least once during the night. Herbert's resultant concern over my health combined with his irritation that I was making this film at all strained our marriage almost to the breaking point many times before the picture was finished.

Things were almost as difficult at the studio as they were at home. Wallace Reid, the male star, was a cause of constant anxiety to me. I heard endless rumors that he was an addict, and although I never saw him take drugs, his behavior never seemed quite right during *Anatol*. He was forever offering me rides, and once he sent his valet to my dressing room to ask for a photograph of me. I always found ways to refuse him politely, but he gave me the jitters.

The publicity department pestered me every day to bring little Gloria to the studio for a morning so that reporters could interview me with her and take pictures of us together. When I said I would do no such thing, because I hated such exploitative nonsense where children were concerned, the publicity people confessed to me that the studio was pestering *them* because they wanted to squelch rumors that my baby was deformed or retarded. Otherwise, reporters had asked, why should I be so protective of her? I told them she was perfectly gorgeous, but that they would have to take my word for it because they would never see her after that, and then I ordered them out. Instantly word spread that I had become cross and irritable since my confinement.

The straw that broke the camel's back was a remark of Jeanie Macpherson's. She was a powerful figure in Mr. De Mille's creative world, and according to the gossip columnists, in his personal world as well. She had no husband or children and had always been jealous of my relationship with Mr. De Mille. As a scenarist, she had no business whatever in the wardrobe department, but during *Anatol* she seemed to make a point of standing around for all of my fittings. It annoyed and embarrassed me but I said nothing, until one day in front of everyone she said with a cutting edge, "Goodness me, but you do stay on the plump side, don't you, Gloria?"

"You'd be plump too if you were nursing a baby," I said and stomped out of the room.

I went straight to Mr. De Mille and asked him if the costume looked all right. He said it looked fine. Then I asked him if I looked all right. He said of course.

"Well, Miss Macpherson doesn't seem to think so," I said, and I could feel my lip trembling.

He came over and put his hands on my shoulders. "That's because you're a star, young fellow, and Miss

Macpherson isn't," he said. "As a star you have to learn to
hear what you want to hear, ignore what you have to ignore.
You have to learn to take the cream and leave the milk.
Always remember that."

Whatever *The Affairs of Anatol* cost me, that moment more than made up for it.

171 • SWANSON ON SWANSON

CHAPTER 9

No one, not even the starriest of [the great stars] *has everything!* Some have more personal advantages than others. Oh, yes! We'll all agree on that. But just glance over the foremost constellation and see what you'll see. Everyone in the group has, perhaps, several points of attractiveness but you will note that in each case, one of the *six great essentials* to success has been featured to a more striking degree than any of the others.

. . .

But you are getting impatient to learn what are the *six great essentials.* And you shall have them. First of all, you know I'm going to say *beauty.* That, of course, needs no explanatory remarks. Another one is *personality.* Another, *charm* (there's a difference between these two that you'll understand later). Next there is *temperament,* then *style,* and sixth, *the ability to wear clothes.*

The most striking, and perhaps the most interesting way to force this truth upon your minds, is to point to six great favorites who have not only made a sensational hit but who have by subsequent achievements proved that their popularity is not a thing of the moment, but is based upon qualities and characteristics that are sure to attract today or a hundred years from today. There are many that we could choose as graceful embodiments of one or more of the *six essentials,* but after conscientious, impartial consideration of the screen's great galaxy of artists, we have selected what are perhaps the most striking examples.

For sheer *beauty,* perfection of features and a portrait-like magnificence, who can call forth more admiration than Katherine MacDonald? . . .

Hardly have we written the next essential, *personality,* when the magnetic name and presence of Mary Pickford flashes before you. . . .

Charm is a more quiet, a more subtle expression than is personality. It is nonetheless attractive, however, to many fans, as witness one of the most popular of its possessors, Elsie Ferguson. . . .

You are probably thinking that Norma Talmadge should have been included long before now, but an analysis of this attractive star's success places her in the forefront of those who hold their admirers through *temperament.* . . .

Style, a semi-mental, semi-physical quality, is more superficial than the above characteristics. It depends not merely upon clothes, but upon an innate knowledge of how to walk, how to stand, how to conduct oneself generally. A number of comediennes can boast of it, but none more rightfully than Bebe Daniels. . . .

The *ability to wear clothes* is no small asset. Is there anyone who can flaunt a superb wardrobe with more dash than Gloria Swanson? To the smallest detail of ornament such as a buckle on a headdress or a wrist trinket, this young woman has a knack of lending to her apparel a certain significance of modernity that makes you unconsciously think that whatever she happens to put on is, of course, *the very latest thing.*

The important question is, which one of the *essentials* is yours? . . .

Study your mirror with a candid eye, and be sure, be very sure, that you are not too modest.

—MARSHALL NEILAN,
"Acting for the Screen: The Six Great Essentials,"
in *Opportunities in the Motion Picture Industry,*
Photoplay Research Society, Los Angeles, 1922

During the summer and fall of 1920, Mr. Lasky and I had worked out the terms of my new contract. Although I consulted with Herbert, I knew that if I once let him take over the negotiations, he would not only try to take over the management of my whole career but also create hostilities between the studio and me; therefore, Mr. Lasky and I did the actual bargaining. At first Mr. Lasky proposed that I make five pictures a year for two years, for which the studio would pay me $2,500 a week. After that they would have the option to renew the contract for three more years at $5,000 a week. That was ten and twenty times, respectively, the salary I was then making, and it was all I could do to keep myself from jumping up and down and clapping my hands and grabbing for the pen on Mr. Lasky's desk; but in my mind I kept hearing Mr. De Mille say, "Ask them for the moon" and "Take the cream and leave the milk." I said I would think it over. I then proposed $6,000 a week during the fourth year and $7,000 during the fifth year. They finally agreed to that, but they still wanted five pictures a year. I said I thought it should be three. It took a month before we settled on four. "Take the cream," Mr. De Mille's voice kept whispering inside my head, so I began to list extras, starting with a star bungalow on the lot, built to my specifications. Agreed, said Mr. Lasky. And musicians on the set. Agreed, said Mr. Lasky. And Hattie when I needed her, and a number of incidentals, including studio cars when I wanted them. Agreed. We signed.

When I got my first check for $2,500 in January 1921, I bought a beautiful horse from Revel English and a riding habit from Hooks, the people who outfitted Mr. De Mille. I was determined to get my figure back to normal for my first starring vehicle, and I had missed riding ever since I left Puerto Rico at fifteen. Peggy Urson said if I'd asked for a horse and corral adjoining the bungalow before I signed the contract, she was sure I would have got it, and judging from the way negotiations had gone, she was probably right.

Mr. Lasky himself went to Europe to scout out an important writer for the first picture and he came back in triumph. He had bagged Elinor Glyn, the author of *Three Weeks,* which some people considered to be the most shocking book ever written—and written by a woman to boot!—and other people praised as the bravest, most thrilling book within memory. In it a noblewoman seduces a younger man and has a torrid affair that lasts three weeks. When she returns to her normal life she does not die for her sins; on the contrary, she is proud of them and even makes perfectly plain that she has *enjoyed* her amorous conquest, and that love-making is an art like any other. I couldn't wait to meet Mrs. Glyn, and she was not a disappointment.

Her British dignity was devastating. She was the first woman I'd ever seen wearing false eyelashes, and although she was old enough to be my grandmother, she got away with it. She had small, squinty eyes and took tiny steps when she walked. Her teeth were too even and white to be real, she smelled like a cathedral full of incense, and she talked a blue streak. Her hair was the color of red ink, and she wore it wrapped around her head like an elaborate turban. She was something from another world.

Her suite at the Hollywood Hotel looked like a Persian tent, with divans, scarlet drapes, purple pillows, gongs, Buddhas, crystal balls, tarot cards, yarrow sticks, Oriental rugs, and a giant tiger skin that reportedly went everywhere with her. Two women also went everywhere with her, one whom she always referred to as Blinky, who was her secretary and personal maid, and one called Miss Morgan, who was her dressmaker. Miss Morgan created the exotic wardrobe Mrs. Glyn dreamed up for herself. Mrs. Glyn said she would not think of buying so much as a hat in a store, for her role was to set fashion on its ear, not to follow it.

"Egyptian!" she pronounced, pointing at me with a hand covered with rings and bangles, at our first meeting. "Extraordinary, quite extraordinary. You're such a tiny, dainty little thing. But of course if your proportions are perfect, they can make you any size they want, can't they? *But . . . my . . . dear,*" she said, spacing the words exaggeratedly, "your proportions are Egyptian; anyone can see that when you turn your head. *You have lived there in another time.* Definitely Egyptian, no doubt about it."

"Mr. Lasky and I are thrilled you're doing the story," I said.

"Are you? Mr. Lasky told me you didn't want to be a star. Well, now you will have to be, because here we are, thrown together. There are no accidents, my dear. We simply live out what was meant to be."

"Do you like America?" I asked.

"People in America are very direct, I find. Since I've been here, I've received over forty proposals of marriage. Gentlemen send me their photographs and copies of their bank statements. I rather like that. I'm very direct myself. It saves enormous amounts of time. And at my age, time is very precious to me."

When I told her I had a baby daughter, she wanted to see her right away. She adored babies and said she could tell by looking at them what they had been in former lives.

"Mr. Lasky told me last year that having a baby would ruin my career. He said I'd lose my sex appeal," I told her.

"Rubbish, my dear, absolute rubbish. Miss Pickford, perhaps, might have problems with public acceptance, but you're the new kind of woman altogether—daring, provocative, sensuous. I'm sure religious-minded people will be *reassured* to learn your love life takes a normal course."

I said I hoped she would mention that to Mr. Lasky. "Indeed I shall," she replied confidently. "If motion picture producers knew what sex appeal was, they'd have no need of me, now, would they?"

She was an aristocrat, friendly with several of the royal families of Europe. "The Prince of Wales absolutely adored you in *Male and Female*. Did you know that?" she asked. I said it had never occurred to me that royalty went to the movies. "But of course they do," she said. "I'll be able to dine out for weeks in London when I get back, telling them all about Hollywood. You children don't realize yet what has happened, I know. But you will. Motion pictures are going to change everything. They're the most important thing that's come along since the printing press. What woman can dream about a prince anymore when she's seen one up close in a newsreel? She'd much rather dream about Wallace Reid. People don't care about royalty anymore. They're much more interested in queens of the screen, like you, dear."

The story she had in mind for me was almost as controversial as *Three Weeks*. Called *The Great Moment*, it was about an English girl from a titled family who falls in love with an American engineer. At one point the girl is bitten on the breast by a rattlesnake, and in order to save her life the engineer has to suck out the poison. The studio was in an uproar over this scene. New York distributors, terrified that the film would be banned, urged Mrs. Glyn to move the snakebite to my wrist. But Mrs. Glyn, who thrived on publicity, sensation, and scandal, held out for the bosom or at least an area unmistakably nearby. That area eventually turned out to be low down on the shoulder, which was good

enough for Elinor Glyn, for by then—before a foot of film
had been shot—she knew that she had the public hanging on
her every word.

Milton Sills, a handsome, fine-featured actor who had won
acclaim in a film called *The Faith Healer*, played the engineer,
and Sam Wood, Mr. De Mille's favorite assistant director for
years, was the director. I felt safe in his hands because I knew
that if we were stuck or uncertain about anything, one or the
other of us could quietly seek advice from Mr. De Mille. The
costume department broke all records for Hollywood lavish-
ness by coming up with an evening dress ending in a four-foot
train composed entirely of pearls and ermine tails.

Everyone working on the film was terribly excited. Everything was new. We were all on trial, and everyone was
determined to come up with something bold and adventurous
and at the same time glamorous. Although everything in the
film was geared to me, no one resented the fact, probably just
because it *was* a fact. That was how pictures worked. If I
succeeded, they knew they would all succeed richly because
of me. If I failed, the failure would be mine alone, and they
could all move on to something else.

Intense and exciting as my days at the studio were, my
evenings and weekends were becoming more and more of a
strain. This had nothing to do with the baby. She was
beautiful and I adored her. By now she had a full-time nurse,
and I envied the woman the endless daytime hours she could
devote to my child. The problem was Herbert.

He had been right when he said in 1920 that a financial
panic was affecting the whole country, not just him, but by
the early months of 1921 the country was on the upswing
again and he wasn't. He continued to have lunches and talk
business and sound important on the phone every day, but I
kept paying the bills. I resented it terribly, although I made
every effort for Gloria's sake to get him on his feet again.

Meanwhile I kept thinking of Craney Gartz and his millions
and the passion we had felt for each other and the fun we had
had. Herbert and I had never had any fun, and I had never
really loved him. I had merely felt secure with him, and now
only a year later he was the least secure person in my life. I
had made the same mistake with Herbert that I had made
with Wally. I had married someone I admired like a father,
not someone I wanted for a husband and lover; and in both

cases, once my trust vanished, so did my warm feelings. In fact, I began to feel for Herbert the most deadly feeling of all—indifference.

He was miserable in our modest apartment, I knew. He felt he should have a better place. He suggested moving to the new Ambassador Hotel, which was about to open on Wilshire Boulevard. Through his mother's sister he was related to the Strauss family, who had built the hotel, and he said they had offered us a special rate for a furnished bungalow. I allowed him to talk me into making the move, against Peggy Urson's advice, and as soon as I saw the first month's bill, I was appalled. It was costing me a fortune in order for Herbert to put up a front for the wealthy side of his family and his friends in the motion picture business. I called Peggy and told her to find us something more reasonable.

The Beverly Hills Hotel, she discovered, also had bungalows, which were attractive and cost half what the ones at the Ambassador did. Also, the Beverly Hills Hotel was out in the open, surrounded by trees and fields. It was healthier for the baby and closer to the studio for me. When I insisted on moving for the second time in a month, I brought things to a crisis between Herbert and me.

He began to be irritable and pick on me. He resented being closed out of my professional life, and as a result he began to criticize my every move. I finally snapped over a remark he made about the number of internal baths I took. These were a necessity caused by Gloria's difficult birth. The doctor had recommended surgery immediately, but I developed a terrible cold and he was afraid I might get pneumonia, so he postponed surgery and ordered me to take internal baths. Then I had to return to work in order to support us, and surgery was postponed a second time. Therefore, when I heard Herbert make an insinuating remark about something as delicate as that, I knew the end was in sight.

Nevertheless, I waited until the picture was finished. Then, in May, I packed up the baby and the nurse and moved to a little inn near Silver Lake, leaving the Beverly Hills bungalow to Herbert. In a few days I called the hotel for messages, and they told me he had moved out. He sent me a sad, short letter saying he had left for what he hoped would be the good of all of us, especially baby Gloria. He hoped I would be generous in allowing him to see her regularly, he wrote, as he expected to remain in California.

I had learned one thing from my first divorce. Legally, in

spite of everything that had happened between Wally and me, I had left him, and therefore had no grounds for a speedy divorce. This time, because the Beverly Hills Hotel was our legal home, Herbert had left me, and with his letter I had grounds for divorce on charges of desertion. I knew that would be the first thing Mr. Lasky would ask me when I told him I wanted a divorce. It was just a matter of finding the right time to ask him.

Once *The Great Moment* was an established success, Elinor Glyn seemed to take over Hollywood. She went everywhere and passed her fearsome verdicts on everything. This is glamorous, she would say. That is hideous, she would say. As she baby-stepped through this or that dining room or garden party, people moved aside for her as if she were a sorceress on fire or a giant sting ray. After Herbert moved out of my life, Elinor got in the habit of taking me with her on her social rounds. Since I was turning out one picture after another, I welcomed the diversion. Going places with Elinor was never dull.

She loved attractive young men and she loved all the new dances, and in the summer of 1921 her favorite young man was an actor from Oklahoma named Dana Todd who danced marvelously, and her favorite haunt was the Patent Leather Room in the Ambassador Hotel. The Patent Leather Room put everything else in Southern California to shame when it came to elegance, and it was always impossible to get in without a reservation unless you were Elinor Glyn. One night in August a group of four or five of us arrived there on a Sunday night to find the room packed. Elinor simply looked shocked and imperious until, as if by magic, a front table materialized and we all sat down.

Max Fischer, the violinist who played on the set for Mr. De Mille, was the leader of the orchestra, and that night, as usual, he began to play tunes he knew I liked. Elinor announced that the studio was considering Dana for the leading man in the film version of *Three Weeks*, and we all chattered enthusiastically about that for a bit. Then we danced. When Dana and I returned to the table, I found a note at my place. It said: "Your M.A.N. is here. Look up." When I did, I found myself staring into the mischievous Irish face of Marshall A. Neilan.

"Hello, Dana," Marshall Neilan said. They knew each

other because Dana had been in several films directed by William Desmond Taylor, Mary Pickford's other important director.

"Mickey! How are you?" Dana said.

Marshall Neilan didn't speak to me. He just held out one hand and walked a step ahead of me onto the floor, like the Pied Piper. Then he turned and took me in his arms. I hadn't seen him in a year and a half, but in an instant I was in love again.

Max Fischer was playing "They Didn't Believe Me." As the song ended, Marshall Neilan whispered, "Two hundred and ninety-seven."

"What?"

"In two hundred and ninety-seven days I'll be free to marry you." I could tell he had been drinking, but he was sober as a judge. "Don't you remember? I told you to put me on the list."

"You said it the night Herbert Somborn proposed. Do you remember *that?*"

"Of course I do. I also said it wouldn't last."

"This time I'm not even between marriages. I'm still married."

"Well, talk to Jesse Lasky. I'll call you next week. But let me be very firm: I love you." With that he smiled and left, as quickly as he had the first time I met him, only this time I knew it would be days, not months, before I saw him again.

"Wasn't that Marshall Neilan, Gloria?" Elinor asked when I sat down.

"Yes," I said.

"Well?" she urged, like an empress ordering her minion to tell her everything she knew.

"Elinor, please!"

"Oh, very well, be coy. *But . . . my . . . dear,"* she said, squinting fixedly, "nab him."

Everybody adored dashing, brilliant, madcap Mickey Neilan, from ZaSu Pitts to William Randolph Hearst. Following D. W. Griffith and Cecil B. De Mille as Mary Pickford's director, his very first film with her turned out to be her most successful one—*Rebecca of Sunnybrook Farm,* made in 1917, when he was twenty-six. Good-looking enough to be cast as a juvenile lead the day he arrived in Hollywood from San

Francisco to deliver a car to director Allan Dwan two years before that, he had been the prey of the gossip columnists ever after, and his name was most persistently linked to that of beautiful, vivacious Blanche Sweet, whom he also directed. The omnipresent playboy, Mickey always knew where the good gin was hidden, where the best party was going on, where the best band was playing. Elinor Glyn called him a child of the age, a hero out of F. Scott Fitzgerald, whose first book had cast a spell over the nation in 1920. Old, young, male, female—Mickey Neilan captivated them all.

Wallace Reid told a wonderful story about him. A friend of Wally's had entrusted him for a day with her niece, a child who was interested in motion pictures. By lunchtime the little girl was bored and Wally was out of patience. Remembering that Mickey, a father himself, loved kids, Wally went next door and asked him if he could possibly keep the little girl on the set of *Rebecca of Sunnybrook Farm* for the rest of the day. Mickey said he would love to have her. He talked to the child for a minute and then plunked her down smack in the middle of a scene of children he was directing. She was so good in the rushes that Mickey kept her on for the rest of the summer and paid her a salary. Thus she joined the army of children who worshiped Uncle Mickey.

He had a beautiful home and he entertained lavishly. He started the fad of having Oriental houseboys for servants, and his house was the first in Hollywood to have a built-in pipe organ. He played by ear and could compose songs at a moment's notice for this friend's birthday or that friend's anniversary. His mother lived with him, and his child, a little boy, visited often after Mickey's separation. Mickey lived like a young lord. He didn't give a rap for convention. He was utterly debonair.

After Herbert, how could I not love him? After one afternoon with him, how could I not forget Craney Gartz and every other handsome man who had ever tempted me? As Mickey Neilan waltzed me into my first real love affair, it never occurred to me to utter a syllable in protest. I was enjoying myself too much.

Early in September, before I had decided on how to approach Mr. Lasky on the subject of a divorce, he made an appointment with me to talk about clothes.

"We know why *Under the Lash* was not successful," he

began, "and I assure you, Gloria, we won't make the same mistake again."

Under the Lash was the title of my second starring picture. Based on a novel called *The Shulamite,* it was about a domineering Boer farmer in South Africa and his much younger second wife, and a visiting Englishman who finally rescues the heroine from her stern, cruel mate. The studio had chosen this drab rural story as a startling change of pace for me after *The Great Moment,* but their plan had backfired. It was the only picture of mine in over two years that had not made money. The studio had quickly made up for any losses, however, by releasing a picture called *Don't Tell Everything,* which was nothing more than leftover footage from *The Affairs of Anatol.* To the public it was a totally new film reuniting Wallace Reid and me, especially since Sam Wood was credited with direction, not Mr. De Mille. It was very popular.

"Do you know why *Under the Lash* failed?" Mr. Lasky asked.

"Not really," I said.

"Because women didn't go to it," he said. "And women didn't go because you wore dull, gray, buttoned-up house dresses through most of it. Women refuse to accept you in homely clothes. Isn't that interesting?"

"I guess so," I said.

"Well, we won't let it happen again. Starting right now, with *Her Husband's Trademark,* anything you want in the way of fancy clothes, you can have. Never look drab again, because the public won't stand for it. In fact, I've already spoken to Elinor Glyn about your next picture. I told her to come up with an elaborate costume drama. What do you think?"

His glasses twinkled. By saying that he had solved all our problems and that I could buy out the store, he had put himself in a good mood. And while he was in it, rather than debate the issue that dressing up is not the same as acting, I decided to tackle the subject that mattered much more to me just then.

"I'm sure you're right," I said. "I'll have a wardrobe session tomorrow before the picture goes any further." Then I added, without changing my tone a fraction, "Mr. Lasky, there's one other thing I'd like to discuss." I told him I wanted a divorce on the grounds of desertion and explained the circumstances of Herbert's leaving in May.

Mr. Lasky stopped smiling. "Impossible," he said.

"Why?" I asked, bristling.

"Why?" he repeated, in an excited yap. "Because after Fatty Arbuckle's little escapade last week, we are sitting on a keg of dynamite. We can't afford the slightest whiff of scandal. That's why."

For a week nobody in Hollywood had discussed anything but the horrible death of Virginia Rappe allegedly at the hands of Fatty Arbuckle at a drunken party in San Francisco over the Labor Day weekend. Nevertheless, without meaning to be unsympathetic, I asked what Fatty Arbuckle had to do with me.

With almost paternal sincerity, Jesse Lasky explained. He said Fatty had given every church group and ladies' club in America a taste of blood. The newspapers had proved in less than a week that the public got a much greater thrill out of watching stars fall than out of watching them shine. One day Fatty Arbuckle had been their most beloved comedian next to Chaplin; the next day they were screaming for his head. He predicted that there would be a rash of scandals because now everyone was looking for them; and whose life, he asked, could stand close scrutiny under a microscope or in the hands of a rabid columnist? Why, look at poor Francis X. Bushman, he said; all he had had to do was divorce his wife and marry Beverly Bayne and his public had dropped him like a hot potato. No one hired him anymore. He reminded me that in my own case, I would be divorcing for the second time and less than a year after having a baby. Did I think the public would swallow that? Or did I think Herbert Somborn would give me a quiet divorce when he had everything to gain by making a stink? What was more, Mr. Lasky said, my screen image was not exactly Mary Pickford's.

"In the public's mind," he said, "you stand for love, passion, glamour, the whole sophisticated atmosphere of Cecil B. De Mille and Elinor Glyn, and they eat it up. But they could turn in a minute. Believe me, Gloria, you're living on the very cusp of scandal. We all are."

There was an edge of warning in his voice, and I wondered if he could possibly know about Mickey and me. I looked him straight in the eye, but he was imperturbable.

"After that, Mr. Lasky, do you still want me to go on wearing the most glamorous, sumptuous, seductive clothes money will buy?" I asked.

"It's too late to change," Mr. Lasky said, announcing a fact. *"Under the Lash* proved that."

Mr. Lasky was right. Fatty Arbuckle had drawn down the lightning on us all. Scandal hung on like a fever through the fall and winter, as his series of trials stretched out, trials in which the evidence was considered so vile, so unspeakable, that much of it was passed around silently, in typewritten notes. People at parties joked feebly that the only person who could breathe easily was Marion Davies, not because she was free of stain—on the contrary; but because William Randolph Hearst, whose mistress she had been for years by then, controlled the very newspapers that might otherwise have chosen to pounce on her. Nobody knew who would be next.

Having an affair with Mickey Neilan, the most popular man in town, in those days was a bit like playing cops and robbers with loaded guns, especially when the studio insisted on sending out releases to advertise my pictures in which they quoted me as saying such things as the following:

The marriage contract should be the strongest tie in the world. It is the foundation upon which civilization is built, and the hope of the future. I have no sympathy with those advocating the freedom of love. The happiest marriage is where it is founded upon love, but when it isn't, regrettable as the consequences are, the marriage contract must prevail.

Greater than even love is a clear conscience and the happiness of knowing you have done right. Therefore, under no circumstances, do I think, is there reason sufficient to prompt a woman deserting a man she has married for one she learns to love while living as the wife of another man.

Naturally, the columnists picked up on this nonsense and published over and over the fact that I had been separated from Herbert, my second husband, since May. The persistence of the press on this issue began to worry the studio.

But then, by the strangest coincidence, my mother, who had always abhorred all the publicity aspects of my life, managed to draw any possible fire away from me. Her late husband had left most of his estate to her, except for small bequests to other relatives. Now, a year later, taking advantage of the scandal epidemic, his relatives tried to break the will. They filed a legal action against Mother, charging her with ensnaring her second husband, and in order to make a public issue of the matter, they dragged me into it, obviously hoping they could blackmail me into paying them off. They charged that Matthew Burns had been in love with me, not my mother, and that my mother had used me as bait to lure him. All the Los Angeles papers gave headline room to the stupid case. The sleazier ones took to referring to me as the Baby Vamp, although it was a simple matter to show that at the time of my mother's marriage I was a married woman myself, playing sophisticated grown-ups in films directed by Jack Conway. The trumped-up story was so patently ridiculous that I urged Mother to fight it out in court if it took all year, and she did. Along with all the respected names it could muster, the studio rushed to my defense; eventually the judge threw out the case and dismissed all the charges. By then the public had forgotten about my separation. All they remembered was my bravery in helping to clear my mother's name.

One evening late in October, Elinor Glyn and I were in the lobby of the Hollywood Hotel. Elinor had been hired to write my next screenplay, so we saw each other frequently. With all of her usual theatricality, she gestured me to bring my head nearer to hers, squinted to the right and left, and then even turned her head to look behind her before she spoke. "My dear, I have the most thrilling news, but I'm not supposed to tell."

"Oh, come on—what is it?"

"Well," she said, rolling her eyes, "don't reveal your source, but do you know whom Jesse Lasky wants to cast opposite you in the picture?"

"No. Who?"

After a great intake of breath and another look around, she whispered, "Valentino."

"Really?"

"Yes. He told me so today. He's going to speak to you about it this week. Isn't it exciting?"

Elinor was such a gossip that I didn't pursue the subject further with her. I had no intention just then of telling her that I even knew Rudy Valentino. But later that night at my place I repeated the conversation to Mickey, and it wasn't hard to figure out what Mr. Lasky was up to. He wanted Rudy to make one more sure-fire picture at a modest salary before the studio had to give him a star contract or lose him. Rudy was in somewhat the same position I had been in when I agreed to make one last film with Mr. De Mille. After that, the sky would be the limit for him. For the moment, however, because I was already a star, Mr. Lasky would have to get my permission.

"So you want to work with him?" Mickey asked.

"Oh, yes. I adore him," I said.

"O.K., just don't let Jesse Lasky know that. Make him think you're doing him a favor and get something in return. Treat him like Ma Pickford used to treat Adolph Zukor when Mary was still at Famous Players."

"How was that?"

"Just before it was time to sign a new contract, she'd quietly mention something expensive Mary would like. That meant Zukor had to throw in whatever it was or Mary wouldn't sign. Do the same thing with Lasky."

The next day Mr. Lasky called me in and told me Elinor Glyn very much wanted Rudolph Valentino to be in *Beyond the Rocks*. In fact, she had told him she had Valentino in mind when she wrote the role of Lord Hector. Mr. Lasky said he had told her he couldn't say yes unless I agreed. After all, I might not want such a big name playing opposite me. He was teasing me, prodding me into a defensive position, but I didn't let on that I even surmised that.

"What does my contract say?" I asked. "Are you allowed to co-star someone in one of my pictures?" We both knew perfectly well he was not, but only after a few minutes of pinching his glasses nervously did Mr. Lasky say no.

I was astonished at how easily my next words came out. "I see. Does my contract say anything about my going abroad and your paying me while I'm away?"

Mr. Lasky started smiling. He released the pressure from his glasses and said no, it didn't.

"Well, then, if I agree to let you co-star Valentino with me, it seems to me you might send me on a nice trip to Europe in the spring when the picture's finished."

Mr. Lasky didn't seem shocked at all, just relieved. He said he would let me know, and sure enough, a few days later he sent me a memorandum agreeing to a vacation with pay. I promptly picked up the phone and shared the joke, first with Mickey, then with Rudy. Mickey told me I was brilliant and said he would meet me in Paris when I went. "I was counting on that when I asked Mr. Lasky for the trip," I said.

I had met Rudolph Valentino in January, nine months earlier, right after the studio had made me a star. The second time I went to the stable to get my new horse, he was there. He smiled and called me Mrs. Somborn, and I recognized him as the good-looking Italian in *Eyes of Youth*, the Clara Kimball Young picture Herbert had screened for Bea and me just before we were married. After that we frequently rode together in the Hollywood hills on Sunday mornings, not as a regular thing but more often than not. Each of us knew the other would be there if one of us felt like having company.

Friendly but not outgoing at first, Rudy spoke with a delicious accent and he was an excellent horseman. We would ride for an hour and then sit on the cliffs overlooking Hollywood and Los Angeles and talk.

It gave me a start when he mentioned how much he admired Clara Kimball Young and how sad he felt about what had happened to her, for it was just about then that I had become aware of how precarious Herbert's finances were. Rudy explained that he had made two pictures with her, three years apart. During the first she was still a star for Lewis Selznick, and things had been wonderful. Then she had divorced her husband and met Harry Garson, who had become her manager and lover and persuaded her to produce her own pictures. She had been so naïve, Rudy said sadly. The studios fought them and the distributors gave them trouble. In the last year she had fallen into terrible financial difficulties and had even had to sell her beautiful jewelry. The studios wouldn't touch her.

From then on I trusted Rudy, and we discussed our problems with each other. I told him how Herbert had taken me to dinner that night at Miss Young's and how impressed I had been, and Rudy told me her business was already in disastrous shape then. The other man at dinner that night had of course been Harry Garson, whom everybody seemed to dislike for what he had done to Miss Young.

Gradually we confessed that we were both miserably married, Rudy to an actress named Jean Acker, and I to Herbert. We were never romantically attracted to each other, except on the surface, as nice to look at; rather, we were friends, professionals, two people with a lot in common. He was worried about his career, although he had hopes for a Rex Ingram film he was working on at Metro. I had fears I would fail as a star and have either to take several steps backward or change studios. We comforted each other and soon came to look forward to our Sunday rides.

The first week in March *The Four Horsemen of the Apocalypse* opened in New York, and within days Rudolph Valentino had become second only to Douglas Fairbanks. The following Sunday he wasn't at the stable, which didn't surprise me, but the Sunday after that he was. Before I could tell him I had seen his picture and loved it, he shyly presented me with a birthday gift, a riding crop with my monogram on the silver handle. I was dumbfounded: How did he know my birth date? I asked. He said I had once told him I was an Aries and he had found the exact date in a published interview. He wanted me to have the riding crop because he thought I had brought him luck. Only then did I get to tell him I had loved him in *The Four Horsemen*.

We rode together less often after that, because he was suddenly the most sought-after guest and celebrity in Hollywood. Distributors started showing his old films, in which he had played bit roles, with his name above the title. Women screamed and wept and tore their hair at the sight of him, so he was no longer free to move around easily. Moreover, both of us had a busy spring and summer, which we discussed whenever we did ride together. Rudy's next picture for Metro was *Camille*, with Nazimova. The set designer was an icy beauty by the name of Natacha Rambova, whom he fell hopelessly in love with. In May *The Great Moment* was a huge success and I broke up my marriage with Herbert. Within a month Rudy, who had felt underpaid at Metro, signed a contract with Jesse Lasky, so while I made *Under the Lash* and *Her Husband's Trademark* on one Paramount lot, Rudy made *The Shiek* on another. Soon the most popular song in the country was "The Shiek of Araby," which capitalized on Rudy's image. Just about that time, he asked his first wife for a divorce because he wanted to marry Natacha, and I met my once-for-all wild Irish love, Mickey Neilan. And now, suddenly, Jesse Lasky was bribing me with a trip to Europe, which I would spend with Mickey, in order that I would consent to be in a picture with a man I was crazy about. No wonder Rudy, Mickey, and I roared when we discussed it. I told Rudy that after *Beyond the Rocks* he should do exactly what Mr. De Mille had told me to do after *The Affairs of Anatol*: Ask for the moon.

Everyone wanted *Beyond the Rocks* to be every luscious

thing Hollywood could serve up in a single picture: the sultry glamour of Gloria Swanson, the steamy Latin magic of Rudolph Valentino, a rapturous love story by Elinor Glyn, and the tango as it was meant to be danced, by the master himself. In the story I played a poor but aristocratic English girl who is married off to an elderly millionaire, only to meet the love of her life on her honeymoon. Elinor introduced historical flashbacks so that Rudy and I could wear costumes of some of the most romantic periods of European history. For the tango sequence, the wardrobe department made me a gold-beaded and -embroidered lace evening gown so shimmering and beautiful that moviegoers talked about it for the next year. I also wore a king's ransom in velvet, silk ruffles, sable, and chinchilla, all dripping from shoulders to floor with over a million dollars' worth of jewels.

The picture could never be as sensual in character as the studio and the public had hoped because it was one of the first big films to be supervised by censors. At the start of 1922, for fear the mounting number of Hollywood scandals would eventually ruin the whole motion picture industry, Mr. Lasky and other movie executives set up their own internal censorship bureau. They hired Will H. Hays, who had served a year under President Harding as the Postmaster General, and brought him to Hollywood to create the Hays Office and assure the American public of a rigid standard of decency in the films Hollywood put before them. One of the first stipulations of the office was that kisses should run no longer than ten feet of film. So we shot each kiss twice, once for the version to be released in America and once for the European version. Poor Rudy could hardly get his nostrils flaring before the American version was over. Only Europeans and South Americans could see Swanson and Valentino engage in any honest-to-goodness torrid kisses. American fevers were now controlled by a stopwatch.

Sam Wood, the director, made most of his money as a real estate agent; there was nothing of the temperamental artist about him. In this, his second film with Elinor Glyn, his nerves were beginning to wear thin in regard to her bizarre and erratic demands. Therefore, the best time for all of us was a brief period on location on Catalina, which Elinor decided sadly we would have to shoot without her because she had other irons in the fire in Hollywood. On Catalina we had to shoot a rescue sequence over and over again because we could never get it right. In the scene, I tip over in a rowboat "beyond the rocks" and the English lord Rudy plays has to rescue me and carry me, unconscious and dripping, to the shore. Given my lifelong fear of ocean swimming, the scene made me jittery and uncomfortable, but the patience and fortitude of Sam and Rudy made everything work at last. The nights in the hotel were great fun. We had long, wonderful dinners, and frequently afterward, pillow fights in the upstairs corridors. I never saw Rudolph Valentino so relaxed and happy.

Before and after Catalina, he was frequently anything but relaxed. He was in the throes of a divorce case in which it turned out that the marriage of the Shiek had never been consummated. This was all owing to the neurotic capriciousness of Jean Acker, the first Mrs. Valentino, but the columnists had a grand time with the trial until the judge finally decided wholly in favor of Rudy. Once *Beyond the Rocks* was finished in January of 1922, Mr. Lasky announced that Rudolph Valentino would thenceforth be a Paramount star, with his name above the title, and his first starring film was *Blood and Sand*. Several months later he married Natacha Rambova, and from then on he and I saw each other seldom.

Although the studios all pretended to be on a strenuous decency campaign after the appointment of Will Hays, they nevertheless continually flirted with scandalous and titillating subjects, because they made money on them. Hollywood was, after all, the glamour factory, the beauty factory, the dream factory; America was, after all, the land of flappers, bootleggers, jazz, and roadsters. Furthermore, as filmmakers grew aware that Europeans dealt quite explicitly with sex and decadence on the screen, and with great success, they became more and more fascinated by directors like Ernst Lubitsch and stars like Pola Negri. Also, they continued advertising their own films as temptingly as they could without actually crossing over the line into vulgarity, urging, for example, the average American woman, who was already sighing at the very thought of Valentino, to "Shriek For the Shiek Will Seek You Too!"

In spite of all their efforts to convince America that the Hollywood product was essentially healthy and uplifting, scandal spread. Before they could put it out in one studio, it flared up in another, and each time the newspapers fanned the flames. In February 1922 William Desmond Taylor, one of the industry's leading directors, was murdered. The last person to see him alive, the journalists reported, was Mabel Normand, and a nightie found in his closet bore the initials of another well-known star, Mary Miles Minter. The headlines raved on for weeks, and no sooner had they abated than the final Arbuckle trial was convened. Although it ended with an acquittal for Fatty, his great career was finished. So was Mabel Normand's. So was Mary Miles Minter's. And how many of the stars who continued to glitter had been just plain lucky? No one knew, but the newspapers never stopped poking and prying. As a twice-married star in love with a married director, I was on slippery ground.

In April, when I finished *Her Gilded Cage*, in which I played a French actress in lots of naughty sequins-and-lamé outfits, I breathed a sigh of relief as I packed my trunks for Europe. I would have to be separated from little Gloria for six weeks, and I dreaded that, but after seven years in one place, not to mention two marriages and thirty-two pictures, I felt I had earned a vacation.

Mr. Lasky came to the set the day before I left to wish me bon voyage and to ask me to agree to make five pictures a year before the studio picked up their option starting in January, which would raise my salary from $2,500 to $5,000 a week. I was aware that his salesmen were already insisting that exhibitors take six other pictures for every Swanson picture they got, so I knew they would pick up the option anyway, but I said I would think about it.

Of course I couldn't travel alone; therefore Peggy Urson got a free trip to Europe too. I had arranged to meet Mickey in Paris. After speaking to a flock of reporters in the Los Angeles station, I boarded the train with Peggy. At every major stop on the five-day trip to New York I gave interviews, and a whole platoon of photographers and columnists were waiting when we checked into the Plaza Hotel.

There was a message from the Paramount office in New York saying that Mr. Lasky was arriving in the morning and would like to talk to me before I sailed. We met before lunch, and Mr. Lasky handed me a new contract to sign. Just by glancing at it, I could see it was deliberately vague regarding the number of pictures I would make as of January. Furious at all this speeded-up, polite coercion to get something for nothing, I said very sweetly I would read it over and send word to him before I sailed.

In the hotel suite that evening, I wrote him the following letter:

Dear Sir:

Regarding the subject discussed in your office yesterday, this is all covered in my contract of August 12, 1920. I signed this contract in good faith and I intend to live up to it. Either you may renew your option on my services sometime before January 1 of this year according to the terms of the contract or not. You may do as you like. Thank you very much.

Gloria Swanson

I had the letter in my purse when Peggy and I boarded the *Homeric*. A dozen reporters were waiting outside my stateroom, and I had to pose for pictures. The studio had arranged the press conference, they told me. When it was over, I asked for a Western Union messenger. I told him to wait until just before they pulled up the gangplank and then to deliver my letter to Mr. Lasky. I had kept my word. We were off.

We had a glorious month of first-class everything: the captain's table on the ship, Claridge's in London, the Crillon in Paris, and the Adlon in Berlin. No matter what we wanted, we had only to pick up the phone and ask for it. Studio representatives and guides were available around the clock. We saw every tourist sight there was to see, and bought everything we could carry or have delivered. I had never tasted trifle or croissants or had pancakes with whipped cream for dessert. I had never heard an English actor doing Shakespeare. I had never seen the cancan with splits, as I did in Montmartre, or a cabaret act of men in women's clothes, as I did in Berlin. I had never seen real French fashions on beautiful women strolling naturally along grand boulevards. I had never seen a Cubist painting or heard of Dada. I had never been in anything like Westminster Abbey, or Notre Dame, or the Charlottenburg. I had never sat at a café sipping mineral water or a stein of beer. I had never used a bidet.

And I never wanted it to end. No wonder, I thought, Dana Todd and everyone else who wasn't tied down headed for San Francisco every weekend they were free. There was some culture there, some sense of a real city. Mickey had been so right, it was time I saw Europe. The glamour of Hollywood illusion dimmed to nothing beside the real glamour of the European rich, whether they were heading for Ascot or driving through the Bois de Boulogne in a Hispano-Suiza.

Everywhere I went, people recognized me, but Europeans didn't scream and point and block the street the way Americans did. It was as if Europeans had already seen everything. They merely smiled or nodded or tipped their hats and walked on.

Peggy and I had barely entered my suite in Claridge's when a letter was delivered from the London office of Paramount-Famous Players-Lasky. I expected it was a schedule of interviews I had to give, but no, it was a letter notifying me that Mr. Lasky was taking up my option for another three years at $5,000, $6,000, and $7,000 a week. They had given up on five pictures a year. In January my salary would be doubled as per my contract. A copy of the letter was delivered to me twice more, in Berlin and Paris. Mr. Lasky obviously didn't want me to make any other arrangements.

I asked the Lasky office in Berlin to arrange a visit to UFA, the studio where Ernst Lubitsch and Pola Negri had made *Passion*, but I didn't meet either of them. The studio was interesting; so were the great museums, but for the most part Berlin was, to me, more frightening than exciting in 1922. You almost needed a wheelbarrow to carry a hundred dollars' worth of marks. Everywhere you looked, Berlin was either poor or decadent. When I realized that I could buy a motion picture studio or a hotel or a château for a few weeks' salary, I shivered to think how war could reduce people. I felt guilty spending money in Berlin.

Not so in Paris. If Mickey hadn't joined us and arranged visits to the Louvre and Versailles, I think Peggy and I would have bought out Panquin and Worth and Poiret and Lanvin and all the rest of the great couturiers. I was supposed to be the world's foremost clotheshorse when it came to films, but the styles and cuts and fabrics in the best Paris showrooms took my breath away. What's more, everyone in them knew me, and they were all as thrilled as I was every time I went into one of them.

In many ways Paris seemed like home to me. Perhaps because of my Alsatian relatives, I felt that I belonged there. The flowers, clothes, foods, perfumes, wines, all delighted me. With Mickey there, the gorgeous city provided the honeymoon I had always wanted, the honeymoon that somehow seemed too good to follow either of the weddings I had had. In fact, Mickey Neilan was the only person to spend a Paris honeymoon with, I kept telling myself. He knew where the flower markets were, and the Flea Market, and where Sylvia Beach's English bookstore was, and where you got tickets to hear Mistinguett sing.

One evening, however, he was over an hour late getting back to the suite before dinner. He hadn't changed clothes since morning, and it was obvious he was quite tight. I was furious. I had on the most beautiful dress I'd bought in Paris and we had planned on a long, marvelous evening.

"Mickey," I said, in an annoyed tone, "where have you been?"

"Drinking with Roy Aitken," he said. "I ran into him on the street and he asked me to have a drink."

"*A* drink?" I said sarcastically.

"Several drinks. As many as I wanted. I could hardly tell the producer of *Birth of a Nation* that I had to run because you and I are living in sin in the Hotel Crillon, could I? Especially when I'm checked into another hotel to avoid scandal."

Before we could stop ourselves, we were into our first bad fight, full of recriminations about our respective serious intentions, our doubts, all the little annoyances we had been saving up. I told him it was ridiculous to kowtow to Roy Aitken if it meant standing me up. He told me I had been kowtowing to Jesse Lasky for two years; what was the difference? After all, who was the free one—he or I? He had managed to get his divorce, hadn't he? What about me? I was still at least a year from getting mine. I hadn't even *started* getting mine, he snapped.

"You could always go back to Blanche Sweet," I said.

"Or you to Craney Gartz. How about that?" he said.

"Oh, be quiet," I said. "You're drunk."

"And you don't love me when I'm drunk, is that it?"

"Yes, that's it."

With that, he walked to the French windows, threw them open, and stood teetering on the little balcony, poised for flight. He expected me to panic and plead with him, but instead I calmly announced that we were on the third floor; if he was really serious, he ought to go to the roof. That so

enraged him that he climbed down off the little ledge and
started toward me, calling on all the Irish saints to keep him
from strangling me.

He turned around, looking for something to smash, and
when he could find nothing at hand he grabbed a beautiful
monogrammed cane that I knew he loved dearly. He went to
break it over his knee, but it was bamboo and didn't shatter.
Instead, it bent like a bow, flew up and struck the ceiling, and
came right back down and hit him on the head. That made me
laugh so hard that I missed the chair I started to sink back on
and fell flat on the floor. Seeing me laugh so enraged Mickey
that he flew to the door and yanked the Limoges doorknob off
trying to open it. Then he brought one leg behind him in a
spasm, but before he could kick the door open, he fell
forward against it, laughing uncontrollably. He walked over
and picked me up, and we fell into each other's arms. We
couldn't stop laughing. Drunk or in a rage, I thought, he was
still the most gorgeous thing in Paris.

He got dressed then and we headed for Montmartre. We
had a fabulous dinner in one place, the best champagne in
another. The place after that had a piano, so Mickey sat down
and played American jazz and show tunes for everyone. He
was so good they wouldn't let him stop. Hours later we pulled
up in a cab to a bistro in Les Halles and had the scalding,
sticky onion soup. By then I was high and Mickey was quite
drunk again. He bought the biggest armful of roses he could
carry for me, and we climbed back into the cab. It was broad
daylight when we got back to the hotel, where for hours we
were entwined in each other's arms.

The next day we fought again and of course loved making
up again.

Two days later he left Paris. We obviously could not arrive
in New York together, so he was booked on one boat, and
Peggy and I had to take another. I was sure I could never love
anybody else as much as I loved Mickey, but the honeymoon,
I knew, was over.

If Mickey had made me see Paris, Paris had also made me
see Mickey. I did more thinking and soul-searching on the
six-day boat trip back to New York than I had ever done
before in my life, probably because I loved Mickey Neilan
more than I had ever loved anyone before in my life. He
needed saving because he drank too much and his career was
slipping. It was three years since he had last directed Mary
Pickford. He kept saying he wanted to direct me in a picture,

but I knew Mr. Lasky would never allow it. In fact, I was fairly sure Mr. Lasky surmised everything about Mickey and me already. Also, the incident with Roy Aitken, my old boss at Triangle, convinced me that Mickey was as nervous and defensive as I was about the constant threat of ruinous scandal. What he needed was someone to look after him, and it was clear that he and I could not possibly live together in Hollywood. The columnists could destroy us both in a month, or less, if they chose to. It would take at least a year for me to get a divorce, and during that time the studio executives would be watching me like hawks because starting in January they would be paying me over a quarter of a million dollars a year. For little Gloria's sake if for no one else's, I couldn't afford to throw away that kind of security.

And Mickey needed someone now. Slowly I began to think of Blanche Sweet, whom I didn't really know at all. D. W. Griffith had made her a star, and Mickey had later directed her in a series for Goldwyn. She was beautiful, and she and Mickey cared for each other deeply. Wasn't she the woman for him now, if she loved him and wanted to marry him? I remembered he had said the night we first met that we would both marry a number of times—that he merely wanted to be on my list. I decided to hold him to that, for his own good and perhaps for everyone's.

There were reporters waiting for me in the harbor, and more at the Plaza Hotel when Peggy and I got there. It was hours before it was safe for Mickey to come up to the suite. He was checked in at another hotel nearby.

I kissed him and told him I thought he should marry Blanche. He was speechless at first. Then he said, "I suppose this is your idea of tidying things up?"

"You know I'm right," I said. "Hollywood isn't Paris, Mickey. I'm less free than I was a year ago because I'm more valuable to the studio."

He didn't argue. He simply asked, "Will you marry me if I marry Blanche?"

I told him I had always promised to marry him sometime. If we were ever both free again at the same time in the future, he could marry me then. In the meantime I would go right on loving him; for that, there was no help. I smiled tenderly as I said it. He stared at me to see if I was going to back down, and then he picked up the phone and called Blanche. Mickey loved to tell me that I was being ruined by weak directors like Sam Wood, and that he would never make a picture with me unless he was the boss. Yet he seemed almost excited at that moment to be reading my lines and following my direction.

Blanche accepted. They decided that since it would take five days for her to get from California to New York, Mickey would meet her in Chicago and they would be married there. He told her to leave in the morning.

"Will you come?" he asked me.

"Of course, if you want me to."

I sent Peggy ahead to California, and Mickey made reservations for us to leave on the same train to Chicago. Blanche needed two days' head start. We all arrived in Chicago the same morning.

I never knew what Mickey said to Blanche, nor did I want to know. They were married that afternoon. Then he spent four hours with me the following morning and took me to the railway drawing room I had reserved to Los Angeles. He and Blanche returned to California via New York.

They were on again, off again, and then separated after two months. I was still many months from being divorced myself when they separated. But in Mickey's mind, and in mine too, I was back on his list, or he on mine, whichever.

As for the gossip columnists, they were nosy at first, then intrigued, then utterly baffled. They could put us all in the same columns by way of innuendo, but their barbs had no real sting. In August a flurry of short pieces like the following from the Oakland *Tribune* appeared in local newspapers, but then the gossip peddlers, defused and defeated, dropped the whole affair.

GLORIA SWANSON, BLANCHE SWEET, MATES SEPARATE

MOTION PICTURE ACTRESSES ADMIT THEY LIVE APART FROM HUSBANDS

Los Angeles, Aug. 9—Gloria Swanson and Blanche Sweet have improved the old Fannie Hurst theory of "husbands by appointment," it would seem.

The theory has been extended to the point of refusing the appointments.

At least both of the beautiful screen stars are now occupying homes separate from their elected mates, it was learned today.

Herbert Sanborn [*sic*], husband of Gloria Swanson

and incidentally a wealthy Pasadena man, admitted that he and his wife "had separated," but said "the separation has never come to discussion with attorneys."

Blanche Sweet would not discuss the report that she had separated from Marshall Neilan, to whom she was married after rushing across the continent to meet him June 7.

She admitted, however, that Neilan lives in Hollywood and that her present home is the Ambassador hotel.

In the fall of 1922 I finished one film with Sam Wood, *The Impossible Mrs. Bellew,* and started another, *My American Wife.* We had clearly found the formula for success in these romantic comedies of marriage and intrigue laced with a series of handsome leading men and a never-ending parade of fabulous gowns. In fact, we couldn't turn out enough of them to suit the public. It was all I could do to hold the quota at four a year.

A girl Mickey knew was in the second film. Her name was Aileen Pringle and we became close friends. She was about my size, with yards of auburn hair and a scorching wit. She had played on Broadway in 1921 with George Arliss in *The Green Goddess.* One day I asked her what she thought of my leading man, Antonio Moreno, a Latin type the studio hoped to launch as another Valentino. "Not much," Aileen said. "Obviously he's never had an idea above the waist." From that moment on, she was one of the few people I could both work and socialize with. She spent lots of time with Mickey and me, often, in fact, acting as referee when we quarreled, and she was always a joy to have around. She was true blue. She turned down a contract with Mr. De Mille because she had heard him berate Pauline Garon on the set one day in front of fifty people about the way she was holding her hand and then order her to go to a projection room and study old scenes of mine. She said De Mille had become a tyrant, and she could not tolerate that. She asked Hattie, who was present, if that wasn't true, and Hattie, loyal as she was to "the Chief," nodded her head yes.

We next enlarged our little group to include Lois Wilson, a marvelous actress I had first met on the set of *Male and Female.* An ex-schoolteacher from Alabama, Lois had real star quality. Everyone who met her knew it was just a question of time until the right part came along. She never stopped working.

Given that my social circle was growing, that my salary was about to double, and that I would eventually be divorced from Herbert and married to Mickey, I made two momentous decisions that fall. First, I told Peggy Urson, who handled all my affairs, to look for a big house in Beverly Hills that I could afford, because I wanted to leave the bungalow Herbert and I had shared at the Beverly Hills Hotel, which I still lived in. Second, to everyone's amazement, I set out to adopt a baby brother for Gloria. I didn't want her to be an only child, even temporarily, and I loved children so much I felt I could never have too many. Since I was a twice-married movie star who appeared frequently in the gossip columns, I naturally had a harder time getting an adoption service to surrender a baby boy under a year old than Peggy had finding a house, but in the course of a few months we managed to get both.

As to my first decision, it was actually Mickey who learned that the mansion King Gillette had built for his sister on Crescent Drive right across the road from the Beverly Hills Hotel was up for sale. Since *The Danger Girl*, that place had had a certain fascination for me, and its park-sized lawns, its private elevator, and its majestic indoor staircase all proved irresistible when I saw them. Peggy Urson had most of my money invested in real estate, but I knew I had to have the Gillette house, so Mickey lent me $18,000 for the down payment. Then we threw ourselves into bringing it to life in anticipation of the time when we would be openly sharing it. We hired a butler and a maid and a cook, and I spent weeks furnishing the elegant, spacious rooms. Mickey said he was giving me an early birthday present and hired a crew of men to turn one of the basement rooms into a lounge with a projection booth for screening films.

When Sam Wood saw the place he immediately wanted to use it for location scenes for our next picture, *Prodigal Daughters*, and I said he could. The cast included Maude Wayne from Keystone and a cousin of Jesse Lasky's named Mervyn Le Roy who played a newsboy. By the time we got to shooting, all the women in the cast spent half of their time making noises at the new baby.

I had first thought to look for a second child sometime in August. One day when I came home from the studio, late as usual, I could see Gloria and her nurse under the palms in front of the bungalow. I had always considered Gloria a happy, normal child, and in order to keep her that way, I had been very lenient with Herbert about when and how often he could visit. That day I walked slowly out onto the lawn until she saw me. She laughed and left the nurse and started running toward me. I squatted down waiting to embrace her, but before she reached me, she slipped and tumbled in the grass. Whimpering, she got to her feet, turned around, and then ran back sobbing into the arms of her nurse.

This knocked the wind out of me. I vowed then and there to devote more time to her every day and to give her a greater sense of family.

I contacted all the local orphanages. I sent them gifts and I called them often, insistently, until some of them grew nervous and suspicious. I wanted every child I saw in every orphanage. I loved the smell of babies, and their little bodies. Their sweet, delicate fingers reminded me of angels.

At last an institution in Los Angeles called to say a four-and-a-half-month-old boy was being transferred from San Francisco. I begged them to let me see him as soon as he arrived, and they agreed. Peggy Urson went to pick him up at the orphanage, and as soon as I saw a car pull in and park in my driveway I ran out and climbed into the back seat. Peggy was in the front seat with a woman from the institution. She turned and handed the baby to me.

He was wide awake. We stared at each other intently, without moving a muscle, as if we were inspecting each other's souls. His violet-blue eyes seemed slowly to be passing judgment on me. I could feel my heart pound, almost stop. Then he smiled, and I cried with joy as I began kissing his tiny fingers. I jumped out of the car with him and called to the nurse to bring Gloria over. He laughed when he saw her, and the two of us, little Gloria and I, started calling him Brother then and there.

The orphanage let me have him, but they told me we would both be on probation for six months to see if things worked out. That was normal procedure. Brother loved Gloria from the start, and she watched him and played with him by the hour.

Lois Wilson was the first stranger to see him. I took her upstairs and told her not to expect too much. He had a fever and ear problems just then, and he was a bit undernourished, which I said I suspected was because he had not been breast-fed.

"Do you know anything much about him?" Lois asked.

"Just that his real name was Sonny and that his father was Irish from San Francisco. I'm changing his name, though. I'm calling him Joseph, for my father."

As Lois and I stepped over to the little crib, the baby turned his head. Then he smiled and held out his hands to Lois. When she took him in her arms, it was love at first sight, and so genuine that I couldn't feel the least bit jealous.

"Tell me, Lois," I said as we went back downstairs, "did you happen to spend a weekend last August with an Irishman in San Francisco?"

That became a running joke, because every time Joseph saw her, he went into ecstasies. She loved him dearly too, and almost killed some woman at the studio, according to Hattie's report, who said she heard the baby Gloria Swanson "adopted" looked just like Cecil B. De Mille. I had a true friend in Lois.

I also got a rival, according to the press, in the fall of 1922. Pola Negri, Berlin's *femme fatale* of films, arrived from Germany to make pictures in Hollywood. She had roughly the same screen image as mine, so in order to publicize her, the studio implied that she intended to put down all the other *femmes fatales*—but mostly me—and take over Hollywood as her domain. They did everything they could to promote a feud between us, but in fact we didn't know each other and felt no real rivalry of any kind. Given the phony feud, however, Pola Negri made hay of it. She asked for a bungalow as big as mine and set her cap for two of the biggest stars in Hollywood—Charlie Chaplin and Richard Dix, none of which bothered or concerned me in the least.

In fact, to put an end to all the foolishness, I had a dinner party shortly after her arrival and invited her, along with Charlie Chaplin, Sam Wood, Aileen, Mickey, Lois, and Lois's sister and brother-in-law, the director George Fitzmaurice. We all had a wonderful time. But I never allowed photographers into my house and I didn't notify the press, so as far as the world knew, instead of sitting down to a fancy dinner at the old King Gillétte mansion, Pola Negri and I had spent that night, like every night, writing poison notes to the press and dreaming up hateful things to do to each other.

Movie magazines that fall told readers across the nation that all the females on Hollywood Boulevard were clearly divided into two camps. The Pola Negri bunch wore white faces and red lips, and my team used no powder at all and wore a single earring. That was because at one point I had lost an expensive earring I liked and refused to retire the mate. I wore it alone. Once the press picked up on it, however, another signature fashion was launched and Pola Negri was on the defensive again.

Pure nonsense.

Shortly before the San Francisco orphanage found Brother for us, I was driving to the studio one morning in my new Pierce-Arrow. It was a perfect day, and I was cruising slowly in order to enjoy it. As I pulled up to a stop sign two girls on the sidewalk called out my name and waved. I waved back, unaware as I did so that another car had pulled up beside mine.

"Hello, Gloria," a familiar voice said dramatically. It was Wallace Beery. "How are you?" he asked.

There was a note of stagy concern in his question, as if he wanted to indicate that he sympathized with me over my separation from Herbert and the endless whispering about Mickey and me. There was also a hint of smugness. Wally had just been featured in *Robin Hood*, a big United Artists film starring Doug Fairbanks. After considerable struggle, his career was booming again.

His smiling face made me bristle with old, painful memories.

"I'm just fine," I said. "So is my baby girl."

He looked at me as if he had been shot. Then he roared off down the street, tires screeching.

Peggy Urson always opened my mail. One day in March 1923 she was pale when she handed me a legal document bound in blue headed *Somborn* v. *Somborn*. Good, I thought, when it dawned on me what it was; Mr. Lasky won't let me file for divorce, but he can't control Herbert. Peggy watched me read it. I saw lots of names in capital letters, arranged alphabetically: CECIL DE MILLE; three Paramount executives (known as the KKKs), ROBERT KANE, SAMUEL KATZ, and SIDNEY KENT; JESSE LASKY; MARSHALL NEILAN; SAM WOOD; ADOLPH ZUKOR—fourteen names in all, ranging from people I didn't even know to the man I loved. "Oh, my God," I gasped when I finally realized that Herbert was suing me for divorce on the grounds of adultery with fourteen men.

There was more to it than that. Peggy picked up the blue paper and read another section. Herbert was demanding a settlement of $150,000, claiming he had obtained a contract for me worth more than $1 million over the next three years. In January my salary had doubled, which meant he had waited until I was earning $5,000 a week before he made his move. I told Peggy to get him on the phone.

"Herbert, I have just seen your papers," I said angrily. "You know it's all a pack of lies."

"Not all of it," he said assuredly, "and it will take you six months to disprove the rest. What will happen to your career in the meantime?"

"I'll deal with that. But blackmail? Never!" I hung up.

Next I received a call from Mr. De Mille, who asked if I would come to his home the following afternoon. When I arrived, Mr. De Mille led me to his library and closed the door. He unlocked his desk drawer and pulled out a copy of the document. "I'm sure you know about this," he said and sat me down. He told me he knew how I must feel, but he said that no matter how angry I might be, we had to keep this out of the papers. The columnists had all been predicting, he said, that Herbert Somborn intended to sue for divorce, and they had hinted broadly that he expected his suit to be bitterly contested.

"I'm not afraid to fight," I said, "and I'm sure I can win. This is irresponsible mud-slinging. Why, Mr. De Mille, you're on that list yourself. You know it's a pack of lies. And poor little Mr. Zukor. Now, really."

"Mickey Neilan is also on the list," he said quietly.

That was a low blow. Defensively, I said I would have had a divorce on the grounds of desertion a year ago if Mr. Lasky hadn't been so terrified of scandal that he insisted I wait. In that sense, I said, this was all the studio's fault. "Furthermore, I will not be a party to blackmail," I told him.

He said he agreed, and he was sure Mr. Lasky agreed, but he would like me to think it over for a day. There was nothing more to say. He put his arm around my shoulder and saw me out. As he opened the front door, a Western Union boy was standing there with a telegram. Mr. De Mille excused himself and read it. Then without a word he handed it to me.

The telegram said in effect that the Swanson matter had to be settled out of court, since it jeopardized not only Miss

Swanson's career but the entire motion picture industry. It was signed "Will Hays."

I felt as if I had been hit in the solar plexus with a sandbag. I was weak in the knees. I handed the telegram back to Mr. De Mille, told him I would think about it, and slowly made my way to the car.

"Drive carefully, young fellow," Mr. De Mille said as he closed the car door, but once alone out of his sight, I was in such a state of emotion—rage, embarrassment, disappointment, most of all a sense of complete despair—that I could hardly drive at all.

As I pulled into the drive I saw Daddy on the lawn with Gloria and Joseph. I had completely forgotten that he was arriving to spend the weekend. After nearly three years in Texas and Oklahoma, he was back at Fort MacArthur. God, how I needed him just then! I ran and threw myself in his arms as if I were six and had just skinned my knee.

"Oh, Daddy, Daddy," I sobbed, "the most awful thing has happened."

"What's happened, Glory? What's so awful?"

"I'm being blackmailed and I don't know what to do."

"Now, now, Glory," he said tenderly, holding me tight and patting my back. "Tell me all about it."

I stammered, "Herbert is suing me for divorce, and they say it will hurt the whole industry if I don't give him a hundred and fifty thousand dollars so he won't mention fourteen men he says I— But it's not true! It's all lies. Oh, Daddy, what shall I do?"

"Glory, baby, calm down so we can think straight. Tell me from the beginning."

The nurse took the children inside and we sat down on the lawn. He held my shaking hands in his, and slowly I became his little girl again. How good it felt! Growing calmer, I told him the whole story.

"Here," he said when I had finished, and handed me his handkerchief. "Blow your nose. You're right, it's an awful story. And I can understand, Glory, why the industry is concerned. What do you think you should do?"

"I don't know yet, Daddy. I only know I can't—I won't— give in to blackmail."

"Wait a minute, Glory. Stop and think. First of all, you owe something to an industry that's been very good to you."

"But it was the studio that kept me from getting a divorce on the grounds of desertion. Oh, how can Herbert do this?"

"That's his problem, baby, not yours. But listen, Glory, forget Herbert and the studio for a minute. What about the children? Those are the only two people you really have to think about. You don't want them to suffer, do you?"

"No," I sighed.

"Well, then,"' he said with assurance.

He was right. The children were the only people I should consider, and a scandalous divorce was bound to hurt them. It was as if he had bandaged my knee with his big white handkerchief. Slowly my hurt and fury began to subside, and all the while his soothing voice kept reassuring me that the best thing I could do for the people I really cared for was to compromise.

"I will, Daddy. You're right. I could never hurt Gloria and Joseph."

"Of course you couldn't," Daddy said.

That evening Mr. De Mille telephoned. He urged me again to settle out of court, and even said he thought the studio would help cover the costs. "I'm sure if you agreed to make another picture or two," he said, "they'd have the whole thing cleared up for you, once and for all."

I didn't want to hear any more about it ever again if that was possible, even if it meant making that hateful extra picture that I had managed to fight free of for the past year. "All right, Mr. De Mille," I said. "Tell Mr. Lasky I'll settle."

I told him to have Mr. Lasky's lawyers haggle with Herbert, and I would sign whatever was necessary. When the papers were drawn up, my temptation was to sign them without reading them and getting upset all over again, but I forced myself. I almost gagged at the first provision, the face-saving fiction that, because Herbert had "assisted in procuring" my contract with Mr. Lasky, he was being paid $35,000 in cash and another $35,000 in installments to be deducted from my salary at a rate of almost $500 a week. Furthermore, I would be obliged to make one extra picture. Thus my divorce was costing me six weeks out of my life and some cash, but the lawyers had cut the original demands in half and the studio had paid the fee and hushed everything up.

In addition, however, there was also a new contract for me to sign, containing a little clause that had never been mentioned up to then, a clause relevant to my future conduct. My original contract had contained no "morals clause." In the days before the Hays Office became a Hollywood institution,

morals clauses were unheard of. Now they were routine.
Mine read:

> FOURTH: Third Party [Famous Players-Lasky] agrees to,
> and hereby does, waive any and all rights (if any it has)
> to discharge First Party [Gloria Swanson] from her
> employment under said written agreement by reason of
> anything First Party has done or anything that has
> happened prior to the date of the execution of these
> presents; Provided, however, that in the event that at
> any time in the future, through no fault of Third Party
> and/or without its connivance and consent, First Party
> shall be charged with adulterous conduct or immoral
> relations with men other than her husband, and such
> charges or any of them are published in the public press,
> the waiver herein contained shall be null and void and of
> no force and effect. . . .

In other words, the studio was putting me on a tight leash.
They were scaring me into being a well-behaved star, telling
me that unless I toed the line, they could cut me off. I was
angry and humiliated, but I signed everything. If I wanted to
keep Joseph, I had to. And after I signed, everyone hugged
me and kissed me and told me how brave I had been. Now
that I was divorced, nobody seemed to care how much I saw
Mickey or anybody else. I could go dancing every night. As
long as Herbert couldn't sue me again, and nobody else had
any reason to, we were all in clover once more.

A couple of months after the case of *Somborn* v. *Somborn*
was settled out of court, Mr. Lasky asked me as a special
favor to him to attend an industry banquet. I hated all such
affairs, but since I had said no so many times before, I said I
would go. When I arrived, I was escorted to the dais and, to
my horror, given the honored position next to Will Hays.

He spoke to me, and I gave him an icy hello. I didn't look
past him, the way Louella Parsons did when she wanted to cut
somebody; I could look right over the top of his head because
he was one of the few people in Hollywood who was shorter
than me. I spent the whole evening talking to the man on my
right. Mr. Hays put up with it until the table was cleared and
the coffee was served. Then he asked if he could talk to me.
Being as coldly correct as I knew how, I said I didn't think we
had anything to say to each other.

"I don't understand," he said. "I am a great fan of yours,

and you have given me the cold shoulder all evening. What have I done to deserve it?"

"Only one thing," I said. "You sent that telegram to Mr. De Mille."

"What telegram?"

"The telegram that concerned me and my divorce."

"But I never sent any telegram to De Mille about you *or* your divorce."

"Mr. Hays," I said reprovingly, "I saw it. Mr. De Mille showed it to me. You said if I contested my husband's suit for divorce, it would endanger the entire motion picture industry."

"When did you see it?"

"In March," I said.

"Miss Swanson—Gloria—I give you my word," he said, "I never sent any such telegram."

"Then I apologize for my behavior, Mr. Hays," I said. But I added, "Are you sure?"

"Positive. Call my secretary if you like. She can check the files."

I told him that would not be necessary. His word was good enough for me.

The moment I got home I called Mickey, but he was drunk, so I didn't tell him anything. I just lay awake most of the night and thought. I didn't lose sleep over Jesse Lasky; I had long ago figured him out. What shattered me was that Mr. De Mille must have been a party to the scene staged at his home. Mr. De Mille was my idol, on another plane altogether from the rest of Hollywood. Since the first day I walked into his office, he had been the standard by which I judged everything else in the motion picture industry. No matter who criticized him to me—Craney, Hattie in rare moments, even Mickey— my opinion of him had never changed. I had never been able to think of myself even remotely as his equal.

Had he known the telegram was a fake? Of course, he must have. Nevertheless, I couldn't bring myself to accuse him or have an ugly scene with him. Mr. Lasky would do for that.

The next morning I asked Hattie to find out if Mr. Lasky was in his office. She came back and said yes, he had just ordered his lunch. I strode from my bungalow to his office in full make-up and costume, walked past his secretary without speaking, and found him sitting down to lunch with a visitor. I didn't care if the man with him was the President of the United States. I just stood and glared.

"Gloria!" Mr. Lasky said. "What a marvelous dress. What picture is *that* for?"

"The picture is *Bluebeard's Eighth Wife*, but that isn't what I'm here for."

In the voice of the concerned diplomat and executive, he said, "Is anything the matter?"

"Yes, there is," I said. "I talked to Will Hays last night about a certain telegram. I could have you put in jail."

His eyes were popping, but he quietly asked his guest if he would mind waiting in the next room for just a moment. That was fine with me. The guest, whoever he was, had heard the important part.

When we were alone, Mr. Lasky said he could understand my feelings, but I had to believe that he had done what he felt was right. Mr. De Mille had told him I had plans to fight Somborn in court. That would have meant the ruin of a great career.

"Stop right there, Mr. Lasky. I just wanted to hear you admit it. That's enough for one day," I said and left.

The problem was, I didn't know what to do next. Leave the studio? Sue the studio? I remembered Clara Kimball Young. She had broken with the studio system, and they had finished her as well as Herbert and the other people who worked with her. They had done the same thing to Charley Ray. If they decided to finish you, you were finished.

And then I remembered the story Herbert had told about Pat Powers, about the policeman who caught the butcher with his hand on the scale. He had nothing to gain from arresting him. So he let him off and had him deliver free meat to him for the rest of his life. If information was power, what could I ask Mr. Lasky for?

I could ask him for a chance to make better pictures, that's what. I could say I wanted to make a picture with Marshall Neilan. That would fix them. Sam Wood was all right, but he was a real estate dealer at heart. We had been grinding out pictures since *The Great Moment*, and each one was worse than the last. The only things that changed were the number and length of dresses I wore and the face of the leading man.

Mickey said the idea was brilliant, but he was in the middle of a picture and he had signed to do another. Then he recommended Allan Dwan, who he said worked with everybody in the business. He was the man who had cast Mickey in his first Hollywood movie and who had taught him to direct. He was also a genius of an engineer. He had invented half the special equipment in the studio. He was under contract to Famous Players-Lasky, and Zukor always gave him everything he asked for. He was afraid to refuse him for fear Allan would quit and they wouldn't be able to run the studio without him. Best of all, however, Allan Dwan hated Hollywood so much that in order to keep him, Zukor had had to build him a studio in the East, in Astoria, Long Island. That's where he worked.

"And that's where you should be," Mickey said. "In New York. When all is said and done, Hollywood is nothing but sunshine, and eventually that fries everybody's brains. Just look around. With modern lighting, nobody needs three hundred days of sunshine a year anymore to make movies. They all stay because they don't know enough to go."

"What shall I tell Lasky?" I asked.

"Nothing until I've talked to Allan. I'll call him tonight and see what he's up to."

Allan Dwan told Mickey he had just talked Adolph Zukor into buying a play he liked, by Mrs. Leslie Carter, that had been done on Broadway. It was called *Zaza* and it would be perfect for me. He would like to talk to me.

As soon as *Bluebeard's Eighth Wife* was finished I told Mr. Lasky I had needed minor surgery since Gloria was born and that I had made arrangements to have it done in New York City. It was the truth but with some stretchers, as Mark Twain would say. Mr. Lasky was nervous with me at best after I had burst in on him at lunch that day, so he quickly agreed, and in July I boarded a train for New York, presumably for two weeks to undergo corrective surgery. I suspected it would be much longer.

Mr. De Mille had been my gold, and he had tarnished. The rest were brass, as far as I was concerned. I would not miss them for a minute.

After I left, scandal broke out once again over Mother and the issue of Mr. Burns's sanity at the time he made his last will. It was all unfounded, as it had been the first time, but before it was over, my name was again on all the front pages along with hers, and Mickey was frequently named in connection with me. The big scandal epidemic was then in quietus, however, and now that I was divorced, everyone but a few hack journalists considered the Swanson-Neilan romance old hat.

One day, two such hacks followed Mickey home from the studio. When they knocked on the door and asked for a statement, Mickey airily had his Japanese houseboy tell them, "The master is out." Then Marshall Neilan, the most bewitching man in Hollywood, poured himself a second double Scotch, sat down at his custom-made, built-in pipe organ, and composed a beautiful song called "My Wonderful One," which he published and dedicated to me.

CHAPTER 10

My first night in the city, I had dinner with Allan Dwan. Mickey had told me I would remember Allan from parties at Mickey's house, but I didn't. In the last three years, since I had been a star, I had been to so many Hollywood parties that I had become as bad as all the other people in Hollywood when I went to them; I forgot everybody who wasn't above the title as soon as I shook his or her hand and thanked him or her for the kind remarks about my pictures. Allan Dwan was easy to forget in that he was inconspicuous in appearance—short, balding, in his late thirties, with a thick waist and a little round pot—but before we had started the first course, I knew that Mickey Neilan was right as usual: Allan Dwan was a genius.

The more I learned about him that night, the more astonishing it became that we had not spent time together before. He had worked with almost everyone in Hollywood, including all the men I was most closely associated with personally. He had directed Mickey in 1915 in *A Girl of Yesterday*, a successful Pickford film that also featured Jack Pickford, Mary's brother, and in the course of it he had taught Mickey all the fine points of directing. Allan was also the favorite director of Mary's husband. He had directed nine of Douglas Fairbanks' pictures, including the most recent, *Robin Hood*, so he knew Wally, my first husband. In addition to all of his other achievements and connections, Allan had directed two Clara Kimball Young films in 1919, just at the time she was leaving Lewis Selznick and becoming an independent producer involved with Harry Garson, so he knew

Herbert, my second husband, as well. That all proved what a small town Hollywood really was. Allan said he tried to direct as much in New York and as little in Hollywood as possible because in Hollywood he felt trapped in the glamour system, whereas in the little studio in Astoria he had to cut corners and force himself to be truly creative.

He had great hopes for *Zaza*, the story of a brash, tough little French soubrette who falls in love with a distinguished gentleman and gives him up when she discovers he is a husband and father. Allan said he had hired H. B. Warner, the New York stage actor, to play the aristocrat and a couple of very talented boys to do my costumes. "Not that I want this to be a costume picture, in the wrong sense of the term," Allan said; "not at all. And surely you've had enough of all that by now, haven't you? I want your costumes to be authentic and exciting, sassy and vulgar, and Norman Norell will give me exactly what I want." He had also found a mansion out on Long Island that he could shoot to look like a château in France, and an apartment on Park Avenue for me to live in while I made the picture.

"Well?" he asked, at the end of an hour.

"I can't wait to start," I said.

"Wonderful. I'll try to telephone Adolph Zukor tonight; otherwise I'll wire him. Tomorrow morning you go and look around the Paramount office and get a script from Walter Wanger. He's the head of the story department."

The next day Wanger looked at me blankly when I asked for the script, and said, "But, Miss Swanson, they said on the Coast you were here for an operation and that there should be no publicity."

"That's right," I said.

"But don't you have to be in a hospital?" he asked, more confused than ever.

"After *Zaza*," I said, taking the script from him.

With difficulty Allan Dwan convinced Mr. Lasky and Mr. Zukor to let me try just one realistic picture with a role I could get my teeth into. He promised that he would speed up the shooting schedule so that my whole trip east, operation included, would not take longer than it took me to prepare and film a picture in Hollywood, and he promised them that they would not be sorry. The minute they said yes, I moved into the apartment Allan had found for me. It belonged to Richard Bennett, the actor.

Every day we all drove across the Queensboro Bridge to

the new studio in Astoria in the borough of Queens. It was
certainly not another Hollywood. The place was full of free
spirits, defectors, refugees, who were all trying to get away
from Hollywood and its restrictions. There was a wonderful
sense of revolution and innovation in the studio in Queens.

Zaza turned out to be the fastest, easiest, most enjoyable
picture I had ever made. Allan and I worked together like
Mutt and Jeff one day, like Maggie and Jiggs the next, but we
both loved every second of it. If anything we needed didn't
exist, Allen invented it. He was a tinkerer, a fixer, a doer.
When the New York summer heat hit us, nobody wilted.
Allan simply ordered giant blocks of ice, placed huge fans
behind them, and created his own cool air. He prepared
everything with such care that the first take was often the best
one, and he had the confidence to know that and shoot a
whole long sequence at once. When we went to the "château"
out on Long Island for location scenes, we traveled in open
cars like a band of gypsies, as I had in the old days at
Keystone with Bobby Vernon and Clarence Badger.

Allan used a script like a blueprint. The best things in the
picture we made up as we went along. We were always
stretching, always trying to improve the scene up to the last
minute before we shot it. Watching the rushes, I could see
that the energy level of *Zaza* was higher than in any other film
I'd made in years. Allan had found some mysterious way of
unleashing me. There was a long, elaborate fight scene in the
picture, for instance, and he made Mary Thurman and me do
it in one take. We had to make it good just by our acting. We
couldn't depend at all on sets and costumes. And Allan
convinced us we could. In a minute, he could push the most
phlegmatic member of the cast to peaks of excitement. He
was extraordinary.

I couldn't wait to do another picture with him. Everything
Mickey had said about him was true. Before *Zaza* was half
finished, I knew that Allan and New York represented some
kind of rebirth for me. I had been getting stale in Hollywood
and I hadn't really been aware of it. But in the sweltering heat
of a New York summer, I suddenly felt the bracing thrill of
spring again.

In addition to being a stylishly dressed twenty-four-year-old
female, I was one of the most recognizable celebrities in
America. I was leading all the box-office polls in 1923, and

many of the film magazines had begun calling me the Queen of the Screen. An average of ten thousand fan letters a week arrived for me at Paramount in Hollywood. There was no way I could live alone or go about by myself in New York City. Paramount got me a maid and a secretary, and Famous Players-Lasky assigned a young woman named Jane West to be my companion and chaperone while I made *Zaza*.

Jane was a society girl from Boston, very prim and proper, a few years older than me. She had never been married. Her job at Paramount was merely a source of pin money, a means of living independently away from her family. It was obvious at once to Allan and me that the studio executives intended to use Jane as their spy, thus preventing me from making any more unpredictable leaps like *Zaza* without their knowledge. So we did everything we could to woo Jane over to our side, and although the role of counterspy was distasteful to her, within a matter of weeks she was performing it beautifully. With her help we could always stay a jump or two ahead of the studio. Through Jane we found out that Mr. Lasky was anxious to get me back to Hollywood as soon as possible, but through her, too, we knew they hadn't yet chosen a new script for me. Therefore, I told Allan and Jane that we had to find a new script ourselves immediately that would keep me in New York. Both of them agreed that the person to ask was Forrest Halsey.

Forrest and I hit it off perfectly. A cultivated Southern gentleman, he was a scenario writer by day and a bon vivant by night. He was also a homosexual, one of the first I knew who was not the least bit embarrassed or secretive about the fact. If a group of us went out in the evening, Forrest frequently had a younger male friend in tow. These young men came and went with regularity and caused Forrest endless anxiety, which he would discuss at length when he was drunk. He was a wonderful friend to me and a formidable intellect. He had superb literary judgment.

When I told him I was looking for a script that would keep me in New York, he immediately mentioned one he was working on for Sidney Olcott, the distinguished cinema veteran who had made the original one-reel version of *Ben Hur* in the first years of the century. Called *The Humming Bird*, it was about a gamine Paris pickpocket. When the newspaperman she is in love with is assigned to the front during the war, she puts on men's clothes, enlists the help of all her old friends, the thieves and cutthroats of Montmartre, and goes off to the trenches to save him. Forrest said it would be a fantastic part for me, and that furthermore it would put me right in line to play another great britches part, which Mr. Lasky and Mr. Zukor were just then in the process of acquiring—*Peter Pan* by J. M. Barrie, the author of *The Admirable Crichton*. If anything could convince the studio that I would be right to play Peter Pan in a film version, at the same time that Marilyn Miller was performing it on the New York stage—which she was scheduled to do—it was *The Humming Bird*. I said I thought it was an excellent idea, if Mr. Olcott agreed, and he did, heartily. Together he and Allan persuaded the studio to let me stay in the East for one more picture, and Mr. Olcott asked me how soon I could start. As soon, I told him, as I could get into a hospital and have my insides repaired.

I consulted a number of doctors before I picked a surgeon and entered a hospital. All of them assured me that the operation would be a very simple one to perform. When I came out of ether, however, I was in terrible pain, and the surgeon, who was looking down at me, had a strained smile on his face. He told me that in the three years since I had had Gloria, an abscess had formed on the tissue between the vagina and the rectum. He told me he had removed it, and there was now a small hole in the tissue. He proposed to heal it by means of drugs, and if that didn't work, he would perform further surgery.

I was amazed that he could announce that so casually, and at once I could feel myself bristling with skepticism. "I don't want any drugs or any more surgery," I said. "What are my chances of having this heal by itself?"

"One in ten thousand," he said flatly.

"Why can't it heal like other tissue?" I asked.

"Because it's interior tissue, and it's constantly prone to infection."

"What if I exposed it to the healing powers of the sun?" I asked.

"I have no idea, but I wouldn't recommend it," he said. "You certainly don't want infection to set in."

It was the end of summer. I decided to give Mother Nature, or Mrs. God, as I called her, a chance to heal me before I took the alternative chance, of becoming addicted to morphine or some other drug, or worse, of losing the ability to have more children.

I called Allan Dwan and said I needed a house with lots of sunshine and lots of privacy right away. Allan telephoned the producer Joe Schenck, who had a beautiful seaside house in Bay Shore, on Long Island, and Joe said I could use the place for as long as I wanted. Allan drove me and my maid out there the following morning. Then I asked Allan to send for my children. The house was huge, and I wanted them with me.

I had the maid buy a box of medicine droppers and a large bottle of sterilized salt water. I lay on the terrace for hours with my legs propped up by pillows and stretched apart so that the sun could shine where it would not otherwise reach unless I were strung up upside down on a clothesline. Every ten minutes the maid handed me a medicine dropper full of sterilized salt water and I cleansed the tissue. I ached all over from the position I was in, but after a few days I knew that the treatment was working. Maybe it worked only because I believed it would. I just lay like a scissors day after day, covering my face and shoulders with an enormous beach hat. My temperature stayed normal. The pain gradually went away. I knew I would be the one in ten thousand. I also knew I would be forever leery of doctors and surgery. Why, suddenly, I asked myself as I lay there, had it become normal practice to want to rid people of their tonsils, adenoids, appendix, ovaries? Why should surgery always seem to doctors to be the answer?

In a week the children arrived, and they alone were enough to finish the healing process. I hadn't seen them in two months.

After three weeks I felt ready to go back to work. First, though, I returned to the surgeon and asked him to examine me. When he finished, he smiled. "It's perfectly amazing. It's sealed beautifully," he said. "In fact, you look like a virgin again."

When I left Richard Bennett's apartment I rented a string of three suites at the Gladstone Hotel, one for me, one for the children, and one for friends and guests and parties. Once I had us all moved in, with our maids and nurses and secretaries, I called Mr. Olcott and said I was ready to start *The Humming Bird;* I was well again.

On October 2, before we were half finished with the picture, the Paramount office in California telephoned the studio in Astoria to tell me that Daddy had died that morning at Fort MacArthur of an acute heart attack. He was fifty-two years old. They told me he had wished to be buried in Chicago, and that the army would arrange a military funeral there if that was agreeable with me. I wired my consent and took the train to Chicago on the sixth. Jane West went with me.

It was the first time I had encountered death in the fullest sense; that is, death the news of which makes you weep involuntarily and uncontrollably at first and leaves you with deep philosophical questions afterward. I could not count my grandmother's estranged husband or my great-grandmother or Mr. Burns in the same company; I had not known any of them well enough to rain tears over them or sit and wonder when I stopped crying. But Daddy was the most complicated figure in my life, probably. I had adored him until I was fifteen, and then had felt for him a mixture of love and pity during the nine years since. I had somehow tried to replace him with the two men I had married, but without success, for in my grief I knew that for me he had always been a full presence, a total reality, someone different from everyone else, someone no one could ever replace. If our relationship had been incomplete, then perhaps it was time I understood that all relationships are incomplete to some extent. No two people can ever know each other completely. My father's life had been his to live. He had made all his own choices. I had no right, as another person, even as his only daughter, to question the choices he had made, just as I felt no one had any right ultimately to question my choices regarding my own life.

Relatives I had not seen for years, like Aunt May and Uncle Charlie, came to the chapel and cemetery, and together we listened to the prayers and the volley of guns and the sad bugle. It was clear that his death meant something different to each one of us, and that it could not knit us back to closeness. I suddenly had some notion of what time is and what it does. Daddy's relatives were strangers to me now, but we all pretended to be close for the time it took to bury him, and I liked that. It was his force at work in us.

The press pestered me in Chicago until Jane and I were on our way back to New York. On the train I had two more days to think. The thoughts were easier and fewer. I was sorry I had not seen more of Daddy. I was happy he had been happy whenever we did see each other. I was sorry he had never been able to love anyone but Mother, or old-fashioned enough to believe so. I was happy he had seen not his replacement but his namesake in little Joseph and had had a chance to love him for almost a year.

I saw quite clearly on the train that that is all life is: love.

Once I had adapted to the Astoria work routine and got my children settled in with me, I set out to discover New York, the biggest, most exciting city in the world. In November I called up Sport Ward, the brother of Sylvia Joslin, the only girl besides Bea La Plante I had ever truly liked at Court Corinne during my Triangle days. I had spoken to Sylvia before I left for New York, and she had told me to call Sport because he knew everybody. "Sport will be your oldest friend in ten minutes," she had said. "He's like that."

Handsome and tall, with a black mustache, Le Roy Pierpont Ward wore a white tie and tails as if they were his everyday work clothes. An architect by profession, he was the unofficial master of the most fashionable midnight revels in Manhattan. Everybody called him Sport. He was a close friend of Jimmy Walker, the debonair young state senator, and called most of New York society by first names. Follies girls waved to him from the stage, and speakeasy doors flew open at his approach. You were nobody until you had been the butt of one of Sport Ward's elaborate practical jokes: until he had sent a furious plumber to your apartment at midnight or a live turkey to the set when you were in the midst of filming a love scene.

Sport was happy to take over my social life and turned my apartment at the Gladstone into an open house on Sundays. He invited half the interesting people in the city to drop by, from Edward Steichen the photographer to Condé Nast, who published *Vogue*, from James Hilton the writer to Jimmy Walker, and they in turn invited the other half. In a month, I was one of the smart set.

After California, New York was a wonderland—an endless array of things to see and places to go. A group of six or eight of us would convene at someone's apartment in black tie and evening dress for a drink, then go to the theater, and then dine late in a little restaurant with candlelight and music in Yorkville or the Village, or at "21," or at the Colony. If everyone was still lively after that, we would go on to Harlem to listen to jazz. Nineteen twenty-three was the year Bessie Smith made her first record, "Down-Hearted Blues."

No matter how often you went to the theater, there were always twenty things still to see. I saw Fanny Brice in the Follies, John Barrymore in *Hamlet*, Jeanne Eagels in *Rain*, Walter Huston in *Desire under the Elms*, Richard Bennett, my ex-landlord, in *They Knew What They Wanted*, and the Lunts in *The Guardsman*. At *Kid Boots*, Eddie Cantor apologized to me from the stage for a joke he had cracked about me the week before, and everyone applauded. People also stood up and applauded when I entered a box at the Metropolitan Opera House to see Eleonora Duse in *The Lady from the Sea*. She was magnificent, riveting, the greatest actress I had ever seen, even in her sixties. I had no idea how ill she was. I made my escort take me backstage, but she could not receive visitors. She drove herself so hard at the eight matinées she gave in New York that they had to have an oxygen tank ready in her dressing room after each performance to revive her.

The biggest theatrical thrill of all for me was seeing June Walker, my darling friend from Chicago, still loaded with personality, now a big star on Broadway, playing with Otto Kruger in *The Nervous Wreck*, and in another play called *The Glass Slipper*. She was married to an Englishman named Kerr, and we visited each other often. With her marvelous, plaintive, cello voice she was at last where she deserved to be—on the New York stage. I told her she was better off than she ever would have been in movies.

In Hollywood, there was no classical music. In New York, practically every orchestra, ballet company, and performing artist in the world appeared regularly. I met Jascha Heifetz after I heard him play at Carnegie Hall, and later that winter I went to hear George Gershwin play his *Rhapsody in Blue* with Paul Whiteman's orchestra. But the joy of joys for me, who had once thought I would be an opera singer, was to hear the world's great voices from the Diamond Horseshoe of the Met: Galli-Curci, Maria Jeritza, Martinelli, Gigli, Chaliapin in *Boris Godunov*, and—as often as I could, because she was the greatest singer-actress of them all—Rosa Ponselle. She was two years older than me, but when I got to call Rosa by her first name, and I did that year, I knew that even Mother could be rightfully proud of me.

I experienced more art and culture in six months than I had

seen in my whole life. Whenever the atmosphere of the arts got too rich, however, or too thin, four or five of us could always drive to Belmont to the races, or to the stadium to see Babe Ruth and the Yankees, or to Forest Hills to watch Bill Tilden play.

By January I knew I had to stay. I couldn't go back to Hollywood, not even for Mickey, not yet. I told Sport to look for a house in the country for me so that the children could enjoy fresh air and a lawn, and when a friend of his discovered a marvelous place for sale in Croton-on-Hudson, forty miles from the city, I bought it.

By the time *The Humming Bird* was finished, in November, the Paramount executives had all seen *Zaza* and recognized the fact that Allan Dwan and I were a winning team. They said they had no objection to our making another picture right away, but they urged me to make sure it was one in which I could wear plenty of lavish costumes.

Paramount vice president Sidney Kent, a genius at sales and distribution, came up with a crackling idea for a title. While reading over a list of things forbidden by the Hays Office code, he discovered an injunction against depicting the act of manhandling on the screen. He thereupon proposed calling our next film *Manhandled*, which there seemed to be no rule against, and told us to find a story zippy enough to live up to that title without outraging the guardians of public morals. Allan asked Frank Tuttle, a studio writer, to see what he could come up with, and Frank suggested a *Saturday Evening Post* story about a department-store salesgirl who leaves her inventor boyfriend for a fling in high society but returns to him when she finds the morals of the upper crust don't match their fancy clothes. Since I had had my hair cut short for *The Humming Bird*, it would look fine for a pert, gum-chewing clerk, so Allan and I both agreed to use the *Post* story as a basis for the film.

Allan, Frank, Jane West, and I sat up night after night working out the details of the screenplay, but it never seemed just right. I finally suggested that a change of scenery might stimulate us.

"Where shall we go?" Jane asked, assuming I meant moving then and there to her apartment or Allan's.

"How about Florida?" I asked with a gleam in my eye. "Couldn't we all use a vacation? And heaven knows, we're sure to be twice as productive if we can just get out of the cold for a week."

Jane protested feebly, but soon the little conspiracy took wings. Allan was all for showing his new girl friend a good time at studio expense. We decided to say we wanted to look for locations for the story, which we would then duplicate in a studio. Allan wired Mr. Zukor, who agreed, and two days later we all left for Miami.

The weather there, however, was almost as bad as the weather in New York, so on the second drizzly night I said with the utmost casualness, "Look, why don't we just go on to Havana?" Eyes sparkled around the table. Havana with its luxury hotels and cocktail lounges and casinos was just then the preferred vacation spot of rich New Yorkers, and none of us had ever visited it. We decided it would be time enough to tell Mr. Zukor when we got there, especially after Jane volunteered that her brother, who was an executive of the United Fruit Company, might pull strings to get us passage on a boat that night or the next.

She telephoned him in New York, and he got us berths the next day. He wired that an acquaintance of his named Aitkens would meet us in Havana and book us into a hotel.

When we got to Havana, the captain of our boat summoned me out on deck, pointed to four Rolls-Royces with drivers lined up on the dock, and said he had been told to tell those cars belonging to Mr. Aitkens were at my disposal.

"Four of them?" I asked with astonishment.

"Two are for your luggage," the captain said calmly. "Mr. Aitkens says there is a gala tonight on the roof of your hotel. He will call for you and your friends at nine o'clock."

Everything about Havana, from the old fortress to the colonial administration buildings to the Spanish churches, reminded me of San Juan when I was a girl. It felt good hearing Spanish and smelling tropical flowers again. People stared at me as they had in Puerto Rico years before, and I told Allan Dwan how my friends used to call me the Cuban Princess. "It's because of my blue eyes," I added.

"Not any longer," Allan said. "Don't you realize that except for Chaplin you probably have the best-known face in the world? Everybody who could beg, borrow, or steal a ticket went to see you and Valentino make love in *Beyond the Rocks*."

Mr. Aitkens had booked rooms for us in the brand-new annex of one of the luxury hotels. Everyone on the staff of the hotel gave us the most special treatment. When Mr. Aitkens arrived at nine, he said he had invited a few friends who would like to meet me to the party on the roof garden.

He was a quiet, dignified man who bore himself stiffly and formally, and I could see, as the door of the elevators opened and we walked out under the stars, that he was typical of the exploding new wealth of Cuba since the war. A whole class of planters and speculators and gamblers had acquired huge fortunes almost overnight. Their *palacetes* outside the city were said to rival the opulence of the Capitol and the Presidential Palace. In a few short years they had turned Havana into a glittering oasis of pleasure and ostentation. There were few women to enjoy the Latin band on the terrace that night, and the men who lined up to meet me were of the weirdest ethnic mix. Invariably, the ones who looked as fair and Irish as Mickey Neilan had names like Ramírez and López, whereas the ones who seemed totally Latin called themselves Riley and Aitkens and O'Rourke. One little man with a waxed mustache and several diamond rings on his hands presented me with a set of keys to a Rolls-Royce he wished me to have, but I managed to convey to him that we already had more than enough Rollses thanks to Mr. Aitkens.

Allan and his lady love danced together most of the evening, but Jane and I had new partners waiting each time the orchestra ended a song. Most of them were fabulous dancers. Between dances we would stroll to the edge of the terrace and look out over the beautiful harbor glistening under the stars. I received a hundred invitations to see this or that tourist attraction, but I turned them all down because something in the smoldering, confident stare of Cuban plantation owners made me realize that they saw me not as a straitlaced American girl who made her own living, but as the *femme fatale* they wanted me to be, one who wore shimmering transparent gowns and bobbed her hair and rode with the Sheik. When Mr. Aitkens escorted us back to our rooms at two in the morning, he said ex-President Mario Menocal had instructed him to invite us to a gala in our honor at his home the following evening, and since that invitation seemed safe to accept, I said yes.

When I returned the next afternoon from having my hair done for the gala, Jane West was in a state of shock. In the process of opening the stack of mail and messages that kept arriving for me, she had come upon a most unusual letter. Two cut rubies fell out of the envelope, and a note signed

"Señor X" laid out in the most lecherous, pornographic detail and the worst English certain activities the señor would like to engage me in. The handwriting was bold and slanted, and many words, even the four-letter ones, were misspelled. Although I was not a proper Bostonian like Jane, the letter made me angry, and uneasy too, and I asked Allan if he thought I should notify the police. He said, "Good heavens, no; don't make an incident of it."

"All right," I said. "I'll turn the jewels over to a worthwhile charity before we leave."

Many of the men we had met on the hotel roof were at the gala, but many of them this time had brought their wives. In halting English, ex-President Menocal greeted me and shortly inquired after the health of Isadora Duncan. I said I didn't know the woman. Slightly embarrassed, he then asked me about President Coolidge, J. P. Morgan, and Orville Wright. I said I didn't know them, either. "You are joking," he stated as a fact, not a question, and when I assured him I was not, he said, "But you are a famous American, and they are famous Americans. Don't you know them?" Allan and I told him America was too big for that, at which point he took in the dining room and adjoining terrace with a small, sweeping gesture and said, "Aha, so? Because all of Cuba that counts is here tonight in this little place. I hoped you might know Orville Wright."

At that moment a distinguished-looking Spanish grandee approached, and Señor Menocal introduced him as Señor De Mesa. The man smiled charmingly and motioned for all of us to follow him into the garden. By the light of torches and a thousand lanterns, couples were dancing the most erotic, sensual dance I had ever seen. The rhythm was unfamiliar too, and so were the instruments the musicians were playing —sticks they banged together and straws they scraped on notched gourds and gourds they shook like rattles. Whatever it was, it made the tango and the Charleston seem as sedate as the waltz. "There," Señor De Mesa said, indicating the dance floor as he watched for our reaction. "That is what all Americans come to Cuba to see: the rumba. It is not done in polite society, except tonight. President Menocal arranged it for you. You are not shocked, are you?"

We all said no, of course not, but Jane West was crimson. Frank Tuttle whispered to me that although we might call our picture *Manhandled*, we could never put anything like that in it. Will Hays would fall over dead.

Señor De Mesa, it turned out, was one of the biggest of the
Cuban sugar magnates. He invited us to see his refinery the
next day and one of the large gambling casinos in the evening.
Allan and his girl friend politely declined, but Jane and Frank
and I accepted enthusiastically.

He arrived at the hotel driving an open Rolls touring car.
He put Jane and Frank in the covered back seat and
ceremoniously helped me into the open front seat beside him.
For two hours we drove through the country outside Havana,
and it seemed that everything I pointed at could be identified
shyly by Señor De Mesa in a word: "Mine." At his hacienda,
a Spanish-style building almost on the scale of Versailles, an
army of servants scrambled to serve us lunch. Then we set out
back to Havana, but when we were about halfway, the sky
turned black and thunder rolled overhead.

In faltering English, Señor De Mesa told me not to worry;
we could beat the storm. Then he pressed down on the
accelerator and drove like Barney Oldfield. "Take hold of
me," he shouted while Jane and Frank kept banging on the
partition to tell me to ride in back with them. Never, since my
first days behind the wheel when Wally taught me to drive,
had I had such a thrill in a car. Scared as I was, I couldn't help
admiring how that man could handle an automobile. As
Havana came into sight, a slight drizzle began to fill the air,
and before Señor De Mesa could get over an aqueduct with
trolley tracks on it, the car went into a skid and crashed
against a brick wall. We all sat stunned. No one was hurt in
the least, but the damage to that magnificent car was considerable. He didn't even get out to look. Surveying our faces
with a gentle, apologetic smile, he backed up and drove to a
magnificent house in the city. It was obviously his, we
realized, when servants rushed out with umbrellas to convey
us to the great portico. Señor De Mesa spoke rapidly to them,
and a moment later another Rolls, a closed one, rolled up
behind the touring model.

"If you are ready, my friends," Señor De Mesa said to us,
"we can go to the hotel now. It would not be fitting to bring
Gloria Swanson home in *that,*" he added, pointing to the
dented car with contempt.

That night he took us to a casino and lost a great deal of
money without the slightest complaint. At parting he invited
us to his yacht the day after next, but I told him ex-President
Menocal had already invited us to his hacienda.

The next day we all went sightseeing. At lunch we sheepishly admitted that this was no way to complete the script, and Jane got reservations back to Miami for us in two days' time. I was not sorry, inasmuch as the afternoon brought another letter from Señor X, filthier than the last, wrapped around two largish diamonds. That night we saw Mr. Aitkens again, and Allan ever so casually mentioned the mysterious letters to him.

"I think it must be a hoax," he said. "I do not know any Cuban who would do it seriously."

The next day ex-President Menocal arrived at the hotel with two cars, both Rolls-Royces. He motioned Jane and Frank into one car and then seated me between him and a man he introduced as his son in the back seat of the other. We smiled a great deal, and I chattered on about how beautiful I thought Havana was.

I was startled after we had gone a few blocks to see through the window between the back and front seats a large police dog sit up in the seat beside the driver. As we drove through the outskirts of the city, I turned to make sure the other car was close by and realized to my dismay that it was nowhere in sight. Furthermore, in turning I had brushed my knee against ex-President Menocal, and as I resumed my position facing front, I felt his knee pressing firmly against mine. When I demurely removed my legs to the left, the man on my left pressed his leg against them. Oh, my God, I thought, Señor X is the ex-President! I forced myself to look out the rear window again. The other car was not behind us.

"Where are we going?" I said, trying to conceal my fear.

Ex-President Menocal smiled and said, "To the yacht club first. Then we'll join your friends at the hacienda."

Of course I didn't believe him. "No. I have to go back," I said. "I forgot something."

"You can get it later," Señor Menocal's son said. The look he gave me indicated clearly to me what he thought of actresses. They could all be bought.

I knew I had to put on the show of my life. "Stop the car!" I said, rapping on the window. "I said, 'Stop the car!'"

The ex-President had the driver stop. I could hear the police dog whine impatiently. Both men looked at me as if to say, Stop playing games.

In steady, angry tones I said, "You know, my friend Miss West is the sister of the president of the United Fruit Company. *The United Fruit Company!* If I am not back in fifteen minutes, she will call the police. Do you understand?"

The two men spoke so rapidly in Spanish that I could not catch a single word. I sat rigid as a poker and glared furiously in front of me. After a minute, during which I sweated blood, they had the driver turn the car around and we drove back to the hotel, where Jane and Frank had been deposited.

Ex-President Menocal bowed politely and said he hoped I might be free another day. I said furiously I was sure I would not and marched into the hotel lobby. My legs were shaking so that I could hardly walk.

I told Jane and Frank and Allan what had happened, but we decided not to summon the police. Instead I had the hotel manager contact a charitable organization and I gave them the jewels—two rubies and two diamonds, and two emeralds which had arrived that morning. That night none of us left the hotel.

Before we left the next day we called Señor Aitkens and Señor De Mesa to say good-bye and to ask them to excuse us for not seeing them on our last night in Havana. I said nothing about my adventure with ex-President Menocal. Señor De Mesa sent a note and a velvet box to the boat. In the box was a gorgeous stickpin in the form of a fox's head, made of diamonds, with rubies for the eyes. The simple little come-back-soon note was only a dozen words in length, if that. What struck me about it was not the message, but the handwriting.

"Jane," I said, as we stood at the rail, "look at this. Carefully."

"Oh!" she gasped immediately. "It's the same, isn't it?"

"Unmistakable," I said. "Furthermore, he must know we know, and that means he's not concerned. I guess in Havana, an actress—*any* actress—is simply considered a prostitute, Jane."

At dinner I said I thought we had our *Manhandled* plot. Our little department-store salesgirl could get into society and then get abducted—manhandled—by the richest, most dignified, most distinguished man in Cuba, or perhaps even by the ex-President, while she's on a cruise.

My three companions all felt that although it had happened, it was too unbelievable for a movie plot. Even Allan's girl friend said nobody would swallow anything as far-fetched as that in 1924.

"Maybe we should just stick with the *Post* story and keep her lover an inventor," said Frank Tuttle. "Better to be a bit prosaic than to come up unbelievable, don't you think, Allan?"

Before *The Humming Bird* was released, a disconcerting rumor had spread that I was dead and the studio was using a double to finish the last scenes of the picture. Reporters looking at stills from the film said they were not all of me. No one knew who had started the rumor, but every time Paramount called the papers to squelch it, they only managed to arouse more suspicion.

Spiritualism was on the rise that year. Harry Houdini made news over and over again by attempting to expose fraudulent mediums at the same time that he and others explored the possibility of communicating with people who had died; and the popular Broadway play *Outward Bound,* about a mysterious boatload of people who all slowly discover they are dead, packed audiences in nightly. The newspapers, in such a year, were not anxious to bring me back to life with undue haste.

The Associated Press finally suggested an interview. A reporter and a photographer came to the Gladstone, and we enacted a little drama that was right out of Pirandello, whose fascinating plays had first hit New York the year before.

"I guess the easiest way to convince you," I told them, "is to let you touch my beauty mark. It's also my trademark, as you know."

They touched it and agreed it was a real mole, all right, but they still seemed doubtful.

I then said with some exasperation, "Well, if I'm not me, who am I?"

"You could be the double," one replied. "It could be a trick."

"Look," I said, "no one could keep a trick going. But I've already started work on my new picture. I may be a *new* Gloria Swanson in each picture; in fact, it's very deliberate on my part. But I'm not a *different* Gloria Swanson. And I certainly would never let a picture be released in which I seemed to be *two* Gloria Swansons. That would mean I was bad in it. Don't you see?"

After a pause the reporter said, "Is there anyone else we could ask? Like your children?"

"I never expose my children to the press."

"How about your mother?"

"She hates pictures. She would never let you in the door. Besides, she's in California."

"Isn't there anyone?"

"Yes," I said, fed up at last. "Ask the public. Ask anyone who buys a ticket to *The Humming Bird* as soon as it's released. After forty-two pictures, I assure you the public knows me, or they wouldn't keep coming back!"

Whether that convinced them or not, they went away, and just before we started shooting *Manhandled*, the Associated Press informed the American public that I was genuine.

Allan hoped to capture some real New York texture in *Manhandled*. He decided that if the girl I was playing worked behind the counter of a department store, I should do the same for a couple of days to get the feel of it. Sport Ward pulled strings so that I could work incognito behind a soap counter at Gimbels for two days. I borrowed a blond wig from the studio, stuffed cotton in my nose to change its shape, powdered out the beauty mark, and painted on new eyebrows and lips. After I had put on a five-dollar dress and padded my bra, even the children didn't recognize me, and because of the cotton in my nose I sounded like a rubber duck. Sport gave me three packs of gum to chew, and the chauffeur dropped me off one block from Gimbels.

I sold toilet soap on special, and after an hour I was quite good at it. I also had the floorwalker down pat and could do a perfect imitation of him eyeing me haughtily. On my ten-minute breaks I would scoot to the ladies' room and there I got a whole education in how to deal with guys who got fresh and took girls for granted. The whole first day, everything worked like a charm.

The second day, while I was in the ladies' room, one salesgirl said to another, "Have you heard the rumor? Gloria Swanson's in the store."

"No! Who told you?"

"Lillian." Then she turned to me and said, "Hey, did you hear that? Gloria Swanson's supposed to be in the store."

"Really?" I said like a duck, and with that I headed downstairs and out the side door. My field work was over.

Allan wanted a wild New York party scene in the picture, so he set up a real party, as nearly as he could, in the studio. At the rehearsal he told everyone to let go and improvise. He hired Ann Pennington from the Follies for the scene, and she shimmied and did the Charleston like a miniature whirlwind while Allan kept yelling, "Come on, everybody, react! You're there! It's a party!" In the midst of the activity I took a black derby from one of the crew and put it on. Then I grabbed a cane from somebody and started wobbling around in an impersonation of Chaplin. People laughed and clapped, and Allan said to keep it in. The next day we got a more accurate Chaplin costume for me and shot the whole sequence in an afternoon.

Allan was so excited by this improvisation that he decided to shoot the trial scenes in our next picture, *A Society Scandal,* on location in a courtroom in Brooklyn. Moreover, he wanted some real, identifiable New York society people in the picture. After a careful look around, he cast the beautiful Morgan twins, Thelma and Gloria, who would shortly become Lady Furness and Mrs. Vanderbilt, in small parts, and the newspapers gasped when the picture was released. Allan Dwan loved flirting with reality in this way, and both of these pictures were discussed at length by the critics for their daring authenticity.

A Society Scandal was based on a play called *A Laughing Lady,* in which Ethel Barrymore had starred. The story involved a society woman, her husband and his possessive mother, who sows the seeds of divorce in her son's mind, and a handsome attorney. Forrest Halsey wrote the screenplay, and he had strict orders from Hollywood to have lots of scenes where I could wear lots of beautiful clothes. Mr. Lasky said they demanded one fancy-dress picture from me a year, because the public demanded it, and he said they had certainly not had one yet. They had said under my picture on all the *Manhandled* ads and posters, "More gorgeously gowned than ever!" but everyone knew that it was not true. Therefore, they wanted me to look fabulous—nothing less—in *A Society Scandal.*

To keep the film from becoming a "costume picture," however, Allan told Forrest to keep the story intense and passionate.

Allan knew I was at my best playing opposite very strong actors, and in this picture he was able to cast not one, but two actors who were both beyond a doubt destined for stardom, Rod La Rocque and Ricardo Cortez. They were both Valentino types, as handsome Latins were called in the wake of *The Four Horsemen* and *The Sheik*, although Rod La Rocque was French-Canadian and Ricardo Cortez was from Brooklyn. Before Valentino, dark, lithe types like them had always been cast as villains, and heroes had always been rugged, heavy, preferably fair, and even a bit on the clumsy side, but Rudy had broken the mold. The two big men's roles in this picture were both rich ones for actors, especially Rod La Rocque's part.

Rod La Rocque had attracted lots of notice playing Richard Dix's brother in Mr. De Mille's *Ten Commandments,* but I had never met him before he appeared on the set the first morning in Astoria. He was taller than Rudy, I noticed, and much more handsome, I thought. For reasons of scheduling, Allan had to shoot the picture out of sequence, and that morning, it turned out, we were filming one of the big love scenes. For most of the day, Rod and I made love while the cameras rolled, and by mid-afternoon, for the first time in almost ten years in pictures, during which I had made love to such matinée idols as Wallace Reid, Tommy Meighan, and Rudolph Valentino, I didn't want the day to end. Within three days I was in love. Within a week Rod proposed.

He was physically irresistible and had a brilliant mind. In spite of Mickey, in spite of everything, I wanted to be with him every minute. For almost a year I had not had anyone near to love, and that was a long time. Rod La Rocque seemed to be everything I had missed, and I was just on the verge of saying I would marry him.

Then, one Sunday, as rapidly as our affair had started, it ended. Sundays I spent with my children, unless they were in the country and I couldn't get to them because of other engagements. The Sundays I was in the city alone, I had open house in my suite at the Gladstone. The first time Rod arrived to join my little salon, it upset him terribly to find that it was composed mostly of men and that I was enjoying myself enormously. Allan and I were set to film a Mary Roberts Rinehart story next, so her son, John Farrar, was there, along with Jimmy Walker, Frank Crowninshield, Edward Steichen, Beverly Nichols, Sport Ward, and several others. Rod had nothing to worry about; he was a match for the best of them in almost every department. But his jealousy was painful to see. It was torture for him to share any part of me with my dearest friends. We tried to talk it out, but he simply couldn't understand that I liked to have lots of people around me, and that the people I enjoyed most were invariably men—the brighter, the better. In fact, one friend had called me a mental vampire. He said I crept off to a corner with some brilliant man and drained him of all I could learn from him, and then went off to another corner with another brilliant man to do it all over again. I considered that a compliment. However famous I might be, I had a lot of intellectual catching up to do, and New York was the place to do it. I couldn't get enough of brainy, interesting people. And Rod could not understand that need in me, or accept it. He couldn't share a wife.

With that settled, we were obviously not suited for marriage or inclined to pursue an affair. We did what I had never thought a man and a woman could do—gently drifted beyond passion into deep friendship, which both of us knew would last. Two months after Rod La Rocque proposed to me, I was treating him like a brother.

Ricardo Cortez, the other Valentino type in *A Society Scandal*, had been married to Alma Rubens, who had been a big star when I was at Triangle, and whose untimely death many attributed to drugs. Shortly after our picture together was finished, I began to hear vicious rumors about Ricardo similar to those that had circulated for years about Rudy. People said he was a gigolo, an operator, involved in shady, even crooked doings. I decided he was too talented to be destroyed by such rumors if they were untrue, so one day I called up the Los Angeles district attorney, whom I had met, and asked him to check through his files and find out if there were any indictments against Ricardo. He called me back the next day and assured me that all the stories were completely baseless. Therefore, I made Ricardo my escort for a few weeks and always made sure we were in the company of the most respectable and sophisticated people I knew. Within a month all the fires were out. It was a wonder, however, that new ones didn't spring up about me, who was seen everywhere for a short, dazzling period with not one, but two of the most handsome men in the world—both Valentino types.

All the while I was making *Her Love Story*, a romantic costume picture based on a Mary Roberts Rinehart story about a Balkan ruler who is forced into a political royal marriage when she is already married to a guardsman, I was furious that Mr. Lasky didn't offer me *Peter Pan*. It was obviously going to be an important picture. Everybody had been talking about it for a year. I felt I shouldn't have to ask for it. After all, I had made *Male and Female* by the same author, I was Paramount's top star, and *Manhandled*, which was playing all over the world, was a bigger success, critically and at the box office, than anything I'd done since my days with Mr. De Mille. I remembered what Mr. De Mille had told me, that the studio liked to put only one egg in each basket, that a picture could have a star director *or* a star performer *or* a prestigious story, but not two together. That was throwing money away, the studio felt. Nevertheless, I thought in this case Mr. Lasky might make an exception. I had mentioned the role to him on several occasions, and he had always been evasive.

Forrest Halsey felt so strongly that I was right for *Peter Pan* that he thought I should take the bull by the horns and go to England and talk to J. M. Barrie personally. He said I had to convince Mr. Barrie that I could play the part and then get him to suggest me to Paramount as his choice for the role. I should remind him, Forrest said, that more people had seen me in *Male and Female* than would see *The Admirable Crichton* in a hundred years, and that I had just played a tomboy pickpocket to perfection in *The Humming Bird*.

"I'll do it," I said. "I'll tell Mr. Lasky I need a month's rest before I start another picture. He'll say yes because he's afraid to say no."

"Before you go," Forrest said, "I want to show you another play you should try to get film rights to when you're over there. It's by a famous playwright named Sardou and it's called *Madame Sans-Gêne*."

"What's it about?"

"A washerwoman who is elevated to the nobility by Napoleon."

That didn't sound very promising, but I trusted Forrest's taste completely, so a few days later I set aside an evening and asked him to read it to me. I loved it. It was a rich, funny story and it had a great woman's role. Sardou had written it for the famous French actress Réjane. The more Forrest and I talked, the more we felt it couldn't be done in Astoria or Hollywood. It should be done in France with a French director on the actual locations—the palaces and châteaus Napoleon had lived in.

"What do you think the French will say to that, Forrest?"

"Ask them," Forrest replied.

Mr. Lasky agreed to a trip. I told him I wanted to go to London and Paris, and he told me to contact the Paramount office in both cities to arrange for interviews to promote my last three pictures. I never mentioned *Peter Pan*.

Jane West and I sailed in June. We checked into Claridge's in London, and I gave interviews for two days. When the press asked me the purpose of my trip, I said it was purely for pleasure. Before I could contact Mr. Barrie, however, all the British papers came out with the news that a young American actress named Betty Bronson had been chosen personally by Sir James M. Barrie to play the role of Peter Pan in the film of the same name. The papers said Herbert Brenon would direct the film. Although I was deflated, there was no doubt but that the studio had stuck with the old formula: the only egg in the basket was the well-known play. I was also grateful that, having made the trip to Europe, I had a second egg in my own basket, thanks to Forrest Halsey.

We stayed in London two more days and then made the Channel-crossing to France. When we got to the Hotel Plaza Athénée, there was a message from Adolphe Osso, the head of Paramount in Europe, saying he wanted to see me, and another message from André Daven, cinema critic of *L'Aurore*, requesting an interview. I told Jane to invite Mr. Daven to lunch and to tell Mr. Osso that I would contact him in a day or two.

After an hour with André Daven, I trusted him perfectly. Small, intense, and extremely handsome, he spoke excellent English and knew more about my pictures in detail than I did. Therefore, I came directly to the point. I told him I was burning to make a film of *Madame Sans-Gêne*, and that I wanted to make the picture in France. Before I approached my studio about such a project, however, I had to be certain of two things: that the French artistic community would accept me, and that France would not feel I was impudently treading on hallowed ground by undertaking a role that was so utterly and so significantly French.

André said he thought there was every chance the government would give me permission and that French artists would see such a venture as a capital break for the French film industry. French audiences spent millions of francs each year to see American movies, but French movies were never seen in America. Usually when Hollywood came to Europe, he said, it was to raid Europe of its talent, not to let it work where it could produce the most fruitful results. In this case the French establishment should be thrilled because I would be bringing American capital to Paris to employ French talent and give it a chance to be seen all over the world. He said he would contact every important person he knew in government and the arts and write a long lead story in *L'Aurore*.

"Never fear," he said, "if the French don't like the idea, they will not be shy about letting us know. But I'm sure they will like it."

Now I was ready for Mr. Osso. No sooner had I told him what I wanted to do than he announced curtly and pompously that any such scheme was absolutely impossible. He said the French would never give an American the rights to film *Madame Sans-Gêne*. He said the government would never let us film on the actual locations because they were all official historic monuments. He said that UFA, the powerful German film company, had tried to obtain such clearances repeatedly and had always been refused.

"Impossible," he repeated, "without question."

"I see," I said.

"You do not know the French," he said, "but I do."

He clearly did not know André Daven, whose story in *L'Aurore* changed everything. Beautifully written, it was a lesson in diplomatic tact and salesmanship. Paramount came out smelling like a bunch of French violets, and Mr. Lasky and Mr. Zukor loomed as potential great ambassadors of culture. André was besieged by letters from directors, actors, designers, and politicians, all saying they thought it was a brilliant idea. Within two weeks Hollywood surrendered, and Mr. Osso was on the phone day and night making arrangements for the picture he had declared flatly was impossible even to think about. Mr. Lasky agreed to give me everything I wanted if I would first return to Astoria and make one more picture there. Allan would direct it, and Ben Lyon would be the leading man. It was called *The Wages of Virtue*. It would take six weeks to make. I told him I would be delighted.

I cabled my undying thanks to Forrest Halsey for his idea and told him we would use his treatment for the screenplay. André promised to take a leave of absence from *L'Aurore* and work with us during the making of the film. And we all agreed that we would start work at the end of October, in three months' time. Then Jane and I bought everything we could lay our hands on for the children and booked passage back to New York on the *Leviathan*.

I could hardly believe I wasn't dreaming.

Jane had booked us as Mrs. H. Somborn and secretary so that I wouldn't have to smile at total strangers and sign autographs for a week. We ordered all meals to be delivered to the stateroom. The first night out, the steward entered at dinnertime with a lighted candelabrum. While the waiter with him poured champagne for Jane and me, the steward, without asking me, dimmed the lights, struck a languid pose against the cabin door, and began to play passionate gypsy music on a violin. I didn't even have to look up. Only one person in the world had ever played a violin like that. I ran across the room, flicked on the light, and kissed Jascha Heifetz.

After a year with Sport Ward, I fancied myself the queen of the practical jokesters, but Jascha had us all beat. He sat down and we had dinner and discussed our friends. Over coffee, he told me Mary Pickford and Douglas Fairbanks were aboard, and together we planned a little pre-breakfast surprise for them.

At eight the next morning we met in front of their stateroom. Jascha was in his steward's outfit and I was got up as a stewardess, with a huge frilly cap covering most of my face. We knocked lightly on the door of their suite and entered before they could say anything. The stateroom was dark, and we could hear their heavy breathing. I pulled back all the drapes and Jascha opened several portholes. Then we began talking in normal tones in a sort of bastard French we had rehearsed while we pushed furniture around. Still asleep, Doug turned over and buried his head under his pillow. When Mary's head emerged from under the covers, I could see out of the corner of my eye she was wearing a chin strap. Putting her finger to her lips to tell us to be quiet, she beckoned for us to close the drapes and get out. As she turned over, I chattered cheerfully to Jascha in our mock language and knocked over a big vase of red roses. Then Jascha scolded me loudly and began shaking out blankets and emptying ashtrays.

Mary opened her eyes again and tried to communicate by means of a couple of French phrases. We ignored her and went right on talking. Then she shook Doug awake and told him to ask us to leave. In careful French, Doug asked us to go away, but we pretended we couldn't understand. Then Doug started laughing at their predicament, and Mary said it wasn't funny. By that time we had made a shambles of their stateroom, and just as we were about to strip the satin comforter off their bed, Doug recognized me by my nose. Then he recognized Jascha and started laughing so hard that he couldn't tell Mary what was so funny. When Mary finally figured out who we were, we all laughed until we couldn't laugh any more. We ached as we pushed furniture back in place and ordered breakfast, but we all knew we were in for a wonderful crossing.

Because of Marshall Neilan, I had been with Doug and Mary many times but never for such a long stretch. I knew that since I had left Hollywood, Mary had made two films, *Rosita* and *Dorothy Vernon of Haddon Hall*, the first with Ernst Lubitsch, the second with Mickey, and that neither had been very successful. It made me worry for Mickey, because *Dorothy Vernon* was the first Pickford film he had directed in five years and I knew he had had great hopes for it. When I asked Mary how Mickey was, she was sweet but evasive. I read easily in her manner that he had disappointed her this time, that—probably because he was drinking too much—in her eyes he was not the director he had been once. After *Rosita* she had needed a great success, and he had not managed to obtain it for her. It was funny: the more she talked, the more I yearned to see him again soon. Now that Blanche Sweet had left him for good, Mary and I were surely the two people who cared most for him in the world, and we both had our reservations about the wild, beautiful devil.

When I told them I was going right back to Paris to make a picture in October, they were madly jealous, but they thought it was a great idea. I said we would probably get permission to use the actual palaces of Fontainebleau and Malmaison, which even Paramount could not conceive of building or buying, and Doug recalled how he and Allan Dwan had spent a fortune to construct the castle for *Robin Hood* outside Hollywood. Even Charlotte Pickford, Mary's mother, who was traveling with them and who had built a reputation by outmaneuvering studio heads, thought I was on the right track. Then Doug asked me when my Paramount contract was up, and I told him in a little over a year. He said he and Mary and Chaplin and D. W. Griffith had all discussed it, and when that time came, they would like me to leave Paramount and join them in United Artists. He said if I could do what I had just done in Paris all by myself, I certainly didn't need Jesse Lasky anymore.

Then Mary said she really had it in for Paramount because they hadn't given her *Peter Pan*. I gasped and said I had hinted as broadly as I could to Mr. Lasky that *I* had wanted *Peter Pan*, and that he had never even discussed it with me. Mary said I should consider myself lucky; Mr. Zukor had told her she could have it only if she agreed to do two other pictures for Paramount. Then she said with a wicked little smile, "But you know, of course, who was absolutely sure it was hers, don't you?"

"No," I said. "Who?"

"Lillian Gish. Everyone says there was not a doubt in her mind."

CHAPTER 11

A tous ceux qui aiment la France, son passé de grandeurs et ses trésors de beauté, j'offre l'hommage de ce film né d'une cordiale collaboration franco-américaine.

—LÉONCE PERRET

Madame Sans-Gêne, *magistralement réalisée par* Léonce Perret, *le premier grand film né d'une collaboration franco-américaine, est non seulement un triomphe, mais également l'avocat le plus éloquent que puisse trouver cette cause riche d'avenir.*

—Le Journal

Il était essentiel, pour le succes commercial du film, d'avoir une interprète faisant vedette à l'écran, aussi bien en France qu'à l'étranger. C'est pourquoi MM. Lasky *et* Osso *m'ont offert la collaboration de l'étoile la plus brillante de la* Paramount: Miss Gloria Swanson.

—LÉONCE PERRET

Pour Madame Sans-Gêne [Léonce Perret] *rassembla toute une constellation de vedettes et composa un vivant album de nos merveilles historiques et de leurs scènes mémorables. . . . Le rôle principal est tenu par* Mme Gloria Swanson, *star des stars d'Amérique.*

—Le Cinéopse

When I sailed for France in October 1924, I was traveling like a diva. My retinue consisted of Mother and the children, Jane West and her mother, a governess, and Ethel, my New York maid. Forrest Halsey was also on board, as script writer and consultant, and he had with him a pale young man he called his secretary. To Mother's chagrin, Allan Dwan and some Paramount executives and a battalion of reporters and photographers stayed on the boat until sailing time, and an hour before that, our long string of staterooms had reached the point where they could not contain one more basket of flowers or one more giant inverted cone of fruit wrapped in cellophane. The publicity that this first big Franco-American film venture had created had so thrilled Mr. Lasky and Mr. Zukor that they were happily paying most of the bills. The rest I was willing to pay myself—Mother's trip to Europe, for instance—especially since my salary would be $7,000 a week starting January 1.

André Daven met us in Cherbourg, with the warning that Adolphe Osso had announced my arrival to the press and that we had therefore better be prepared for crowds of fans at the Gare St. Lazare and the Crillon. André had booked two complete cars on the boat train to Paris, and he apologized because he had not been able to exclude the press entirely on account of Mr. Osso's determination that I get full coverage every minute. I said I would talk to them on the train if they promised not to bother Mother and little Gloria and Brother, so most of the way to Paris I answered reporters' questions, trying out when I dared an occasional word in French. By the time we reached the city I had realized that the first thing I would need in France was a combination escort, translator, and interference runner so that I could move around and communicate, and André said he would find somebody suitable.

A mob at the station cheered when I stepped off the train, and a crowd of several thousand surrounded the string of Renault limousines lined up to transport us to the hotel. Clearly, I could no longer get around anonymously in Paris as I had two years ago with Mickey—not after *Beyond the Rocks* and *Zaza*. At the Place de la Concorde two dense lines of people watched us file into the lobby of the Crillon, where Adolphe Osso was waiting to greet me on behalf of Paramount in Europe.

Later in my suite, Mr. Osso introduced me to Léonce

Perret, who would direct *Madame Sans-Gêne*. Mr. Perret was a revered pioneer of cinema in France. He had spent several years before the war in a little studio on the Hudson outside New York studying American filmmaking and had returned to France during the hostilities to put the techniques to use in propaganda movies. Mr. Lasky and Mr. Osso had chosen this prestigious figure for his obvious international link, and I had approved of their choice before I left New York. A number of years before, Mr. Perret had invited me by letter to be in a film of his called *Koenigsmark*, but I had not been free.

He was a dark, svelte man of middle age, and I liked him immediately. His wife, a former actress, was a tiny blonde with a candy-box face and a plump, corseted figure who had seen better days as the mistress of a titled nobleman, which she referred to proudly as often as possible. She insisted on acting as translator between us, but her contribution consisted mainly of henpecking him and flattering me, so I indicated again to André when I could that the first thing on my list of requirements was a dignified, socially adept translator who could take such people as Madame Perret and Mr. Osso off my hands. This picture, I determined, was going to be mine, not theirs.

Mr. Perret told me they had permission to shoot in and around Napoleon's three favorite residences, but he warned me that time was of the essence. The weather in November could turn bad in minutes and could stay bad for weeks, and the number of days we had been given to take over the great historic monuments was limited. Therefore, they had taken the liberty of selecting a tentative cast and of finding a costumer for me (subject, of course, to my approval), and they had arranged, for purposes of press relations, a large reception the following evening at which I would meet *le tout Paris*, as they called the establishment of diplomats and artists who dictated the cultural affairs of the great capital. As soon after that as we could get my first costumes built, we should start the location shooting, so that by the time the Paris winter set in, we would have only studio scenes left to do. I was impressed with Mr. Perret's taste, good sense, and efficiency, and happy to be able to agree with everything he suggested.

The following evening, at the reception in the ballroom of the Crillon, I walked for two hours beside André Daven, who was just short enough to make me look tall, and met everyone who mattered in Paris. These were the people whose approval would turn the filming of *Madame Sans-Gêne* into a pleasure; whose disapproval would turn it into a costly agony. I was all in white and carried a white beaded bag and a red carnation exactly the color of my lip rouge. Hundreds of snobbish Parisians I would probably have been terrified to meet under any other circumstances—the men arch and suave and covered with ribbons and decorations, the women in the most beautiful clothes money could buy, forming a bouquet of the world's most expensive perfumes—waited patiently in turn to touch me and hear me talk, to tell me that all of France was enthusiastically behind me, to ask me discreetly what people did at parties at Pickfair and what kind of pomade Rudolph Valentino wore on his gorgeous hair. They were, when it came right down to it, touching me to see if the shining silver and black-and-white image they had seen on the screen was real. That seemed much more thrilling to them than finding out whether or not I could play a French laundress. When the reception was over, André Daven kissed me ecstatically on both cheeks and told me that what he had been sure of in July was now confirmed: Paris was mine.

Mr. Perret had cast the film impeccably, and with a delicate sense for the international character of the production. There would be two final versions, an English one and a French one, and the producers naturally wanted the picture to be successful around the world. The leading male roles, therefore, had been assigned to Charles de Rochefort, who had acted both in America and France; Emile Drain, one of the major players of the Comédie Française; and Warwick Ward, an Englishman. Charles de Rochefort was playing my husband, Emile Drain was playing Napoleon, and Warwick Ward was playing Neipperg, the Austrian diplomat. Except for me, all the actresses in the film were French.

The young costumer Mr. Perret had mentioned, whose name was René Hubert, brought me sketches the day after the reception, and I accepted them on the spot. Combining the elegance of the Empire line with a delightful, innocent vulgarity, Hubert had created the perfect wardrobe for the most beloved example of the *nouveaux riches* in French literature. In every single one of his designs, he had underlined Sans-Gêne's character in the most tender, captivating way. He said that he estimated the ermine mantle he had designed for a scene at Fontainebleau might run as high as

75,000 francs, but when he assured me it would be unforgettable, I told him to go right ahead. I knew Mr. Lasky would love it.

Just before we started shooting, André and Forrest Halsey told me they had agreed on the person to be my interpreter. In fact, they said, he was the man who had recommended René Hubert to André. One of a group of smart Paris swells who frequented the Ritz bar, this fellow, according to Forrest, spoke English like Bernard Shaw, had the body of an athlete and the face of a matinée idol, and carried the title of marquis.

"Then why in the world should he want to work for me?" I asked.

"Because he's an impoverished marquis, like so many," said André. "His uncle is Hennessy and his grandmother is Lady Douglas, but Henri himself runs a little insurance business. I'll bring him to meet you tomorrow."

The next morning André returned with a man in his late twenties whom he introduced as the Marquis de la Falaise de la Coudraye. The marquis was handsome and reserved, every inch the aristocrat, in perfectly tailored clothes, the kind of dapper person who wore well-chosen suede gloves and carried a walking stick as if it were second nature to do so. He spoke English well enough to be witty in it and said he could begin immediately, so when we settled on a salary for the two months he would work for me, he sat right down and started straightening out a hundred aggravating details regarding scheduling and government permissions.

Before I knew it, he had become indispensable. He picked me up and drove me to the studio at Joinville when we were shooting there, he knew how to dismiss the press politely when I was tired, and he delighted in showing me the Paris tourists never see. He chummed with the best of Paris society. His friend Bob turned out to be a baron, and his friend Paul was a count. Henri knew that the quickest way through bureaucratic channels was often to send flowers to this minister's wife or a small gift to that one's mistress, and he could overcome the toughest obstacles with charm and grace, leaving everybody involved feeling that he or she had performed the one act that made everything else fall into place. When, at one point, for some mysterious reason, we lost the permission to shoot on location at one of the châteaus we were using, Henri arranged everything with a dozen phone calls and without losing a day in the shooting schedule.

He even got me out of the Crillon and into a private mansion. One day when he was driving with me to a fitting, I pointed to a beautiful house that looked like a small palace and asked if it was ever possible to rent a place like that. He said he would see. The house, he found out, belonged to the Marquise de Brantes, whom one of his friends knew. He spoke to her butler on the phone and found that the marquise was about to leave for the south of France for the winter months. He then contacted her, assured her of my good character, and told her I was miserable at the Crillon, where reporters plagued me and where the children had no place to play inside. As soon as the marquise heard that I was a mother to whom privacy was sacred, and that I was the famous ambassadress who had set in motion the great international venture to film *Madame Sans-Gêne,* she turned over her house and staff to me for the rest of my stay and decamped. She never so much as asked to meet me. She simply made the grand gesture out of a sense of noblesse oblige, as a marquise appealed to by a marquis. In two phone calls, Henri had obtained for me one of the most beautiful *hôtels particuliers,* as such private mansions were called, in all of Paris.

The house was on the Place des Etats Unis, a five-minute walk from the Arc de Triomphe. A splendid marble stairway surrounding a delicate bird cage of an elevator connected the five floors. On the second floor was a drawing room fifty feet long, with an enormous fireplace at either end and a series of Gobelin tapestries between, and a paneled dining room overlooking a charming garden. The third floor was my private suite. It consisted of a library, a bedroom, a dressing room, and a small lounge. The bedroom was lacquered in black; the bed was Chinese, and unlined beige taffeta drapes created an extraordinary, delicate light in the room. The tub in the dressing room was probably large enough to hold a bridge table and four players without crowding. The fourth floor had beautiful apartments for Mother, the children, and the governess. The first and fifth floors were the domain of Alexandre, the Marquise de Brantes's imperious butler, and the rest of the large staff.

One evening shortly after we moved in, I invited Henri and a friend of his, the Comte de Chambrun, to dinner. The count was impressed with the great house and asked me what I knew about the marquise. I said I imagined she was between forty-five and fifty, that she had had a very austere upbring-

ing, some of it at least in a convent, and that her last lover was
an artist, younger than herself.

"How do you know all that?" Henri asked.

"By living in her house," I said, "with her books, her
pictures, her furniture—you know. I say a young lover
because her bedroom and bath on the third floor have been
done over in a modern style quite different from the rest of
the place. I say a convent because there are lots of delicate
little religious objects thirty years old or so placed lovingly
here and there."

"You're a detective," Henri said with fascination. Then his
friend called the prefect of police, whom he knew, and the
prefect corroborated everything I had said. Both men were
amazed, and while I was pleased to have made a favorable
impression on the count, I was more pleased to have scored
points with the marquis. He was a joy when he smiled.

Through the artistry of Léonce Perret and the diplomacy of
Henri, *Madame Sans-Gêne* became a marvelous experience
for everyone involved. Even the scenes of Sans-Gêne's early
life in the laundry, which had to be shot in the drafty studio in
Joinville, turned out beautifully. The location scenes proved
so moving to the French actors in the company that they
frequently actually got tears in their eyes to think of where
they were. One day a young extra was knocked out acciden-
tally in a fight scene. When he came to, he didn't say he was
going to sue. Instead he bowed to me and apologized to
Léonce Perret for delaying the morning's work.

At Compiègne we shot scenes in Napoleon's own library
and had for props his own books, bound in leather with his
coat of arms on them. Emile Drain used the quill pen the
emperor had used to sign actual treaties and blotted the ink
with blotting paper the emperor had with him in his little
campaign chest in Prussia. At Fontainebleau we filmed
Sans-Gêne's presentation to the emperor in the Salle Henri
II, and in Louis XV's game room we filmed a chess game on a
set that had belonged to the emperor of China before the
Christian era. Suzanne Bianchetti, who played the empress,
awoke before the camera in a royal bed where Marie de
Médicis, Maria Theresa, Josephine, and Marie Louise had all
slept with sovereigns. The jewels I wore were reproductions
of originals in the national treasury lent us for copying
through the courtesy of the great museums of France.

For chief cameraman, I had insisted on George Webber, an American, and his work pleased everyone. I made one other link between France and the United States by recommending Arlette Marchal, who played the Queen of Naples, to the executives of Paramount, who gave her a contract immediately for a series of films in America.

With all of the patriotism and pageantry and diplomacy involved, everyone felt he was working to produce a film of international importance. The experiment in having two countries cooperate to achieve an artistic unity was totally successful. At each of the major locations, official representatives greeted us before the press and made a ceremony of opening the huge doors to us. They also presented me with several awards and medals, and each time Henri primed me with all of the right responses and the proper gestures. At all the banquets and receptions in my honor, he stood beside me and prompted me in what to say. If French officialdom fell in love with me during those months, it was largely because of Henri's flawless choreography. He knew French snobbery and decorum and protocol down to the most minute detail, and he never allowed me to miss a beat. In response to any question I was in doubt about, I repeated one long French phrase I had learned by heart: *"Vous n'avez qu'à demander au Marquis de la Falaise de la Coudraye."*

In November, when we had finished most of the location shooting, Mr. Osso asked me if I would go to Brussels and make an appearance at a U.S. embassy function and pay visits to several orphanages and hospitals, all in conjunction with a Swanson film festival he was arranging in the city. Since I had never been to Brussels, I thought it would be a nice break. To help me with the press and diplomatic corps, I took along Jane West, Henri, Forrest Halsey, and Madeleine Guitty, one of the French actresses in the film. Forrest, in turn, took his young "secretary." We traveled on the deluxe express, had its famous lunch between the two capitals, and when we got to Brussels, the usual police cordon and line of studio cars were waiting for us. On the way to the hotel, the limousines snaked through the city in order to pass before all the bunting-draped theaters that were showing my pictures. Crowds roared as we went past a series of enormous billboards which traced loosely the past six years of my artistic career, starting with

the major De Mille pictures. It looked as if half the city had
stayed home from work to wave at me and cheer each time I
waved back. Henri was in the first car with me, and between
the batches of kisses I blew to the people on the streets, he
asked, "How long has it been like this for you, Gloria?"

"Too long," I said with surprising honesty. "I was nineteen
when I made my first really big film."

I then began telling him the story of my life, backward,
and to my amazement he compared his own experiences with
mine. He had never spoken about himself before. He was
four years older than me, I found out. The year I had made
Don't Change Your Husband with Mr. De Mille, he had
received the Croix de Guerre for bravery in battle. While I
was making awful spy pictures at Triangle with Albert Parker
and Lightning Hooper, he was in a hospital in Flanders, lucky
that they didn't amputate his leg there. When I was at
Essanay, he was already in the trenches.

"How old were you then?" I asked.

"Twenty," he answered modestly, with some embarrassment, and immediately snatched at the first occasion to
change the subject. We were passing a poster of *Beyond the
Rocks,* with writing in Flemish, and he said, "I had forgotten
you made a film with Valentino."

"To be perfectly correct," I said with a teasing smile, "he
made a film with me. You see, he wasn't a star yet." Then I
asked, "Did you like it?"

"To be perfectly honest," he said, "I didn't see it." He
reddened and turned away.

"Why are you blushing, Henri?" I asked.

"Because . . . because . . . Well, I may as well tell you. I
have never seen a single one of your pictures. In fact, I have
seen only two or three pictures in my life, when I was in the
army."

"Is that true?" I said with amazement.

"Perfectly. I could not lie to you."

"Why not?"

He paused, and we exchanged a long look. Then, with a
light tone, he said, "Because you are my boss, *ma patronne.*"
Nervously changing the subject again, he said, before I could
speak, "Oh, look! They are waving over there. Shouldn't you
wave back?"

We did not speak on a personal level again until the next
afternoon. All of us had appeared at the embassy and had

visited a veterans hospital. Henri was very much the soldier, the comrade, with the sick and mutilated men there. Many of them had seen my pictures because they had movie nights in the hospital, and they liked *The Humming Bird* especially, because of its French subject. Moreover, they were happy to talk to me in person. But I could tell they felt more comfortable and more in tune talking about the war with Henri than they did talking about motion pictures with me, and that only pointed up the relative unimportance of the latter in my mind. "Don't feel that way," Henri said. "Remember, the war destroyed over one and a half million young Frenchmen; motion pictures didn't."

That night I had to make appearances at one theater after another where my pictures were playing. At each one they turned a spotlight on me and played "The Star-Spangled Banner" and the Belgian national anthem. Then our small party left, each time before the picture had even started. Henri was always at my side.

Later, sitting at a large table in a night club with the rest of our movie people, I made Henri tell me about the war. He described life in the trenches and the occasional short, agreed-upon truces when Germans and French would put down their guns and wash and swim together in the same river and talk and laugh like friends and then go back and start shooting at each other again. Those brief hours, he said, pointed out so clearly the folly of war. "That's what war movies should be about," he mused, "—about the folly of war. Not about spies and patriotism." Then he got embarrassed to be talking seriously and asked me to dance.

It was our last night in Brussels, and it was late when we got back to the hotel. Jane and Madeleine went to their rooms, but the rest of us went to the bar for a nightcap. There Forrest and his secretary got into a fierce lovers' quarrel. The secretary stormed out to the elevator, and Forrest followed right behind him. They hissed like snakes at each other and called each other the most frightful names. They were still raging when they got into the beautiful open Art Nouveau elevator and ascended to their room. Henri and I sat in the bar laughing at the outrageous but sad scene until their voices disappeared in the upper stories.

Then we became very quiet. Without a word Henri paid the bill. Once he tried to speak but checked himself. Still we sat. Finally he said, "I am sorry I have nothing to offer you, Gloria."

"Such as?" I said, almost in a whisper, not wanting to stop him from saying what I wanted to hear.

"Money. I have none," he said. "I am sorry."

I stared at him sitting there—war hero, aristocrat, young god of an athlete—for a full five minutes. During that time I had a few fleeting thoughts of Mickey Neilan, too, and ended them by saying good-bye to him, taking him off my list. There was no list now. There would never be again. There was only Henri de la Falaise de la Coudraye.

"Don't be sorry," I said. "Be happy instead."

I reached for his hand and we took the fairy-tale elevator up to my floor. Then slowly we walked to my door. If the presidents of France and America and the whole of the Belgian press and Will Hays himself had been there in the corridor, I would have swept past them proudly and closed the door of my suite behind us, but at that hour there was no one. The corridor was empty.

December of 1924 was the happiest month of my life. For the first time ever, I was in love with a man quite near my own age, and he happened to be a handsome, *galant* French nobleman, the kind every American woman dreams about. He had no faults that I could find; he wasn't in pictures, he didn't drink, and he didn't have a string of marriages behind him. I contacted my lawyer in California to find out when my divorce from Herbert would become final, and when he informed me I would be free in mid-January, I decided to stay in France until then and be married in Paris. All I wanted in the world was to become the Marquise de la Falaise de la Coudraye and eventually make Paris my home.

The pressures of filming lessened each day. We were through with governmental red tape and worries over the weather. It was all studio shooting in December, and the cast worked efficiently and harmoniously, for they felt themselves nearing the end of a project they were sure would be a stupendous success. *Madame Sans-Gêne* was scheduled for release in America in early spring, and plans there were under way for premieres in New York and Hollywood and gala openings across the country. Paramount had already picked my next screenplay, entitled *The Coast of Folly*. Mr. Lasky notified me that he wanted Allan Dwan to direct it, so I wrote to Allan to come to Paris in order to discuss the script and meet René Hubert, whom I wanted to launch as my costumer in America. Allan said he would arrive early in January.

All during December I splurged. I owed France a great deal, more than I could ever repay. The French had greeted me with open arms. That fall and winter could with no exaggeration have been called the Swanson Season. Never had a picture created such excitement on the Continent. Never had the French press treated a star more lovingly or covered one more fully. Until Josephine Baker arrived and danced the Charleston and stole half of the limelight, I was the toast of Paris. Therefore, with the help of André and Henri, I planned a series of elaborate costume parties in the Marquise de Brantes's gorgeous house in December and early January and invited everyone who had worked with me, played with me, and done favors for me in my two packed months in the City of Light.

The idea for costume parties arose right after I returned from Brussels. One morning I heard someone whistling beneath my bedroom window in the garden, and when I looked out I saw a street cleaner in blue coveralls at work in the alley. As I started to pull my head back in, he smiled and waved and blew me a kiss. He then pulled off his big droopy mustache and revealed himself as Henri. Laughing, I motioned for him to come up and show the children his getup. Gloria and Brother were so delighted that we spent half the morning playing hide-and-seek in the enormous house. When it came my turn to hide, I ran upstairs and got the maid to give me her dress. Then I called, "Ready!" When little Joseph toddled into the bathroom looking for me, I was on my knees scrubbing the floor, and as he walked past me, I pinched him. He froze in place and then ran to Henri to tell him what the maid had done. Gloria squealed with laughter when she found out I had done the pinching, so next I had to let her wear a dress of mine and hide. Henri and I, of course, had at least as much fun as the children, so in the end we planned to have a costume ball.

I invited fifty people and hired caterers and a band. René Hubert made me a fantastic schizoid costume. I was bare to the waist in back with the usual beaded train, but when I turned around and lowered my fan, I became a pot-bellied man with a vin rosé nose. It was perfectly ingenious. No matter how many times I turned around, Joseph and Gloria never tired of the switch. It was hours before the governess could pack them off to bed. The party was such a huge success that I planned another one, on a somewhat more elaborate scale, for Christmas.

I invited everyone who had worked on *Madame Sans-Gêne* and made a deal with the film crew during the last days of shooting to make a sort of French Keystone comedy of all of us. I played Napoleon in it in one of Emile Drain's costumes, and other cast members did equally zany things. It was hilarious and proved to be the great hit of the whole party, because many members of the cast had never realized it was being shot. Whenever I had a few hours free in the weeks before Christmas, Henri and I would race to Cartier's to buy gifts. I got something for everyone in the company, until Henri finally said with concern that this party was costing me a fortune. I told him not to worry, because starting January 1 I would be making $1,000 a day, including Sundays. He was absolutely stunned.

The party was indeed lavish. I had the house decorated inside and out and hired three dance bands. Stories about the elaborate affair appeared in all the newspapers in Hollywood and New York as well as in Paris. I learned from Aileen Pringle and Peggy Urson that people were saying I had gone completely mad with excess in France. There was no doubt I was spending large amounts, but I had never had such a good time spending money. When Allen Dwan wrote details of his arrival in January, I could tell by the tone of his letter that he was worried about me. I had leaked stories to the press that I was remarrying as soon as my divorce was final, and columnists were already hinting that I was marrying a millionaire and quitting pictures. Obviously Mr. Zukor had told Allan to get right over to Paris and find out the truth before I made some awful mistake. Their consternation gave me the chance to arrange the greatest practical joke in the world for my dear friend and director. Together with Jane and André and Henri, I planned a charade so elaborate I knew Sport Ward and Jimmy Walker would talk about it for years to come.

In the middle of our preparations for the great joke, however, I made a worrisome discovery. I was pregnant.

I spread my contract out before me on the table and turned to the morals clause.

. . . Provided, however, that in the event that at any time in the future . . . First Party shall be charged with adulterous conduct or immoral relations with men other than her husband, and such charges or any of them are published in the public press, the waiver herein contained shall be null and void and of no force and effect. . . .

Technically, I had already broken the contract, but no one would know that if I married Henri immediately, which I could not do. Before my divorce from Herbert was final, as much as a month could go by. After that, it would be easily provable that I was pregnant when I married Henri, and in the eyes of the press and the public, that would be enough to finish me.

Moreover, if the press didn't destroy my career, Mr. Lasky could. If he didn't, however, he would be able to renegotiate my contract while holding all the trumps in his hand, because I would have broken my contract, with four pictures still to do in 1925. Mr. Lasky could therefore rewrite the contract on his terms, at his price. The awful part was that he could dictate terms to me just exactly at the point when I was at my peak, just exactly when he would otherwise have to accept any terms I chose to name—double my salary at least, plus many dividends.

By having Henri's child under the terms of my present contract, I would forfeit the chance to become one of the highest-paid performers in history. I would also, probably, lose Henri, because we had both gone past the stage where we could be happy in a garret.

By not having the baby, on the other hand, I could begin *The Coast of Folly* on schedule and complete my contract in a year, I could be free to dictate my own terms after that or leave Paramount altogether, and I could provide a rich, happy life for Henri and me.

The contract was a devilish trap. It always had been. But I had helped to build the trap by letting the studio persuade me not to sue Herbert for divorce but to wait until he sued me.

I knew I needed to confide in someone. I couldn't handle this decision alone. The person I trusted most was André Daven. I called him, and when he came to the house late in the afternoon, I showed him my contract and explained the awful dilemma. When I finished, I told him I thought I had to have an abortion.

André said, "You are absolutely right. The situation must be regularized. It is easier perhaps in Paris than in New York or California. You and Henri are both very young. You have all the time in the world to have another child."

The words went through me like an electric shock. They'd been said to me before, by the nurse in the Hollywood hospital after Wally gave me the awful medicine to take, when I was seventeen. I had judged Wally harshly at the time and had held that judgment against him ever since. I had thought he had done the most monstrous thing in the world, and now I was preparing to do it myself. Furthermore, I was doing it for the same reason Wally had, probably—to save my career.

"Have you told Henri?" André asked.

"I've told no one but you, André," I said. "I can't burden Henri with the price of my career. It would change our relationship totally."

"I know."

"But I just had to tell someone, André, that I have such a bad conscience about doing what I'm thinking of doing."

"You musn't blame yourself," André said. "Leave it to me. I will arrange everything. I promise to get you the very best doctor in France. No one need ever know."

"There's no other way, is there?" I asked.

"Of course not, Gloria," he said.

His voice was reassuring, and I smiled feebly at him in gratitude. Then I heard another voice speaking very clearly. "Don't do this," it said.

The voice, I knew, was inside me. It was the voice of my unborn child. I tried not to listen.

"Your heart is pounding," the voice said. "I know you hear me. Listen to me. I want to live. I am frightened of the sewers."

I shuddered and started to sob convulsively. André came over and held me tightly in his arms. He didn't ask me what was wrong. He thought he knew. But of course he didn't know at all, and I could never tell him what I had just heard.

"I will arrange everything," he repeated. "Do not worry. You are doing the right thing. You are choosing for many people besides yourself."

When he had left, I pulled back the taffeta curtains in my bedroom and stared into the gray, foggy Paris dusk. A face was looking at me from the darkness. It was not a baby's face. I could not have stood that. It was the face of death, beckoning or warning, I couldn't tell which.

I pulled the shades.

Then I got into evening clothes and went downstairs. At eight Henri arrived to take me to dinner.

"You look beautiful," he said, kissing me. "Are you ready?"

"Yes, darling," I said, "I'm ready."

Our surprise for Allan Dwan began the moment he and his assistant director, Richard Rosson, got off the boat train at the Gare St. Lazare. Forrest Halsey was there to meet him, looking pale and worried. He told Allan he had arrived just in the nick of time. He said I had gone completely mad and was spending money like water. Worse yet, Forrest told him, I was hopelessly in love with an Indian maharaja and was making myself a ridiculous fool over him. I had become the talk of all Paris.

As they emerged from the station I pulled up in a chauffeur-driven car. André Daven had borrowed the longest Mercedes in Paris for the joke, and René Hubert had filled the back seat with leopard-skin rugs and pillows. The chauffeur wore a sky-blue uniform the color of the car, and when I stepped out, I was dressed in gold satin. I had on most of the expensive jewelry I owned, as well as a few large pieces of Mother's, and I was carrying an intricate little filigree fan Arlette Marchal had used in one of the ball scenes in *Madame Sans-Gêne*. Being cautious not to overdo it and give the whole thing away, I snapped something unkind in French to the driver and waved grandly at the crowd gathering around. Then I smiled sweetly at Allan and let him kiss me on the cheek. I was very reserved with Richard Rosson. I told them I was dropping them at their hotel so that they could bathe and change, and that I would have them picked up at eight for a small dinner I was giving in my home in Allan's honor. As Allan was getting out of the car, I said, "Darling, it's black tie. You don't mind, do you?" He gave me a look of pity mixed with scorn and said they would be ready. "Oh, and Allan," I said in a voice so affected I admired him for not throwing up at the sound of it, "please don't mention pictures tonight. My friend—he's a maharaja—hates them. O.K.? See you later."

That night Forrest picked them up at the Ritz bar, and Allan confessed he was shocked at the change in me. When he saw the mansion on the Place des Etats Unis he was more shocked still, and Alexandre, the butler, played the role of the haughty servant to perfection. He could make anyone acutely uncomfortable with a sidelong glance. When Allan and Richard walked into the library, they had a further shock. Jane West stood before them looking like a French countess, her hair skinned back in a bun and topped by a tiara and wearing a gown cut to the lowest possible decent point on her back. My mother and Jane's were dressed to kill as well. I entered with Arlette, both of us in dresses to the floor, chattering snobbishly in French a mile a minute. We had actors from the cast whom we introduced as visiting royalty, and there were a few real dukes and counts for good measure.

While a dozen waiters served canapés and champagne, Henri appeared, dressed as an Indian maharaja, with a large emerald in the center of his turban. His make-up was flawless, and it worked perfectly with his little mustache, which was real. I curtsied low to him. Then he passed before each person in the room and waited for each one to bow—including the boys from Astoria.

When Alexandre announced dinner, we paired off and passed formally to the dining room, where the beautifully laid table gleamed in the light of a hundred or so candles. The maharaja sat on my right, and Allan and Richard were far down the table between guests who pretended to speak no English at all. Forrest sat two seats down on my left so that we could play out the little drama we had arranged.

The meal was the most intricate imaginable, served on an endless series of gold-edged plates, and it went on for two hours, during which everybody spoke mainly French.

When the time came to drink a toast to the maharaja, I rose and several servants rushed over to arrange my train. I rattled off a long toast Henri had taught me in French. That was the signal for Forrest Halsey to pretend to be drunk and start a disturbance. As we all raised the toast and the maharaja smiled unctuously at me and bowed, Forrest broke into tears, staggered to his feet, and shouted in plain English with his pronounced Southern accent, "My God, Gloria, you can't marry this son of a bitch. He's black as the ace of spades."

The guests gasped. Jane screamed. The maharaja threw a glass of wine in Forrest's face, grabbed a knife from the table, and chased Forrest from the room. Two dukes followed, but before Allan or Richard could move, I said, "Please, everyone, sit down. It is nothing. It has happened before."

From the outer hall there was shouting and then a shot, but I ignored it. Turning calmly to Alexandre, I ordered him to serve the dessert and more wine. At that point Forrest staggered back into the dining room wiping blood off his shirt and said, "Well, that's one dead Indian!"

Then we all broke into hysterics, and I was finally able to run to Allan Dwan and kiss him properly. "Tell everybody back home I'm not really crazy, will you?" I said. "And that my bathroom fixtures are not solid gold. That's another house altogether."

When Henri entered in his normal clothes, I introduced him as my fiancé and Allan complimented him on his wonderful maharaja.

We danced until the wee hours of the morning and had a fabulous time. André Daven stayed until the bitter end, and I realized he had something to tell me, so I led him up to my dressing room.

"I have spoken with the surgeon," he said.

The voice inside me cried "No!" once, like a fist slamming on a table.

I had to struggle to ask, "When?"

"He can give you the appointment on January 29. He will take no other patients that day."

"All right."

André touched my hand. "You will feel confident once you meet the doctor," he said. "I will make the appointment."

I told him Henri and I planned to be married as soon as it could be arranged.

"Wonderful," André said. "I am so happy."

"I want to have lots of babies with Henri, André."

"You will."

"As soon as I am pregnant again, in a year or six months, I am going to tell him everything."

"Not before?"

"No, André, not before."

At first the authorities would not accept newspaper dispatches as evidence of my divorce, once it was announced, so day after day we waited for the official papers to arrive from California. When two weeks passed and still nothing came from the lawyers, I assumed the documents had been lost and there would be even further delay. Delay would in turn cause traveling problems because Henri and I had made reservations to return to New York on February 11 but we couldn't travel together if we were not married.

Finally Henri persuaded the municipal council of the sixteenth arrondissement to waive the legal obstacles if we had an official U.S. representative on hand to vouch for me. He rushed to tell me we had permission to be married in Passy in two days' time, on January 28.

I shivered when he told me the date—the day before André had arranged for the abortion—but I couldn't back down now or arouse Henri's suspicions, so I said nothing.

In order to avoid a circus or a full Paramount production, we agreed to tell no one—not even my mother—except for the handful of people we wanted at the town hall. We said we wished the ceremony to be kept absolutely secret, and the mayor of Passy agreed. All he asked was permission to invite his wife. I went to three dress-makers and finally found a beige suit with gold embroidery and little gold tassels on the sleeves. I ordered a hat to match and they promised it for ten in the morning on the twenty-eighth. It arrived one minute before we had to leave for Passy.

Our small group of friends and witnesses consisted of André Daven, René Hubert, and Baron d'Aiguy, Henri's brother Alain, Léonce Perret and his wife, the mayor's wife, and Hewlett Johnson of the U.S. embassy, who served as my witness in lieu of official documents.

The ceremony was in French; Henri translated for me. When it came to the vows, Henri answered "Oui" and I said "Yes." The mayor then pronounced us man and wife, and we kissed. Our friends crowded around to embrace us, and when I saw Madame Perret and the mayor's wife both patting their eyes, I cried right along. Then we headed for a private reception at the Hotel Plaza Athénée, where I agreed, at André's suggestion, to a brief interview with Basil Woon, William Randolph Hearst's chief cultural correspondent in London and Paris, just to make sure that for once the facts printed were correct when Mr. Lasky and all the others read the news the next morning.

After lunch at the hotel, Henri and I returned to the big house. I had warned Alexandre the night before to be ready for a few friends in the late afternoon, and I had called Mother from the Athénée to tell her the news. She was furious that I had not let her know, and told me flatly she thought I had made a terrible mistake marrying a penniless Frenchman, no matter what his name was. She behaved like an iceberg at the reception and made arrangements the same day to travel back to America alone.

Henri and I booked a suite for our honeymoon at the Plaza Athénée. Before we left we had supper alone with the children. Gloria knew what it meant to have a daddy, but it was something new for Brother. He was overjoyed when I explained that Henri was going to live with us in America. I told him he could call Henri papa.

The first time he said the word *"Papa,"* in the French fashion, with the accent on the last syllable, I thought I would melt.

Joseph asked me why I was crying. "Because I'm happy," I told him. "Girls often cry when they're happy." He thought that was strange and kept trying to dry my eyes.

When we got to the hotel, stacks of cables were waiting for us, baskets of little blue envelopes. On top was one from Adolph Zukor, saying he was coming to Paris with Mrs. Zukor on Thursday. Basil Woon had also delivered a carbon copy of his interview with me that morning, so that I could see what the news services were carrying.

"You see? It's started," I said. "Don't open them tonight. You can read them in the morning. By the way, darling, I forgot to tell you I have to be out most of tomorrow. André is picking me up early to go to approve the press releases and the editing arrangements for the film. I'll be back late in the day, and then we'll start our honeymoon properly."

I wanted to go to sleep in Henri's arms. Instead he dozed off in mine. For me it was the longest, darkest night of the year, and the dawn was gray and bleak too, without a sliver of sunshine. I made a great effort not to waken Henri because I knew I couldn't trust myself to say good-bye. I hurried to put on a dress I had laid out the night before and slip out the door.

André was waiting downstairs. I could tell from the look of him that he hadn't slept either. I followed him to the car, and we drove most of the way to the doctor's without speaking. We took the elevator to the third floor of an elegant apartment building in which the doctor had his offices. In the waiting room, a nurse offered us chairs, and André sat me down and held my hands. He spoke to the nurse in French. She left the room, and when she returned she beckoned for me to follow her. André walked me down the hall to the last door, which the nurse and I entered. Inside the office she helped me off with my clothes and then helped me into a white hospital gown. She had me lie down on a table and she strapped my hands down and put my feet in some sort of stirrups. Then the doctor came in and spoke a few words of heavily accented English in a beautiful voice. He told me to breathe deeply, and as I inhaled the familiar ether, his voice faded to nothingness.

When I came to, André was with me. I could feel my hand in his. My wrists were free. He kissed me on the forehead. I knew from the pain that the awful deed was done. The nurse wanted to give me something for the pain, but I refused. No pill could remove the real pain I felt, of that I was sure.

They helped me to sit up. The nurse slipped on my shoes. I was surprised to find I could walk. The nurse spoke to André and he asked me if I wished to speak to the doctor.

"Oh, no, André," I whispered, "I can't. I don't want to see him."

André assured me he had taken care of everything. He had also telephoned Henri to tell him we would see him at the hotel sometime after lunch. He led me out to the car and took me for a long drive. When I felt recovered, we went back to the hotel.

The room was in chaos, and boxes and baskets of flowers lined the corridors in all directions. Both phones were ringing and cables were piled on the bed. Henri put down one phone long enough to kiss me and ask me if I'd had a good lunch. Jane West was on the other phone. She held her hand over the mouthpiece and said Paramount was furious they hadn't known about the wedding. They wanted to know if we would do it over again so they could film it. My name was on the front page of almost every paper in America.

I asked Henri if he had had lunch. He said no and kissed me again. Then I told André to take him to lunch at the Ritz and I told Jane to have the switchboard turn off the phones and go home. I said I was tired and needed a nap. They argued, but I pushed them out. I said they could all come back in two hours and we would start celebrating again with champagne. But first, I said, I had to have a little sleep. I locked the door after them.

All the Paris newspapers were stacked up on the floor, but I couldn't read them. The carbon copy of Basil Woon's article was still on the night table, however, and I knew it was the sole source for all the front-page stories. I stretched out on the bed and read a few paragraphs, starting somewhere in the middle.

> Gloria is now a full-fledged marquise. She has joined the oldest aristocracy in Europe. Her title goes back to the days of Napoleon.
>
> She is conscious that she is going to be accused by the jealous minions of Hollywood of marrying for a title. She knows the ordeal that is facing her. But, as she clasped her Marquis to her heart unashamedly before me in their bridal suite at the Plaza Hotel here, she looked the happiest woman I have seen in years.
>
> Gloria had cried at the culmination of today's ceremony. Her husband is only twenty-nine. He is blonde and handsome and comes of one of France's oldest families. He hasn't much money. But—well, let Gloria tell it as she told it to me, with her face gloriously flushed, after the ceremony:

> > "I have had everything in my life. I have had hard knocks and I have had success. I have had passion and I have had heartbreaks. All I wanted was devotion—and I have found it.
> > "I want babies!"

> Such was her own, unorthodox remark. She went on defiantly:

> > "Yes, I want babies. I'm wise enough to know that while I may be a star now it will be all over with when I am thirty-five, and that is not a century off.
> > "What will be left then?"

I couldn't read any more. I was crying. There were four or five baskets of flowers in the room, mostly roses, and the sweet smell was almost unbearable, but I was too tired to put them out in the hall with the others. I pulled the shades and turned out the lights. Then I lay down on the bed, rolled over on my stomach, and buried my face in the pillow.

I could hardly move my parched tongue. I was awake again. Henri was smiling at me. "Give me some water" was all I could say. For three days I had stayed in the room. Everyone said I was exhausted. René Hubert had had to go to

Cherbourg on the train with Mother. Jane was with the children. André was also in the room with me. He was alarmed. He told me in a low voice that the doctor we had gone to was in St. Moritz, but that he wanted to call another. I refused and started crying. Finally he showed me a thermometer and shoved it in my mouth. I didn't understand the numbers in centigrade, so I gave it to Henri. His face fell and he went to the telephone and called Bob, the Baron d'Aiguy, to get a doctor.

Dr. Vodéscal, when he arrived, took my pulse and told Henri to tell me I had a remarkable constitution. He gave me some pills and more water. I went back to sleep. Each time I stirred, Henri gently woke me and gave me another pill. Then the doctor came back and took my pulse and my temperature. Henri told me he said the fever was coming down. Henri wrapped me in a blanket and carried me to the other bed. It was cold and dry. A maid carried out the soaking sheets from my bed.

By morning my fever was nearly normal. I wanted pots and pots of tea, but I still couldn't eat. Then I went to sleep again.

It was dark, and I knew without asking that the fever was back. Dr. Vodéscal looked worried and spoke with Henri. Then the doctor went into the other room and Henri sat down beside me. He told me we were going to the hospital. The doctor was alarmed at the fever. I asked what I had. Henri said blood poisoning or—he stumbled on the word—tetanus. He said I would be fine once I got to the hospital.

In the hospital room, after the stretcher and the tiny ambulance, I could hardly whisper. I touched my sweet husband's hand and said, "Henri . . . darling Henri, I have committed the most awful sin of all. Our baby . . . I knew I would be punished."

He smiled tenderly and asked me not to talk. He kissed me. I could hear people whispering. The light dimmed. Death was in the room. Mine, this time.

When I opened my eyes, they gave me water. Day after day they jabbed my arm with needles. If they spoke, I was too tired to hear them. Too tired to move. Too tired to breathe.

Dr. Vodéscal was actually weeping when I opened my eyes. I could see my stomach moving ever so slightly as I looked at the foot of the bed for Henri. He was not there. He was beside me, whispering in my ear. "You have fooled them all," he was saying.

Chattering nurses roused me. Later Henri lifted me from

the bed and tried to get me to stand up. I couldn't. The next day it was the same. My feet folded under me like a tiny baby's. The next day Bob, Henri's friend, arrived, and the two of them tried again. I could stand, but my legs wouldn't move.

The next day Bob brought a thermos of soup he had made himself. I drank it sitting in a chair. I was beginning to move my toes. Henri was delighted.

"What happened to my hair?" I asked. The two of them were so astonished to hear me speak that at first they forgot what I had said. Then they told me the nurses had cut it off so that they could wrap my head with a towel in order to keep it dry of perspiration during the long days of high fever.

One day Henri wheeled me to an old-fashioned horse-drawn carriage outside the hospital for a little drive. He pointed to the café across the street where reporters had sat all during my illness, trying to bribe nurses and servants for news. They had kept the death watch for two whole weeks, smoking cigarettes and drinking coffee and beer and taking regular turns at the telephones. Every paper in Europe and America had carried my fever count and the daily small signs of my recovery.

The next day we went to the palace at Versailles. Bob and Henri put me down beside a table in the Hall of Mirrors. To their great joy I managed to take a few steps to the next table, and after a rest I made it to the next. After a week I could walk the length of the corridor on Henri's arm.

One day early in March, when I was feeling much stronger, Henri drove me out for a farewell look at the palace of Fontainebleau. It was a blustery spring morning. We would be leaving for America in ten days. A guide was taking a group of students through the museum. From the far end of one gallery, I thought I heard the guide down at the other end mention my name. Henri smiled and hugged me. "Listen," he whispered, "the guide says that that carriage of Napoleon's was used by Gloria Swanson in her last cinema, *Madame Sans-Gêne*."

We had planned to sail on the *Berengaria* on February 11, but because of my illness Henri had had to change our reservations twice. We finally sailed on the *Paris* the third week in March. I was still terribly weak, but Mr. Lasky and Mr. Zukor beseeched me not to postpone our sailing again, or we would not be in New York to attend the premiere of *Madame Sans-Gêne*.

I knew that Famous Players-Lasky-Paramount would put on a real show when we arrived. Through my marriage to a nobleman and my long battle with death, I had provided the studio with millions upon millions of dollars' worth of free publicity. I had stayed in the world's headlines for six weeks. During that time the studio had speeded up the completion of the American version of *Madame Sans-Gêne* so that they could synchronize the opening with my triumphant return into New York Harbor. After that they had already arranged to whisk me to California for the West Coast opening. I could tell from their cables that they were licking their chops; that they were prepared to pay whatever it cost to buy me once and for all and make me the biggest star in the world—bigger even than Charlie Chaplin.

I determined to spare the children all of the vulgar hoopla that such plans would certainly entail. I sent them on ahead on another ship with René Hubert, and I asked Mother to stay with them at the house in Croton-on-Hudson until Henri and I were settled.

Once they had sailed, our friends all planned elaborate festivities for Henri and me, but the series of parties tired me. Henri was constantly in a nervous state over my health. He became very protective and clung to the foolish notion that I would be able to relax once I got back home to the United States. Also, he couldn't wait to see America, which he had dreamed about visiting all his life, whereas I couldn't bear to leave Paris, which I loved more than any other place I had ever known. And while I had some inkling of what the reception in America, as engineered by Paramount, would be like, he had no idea whatsoever.

In addition to everything else, California would be *so* dull after Paris that spring. The new word for 1925 was "chic," which everybody repeated constantly but nobody could define. Some said it had to do with dress; others said it was a state of mind. The great couturiers—Callot, Jenny, Lanvin, Poiret, Schiaparelli—were all competing to raise women's skirts until they actually got up to the knees, and two artists who appeared from nowhere—Van Dongen and Vertès— recorded the new look in a new way and became famous overnight. Antoine was *the* coiffeur for the new short haircuts that spring, and the Gillette company knocked the bourgeoisie for a loop by placing the very first ads in fashion magazines for razors with which to shave the armpits. "Surrealism" was another new word, and all of our artistic friends said the biggest revolution since Cubism would occur in July, when the exposition of *arts décoratifs* was scheduled to open. The atmosphere was delightful, exciting, enchanting, and I wanted to live in that world of art and flowers and fashion forever.

We couldn't stay, though, as I reluctantly told Bob and André and all the others, because Mr. Lasky was waiting.

Just before we left, we went to see *The Covered Wagon*, the latest American picture that had opened to tremendous acclaim. It was the film that had finally elevated Lois Wilson to stardom, and she was wonderful in it, and everyone raved about her. At last my dear friend was on the skyrocket to fame. I could have given her lots of advice at that point, I knew, but I also knew she wouldn't listen. She couldn't. Fame was too exciting at first.

Similarly, nothing I could have said to Henri would have prepared him for the tumultuous reception awaiting us in New York, or the cross-country trip on the private train, or the grandstand of luminaries in the station in Hollywood. Crowds everywhere flocked to see the greatest attraction since P. T. Barnum's half-dead whale on the flatcar: the girl with the big eyes and the mole who had married the prince and risen from the dead. Through it all Henri behaved magnificently, right up to the Hollywood premiere of *Madame Sans-Gêne*. As we were hustled out through the orchestra pit and backstage right after the picture started, I smiled to think that my husband had still not seen a whole Swanson movie. Thank heaven for that, I said to myself. At least I knew he had not fallen in love with—or married—That Woman Up There on the Screen.

In the car on the way home Mother was saying, "Glory, you're so quiet. This should be the happiest night of your life."

"No," I heard myself saying, "it's the saddest. Don't you see, Mother, that all of that cheering tonight had nothing to do with my acting? It was all publicity. They weren't cheering me as an actress. They were only using me to make money. I'm just twenty-six. Where do I go from here?"

I knew where I wanted to go. I wanted to go to Paris and make love to the wonderful man beside me and present him with children, lots of them, to make up for the one I had destroyed. I took Henri by the hand. I'm sure he knew what I was thinking.

He had never seen me in a movie. What a luxury to be loved by someone like that! To all the others—Mr. Sennett, Mr. Lasky, yes, even Mr. De Mille—I was money. Their money. That's how they saw me. They would never let me do anything to diminish my value or hurt the industry. They would lie first, just in order to control me. They cared only about That Woman Up There on the Screen. But to me That Woman was not worth a baby; that much I knew after ten years in pictures.

Out of the blue I remembered kissing Daddy good-bye in Grand Central Station in 1914. The Essanay job at $13.25 a week, whether I worked one day or four, was dangling before me then; however, I was afraid to tell Daddy for fear he would say no. But I loved him too much to lie, so I hinted. And he loved me too, because he said although he must have known it would disappoint me, "Take your time, Glory. Remember, life is ninety-five percent anticipation and only five percent realization." He meant that life *should* be ninety-five percent anticipation; that something was wrong if it wasn't. And he was right.

Before we reached the Gillette mansion, which was now just my West Coast home, I determined that I would make the four films I was still bound by contract to make and then leave pictures.

Ten years was enough.

I had no wish to live through ten more, no matter how much Mr. Lasky was prepared to offer me.

Part
Two

CHAPTER 12

DATELINE: The St. Louis *Post-Dispatch*,
February 13, 1951

BETTE DAVIS AND GLORIA SWANSON
LISTED FOR BEST-ACTRESS OSCARS

Hollywood (UP)—Bette Davis and Gloria Swanson, both movie veterans, were nominated last night for best-actress honors in the 1950 Oscar awards, along with three younger actresses—Judy Holliday, Eleanor Parker and Anne Baxter.

Two films about aging actresses—*All About Eve* and *Sunset Boulevard*—won most listings in the academy nominations. *All About Eve*, a satire of theater life, brought 14 nominations. *Sunset Boulevard*, a murder story about a faded film star, was listed 11 times.

Nominated for best-actor awards were Louis Calhern for *The Magnificent Yankee*, José Ferrer for *Cyrano de Bergerac*, William Holden for *Sunset Boulevard*, James Stewart for *Harvey*, and Spencer Tracy for *Father of the Bride*.

Best pictures nominated were: *All About Eve, Born Yesterday, Father of the Bride, King Solomon's Mines* and *Sunset Boulevard*.

DATELINE: The Brooklyn *Eagle*, February 18, 1951

"20TH CENTURY" STARS SET B'WAY RECORD IN OSCAR LISTINGS

Broadway history of a sort was made last week when, for the first time, both stars of a current play were nominated for the best actor and actress awards in Hollywood's "Oscar" sweepstakes. The players are José Ferrer and Gloria Swanson in *Twentieth Century,* hit comedy revival at the Fulton.

By an amusing coincidence, as part of its factional plot, one scene of the Hecht-MacArthur farce has Miss Swanson proudly displaying to Ferrer an Oscar she had won, and he sarcastically inquires, "What did you get that for, bowling?"

Ferrer, who stands an excellent chance for the Academy Award for his portrayal of the long-nosed Cyrano de Bergerac, is a comparative newcomer to films.

Miss Swanson, in films for many years, has yet to win her first Oscar. Her *Sunset Boulevard* performance carried her back to the top of the Hollywood ladder.

DATELINE: The Los Angeles *Herald-Express,*
March 1, 1951

SWANSON, FERRER FILM PAIR GET WRITERS' AWARDS

Gloria Swanson and José Ferrer today were possessors of "Golden Globes," awarded annually by the Hollywood Foreign Correspondents Association for the best performances by an actress and actor during the year.

Miss Swanson received her award at the ninth annual Golden Globe Awards Dinner at Ciro's for her performance in *Sunset Boulevard* and Ferrer was honored for the title role in *Cyrano de Bergerac.*

Other awards by the 70 Hollywood reporters, representing 55 nations:

Best picture, *Sunset Boulevard;* best actor in a musical, Fred Astaire in *Three Little Words;* best actress in a comedy, Judy Holliday in *Born Yesterday;* best supporting actor, Edmund Gwenn in *Mr. 880;* best supporting

actress, Josephine Hull in *Harvey;* best director, Billy
Wilder for *Sunset Boulevard.*

DATELINE: The Louisville *Courier-Journal*,
March 25, 1951
BY-LINE: Bob Thomas

IT'S A TIGHT RACE (AMONG THE FILLIES) AS OSCAR DERBY HEADS FOR HOMESTRETCH

Hollywood—Movietown's "Run for the Roses"—the
annual Oscar derby—comes down the homestretch next
Thursday night and it's still a wide-open race, particularly among the fillies.

The Academy Awards—the entertainment world's
Kentucky Derby—will be dealt out amid glorious trap-
pings at the Pantages Theater on Hollywood Boulevard.
The contestants are the subjects of as much touting as
any prize crop of 3-year-old nags.

Everyone in Hollywood has his own ideas about who
will be crowned the year's movie champions. Here is a
consensus of the current trends, as well as some observa-
tions of my own:

Female star performance—ah, here's the toughie.
Seldom has there been a tighter race in this division, and
it's continuing right down to the wire. It's largely a
three-filly struggle among Gloria Swanson *(Sunset
Boulevard)*, Bette Davis *(All About Eve)* and Judy
Holliday *(Born Yesterday)*.

Miss Swanson may very well nab the honors. As the
aging film queen, she gave a striking, if stylized performance. Her comeback is perhaps the greatest in film
history, and she will snag the sentimental vote, which is
considerable.

Many of the Academy voters may plunk down for
Miss Davis because of sentiment and because of her
sheer artistry. The two-time Oscar winner came back
brilliantly in her role as another over-age actress. The
great popularity of *All About Eve* might well make her
the first star to win three Academy Awards.

Judy Holliday is pushing the two older stars for
contention. Her dumb-blonde role made her an immediate star, and her rise has been called the swiftest since

Mae West. She could upset the dopesters and walk home with the statuette.

Anne Baxter *(All About Eve)* and Eleanor Parker *(Caged)* are strong entries, but probably will be outdistanced. Miss Baxter could be dubbed the dark horse, because of her adept portrait of the stage aspirant.

Selection: Gloria Swanson.

DATELINE: The Chicago *Daily News,* March 27, 1951

IT'S GLORIA, BETTE IN STRETCH

(Sam Lesner, *Daily News* film writer, has gone to Hollywood to cover the awarding of movie Oscars Thursday. This is his first dispatch.)

Hollywood—The beautiful sunset over Los Angeles didn't jibe with a movie poll taken among passengers on our plane as it approached the film capital.

Ballots handed out by the plane's stewardess showed Bette Davis, instead of Gloria Swanson of *Sunset Boulevard* fame, as the top actress of 1950.

The 1,850 members of the Academy of Motion Picture Arts and Sciences will decide this at a gala "Oscar" dinner here Thursday.

But I do not believe Miss Swanson's role of the aging actress trying for a screen comeback in *Sunset Boulevard* will be eclipsed by Miss Davis' role of an aging legitimate stage actress in *All About Eve.*

. . .

At an altitude of 18,000 feet (when this was written) one is apt to be a bit lightheaded. Here's the final word on the Oscar derby until Thursday:

—Gloria Swanson, best actress.

—William Holden, best actor.

—*All About Eve,* best picture, best screenplay and best direction.

Tennessee Williams arrived at the apartment a few minutes before eleven the morning of the Academy Awards. I took him into the library, where the engineer was setting up the microphones and the recording machine, and showed him where we would sit during the interview for my radio show. Once we were settled in comfortable chairs, the engineer switched on the wire spool and went into the next room, closing the door behind him.

The fifteen minutes flew. Mr. Williams was a gifted talker with a beautiful accent and we had lots of things in common, among them Key West. His house there was near the army base where I had lived when I was little. By the time we had said something about work habits and a few of the directors he admired and he had given a quick synopsis of his newest play, *The Rose Tattoo,* our time was up. To indicate that we were in the last two minutes, the engineer reentered the room. As I was ending the interview Mr. Williams wished me luck in the Academy Awards race.

After I had seen him to the door and thanked him for coming, I went back to the library and wound up the program with some tips about fashions and cosmetics. Then the engineer started to put the equipment away. Often I did two or three interviews in one day in order to have whole days free to read and prepare for guests I didn't know personally, but today was probably going to be full of interruptions, so I had arranged just the one, and an easy one at that. Before the engineer left to go back to the radio station, I called in my secretary so that we could go over the following week's schedule. We'd do two interviews on Monday—Paul Lukas and Lisa Kirk—and on Wednesday, my matinée day, we'd do one in the morning—Robert Stack. The engineer made notes of the times, wished me luck, and hurried out.

For an hour or so, I answered correspondence with the secretary. When I got to a long, funny letter from Clifton Webb, I reread it. He said he had been told that I was skipping one theater performance in New York and that the studio was flying me to California for the Oscars, so he wanted to get together with me. We had seen a lot of each other again when I was making *Sunset Boulevard,* and since then we had stayed in close touch. He hadn't been well for the past month, but near pneumonia hadn't dulled his tongue.

As yet I have not taken a quiet ride to Forest Lawn. But I have had one hell of a siege. . . .

Now that you are the new "Baby Wampas" star on the silver sheet, "La Reine du Théâtre," "Empress of the

Air Waves," and the "Little Princess of Publicity," will
you please saturate your beautiful body with some of
that Jergens lotion and get the hell out here. I want to
see you get your satiny little hand on that nude little
Oscar. After it is all over we can elope to that famous
Pasadena clinic and you can teach me the joys of high
colonics and fruit juices.

I wrote Clifton that I'd be back in Hollywood in July for my
next picture and see him then. While I was dictating telegrams inviting people to be on the radio show, I remembered
that I hadn't contacted Mary Pickford since she had come to
see *Twentieth Century* the week before, so I dictated one to
her too.

YOU'RE A NAUGHTY GIRL FOR NOT COMING BACKSTAGE   LOVED
YOUR WIRE THOUGH, WHICH WAS THE NEXT BEST THING TO SEEING
YOU

I laughed when the secretary read it back, because it sounded
funny to hear someone else say it.

"Do you want me to change it?" she asked uncertainly.

"No," I said sharply. "That's the way we talk to each
other."

At one-thirty I had the usual Dr. Bieler special: steamed
celery and zucchini, string beans, and two slices of toasted
homemade bread without a lot of junk in it. Then I phoned
Mother. I told her Michelle—my youngest child—would pick
her up and bring her to the theater at ten o'clock. Then the
three of us would go to the party at La Zambra together and
listen to the Academy Awards on the radio.

Ordinarily Mother would have refused to do any such
thing, but she was absolutely crazy about José Ferrer and had
accepted with alacrity when he'd invited her the week before.

"I'm wearing a dark dress, Glory," she said. "What are
you wearing?"

"A dark dress too," I said. "We'll look like twins."

"It's supposed to rain," Mother said. "And I don't think I
want to eat that late."

"Well, eat before you come, then," I said. "I'll see you at
the theater."

"All right," she said and hung up.

The manicurist came at four and did my nails. Studying my

hand, she said, "Mr. Ferrer broke another nail." She never tired of hearing me tell how Joe threw me around in the play, how we had to hiss and claw at each other like a couple of cats for two and a half solid hours eight times a week. She wished me luck when she left, and told me shyly to wish Mr. Ferrer luck too.

Michelle got back to the apartment just before I had to change and leave for the theater. The two months of study in London had been good for her, and she was all revved up about being an actress. I told her I'd send my car back from the theater for her and that she should pick up her grand-mother at ten.

At half past six the chauffeur drove me to the Fulton. It was raining lightly.

The play went well, and the people in the audience seemed determined to make this a special night. When I brandished the fake Oscar in Joe's face, they sent up a prolonged cheer, as if they wanted Norma Desmond, my character in *Sunset Boulevard*, to step out of Lily Garland, my character in *Twentieth Century*, and take a bow or do a turn. They went wild again during the curtain calls, particularly when it got down to just Joe and me, hand in hand. They all leaped to their feet and started clapping in unison, through five calls, until the house lights came up.

"I'll see you at La Zombra," Joe said as we came offstage.

In my dressing room, Michelle was reading through a pile of telegrams and Mother was sitting primly on the chaise, holding her purse on her lap with both hands. I hurried to get off my stage make-up. Then Carrie, my little maid, helped me on with a sleeveless black dress with a halter top and laid out long black kid gloves, a beaded hat with tall feathers, and a little white fur jacket. While I was doing my street make-up, Mother said, "Hurry up, Glory. We don't want to be the last ones there."

"We won't be," I said. "We have plenty of time. Carrie, where are the flowers?"

Carrie reached for a small florist's box, pulled out two red carnations, and handed them to me. I gave a white one to Michelle and asked Mother if she wanted one. She said no, so I gave a second one to Michelle.

"All right, let's go," I said. "Good night, Carrie."

"Good night, Miss Swanson. Good luck."

Carrie had bet me $50 that I would win the Oscar, but I had

somehow known in my bones from the beginning that I wouldn't, so as we went out the door I turned back and said, "I'll see you tomorrow—have your money ready."

There seemed to be double the usual number of autograph hounds in the alley in spite of the rain, but I told them I couldn't stop for any signatures at all, that I was in a terrible hurry, that they'd have to come back another night. A couple of them yelled "Happy birthday," and a few others called "Good luck," as the doorman and the stage manager held huge umbrellas over Mother and Michelle and me and walked us to where the Cadillac was parked, just in front of the theater. It was five minutes to the Spanish night club.

The place was dark and smoky and packed. Half the people there were media types with microphones or note pads in their hands or with cameras strapped around their necks. I didn't recognize anyone until a waiter led us to a table against the wall where Joe and some of his friends were seated.

"Is it all over?" I asked gaily as we sat down.

"No," a man next to me said, "they're still awarding songs and special effects and short subjects—all that stuff."

"Waiter!" Joe called, and then asked us, "Do you want something to eat?"

Mother and Michelle had eaten, and I wasn't hungry. I smoked several cigarettes and had to smile to see how contented Mother was just to be sitting at the same table as José Ferrer. Everything he said delighted her.

Beside me, a columnist wanted my mother's name for his column.

"Mrs. Woodruff," I said and spelled it.

"And that's your daughter, isn't it, Miss Swanson?"

"That's right. Michelle Farmer. Two l's in Michelle."

A second reporter chimed in: "Is your other daughter here, Gloria?"

"No, she's home with her children." Anticipating the inevitable next question, I added, "And my son is doing graduate work in California."

"Are you nervous?"

"Not in the least," I said quite truthfully. "I've been through all this before, and I don't expect to win. I couldn't pick the winners myself if you asked me to."

Intermittently people had been calling for quiet, but the din

of shouts and laughter and barmen's orders went right on.
Suddenly, however, there was a unified surge of noise and
excitement through the whole place, and someone rushed
over to our table to say that Sam Jaffee, who was in the room
and who was up for best supporting actor, had just lost out to
George Sanders. Quickly the press and radio people asked
the rest of us who were up for awards to sit together at a
well-lit table in the center of the room. Judy Holliday and I
laughed and shook hands when we got there and saw each
other. Then we sat down and Joe Ferrer sat between us.
Celeste Holm sat on my left. The radio was turned up full
now, and the broadcasting crew said that winners could make
their acceptance speeches by special hookup with the Coast if
they wished. A voice on the radio was reading the nominees
for best supporting actress. These included Celeste Holm,
who, when the winner turned out to be Josephine Hull for
Harvey, moved back to her original table, and George Cukor
came and sat next to me. We were old friends, but as the
director of *Born Yesterday* he was certainly rooting for Judy
Holliday, his star.

"What a sleazy affair," George said to me. "You can't hear
yourself think. Are you going to make a speech if you get
it?"

"Heavens no," I said, "but they pestered me right up until
three days ago for a written statement."

George smiled past me at Judy Holliday, who smiled back
nervously.

As the names of the nominees for best actor came over the
air, a hush descended on La Zambra: Louis Calhern, Jimmy
Stewart, Spencer Tracy, William Holden, and Joe. Bill
Holden was my co-star in *Sunset Boulevard* as well as Judy
Holliday's in *Born Yesterday*, but he was up for *Sunset
Boulevard*. He was brilliant in our picture, and I adored
him. But Joe was brilliant in *Cyrano* too, and I adored
him. Neither one of them could have played the other's
part. That was what was so stupid about awards and con-
tests.

Many people thought Joe Ferrer couldn't possibly win,
because he had been pointed out as a Communist sympa-
thizer in the hearings being conducted in Washington under
Senator McCarthy and had been subpoenaed to appear
before the House Un-American Activities Committee in a
month. No matter how wonderful his performance was,

people said, too many members of the Academy would vote against him just on account of that.

But to everyone's astonishment he did win. I let out a war whoop and threw my arms around him. So did Judy Holliday. The whole room stood and clapped and cheered. When announcers with mikes appeared to ask Joe if he would like to make a statement, he said he most certainly would. During his acceptance speech I could hear his real voice behind me and his radio voice coming over the air. He said he accepted the award as an act of faith and a vote of confidence, and Joe was too good an actor not to ring all the overtones out of the statement. Nevertheless, as he started to sit down again, one reporter dully asked him if he was making a political reference. "You're goddamned right I am!" Joe said. "I meant it as a rebuke to all the people who tried to affect the voting by referring to things that are (A) beside the point and (B) untrue."

And when wasn't that the case? I thought. Who, after all, were Academy members but individuals shaping careers and protecting investments? As Mr. De Mille had said so often, only the public can judge. Mr. De Mille had never got an Oscar. Neither had Erich von Stroheim. And D. W. Griffith had got only an honorary one, when his career was finished and he was too sad and bitter to enjoy it. Yet without those three, pictures would never have made it past the crawling stage.

Someone had plunked the fake Oscar from our show on the table. The photographers asked us to pose with it. First they asked Joe to sit and smile behind it while Judy and I kissed him on either cheek. Then they asked Judy and me both to reach for it, to ham it up, while Joe looked playful beside us. It was a tasteless exercise, even for the press, and Judy and I were both acutely embarrassed to go along with the galumphing horseplay, which, thank heaven, couldn't go on for long because the next fraught moment had come.

"The nominees for best actress *are:*" In a second the room was as quiet as a hospital ward. Gloria Swanson, Bette Davis, Judy Holliday, Anne Baxter, and Eleanor Parker. Now it's my turn, I thought. Every poll had said Joe couldn't win. For three months every poll had said I couldn't lose. How were the 1,850 Academy members going to surprise me?

I wondered what Bette Davis was thinking. Our paths had crossed several times before. In 1935 Warners had bought the rights to my first talking picture, *The Trespasser,* from me in order to remake it with Bette Davis.

"And the winner *is* . . . Judy *Hol*liday!"

Judy was overcome. She stood up and turned this way and that and couldn't speak. I said, "Judy, darling," and reached for her. She looked lost, as if she didn't recognize anyone. She was laughing and crying at the same time, and everyone was applauding her. Her father and her husband rushed up to her, and George Cukor went and stood beside her. We were all talking at once and a hundred flashbulbs were going off, blinding us.

I hadn't thought I would be greatly affected one way or another, and I wasn't. I knew Hollywood too well. Every year the losers all said they knew why they had lost, and the winners all said they couldn't imagine how they had won. Nobody had ever died of grief or left pictures because someone else's name was in the envelope, though. I had been through this all before, at times when winning might have been considered crucial to any other person. Both times I had shrugged and moved on. The simple truth of the matter was, I just happened to be the sort of person who couldn't be motivated by competition or prizes.

As I was about to drop anchor in this philosophical calm and smile out what remained of the evening, I realized, however, that the people around me were expecting me to react differently. Even in the people I knew there was a barely perceptible change. Joe turned and gave me a big consolation hug. Michelle came and stood protectively at my side, drying her pretty eyes at regular intervals. Judy Holliday, when she dared to look at me at all, seemed to be pleading for forgiveness.

The press was much less subtle. Even while the last awards were being announced—best director, Joe Mankiewicz; best picture, *All About Eve*—they hung around me, plainly waiting for a delayed reaction that would provide them with the story of the evening. Their questions had a certain eerie tone to them: Would you care to make a statement, Miss Swanson? What's next on your schedule, Gloria? You were nominated the very first year they gave Oscars, weren't you? You were also nominated for your first talkie, right? It slowly dawned on me that they were unconsciously asking for a bigger-than-life scene, or better still, a mad scene. More accurately, they were trying to flush out Norma Desmond. In the final analysis, from the moment Judy Holliday was announced, they had been waiting, and rather hoping, to see the *Hindenburg* go up in flames.

George Cukor broke the spell. He stepped over and took my hand. "Sorry," he said. "Look, we're going around the corner for a decent meal. Are you staying?"

"No, I'm going," I said. "I have to do my radio program in the morning."

I waved good-bye to Joe Ferrer and motioned to Mother and Michelle.

The rain had stopped. On the drive uptown my mother and my daughter were both still as stones, as if they were willing the ride to be over so that I could be alone and give vent to my anguish. I wanted to tell them they were completely off base, but I was tired and it was easier to say nothing. When we dropped Mother off, she patted my hand tenderly and said she would phone in the morning. As Michelle kissed me good night, I caught her smiling bravely. Even my family, I could see, was altered in the drama of the comeback, or, as all the papers and magazines called it invariably, the greatest comeback in the history of pictures.

After nine years of obscurity in pictures, I was in the glaring spotlight again, thanks to Billy Wilder and a brilliant script. I already had another picture and another play lined up. Five unsuccessful marriages were, thank heaven, behind me. And with Dr. Bieler's help, I looked pretty good for fifty-two. But tonight I had seen for the first time with perfect clarity that I had a huge specter in the spotlight with me. She was just about ten feet tall, and her name was Norma Desmond. During my years of obscurity, the public had forgotten Gloria Swanson. In order to spring back to them in one leap, I had had to have a bigger-than-life part. I had found it, all right. In fact, my present danger seemed to lie in the fact that I had played the part too well. I may not have got an Academy Award for it, but I had somehow convinced the world once again of that corniest of all theatrical clichés—that on very rare occasions the actor actually becomes the part. Barrymore *is* Hamlet. Garbo *is* Camille. Swanson *is* Norma Desmond.

It was a chilling thought, yet most of the scripts I had been offered since finishing *Sunset Boulevard* dealt with aging, eccentric actresses. It was Hollywood's old trick: repeat a successful formula until it dies. The problem for me was that if I had played the part at a spry fifty-one, I could obviously go on playing it in its many variations for decades to come, until at last I became some sort of creepy parody of myself, or rather, of Norma Desmond—a shadow of a shadow.

I had said at my peak in pictures that I could take them or leave them alone. Maybe it was time to say it again, while I was close to the top again, before I met another Joe Kennedy and lost everything again, or before I became the world's most dazzling, glamorous ghost. At the very least, I should have alternatives.

And what, I asked myself as I turned out the light and got into bed, might they be?

Painting?

Sculpturing?

Writing?

Dress designing?

Why not? I had come into this world with nothing at all and had risen by the age of twenty-six to the point where I could turn down a salary of one and a quarter million dollars a year. If life was that capable of change once, why couldn't it be again? Why couldn't I paint or design dresses? The only thing it was too late to become was the first thing I had ever decided to be—an opera singer.

CHAPTER 13

At twenty-six I felt myself a victim rather than a victor in the realm of pictures. Weak, run-down, confused, full of guilt and bitterness, I dreaded nothing so much as making four or five more films in rapid succession, especially in Hollywood. I missed Paris and New York and the children, and I envied all the sane, contented people who lived interesting lives in other spheres. The remainder of my contract loomed before me like a cold stone wall, and Mr. Lasky's shadow fell across me like a prison warden's. The ghosts of my past crouched around every corner. The very thought of the Hays Office and morals clauses made me ill. Not since those months right after I left Wally and Mack Sennett had I felt such sadness and frustration. Worse yet, my mood seemed almost palpable; I could sense it infecting and subjugating Henri. For a solid week the phones rang and invitations poured in, to parties, dinners, screenings, and for a week I ignored them and let Henri nurse me and indulge me. I wished I belonged to a species that hibernated naturally for long periods. I wished the whole world of motion pictures with all its sad reminders would go away.

Once again, however, the forces resident in Aries shook me awake before I could roll over into despair, just as they had done after I lost my first baby in 1916. One morning in mid-April I said angrily to myself, "Gloria, if you're going to die, die and get it over with. If not, stop making life miserable for yourself and everyone around you. Instead of moaning about the remaining pictures you have to make, make them

*F*ather and Mother and the house on 341 Grace Street, Chicago, where I was born in 1899.

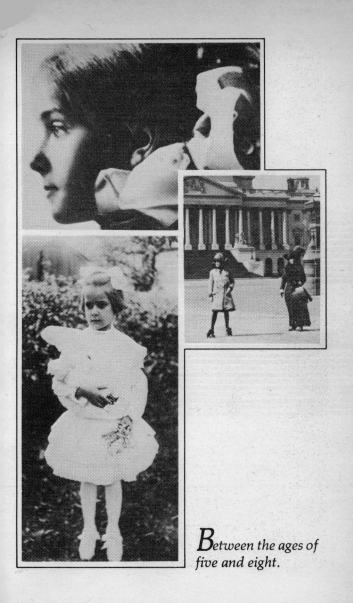

*B*etween the ages of
five and eight.

*P*uerto Rico in 1912,
with Father and Mother.

*G*uaranteed extras
at Essanay Studios,
Chicago, which I joined
in 1914.

*L*earning the
tango and
working with
Chaplin in 1914.

Wallace Beery and I elope in 1916 with Mother in tow.

Disguised as a young man in The Danger Girl, *1916.*

*O*n location with Cecil B. De Mille and in his productions of **Why Change Your Wife** *and* **Don't Change Your Husband.**

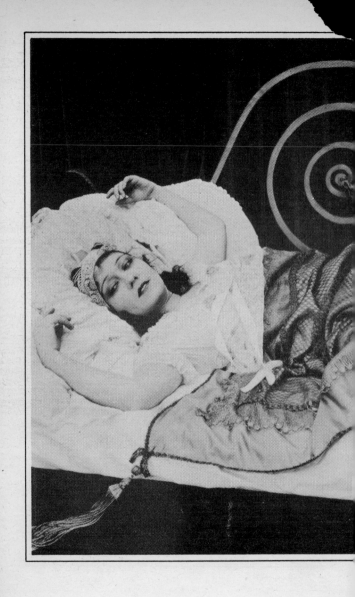

In Cecil B. DeMille's Male and Female, *1919.*

*S*etting the fashion, and an unforgettable moment in Male and Female.

At home with baby Gloria.

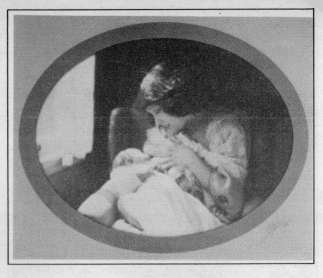

*N*ursing baby
Gloria, 1920.

*Her father,
Herbert K.
Somborn, my
second husband.*

*O*utside the studio bungalow
built for me by Famous Players-Lasky, 1920.

*I*mpersonating a
young man in the
Humming Bird, *1924*,
and riding in the
Hollywood hills.

On location with director Sam Wood.

*W*ith *Rudolph Valentino*
between takes in Beyond the Rocks, *1922.*

*With scenarist
Elinor Glyn.*

*C*ontinuing to set the fashion in Zaza, 1923, and posing with little Gloria.

Steichen's portrait, 1924.

*D*irector
Mickey Neilan.

*Impersonating
Chaplin with
Allan Dwan on
the set of*
Manhandled,
1923.

*T*he house in
Beverly Hills.

On the set with
little Gloria and
brother Joseph,
1924.

On location at Fontainebleau for
Madame Sans-Gêne, *1924.*

As the washerwoman and with my interpreter, Henri de la Falaise.

The Marquis Le Bailly de la Falaise de la Coudraye, my third husband, 1925.

My unforgettable
journey back to America,
1925.

*A*s Sadie Thompson
with director Raoul
Walsh, 1926.

sept. 12 1928

Musqueteers! ... in
Biarritz

*Joseph P. Kennedy
with Henri at Biarritz
and with Jesse Lasky at
Harvard.*

With Henri at the London premiere of The Trespasser, *1929.*

As Queen Kelly under the direction of Erich von Stroheim.

*E*dmund Goulding,
Noël Coward,
Laura Hope Crews,
and with my dog,
Ping.

Michael Farmer, my fourth husband, and Clifton Webb, 1931.

In Cannes with Michael.

My children Joseph, Michelle, and Gloria in Beverly Hills, 1934.

Laurence Olivier in Perfect Understanding, *London, 1932, including a scene with Michael Farmer.*

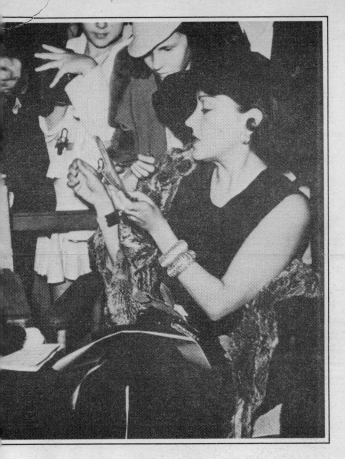

*In public with Herbert Marshall and at
my company's headquarters, New
York, 1939.*

New York, 1946, with Henri, his third wife Emmita, and Sport Ward, and in 1950 with my daughter Gloria and my first grandchild.

Dining with Michelle and Joseph and with my fifth husband, William Davey, 1945.

William Holden, Cecil B. De Mille, and impersonating Chaplin once again in Billy Wilder's Sunset Boulevard, *1949.*

José Ferrer, Mother, and Michelle on the night of the Oscars, 1951.

*O*n Broadway,
1970, and on The
Carol Burnett
Show, *1973.*

*William Dufty,
my sixth husband.*

A self-portrait in bronze, and my First-Day Cover for the United Nations Decade for Women.

and then move on. After all, you signed the contract; nobody else did. So finish what you've committed yourself to do and then do something else if you want to. But do *something.*"

In an hour I was living again, back on the horse. In fact, I got myself so fired up that first morning that I tried to do *everything* and almost had a relapse, but I recognized good old healthy exhaustion, the first I had felt in three months, and I welcomed it. I told Henri to get on the phone and make arrangements for the governess to bring the children on the train from New York right away. I wanted them with me to speed up the healing process. Then I handed Henri a stack of stiff white envelopes, all obviously invitations and all unopened, and said, "I'm sure everybody important in Hollywood is in there somewhere, all dying to be the first to entertain a real marquis. Pick out the ones you want to meet, darling, and we'll RSVP no to the rest." After that I called Allan Dwan and asked him to lunch the next day to discuss the shooting schedule for *The Coast of Folly.*

Allan studied me closely across the table and said, "You seem fine, but are you? If you don't feel well enough to start, Gloria, say so and we'll wait."

"I'm fine, Allan," I said. "The only way to get over boredom and depression is to give yourself a kick and throw yourself into work."

"All right, we'll start next week. We've lost Rod La Rocque, you know. He waited two months but finally he signed for another picture."

"I don't mind. There are too many memories in Hollywood as it is. I just want to work and get this contract behind me. I don't want to keep cranking out one picture after another. It's killing me. Instead I'd really like to concentrate on acting in this one."

"What's wrong with your acting?"

"You know what I mean. I want to grow. I want to have alternatives, options. From now on, I want to be proud of pictures I make or I want to stop making them. From now on, I want every picture I'm in to interest me. *The Coast of Folly* is a good place to start. I've never played two parts in a picture before, and the old countess will be my first real character part. From now on, I want people to judge my performance, not my personality. I don't want to belong to the public or be dictated to by the studio. I just want to do a job and do it well and have my own life when I'm through each day."

"That's the kind of talk that gives people like Lasky and Zukor heart attacks, you know. If the public likes you the way you are, that's exactly the way they want you to stay."

"Look who's talking," I said. "Who taught me to fight the studio in the first place? You and Mickey. The average career lasts five years. I've already been going for ten. It's time to enlarge or quit."

"You'll never quit," Allan said. "You can't. Not when they're on the brink of offering you the moon."

"Are they?" I asked.

"Yes, they are," he said. "Just wait."

"You know as well as I do, Allan, that the only time they offer anything is when they're scared. If it weren't for Herbert Somborn, they would still be paying me three hundred and fifty dollars a week. I can wait."

That afternoon I had a meeting with a man named Maurie Cleary who had sent messages to the Ritz every day Henri and I were in New York and who had been phoning the house every day since we'd been in Beverly Hills. He was short and lively, with a sharp beak of a nose, and he came straight to the point. He was authorized to invite me to join United Artists as soon as my contract at Famous Players-Lasky terminated in a year. As a member of UA, he told me, I would be my own producer, choose my own pictures and directors, and arrange my own schedule.

"I believe Doug Fairbanks proposed something of this sort to you about a year ago, is that correct?" Mr. Cleary asked.

"Yes, he did," I said, "but I was too busy at the time to think much about it, and since then I've remarried, as you know, so at the moment I'm quite uncertain about my future. In fact, Mr. Cleary, I have been considering leaving pictures when my contract is completed."

"Are you serious?" he asked in a startled voice.

"Yes, but perhaps not entirely. I'm serious, certainly, when I say that my husband will figure importantly in any decisions I make from now on, and the bulk of his experience is not in motion pictures. But do go on. Producing, I must say, has always interested me."

He told me that the producer-artists of UA—Doug, Mary,

Charlie Chaplin, and Mr. Griffith until his recent removal to Paramount—made no more than one or two pictures a year and so could concentrate on quality in their films. Together with Joseph Schenck, the business head of the company, they agreed that I was one of the few Hollywood stars big enough to run my own show. I would own stock in UA, but I would produce autonomously. I could ask for advice from Doug and Charlie and the others, but I would never be bound to take their advice. They would simply expect me to sign on with UA for a certain number of pictures, six probably. And now that the initial founders had run all the risks of making the company solvent, I could expect to make much more than I made working for Mr. Lasky if my pictures pleased the public and made money, which they had never failed to do.

"How soon does UA want an answer?" I asked.

"Yesterday," Mr. Cleary said with a laugh. "Seriously, Miss Swanson, we want you without reservations. When can we talk again about this?"

"In a week?" I asked. "In the meantime I can discuss the situation with my husband."

After Mr. Cleary left, I sat all alone in the study for over an hour, and for the first time in weeks and weeks I was not despondent, or merely forcing myself not to be despondent; rather, I was hopeful, almost excited, because I could see light at the end of the tunnel.

Until then I had been firmly resolved that if I was ever going to find happiness, I would have to leave pictures. Pictures had become a trap, a treadmill, a prying spotlight that glared day and night. Who could give interviews every day and have secretaries answering ten thousand fan letters a week and still have a relaxing evening out? Who could have her picture in twenty magazines every week and earn $1,000 a day and still hope to make some man a wonderful wife? Who could make four pictures a year and still find nine months to have a baby? I had long ago determined that no one could.

Furthermore, the rewards were illusory. Fame was thrilling only until it became grueling. Money was fun only until you ran out of things to buy. Hollywood abounded with the victims of both—driven creatures endlessly looking for solace or compensation in alcohol, drugs, and sex. Even Pickfair and San Simeon were, in a way, prisons. Prisons of luxury.

At twenty-six I was a victim myself. How else could I explain two marriages to men I hadn't loved or the deaths of two children I had wanted to have? Or a life style and a string of liabilities I couldn't possibly pay for except by acting in movies?

I often tried to blame these things on Mr. Sennett or on Mr. Lasky or on Mr. De Mille or on "the studio," but when you came right down to it, the villains of the movies were invisible. They were everywhere. They were sitting out there in twenty-five-cent seats in the dark just as surely as they were sitting behind the big desks on the studio lots, for wasn't it just as villainous to buy someone else's glamour as it was to sell it? In neither case did you own it; you simply tyrannized over it.

And weren't the victims villains too? Hadn't they asked for everything they got and been all too eager to get it, even if it destroyed them?

I was not out of the tunnel by any means, but I felt I was headed out at last. I felt sanguine recognizing my enemies, even if I myself was one of them.

I smiled.

If I had surrendered to the system, I thought, perhaps I could also conquer it. By ending my slavery, I might also attain my freedom. If every victory is also a defeat, I thought, then why can't every defeat also be a victory?

I would never know anything as well as I knew pictures, I reasoned, so why should I leave them if I could change the things I hated about them? For instance, I hated making four pictures a year. At UA I could make one or two a year, according to Mr. Cleary. I hated making silly formula pictures to please the studio or the public. At UA I could choose my own stories. I hated contracts and red tape and tight leashes. At UA I would make up my contract as I went along. I hated bosses. At UA I would be my own boss and the equal of the founding artists. The irony, it turned out, in view of my talk with Allan, was that it was not Mr. Lasky who could offer the moon, but UA.

After years of negotiating, I felt bitter and resentful about Mr. Lasky and Paramount and I knew I always would. Although I could understand their motives, I would never forgive their tactics. It would be healthy for me to end the association. But I didn't have to leave pictures. In fact, it would be stupid for me—Gloria Swanson—to leave pictures, and I detested stupidity in anyone. I could simply enter a new area of pictures. By ending my association with Mr. Lasky, I would be ending what I disliked about films and beginning what might be the best part of films.

Most important of all, I would be moving forward, ending something and beginning something else.

I smiled again.

Maybe every defeat is not a victory, I thought, but every end is surely a beginning. Every Aries feels that long before he or she articulates it.

I was ready to start again.

I only had to be certain that Henri had a place that suited him and pleased him in the new arrangement.

Hollywood's scramble to meet the marquis accelerated the minute we said we'd have dinner at Pickfair, and in the ensuing string of parties in our honor during the following weeks, everyone took Henri's measure and found him perfect. Elinor Glyn approved. Louella Parsons approved. Marion Davies approved. Mary Pickford approved. So did their mates and escorts. No one could resist the athletic figure of Irish and French descent whose English was so good that most people quickly called him Hank, or Henry with the English pronunciation, as I myself usually did. Henri could talk noble lineages with Doug Fairbanks and history with Charlie Chaplin, who was deeply interested in Napoleon. Mr. De Mille discussed the war with him. Mr. Zukor discussed *Madame Sans-Gêne* with him. By the time I started work on *The Coast of Folly,* I was sure Henri could work in the movie industry if he chose to or in almost anything else if he chose to. He charmed and impressed the widest variety of people the minute he met them. He also inspired people to want to include him. I abandoned my fears that he would be eclipsed by me or be cast as my satellite.

Also, he loved little Gloria and Brother. With their return, the big house in Beverly Hills sprang to life again. Gloria was four and a half; little Joseph was walking and talking. They clung to Henri and made demands on him and he thoroughly enjoyed it. He seemed to possess all the parental instincts. The dream I had had when I bought the place was materializing a bit more each day.

Meanwhile Allan Dwan managed to make *The Coast of Folly* a memorable work experience. In the story, a woman abandons her home and child for the pleasures of a snobbish, frivolous life of ease. Years later on the French Riviera, after she has become the bored, jaded Countess de Tauro, she meets her daughter, who is about to ruin her own life after the fashion of her mother, and saves her. I played both roles, and for all of the script's sentimentality, it gave me great opportunities to show my versatility. I assembled the Countess de Tauro out of bits and pieces of everyone in the genre I knew: Elinor Glyn, Fannie Ward, even a hint of Mother. Not since the days at Essanay in Chicago had I played a part so far out of my age range. I made the daughter a vigorous, athletic type, and the difference between the two creations was truly amazing. I had not stretched so far in years, and the exertion gratified me.

In a variety of wicked ways, Allan took his revenge on me for the maharaja evening in Paris. A renegade back in the city he loved to kid, he played the Hollywood game to the hilt during the shooting, and I relished helping him. One day he made everyone on the set address me in full, whenever they spoke to me, as Madame la Marquise de la Falaise de la Coudraye, and he made sure, that same day, that plenty of columnists were present to record the new Swanson image. Another day he had four footmen transport me in a sedan chair emblazoned with a coat of arms from my bungalow to the set, where an enlarged band of musicians played the "Marseillaise" and every member of the cast and crew bowed to the ground. Then when he heard that Pola Negri had complained that the noise disturbed her in her bungalow, he did it all over again the next day with double again the number of musicians, enlisted from the University of Southern California marching band. But all the time that we were pulling Hollywood's leg and letting the public in on the joke, we were also doing the industry proud with our work and we knew it. We set a pace we hadn't kept since *Manhandled*, and we both came out of it feeling years younger.

Between our shenanigans on the set and my appearances at parties with Henri, I claimed a goodly share of the Los Angeles newspaper space for a month and more. My marriage, my illness, my recovery, and my return to Hollywood had combined to send my popularity soaring. As a result, Mr. Cleary soon made a second visit to my bungalow to persuade me to sign a tentative agreement to join UA without delay. He assured me that the number of pictures demanded of me per year would be adjustable. He guaranteed me the full profit of the sale of my films after costs, plus preferred stock options and a percentage of distribution profits. He told me that Norma Talmadge and Rudolph Valentino and Sam Goldwyn were joining the company, and that Mr. Schenck also had feelers out for Ronald Colman and Vilma Banky. At UA, therefore, I would belong to the brightest galaxy of talent in the world. I told him I needed a bit of time to think over his proposal.

The papers were buzzing with UA's hopes of enlisting me as a full partner, so naturally Mr. Cleary's visit did not go unnoticed by Mr. Lasky, who arrived without fanfare on the set the following day and asked me if we could have a word in private. I had waited two years—since the surreptitious insertion of the morals clause in my contract—for the moment when I would sit down to cards with Jesse Lasky and know that I held all the high trumps. That moment had come. I was at the end of a contract, not the beginning, and I was a walking gold mine in the eyes of Paramount's shareholders. I also had a firm, enthusiastic offer from United Artists. I had absolutely nothing to fear. Furthermore, I had a score to settle.

"Is this about business, Mr. Lasky?" I asked.

"Yes," he said. "It won't take long."

"Well, I'd prefer to discuss any business at home in front of my husband. Can you come there tomorrow at three?"

He turned to ice but he didn't shift his gaze. I knew just what he wanted to say: How come you see Maurie Cleary on this set, which I built, and not me? But he couldn't say it. He could only say, "Of course, Gloria. I'll see you then."

When he arrived the next day he had two lawyers and an accountant with him. The butler showed them to the library, where Henri and I were waiting. I had told Henri to sit behind the desk in an officiating position, and I sat in a comfortable chair to his right. After Mr. Lasky and I introduced everybody, the visitors sat down and the butler served sherry. Then Mr. Lasky began.

"Gloria, we're coming to the end of seven great years. You started your first Paramount picture with Cecil B. De Mille in 1918. All that time you've been our biggest star, and Mr. Zukor and I want to keep it that way. We feel you're where you belong. I'm here today to offer you unprecedented terms."

"I'm anxious to hear them, Mr. Lasky," I said. "But first, my husband and I are very unhappy about another matter."

"Really? And what is that?"

"*Madame Sans-Gêne* and what Paramount is doing to it. Henri, why don't you explain our position in the matter."

I had prompted Henri to take over as much of this

discussion as he could, and I had pointedly begun it by introducing a subject about which he felt strongly and in regard to which Mr. Lasky could have no defense. In recent weeks Léonce Perret had sent him a string of worried letters from Paris about the cut version of *Madame Sans-Gêne* that was being shown all over the United States. In order that theater owners be able to squeeze in five shows a day instead of four, Paramount, after the premiere in California, had chopped thirty minutes out of the film, thus reducing it to a series of barely related scenes mainly of me in fabulous costumes. As a result, many of the critical reviews were bad and the French were apprehensive about the coming Paris premiere in December. They wanted guarantees that Paramount in Europe would not cut a single minute out of the French version. Mr. Osso, however, had been evasive whenever Mr. Perret approached him on the matter, so Mr. Perret had appealed to Henri to do something.

Henri explained all this in a tone of grave concern. "*Madame Sans-Gêne*, gentlemen," he concluded, "is a very important work in the hearts of the French, and during the filming they were given constant assurances that it would not be altered in the hands of foreign producers. Mr. Perret requests that Paramount send my wife and me personally to Paris to tell the French that they will see the complete Sardou play on the screen."

Mr. Lasky nodded enthusiastically. "A very good idea," he said. "You realize, of course, Marquis, that the only reason the film is cut here is because audiences get restless in the historical parts. Be that as it may, I would be delighted to have you and Gloria go to Paris as studio representatives before the premiere and tell your countrymen we won't cut a frame over there. You could function as our official, salaried, international appointee to handle the matter. Would that be agreeable to you?"

"Perfectly," Henri said.

"Then I will arrange everything," Mr. Lasky said.

"Thank you," Henri said in a pleasant mixture of satisfaction and gratitude.

Poor, dear, sweet Henri, I thought. He had fought battles in the war, but not with sharks or businessmen. Mr. Lasky had retired him from the field in a minute merely by accommodating him. He had offered him a job, and Henri had graciously accepted it, not realizing that whatever Mr. Lasky paid him, he would get back hundredfold in free

publicity if Henri and I promoted the film in Europe. Henri
was too noble in every way for Hollywood. He was not Mr.
Lasky's kind of fighter. He did not see that Mr. Lasky was
happily yielding to him in hopes of being able to put pressure
on me.

By now the room was full of nervous cigarette smoke, but
Mr. Lasky was smiling. He turned to me and said, "Gloria
—not to string this out, we're prepared to double your salary."

"Fourteen thousand a week?" I said. "Why, Mr. Lasky, for
two months all the columnists have been naming a higher
rumored figure than that."

"Has—anyone else offered you more?" Mr. Lasky asked.
He was not in a mood to be played with.

Neither was I. "United, you mean?" I replied. "They're
offering me complete artistic independence—free of extra
pictures and morals clauses, for example."

You could hear the clock tick. Mr. Lasky's voice had a
parched sound when he finally spoke, in affected good-
naturedness. "As of right now, those are both dead issues,"
he said. "Let us never mention them again."

I knew that was my cue to thank him, but I said nothing.
The clock ticked.

"Well, Gloria?" he finally said.

"My husband and I will have to discuss it."

Mr. Lasky looked at the two of us as if to say, if only I were
dealing with the husband, I wouldn't have a problem in the
world. That look annoyed me, and almost unconsciously I
picked up a pipe of Henri's that was on the desk and pointed
it like a gun at the carpet near Mr. Lasky's feet.

To Henri, Mr. Lasky said, "Write to Mr. Perret that he has
my assurances. Call me and we'll work out the details." After
a pause he said, "Gloria, I can go as high as eighteen a week.
And I'll tell you right now, I had no intention of naming such
a figure today."

I realized I was still holding the pipe in a threatening
position. Putting it down, I said to the accountant, "Is that a
million a year?"

Mr. Lasky answered for him. "Not quite."

"Well, gentlemen," I said, "let us think about this for a
week or so." With that I rose. So did they. So did Henri. The
interview was over. I was pleased to note that I was not
salivating at the thought of making a million a year. Mr.
Lasky's lawyers and accountant had said virtually nothing but

hello and good-bye, and I was sure he had had greater
expectations than that for them or he wouldn't have brought
them along. That meant I had proven stronger than Mr.
Lasky had given me credit for, and I was glad. On the other
hand, Henri had proven even more courtly and diffident in
the meeting than I had feared. He could have demanded
anything and got it in the discussion about *Madame Sans-
Gêne*. Instead he had avoided going into particulars. He has
enough nobility for the two of us, I thought with an inward
sigh.

While Allan and I shot the last of *The Coast of Folly,* we were
already at work on our next script, a funny, wistful story
about a small-town waitress who dreams of becoming a
famous actress and winds up on a showboat on the Ohio
River. We picked out a small village near Wheeling, West
Virginia, for the location scenes. Both of us were dying to get
out of Hollywood and back to New York. Henri had still not
seen the house in Croton-on-Hudson, and even I had not seen
my Manhattan penthouse completed, the work of the master
builder himself, Sport Ward. I had bought if before leaving
for Europe to make *Madame Sans-Gêne*. It was originally a
large set of servants' and utilities quarters on the top floor of
the Park Chambers Hotel at Sixth Avenue and Fifty-eighth
Street; Sport had converted them in the course of a year into
a splendid penthouse. Recently he had written that they were
ready whenever I was.

Before leaving Hollywood this time, I wanted to decide
once and for all about my future. Late in June I invited Mr.
Cleary to spell out the United Artists proposal in front of
Henri. We sat in the library. Over drinks, Mr. Cleary
explained what my situation at UA would be. He told Henri
that UA was primarily a film distribution company, owned
jointly by the founding members and any additional partners
who joined the company, of which I would be one. As an
independent partner, I would have the opportunity to buy
$100,000 worth of preferred stock in UA and so profit from all
the films the company distributed. A separate affiliated
company called Art Finance Corporation lent money to the
member artists to produce their films. Once I made a film my
only obligation was to pay back the Art Finance Corporation
loan with interest. As for the sale of the picture, I could sell it
to any distributor I chose. I was under no obligation to sell all

or any of my films to UA to distribute, even though I was a
stockholder.

From the beginning, Mr. Cleary explained, the whole point
of the company had been to allow certain sure-fire artists to
be their own producers. For that reason, the only stars UA
was interested in absorbing were those whose ongoing success
was established beyond a doubt. Why should such stars make
producers and middlemen like Mr. Lasky and Mr. Zukor
more money than they made for themselves? In six short
years in spite of temporary difficulties along the way, the
member artists had proved that there was no reason whatsoever for artists not to be their own producers. In my own
case, for instance, a Swanson picture cost no more for me to
make than for Mr. Lasky to make, so why should I not do the
organizational work and take Mr. Lasky's profit as well as my
own? And once I did that, there was no longer any need for
me to grind out four pictures a year. If I made the full profit
from my pictures instead of less than half of it, I could afford
to make only one or two pictures a year. And that, Mr.
Cleary concluded, was the ultimate reward for artists in
UA—creative freedom from studio pressure to make formula
pictures. Of course, producing meant additional work, Mr.
Cleary pointed out, but work in a field where I knew
everyone. I would need additional "hands," he said, but he
presumed my husband would be able to supply them. Family
members often made the best producing partners, he said.

As he talked he filled me with worries, for he was talking
about millions of dollars. For years I had blamed the greed in
others for everything wrong in my life. Now, before I dared
to cut the ropes and be free, I had to know if I honestly had
faith in myself. Was I real or was I the creation of a few good
directors and a few ruthless businessmen? Was I capable or
was I just intuitive and lucky? Could I run my own life? If I
couldn't, could Henri? He had a small insurance business in
Paris, but could he adapt to another kind of business? If he
could indeed be my "hands," how soon could he prove it?
And if he couldn't, would I ever have the courage to tell him
so? Mr. Cleary had just linked us in a way I had dreamed of
our being linked, but the vision made me nervous. Hand in
hand, stripped of everything but my acting talent and his
business judgment, we would have to jump into a tank of
sharks.

"You are interested in producing, I presume?" Mr. Cleary
was asking cordially.

"Oh, yes. Yes, I am," Henri said, and he smiled and took my hand.

"We're leaving for New York in three weeks, Mr. Cleary," I said. "I'll let you know definitely before then."

After he left, I said to Henri, "Do you really want to get involved in pictures?"

"Yes, but only if you want me to."

Too polite, I thought, too uncertain to battle with sharks.

"Do you want me to?" he asked.

Did I? I loved him, I knew that. And I had no one else in the whole world, I also knew that. Deep down I was terrified for both of us, but I was also furious at myself for being terrified. Could I be such a coward as to refuse the moon when it was offered, just because I didn't know if I could take responsibility for it? How could I ever know anything unless I tried? If Charlie Chaplin from the London slums could produce; if Mary Pickford with no education at all could produce—why shouldn't I try, and why shouldn't I feel confident leaning on a French marquis who wore the Croix de Guerre?

"Of course I do," I said. "I don't want to do anything without you, ever again."

My knees were shaking, though, and they all but buckled under me a few days later when Allan Dwan told me Mr. Lasky had asked him to feel me out and, if necessary, tell me he was prepared to go as high as $22,000 a week.

Way over a million.

"What would you do, Allan?" I asked.

"Take it, probably, but I know nobody will ever offer it to me. The question is, Gloria, do you really want to produce?"

"I don't know," I said. "It would be truer to say that I have come to the point in my crazy life where I think I have to. I once dived off a pier into sixty feet of water at night for Jack Conway rather than confess I couldn't swim. In some strange way, I'm on that pier again, and this time Jesse Lasky is watching me, Allan."

What I didn't tell Allan was that I couldn't go on making four formula pictures a year forever and not go stale. I was worth a million plus to the studio only until the public tired of me. Once that happened, the studio would dump me and I would be finished. Thousands of bright young things were lined up at the casting grille to replace me. No one was more aware of that than I was. I knew that I had to change or expand my image soon or face the consequences.

On July 15 I met with Mr. Cleary and signed an agreement to join United Artists and produce six pictures.

Two weeks after that, without speaking to Mr. Lasky in the interim, I boarded a train for New York with Henri and the children.

Two weeks after that, Charlie Chaplin's film *The Gold Rush* opened in New York City to a roar of applause. A founder of United Artists, Charlie made only that one picture in 1925. He took his time. He pleased himself. He listened to no one. He also probably died of insecurity a thousand times along the way. But he came up with a masterpiece—produced by Charlie Chaplin, directed by Charlie Chaplin, story by Charlie Chaplin, starring Charlie Chaplin.

If I could do just half that much: produce and star. And I probably could. After all, just ten years before, when Charlie had kicked me in the seat in Mr. Spoor's studio in Chicago, I hadn't thought he was funny and he hadn't thought I could act.

Governor Howard Gore of West Virginia declared the day we arrived in New Martinsville to start filming *Stage Struck* an official holiday, and half of the town, which numbered less than 5,000, was at the station to meet us. The mayor presented me with flowers, and the high school band played as we got into a line of cars with bunting draped over the sides and crepe paper woven into the spokes of the wheels. They paraded us and the whole crowd through the main street in the August sun, and then the little cavalcade, with the townspeople walking behind and at the sides, turned down a tree-lined street to the big old house that would be our home for the next two weeks. A large woman in a powder-blue dress seated at a piano in the middle of the front lawn played a stately processional as we walked from the cars up onto the front porch, where the mayor made another speech and I made one back. Everyone clapped and stared. Never could the residents of that sleepy little river town have witnessed a rarer group of birds on one porch: a Hollywood movie director, a French marquis, a French dress designer (René Hubert), a Mack Sennett villain (Ford Sterling), a six-foot blond siren (Gertrude Astor), and the Queen of the Screen herself, weighed down with garden flowers and looking like a dwarf beside Gertrude. Next we all filed into the house, where a group of church ladies had prepared a buffet for us in the dining room and parlor.

The days ahead in that house were awkward and funny and sometimes downright hilarious. Every hour, it seemed someone appeared at the front door to present us with a cake or a jar of pickles, and three young citizens instantly volunteered to serve as our staff for the course of our stay. The more we protested, the more they pleaded, and when we finally gave in, they showed up looking like two maids and a butler in a stock-company farce. They then hung on our every word, until more and more Henri and René resorted to speaking French, which frequently consisted of risqué remarks about the two young maids, calculated to delight the rest of us. In addition, everyone who came to call seemed so churchy and staid that we literally had to crawl on our hands and knees past the large open windows in order to smoke a cigarette for fear they would see us from the front lawn, where they often gathered to catch a glimpse of us. We were hardly proper residents of that world of church socials and ladies' clubs and the picture show on Saturday night, but we had a wonderful time. As for our servants, whom we couldn't help joking privately about, the joke finally turned out to be on us. Halfway through our stay we discovered that both of the girls who slaved for us as maids, for nothing, were university students, and that one of them was a French major.

Allan had scheduled our stay to coincide with a local fair and carnival, so we spent two busy weeks filming in houses and stores, on a paddle-wheel steamer on the river, and on the fairgrounds, where we drew much bigger crowds than the freaks in the sideshow did. Ford Sterling enchanted the kids wherever he went, and no one in New Martinsville ever seemed to tire of hearing Henri and René speak French to each other. In order to build my part I tried to study local girls in work situations, but as soon as I approached one, her jaw would go slack and she would stop what she was doing and stare at me, fascinated, so I finally had to make up the little waitress-heroine from whole cloth.

The script called for broad comedy, which I hadn't played in years. Gertrude Astor, as the star of the showboat company, and I even had a long fight scene, in which both of us wore boxing gloves and swimsuits. When I lose the fight I am so humiliated, and so fearful I have lost my beau as well, that I attempt suicide by plunging into the Ohio River, but I am foiled by the elastic in my bloomers. A hundred townspeople stood on the riverbank and roared when we shot it. Ford Sterling played the manager of the showboat company and Larry Gray played my all-American boyfriend and fellow worker in the restaurant, and together under Allan's direction we achieved moments even Buster Keaton could have been proud of.

Then the whole town saw us off and we headed back to New York. Allan had decided to shoot the major dream sequence there—in which I imagine myself as Salome—in color. The first experimental film in color had been shown in New York three years earlier, in 1922, but no one had yet tried color in a popular Hollywood-type picture. It worked perfectly, and when we watched the rushes I knew the picture would cause a sensation. Once again Allan had proved himself the great innovator.

The day we finished shooting, Henri and I started packing for Paris. Even though I had signed up with UA, Mr. Lasky had not released Henri or canceled our trip. During our last week in New York I invited Allan for dinner so that he could see the new penthouse—the $100,000 bungalow in the sky, as the papers had referred to it. Allan admired Sport's handi-work in one room after another, and then we sat down to eat. As Henri was pouring the wine Allan said, "I heard from Jesse Lasky today. He wants me to recommend someone to direct your next picture."

"Really?" I asked. "Is that to punish me?"

Allan was silent. "I'm going to suggest Frank Tuttle," he said at last.

"Frank Tuttle's a writer," I said. "I haven't seen him since we all went to Havana with Jane West."

"Well, he's a director now," Allan said, "and he doesn't want to leave New York, so I think he's your best bet."

"All right, if you say so. It's infuriating, isn't it?" I added.

"At least we got to do *Stage Struck*," Allan said after another pause.

"And *Zaza* and *Manhandled*," I said.

"That's right," Allan said, raising his wineglass. "We did a lot for Paramount from Manhattan to New Martinsville, in black-and-white and color. Let's drink to us, Gloria."

We had spent our first honeymoon in Paris in a hospital room. This one we spent mostly traveling around France, mainly on the Côte d'Azur and often in the company of André Daven.

Everywhere we went we gave interviewers Paramount's word that the long-awaited French version of *Madame Sans-Gêne* would not be cut or altered. The press praised Henri for this and referred to me over and over again as "the Franco-American star." In every city we visited, crowds cheered and theater owners showed my pictures, with titles, of course, in French: *Bluebeard's Eighth Wife* was literally *La Huitième Femme de Barbe-Bleue,* but *A Society Scandal* was *Scandale!*; *Manhandled* was *La Tricheuse; The Humming Bird* was *Les Loups de Montmartre;* and *Her Love Story* was *Les Larmes de la Reine* ("The Queen's Tears").

This last film was playing at the Salle Marivaux on the Boulevard des Italiens when we got to Paris, and the Paramount office called to tell us to go and take a look at the theater because it was where *The Gold Rush* would play next, and *Madame Sans-Gêne* after that. I had always thought that *Her Love Story* could never move anyone. It was the kind of silly costume picture I was a bit embarrassed to make. But the advertisement for it outside the theater seemed to shake the ground under me and confront me with the fire of truth itself. To dramatize the dilemma of the Balkan ruler in the story, it showed a gigantic throne against a backdrop of purple velvet. Before the throne was a huge question mark, and over the throne was an enormous set of scales, driven by a motor so that it was in constant teetery motion. On one scale rested a jeweled crown and on the other lay a baby. The message was clear. Your throne or your baby? I had such a violent reaction when I saw it towering over me that I almost fainted. Henri rushed me back to the hotel, where I wept for hours. Only three people in the world could have read the message on the billboard as I had—Henri, André, and I—but that was no consolation. The jolt had gone clear through me. I could still feel it two days later, when André called to say the picture had closed and the sign was down.

Paris seemed to be jinxed again for us a few days after that. One after the other, two stories broke in America that made us the prey of the French press. First, some American paper had stupidly reported that Gloria Swanson's husband was not a real marquis—that his title was a fiction created by the studio. This confusion probably arose out of the simple fact that Henri, because he was not a U.S. citizen, had to return periodically to France in order to have his visitor's permit renewed. In fact, that was one of the things he had to arrange for in Paris during this trip. Nevertheless, papers all over the

States had picked up the phony nobility story, and indignant letters were pouring into Paramount by the thousands. The publicity department called Mr. Osso. Mr. Osso called us. We called André, who quickly arranged a large press conference at which Henri presented his credentials, which went back in the records office in Rouen to 1271. The French press cheered him, and reporters all over America printed apologies. But it was an aggravation.

Next a story spread that I would be fined or jailed for ignoring a subpoena. Just before Henri and I left New York, the wife of Dr. Richard Hoffman, a friend from my Sunday-salon days in New York, had had me subpoenaed as a witness in her divorce suit, which I had ignored. I had never even opened the subpoena. Richard Hoffman was a brilliant, wealthy psychiatrist who had attained considerable notoriety in the Leopold-Loeb murder trial the year before. I had not seen him in over a year, and I had never met his wife. In a court battle over custody of a child, Mrs. Hoffman was obviously attempting to damage his character. The situation was all too familiar to Hollywood stars. I had been named in innumerable lawsuits involving people I didn't know, usually because a wife discovered a picture of me in her husband's wallet. In this case I refused to make a statement to the press, and evidently Mrs. Hoffman's lawyer advised her to drop the issue because in the end I was never called to court. In fact, all that happened was that the press rallied around me and showered me with praise for my good sense and fortitude.

I could not tell whether it was in spite of these happy-ending scandals or because of them that Mr. Lasky forwarded one last offer to me via the Paramount office in Paris. He said he would match any arrangement I had made with United Artists if I would stay with Paramount. He also offered me a share of distribution profits of all my pictures at Paramount. He even offered Henri a permanent position in charge of distribution of all Swanson films in France. I told the Paramount office that it was too late; I was firmly contracted to UA.

When Henri and I returned to New York in October, we were heroes once again. We had defended the honor of France against Hollywood. We had also defended Henri's nobility and my decency. The time seemed right to hint to the press that I was soon to become an independent producer and that my husband would control many of my business interests, such as distribution of my films in Europe.

In expectation of being my business partner, Henri opened an office in New York that fall. The press mistakenly took him for my agent, so from the day he moved in, he was deluged with scripts for me to read and with requests for interviews. Until I finished my last two pictures for Paramount, his role could not be clear. We both knew that. But at least he could begin to see a few of the problems of being a star-producer.

The happiest result of our trip was the tumultuous reception of the full-length *Madame Sans-Gêne* in Paris in December. André Daven sent us every single review, and aside from the predictable carping made by certain reviewers that the leading role should rightfully have been played by a Frenchwoman, the picture was a huge success. *Action Française* described the opening-night audience as one of the most enthusiastic in memory. *Paris-Soir* called the film adaptation "absolute perfection." Léonce Perret was in seventh heaven.

Henri translated all the reviews and articles aloud for me. The author of one magazine piece had questioned certain members of the premiere audience when the picture was over. When asked what Réjane, the actress for whom the role had been written, would have done if she were present, Jacques Porel had replied, "She would have joined in the applause."

"Does that please you?" Henri asked.

"I don't know," I replied. "Who's Jacques Porel?"

"Réjane's son," he said.

I had no sooner started *Untamed Lady* with Frank Tuttle than I was informed that my last Paramount picture would be directed by Richard Rosson, who had up until then been Allan Dwan's assistant. There could no longer be any doubt that even if I was not being punished by Mr. Lasky, at least the studio had reverted to the old formula of one egg per basket—in this case, me. They obviously intended to make as much money as possible off my last two pictures by eliminating any other large expenses: no co-stars, no big directors, no expensive stories, no large casts. My initial reaction to such stinginess was to breeze through the two films without any undue effort and be done with it, but I found that I couldn't do that. For one thing, Allan and I had cranked each other up to such a high pitch of professionalism in our last two pictures together that there was no way I could walk through a picture again—if I ever had. For another thing, I decided that if the studio was determined to throw me into rote parts in my last two films for them, I would take all the extra energy I might have used in more demanding roles and devote it to learning how to make pictures. In other words, I would turn Paramount into my producing school if I could.

Untamed Lady was based on a thin Fannie Hurst story about a spoiled rich girl who almost ruins her life with her willfulness but who is rescued before it is too late by a young man who truly loves her in spite of her faults. Larry Gray, who had played my beau in *Stage Struck,* played the young man, and we got on wonderfully together.

I had not seen Frank Tuttle in nearly two years, and this picture was an early directing experience for him. Out of insecurity, therefore, he pretended to be utterly confident at all times, the dapper Ivy League type who always had the answer ready before the question was asked. Exasperated by that posture, I went over his head ten times a day. I redirected scenes, asked the cameraman how he would shoot certain sequences, made changes in the script, and consulted with all the technicians. In two weeks I learned more about producing than I had bothered to find out in the last ten years, and I had been on sets long enough to know that the picture was the better for my impositions.

Frank Tuttle certainly grew to doubt that in the course of the shooting, particularly in one instance, where I must have seemed more willful than the girl in the script. We shot much of the picture at a fancy country club in Pinehurst, North Carolina, because the script called for me to ride horseback. I told everyone how eagerly I was looking forward to the riding scenes, and I made the grooms at the stable show me a dozen horses before I picked one that suited me. After ten minutes in the saddle, however, I stopped the horse in its tracks, dismounted, and walked it back to the corral. I told Frank Tuttle we would have to write out any actual riding scenes because I could not go through with them. He did not ask me why, and I did not tell him, but I had had the clearest premonition of tragedy as I rode, a voiceless warning that I must never ride again. I knew that Henri's father had died after a riding accident, but the feeling I had had admitted of no such logical connection. It was a command of terrifying force, and as explicit as the vision I had experienced on Santa Cruz during the filming of *Male and Female.* I couldn't dream of ignoring it. Moreover, I knew that nothing would ever induce me to ride again.

I was then ready for my last Lasky assignment. This, my last Paramount picture, entitled *Fine Manners*, was about a wealthy gentleman infatuated with a girl who works in burlesque. He persuades his aunt, a formidable socialite, to educate the girl to a life of wealth and refinement, but when her education is completed, he finds he liked her better as she was. Richard Rosson turned out to be a delightful surprise. Since he had learned his directing from Allan, he was a superb technician. He had also been present at the famous maharaja dinner party in Paris before my marriage, so we knew we could have fun together at the studio in Astoria. In addition, he was a bright, creative person. If he wasn't an Allan Dwan yet, he was on the way.

Eugene O'Brien was my leading man, and Helen Dunbar was cast in the role of the dowager aunt. Helen Dunbar. She had been there when the egg cracked open and I emerged. The first day I ever wept buckets on cue, at Essanay in 1915, Helen Dunbar had said to me, "You know, young lady, one day you'll be a good actress," and I replied, to my everlasting shame, "Yes, I know. I'm going to be very famous." We had worked together several times since, but we had never again discussed my acting ability or my fame, and we didn't now. We didn't have to. We were two old pros in *Fine Manners*, and both pretty good.

When Mary and Doug and Charlie Chaplin and D. W. Griffith formed United Artists in 1919, someone said jokingly that the lunatics had taken over the asylum. In spite of setbacks and intramural squabbles, the company had grown, and with the appointment in 1925 of Joseph Schenck as president and chairman of the board, UA acquired a tough, aggressive executive who was out to make millions and who knew the business of financing and distributing movies inside out.

In my talks with Maurie Cleary a year before, I had naïvely imagined that being one of the select "united artists" would mean board meetings over coffee on the terrace of Pickfair and help in a jiffy if I should ever need it. I soon learned that what it really meant was trying to hold my own in long, grueling business sessions in New York with Joe Schenck and a shrewd gang of lawyers, accountants, and bankers. Joseph Schenck, a squat, homely man who looked like a secondhand-furniture salesman and who had risen from the bottom of the movie business to marry Norma Talmadge and become head of UA, knew more about the underside of corporate success than I could learn in a lifetime. It was he who had lent me his house on Long Island in 1923, through Allan Dwan, and every time we were together now I remembered a story Allan had told me then. Allan had directed Norma Talmadge in several pictures and had also introduced her to Joe Schenck when Schenck was in charge of booking pictures for Marcus Loew's theater chain. One morning Norma arrived late on the set, and because it was unlike her not to be prompt, Allan asked her if anything was the matter. Norma told him a terrible thing had happened to her on the way to work. "I married Joe Schenck," she said.

For me Joe Schenck turned out to be a worthy adversary and a masterly teacher. Being twenty-seven and a woman, and three thousand miles from my fellow united artists, I had to learn fast or go under. In addition, within a month I saw clearly what I had refused to face earlier: Henri could be of no help whatsoever at a bargaining table. Diffident and trusting by nature, a war hero saturated with honor and dignity and French good taste, he was no match for the men Joe Schenck brought around to negotiate loans and contracts. We soon established that Henri could concentrate solely on the foreign translation and distribution of my films, when that time came. In the meantime, I had to trust and fear Joe Schenck all alone. When things got too tough for me, I would say to him, "Look, do you want me to succeed or to fail? Because if you want me to succeed, then you'd better help me understand what I'm doing."

Joe Schenck advised me to make my first film in Hollywood but I wanted to stay in New York. Preliminaries took months. Before Art Finance Corporation (which was absorbed into Art Cinema before the year was out) could finance my picture, it needed collateral on which it could borrow money from the Bank of America to lend to me. It therefore required me to take out over a million dollars' worth of life insurance to protect its investment in case anything happened to me. Joe Schenck warned me to beware of the doctor I chose to examine me because doctors in such cases were often thoroughly unethical, ready either to diagnose an ailment they knew the examinee would pay them to conceal or to charge for passing over an ailment that would prevent the

examinee from obtaining the insurance policy. After the
examination the insurance company refused to take my word
for my age, so my mother and Grandma Lew had to travel
from California and vouch for me. Then, before I could set up
a company, I needed a board of directors, and since Henri
was not a citizen, Mother had to sign on—most reluctantly—
as an officer of Gloria Swanson Productions, Inc.

I soon understood that as a producer I could never expect
to do anything simply again. In order to rent a studio that
William Randolph Hearst had built in Harlem so that Marion
Davies could make films on the East Coast when she wanted
to, I couldn't just pick up the phone and call Marion and say,
"Will you do me a favor and rent me the Cosmopolitan
Studios for two months?" Instead my lawyer, after contacting
several studio rental agencies to see if Cosmopolitan was a
good deal, had to call Mr. Hearst's lawyers to settle on a sum
and to arrange for special fire insurance and workmen's
permits and labor contracts, which in turn called for the
services of three or four more lawyers. It took three exhausting months from dawn to dusk to set up the company,
negotiate loans, and rent studio space.

By mid-July 1926, when that much was behind me, I was
only just beginning to be aware of the greatest difficulty of all.
Movies, for the first time in their short history, were in a
serious crisis at the box office, owing to the recent phenomenal growth of radio. Broadcasters were sending out variety
programs three and four hours long, and in one year Americans spent $500 million on radio sets and parts. The only
solution, everyone in the movie industry agreed, was to make
better films and build more glamorous theaters to show them
in and hope that the radio craze was temporary.

For me, it was too late to turn back. I had to spend the
money I had borrowed and make the best film I could make.
What that film would be, I was slow to decide, and while I
worried about it, everyone I knew confused and worried me
more by offering advice and suggestions. I finally decided not
to try anything too adventurous on my maiden producing
venture. Three months of talk about costs and distribution
patterns and opinion polls had left me with little courage to
be rashly experimental. Rather, I settled for the kind of film I
was sure I could make well and that audiences had never
failed to respond to: a romantic story with several handsome
leading men and a variety of love scenes and a wardrobe of

dazzling creations. Just the kind of picture I blamed Mr. Lasky for making, I realized; but I was scared, and I convinced myself that I would improve on the formula, at least, or never make another picture.

Late in July I acquired the rights to a 1917 play called *Eyes of Youth*, which had made a star of Marjorie Rambeau. That was the play Clara Kimball Young had made a film version of in 1919, featuring Rudy Valentino, and I well remembered Herbert screening it for Bea La Plante and me shortly before I married him. But remakes of good stories were very common, and seven years was a long time. I hired a writer named Earle Browne to adapt it for a new screen version. The story opens with a prologue in which a Roman maiden flings herself into a flaming abyss rather than submit to an Egyptian brute. Then the story shifts to the present time, and the maiden is a modern woman indecisive about which man in her life she should choose for a husband. The Egyptian reappears as a magician, and in order to atone for the crime he committed thousands of years before, he allows the heroine to see the future in a crystal ball. In fact, he shows her all three of her possible futures, and she chooses the one that will make her happy.

I wanted a good director, but most of the ones I knew, like Allan Dwan, were under contract and so were either not available or too expensive to buy away from the studios. At last I chose Albert Parker, who had directed me in *Shifting Sands* and *The Secret Code* at Triangle, and who had also taken a black eye from Wallace Beery that day long ago in 1918. He was an amusing, gifted man who was scheduled to direct Doug Fairbanks's next picture and who, which was more important for me, had directed the original screen version of *Eyes of Youth* with Clara Kimball Young. That meant he knew the work well and would want to top himself a second time around. His lawyer insisted on a two-picture deal for the price of $100,000, and although that seemed terribly steep, I felt I needed a director this first time out whom I liked and trusted. Moreover, I remembered Mary Pickford's formula for survival as an independent producer: Find the best people, pay them well, and keep them under contract. "Sign him up," I told my lawyer.

Then Albert and I spent weeks casting the picture. I recommended Ian Keith, whom I had worked with, for one role, and Albert suggested an English actor named Hugh

Miller for another. We also cast Andres de Segurola, the former Metropolitan Opera star, and Pauline Garon, the woman Cecil B. De Mille had once ordered to a screening room to study my acting, according to Aileen Pringle. We picked Raymond Hackett for my brother, and gave Flobelle Fairbanks, a niece of Doug and Mary's, a bit part in her first film. All we needed was a leading man and I was determined to introduce someone who had not been in pictures before. That's what every producer and director always tried to do—find talent—and it would be a great coup if I could discover someone in my first production. I started going to the theater night after night, until I spotted a man named John Boles singing in a Broadway show called *Kitty's Kisses*. He was tall, handsome, and more exciting then Milton Sills, and he could act and sing, so I went backstage to talk to him. He was a refined Southern gentleman with a beautiful accent, and his enthusiasm at the thought of making a motion picture promised that he would be willing to work his head off to compensate for his lack of experience. Up close, his ears seemed to stick out, but I knew they could be held down with tape. Three days later I signed him to a contract.

I went over the script with René Hubert and told him I was counting on him to turn the world of fashion upside down and set America on fire with a barrage of fantastic gowns. "We have to dazzle them," I said. "I know you won't disappoint me."

Before we went into production I had a call from S. L. Rothafel, the Sid Grauman of the East Coast, better known as Roxy, who was then constructing the Roxy Theatre at Seventh Avenue and Fiftieth Street, the ultimate movie palace, the "cathedral of the motion picture," as he called it. It would open in March, he said, and he wanted my first production to be his initial offering. He told me he would see to it that the premiere would be remembered forever as the biggest night in movie history.

"Is it a deal?" Roxy asked.

"Absolutely," I said.

Then he asked me to visit the construction site that week and sign my name in huge letters on the gold-leaf dome. When I left the site, I trembled at what I had done. I had borrowed over $200,000 and promised a picture for the spring to the greatest showman in America for the biggest opening night in the history of New York, and so far I had not one foot of film to back me up. At least, though, I thought, swallowing with difficulty, I had a deadline.

In July, Henri's visitor's visa was up once more, and he had to return to France to have it renewed. I saw him off on the ship, where we ran into Rudy Valentino, who was seeing his brother off. Rudy was in New York for the opening of *The Son of the Sheik,* his second film to be released by United Artists. We had come a long way since *Beyond the Rocks.* His marriage to Natacha had ended in divorce, and my romance with Mickey Neilan was long dead. We chatted for a while, but we were both preoccupied with our own farewells.

Henri returned on the *Olympia* on August 19, and because he could not disembark until he was cleared by immigration, I was allowed to spend the night in his stateroom with him. He asked me about Rudy because for three days the papers had been full of reports of Valentino's collapse as the result of a ruptured appendix and a perforated ulcer. I told him the papers said he was much better. Then, on August 23, Rudy died. His death enraged me and his funeral sickened me. A month before his death his physician in Hollywood had examined him and said he was in perfect shape, and up to the very end his doctors in New York were broadcasting encouraging reports about his recovery while they kept him sedated and flat on his back. People lined up for ten blocks to file past his corpse, and mobs of women in the street in front of Campbell's funeral parlor screamed and tore their hair. Pola Negri took center stage and claimed to be the only woman Valentino had ever loved.

He haunted me for weeks. Dead at thirty-one, of success and pressure and medical negligence. When I had had the premonition about riding in North Carolina, I was holding the riding crop he had given me five years before, and I had almost called him then, because I had been worried about him as well as myself. I regretted that I hadn't. His ghost stirred beside me every day for the next three months too, because the first thing we had ever discussed at length, Rudy and I, was *Eyes of Youth.*

We began shooting in early September. Although *Eyes of Youth* was my fifty-second featured film, it was the first one I had ever produced, and it was not a simple picture to make. The plot was really four plots, seen in a crystal ball, so the film called for lots of dramatic climaxes and lots of special effects and trick photography. Dudley Murphy, in charge of these effects, was, I discovered, not an engineer like Allan Dwan. On the contrary, he foundered at each technical problem, and soon we were running behind schedule in a rented studio with an unfamiliar crew. Bills mounted, and I was so busy trying to cope with the mechanics of producing that I had to steal time to prepare my role. Moreover, Flobelle Fairbanks and John Boles needed special attention because they had never acted in front of a camera before. I panicked at the thought that I might fail in the dramatic as well as the technical aspects of this picture and be a laughing-stock. I began working sixteen- and eighteen-hour days, and the only results seemed to be more delays and second-rate effects. "Do it over," I would say with control to Albert Parker and the crew while screaming hysterically to myself, "You turned down one and a quarter million dollars a year for this misery, do you realize that, you idiot!"

Suddenly, however, just as I felt I was about to go totally mad, someone recommended a strange Russian refugee to help Murphy with the special effects. His name was George de Bothezat, and he was an engineer and inventor. He had been working for years on a design for an aircraft that would take off vertically, he told me modestly, and I later learned that he was considered a great pioneer in aeronautics. I turned over all the technical problems to him, and he immediately came up with brilliant, unconventional solutions. He had never worked in pictures before, so he had no idea what was considered impossible and what wasn't. He just went ahead and did everything. From the day he arrived I lost the smell of fear and defeat, and Albert and I started at last to concentrate wholeheartedly on the dramatic structure of the picture.

By November we were running over budget as well as behind schedule, but I borrowed more money and we finally finished shooting in early December. At that point I was too exhausted to do anything but call a break. Henri and I took the children to Croton-on-Hudson and had a long, peaceful Christmas. In January we started editing and titling, and Henri began working on the French titles for the European version. In February we screened the first rough print for a small group of friends, who made a million suggestions for small changes I knew there was no time to make. Then Albert and I finished the editing and turned our attention to the last big problem: the title. From the start nobody had liked the sound of *Eyes of Youth*. I wanted to call it *The Secret of Life*, but everyone said that sounded like a biology textbook. In the end we submitted a list of titles to Roxy, and he picked *The Love of Sunya* and I said fine.

I was not satisfied with the picture. I knew it could be better. But it was certainly not bad. It had many good things in it, I told myself, and after all, a deadline was a deadline. We had done our best. I had learned a lot. I would know how to avoid the same mistakes in my next five pictures, I was convinced, and if I had to go back to Hollywood to make good pictures, well, I said to myself, I would do it.

I was hooked. I was thinking like a producer.

A few weeks before the opening of the Roxy, I happened to be in the apartment alone one afternoon after a business conference. Henri was out, and the governess had not brought the children back from the park. I turned on the radio and sank into a sofa in the living room. After a minute I felt like a hot cup of tea, so I got up and rang for the butler. While I waited for him to appear, I fiddled with the radio dial to get some music. He didn't come, so I rang again, and when he didn't appear that time, I walked to the pantry to look at the indicator on the wall. The indicator was working, but the kitchen was empty. The butler was out. So were the cook and maid. So was the secretary. I forgot all about the tea and went back to the living room to do something about the radio, which was emitting the most awful static sounds. I reflected on something I had read—that sound travels across great distances on waves. Suddenly it occurred to me that the indicator in the pantry was adequate as a signal only if the butler was right there to see it drop. But what if he was in another part of the large apartment or in the basement? He wouldn't get my message until he came back to the pantry and looked at the indicator on the wall. So, I thought, what if the indicator could send out sound waves? And what if each of the servants wore a little gadget on his lapel to receive the waves? In the form of little beeps. One beep for the butler. Two beeps for the maid. A long and a short for the secretary. A sort of Morse code.

Then I thought that if such a contraption would be useful in a penthouse, it would be an absolute godsend in a studio or a big house like the one in Beverly Hills. I was beside myself with excitement. I had invented something! Or at least I thought I had. In any case, once again I felt myself using muscles I had never used before, and moreover, I felt a mysterious certainty about what I was thinking.

I dug out Mr. Bothezat's number and phoned him. Did it sound crazy? I asked. Was it something he could get down on paper for me? Was it something that would work? When he didn't discourage me, I began naming ways I thought it might be used. I had only three or four servants, I said, but Mayor Jimmy Walker, for instance, had thousands of firemen, policemen, civil servants. Crews building skyscrapers had no easy way of communicating except for a few phones. Did a portable device sound possible? I asked.

Mr. Bothezat said it sounded like a remarkable idea. The next day we talked some more, and he said he would make drawings and that I should hire a patent lawyer to protect the idea. He told me not to be discouraged if my invention didn't take shape right away. He had patented all his aircraft designs, even though as yet no plane with an overhead propeller was actually in the sky.

"I'm sure," I told him, "all of this rubbed off on me from watching you in the studio. But the combination of the radio dial and the missing butler made me leap to a solution—just like that. Is that crazy?"

"Not in the least," he said in his heavy accent. "That is inventing."

The Roxy, which seated 6,214 people and cost $10 million to build, opened on March 11, 1927. First-night tickets sold for $11, and scalpers in the last days before the opening were getting five times that. Nothing had so captured the imagination of New Yorkers since—according to which paper you read—the opening of the Brooklyn Bridge (which had cost $1 million less to build than the Roxy) in 1883 or the presentation of Jenny Lind at Castle Garden by P. T. Barnum in 1850.

René Hubert had designed a marvelous black evening dress for me, and I wore my hair lacquered down flat against my head the way I wore it in several long sequences in *The Love of Sunya*. A limousine arrived for Henri and me at seven-thirty, and the short drive from Sixth Avenue and Fifty-eighth Street to the theater at Seventh Avenue and

Fiftieth Street—ordinarily less than five minutes by car—took half an hour, owing to the traffic congestion caused by the sea of people that had been building up around the theater since late afternoon. Policemen on horseback spotted our car and slowly cleared the way for us. The driver told Henri that Mayor Walker had put a hundred extra cops on just for the opening and that the cops had told him that the crowd in the street numbered well over ten thousand.

When we pulled up under the marquee and got out of the car, a tremendous roar went up. In the blinding glare of a double row of klieg lights trained on the shiny new building, I turned and waved, and before I could turn back again and enter the theater, an unstoppable wave of people surged forward and almost knocked us over. In spite of the efforts of the police, we had to fight our way into the lobby in order not to be crushed against the closed doors and walls.

Inside the monumental foyer, in front of an inclined bank of red and white carnations that spelled out his name, Roxy stood with his family, being photographed with celebrities. Henri and I joined them to kiss and shake hands with the people we knew in a steady blaze of flash powder. Roxy had pulled out all the stops. The parade of notables included four U.S. senators, three U.S. generals, three consul generals, two borough presidents, the governor of New Jersey, and the minister of Lithuania, as well as Adolph Ochs, Mrs. Otto Kahn, and Mr. and Mrs. Jimmy Walker. The crowd almost broke down the doors when Charlie Chaplin tried to sneak in unnoticed, and they went wild again when they recognized Harold Lloyd and his wife. We stood there for twenty minutes and greeted an endless stream of people with engraved invitations: the Shuberts, Irving Berlin, Lois Wilson, Sport Ward, Hope Hampton, Tommy Meighan, Joe Schenck, Walter Wanger, Will Hays—even Jesse Lasky. Then we all took our seats down front in the great auditorium, and the show began.

After a short concert played on three organs, an actor read a solemn invocation, ending with: "Let ev'ry day's toil be forgotten under thy sheltering roof, oh glorious, mighty hall; thy magic and charm unite us all to worship at beauty's throne." Then the hundred-piece Roxy Symphony Orchestra led by four conductors played a tone poem to a pageant onstage depicting the writing of "The Star-Spangled Banner," at the end of which a glowing orange sky of dim stars slowly metamorphosed into the Stars and Stripes. Next the forty-member Roxy Ballet Corps performed a floral fantasy, and the prima ballerina, Maria Gambarelli, made famous to large audiences all over America by Roxy as Gamby, brought the house down as the Fairy.

Filmed greetings from President Calvin Coolidge, Mayor Walker, Vice President Charles G. Dawes, and Thomas Alva Edison, with printed titles, appeared on the enormous screen. Then came a medley of Southern songs performed by the Roxy Chorus and Ensemble, with pictures of magnolias and cotton fields projected on a special transparent screen. After that there was a newsreel. Then Gladys Rice and Douglas Stanbury, backed by the Roxy Chorus, sang "A Russian Lullaby," written for the opening of the Roxy by Irving Berlin. Next there was a demonstration of Vitaphone, a filmed performance with sound of selections from *Carmen* performed by Giovanni Martinelli and Jeanne Gordon. The sound was tinny and distant and unreal, a bit on the order of voices as they sounded on the radio. Then an actor read a prologue written especially for my film, a giant organ began to play, and the house lights dimmed for *The Love of Sunya*.

For the first time ever, there were no titles to introduce a picture. The story started immediately, and a thin mist concealed the edges of the screen and seemed to float the opening sequence, set in ancient Rome. Thanks to Mr. Bothezat's inventiveness, all the special effects looked spectacular, and the audience actually applauded when I appeared in a number of René Hubert's creations, particularly a dark sleeveless gown with jeweled straps and matching Art Deco jewelry. At the end of the picture the audience stood and cheered for five minutes, and Henri and I held hands and I almost burst with joy.

The first-night program ended at twelve-thirty. The next morning stacks of telegrams arrived, and the New York critics were wildly enthusiastic, about the picture as well as about the "cathedral of the motion picture." Harriette Underhill in her review alone swept all my fears of failure away.

For the opening program Sam Rothafel chose Gloria Swanson's first United Artists' picture, *The Love of Sunya*. This is a screen version of *Eyes of Youth*. We had feared that we weren't going to care for the picture, and we ardently desired to do so. This fear, we know now, was founded on the fact that *Eyes of Youth* was an exceedingly interesting play. Invariably, we find that if one enjoys a play one is woefully disappointed in the screen transcription.

However, the picture had not been on the screen five minutes before we entirely forgot the play. *The Love of Sunya* is so engrossing that one hasn't a chance to think of other things. It is a superb picture. Also, Miss Swanson does more whole-souled and convincing acting than ever we have seen her do in all the years we have admired her.

Furthermore, we never had any idea that she was so beautiful. In the episode where she is the love as well as the business partner of the great impresario, so dazzling is Miss Swanson that words fail one. However, we decided the only way to describe her is to say she is at least three Greta Garbos, and let it go at that.

No review of *The Love of Sunya* is complete without reference to the exquisite composition and the fine direction. Scene after scene is of such beauty that it leaves you gasping as it hurries on.

Dudly Murphy has furnished the mechanical devices which produce the weird effects of the soul being wafted from the land of reality to the crystal land of the future. They are impressive as well as beautiful. We've never seen such things so well done before.

And the cast is perfect. John Boles, who plays the lover, never has been on the screen before. Every one was saying, "He's beautiful, but has he It?"

Well, he has! . . .

Sunya had taken me nine months to make instead of six weeks, and I could find many more faults in it than all the critics put together ever would, but it was not a failure or an embarrassment even for me in my most self-deprecating mood. For one thing, I felt I had made René's fortune from now on as a designer. I had also unquestionably launched John Boles as a star. And as far as my own performance was concerned, all the critics agreed that I had out-Swansoned Swanson. There was life in the old girl yet. I was out of the tunnel.

Only two people might have been unhappy with Harriette Underhill's review: Greta Garbo, another Swede, who at twenty-one was just starting her career in Hollywood and who would surely never read the review anyway, and Jesse Lasky.

CHAPTER 14

The Gloria Swanson picture that opened in Roxy's theatre the other night may have rented in that theatre for $50,000 for ten days, but nine months from now it will rent in Oshkosh or somewhere else for $7.50. . . . You are always running a race with the calendar. . . .

The motion picture industry has attained a standing and a volume that makes it impossible for serious students of industrial conditions to overlook it. It is already the fourth largest industry in the country. Yet it is an industry that has developed only within the last ten or twelve years. . . .

When I was in England this summer I talked with one of the men who represented England at the peace conference in Berlin. He told me that one of the most formidable trade obstacles that foreign countries are facing today was the fact that American films were serving as silent salesmen for other products of American industry.

—JOSEPH P. KENNEDY,
speaking at Harvard
March 14, 1927

From the first day I joined United Artists, Joe Schenck had urged me to make my films in Hollywood, but I had strongly resisted being drawn back into the suffocating atmosphere of the movie establishment. However, once *Sunya* was finally on the screen, and I had bruises everywhere to show for my stubbornness, I reluctantly admitted that perhaps Joe Schenck was right. Much as I loved New York and mistrusted Hollywood and wanted to be a rebel like Allan Dwan, the agonies of producing totally on my own in rented space with an inexperienced crew convinced me that Hollywood was worth a try. Moreover, UA had just completed its huge new studio lot, which included a private office and a bungalow for me, and everyone I knew, down to the staunchest holdouts for freedom in the East, told me I would be foolish not to take advantage of the marvelous new facilities and all the attendant publicity I would get from working in them for the first time as a star-producer. Besides, if Mary and Doug made their films there, they must have good reasons, I thought, so right after Christmas I swallowed a mouthful of crow and started making plans to move to Hollywood.

Once I made the decision, I knew I had to live with it, for whereas as an actress I had once been able to dart here and there with only a maid and a secretary, I was now obliged to transplant a considerable household and the nucleus of a company with me wherever I went to work for any length of time. In January I notified Irving Thalberg, the head of Metro-Goldwyn-Mayer, who was renting my house in Beverly Hills, that he would have to vacate it by the middle of March. Then I told Henri and the secretary and the company accountant to arrange for the mass exodus of Gloria Swanson Productions—twenty-five people in all, including little Gloria and Brother—to the other side of the continent. On March 19, eight days after *Sunya* opened at the Roxy, Henri and I boarded a train for California to attend the Hollywood premiere of *Sunya* and repossess the house.

Hollywood had not changed much in two years. As a matter of fact, Henri and I had both been back for short business trips, but never for longer than a few days. In one case the Peugeot company had approached Henri to assume the franchise for the sale of its automobiles in California, but he had declined in order to take responsibility for the European distribution of my films. If he had chosen to be a car importer, however, I would have been no more surprised than I was to find that Herbert Somborn, in my absence, had become a restaurateur. He had opened the fashionable Brown Derby across from the Ambassador Hotel on Wilshire Boulevard, and according to Lois Wilson, he was very successful. Lois advised Henri never to go there because it was said to be a favorite lunch place of Wallace Beery's, and the very notion of my three husbands sitting down to a meal together made her dizzy, she said. I seconded her. Nevertheless, as soon as little Gloria was settled in her new California life, I made arrangements once again for Herbert to see her on a regular basis. In spite of my feelings, he was her daddy still and she loved him very much.

The Hollywood of the movies, one year after the radio scare, was going stronger than ever. Buster Keaton's film *The General* and Mr. De Mille's *King of Kings* had been the outstanding hits of 1926, and according to Elinor Glyn, unless I came up with a new picture soon, *the* film of 1927 would doubtless be *It*, starring Clara Bow, with a script by the high priestess of "It" herself. At a glance around the studios, I could tell that the moviemakers were all at a high pitch of productivity. United Artists, at least, was certainly booming.

Once the dust settled after our arrival, I began to take stock of my situation. As an artist I was at the stage I had always dreamed of achieving, in the sense that, for the first time in my life, I had made only one picture in a year. As a producer, however, I was advised by all the partners in UA to get cracking. Even if *Sunya* turned out to be a gigantic success, which was not likely, considering it was my first picture, it would take time for it to show a profit. By the same token, I would be mad not to have another picture ready before *Sunya* was out of the minds of the public. In other words, until I could be sure that every picture I produced was a great success, I could never afford not to have another picture cooking on the back burner. I appreciated their concern and I knew they were right, but I refused to be rushed. After *Sunya*, I knew that an "easy," so-so picture took just as much out of a producer as a brilliant, creative picture did; therefore, I made up my mind that from now on I would settle for nothing but the best. If I failed, I could go back to working for someone else. But before I failed, I wanted to make my *Gold Rush*. I wanted to stretch to my fullest height and then some.

Joe Schenck did everything he could to persuade me to pick *The Last of Mrs. Cheyney*, a very successful romantic comedy in which Ina Claire had starred on Broadway two years earlier. He was even ready, he said, to pull corporate strings in order to get Allan Dwan to direct it. However, the gushy story sounded a bit too formula to me, and my memories of the only other Ina Claire role I had performed on the screen, the young bride in *Bluebeard's Eighth Wife*, did not tend to make the project auspicious. Henri and I, in the meantime, had been screening all the recent Hollywood films in order to get ideas of our own, and one picture above all others made us bite our tongues with excitement—*What Price Glory?*, the cinematic adaptation of the war play by Maxwell Anderson and Laurence Stallings. Henri sat through it three times, and each time he said with assurance that it was a masterpiece. Therefore, when Joe Schenck impatiently approached me yet again about *The Last of Mrs. Cheyney*, I stopped him before he could get halfway through his pitch and said, "Tell me about Raoul Walsh."

"He just directed *What Price Glory?*" Joe Schenck said.

"I know that. I also know he directed *The Thief of Bagdad* and pals around with Allan Dwan and Doug Fairbanks. What's he like?"

"He's a crazy Irishman who wandered into movies by accident, like Mickey Neilan. He played John Wilkes Booth for Griffith in *Birth of a Nation* and later started directing. He's a man's director," Joe Schenck added forcefully, as if to terminate the interruption.

"He didn't do too badly by Dolores Del Rio in *What Price Glory?*" I said. "It made her a star."

"Well, anyway," he said, "he's under contract at Fox, in case you have any ideas."

"I just want to talk to him," I said.

I called Raoul Walsh that evening, and the next morning he came to the house and we had breakfast in the garden. He was tall and robustly good-looking, with a huge, boyish grin and a shock of curly fair hair, and so shy that he blushed when Henri and I started to praise *What Price Glory?* I told him that the wonderful thing about the picture was its frankness, its naturalness, and I asked him how he had been able to preserve that. How had he managed to make a film of a play containing language that had shocked even Broadway audiences and situations that were clearly circumscribed by the Hays code and still keep the feel of it? He said he had assumed that audiences would forgive fighting marines for acting like men at war, because there was no other way they *could* act. If audiences wouldn't accept them as such, he had felt, there was no point in making the film. It turned out he had been right. Audiences everywhere went crazy for Captain Flagg and Sergeant Quirt. He laughed and asked if we had been able to lip-read Quirt when he said "son of a bitch" once, and we said yes. He said he was surprised that the censors had let that go by.

The man was amazing. Within two hours we were talking like old friends. No wonder he and Allan Dwan were close, I thought; they were totally kindred spirits. I finally told him quite bluntly that I was looking for a challenging script and an exciting director. I said I was aware he was under contract to Fox, but if we could borrow him, was he interested in directing me and did he have any suggestions for a screenplay?

"You mean like *What Price Glory?*" he asked.

"Not necessarily," I said, "but something solid and real like that. I don't want to spend the rest of my life making fancy-dress pictures."

"Well, there's always *Rain,*" he said, with a blush and a grin.

In any discussion of frankness and censorship in Hollywood, the play *Rain* inevitably came up. Written by John Colton and Clemence Randolph, it was based on a wonderful story by W. Somerset Maugham entitled "Miss Thompson," in which a sadistically puritanical minister named Davidson in the South Seas tries to reform a prostitute named Sadie Thompson. Instead of saving Sadie, however, he falls prey to her charms and kills himself, and Sadie leaves for Sydney with a lovable marine named Handsome to find a better life. Jeanne Eagels had played Sadie when *Rain* was on Broadway. Raoul and Henri had never seen it, but I had, twice, the second time in order just to study Jeanne Eagels, who for the run of the play was that rarest of phenomena—a great actress in a great role that suits her perfectly. Every actress in America with a brain and a figure still wanted to play Sadie, and every producer had secretly dreamed of filming the work. But everyone knew that the Hays Office would never give the nod. The two major problems with filming *Rain*, as Raoul said, were that the minister in it was a secret lecher and the heroine talked like a sailor on leave. Such things might be all right for theater audiences, Hollywood censors felt, but movie audiences must be spared.

As we sat in the sun-speckled garden and talked, we kept coming back to *Rain*. At one point Raoul remarked that it was absurd, when you stopped and thought of it, that there should be different criteria for what could be shown to theater audiences and to movie audiences. "In the old days Blanche Sweet played a whore in *Anna Christie* and nobody batted an eye," he said.

"Yes," I said, "but that was in 1922, before we had the Formula." The Formula was a decency code drawn up by Will Hays and agreed upon by all the major film studios, which included a list of books and plays that had been banned from consideration for film treatment. *Rain* was at the top of the list.

"Why should Will Hays be the judge of what is decent and what isn't?" Henri asked indignantly.

"He's not," I said. "The industry hired Will Hays to protect itself. After the Fatty Arbuckle scandal, Hollywood overnight had such a terrible reputation for sin throughout America that the producers thought the public would burn down all the theaters. So they set up a special office headed by an ex-Cabinet member to tell Mr. and Mrs. America that Hollywood was clean and reverent. The point is, they overdid it. And the proof is that every single producer walks right up to the line whenever he can and suggests in all his advertising that he has daringly crossed over it. In short, Hollywood 'morals' are usually hypocritical at best, darling."

"Your wife is absolutely right," Raoul said loudly, making a doubled fist and hammering the air with it once.

Then we talked about other properties, but without much interest. We were all thinking the same thing: how to get around the Hays Office and film *Rain*. Filming *Rain* in 1927 was the maddest idea in the world, but every other idea suddenly seemed dull. Raoul Walsh and I sized each other up with searching looks.

After a long pause I asked, "Do you think I could play Sadie?"

"Sure, you'd be perfect, if anybody would let you," he said.

"Who's anybody?" I asked.

"The pinochle club." To Henri he explained, "That's the nickname for all the producers who made up the Formula the Hays Office goes by. They're all buddies."

"I'm a producer," I said with meaning, "and I'm not a member. I didn't sign anything."

Raoul smiled a smile as wide as his face and said, "This is crazy, isn't it? Do you have a copy of *Rain* I could borrow?"

"No," I said, "but I've got a copy of the Maugham story.

That may be even better. The code mentions plays, but it doesn't mention stories, does it?"

"I don't know. I'll dig it out and see."

By that time we were so fired up that we had a real drink and some lunch. Then I lent Raoul my copy of *The Trembling of a Leaf,* Somerset Maugham's collection of short stories that included "Miss Thompson," and asked him, "Are you free tomorrow?"

"Free as a bird," he said, his shyness gone. "Same time?"

"Same time."

The next morning, while the children piped to each other like little birds and ran and played on the lawn with their governess, Henri and Raoul and I sat around a table under the trees and conspired about how best to break the Hays code.

First we read a recent statement made by Will Hays about the Formula:

> . . . The motion picture theatre is a community meeting-house. There gather the families—fathers, mothers, and children. Motion picture success is based entirely upon ability to please the entire family, and the success that has come to the industry, the real affection with which it is regarded by the millions, is genuine proof that we are succeeding in that effort.
>
> There has become rather prevalent of late a certain type of book and a certain type of play that deals in theme and situation with certain topics which in previous years were discussed only in whispers. Many persons have asked, "Why haven't we seen these in the movies?" The reason is very simple. We [the Association of Motion Picture Producers and Distributors of America] were determined that this type of book and play should not become the prevalent type of motion picture and to prevent this we set up what we call "The Formula."
>
> "The Formula" is this:
>
> When any member company is offered the screen rights to a book or play of a probably questionable nature, its representatives immediately inform the offices of our Association, representing about eighty-five per cent of the producing elements. If the judgment of the

member company to the effect that the picturization of the subject matter is inadvisable is confirmed, a notice is sent to all the other member companies, giving the name of the objectionable book or play. Such company members, thus having their attention directed to the subject in question, have the opportunity of avoiding the picturization of the novel or play.

More than a hundred and fifty books and plays, including some of the best sellers and stage successes, have thus been kept from the screen.

Our method, which is of course thoroughly legal and which has proved efficient, is not censorship in any sense of the word. No censorship could have brought about the results which have been attained. At the same time, our formula does not by any possible interpretation limit the production of vital or artistic pictures. Any method which did that would fail absolutely. Some pictures have been made which might very well have been omitted. A few have been made which should not have been made at all. But the standard of the whole is very definitely advancing. . . .

"You see, it's not censorship at all," I said, and we all smiled wryly at each other. "Technically, we're safe anyway," I said, "because it says 'books and plays.' It doesn't say anything about short stories."

"Or classics," Raoul said. "We can make a case that Maugham is considered great literature. They're not fussy about classics. Irving Thalberg got permission just last year to get *The Scarlet Letter* taken off the list so Lillian Gish could make a film of it. He argued that the purpose of it was moral even though the subject was adultery."

"Well, so is *Rain* moral in purpose," I said.

"Of course it is," said Raoul. "Better and better."

Next we pulled out the resolution drawn up by the Association of Motion Picture Producers and Distributors of America and turned to the passage on things forbidden to be shown in pictures.

BE IT FURTHER RESOLVED that those things which are included in the following list shall not appear in pictures produced by the members of this Association, irrespective of the manner in which they are treated:

1. Pointed profanity—by either title or lip—this in-cludes the words, God, Lord, Jesus, Christ (unless they be used reverently in connection with proper religious ceremonies), Hell, S.O.B., damn, Gawd, and every other profane and vulgar expression how-ever it may be spelled;
2. Any licentious or suggestive nudity—in fact or in silhouette; and any lecherous or licentious notice thereof by other characters in the picture;
3. The illegal traffic in drugs;
4. Any inference of sex perversion;
5. White slavery;
6. Miscegenation (sex relationships between the white and black races);
7. Sex hygiene and venereal diseases;
8. Scenes of actual childbirth—in fact or in silhouette;
9. Children's sex organs;
10. Ridicule of the clergy;
11. Willful offense to any nation, race or creed. . . .

The sticklers, of course, were items 1, pertaining to profan-ity, and 10, pertaining to the clergy. However, we decided we could easily get by without using any actual profanity and that Davidson didn't have to be a minister. He could simply be a misguided, overzealous moralist—*Mister* Davidson instead of *Reverend* Davidson. What we had thought would be the biggest problem of all—the treatment of prostitution—came under another heading altogether in the association's resolu-tion:

BE IT FURTHER RESOLVED that special care be exercised in the manner in which the following subjects are treated, to the end that vulgarity and suggestiveness may be eliminated and that good taste may be emphasized:

. . .

17. The sale of women, or of a woman selling her virtue;

. . .

26. Excessive or lustful kissing, particularly when one character or the other is a "heavy."

"Who's to say if we treat it with taste?" I asked.

"They are," Raoul said, pointing to a list of the studio members of the association, which together represented the entire movie industry worth talking about. "If we make *Rain*, we'll be taking them all on." The list included:

Chadwick Productions
Christie Film Company
Cecil B. De Mille Pictures Corporation
Educational Studio
F.B.O. Studios, Inc.
First National Pictures, Inc.
Fox Film Corporation
Samuel Goldwyn, Inc.
Harold Lloyd Corporation
Metro-Goldwyn-Mayer Corporation
Metropolitan Pictures Corporation
Paramount Famous Lasky Corporation
Hal Roach Studios, Inc.
Mack Sennett Studio
United Artists Studio Corporation
Universal Pictures Corporation
Warner Bros. Pictures, Inc.

"The funny part of it is, they'd all love to do *Rain* themselves," Raoul said, laughing. "But none of them has ever figured out how."

"Can we?" I asked him.

"I don't know," he said. "Where do we start?"

"With Will Hays," I replied. "Henri and I will have him to lunch, and I'll see if I can get his blessing."

A few days later we invited Will Hays and a few business associates to the house. When lunch was over and the guests began to move out to the terrace for coffee, I detained Mr. Hays for a few minutes in the dining room. I told him I had a quick question.

"And what is that, Miss Swanson?" Mr. Hays asked in his reedy Indiana twang.

I said I had so far produced only one picture and had not as yet been asked to join the Association of Motion Picture Producers and Distributors, but I was anxious not to transgress against the code. I said I had found a marvelous short story about a fanatical missionary intent upon punishing a social outcast who is trying to make a new life for herself. It was a powerful story about tolerance and reconstruction, I said, and I thought it would make a beautiful film. The hitch was this: since the missionary was a clergyman, unfavorable treatment of him might go against the code; but on the other hand, if I made him a reformer but not a man of the cloth, I was afraid the author might not sell me the rights to the story.

Therefore, I said, would it be all right to use his name in trying to persuade the author?

"Of course, Miss Swanson," Will Hays said, smiling. "What is the author's name?"

"Somerset Maugham, the Englishman. He's supposed to be very strict when it comes to altering his stories."

"And what is the name of the story?"

"It's called 'Miss Thompson.' Have you read it?"

"No, I don't believe I have."

"You should. It's a classic. I suppose you're not much concerned with magazine stories, though, are you?"

"Not really. But I recognize Maugham's name."

I held my breath.

"And you're right," Mr. Hays continued. "Some of his works are classics."

"So I may use your name, Mr. Hays, when I tell him I must make Reverend Davidson just plain Mister Davidson?"

"Of course you may. And good luck." Then he apologized for the fact that I had not been asked to join other independent producers as a signatory to the code and said he would endeavor to find out why.

"No rush," I said. "You've done enough for one day. Let's go and have some coffee now."

I threw my arms around Henri and kissed him as the dear little man was driving away later. "We're over the first hurdle, darling," I said.

The next step was to acquire the property. Since it would be easier for me to rob the U.S. Mint than to buy the rights to "Miss Thompson" without anyone's finding out, I obviously needed a secret agent, some lawyer who had no connection with me or even with United Artists, and in order to obtain one, I realized it was time to show my hand to Joe Schenck. When I told him of the strategy I had used on Mr. Hays, he said he should fire his lawyer for not having thought of it sooner. He said it was brilliant, because any version of *Rain* was bound to be big box office. But what, he asked, if Mr. Hays caved in under pressure? Every studio in town would like to film *Rain* without breaking the code, and they would all be furious to find that I had got permission. They would certainly bring pressure to bear if word leaked out of what we were up to. Therefore, any publicity would be fatal. The asking price for the play was, as everyone knew, $100,000. That was more than Jesse Lasky had paid for *An American Tragedy*, and Jesse Lasky had been forced to shelve the Dreiser novel once the association bore down on him. The same thing could happen to us, Joe said, if Mr. Hays was pressured into changing his mind.

"I'm sure he won't go back on his word," I said. "Everything I told him was true."

I suggested to Joe, however, that we buy both the short story "Miss Thompson" and the play *Rain* in order to pre-empt all comers. Joe, who was a signatory to the Hays code and president of United Artists, could hold the rights and title to the play as protection for me, thereby leaving Gloria Swanson Productions, which was not a signatory to the code, free to go ahead and make a picture based on a short story which in itself was not banned, or even mentioned, in the Formula.

Joe said he admired the plan. He went ahead and contacted a Los Angeles play broker to negotiate secretly for us. He had the broker get in touch with Maugham's agents and Sam Harris, who was the producer of the Broadway play and who acted as representative for the playwrights. Joe told him to try to get the story and play for less than the asking price, since we would not be using the play, which was supposedly the valuable property, to concoct the script. He also told him never to reveal our identity and to refer to the play in his communications as the Maugham Colton Randolph play, never as *Rain*. Before the broker left for New York on May 10, he sent the last of many low-key telegrams to Maugham's agents.

HAVE INDEPENDENT DIRECTOR NOT ASSOCIATED WITH HAYS ORGANIZATION WILLING TO TAKE CHANCE AND MAKE THE PICTURE STOP NOT WILLING TO RISK A GREAT DEAL OF MONEY STOP I THINK YOU PEOPLE SHOULD NOT MISS THIS CHANCE TO GRAB SOME MONEY STOP GET HARRIS AND THE AUTHORS LINED UP BY THE TIME I REACH NEW YORK MONDAY

All communication between the broker and us was in code. I received an encouraging telegram from him dated May 20, and then nothing more for nearly a week. While I held my breath, the greatest event in my recollection occurred: Charles Lindbergh flew the Atlantic. At twenty-five he became America's new god, and everybody wanted wings. I remembered my only flight and the thrill of it and my terrified father on the ground when it was over, and I realized that the promise I had made then never to fly again could now be

broken. Flying was no longer a dangerous thrill. The airplane
was one of man's most brilliant inventions to conquer time
and distance. We would all be flying, routinely, I imagined, in
my lifetime.

On May 25, the following telegram in our agreed-upon
code arrived:

VERY HAPPY TO ADVISE YOU ARE NOW OWNER OF THE TWO
MOLEHILLS OF NEBRASKA WHICH COST YOU SIXTY THOUSAND
STOP   MAY I SUGGEST THAT A COPY OF ANY PUBLICITY THAT MAY
BE GIVEN OUT BY ANYONE REGARDING THIS NEWLY ACQUIRED
PROPERTY SHOULD BE FILED AS PROOF AND PROTECTION THAT AT
NO TIME DID ANYONE CONNECTED WITH YOU REFER TO THE PLAY
BY NAME

That meant I had the rights to both the story and the play and
that no one knew it was I who had purchased them. I replied:

BRAVO AND MANY THANKS STOP   HAVE WALSH STOP   IS IT
POSSIBLE TO GET COPY OF PLAY   REGARDS
    GS

By the time the telegram from New York arrived, Raoul
and I had been working on the script for a week in my garden,
and all we had to work from was the short story. Joe Schenck
had arranged for the loan of Raoul from Fox, I found out, by
calling in an old IOU from another member of the pinochle
club, and thanks to the fact that Raoul's agent, Harry
Wurtzel, happened to be the brother of Sol Wurtzel, general
manager of Fox Studios, another member of the club, the
deal had been made most amicably.

When our secret agent returned from New York with all the
legal papers, plus a copy of the play, Joe had them examined
by his experts on copyright. The story belonged to me. Joe
held the rights to the play. Everything was in order. We were
in the catbird seat. While the newspapers were still full of
Lindy and his flight, we placed a discreet announcement in
the back pages of the newspapers saying that Gloria Swanson's second production for United Artists would be based on
Somerset Maugham's story "Miss Thompson." We never
mentioned the words *Sadie* or *Rain*, but someone figured it all
out soon enough, because two days later headlines screamed
that Gloria Swanson was going to play Sadie Thompson in
Rain, in defiance of the Hays Office ban.

The roof fell in. Attorneys for Maugham, Colton and Randolph, and Sam Harris charged the broker who had made the purchase for us with misrepresentation and threatened to sue Joe Schenck and me and to stop the picture before we could even get it started. Worse yet, Joe received a virulent two-page telegram signed by a list of studio chiefs and representatives of every big chain of theaters in the country, charging us with endangering the entire film industry and hinting at foul play and retribution. The pinochle club was plainly out for blood.

NEW YORK JUNE 10, 1927

    JOSEPH SCHENCK
    UNITED ARTISTS STUDIO
    HOLLYWOOD CALIFORNIA

WE THE UNDERSIGNED IN MEETING ASSEMBLED TODAY DESIRE TO VOICE THE STRONGEST PROTEST OF WHICH WE ARE CAPABLE AGAINST THE MAKING OF RAIN EITHER UNDER THE NAME OF SADIE THOMPSON OR ANY OTHER NAME OR THE MAKING OF THIS STORY EVEN WITH VARIATIONS AND CHANGES STOP   A YEAR AGO IT WAS AGREED THAT THIS STORY WAS BANNED AND ON THE STRENGTH OF THIS EVERY PRODUCER LAID OFF THE MAKING OF CERTAIN MATE-RIAL STOP   IT WAS FURTHER UNDERSTOOD THAT IF SUCH MATERI-AL WAS PRODUCED BY ANYONE THAT MEMBERS OF THE ASSOCIA-TION IN ORDER TO PROTECT THEMSELVES SHOULD REFUSE TO EXHIBIT THE SAME STOP   FOR THIS SUBJECT TO BE PRODUCED AT THIS TIME WILL OPEN UP THE ENTIRE QUESTION AGAIN AND CERTAIN BOOKS AND PLAYS NOW BANNED WILL BE PRODUCED BY THIS ASSOCIATION AND WE WILL LOSE FOR OURSELVES EVERY-THING THAT WE HAVE GAINED IN PUBLIC RESPECT AND CONFI-DENCE FOR THE PAST FOUR OR FIVE YEARS STOP   AS MEMBERS OF THE ASSOCIATION AND AS PERSONAL FRIENDS OF YOURS WE BEG YOU TO STOP THE PRODUCTION OF THIS PICTURE AT ALL COSTS STOP   WE DO NOT BELIEVE THAT ANY INDIVIDUAL MEMBER HAS THE RIGHT TO JEOPARDIZE THE INTERESTS OF ALL THE MEMBERS NO MATTER WHAT THE FINANCIAL GAIN MIGHT BE BY TAKING ACTION WHICH WILL PUT OUR ENTIRE ASSOCIATION AND ALL OF ITS MEMBERS IN DISREPUTE WITH THE PUBLIC OF THE COUNTRY STOP   OUR REFUSAL TO PRODUCE SALACIOUS BOOKS AND PLAYS AGAINST WHICH THERE IS AN OVERWHELMING PUBLIC OPINION AT THIS TIME HAS BEEN THE CORNERSTONE UPON WHICH THE PRO-DUCERS ASSOCIATION HAS BEEN BUILT AND TO DESTROY THAT AT THIS TIME WOULD IN OUR OPINION BE AN ACTION UNFORGIVABLE AND UNWARRANTED AND A DIRECT VIOLATION OF PROMISES WE

HAVE MADE THE PUBLIC THAT MATERIAL OF THIS KIND WOULD NOT
BE MADE   KINDEST REGARDS FROM

WILLIAM FOX	JOE KENNEDY
WINNIE SHEEHAN	SAM KATZ
ABE WARNER	JOHN MCGUIRK
J J MURDOCK	S R KENT
MARCUS LOEW	ADOLPH ZUKOR
ROBERT RUBIN	JESSE L LASKY
ROBERT COCHRANE	SAM SPRING

RICHARD ROWLAND

Raoul and I studied the ultimatum with concern. The first
two signatories were his bosses at Fox, William Fox himself
and studio chieftain Winifield Sheehan. That meant I could
very well lose my director. Then there was Marcus Loew,
head of Metro-Goldwyn-Mayer. Abe Warner of Warner
Bros. Jesse Lasky and Adolph Zukor of Paramount, to be
sure, plus two of the three KKKs, Sidney Kent and Sam Katz.
The head of Universal, two moguls from First National, and
J. J. Murdock, the new head of the Keith Albee theater
chain, plus a few others. All together, they represented
thousands of theaters across the country, the biggest and best
of them, in fact. Between us we could identify every signature
on the telegram but one. Raoul underlined the Irish name.
"Who the hell is Joe Kennedy?" he asked me. I had no idea.
The rest of them were old-time distributors and producers.
He was new.

What infuriated me was that the studios represented by
those signatures had themselves produced pictures the moral
content of which was at least as questionable as that of *Rain*,
pictures like *What Price Glory?*, *Cradle Snatchers*, *Carmen*,
Silk Stockings, *Flesh and the Devil*, *The Wedding March*,
Forbidden Paradise, and *Camille*. The real reason they were
out to get me was that I had reached up and picked the
biggest plum of all, but they were too dishonest to say so.

While I was debating what I should do, Doug Fairbanks,
Jr., arrived at the house in a marine uniform and said he
would like to test for the part of Handsome O'Hara if I was
really going to film *Rain*. He obviously heard the news
from Doug Senior. He had been in a couple of pictures, but
since I knew he was not yet seventeen, I kept a straight face
and thanked him for his enthusiasm. I said I would let him
know, once Raoul and I got around to casting. After he had

gone, Raoul and I laughed uproariously at the thought of
what reprisals the pinochle club might suggest if Sadie
Thompson left for Sydney at the end of the film in the
company of a minor.

Just then Joe Schenck arrived with a letter he had received
that morning from Will Hays. It included the strongest
statement yet from the pinochle club.

Hollywood, California
June 11, 1927

Mr. Joseph M. Schenck
United Artists Corporation
7200 Santa Monica Blvd.
Hollywood, California

Dear Joe:

With further reference to "Rain." I just have the
following night letter:

> We the members of your Association have today
> sent the following nightletter to Joseph Schenck quote
> We the undersigned in meeting assembled today de-
> sire to voice the strongest protest [etc., to the end of
> the telegram Joe had received the day before] unquote
> end of wire stop

> We wish to protest to you with all the force of which
> we are capable against United Artists making or
> releasing the production Rain under any change or
> subterfuge story by another title and with or without
> the original characters of the stage play stop   This
> play was banned a year ago and the agreement was
> that if it was made by anyone outside it would not be
> exhibited by the members of the Association stop   If
> this play is produced in any form other members of the
> Association will produce other plays as detrimental
> and harmful as this one and we feel the entire work of
> our organization which we have struggled to build up
> will be lost and that we will forfeit public confidence
> stop   We request that if this play is produced that
> you use every power that you possess to prevent its
> exhibition by the exhibitors of this country as its
> release would be a blow against every member of the
> Association who has abided by the policies that you
> have outlined for us all stop   We believe that no
> action is too strong for us to take to protect our

individual and collective interests in the handling of a matter that is a direct violation of every understanding and every pledge that we all made to you and that you in turn made to the public and we are determined individually and collectively that no one shall risk the investment that we have made in trying to win public opinion public goodwill and respect and further insist that no one has a right either for financial gain or any other reason to jeopardize the structure of the entire business because of the disregard of a promise or policy of any one member either directly or indirectly associated with this organization stop   We all have in our possession material bought and paid for in times gone by which at your request we have refrained from making and there are also in the market many plays no more offensive than this one that there can be no justification for refusing to make if this one goes through because the making of this will tear down in our opinion everything that we have all stood for

Kindest regards William Fox Winnie Sheehan Abe Warner J J Murdock Marcus Loew Robert Rubin Robert Cochrane Joe Kennedy Sam Katz John McGuirk S R Kent Adolph Zukor Jesse L Lasky Sam Spring Richard Rowland

I again urge most earnestly that you follow up the inquiries in my recent letters. We should be able definitely to know whether or not there have been positive misrepresentations in the situation. I will appreciate it personally very much if we can ascertain exactly what the situation is.

With kindest personal regards, I am

Sincerely yours,
Wm. H. Hays

After we read the letter, Raoul said, "There's that name again. Tell us, Joe, who is Joe Kennedy?"

"He's an Eastern distributor," Joe said. Then he looked quite serious and said, "All right, friends, what do we do now?"

"I'm going to reply to them," I said, "even if they didn't have the courtesy to address their protest to me." The two of them sat mute because they could tell from the tone of my

voice that I was furious. *"I'm* producing this picture," I
continued. *"I* talked Will Hays into saying it was all right. *I*
paid sixty thousand dollars for the rights. So why are they all
sending their telegrams and letters to you, Mr. Schenck? I'll
tell you why. Because I'm a woman. They refuse to recognize
me as a producer. They expect you to handle me like a silly,
temperamental star. Well, I'm not going to let them get away
with it."

I told them I had two choices. I could either appeal to the
newspapers for support or I could put my case directly before
my adversaries. In either case I would have to put Will Hays
on the spot for leading me to believe I had permission in the
first place. For that reason I chose to keep the debate out of
the papers, for the time being at least. Raoul helped me word
the reply, and I sent it off two days later, again in the form of
a telegram.

JUNE 13 1927
PLEASE SEND THE FOLLOWING WIRE TO THE FOLLOWING PEOPLE:

WILLIAM FOX	850 TENTH AVENUE	NEW YORK CITY
WINIFIELD R SHEEHAN	850 TENTH AVENUE	NEW YORK CITY
ABE WARNER	1600 BROADWAY	NEW YORK CITY
J J MURDOCK	KEITH ALBEE CIRCUIT PALACE THEATRE	NEW YORK CITY
MARCUS LOEW	1540 BROADWAY	NEW YORK CITY
J ROBERT RUBIN	1540 BROADWAY	NEW YORK CITY
ROBERT COCHRANE	UNIVERSAL PICTURES 730 FIFTH AVE	NEW YORK CITY
JOE KENNEDY	F B O 1560 BROADWAY	NEW YORK CITY
SAM KATZ	FAMOUS PLAYERS	NEW YORK CITY
SIDNEY R KENT	FAMOUS PLAYERS	NEW YORK CITY
ADOLPH ZUKOR	FAMOUS PLAYERS	NEW YORK CITY
JESSE L LASKY	FAMOUS PLAYERS	NEW YORK CITY
JOHN MCGUIRK	STANLEY AMUSEMENT CO	PHILADELPHIA PA
SAM SPRING	FIRST NATIONAL PICTURES 383 MADISON AVE	NEW YORK CITY
RICHARD ROWLAND	FIRST NATIONAL PICTURES 383 MADISON AVE	NEW YORK CITY

MR SCHENCK CALLED MY ATTENTION TO YOUR PROTEST AGAINST
MY PRODUCING SADIE THOMPSON STOP   AT THE OUTSET I WANT
YOU TO KNOW THAT I AM IN SYMPATHY WITH THE HAYS ASSOCIA-

TION AND IN SYMPATHY WITH ALL OF THE PRODUCERS AND THEIR
PROBLEMS I ALWAYS TRY TO BE CONSTRUCTIVE AND NEVER WANT
TO BE DESTRUCTIVE STOP   SADIE THOMPSON IS A MAGAZINE
STORY BY SOMERSET MAUGHAM AND ALTHOUGH I WAS FULLY
AWARE OF RAIN HAVING BEEN BANNED AND ALSO AWARE OF THE
FACT THAT RAIN HAD BEEN ADAPTED FROM THE MAGAZINE
STOP   NEVERTHELESS I FELT AND I STILL FEEL THAT THE PRO-
DUCTION OF SADIE THOMPSON PROVIDING THE PICTURE IS PRO-
DUCED IN A CLEAN MANNER WITHOUT OFFENDING THE CLERGY
AND THAT IS WHAT I INTEND TO DO AS I AM NOT USING EITHER A
MISSIONARY OR A CLERGYMAN IN THE PICTURE WILL NOT IN ANY
WAY INTERFERE AND BREAK DOWN ANY RESOLUTIONS MADE BY
THE MEMBERS OF THE ASSOCIATION STOP   I SAW MR HAYS AND
TOLD HIM THAT I INTENDED TO PRODUCE SADIE THOMPSON AND AS
LONG AS I DID NOT USE THE CHURCH OR CLERGY IN MY PRODUC-
TION OF SADIE THOMPSON BY SOMERSET MAUGHAM THERE WAS NO
OBJECTION STOP   I HAVE SINCE INVESTED OVER TWO HUNDRED
THOUSAND DOLLARS IN THIS PICTURE AND A GREAT DEAL OF TIME
AND THOUGHT OF MY OWN AND I AM IN NO FINANCIAL CONDITION
AT PRESENT TIME TO SACRIFICE THIS AMOUNT OF MONEY I WILL
ASK YOU TO BE GENEROUS AND BROADMINDED AND WITHDRAW
YOUR OBJECTION TO MY PRODUCING SADIE THOMPSON AND TO
FURTHER PROVE TO YOU THAT I WANT TO SUPPORT AND ENDORSE
THE EFFORTS OF MR HAYS AND THE ASSOCIATION I WILL COMMIT
MYSELF DEFINITELY AT THIS TIME WHICH IS MY FIRST COMMITMENT
NOT TO PRODUCE ANY STORY THAT HAS BEEN BANNED BY THE
ASSOCIATION STOP   YOU KNOW VERY WELL THAT AS FAR AS THE
PUBLIC IS CONCERNED SADIE THOMPSON CAN BE PRODUCED IN
SUCH A MANNER THAT THERE WILL NOT BE THE SLIGHTEST
OBJECTION TO IT BY ANY CENSOR BOARD OR ANY RELIGIOUS BODY
STOP   RAIN WAS PUT ON THE BAN ON ACCOUNT OF THE CHARAC-
TER OF THE MISSIONARY STOP   ACCORDING TO THE EXPLANATION
OF MR HAYS AT THE PRESENT TIME IF THE BAN WERE LIFTED FOR
THE PRODUCTION OF RAIN IT WOULD BREAK DOWN THE BARS AND
AS HE SAYS HIMSELF CRACK THE CEMENT STOP   AS FAR AS THE
STORY ITSELF IS CONCERNED IT IS A GREAT LESSON IN TOLERANCE
PLEASE DO NOT THINK I AM USING THE LATTER WORD IN
CONCLUSION TO POINT OUT TO YOU THE NECESSITY OF YOUR BEING
TOLERANT   VERY SINCERELY YOURS

    GLORIA SWANSON

                   CHGE.   GLORIA SWANSON PRODUCTIONS

The next morning I got two telegrams in reply. The first
was useless. The other was from Marcus Loew, chairman of

the board of Loew's Incorporated Theatres and Metro-
Goldwyn-Mayer, probably the most powerful and influential
man on the list.

NEW YORK NY JUNE 14 1927
    MISS GLORIA SWANSON
    HOLLYWOOD CALIF
YOUR TELEGRAM ADDRESSED TO MR. KENNEDY HAS BEEN RE-
CEIVED MR. KENNEDY IS OUT OF TOWN AND IS NOT EXPECTED
BACK FOR TWO WEEKS BUT YOUR COMMUNICATIONS WILL BE
BROUGHT TO HIS ATTENTION IMMEDIATELY AFTER HE RETURNS
    C E SULLIVAN

NEW YORK NY JUNE 14 1927
    MISS GLORIA SWANSON
    HOLLYWOOD CALIF
SENT JOE SCHENCK FOLLOWING WIRE TODAY QUOTE I WAS
PREVAILED UPON TO JOIN IN THE PROTEST BECAUSE OF THREAT-
ENED DISRUPTION OF THE ORGANIZATION STOP   IF HAYS GAVE
HIS CONSENT EVEN THO IT WERE IN ERROR I WILL USE MY UTMOST
ENDEAVOR TO SEE HE IS BACKED UP BY THE ORGANIZATION LETTER
FOLLOWS KINDEST REGARDS UNQUOTE REGARDS
    MARCUS LOEW

What a dear, wonderful, honorable man, I thought when I
read Marcus Loew's telegram. A big man, I thought. And I
couldn't help thinking, besides, that of all the men on the list,
his opinion mattered the most because Raoul Walsh and I
both wanted Lionel Barrymore to play Davidson, and Barrymore was under contract to MGM, Loew's company. I
wrote him a letter of thanks, and he sent another hearten-
ing reply.

July 6, 1927

My dear Miss Swanson:
    I have your letter of the 24th of June, and of course
you know I will do all in my power to straighten out the
situation.
    Were it not for the fact that I have not been well, I
would have tried to avoid having it go as far as it has. I
regret that the whole thing occurred, as we all know
what the organization means to our business. I would
not like to have anything happen to cause a disruption, and I am deeply sorry it happened to you as I

can readily understand how you feel about the whole matter.

Sincerely,
Marcus Loew

I had to take Mr. Loew's word for the deed that he would succeed in calling off the association. Certain members might resent me, but unless they were united they couldn't stop me, and Marcus Loew and Will Hays together were too strong not to have their way in restraining them. I never received any official word that the association acquiesced to my plans to shoot *Sadie,* but since, by the end of ten days, I had not heard anything to the contrary either, I went ahead. I had to. By then I had tied up a quarter of a million dollars of other people's money in the project.

The first thing I did after paying for the rights to the story and play was to write to Somerset Maugham and ask him to create a sequel to the Sadie story. Raoul suggested this as a safeguard and an investment. Based on the success of *What Price Glory?,* he said, he had been commissioned to do two sequels about Captain Flagg and Sergeant Quirt. In the same way, if *Sadie* turned out to be a success, every producer in Hollywood would rush to capitalize on our work and produce a sequel. I only hoped Mr. Maugham was not angry with me for the fact that his agent had sold me the Sadie story and play for much less than the asking price. My letter was very short.

Dear Mr. Maugham:

As you know, I am at present producing a photoplay of your story SADIE THOMPSON. Mr. Raoul Walsh has adapted a script to conform with the needs of the cinema and he is to direct me.

It has occurred to us that a further photoplay might be done about Sadie Thompson, and I, as a producer and actress, should like to do it in conjunction with Mr. Walsh. Could you not write an original story for me, THE LIFE OF SADIE THOMPSON, tracing the woman from the moment she leaves Pago-Pago and goes on with whatever life your imagination has created. I believe that you could make a story as colorful as the one I am now doing as a picture.

I am writing directly to you in order to avoid the troublesome route of agents and commission seekers in the hope that our suggestion may tempt your fancy.

I shall be happy to hear from you at which time details of our play may be further discussed if you consent.

Faithfully yours,
Gloria Swanson

The next job, that of casting the picture and hiring first-rate technicians to film it, was not going to be easy, I knew, since many of the studio heads who controlled the talent were at present furious with me. The industry as a whole was divided into camps. Mary and Doug and Charlie Chaplin and others wanted me to succeed and helped me in every way they could. The opposing camp, consisting of individuals who either thought the film would hurt the industry or resented my audacity in insisting on making it, did everything they could to discourage me and slow me down. The third and biggest group was made up of people who couldn't afford to risk their jobs by expressing any opinion at all.

From day to day Raoul and I held our breath waiting to see whether Fox Studios would order him off the picture, and while we waited, problems multiplied. Rapley Holmes, who had played the fat storekeeper Joe Horn on Broadway, said he would also play the part in the film but then ill health kept him from even making the trip from New York, so we had to recast the role. Our first choice for a cameraman was George Barnes, but he was under contract to Goldwyn, and when we approached Sam Goldwyn for the loan of him, Goldwyn stalled. Just about then the play broker who had purchased the Maugham story and play for me attempted to gain recognition for himself by telling the columnists all about the secret negotiations involved in the deal, and one story after another appeared in the papers which made the whole project appear just a bit shady.

At last Lionel Barrymore, our first priority as far as I was concerned, said he would play Davidson, but at the same time he warned us that he was not in good health, due to an injured leg. Nobody, meanwhile, absolutely nobody, seemed right for Handsome O'Hara, starting, of course, with young Doug Fairbanks, Jr. It suddenly dawned on me that the person I had pictured in the role from the beginning was Raoul Walsh himself, but when I suggested it he blushed purple and flatly refused, mainly because he thought he wasn't a good enough actor. It took a week to persuade him he was perfect. Then other delays piled up. By the time we were sure of George Barnes, July was half gone. That meant there was not a prayer of taking American Express up on its offer to transport cast and crew inexpensively to Samoa for location shooting, which would have meant reams of free publicity. Instead we had to settle for Catalina Island, off the coast at Long Beach, and while one crew turned an end of it into a South Seas outpost, another crew built William Cameron Menzies' marvelous interiors on one of the new United Artists stages. They finally said we could begin shooting in a week.

To my horror, however, as we neared the end of this snarl of preliminaries, I began having terrible stomach pains. I tried to ignore them, but they didn't go away. They increased. I was absolutely certain I had ulcers, the disease of producers, and the more I worried, the worse the pain got. Henri and Lois Wilson begged me to see a doctor, but the only doctor I trusted was in Paris, and knowing me, all of our friends were reluctant to suggest one, particularly after what had happened to Rudy Valentino at the hands of greedy, careless physicians. I was frantic, however, and in serious pain. In no way could I start shooting in that condition. After winning the battle to obtain *Sadie,* and after borrowing a fortune to produce it, all I could think of was that I would collapse on the set the first day with a bleeding ulcer and have to hire Norma Talmadge or Dolores Del Rio to replace me. Finally I called Jane Grey, a friend who worked for *Good Housekeeping* magazine, and she recommended a doctor in Pasadena who had been treating her mother. In fact, she swore by him. When I was no better the next day, I gave in and drove to see him.

The doctor's name was Henry G. Bieler, and his office was so tiny and unassuming that I checked the address again before I went in. There was no receptionist and no nurse, just a simple room with a couple of chairs in it and a sign on the wall that said: NO SMOKING. Oh, no, I thought; had I driven all the way to Pasadena to get a sermon on the evils of smoking? What nonsense. I had been smoking since I was fifteen. The only time I ever quit was when I was pregnant.

Dr. Bieler was a little man, not much bigger than me. He looked more like a bookkeeper than a physician: no white coat, no stethoscope, no smell of medicine or disinfectant about him. I repeated what I had told him on the phone, that I feared I had ulcers and that Miss Grey had recommended him to me. He seemed not to pay much attention to what I said. He just kept staring at me. Then he sat down at his desk and motioned for me to sit down opposite him.

At last he spoke: "Take off your earrings, please."

As I started to reach for my ears I thought, This is ridiculous, and paused. I even considered leaving by the door I had just entered. He gave me an insistent look, however, so I took off my earrings and put them in my purse. Still he just kept looking at me. Then he reached into a desk drawer, and pulling out a long yellow pad and a pencil, asked, "What did you have to eat last night?"

I was still dubious—very—about the earrings business, but at least his second remark related to my stomach, where the pain was, so I hastened to be cooperative. "Oh!" I said. "A shrimp cocktail."

"You didn't have any of those little things before you went to the table?"

"Oh yes, hors d'oeuvres. Well, let's see, I had some toasted almonds, several green olives wrapped in bacon, and a deviled egg."

He was writing everything down. When he got to the deviled egg, he motioned for me to stop until he could catch up. Half amused, I looked at the pad as he wrote. "Deviled egg" wasn't two words. It was a list of all the ingredients: egg, mayonnaise, mustard, paprika, Worcestershire sauce, chives.

"And a bit of pâté and a cheese puff," I said, in a deliberately speeded-up tone in order to convey to him that I was a busy woman and in no mood for games. With no change of pace on his part, he added those things to his list.

"Did you drink?" he asked.

"Yes," I said. "Dubonnet. A sip."

"All right," he said, "now, back to the table. What kind of sauce did you have on the shrimp cocktail?"

You have to guess, I wanted to say, but I controlled myself and said, "Something red."

He stopped and considered for a minute and then added many items to the list. His inquisition continued, course by course, through the whole meal I had eaten the night before with Henri and friends: soup, fish, chicken, the various accompanying wines, the jelly with the bird, the sauce and the stuffing with the fish, the peas, the fresh asparagus.

"Hollandaise sauce?" he interjected and I nodded, and he recorded it.

"How about dessert?" he asked, when we came to the end of the meal.

"I have an English cook," I said, "and she made a trifle."

"I see," he said and wrote down all the ingredients: eggs, flour, raspberry jam, sherry, whipped cream, slivered almonds, maraschino cherries.

"Coffee?"

"No."

"Nothing to drink after dinner?"

"Yes, champagne," I said, "one glass. And several cigarettes," I added, assuming that that was what he had probably been trying to get out of me all along.

It didn't seem to interest him. By now he had covered three sheets of foolscap, and he was scanning them like an accountant.

"I'll tell you what I want you to do," he said. "Close your eyes while I read off each item I've recorded here on your chart. I want you to imagine a plate, empty at first, and then as I call out these ingredients, I want you to visualize them piling up on that plate. Or better still, imagine spooning them into a garbage pail." He read the whole list slowly to me; waves of nausea built up inside me, so that I thought I was going to throw up. When he finished he asked me calmly and matter-of-factly, "Tell me, what animal, including a pig, would eat that combination of things in less than two hours?" I was struck dumb. No one had ever spoken to me like that before. He smiled quizzically at me for a full beat before he drove the nail home. "Why do you treat your stomach like a garbage pail?"

We then exchanged a smile of complete trust. I knew this was the doctor for me and he knew I was salvageable.

In medical school he had been ill himself, he told me, of asthma and kidney problems. His professors recommended all the conventional treatments, but he got steadily worse. At last he came across an out-of-print book on fasting. Having tried everything else without success, he felt he had nothing to lose, except useless weight. As he grew noticeably thinner, his friends and professors expressed concern. They told him he was killing himself. But he didn't feel awful, and once he had lost sixty pounds, he also lost his asthma and his kidney problems. Then he began to read some of the books on natural medicine written by traditional American doctors who had practiced and studied in this country early in the century, before doctors began to prescribe only the standard drugs and medicines produced by the huge international pharmaceutical cartels. At that point he became a maverick and reverted to the good sense of a healthier age.

His words made perfect sense to me. In fact, I felt better just listening to him. At the end of an hour and a half he told me I could put my earrings back on. Then he prescribed a series of enemas and a modified fast of vegetable broth made of zucchini, celery, and string beans, and told me to come back in a week.

"May I ask why you had me take off my earrings?" I questioned him before I left.

"Of course," he said. "I wanted to see your lobes. Long lobes indicate healthy adrenals, and you certainly have them."

I had a few rough days as my body gradually eliminated the poisons built up in it, and Henri protested loudly that surely I was making myself ill, not well, but by the time I went back to Dr. Bieler I felt like a different woman. And by the time we went into the studio to start shooting *Sadie*, my skin was glowing, my eyes were clear and sparkling, and my nerves were calm.

Dr. Bieler was a great doctor because he was a great teacher. He taught me simple things, such as: There are not thousands of physical disorders, only one—toxemia. We poison ourselves and one another. Pain is a divine signal from heaven, nature, Mrs. God, Mother Nature, whatever it is, telling us to mend our ways, to stop poisoning ourselves, to clean ourselves out. If we eat simple, natural food in modest amounts, our wonderful bodies will heal themselves naturally. Each of us is personally responsible for his own health. He said he wouldn't allow his patients to take any medicine or drugs, not so much as an aspirin. To take painkillers and treat symptoms, he said, is as insane as turning off an alarm while the fire rages on unchecked.

In his way, he was a genius as great as George de Bothezat. He completely changed my life. Lacking all pretensions, he was as constant as his fee: $3 a visit.

Raoul Walsh hadn't been in front of a camera in eight years, but in spite of his initial fears about not being able to act the part of Handsome and also about not being able to see himself with the eyes of a director while he was acting, it was evident after two days in the studio that he could do both, that in fact Lionel Barrymore and I were going to have to dust off every trick we knew to keep him from outdistancing us. He exuded all the strength and vitality and raffish good humor the role called for, and as a director he could call out of himself as an actor just the right mix of emotions to score a bull's-eye in one scene after another.

Lionel Barrymore, on the other hand, never displayed any nerves whatsoever. He had been acting too long with the greats ever to doubt how this or that role should be tackled. One of those perfect chameleons of the profession, he would, without any visible effort, turn into Davidson the minute Raoul started calling out directions. A mild, distant, unkempt man in his late forties, Lionel was a slave to painkillers at the time because of an infirmity in one leg. But he could shake off his customary lethargy and disorder in an instant and be a half-mad zealot with eyes ablaze, roaring at Sadie Thompson in a voice big enough for the biggest theater that she would be punished for her wickedness.

With two such partners, who were opposite as the poles in every way, I could not fail to discover many of the complexities and contradictions buried in Sadie Thompson. Acting is like playing tennis in the sense that the better your opponent or your partner is, the better you will play. With a perfect Handsome and a perfect Davidson, how could I be a bad Sadie? I would have been an idiot not to see that this picture was providing me with the greatest acting opportunity of my career. Furthermore, as a producer, I was breaking the primary rule and filling the basket with eggs: two world-renowned stars, a major director, and a great and famous story. Unheard of. And scandal and immorality and an intramural industry war to boot. I felt in my bones from the first day on the set that *Sadie Thompson*—we had settled on that title—was going to be dynamite.

One week into the picture, however, Pierre Bedard, my production manager, came to my bungalow to tell me that we had lost George Barnes, our cameraman. Sam Goldwyn had recalled him to shoot *The Devil Dancer* with Gilda Gray.

I went through the roof. "How could Sam Goldwyn do this to me?" I demanded. "He's a member of United Artists, and we had an agreement in writing. I insisted on that."

"But the agreement allows Barnes to be recalled on three days' notice."

"That's absurd," I said.

"I know," Pierre said, "and I told Joe Schenck so the

minute I saw the agreement. But he said not to bother to get it changed because Goldwyn would never think of taking Barnes away from us in the middle of a picture."

"Is Joe Schenck producing this picture or am I?" I snapped and grabbed the phone. Joe Schenck was out of town, so I told his secretary to find him and have him call me. Then I called Doug Fairbanks, and he said he would do what he could, but it would take a few days. When Joe Schenck returned my call, it was to say he would be back in three days and he would see to matters then.

In the meantime, over a hundred people were sitting around waiting for me to decide what to do next. What I could *not* do was scrap the work Barnes had done in the studio. If I did, we would never finish the film. The trick, therefore, was to find a cameraman who could shoot to match Barnes's work or at least to blend unobtrusively with it. Raoul and I decided to try the man who had worked as second cameraman under Barnes, but he proved too inexperienced to shoot a major picture by himself, and the footage he produced was poor. He was actually relieved when I told him the second day that we had found someone else. Raoul had managed to turn up an available cameraman from Fox. We crossed our fingers, since we were only two days away by then from going on location to Catalina, and there was no way of putting off the departure because postponing the schedule meant losing Lionel and Raoul, who both had other commitments coming up.

After the first day's rushes, however, it was apparent that the borrowed cameraman from Fox would not do, either. By then Joe Schenck was back and phoning people, and Raoul and I were calling everyone we knew. From among the available candidates Raoul next picked a man named Kurrle who had done the camera work for Griffith on *Resurrection*, and told him to be ready to go to Catalina the following day. Just before we left, Mary Pickford volunteered the services of her favorite cameraman, Charles Rosher. I told her to stand by; I would phone her from Catalina in the event that Kurrle didn't pan out.

If I didn't have ulcers by then, I should have got them in the process of moving a cast and crew of nearly a hundred and fifty to Catalina, but by then I was too angry with Sam Goldwyn and Joe Schenck to get ulcers, and too busy. I was so preoccupied with the technical and artistic aspects of the picture that I couldn't even find time to spend with Henri when I didn't have a phone or a script in my hand. For the duration of the picture, I told him, he would have to be daddy and mommy both with the children because if I took off my producer's hat for so much as an afternoon, the whole picture would collapse, and so, probably, would I. Everything I had ever worked for was riding on *Sadie Thompson*, and I was not going to let anything or anyone defeat me.

Kurrle's exterior shots of Catalina were lovely, but to my dismay his interior work was mediocre. Raoul and I both felt that he would never be able to bring the picture together visually the way we wanted it to look. I began to feel that the entire venture was doomed. I told Raoul to call Mary Pickford and tell her to send Charles Rosher immediately. Mr. Rosher duly arrived, and although he was unmistakably a fine cameraman, his sharp, clear images didn't blend at all with the shadowy, impressionistic style that George Barnes had set for the picture in the first days of shooting. If I kept Rosher, we would have to reshoot every foot, so I let him go before the situation became irreparable. Once again I turned to Joe Schenck, who told me he would try to find someone, but that frankly it was time I started learning to make do. I saw red, but I said nothing. When I hung up, I was at my wits' end, exhausted and enraged and desperate. Then, on an impulse, I decided to turn to Marcus Loew, the man who had saved my skin earlier on this picture. They told me at MGM in Hollywood that he was very ill, but I sent him a long, detailed wire, and when he realized the trouble Sam Goldwyn had created for me, he gave orders to MGM to give me anyone I wanted. MGM let me have Oliver Marsh, and he saved the film for me.

The entire stop-and-start process had cost a fortune. Even with the acquisition of Oliver Marsh, I knew we would have to reshoot scene after scene when we returned to the studio. Nevertheless, I felt elated for having survived, and moreover the delays and frustration had in some way worked favorably on the cast and crew. Their adrenaline was pumping for the picture and for me. The rushes looked better each day. I think I could have asked the company to do anything and they would have done it.

The most unusual thing I called on anyone to do on Catalina was to change Lionel Barrymore's clothes. Perhaps because he was in pain much of the time, perhaps because he simply didn't care about niceties—whatever, he worked day after day in the same clothes. It rained frequently on Catalina, and after each drenching he just let his clothes dry on him. My strongest sense is my sense of smell, and I couldn't stand it. On the other hand, I liked him so much and he was so fantastic in the picture that I could hardly walk up to him and tell him that he smelled. I finally told two crew members to go into his dressing room at lunchtime when he was napping and get the clothes he was wearing off him. "When he wakes up without them, he'll put on something else," I said, "and maybe even take a notion to bathe."

The boys never told me what they did or if Lionel woke up, but for the last week on Catalina he was a changed person. Bathing, of course, didn't alter his performance. Clean or dirty, deodorized or pestiferous, Lionel Barrymore had nothing to learn about acting, and the role of Davidson fit him like a spotless glove.

When we got back to Hollywood and started reshooting scenes in the studio, Joe Schenck called and asked if I could come and see him. I was still sore at him, as well as half crazy with work; therefore, I asked, could *he* come to see *me?*

"O.K.," he said, but his voice was not friendly. "How about this afternoon?"

"How about tomorrow afternoon?" I said, trying not to sound quarrelsome.

"O.K.," he said again, in the same flat tone, and the next afternoon he showed up at the appointed time in my producer's office on the lot.

"Sadie isn't finished, right?" he asked, after we had exchanged civilities.

"That's right."

"Well, Gloria, you're over budget. What are you going to do for money?"

"Borrow more," I said confidently. "This picture is going to be dynamite. I know it."

"Well, so far *The Love of Sunya* has not turned out to be dynamite. That was over budget too."

This was pure muscle talk, and I knew it. Stay in line, he was saying. He always took that tone with money because he was president of Art Cinema, the company that lent members of United Artists money to finance pictures, and he was also on the board of Giannini's Bank of America, which lent the

money to Art Cinema that it lent to the members of United
Artists.

He had picked the wrong afternoon to discipline me.
Before I could stop myself, I said, "Look, two years ago you
were all begging me to join United Artists, telling me I
couldn't fail. Now you seem to be saying I can't succeed. I
know I'm over budget, but I also know *Sadie Thompson* is the
best thing I've ever done. *Ever!* Ask Raoul Walsh. Ask
Lionel Barrymore. When Irving Thalberg reshoots a third of
a picture, you call him a genius. When Sam Goldwyn does it,
you say he's maintaining his reputation for quality. But when
I do it, you treat me like a silly female who can't balance her
checkbook after a shopping spree. If you had held Sam
Goldwyn to a responsible commitment in the first place, Joe
Schenck, *as Pierre Bedard asked you to,* this picture would
not only be dynamite; it would be showing in theaters by
now."

After that outburst we could certainly not talk business
amicably. I excused myself, saying I had to be on the set in an
hour. He was furious, but he was a clean fighter in that he let
it show. I knew he would get more money for me. He was too
shrewd a businessman to refuse. But I had a feeling he would
make me stoop to pick it up, and I didn't like the idea. I had
no wish to put polished apples on Joe Schenck's desk through
four more pictures. Therefore, I called Pierre Bedard, my
production manager, as well as Thomas Alan Moore, of the
Guaranty Trust in New York, who was an officer of my
company, and told them to put as much of my property on the
market as it would take to finish *Sadie.* I told them they could
sell the farm in Croton-on-Hudson, the penthouse in New
York, or the property I owned in Malibu. "As much as it
takes," I said. For starters, they sold the place in Croton-on-
Hudson.

Next it was the Hays Office. The minute we started editing
the picture, they hired lip readers to scrutinize every inch of
the film. They also went over the titles with a fine-tooth
comb. In the first scene of the picture it was raining, which
was fine by them, but whenever the word "rain" appeared in
a title, they asked that it be deleted or changed. They also
recommended that we change Davidson's name—which we
had already changed from Reverend Davidson to Mister
Davidson—to Hamilton or Atkinson, but we left it Davidson.

They drove the editors crazy, and Raoul and I had to fight for every word and every foot of film.

We had hoped to release the picture before Christmas, but these delays made that impossible. Also, each delay made my financial situation more desperate. Revenue from *Sunya* was slow in coming in. My accountants told me it might not pay off its cost until it was released abroad. Everyone felt the picture had great potential in Europe, but UA distribution was said to be weak there. Henri had to go back to France to renew his visa in six weeks, so we arranged that when he went, he would investigate the situation and get *Sunya* into European theaters as soon as possible.

I finally heard from Somerset Maugham about a Sadie sequel. By then, the last thing I wanted to do was make another film about Sadie Thompson, but the letter was intriguing in itself for other reasons.

Dear Miss Swanson:

Thank you for your letter of June 20th. I had made arrangements with the Fox Film Co. to write a sequel to "Rain" and I had devised a story in which I was proposing to take Sadie Thompson to Australia and show what became of her, but when I informed the Fox People that negotiations had been concluded for the sale of the film rights of "Rain" they preferred not to go on with the matter. So if you would like me to do a picture for you on these lines I am not only at liberty to do it, but should be very glad to. I think I have abundant material to make a scenario full of colour and action. The price I had arranged with the Fox Film Co. was $25,000.

Yours very sincerely,
W. Somerset Maugham

That meant Fox had already been negotiating for a Sadie Thompson scenario when I made a bid, but they were too cowardly to go for the actual story or play. Instead, to avoid any difficulties with the Hays Office and to save a lot of money, they had asked for a sequel under another name. Not the blasphemous, frightfully expensive play *Rain*. No. Something different by the same author. The same but not the same. The game but not the name.

I had found in two years of marriage to Henri that I could

turn on the Marquise de la Falaise de la Coudraye and be very
cold and grand and formal at will, as, for example, when I
wanted to terminate an interview or get through customs
quickly, or put down a phony. When I finished reading Mr.
Maugham's letter, I turned on Sadie instead. "Those hypocritical sons of bitches," I said out loud. All of them being so
high and mighty, so prim and proper, so protective of the
industry and the American family. And all of them dying to
get rich without getting caught. William Fox and Winnie
Sheehan had headed the list of names on the telegrams to Joe
Schenck and Will Hays.

I showed the letter to Raoul, who, since he was under
contract to Fox, would have directed the sequel if it had ever
been bought for $25,000, and we roared with laughter.

"Hoist on their own petard" was Raoul's comment.

I sent a copy of Maugham's letter to Will Hays, by way of
repaying his favor to let me apply for the story in the first
place, and I would have sent a copy to Marcus Loew, but I
was too late. My champion, my knight in shining armor, the
last great gentleman of the movie business, as far as I could
tell, had died in September.

Henri had to leave for France early in November. I had
planned to travel to New York with him and see about
distribution and publicity for Sadie, but when the time came
for him to go, I still had a hundred small things left to tidy up.
I drove him to the train and told him to hurry back.

I wanted to arrive in New York with a perfect print of the
film to screen and some evidence of favorable audience
reaction to it. In spite of my optimism I couldn't help being
nervous, mainly because at least half of the big producers
were hoping audiences would reject the picture and I would
fall flat on my face for ignoring the Formula.

On November 10 the picture was sneak-previewed in San
Bernardino; that is, the audience saw it free as an extra
picture and were asked to write down their opinions on white
cards. I asked to see the cards immediately. If they were
good, I would take a copy of them to New York by way of
predicting the popularity of my film. If they were bad, I would
try to think up some other strategy to sell Sadie. but I knew in
advance that none would work. As Mr. De Mille had told me,
"It's the audiences who do the deciding. We only guess."

When the cards arrived, I put them in a neat stack on the

table in front of me, took a deep breath, and read the first
one:

Acting was wonderful but as a church member think
religion should be left out of pictures.

I smiled nervously and thought, Even if they don't like it,
they know what it is. It doesn't matter whether you call
Davidson Reverend or Mister; the public isn't fooled. I
looked at the second card.

She's good picture's good.

She. Me. I smiled again. Then I raced through the rest,
pausing and evaluating each one.

Very good. No room for applause one is held so by story.

Disgusting.

Miss Swanson wonderful. Superb Picture.

First picture I ever saw where Gloria didn't wear a
million dollars worth of clothes.

Wonderful. Way ahead of the play at the Biltmore.

A slam on a christian nation.

Show a scene of her in Singapore with kids, etc.

Marvelous acting great photography. But the ending was
a let down. Sadie should turn out either good or bad.

Enjoyed it more than any picture I've ever seen.

Sadie should have used the razor on Davidson's neck.

The best picture of Gloria's ever. She is positively
beautiful. In other pictures her beauty didn't show up so
good.

Splendid, don't cut a scene.

Not interested in that type of a woman unless a REAL
Christian gets ahold of her.

Wonderful. The downfall of the minister may bring the
money in but let him show he's a real Christian by
relenting and let Sadie go to Sidney.

Gloria was right It's a wonderful picture.

Good acting but I've seen Barrymore better than as the Minister.

Gloria's acting was the only good thing about it. Such terrible clothes. Why is it necessary to show the Minister's downfall?

When I finished, I read them again. There were some negative statements, but none indicated indifference. The great majority liked it. I had a triumph on my hands.

A week later I packed for New York full of confidence—so much so that I determined to inquire about investors while I was there. If Joe Schenck was going to be difficult, I would attempt to get my money elsewhere.

By coincidence I discussed this subject with Robert Kane, one of the KKKs at Paramount, just before I left. He had once expressed interest in the property I owned in Malibu, so I had called him to say it was for sale.

"Why?" he asked.

"To pay for *Sadie Thompson*," I said. "Surely you've heard I ran into debt on it. I'm not worried. This picture is going to be a great success. In the meantime I need cash."

Bob Kane told me to relax, that everyone who produced pictures had debts. The money always came in eventually. Then he said he knew a banker in New York who was a consultant to several Wall Street banking houses. They were just starting to invest in motion pictures, and in order to get going they were ready to give the Bank of America a little competition. "When you're in New York, you should see my friend," Bob said.

"I'm leaving for New York tomorrow," I said.

"Will you be staying in your apartment?"

"No," I said, "it's shut up because I've got the staff out here. I'm staying at the Barclay."

"Shall I call my friend and arrange a lunch there?"

"Fine," I said. "What's his name?"

"Kennedy," Bob answered. "Joseph P. Kennedy."

That name again, I thought. "Isn't he a film distributor?" I asked.

"He's also a banker," Bob Kane said. "I'll give him a call."

CHAPTER 15

Robert Kane called to say Mr. Kennedy could lunch on Thursday, so I told the maître d' at the hotel to reserve a table for two off to the side in the dining room and to call me when my guest arrived. I told him expressly to put the check on my bill. I said if the gentleman asked for it, he was to tell him the lunch was compliments of the management. For although Mr. Kennedy might offer to help finance my next film, he had also signed the telegrams to Joe Schenck and Will Hays denouncing the filming of *Sadie;* therefore, I wanted to be under no obligation to him.

When the maître d' phoned to say Mr. Kennedy had arrived, I picked up the envelope of papers I intended to show him and went downstairs. The maître d' led me to the table, and Mr. Kennedy rose and energetically introduced himself. I was amused by his heavy Boston accent, and I could tell he was surprised that I was so tiny.

He didn't resemble any banker I knew. His suit was too bulky, and the knot of his tie was not pushed up tight. With his spectacles and prominent chin, he looked like any average working-class person's uncle. A man of about forty, he still retained a certain boyishness. Apart from his accent, his hands were the most noticeable thing about him. They looked unused to work, and there were wide spaces between his fingers. He gestured often and animatedly with them when he talked.

He mentioned a few familiar names and said he had looked forward to meeting me. He said he had certainly impressed his wife and children when he told them he was having lunch with a famous movie star with a European title. That led us to talk about our children. The Kennedys, I learned, had seven, three boys and four girls. He knew my daughter was named Gloria, and he asked me what my son's name was. I said that Gloria and I had called him Brother for so long that the poor child thought that was his proper name, but in fact his name was Joseph, after my father. I said I just hadn't got around to having him officially christened. Mr. Kennedy could not conceal the fact that he was shocked that a child of five had not yet been baptized, but he smiled agreeably and said that his eldest boy was named Joseph too, after him. Then he turned his attention to the menu.

I surprised him again when I ordered steamed string beans and braised celery and zucchini. He was obviously very much a meat-and-potatoes man, although he ordered a shrimp cocktail to start.

At Bob Kane's suggestion I had brought a memorandum from my accountant outlining the two propositions I had received for financing my third picture for United Artists, one from Joe Schenck, the other from Mr. Giannini at the Bank of America. I handed the sheets to Mr. Kennedy and told him they would give him an idea of the scale of my operation. I said I would be grateful if he would advise me as to which proposal seemed better or if he would come up with an alternative proposal of his own.

Mr. Kennedy seemed relieved to have something to study. He scanned the papers quickly and then began asking questions, about my accountant, about the officers of my company, about the balance sheets. Nobody in Hollywood, he declared, knew how to make a balance sheet that gave a banker what he needed. The motion picture business was so young that nobody in it had yet learned how to keep proper figures. Certainly nobody knew how to depreciate, to amortize, to capitalize—those very things, he said, that spelled success or failure in any other business. That was what fascinated him about motion pictures, he went on, that here was a giant industry but that nobody seemed to realize it.

Then he asked me about my European grosses, and I replied that I could never seem to get accurate up-to-the-minute figures. I told him I had my own office in Paris, because Paramount distributed most of my films there and I didn't trust their figures, or their advertising, or even their artistic integrity. But, I said, there was little I could do, and even my husband wasn't much help, for although he was French, he had no experience with movie moguls. I said I knew from being in France, however, that the distributors were stupid about placing my pictures. The poor ones always seemed to be in huge theaters, while the best ones were run in little out-of-the-way holes in the wall. *The Love of Sunya* had got better notices in Europe than it had in America, I continued, but as far as I knew it was still not showing a profit there. To read the papers, I said, you'd think that nobody in the business made any money except the stars, that the studio chieftains all worked for nothing. Well, no one would ever convince me that I made more money than the president of the Bank of America. I said I understood that out of $800 million taken in at the box office in the past year, $700 million of it had gone to exhibitors and distributors, to say nothing of their friends: the butcher, the baker, and half the world of business, who walked in free. But how could I as a producer stop it? Why, even Mary Pickford's mother, I said, couldn't be in twenty thousand theaters every night counting the house.

Mr. Kennedy registered astonishment and asked, "Does she do that?"

"That's what they say," I replied, "but you couldn't prove it by me because she never took me along."

He broke into peals of laughter at that and began whacking his thigh. His reaction was so large for the Barclay dining room at lunchtime that people began to stare, but he couldn't stop laughing, and he was enjoying himself so unabashedly, so unaffectedly, that I started laughing too.

At last he grew businesslike again and said I should ask Sidney Kent for some old Paramount distribution figures for Europe. With those, he said, he could work out projected grosses for *Sunya* and *Sadie Thompson* for me. "Upcoming play dates should be counted as income, don't you see?" he said, slicing his hands up and down in the air in a parallel emphasis. "In any other business they would be counted as sales, or accounts payable. Otherwise your balance sheet for *Sadie Thompson* for this entire year would be just an inventory of costs—all red ink."

Everything he said was reasonable and convincing. Bob Kane was right; this man did have something to offer, and it wasn't just money for interest. He had a whole theory, it seemed, of movies as corporate business. When I asked him where he had learned about the movie business, he said, "At Harvard. Or I should say," he added quickly, "I studied business at Harvard. I'm just applying the principles I learned there to the movie business because I'm convinced that most people in the movie business don't know how to do that."

I couldn't get over how funny it sounded when he said "Hah-vad" in his Boston accent. I was also trying to think who it was he reminded me of. By the time the waiter had cleared our plates and returned with Mr. Kennedy's pie and ice cream and coffee, I knew. It was Craney Gartz; not Craney Gartz the handsome playboy, but Craney Gartz the passionate intellectual, obsessed with an idea, which he could discuss brilliantly for hours. Craney's obsession had been revolution, Mr. Kennedy's seemed to be success; and whereas Craney was a wild idealist, Mr. Kennedy was a practical realist. But the collegiate thrill that ideas inspired in them made them similar, somehow.

"Tell me," Mr. Kennedy was asking me with a twinkle in his eye, as if he were asking an indiscreet question, "how did you ever get Will Hays to say you could make *Sadie Thompson* in the first place?"

I was amazed that he would ask that. Surely he must sense that I still smarted from the battle over *Sadie*. On the other hand, I thought, perhaps he was paying me the compliment of dealing with me man to man, without any false deference or chivalry. And since the battle was behind me, anyway, and I had won it, I said in my demurest voice, "I just invited him to lunch and asked him."

He rolled his eyes and went off into gales of laughter again, slapping his thigh with the palm of his hand. This time, however, I didn't join in the laughter, because latent in the joke seemed to be the implication that I had vamped Will Hays by pursing my lips into a bee sting and batting my eyelashes, whereas the truth of the matter was that I had outsmarted Will Hays along with the whole pinochle club.

"In fact," I said in measured tones, as I took out a cigarette, "I think I told all you gentlemen as much when I replied to your telegram to Joe Schenck in June. I know you got your copy, Mr. Kennedy, because your secretary or assistant replied."

He reddened, and his embarrassment increased when he realized that he had no match with which to light my cigarette. I didn't fumble in my bag for one; I just held the cigarette in smoking position in front of me until a waiter hurried over and lit it. "Thank you very much," I said to the waiter.

"I didn't know if we were going to get to those telegrams," Mr. Kennedy said awkwardly. "For my part, I was told the issue was cut-and-dried, a mere formality. A number of the other signers had done me a favor. I felt I owed them one in return."

"May I ask what favor they had done for you?"

"Of course. They attended a symposium on the film industry at Harvard that I organized."

I could not refrain from saying, "Adolph Zukor at Harvard. That is an image to conjure with."

At that we both smiled.

"Well," I said, with stagy uplift in my voice after a long pause, "*Sadie* was worth the struggle. I'm very proud of it. Lionel Barrymore and Raoul Walsh are both marvelous in it."

"Oh, I'm sure you are too," Mr. Kennedy said, glad to be off the hook.

"By the way," I said, "you were a great mystery to Raoul and me when we saw your name on the telegram to Joe Schenck. You're a banker *and* a distributor, is that correct?"

"I've also produced," he said, but there was a mildly defensive tone in his voice when he said it, so I could hardly resist asking, again in a demure voice, "Really? What?"

That disconcerted him even more. He mentioned some cowboy pictures he had made with Frances Marion's husband, who was a football player, and then said that his most successful picture was called *The Gorilla Hunt*. I told him I hadn't heard of it. He told me I never would, either; that he himself had walked out on it and couldn't for the life of him understand why it made money, but it did.

We both smiled again with embarrassment.

Mr. Kennedy called for the bill and the maître d' told him our lunch was on the house. By then, after all his grand opening talk, he was going down in total defeat. He recovered, however, and made an effort to seize the day by glancing once more over the memorandum from my accountant. With a certain casualness he advised me to accept Joe Schenck's offer. He said it seemed to him the better of the two. He made no alternative offer of his own.

The meeting, therefore, had been a complete waste of time. I feared I had annoyed him seriously. In spite of the fact that we said good-bye in the most polite fashion, I was quite

certain that we would never see each other again. I would
have to look elsewhere for advantageous loans.

There was a message for me at the switchboard to phone Mr.
Bothezat. When I got him on the line, he asked me about
some papers he had sent to California for my signature. I
knew I hadn't signed any such papers, which meant they had
been stacked or shoved to one side in the hectic rush to finish
Sadie or when I was on location. I apologized to Mr. Bothezat
and promised to call California and have someone find the
papers. I said I would mail them to him as soon as I returned.

"Why?" it finally occurred to me to ask. "What were
they?"

He said they were the application for a patent for my
wireless idea. He had developed the idea to the drawing stage
and sent me the scheme and application to sign.

"When did you send them?" I asked him.

"In June," he said. That was over six months ago.

"Don't worry, I'll find them. I have never lost anything," I
assured him. Then I asked, "Do you mean my idea works?"

"Yes, of course it would work," he replied in his heavy
accent. "Don't forget now. As soon as you get back."

"I'm absolutely thrilled, Mr. Bothezat. Say it once again;
tell me I invented something."

"You did, yes. Now you have to get it patented. That's also
part of inventing."

When I hung up, I was beside myself with joy.

For the rest of the afternoon, I had a meeting in my suite with
the UA heads of sales and distribution. I told them to screen
Sadie Thompson immediately for the big theater owners
while I was in New York and could answer questions. I
assured them that there would be no possible censorship
problems, apart from the terrible delay the Hays Office had
already caused. I showed them the comment cards from
sneak previews, of which by then I had several more sets, all
favorable and enthusiastic. We also arranged for a series of
promotion and publicity interviews. Then I adjourned the
meeting.

I had told the hotel operator not to disturb me, but around
five she called apologetically: a Mr. Kennedy had been

phoning for two hours, and now he was downstairs asking to see me. I was bemused and told her to send him up.

"I hope I'm not disturbing you," he said when I opened the door. "You remember that I told you to ask Sidney Kent about European grosses on your pictures?"

"Yes, I remember."

"Well, I called him myself, and he will give us everything we need. He's calling me back tomorrow."

Us? I thought. Who's us? But before I could ask, Mr. Kennedy said there was also something we could do for Sidney in return. It would require nothing but a phone call. The situation was this: Sidney Kent and his wife were in the process of a divorce. Sidney's lawyer had asked for a postponement, but Mrs. Kent's lawyer was being stubborn. It so happened that Mrs. Kent's lawyer, Milton Cohen, was also my lawyer. Therefore, would I call Milton and tell him Sidney was helping me out and ask him to reconsider.

It seemed a small enough thing to do, and I still felt a bit guilty about my behavior at lunch. I said, therefore, that I would telephone Milton and get back to Mr. Kennedy in a day or two.

"Could you phone him now? I'd like to have an answer when Sidney calls me in the morning."

"All right," I said, "I'll try." Ordinarily I disliked being pushed or coerced, but his urging had an almost playful tone to it, as if he were sharing the fact that it was fun to get things done quickly and efficiently. As luck would have it, the operator got through right away. Milton had entered my life as Herbert Somborn's lawyer in my second divorce case, and he had later called to apologize for the tactics involved and to volunteer to serve as my lawyer anytime. He had been invaluable to me ever since, and he had never sent me a bill for any personal legal matters he handled for me. When I heard his voice, I said I hated to ask favors but I was going to ask one now. Milton paused at the strange request, but he agreed to give Sidney Kent's lawyer a postponement, and I thanked him.

Mr. Kennedy had been standing beside me during the call. When I told him Milton would do what I had asked, he smiled as if I had passed a special test of his devising. He called me a good scout and said he wouldn't forget it. Then he said he had found out from the hotel manager that I had paid for our lunch, so now it was his turn. Could I have dinner with him?

He added in a different tone altogether that he had a proposition to discuss with me.

I had made a dinner date with Sport Ward, but I knew I could cancel. Sport Ward would never lack for something to do, and I had a hunch this dinner with Mr. Kennedy might be important. So I accepted. He said he would call for me at six-thirty. That was a bit early, he said, but he wanted to take me to a special place on Long Island.

After he left, I called Sport and changed our date.

"Jilted!" Sport cried. "Never mind, I'll eat with the mayor. He called me earlier, anyway. I'll just call him and reaccept."

That reminded me that Sport knew everyone. I asked him if the name Joseph P. Kennedy rang any bells.

"Nope," he said after a minute.

The Barclay operator phoned at six-thirty on the dot to say Mr. Kennedy was waiting in the lobby. When I got downstairs I saw him standing beside a large table with another man, who looked like a functionary of some kind or a detective. The man gave him something, which he put in his overcoat pocket. Then they exchanged a few words and the man left. As Mr. Kennedy greeted me he reached for a florist's box on the table beside him and handed it to me with a big smile. I thanked him, opened the box, and imperceptibly winced to find an orchid corsage inside. I hated corsages, and orchids were my unfavorite flowers; they made you look like somebody's visiting aunt or piano teacher. And there was I in the smartest evening suit I'd brought along on the trip. Nevertheless, when he asked if I wanted him to pin it on my fur coat, I heard myself saying in my sweetest voice, "No, please, I'll carry it; that way I won't crush it." Any chagrin I had sensed in him at lunch was gone, and I noticed as he put my coat over my shoulders that he was well scented and all spruced up in dinner clothes.

On the drive over the Queensboro Bridge to Long Island, Mr. Kennedy inquired several times if I was warm enough, thereby indicating that the car had a heater as well as a driver and that he was very proud of it. Despite the cold November wind outside, it soon grew much too hot in the car, but I waited a polite interval before I said I thought the chauffeur could shut it off.

All the way to our destination, a matter of three quarters of an hour, he talked about nothing but motion pictures, and I assumed at first that it was because he thought I might be at a loss if asked to discuss anything else, but it soon became evident that his interest in the subject was bottomless. He questioned me about various directors and expressed great curiosity concerning schedules and budgets and publicity. He finally even dared to ask if I minded telling him why I had turned down $1 million a year from Jesse Lasky. He said he had heard Paramount's version from Sidney Kent but he would really like to hear my side of the story. His enthusiasm was so direct and open and academic that I had no qualms about supplying him with a valid, usable answer so long as I didn't have to go into those deeply personal issues that could be none of his concern.

I said I had taken a certain pleasure in turning down Jesse Lasky's offer, first, because United Artists was waiting for me with open arms, and second, because it seemed the only way to convince Mr. Lasky, and studio executives in general, that their exploitation of stars' lives was ruthless and intolerable. Stars weren't property, and they had better understand that. "I won't deny that I've passed through a few anxious times since I turned down that million, Mr. Kennedy," I concluded, "but all things being equal, I'm sure I'd do it again tomorrow. After all, I would have been the second or third person in movie history to sign a million-dollar contract, but I was the very first ever to turn one down."

That tickled Mr. Kennedy no end. He liked to laugh, and was so affable that I finally found myself deliberately saying things to amuse him. At one point I even said something in a perfect imitation of his Boston accent, and that sent him off into long, loud peals of laughter, at the end of which he wiped his eyes, groaned pleasurably, and asked me to do it again.

Then he would become serious in a minute and ask me a very technical question about filmmaking. He knew nothing about the industry in France, for example, so he asked me to tell him in detail the difference between French and American crews and equipment, and all the while I did, he sat in rapt attention.

The restaurant turned out to be a very elegant sort of place with an orchestra but no dancing and a menu the size of a billboard with no prices on it. Mr. Kennedy seemed disappointed when I again ordered steamed green vegetables, a little rice, and unbuttered dark bread, and he was very put out when the waiter said they didn't have any zucchini. After he had ordered a big meal for himself, he motioned the captain over. Mr. Kennedy explained that I could have wine served in a teacup from a concealed bottle if I'd like some, but I knew from his tone that he didn't drink, and he seemed pleased when I declined. He didn't smoke, either, but when I pulled out a cigarette, he produced matches this time and lit it.

While we waited for the meal to be served he asked me timidly why I ate such bland food. I described my recent ulcer scare and Dr. Bieler's regimen, and Mr. Kennedy said he had stomach problems too from time to time, but when I volunteered to put him in touch with Dr. Bieler, he said, "Oh my, no, I already have the best doctor in Boston working on the case," and laughed. We discussed Prohibition, which was still in force, and he said that although he personally didn't drink, his father had made all his money as a saloonkeeper. "Before he went into politics," he added. He too was very interested in politics, he said, and dropped in passing that his wife was the daughter of the former mayor of Boston.

"This is for you," he said, handing a small, nicely bound book across the table to me. I was startled to see my name stamped in gold on the cover, and his name as well: Edited by Joseph P. Kennedy. The name of the book was *The Story of the Films*. Without doubt, this was what the other man in the lobby of the hotel had been delivering to him.

"How marvelous," I said, a bit bewildered. "Thank you very much. Did you write it?"

"Part of it," he said, adding, "The first essay. Remember I told you I organized a symposium on films at Harvard? This is the printed version of all the speeches given. I edited it and had it published. These are the people who came and spoke." He turned proudly to a page of names arranged in a long box under the heading "The Lecturers." The fourteen speakers were Mr. Kennedy, Will Hays, Adolph Zukor, Attilio Giannini, Jesse Lasky, Cecil B. De Mille, Earle W. Hammons, Milton Sills, Sidney Kent, Robert Cochrane, Samuel Katz, Marcus Loew, William Fox, and Harry Warner. Except for Mr. Kennedy himself, the banker Giannini, and Earle Hammons, who was president of Educational Pictures, all the names on the list were prestigious bywords in Hollywood. The book's title page read in full:

THE STORY OF THE FILMS

*As Told
by Leaders of the Industry
to the Students of the
Graduate School
of Business Administration
George F. Baker Foundation
Harvard University*

*Edited by
Joseph P. Kennedy
President, FBO Pictures Corporation*

While Mr. Kennedy described the symposium and his role in it, I was thinking to myself, This is indeed a clever man. As head of a small distribution company called FBO, he would by all odds have remained unknown forever to the senior members of the pinochle club, but by rearranging his cards a bit, and by bluffing a bit, he had managed to win a hand, and now his ambition was to stay in the game and start winning pots.

He had somehow convinced Harvard, his alma mater, of the importance of the film industry in American economics and had said he thought he might be able to get a few key people like Cecil B. De Mille, Jesse Lasky, William Fox, and Marcus Loew—in short, the great pioneers—to speak to the students of the business school about motion pictures. Once Harvard put up the money, he extended an invitation to a dozen people in the film business he wanted to know to speak about the industry at the great university. Since half of the people in pictures had never finished high school, the chosen top men welcomed the chance to dignify the profession and gain some prestige for it, and they were naturally grateful to the man who had made the honor available to them and who followed up the occasion with a printed edition of their speeches in bound book form with their names in gold on the cover. Within three months after the lecture series, Mr. Kennedy's name was on the telegrams of protest about *Sadie Thompson* that Joe Schenck and Will Hays had received. Raoul Walsh and I might well have asked who Joe Kennedy was; he was plainly someone who might go far in the intellectually innocent world of pictures.

I said I wished I had been a fly on the wall the day Adolph Zukor talked at Harvard, and I imitated Mr. Zukor's heavy Hungarian accent. Mr. Kennedy laughed gleefully and whacked his thigh. I said the notion of Milton Sills as lecturer also exercised my imagination. Milton had been my handsome leading man in *The Great Moment,* so I knew his painful shyness with interviewers was no pose; he could scarcely take the pipe out of his mouth unless he had scripted lines to say. Mr. Kennedy said Milton had read his speech, and very effectively. "One other thing," I interjected. "Why didn't you get a woman to speak?" No one, I said, knew more about the financing of pictures than Charlotte Pickford, for example; she would have given Harvard a real earful. I saw that Mr. Kennedy was about to laugh again, but I stopped him by saying that for the second time that day I had forgotten myself; Mrs. Pickford was very ill and Mary was terribly worried and I shouldn't be joking about her.

Mr. Kennedy immediately grew serious; he took a heavily sentimental view of the family, I gathered, because his tone always changed when he mentioned children or parents. "Oh, I'm very sorry to hear that," he said with feeling. "I should have asked you to speak," he went on brightly after a pause. "You act, you produce, and you make films abroad. The French government presented you with an award, didn't it? Did you have to speak then?"

"Hardly," I said. "Why, if my husband—my fiancé then—hadn't been present, I'd have gone down in shame that day. I was in front of the camera in a dripping wet dress and peasant shoes, with a terrible red wig on my head and a basket of laundry in my hands, and Henri came and said, 'The men from the Academy are here to present you with the Palms.' 'What?' I said. 'It's a special award for foreigners,' he said. Then the men in top hats and cutaways and striped trousers made the presentation, and the director kissed me on both cheeks, and all the time I wanted to sink into the earth. But Henri told me what to say, so I lived through it."

Mr. Kennedy made a gesture of emphasis and said he thought that was a good idea, giving awards. The government or the press should give a prize for the best motion picture and the best performance every year. He asked me if I didn't think that would be good for prestige and publicity.

"No," I said. "I don't like the idea of competition among

artists. If you were to say, 'Who's a better actor, Doug Fairbanks or Charlie Chaplin?' I would say, 'I couldn't tell you and you shouldn't ask.' They're totally different. The same thing with Mary Pickford and me. We're different. It would be like saying, 'Which is better, an apple or an orange?' or 'Which is prettier, red or blue?' "

"I'm just thinking of the commercial benefits," he said. "The real problem is, people don't realize the potential of pictures. Properly advertised, they open limitless markets. Do you know that the United States produces over eighty percent of the films distributed in the world, as compared to only some twenty percent of the world's wheat? Therefore, films are the perfect medium for displaying American products to foreign consumers. I tried to drive that point home at Harvard."

His blue eyes were bright with excitement, and none of it was counterfeit. By the time he had eaten three heavy courses, we were having a fine old time. I usually got bored to death talking about pictures, but not with him. He had the most ambitious view of pictures I had ever encountered; in fact, he seemed to see them precisely as a means of attaining not only wealth but also power. Like his father and his father-in-law, whom he mentioned over and over again, he was intrigued by the manipulation of people and events.

"Take Boston," he would say. "The Cabots and the Lodges wouldn't be caught dead at the pictures, or let their children go. And that's why their servants know more about what's going on in the world than they do. The working class gets smarter every day, thanks to radio and pictures. It's the snooty Back Bay bankers who are missing the boat."

Driving back to Manhattan, he said he was interested in financing my next picture, but he was much more interested in personally handling all the business aspects of it. He said he was sure that together we could make millions. As far as he could tell, he continued, everybody in Hollywood thought small and looked no further ahead than to the next picture. United Artists was not much better than Paramount now, in spite of its promising beginnings. Joe Schenck was not ambitious, not really; like all the other Hollywood types, he worried solely about keeping the exhibitors happy and the theaters full. They all wanted their yacht and their race horses and their girls, but their dream stopped there, stopped short, far short. Nobody who was smart could *lose* money in pictures in their present state of development, he said; the trick, the challenge, was to make a fortune in them and also exploit their economic and political potential.

He said he had wanted to produce an important picture for some time, ever since another Boston banker, by the name of Pat Powers, had financed a picture for Erich von Stroheim.

Pat Powers. I remembered the name well. In 1919 he had been an associate of Herbert's, involved somehow in Clara Kimball Young's production company. Since then he had left his failed colleagues behind him, apparently, like a smart banker, and hooked up with the Austrian everyone said was a genius, albeit a headstrong and capricious one—Erich von Stroheim.

Mr. Kennedy kept repeating the word "important." For instance, he said the title of the next picture I was considering making, *Rock-a-bye*, didn't sound important and therefore didn't appeal to him at all. If he became involved, he would hold out for an important story as well as an important director.

"That's precisely what all the people you got to speak at Harvard would advise you not to do if you want to make money."

"Well, they're wrong," he said. "You told me at lunch your work in *Sadie Thompson* is your best so far because the story is the best you've ever had. If that's true, why would you consider anything but the next logical artistic step forward: a great story *and* a great director? Isn't that what you turned down a million dollars to be able to do, Gloria?"

He was right, and so sure of the fact that in his enthusiasm he had slipped and called me by my first name. Just as confidently, I started calling him Joe. "You've convinced me, Joe. You can almost read my mind. I think we should make a picture together."

"Wonderful!" he said jubilantly, and laughed and clapped his hands together smartly like a college boy.

He began asking me detailed legal questions about my agreement with UA, about my financial obligation to Joe Schenck, about my corporation, my lawyer, my staff. I told him my business and staff were in California, but that I also kept an office on Fifth Avenue. I gave him the address and said I would call my secretary and tell her he had permission to look at all relevant papers and files. In cases where important documents were in California, she could get copies for him.

By then we were back at the Barclay. As he escorted me to

the elevator I told him I was leaving for California in two days' time. I gave him my private number and said he could call me after he'd looked through my New York files. I thanked heaven Bob Kane had put me in touch with this strange hybrid of banker, film distributor, and university intellectual. After *Sunya* and *Sadie,* I knew I was in need just then of someone with business acumen and political savvy, qualities in which Henri and I were both sadly lacking. Furthermore, Joe Kennedy had told me that he was ready to move his whole movie operation to Hollywood. I felt in my bones that I had just passed a significant evening. I had no doubt in my mind that I had stumbled on the right business partner to straighten out my career.

I called my secretary in the morning and told her if Mr. Kennedy or any of his staff came to the office to look over the files, she was to extend them every cooperation; they had my permission. The following day, just before I left the hotel to go to Grand Central, Miss Crossman phoned to say that two men in fedoras had arrived and gone through every file in the office.

"And they're coming back today or tomorrow, Miss Swanson. They—"

"They what?" I asked.

"They were strange, those men," she said, releasing all the possible ominous overtones. "To me they looked like gangsters."

I didn't laugh at her but I didn't conceal my amusement either. "I wouldn't worry about it, Miss Crossman," I said. "The man they work for is a Harvard graduate with seven children, and his father-in-law used to be the mayor of Boston. If he can bring order to those files, more power to him. I'll take full responsibility."

The day I got back to California, Joseph Kennedy telephoned. He didn't waste any time with a lengthy diagnosis or mince any words; he simply said that my affairs were in a mess and that everyone around me was deadwood. He cited as an example a document that showed that my financial adviser in a meeting with Joe Schenck's lawyer had wasted over an hour discussing the salary of the maid who cleaned my dressing room at Cosmopolitan Studios—fighting over whether her $18-a-week salary belonged on the budget of *Sunya* or whether it should be charged to my personal account. Did I have any idea, Joe asked, how much it had cost me in lawyers' fees and lawyers' lunches to settle a matter involving less than $60? And furthermore, the item was typical of the overall mismanagement represented in the combined files of Gloria Swanson Productions. Everybody and his brother, Joe said with indignation, had been taking me for a ride.

"All right," I said, "what do you want me to do?"

"Nothing," he replied. "Let me handle everything. I'm coming out to Hollywood in a couple of weeks to reorganize my own company, and I'll deal with yours at the same time. I'll bring along a few members of my staff and we'll perform some emergency surgery. For now, don't say anything to anybody. Just be ready. Because when we get there, heads will roll. In the meantime, don't worry about a thing. By the way, when is *Sadie Thompson* being released?"

"Sometime in January," I said. "The Hays Office delayed us, you know."

"That's all right," he said. "In fact, it's just as well. By then I should have your company back on the tracks again with a whole new set of books. Don't worry about a thing, Gloria."

The last person who had said anything like that to me with the same utter confidence, I remembered as I hung up, was Cecil B. De Mille.

In early December Mr. Kennedy arrived in California and installed himself and his organization in a house with a tennis court on Rodeo Drive. His FBO studios on Gower Street in Hollywood were in the process of becoming, through merger and conglomeration, a new company called RKO. In addition, in his spare time, Mr. Kennedy began taking over the management of the Pathé studios in Culver City. Originally a French company, Pathé had seen better days and badly needed an overhaul. I asked him how, with all that, he could possibly find time for me and my problems. "You know what they say," he answered, laughing; "if you want something done, get a busy man to do it." With two studios under his wing, he pointed out, he had an army of employees at his beck and call, all on trial, as it were, and therefore anxious to prove themselves. In putting them through their paces, he could give them any number of extra things to do and be certain they would scramble to do them well.

On his first free evening he came to dinner and brought with him his four horsemen, as he called them, four trusted colleagues who had been with him since the days during the war when he had worked as an executive of the Bethlehem Shipbuilding Corporation in Quincy, Massachusetts. Their names were Eddie Moore, Charley Sullivan, E. B. Derr, and Ted O'Leary. I could see why Miss Crossman might have likened any two of them to gangsters in appearance, but they struck me, rather, as four working-class Irishmen who had risen by perseverance to responsible jobs under an Irish boss whom they admired greatly. In fact, they referred to him as the boss, with obvious affection. Whether it was to please him or me I couldn't tell, but within a quarter of an hour they were behaving with me like Snow White's dwarfs. I couldn't mention the word "butler" before one of them had rung the bell to summon him; and every time I reached for a cigarette I all but went up in flames as two or more of them struck matches to light it.

At all times they operated effortlessly and harmoniously, like a well-drilled team. For example, when the children coaxed this captive group of guests to play a game of spin the bottle, they didn't say "Not right now" or "Next time," as most adults would do in such a situation. All four of them got right down on the floor and really played; Gloria and Brother had such a marvelous time with them that before I knew it, Joe Kennedy and I were sitting down and playing too. The second time the bottle pointed at me and I started to get up to do whatever it was the spinner had told me to do, I wrenched my knee and let out a sharp cry of pain. At the sound, the horsemen went into action. One of them quickly and quietly took the children upstairs to the governess. Another went into the kitchen to tell the cook to hold dinner. A third phoned a doctor to meet us at the nearest hospital, and the fourth picked me up and carried me to the chauffeur-driven car out in the driveway. Mr. Kennedy went with us to give orders, and within an hour my knee had been x-rayed and bandaged and we were all back in the house and sitting down to dinner. The incident was slight, but the horsemen's capacity for dealing with emergencies was not lost on me.

They seemed to accomplish everything with dispatch. In the living room after dinner they told me they had gone thoroughly into every aspect of my producing company and had decided there were so many things wrong that the best solution was to dissolve the existing company and form a new one, which they spoke of as a dummy corporation. I reminded them that it had taken me a year to set up the original company, what with lawyers and insurance companies and appointment of officers and conferences over stock and interest and contracts and proxies, and that I didn't want to go through all that again, but they assured me that there would be no such delay this time. It could all be done within a month probably.

I had the reassuring impression that nothing deterred them, or even seriously challenged them, because they knew how to anticipate difficulties and avoid them. Every question I raised brought the same response: They could handle it. What about Albert Parker's contract for a second picture, I asked, which amounted to $60,000? They would handle it; it was no big problem. What about the intermediary who claimed he had negotiated my UA deal and was demanding a settlement? They would handle it; they had all the correspondence. What about distribution arrangements with Joe Schenck over *Sadie Thompson?* They would take care of them when the time came.

My only job was to forget everything and let them set up a proper company for me once and for all. Once I signed a single power of attorney, made out to E.B., E.B. would handle everything. From then on, I would not be plagued with a thousand problems I was not equipped to deal with. I could concentrate solely on acting and other artistic concerns. The four of them would run the company as it should be run, for a change, and the boss and I could devote ourselves to planning my next picture.

Joseph Kennedy was beaming proudly. He had done all this not for me alone, but so that he could become involved in the production of important pictures, and he had done it all in less than a month. Let Joe Schenck or anyone else in Hollywood match that, he seemed to be saying.

I told him I couldn't make a definite commitment about the new company until I had spoken with my husband, who was returning from Paris in ten days, but that for myself I was impressed and grateful. "You're offering me all I've wanted for two years," I said, "freedom from the hassle of business worries. It's worse for me than for most star-producers, because I'm a woman and I'm alone. My husband is less experienced in the financing aspects of pictures than I am. But you've seen the files, so I'm sure you understand. As I say, I'll speak to my husband, but I really don't foresee any difficulties."

By the end of the evening I had the four horsemen clearly separated in my mind. Except for the fact that they were all

Catholics and devoted family men, they were quite distinct as individuals.

Eddie Moore was the boss's shadow, his stand-in, his all-around private secretary and aide-de-camp. Slender, blue-eyed, and gentle, he had a very dry humor, which he employed only rarely and when he was certain of achieving the proper effect with it. He was Mr. Kennedy's chief brain, his auxiliary memory. He kept track of everything that went on.

Charley Sullivan, nicknamed Pat, who looked like a New York policeman, was the silent one. He never seemed to be able to express himself until a pile of papers with digits on them were dropped in his lap. Then he became a wizard.

E. B. Derr was a pleasant man with a noticeably pigeon-toed walk. He could work out any mathematical problem in an instant and give you the answer out of his head. He spoke often about his little girl, who was Gloria's age.

Ted O'Leary, pink-faced and blond, the heaviest of the four, looked like a bouncer, and the Kennedy liquor business was his principal concern. He said I could always reach him at the New York Athletic Club, Fifty-ninth Street and Sixth Avenue.

It was Eddie Moore who called me a few days later to say the boss had got Von Stroheim. He wanted me to make an appointment so that he could bring him over, because Von Stroheim had an idea for a story for me.

Mr. von Stroheim was gracious and charming but at the same time aloof and conceited, an immaculately groomed man in his early forties steeped in Viennese culture and blazing with his recent success in America. Before he started directing, he had played a few roles for D. W. Griffith, most notably that of a Prussian officer in *Hearts of the World*, but with the completion of *Greed* in 1924 he had taken his place as the third in the triumvirate of great directors, the preeminent sophisticate among them, outranking Mr. Griffith in his decline and surpassing even Mr. De Mille when it came to sheer opulence. His films always had a savor of delicate, authentic decadence about them, like the smell of cut gardenias at the end of a party, which no other director seemed capable even of imitating.

We were sitting on my patio with Joseph Kennedy. Mr. von Stroheim, sipping his coffee, expressed his great admiration for *Madame Sans-Gêne* and said he would have given anything to direct it. The taste in costuming he had found faultless, and he declared it an incredible feat on my part to have obtained permission to film on the actual historic locations, for we all knew there was nothing worse than having to make do with plaster palaces. He talked of the idea of a Franco-American production as a milestone in the history of film and praised me for daring to attempt it. He told me not to be concerned if jealous audiences in Hollywood and insensitive audiences in the rest of America failed to appreciate the film's excellence, and remarked that such lack of understanding necessarily went hand in hand with the creation of a classic. He went on to praise my acting ,and declare that it was his fondest wish to make a film with me; in fact, to that end he had, at Mr. Kennedy's suggestion, created a story that he thought would allow me to display my talent to its fullest range.

I wished Henri were present because his natural poise and dignity and his title might have kept Mr. von Stroheim from holding court to the extent that he did. Not that he was anything but deferential with me; he referred to me often as Marquise and fairly often in the third person: If Madame La Marquise were to do this or that . . . But it fretted me that he was a touch condescending with Mr. Kennedy, scolding him like a schoolboy who hadn't done his assignment when he said he hadn't seen *Madame Sans-Gêne*. However, if his manner in that respect struck me as a bit overbearing, it didn't seem to bother Joe Kennedy in the least. On the contrary, each time Mr. von Stroheim made a lofty observation, Joe would look at me and smile broadly enough to show his teeth, like a dog who had run up out of the garden and presented me with a choice bone he had uncovered, as if to say, What do you think of that?

Mr. von Stroheim said he would always be grateful for the wonderful things I had said for publication in Europe about his film *The Merry Widow*. He had sensed a truly generous spirit in my remarks about Mae Murray, for example. I replied that I wouldn't have been able to be nearly so generous if the interviewers had asked me my opinion of John Gilbert, whom I had known for years and always found to be dull as dishwater. "However, Mr. von Stroheim," I said, "even there I will add that you have made a new man of him. Everyone tells me Jack Gilbert has *become* Prince Danilo, as if you had hypnotized him and told him to stay that way until you snapped your fingers." Mr. von Stroheim smiled with amusement while Joe Kennedy tore the air with his laughter.

I told Mr. von Stroheim I was glad he had seen an uncut print of *Madame Sans-Gêne,* and explained that Paramount had butchered it in America. That created a bond between us. He said Paramount was just in the process of doing the very same thing to *The Wedding March,* his newest film, and he resented it terribly.

When Mr. von Stroheim finally got around to telling the story he had in mind, I decided he did not sell Mr. Kennedy short, after all. Like Mr. Kennedy, he was Catholic, political, and ambitious, and he was as ready to make an important original film for someone who could pay for it as Mr. Kennedy was anxious to enter the temple of art in the company of an acknowledged genius. The heroine of this story, therefore, wasn't a Viennese Cinderella like most of his heroines, but an Irish Catholic convent girl, spirited and full of fun, but an innocent virgin for all of that. Her name is Kitty Kelly, and she encounters by chance a dashing young crown prince. The prince is betrothed to his country's mad, selfish queen, but on the night before they are to be married, he plans one last romantic bachelor adventure for himself. He sets a fire in Kitty's convent, kidnaps her in the confusion, and takes her to the royal palace for a midnight supper with champagne. As they declare their love for each other, the mad queen rushes in and discovers them. She drives Kitty, who is still in her nightie and the prince's overcoat, from the palace with a blacksnake whip. Time passes, and after a long, complicated chain of events Kitty Kelly inherits from her aunt a dance hall in German East Africa. The prince, on maneuvers, finds her there, and after a thrilling chase sequence through the African swamplands, the two are reunited in a happy ending. "The working title," Mr. von Stroheim said in conclusion, "is *The Swamp.*"

The strange story reminded me of nothing I had ever heard before, and its creator left no doubts in the telling that it was richly cinematic from beginning to end. Moreover, it was flattering and intriguing to sit and listen to a story imagined especially for you by a major artist, but I hesitated before I said I thought it was wonderful. If I really liked it, Mr. von Stroheim said, he was willing to drop everything and go to work on the script. I paused again. Then Joe Kennedy interjected that he was impatient to choose a property and get

started before he had to go back east, and this one sounded
very powerful to him.

"What are you thinking, Gloria?" Joe finally asked.

I almost said, I'm thinking I'm long in the tooth to play a
convent girl and I don't know what the public will think when
Erich von Stroheim and I, of all people, come up with a film
set in Africa in which my two major costumes are a novice's
habit and a nightie. But I didn't say it, because something told
me this was the film that would change my life.

"I think," I said, pausing for the last time, "that Mr. von
Stroheim should begin at once." Then we all smiled and stood
up and shook hands.

After Erich von Stroheim left, I asked Joe Kennedy if he
was aware that the man of his choice had a growing reputation for being an undisciplined spendthrift, a hopeless egotist,
and a temperamental perfectionist.

"Yes, I am," he said. "But I also know he's our man. I can
handle him."

A week later Joe Kennedy and three of the horsemen
returned east, leaving E. B. Derr in California to mind the
store. The evening before they left, Joe invited me to dinner
at the house on Rodeo Drive. He was still in a festive mood at
having landed Erich von Stroheim, which I took to be one of
the proudest accomplishments of his life. He had gone out for
the best, he repeated several times, and he had come back
with it. To add to his high spirits, RKO and Pathé were both
showing marked improvement every day.

It was the strangest house. An Irish maid took my coat
when I arrived, and another Irish maid served the elaborate
meal. In addition I saw a butler, and there was mention of the
gardener and the cook. Yet the mood of the place, despite its
domestic furnishings, was strictly that of a clubhouse or an
office building. Dinners there were business dinners. Lunches
there were business lunches.

Joe Kennedy told me the first thing on the agenda back east
was to set up my new company. He said Pat Sullivan would
handle all the legal aspects through the FBO office in New
York. Pat would stay closely in touch with E.B., who would in
turn relay news of the progress to me and present me from
time to time with papers to sign. Joe cautioned me not to
discuss the impending change with any of my employees or
advisers or associates. When I asked him why, Eddie Moore

said, "Because if they find out they're going to get kicked off the gravy train, they'll try to set up obstacles and cause delays."

"That's right," Joe Kennedy said. "We've got to sneak up on them while they're asleep, or else we'll be sitting in meetings for a year, the way you did the last time. So don't talk to anyone about it, Gloria, until we've got the company formed."

I was perfectly delighted to be asked to stop doing what I knew I had never done well, anyway, and to turn my thoughts instead to the exciting prospect of working with Erich von Stroheim. Some of Joe Kennedy's enthusiasm had rubbed off on me. Much as I loved Allan Dwan and Raoul Walsh, it had been seven years since I worked with the great De Mille, and although my friends and I loved to indulge in the reverse snobbism of pooh-poohing Hollywood pretensions, there was no feeling quite like making a picture with one of the legendary figures. When UA sent me the premiere schedule for *Sadie Thompson*, I saw that I was a free woman until late January. Therefore, when Henri returned from France the following week, I brought him up to date on the events of the extraordinary two months he had been away and told him he would soon be meeting the director of *Greed;* but first, I announced, we were going to have a wonderful, leisurely, happy Christmas with the children, and I set about arranging it.

As soon as the holidays were over, the funny voice from Boston, the voice I had imitated so often for Henri, was on the phone almost every day. He wanted Henri and me to meet him in Palm Beach in two weeks to discuss the new company and the Von Stroheim film. I told him *Sadie Thompson* was set to open in San Francisco at the same time, and the publicity department from United Artists wanted me there. But Joe Kennedy importuned. He said there was lots to be settled, including an important place for Henri with an office in Paris. I yielded at that, and he said he would have E.B. book tickets for us. At his suggestion I told no one about the trip. I merely informed UA's publicity department that I could not attend the San Francisco opening of *Sadie*.

E. B. Derr came to the house several times with papers for me to sign. The new company was going to be called Gloria Productions, Inc., and the charter for it had been filed in Delaware.

"Why Delaware?" I asked.

"Because Pat Sullivan knows people there. Pat says that never has a corporation been formed faster than this one. He told me to tell you that."

Henri and I were scheduled to leave for Florida on January 14, in the evening. E.B. told me not to worry, everything would be in order by then; and indeed, he brought the last papers for me to sign the afternoon of the day we were leaving. He also had with him a telegram from Pat Sullivan dated that day.

CORPORATION HAS BEEN FORMED UNDER LAWS OF STATE OF DELAWARE KNOWN AS GLORIA PRODUCTIONS INC OF WHICH YOU ARE PRESIDENT AND DIRECTOR STOP   YOU ARE VESTED WITH AUTHORITY AS PRESIDENT TO MAKE ANY CONTRACT WHICH YOU DEEM TO BEST INTERESTS OF CORPORATION STOP   OFFICERS ARE DERR PRESIDENT SCOLLARD VICE PRESIDENT AND TREASURER MALONE SECRETARY EACH OFFICER ALSO DIRECTOR WILL AIR MAIL MINUTES OF MEETING TONIGHT   —

   PAT

Scollard and Malone were business associates of Joe Kennedy's, E.B. told me, and he said that Pat Sullivan had said jokingly on the phone that if he, Pat, didn't go to jail on this deal, he never would. There were people in three states getting signatures that very minute, and the timing was crucial.

"Everything'll be fine, though," E.B. said. "J.P. always knows what he's doing. Nothing ever goes wrong with him. By the way, Miss Crossman in your New York office told Pat that Joe Schenck and Tom Moore have got wind of the new company." Tom Moore was a New York banker and an officer of Gloria Swanson Productions, Inc., the company that was at that moment being dissolved.

"Well, I didn't tell them," I said gaily, signing the final paper, "so don't blame me."

"There's nothing they can do about it now, anyway," E.B. said with a grin. "Have a nice trip, both of you."

We boarded the train for Florida a few hours after that. E.B. had said feathers would fly when the official announcement of the new corporation was made. Therefore, I settled down in our drawing room on the train with the happy thought that by the time Henri and I got to Florida, the commotion would all be over. In the meantime, no one could reach us.

When the train stopped in Yuma, Arizona, however, the conductor brought me a telegram. I assumed it was from Joe Kennedy or E. B. Derr because no one else knew where I was, so I told the conductor to wait; there might be a reply. When I opened the telegram, I found to my surprise it was from Milton Cohen, my lawyer.

A REAL FRIEND SHOULD NEVER BE DESTROYED STOP   REGRET YOUR ATTITUDE EXCEEDINGLY STOP   WISH ALWAYS TO BE YOUR FRIEND BUT NEVER YOUR LAWYER PLEASE ARRANGE IMMEDIATELY FOR OTHER COUNSEL
    MILTON

I felt as though I'd been slapped. Milton had been my lawyer for almost five years. He had volunteered his services after my divorce from Herbert and he had helped me arrange for the adoption of Brother, for which I would be eternally grateful. But in spite of the word "friend," which occurred twice in the telegram, we were hardly close. Furthermore, this message came from an angry man, a bitter man, a man who wished to hurt me or who at least wished for some reason to be on record as having touched base to register his disapproval of my actions, for why else would he communicate anger to me in Yuma, Arizona, where I had no possible means of rectifying our differences, if we had any? I could only imagine that his anger sprang from the fact that he had, in Eddie Moore's words, been kicked off the gravy train. I could not forget, moreover, that Milton had originally represented Herbert Somborn, not me, in a divorce case that could well have meant the end of my career if I had not been persuaded to bow down to blackmail rather than start a scandal. Only after that had he called to apologize and volunteer to do me a favor if ever I needed one.

The conductor was waiting for an answer, but no answer seemed possible to Milton's telegram, which was a cut, an accusation, a dismissal. Therefore, I sent a telegram to E. B. Derr instead.

RECEIVED FOLLOWING FROM MILTON QUOTE A REAL FRIEND SHOULD NEVER BE DESTROYED STOP   REGRET YOUR ATTITUDE EXCEEDINGLY STOP   WISH ALWAYS TO BE YOUR FRIEND BUT NEVER YOUR LAWYER PLEASE ARRANGE IMMEDIATELY FOR OTHER COUNSEL UNQUOTE MAYBE I AM SELFRIGHTEOUS BUT CAN'T SEE

WHAT I HAVE DONE THAT IS SO TERRIBLE STOP   ADVISE WHETHER
I AM TO CUT MY THROAT OR NOT BEST REGARDS
    G S

Eddie Moore and Ted O'Leary, dressed in tropical suits and
white shoes, with candy-striped bands on their straw hats,
were on the station platform to meet us in Palm Beach. I
called out the open window to them as the train came to a
stop, and Henri jumped off one end of the car to introduce
himself and make arrangements for the luggage. It was early
Sunday morning. I was standing in the doorway to our
drawing room waiting for a porter to collect the hand luggage
when I saw Joe Kennedy come charging down the narrow
aisle from the other end of the car like a cyclone. He pushed
me back into the drawing room, said a few excited words, and
kissed me twice. Just as quickly he released me and straight-
ened up to his full height, and in doing so he scraped his head
on an overhead rack and knocked off his spectacles. I started
to laugh when he fell to his knees to retrieve them under the
seat, and I laughed even harder when he stood up and I saw
that the knees of his white pants were dirty and he had
lipstick smeared on his face.

He laughed back, and his blue eyes flashed.

"Now you have lipstick on you," I said, embarrassed
suddenly, and showed him where with my finger.

"I missed you," he said, with no embarrassment at all.
"And I wanted you to know." Then he scrubbed his face with
his handkerchief.

"I missed you too," I said, managing to keep my voice
steady, although my body was shaking as though the train
were still in motion. "Come out and meet my husband," I
added, and stepping to the window, I pointed to Henri and
waved. "He's there, beside Eddie Moore. Do you see?"

"Oh yes, there he is," Joe Kennedy said in a bright,
cheerful, open voice. Then he called down the corridor to a
porter to carry my bags and follow us to the car.

On the platform Joe introduced himself to Henri and
welcomed him to Florida while his horsemen saw to the
loading of the bags into two long shiny cars. Joe beckoned to
Eddie Moore and Ted O'Leary to ride with Henri in one, and
he helped me into the other. On the way to the hotel I
avoided Joe Kennedy's eyes as though nothing had happened
on the train five minutes before. Assuming a businesslike

voice, I asked if he knew that my lawyer had resigned in a telegram delivered to me in Yuma. "Of course I know," he said. "Let's just say he saved E.B. from firing him, along with your business manager and quite a few others. Pat Sullivan is coming down here tonight. He'll tell you what a bunch of worthless passengers you were carrying. Anyway," he said with triumphant finality, "things are going to be different from now on."

The manager of the Hotel Poinciana greeted us at the door and presented me with an orchid corsage. I thanked him profusely, but I could tell by the expression on Joe Kennedy's face that the man was merely following instructions. Then a parade of bellboys and a captain led all of us up to a cool, spacious suite, which in the early morning light could have passed for a florist's shop the proprietor of which favored orchids almost above life itself. A maid was piling extra towels in the bathroom and opening windows along the wall that faced in the direction of the ocean.

"Everybody in Palm Beach is lining up to meet you," Joe Kennedy said. "Eddie typed up a whole schedule for your stay. Give it to her, Eddie. And Ted? Show Gloria Mrs. Stotesbury's flowers." Ted O'Leary moved doubtfully from one bouquet to another before stopping at a large vase of yellow roses. "And, Gloria," Joe continued happily, "just look at all these calling cards and invitations. Here, Marquis, look at this one, right on top." Henri took the envelope and we read the note inside, also from Mrs. Stotesbury. She had arranged a party in our honor, the note said, with the concurrence of Mr. Kennedy.

"People will be arriving from all up and down the Eastern seaboard for it," Joe Kennedy said, leaving no doubt that Mrs. Stotesbury was definitely the big fish, the unquestioned leader of Palm Beach society.

"That's right," Eddie Moore said; "anybody who didn't get an invitation has just one week to commit suicide or leave town." Joe Kennedy burst into laughter at that and banged his hand on his thigh. Then he rose from his chair by the window and announced, "We have to leave right now or we're going to miss late Mass. How about you, Henri? Are you Catholic?"

"Yes," Henri said blithely, "but not a very good one. I'll stay with Gloria and unpack and have a bit of breakfast. We'll see you later, Joe."

Joe Kennedy cleared his throat as if to speak, but he

brushed off his knees instead. "All right, then," he announced, "shall we say one o'clock for lunch?" With that, he and the two horsemen left for church.

For the rest of the day we relaxed, postponing all business discussion until Pat Sullivan would be with us; but by the time he got there that evening, we had all had such a beautiful time doing nothing that we deferred business again until the following day. We dressed for dinner and Joe Kennedy took us all out to one of the big hotel dining rooms—five men and a woman carrying an orchid corsage.

During the days that followed, we mixed business with a round of teas, receptions, and dinner parties. All of Palm Beach scrambled to entertain the Marquis and Marquise de la Falaise de la Coudraye, and throughout these affairs, which after three years were boring routine for Henri and me, Joe Kennedy beamed as if he were P. T. Barnum presenting Lavinia and Tom Thumb or a pair of unicorns. At the same time, he manifested an endearing, boyish pride in himself, by means of which he seemed to challenge all the swells to remember that this was the saloonkeeper's son who was providing them with the thrill of their social life. About his background and his religion he made no apologies whatsoever, and I admired him tremendously for that; after all, I hadn't been a star or a marquise so long that I couldn't remember exactly how much a ride on the trolley cost. Joe Kennedy had the fighting-Irish pride that came of having withstood oppression and endured prejudice and arrived washed and healthy and rich on the speaker's platform, all due to brains and stamina and the political support of a horde of other urban Irishmen. He enjoyed Palm Beach because at forty he could pay for Palm Beach, and give it quite a show. He baldly enjoyed the fact that his kind were newly arrived there, and he made it plain that they would stay as long as it pleased them.

In spite of his sanguinity, however, the horsemen all squirmed miserably at the society parties when they attended them. Nevertheless, they sprang to excited life whenever we turned to business. Pat Sullivan, for instance, informed me that the only significant member of Gloria Swanson Productions who had been allowed to remain on in Gloria Productions was Lance Heath, the chief of publicity for my pictures; all the rest had been retired, and he was able without notes to rattle off a list of specific reasons for each dismissal. As he outlined in detail the corporate housecleaning that had been necessary, I was pleased and grateful to be the boss no longer, and Henri sat beside me in stunned silence. From now on, Pat Sullivan concluded, E. B. Derr would take care of all my business affairs with a handpicked staff of efficient experts. Agreed? Agreed.

Next Joe Kennedy proposed a whopping single deal that would set all of my finances straight. He wanted to sell Joe Schenck the full distribution rights to both *Sunya* and *Sadie*. That would wipe out my debt to Schenck's finance company, which had advanced me the money to produce the pictures; bring my steep interest payments to a halt; provide me with some liquid capital; and solve the tricky distribution problems that would arise over *Sadie*—all in one bold stroke.

"What distribution problems?" I asked, with a defensive edge in my voice.

Joe said exhibitors were already showing signs of being leery about *Sadie Thompson,* even before it was released. Although I had taken the dirty words out and turned Davidson's clerical collar around, religious groups all across America, from the Catholics to the Baptists, were still going to find it pretty hot stuff. "I've seen it," Joe said, "and I've seen all the sneak-preview cards, and I still say it's going to be a hard film to sell. Let Schenck sell it. It opens in New York at the Rivoli on February third. New York critics won't be shocked; they'll love it and give it good notices. E.B. even has a social charity lined up to launch the preview. And that's the time to sell it to Schenck, when you've got all the artistic honors, but before the commercial headaches begin. Arranging distribution for *Sadie Thompson* could turn out to be a gargantuan labor, and I think we're better off investing that same energy in the new picture, which, by the way, Erich von Stroheim told me yesterday is going to be a masterpiece."

"I think *Sadie* is a sort of a masterpiece," I said, sorry to surrender a proud part of me.

"Fine," said Joe. "But take my advice and let Schenck sell it. Even though the Hays Office passed it, they'll never approve it or recommend it." Then he asked, "Have you seen it, Henri?"

"No," Henri said with some embarrassment, "I haven't."

Joe raised his eyebrows critically. "Well, you should," he said flatly.

Then Joe waited for me to speak. In a moment, I had to trust my intuition that the film was going to be a huge success or trust Joe Kennedy's superior business sense and unload the

headaches of distributing it. All I knew was that I had made
mistakes in the past, whereas so far, in his dealings with me,
he had made none. Reluctantly, therefore, I told him he
could arrange the deal with Joe Schenck if he thought it was
the smart financial thing to do.

"I know it is," he said. "I'll have E.B. start on it tomorrow.
After the premiere Joe Schenck will owe you money for a
change instead of you owing him."

The other important matter of business was a position for
Henri. For the three years since our marriage, Henri's
responsibilities had been nebulous. At present he was in my
employ, and that was a poor arrangement; by any standards it
was somehow demeaning for him. With the greatest tact
imaginable, Joe Kennedy offered him a marvelous position as
European director of Pathé studios. It would make him
distinctly his own man, and if he was clever, it could make
him very rich as well. Always left unspoken was the job's
principal advantage: that Henri would no longer be on salary
with me in some vague position with no real authority.

Henri was quick to see he would have to go far to find a
better opportunity. I realized the same at once and flashed
Joe Kennedy a subtle smile of deep gratitude. Without any
hesitation the two men came to a verbal agreement, and Joe
told Pat Sullivan to draw up the papers.

In a few brief sessions, then, we had rearranged the world.
After that, everyone agreed, it was time to enjoy the nation's
finest winter resort. Eddie Moore asked Henri if he would
like to try an afternoon of deep-sea fishing, and Henri said he
would be delighted. The next morning at breakfast Eddie
announced that he had chartered a boat and hired a photographer to be on the dock at sunset to take pictures of them
with their trophies. "We'll leave right after lunch," he said.

"Not me," Joe Kennedy said. "I have business calls to
make that won't keep."

"How about you?" Ted O'Leary asked me. As we were
becoming friendlier, it was becoming customary for the
horsemen to address me as nothing at all, rather than as
Marquise or Miss Swanson.

"Absolutely not, thank you," I said. "I don't feel safe in
anything smaller than the *Leviathan*. I'd much rather shop for
presents for my children."

After they left I bought some gifts in the fancy stores in
Palm Beach and then went back to the hotel, where I got into
a kimono and slippers and stretched out sitting up on the bed.

The maid brought in some dresses she had ironed for me, and as she was hanging them up, the phone rang. It was the hotel florist, warning me of an impending crisis. Owing to Mrs. Stotesbury's party the following evening, there was already an orchid shortage. Mr. Joseph Kennedy had told him to phone me and ask what color dress I would be wearing so that he, the florist, could save me two orchids of exactly the right shade.

"If you have an orchid shortage," I said, laughing, "I know why. I've had orchid deliveries every day I've been here."

"Orders of Mr. Ken—"

"I'm aware of whose orders," I said. While I was talking I nodded to the maid indicating that there was nothing further I needed. "The point is, I don't like orchids. And I never wear corsages, on my shoulder, on my wrist, at my waist, anywhere. What you can do is save me two or three fresh red carnations—no wire, no tinfoil, no pins, no ribbons—just two plain carnations."

"Very well, madam," the florist said.

I hung up, dimly aware that the maid had left. As I stretched back out on the bed, I saw Joseph Kennedy standing in the open doorway. He had obviously arrived as the maid was leaving and had certainly heard the whole conversation with the florist.

"Well," I said with a twinge, "now you know."

He wasn't listening. He just stood there, in his white flannels and his argyle sweater and his two-toned shoes, staring at me for a full minute or more, before he entered the room and closed the door behind him. He moved so quickly that his mouth was on mine before either of us could speak. With one hand he held the back of my head, with the other he stroked my body and pulled at my kimono. He kept insisting in a drawn-out moan, "No longer, no longer. Now." He was like a roped horse, rough, arduous, racing to be free. After a hasty climax he lay beside me, stroking my hair. Apart from his guilty, passionate mutterings, he had still said nothing cogent.

I had said nothing at all. Since his kiss on the train, I had known this would happen. And I knew, as we lay there, that it would go on. Why? I thought. We were both happily married with children. We were ten years apart in age. He was a staunch Roman Catholic, and I was married to a thoroughly unexceptionable man I had no wish to divorce. Furthermore, we had no domestic feelings for each other. In

fact, at that instant we would both probably have liked to
have an extra life to live so that we wouldn't have to forfeit
the one we were already living. All arguments were useless,
however. I knew perfectly well that whatever adjustments or
deceits must inevitably follow, the strange man beside me,
more than my husband, owned me.

In an hour, long before the fishermen returned with their
catch, he got up and dressed. Before he left the room he said
softly, as if reciting a lesson, "No more orchids," and we were
both relieved to have a reason to laugh.

The following evening I arrived at Mrs. Stotesbury's beautiful party with my husband and Mr. Kennedy. Mrs. Stotesbury said everyone was dying to meet us and asked if we
would stand beside her in the receiving line. I was wearing a
blue-gray gown designed by René Hubert, and I carried a
single red carnation—both noted, I could see, by many of the
matrons wearing variegated orchids as they filed past. Henry
and Joe wore red carnations too, as boutonnieres, which I had
put on them in the lobby of the Poinciana.

In two months Joseph Kennedy had taken over my entire
life, and I trusted him implicitly to make the most of it.
He insistently kept all business negotiations in my name
confidential and secret. E. B. Derr handled the paperwork
through the FBO office in California, and Pat Sullivan signed
the checks. From New York, Joe would communicate with me
through channels and always refer to me as "the client." E.B.
would get a telegram saying, "Have your client call me at six
today New York time" or "Inform client I arrive Friday at
four." Whenever Joe was in Hollywood, he was there as the
head of FBO-RKO and the manager of Pathé, never visibly as
the boss of Gloria Productions.

From the outside, my company had not changed at all, not
even in name, for Gloria Swanson Productions and Gloria
Productions began to be used interchangeably, until no one
thought there was any difference. In reality, however, only
Lance Heath remained of all my former staff, and after
getting his orders from E.B., he relayed them to the outside
as if they came from me. If I had been producing three or four
pictures a year, the situation might have been more apparent,
but since I was involved in one big production only, there
would be a period of relative quiet until publicity for *The
Swamp* got under way. As of the spring of 1928, though, Joe

Kennedy's wish was to release no publicity notices about the picture until a male star was chosen and shooting began, in spite of the fact that by then *Sadie Thompson* was getting marvelous notices in New York and other major cities. In the fall *The Wedding March*, Von Stroheim's last picture, which had taken two years to shoot and cost $2 million, would be released, and Joe Kennedy wanted to associate *The Swamp* with *The Wedding March* in the public's mind, not with *Sadie Thompson*. In the meantime, as he said, I was free to enjoy my family.

The family included briefly Henri's aunt, who arrived in Los Angeles with a young lover, to my amazement, and proved indefatigable in making the rounds and seeing the sights. By the time she departed it was time for Henri to go too and take over his Pathé office in Paris. Joe Kennedy had arranged everything, including Henri's departure time, and starting then I had two distinct existences, one with Henri and one on Rodeo Drive with Joseph Kennedy when Henri was abroad. As much as possible, these two existences were kept strictly separate. In late May, for instance, Henri planned to return to Hollywood and bring his brother Alain back with him for a visit. Therefore, Joe Kennedy spent as much time as he could arrange before then to be in Hollywood, and he arranged to be away for the period when Henri would be at home.

After dinner on Rodeo Drive one night in March, Joe finally handed me a copy of the massive completed script of *The Swamp*. Like a college boy wanting to jump for joy but compelled to be serious by the matter at hand, he told me Robert Sherwood, the film and drama editor of *Life* magazine, had read it and pronounced it the best film story ever written. Other knowledgeable literary people had also gone over it and said it was magnificent. "We have the star, the director, and the story now," Joe said, "and I'm hiring two producers, Bill Le Baron and Benjamin Glazer, to keep Von Stroheim on a tight leash and see he doesn't take two years this time or spend two million again. They've both read the script too, and they say it's far and away the best thing he's ever done. Oh, I tell you, Gloria," he said with solemn pride, pressing my hand tightly, "this is going to be a major, *major* motion picture."

Other nights we spent watching films. He had a real academic interest in keeping up with what was being produced, now that he had entered the field with an eye solely to making the best. He said he had still not seen *The Jazz Singer*, the film Warner Bros. was touting as the first talking picture, but he had sent people to see it in New York and they had reported it as an interesting novelty that wouldn't do well in the rest of the country. He wanted to know if I had seen it.

"No," I said, "and I'm in no great rush. There's nothing new about talking pictures. In 1925 when Henri and I arrived in New York from Paris, Lee De Forest asked us to do a talking segment as a stunt for a presentation at the Lambs Club. He got Allan Dwan and Tommy Meighan and Henri and me into a little studio in Manhattan and had us talk to one another while a cameraman photographed us and another technician waved a microphone around on a pole. We all sounded terrible; none of us could believe our own voices."

"Maybe it's been improved since then," Joe ventured.

"It hadn't been as of a year ago. Roxy had a Vitaphone segment of opera singers along with the premiere of *Sunya*, and the great Martinelli didn't sound any better than we had. *The Jazz Singer* is made with exactly the same process—Vitaphone. Believe me, the opening-night audience at the Roxy was relieved when the real picture came on."

At the end of these evenings, after our intimate hours together, Joe would have one of the horsemen drive me home. We rarely saw each other during daytime hours unless other people were present. The first close friend with whom I shared the secret of the house on Rodeo Drive was Lois Wilson. In addition to being a successful star now, Lois was a Catholic convert, so she enjoyed the boss and his horsemen and occasionally drove back from Mass with one or more of them for a Sunday luncheon. She could understand, she said, why Joe kept pestering me to have little Joseph baptized. Since our first meeting at the Barclay, I knew that Joe could hardly bear the idea of an unbaptized child, and he brought up the subject frequently. When Lois began to second him in his concern, I finally gave in. Joe was delighted and said he would throw a big christening party, whereat I consented to a small one, which included the four horsemen, E.B.'s daughter Betty, and some of the Irish community from Beverly Hills: Winifield Sheehan from Fox and his wife, Maria Jeritza, the opera singer, and Allan Dwan and Aileen Pringle. I also allowed Joe to be Joseph's godfather and granted his wish that Joseph have Patrick for a middle name. All in all this made him very happy. Nevertheless, as time passed, Joe spoke less and less of our separate families.

All during April and the early part of May, United Artists sent a steady stream of telegrams demanding to know what my plans were for a third picture. On May 21 E. B. Derr gave the nod to Lance Heath to tell United Artists what was going on.

RECEIVED DEFINITE WORD TODAY SWANSON HAS SIGNED VON STROHEIM TO DIRECT THIRD INDEPENDENT UNITED ARTISTS PIC-TURE STOP   TITLE THE SWAMP BASED ON HIGHLY DRAMATIC ORIGINAL BY VON STROHEIM WITH LOCALE GERMAN EAST AFRICA STOP   BEGÍN PRODUCTION HERE AT EARLY DATE STOP RELEASING   STORY   CONFIRMING   DEAL   FOR   WEDNESDAY PUBLICATION   REGARDS
      LANCE HEATH

Four days later United's publicity department replied with the following:

CAN YOU COMMUNICATE WITH MISS SWANSON AND SECURE MORE ATTRACTIVE TITLE THAN THE SWAMP

We replied that the title was set and approved.
Thereupon, United began sending exhibitors all over the country its official list of coming attractions.

NINETEEN GREAT PICTURES FROM UNITED ARTISTS
(1928–1929)

MARY PICKFORD	Title to be an-nounced	The crowning achievement of Mary's career; directed by Sam Taylor.
NORMA TALMADGE	"The Woman Disputed"	Adapted from the famous stage success; di-rected by Henry King.
GLORIA SWANSON	"The Swamp"	Written and di-rected by Eric von Stroheim.
DOLORES DEL RIO	"Revenge"	An Edwin Carewe Pro-duction.

VILMA BANKY	"The Awakening"	With Movietone by Irving Berlin.
CHARLIE CHAPLIN	"City Lights"	High Life, Night Life, and Low Life.
DOUGLAS FAIRBANKS	"The Man With The Iron Mask"	Sequel to "The Three Musketeers."
D. W. GRIFFITH'S PRODUCTION	"Battle of the Sexes"	Great Cast—Great Exploitation Title.
JOHN BARRYMORE	"Tempest"	Now a Tremendous Hit at $2.00 Top.
RONALD COLMAN	"The Rescue"	Joseph Conrad's famous Sea Novel; directed by Herbert Brenon.
RONALD COLMAN and VILMA BANKY	"Two Lovers"	Fred Niblo's Production of Baroness Orczy's great novel, "Leatherface."
BUSTER KEATON and ERNEST TORRENCE	"Steamboat Bill Jr."	A wonderful combination of comedy stars.
HERBERT BRENON'S	"Lummox"	Fannie Hurst's greatest novel.
D. W. GRIFFITH'S PRODUCTION	"The Love Song"	William Boyd, Lupe Velez, and Movietone by Irving Berlin.
ROLAND WEST PRODUCTION	"Nightstick"	The famous stage melodramatic sensation.
GIGANTIC AVIATION DRAMA	"Hell's Angels"	An epic of the clouds; most stupendous air picture ever conceived.

HENRY KING PRODUCTION	"She Goes To War"	Rupert Hughes' splendid Red Book novel.
REX INGRAM PRODUCTION	"Three Passions"	Alice Terry and a powerful cast of supporting artists.
JOHN BARRYMORE	Title to be announced	An Ernst Lubitsch Production.

The reaction of exhibitors everywhere was that the title of the new Swanson picture was guaranteed to keep people away in droves. They wanted it changed, especially in view of the ongoing success of *Sadie Thompson*. UA then began burning up the wires to Lance Heath, and by the end of the summer things had progressed to the stage where the film was always referred to as "tentatively titled *The Swamp*." More than that, for the moment, Mr. von Stroheim and Mr. Kennedy were unwilling to yield.

When Henri returned from France with his brother at the end of May, he seemed very changed. He suddenly appeared a man of responsibility with an identity all his own. Although in the Hollywood columns he was still known as Gloria's marquis, in Paris he was quickly establishing himself as one of Pathé's top indispensable men, and he talked as if he would be obliged to spend more and more of his time there. When he asked about the picture, I told him we hoped to start shooting soon. If he had any suspicions about my relations with Joe, he never voiced them, perhaps out of gratitude for the Pathé job, perhaps out of a cultivated European good sense to let such affairs run their course, particularly inasmuch as this one could almost certainly never lead to marriage.

In his short stay in Hollywood, however, Henri's own name was brought into question in the area of marital fidelity. While he was dining at a Russian café on Sunset Boulevard with friends one evening, the place was bombed. The police said it was a case of arson with political overtones, and Henri and Charlie Chaplin, who had also been dining there that night, were subpoenaed as material witnesses. Once Henri had been questioned, he was free to leave the country again, but by then several columnists had snidely reported that the marquis was not dining alone when the bomb exploded.

Apart from his business friends, he had had a dinner companion who was not his wife. Neither of us mentioned the stories or their implications. For the time being, we both seemed relieved when the time came for him to return to France. I drove him to the train, and there we kissed good-bye and exchanged endearments, but driving back to the house alone, I felt that we had done so in the spirit of a couple who had been married thirty-five years instead of three and a half.

The last week in July, Erich von Stroheim settled at last on a leading man for the picture, and on July 31 E.B. authorized Mr. Heath to forward the news to the head of publicity at UA. Lance Heath did so in the following night letter:

FOR PUBLICATION FRIDAY PLANTED HERE WITH LOUELLA PARSONS REGINA CREWE AP AND UP STOP   GLORIAS LEADING MAN IN THIRD INDEPENDENTLY PRODUCED FEATURE FOR UNITED ARTISTS RELEASE TENTATIVELY TITLED THE SWAMP WILL BE WALTER BYRON YOUNG ENGLISH ACTOR BROUGHT TO HOLLYWOOD BY SAM GOLDWYN FEW MONTHS AGO STOP   MISS SWANSONS ANNOUNCEMENT OF BYRON AS LEADING MAN FOLLOWED COMPLETION ARRANGEMENTS BY WHICH GOLDWYN AGREED TO LOAN THE PLAYER FOR HER PICTURE WHICH WAS WRITTEN AND WILL BE DIRECTED BY ERICH VON STROHEIM STOP   BYRON SIGNED BY GOLDWYN IN ENGLAND LAST APRIL STOP   JUST COMPLETED LEAD OPPOSITE BANKY IN THE AWAKENING AND THE SWAMP THEREFORE IS HIS SECOND AMERICAN PICTURE STOP   APPEARANCE OPPOSITE BANKY AND THEN SWANSON IS BIT OF GOOD FORTUNE WHICH WILL MAKE HIM MOST ENVIED OF HOLLYWOODS LEADING MEN STOP SWANSON AND VON STROHEIM CONSIDERED BYRON IDEAL FOR THE WILD AND ROISTERING GERMAN PRINCE WHO PLAYS OPPOSITE QUEEN KELLY THE IRISH GIRL WHO SWANSON HAS CHOSEN TO SUCCEED SADIE THOMPSON ON HER LIST OF OUTSTANDING SCREEN PORTRAYALS STOP   THE SWAMP TO GO INTO PRODUCTION AT EARLY DATE POSSIBLY BEFORE FIRST SEPTEMBER STOP   KINDEST REGARDS
    LANCE HEATH

When I remembered what Sam Goldwyn had cost me on *Sadie Thompson* by pulling his cameraman off the picture after a few days' shooting, I asked Joe when he called if he thought we were wise to deal with him again. Joe said not to worry; he had excellent personal relations with Sam Gold-wyn, and besides, Erich von Stroheim had made it quite clear that after testing Walter Byron, he would be most unhappy to have to settle for anyone else. He also told me that Von Stroheim had relented on the title. We would change it. In the meantime, Von Stroheim was at work full-time supervising construction of the royal palace and the convent on the FBO lot, and Wardrobe was making hundreds of elaborate uni-forms and bejeweled gowns for the palace scenes.

Of all these things, only the title concerned me for the moment. Joe said I should think of what I wanted to call the picture. As I already knew, for the whole first half of the film my clothes would consist of a convent uniform, a loose cotton nightie, and the prince's overcoat. My clothes for the scenes in Africa need not worry us yet. From the tone of his voice on the phone, I could tell that Joe was all but bursting with excitement.

"Ask him when we're going to start shooting," I said before I hung up.

"He says soon," Joe said. "Don't worry, Le Baron and Glazer are watching him every minute."

By the end of August, everyone in Hollywood was inviting me to parties, and I was perfectly aware it was because they were all morbidly curious to know what Von Stroheim, the mad genius, was up to. I therefore stayed at home with my children and kept my mouth shut, declining all invitations except for one to a dinner and dance at Pickfair for Prince George, the Duke of Kent, of Great Britain, which I felt I couldn't refuse.

Instead of the sedate affair I was anticipating, it turned out to be a memorable evening. As I left my house I said to Lois Wilson and Virginia Bowker, who were staying with me, "I'll be home early," and laughingly added, "And I'll bring the prince." At the formal dinner for twenty the prince, who was utterly charming, was seated between Mary Pickford and me. At one point he leaned over and whispered that he hoped he would see more of our local night life than just Pickfair on his only evening off his ship. He asked if we might not leave the party early and look for something livelier. I concealed a smile and said I didn't see how. After dinner about a hundred additional guests arrived for the dance. The prince invited me to dance and again asked if we couldn't go someplace more amusing. I finally said all right, I would make my excuses as early as possible to Mary on the pretext that I was expecting an important call from Henri in Paris. I suggested that we go to the current favorite night spot, which was the Fatty Arbuckle in Venice, and I told the prince to indicate discreetly to me as we danced those people he would like to have go along. He gestured toward six or eight people, including Charlie Chaplin, to whom I passed word of our plan, and as early as we could leave without being rude, we made our individual excuses to Doug and Mary and left. The prince had to leave first, of course, because none of us could leave before him.

I went back to my house and filled the car up with champagne, and as I started for the Fatty Arbuckle, I could see behind me a caravan of other cars—containing the chosen deserters from Pickfair. We stayed at the club until nearly three, and the prince enjoyed himself enormously. He knew the lyrics to all the latest American songs and was a perfect dancer. When we left, I suggested we continue the party at my house and invited four or five of the band members to come back and play. I woke Ransom, the butler, and told him to start making preparations for breakfast and to wake Miss Wilson and Miss Bowker and tell them I had a surprise for them.

Lois and Virginia couldn't believe their eyes when they arrived on the scene. Instead of the four or five musicians I had invited, the whole band showed up and played until dawn, and Charlie Chaplin entertained us with skits, in which he played all the parts, *and* all the instruments in the band, for hours. Then we had breakfast, and the prince left to go back to his hotel. Later I drove him from the hotel to the airport, and from there he flew to his ship in Santa Barbara.

I had made everyone promise never to tell Mary and Doug, but in vain. It was all in the papers the next day, and that evening Joe Kennedy called to say he was furious he had been on the wrong coast. At the same time he begged me to come to New York for a few days because he missed me and couldn't leave his business there for at least a month.

"I can't," I said. "The children."

"Bring them," he said. "Please, Gloria."

"What about the picture?" I asked.

"He won't be ready to shoot for three more weeks," Joe said. "I just talked to him. You'll be back long before then. Please, Gloria."

I liked to hear him say "Please" that way, so I said very well, I'd leave on Tuesday.

Joseph was six years old, just the age to fall in love with trains; he played engineer and conductor with the maid the whole way. Gloria and Miss Simonson, the governess, in the meantime, sat quietly like ladies and read the stack of books we had brought along. They had grown up into enjoyable company at last, but I wished every mother's wish, as I watched them and as the golden autumn landscape fled away: that they were still little. In spite of the complications Joe Kennedy had brought into my life, he had nevertheless taken the business load off me for a year and allowed me hours every day to watch my children grow.

Employees of his met us at Grand Central and took us to the hotel, and before we had been in our large suite fifteen minutes, Joe himself bounded in, carrying a stack of presents for the children and me. I was reading a telegram from Lance Heath saying the publicity department of UA in New York wanted urgently to see me and to arrange interviews for me with the press while I was in New York and advising me to spend some time with them. Joe said it was nonsense, this was a vacation, adding, "Where shall we go tonight?"

I told him to be reasonable; in no way could I be seen out on the town with him that night or any night in New York.

"But we're business associates," he said.

"Business is done in the daytime if both associates are married," I said. "Joseph, don't you see it's impossible? If we want to go out, we have to go out with other people."

"I'll call Pat Sullivan," he said.

"Never mind. I have friends of my own I can call," I said. "In fact, I wired Sport Ward to ask him to be free for dinner tonight."

Before I had the sentence out, he was acting as hurt as a sophomore who's been turned down for the prom. He blurted out that he had been faithful to me.

"How can we be faithful, Joe? We're both married."

Then he stunned me by telling me proudly that there had been no Kennedy baby that year. *Our* year was what he meant, for it had been almost a year since our meeting at the Barclay. What he wanted more than anything, he continued, was for us to have a child.

"You can't ask that of me," I said. "I refuse to discuss it. If you so much as mention it again, I will turn right around and go back to California tonight. You can't manipulate the public, Joseph. I would be finished tomorrow."

After that he was a lamb. We dined that night with Sport, and within an hour Joe thought that he was the most amusing man in the world. Joe, in fact, was the perfect audience for Sport Ward, who kept him roaring with laughter all evening. They even found they had a friend in common, Robert Benchley, who had been a classmate of Joe's at Harvard. When Joe learned further that Sport was close with Jimmy Walker, he opened up to him completely. He outlined in all its complexity the latest merger he had just put together in New York and Hollywood and urged Sport to join us in it when a proper time came, telling him he was sure he could make a handy million or so.

He also told Sport that through his merger he now had the equipment to film all or part of our picture in sound, but he knew that Von Stroheim and I both felt sound reproduction was still too crude to spoil a great picture with.

"Maybe next time," he said with a smile in my direction. "The important thing is to be ready to go if sound pictures become more than just a novelty. Well, I'm ready with Photophone. That's what our sound system is called." Listening to him, I marveled once again at what a head he had for business, and how few people in the movie industry were capable of planning ten stages at once in advance the way he was.

We saw Sport often after that. Joe never ceased to be delighted by the stir people caused when they recognized me, and his innocent enjoyment in turn amused blasé Mr. Ward no end. "Della Falaise," he announced to me when Joe was away from the table, "remove your spell from that poor man." Della Falaise was Sport's debunking nickname for me; he said that's what the man on the street thought my name was when he heard "de la Falaise." Then he added, "He's amazingly clever, isn't he?"

A few days before I was ready to leave New York, Joe said he had promised his wife and children that I would bring my children up to their home in Bronxville for a Halloween party. When I realized what he'd said I told him I just couldn't do that.

"Please," he said. "I promised."

There in that strange situation was all of the man's complexity in a nutshell. While he was in control, he saw nothing as impossible or out of the question. I couldn't even argue with him, because it would have done no good. I finally said the children could go but I would not, and he accepted that as the best compromise that could be reached.

Eddie Moore drove the children up with Miss Simonson, and when they got back they reported that they had had a wonderful time. Gloria had just had her eighth birthday party in the hotel, which was not much fun, but she said Bronxville had more than made up for it. She could not get over the fact that one family could have seven children in it. She had taken a particular shine to a boy called Jack, she said, who was a few years older than she was. "He was very interested in Daddy," she said.

"Really?" I ventured. "Why?"

"Because I told him Tom Mix goes to his restaurant for lunch."

That was the end of our socializing. I gave several more interviews and then, on the off chance that there might be news on the wireless patent, I called George de Bothezat. He reported sadly that our application had been submitted too late. Someone had beat us to it.

I said it was all my fault, for having ignored his original letter when I was busy on *Sadie Thompson*.

"It was also your idea," Mr. Bothezat said. "Now you begin to see how important it is to protect ideas."

"If there's ever a next time, Mr. Bothezat, I swear to you I won't miss the opportunity." I meant it.

On the second of November, Joe and Sport saw us off on the train. By then Joe and I had decided, with Erich von Stroheim's approval, that the picture would be called *Queen Kelly*.

In November of 1928, almost a year after Erich von Stroheim had first told the story of *The Swamp* to Joseph Kennedy and me, he began shooting the film under its new name. When I returned from New York I went to the FBO lot, which was now officially the RKO lot, to greet the cast, approve my simple wardrobe, and inspect the beautiful new dressing room Joe had ordered for me. Mr. von Stroheim, courtly and refined, his head shaved almost bald, walked me proudly

through the magnificent sets. Never, he confided, had he felt
so utterly confident in the rightness of every detail in a project
as he sensed around him with *Queen Kelly*. For the first time
in his career, absolutely nothing was wrong; everything
worked. He told me we would start shooting my scenes in
about a week. In the meantime, he and I met each day to look
at the rushes.

Those first rushes were breath-taking. Every scene was
alive with glowing light play and palpable texture. You could
almost smell the thin Havana cigars and taste the Viennese
coffee and feel the dew on the grass. Each image seemed
richer and more dazzling than the one before: the mad queen,
her nakedness covered with nothing but a big pure white
Persian cat, waiting on her balcony in the morning light for
Prince Wolfram to return to the palace; the race to the palace
by the prince and his uniformed companions and a carriageful
of demimondaines in satins and feathers after an all-night
revel; the prince in his luxurious private quarters being
sobered up by his staff in order to be in a condition to answer
a summons from the queen, his fiancée; and, most beautiful
of all, Griffith Park turned in a meadow in Mitteleuropa,
where a double row of convent girls shepherded by nuns
encounters a double file of cavalry on a drill.

"That could be better," Mr. von Stroheim would announce
from time to time as we watched the fabulous rushes, or
"That I will change." Sure enough, two days later I would see
the same scene from a slightly different angle or in a slightly
different cast of light, and as it rolled, Mr. von Stroheim
would purr a gruff approval.

Finally he was ready for me. The experience of working
with him was unlike any I had had in more than fifty pictures.
He was so painstaking and slow that I would lose all sense of
time, hypnotized by the man's relentless perfectionism. A
scene that Allan Dwan or Raoul Walsh would have wrapped
up in an hour might take Von Stroheim all day, fondling and
dawdling over the tiniest minutiae, only to announce late in
the afternoon that he would like to try it once more the
following day. But his exactitude always paid off in the
rushes, and it was a course in the art of filmmaking to hear
him defend his choices and explain his reasons—rare occasions, to be sure, for in general he considered himself to be
his own best audience and only critic. Under his direction
Seena Owen, who played the queen, was marvelous, and

Walter Byron stood to be the next great male star of Hollywood. My own scenes passed before me each day in the rushes like paintings created by a master of a girl I didn't quite know. Erich von Stroheim had stripped a dozen years off me. I looked sixteen.

On my first day of shooting in Griffith Park, I had one of my rare extrasensory experiences. As I checked my make-up in a small hand mirror, I said involuntarily, "I can't see this picture finished." When another actress later asked me what I had meant, I said I didn't know.

We shot the sequence of the convent girls and the man on horseback so many times that I lost count. Even to my trained eye the rushes began to look the same, but Mr. von Stroheim always had a reason for doing it one more time.

One day Ann Morgan came to my dressing room to alert me to something she thought I had missed in the day's shooting. This was the same Miss Morgan who had come to America in 1921 as Elinor Glyn's dressmaker. Since Elinor's return to Europe, Ann had stayed in Hollywood as my personal modiste. When Mr. von Stroheim saw her with me one morning, he remarked on her angelic little face and asked if she might play one of the nuns in the picture. Therefore, for days on end, this quiet stitcher of dresses had been marching up and down Griffith Park in a habit, being photographed over and over again.

"Today was very different," she was saying. "He specifically had Mr. Byron put the panties up to his face."

"He" was Erich von Stroheim, I knew. In the meadow scene, when the prince and his cavalry are filing past, all the convent girls have to stop and curtsy. As I do, my panties drop down around my ankles and I have to struggle with my feet to step out of them. When the prince sees this he laughs gaily, which so arouses my Irish temper that I wad the panties up and throw them at him. He playfully catches them and stuffs them into the jacket of his uniform. When the prince orders his men to reverse direction and file past us again, I plead with my eyes and mouthed words for him to return the panties, and he playfully flips them back to me. Such stuff was typical light Von Stroheim decadence, of the sweet, harmless, titillating sort. We had shot the scene so many times that we could do every movement in our sleep, and it was delightful fun, interspersed as it was with shots of serenely unaware nuns' faces.

Ann Morgan was so shocked that she could hardly speak of this latest variation, but she swore she was not mistaken. Mr. von Stroheim had expressly instructed Walter Byron as Prince Wolfram to fondle the panties, and before stuffing them into his uniform, to pass them in front of his face. The idea of putting such an act into a film was so unthinkable in 1928 as to be unmentionable, even in the Formula. That, in fact, I thought, might be the very reason Von Stroheim thought he could get away with it. And from then on, I began to watch him more closely.

Looking at the rushes, I saw that the action was subtle, but it was there. Mr. von Stroheim made no comment. Neither did I. Since everything else was so beautiful, I decided not to excercise my veto on the matter until the proper time came.

Once we finished the location scenes and moved to the studio, Mr. von Stroheim became more meticulous than ever. I knew that thousands of feet of film must be piling up, and I began counting the takes, but the supervisors, Bill Le Baron and Benjamin Glazer, said nothing, so I assumed we were all right. Next, however, I began keeping track of the number of days it took to shoot a single page of the script, and I knew by mid-December that at the present rate of progress we would probably take several months more and run over budget. But still Le Baron and Glazer held their peace, and Mr. von Stroheim continued to purr through the rushes, so I assumed they planned to speed up in the studio.

In December the United Artists sales organization was having its annual meeting in Chicago, and the studio asked us for statements about the long-awaited film. Mr. von Stroheim and I both sent off enthusiastic reports in night letters shortly before we halted shooting for the holidays:

WHILE YOUR CONVENTION IS IN PROGRESS MAY I EXPRESS MY SINCERE THANKS TO MEMBERS OF THE SALES FORCE FOR THEIR MOST EFFICIENT HANDLING OF THE UNITED ARTISTS PRODUCT STOP   THEIR EFFORTS DESERVE THE HIGHEST PRAISE AND I AM ONLY SORRY IT IS IMPOSSIBLE TO THANK EACH ONE INDIVIDUALLY STOP   WE ARE MAKING EXCELLENT PROGRESS ON MY NEW PICTURE QUEEN KELLY UNDER MR. VON STROHEIM'S DIRECTION STOP   HE TRULY IS THE GREAT VON STROHEIM AND I AM THANKFUL IT HAS BEEN MADE POSSIBLE FOR HIM TO DIRECT THIS PICTURE STOP   MANY KIND THINGS HAVE BEEN SAID IN REGARD TO QUEEN KELLY AND WE ARE DOING OUR BEST TO MAKE A

PICTURE THAT WILL MEASURE UP TO EVERYONE'S EXPECTATIONS
STOP   VERY KINDEST REGARDS
    GLORIA SWANSON

THIS WOULD SEEM TO BE A GOOD TIME TO TELL YOU SOMETHING OF
THE MAGNIFICENT WORK MISS SWANSON IS DOING IN QUEEN
KELLY STOP   SHE IS ABSOLUTELY MARVELOUS IN THE ROLE AND I
KNOW THAT ALL OF YOU WHO ARE INTERESTED IN SELLING THE
PICTURE WILL AGREE WITH ME WHEN THE FINAL PRINTS REACH
YOU STOP   WITH THE EXCEPTION OF JACK GILBERT IT HAS NEVER
BEEN MY PRIVILEGE TO WORK WITH A REAL ARTIST IN A ROLE OF
SUCH IMPORTANCE STOP   IT IS A RARE EXPERIENCE STOP   MY
VERY BEST WISHES
    ERICH VON STROHEIM

Henri returned for Christmas and New Year's, looking
more handsome than ever, and we had a happy, loving time
together, probably because Joe Kennedy was three thousand
miles away with his family. Joe called a number of times, and
I told him I thought we were behind schedule, but he said not
to worry; he'd speak to Bill Le Baron and Benjamin Glazer
right after New Year's. He never once mentioned the colossal
surprise he had arranged for me on the Pathé lot: the most
elaborate bungalow in Hollywood, outshining even the one
William Randolph Hearst had built for Marion Davies, which
people jokingly referred to as the Trianon. Mine had a living
room with a grand piano, a full kitchen, a wardrobe, a fitting
room, and a big bedroom. It also had a private entrance from
the road and a private garage. I could only surmise that Joe
Kennedy was starting to do very well for himself in the movie
business. And that he loved me.

Work on the African sequences began the second week in
January on the Pathé lot, where a dance hall, a street, and
several other sets had been built. In this second part of the
story I was the manager of a low, squalid dance hall. My
costume for this section was a clinging black dress with a high
neck and a rope of pearls. To accentuate the vulgarity of the
locale I wore an enormous ring and big earrings, and two
orchids as big as cabbages on my shoulder. Once again Mr.
von Stroheim said we would not be shooting my scenes for
about a week, and once again we watched rushes together.

As of then, by my rough calculation, he had shot over ten
hours of film in two months, which would have to be edited

down to forty minutes—one third of a two-hour picture—
because according to the script, the African scenes would run
much longer than the ones in the European principality. At
that rate, we had another four months of shooting to go and
twenty more hours of film, most of which would end up on the
cutting-room floor, unless a great change occurred soon. Joe
had told me not to worry, however, and Bill Le Baron and
Benjamin Glazer continued to abide by Erich von Stroheim's
rules.

Nevertheless, as soon as I saw the first rushes of the
African sequences, I knew we were in trouble. First of all,
they seemed utterly unrelated to the European scenes or the
characters in them. Moreover, they were rank and sordid and
ugly, Mr. von Stroheim's apocalyptic vision of hell on earth,
and full of material that would never pass the censors.
Something was terribly, terribly wrong. What was called a
dance hall in the script had unmistakably become a bordello,
steaming and filthy, on the screen. In my first scenes in this
part, my dying aunt is marrying me off to an old man. Erich
von Stroheim had cast Tully Marshall in the part, and not
content to have him old, he had turned him into a leering,
slobbering, repulsive cripple. Mr. Marshall was playing the
part to the hilt, as a sort of demented, twitchy lecher in a
greasy suit. On my third day of shooting Mr. von Stroheim
began instructing Mr. Marshall, in his usual painstaking
fashion, how to dribble tobacco juice onto my hand while he
was putting on the wedding ring. It was early morning, I had
just eaten breakfast, and my stomach turned. I became
nauseated and furious at the same time.

"Excuse me," I said to Erich von Stroheim, and turned and
walked off the set. Once I reached my bungalow, I slowly
took off my make-up and costume. The time had come. I
picked up the telephone and called Joe Kennedy.

"He's in a meeting," his secretary said.

"Well, get him out of it," I told her in a tight voice, "and
have him call Gloria Swanson."

The minute I heard his voice, I poured out everything.
"Joseph, you'd better get out here fast. Our director is a
madman. You and everybody else tried to stop me from
making Sadie Thompson. Well, believe me, Sadie Thompson
was Rebecca of Sunnybrook Farm compared with what Queen
Kelly is turning into. It's ruined! And awful! Now, are you
coming out here and starting to make decisions or aren't
you?"

"I'll be there as soon as I can," he said, trying to calm me. "I'll leave tonight or tomorrow."

After I hung up, I walked the floor. Then I called for my car and went home. I never went back to the set, and Mr. von Stroheim never sent for me. Ann Morgan told me the entire studio was in a panic, but no one came near me. My phone never rang.

When Joe Kennedy arrived, he told me to come to my bungalow and wait for him there. When I got to Pathé, the gateman told me Mr. Kennedy and his friends were in the projection room. An hour later he charged into the living room of the bungalow, alone, cursing Von Stroheim and Le Baron and Glazer. Stopping abruptly, he slumped into a deep chair. He turned away from me, struggling to control himself. He held his head in his hands, and little, high-pitched sounds escaped from his rigid body, like those of a wounded animal whimpering in a trap. He finally found his voice. It was quiet, controlled. "I've never had a failure in my life" were his first words. Then he rose, ashen, and went into another searing rage at the people who had let this happen. But he was too hurt and stunned to get properly angry. He yanked me into his arms, and soon my face was wet with his tears.

Bravo, I wanted to say. If you're forty years old and you've never had a failure, you've been deprived. Failure is a part of life too, so better late than never, even though it had to be *Queen Kelly*. But I didn't say it.

"Don't cry" is what I said. "We'll try to save it."

"I don't want to see any of them again," he moaned.

"Then we'll try to save it without them."

Two weeks later, while we were calling up people for suggestions on how to salvage *Queen Kelly*, the newly founded Academy of Motion Picture Arts and Sciences presented its first Oscars at a dinner in Hollywood attended by two hundred people.

I had been notified in advance that I was in nomination for my performance in *Sadie Thompson*, but I had not even informed Joe Kennedy of the fact, just as I had not shown him a telegram from Henri informing me that *Sadie Thompson* was on the list of the ten best pictures of the year. *Sadie Thompson* was the last thing in the world to mention to Joe just then—first, because he refused to identify me with the image I projected in it even though he was attracted to that image, and second, because he had manipulated me into selling the distribution rights to Joe Schenck. The last thing he needed to hear, now that *Queen Kelly* was nothing but $600,000 worth of unresolved footage, was that *Sadie Thompson* was what I had claimed it would be—a triumph.

I did not attend the Academy dinner, but in report it bore out all my feelings about awards and prizes, particularly those given within the industry.

Louise Dresser and I lost out to Janet Gaynor, who at twenty-one was where I had been at twenty-one, making three or four pictures a year. She was nominated for three pictures.

Richard Barthelmess and Charlie Chaplin lost out to Emil Jannings.

Oranges and apples. How could anyone honestly see Charlie Chaplin and Emil Jannings in competition, or Janet Gaynor and me?

The best picture, according to the judges, was *Wings*, produced by Adolph Zukor. Best director: Frank Borzage for *Seventh Heaven*—the Frank Borzage who had directed me in *Society for Sale* at Triangle, one of my worst pictures. Best adaptation: Benjamin Glazer for *Seventh Heaven*—the Benjamin Glazer who had not kept a tight leash on Erich von Stroheim.

At the dinner, a talking film made in New York was shown; it was a dialogue between Adolph Zukor, producer of *Wings*, and Doug Fairbanks, president of the Academy. In addition, a special award went to Warner Bros., maker of *The Jazz Singer*, for—as the judges said—revolutionizing the industry.

Maybe Joe Kennedy had been right.

CHAPTER 16

The picture has suffered from the lack of sound exactly as the radio now suffers from the lack of sight.

. . .

I do not believe that the talking pictures now to be seen in New York City, with the exception of the news reels, give much of my indications of the talking picture's possibilities. I scarcely think they indicate, at all, what it will be.

Actually, they are but silent motion pictures accompanied by synchronized, but wholly mechanical and artificial sounding voices or instrumental music. Their novelty may be called the only element which invites attention to them. They are scarcely even samples of that which is to come. They are old-style movies with a little sound superimposed upon them.

. . .

The girl who in a close-up can sing a soft lullaby to her baby and whisper—"Good night, my darling," in such a way that the camera might be listening in through the key-hole—she will be the new star.

—EDMUND GOULDING,
"The Talkers in Close-up," in *National Board of Review Magazine* (July 1928)

389

For weeks Joe Kennedy was like a beached whale, all his tremendous energy drained, all his lust for ambition mortified. His business enterprises went on as usual, but he took no interest or pleasure in them. They were routine for the bright Harvard business graduate; Joe wanted to fall asleep and dream again.

I was not nearly so unaccustomed to crises. Therefore, the more Joe languished, the more determinedly I forced myself to action. I contacted various people I knew and asked them if they would look at the unedited film and say whether they thought it could be revised or reworked for distribution. All the ones I really trusted—Mickey Neilan, Allan Dwan, Raoul Walsh—were either on location or too deeply immersed in ongoing projects of their own to get involved in mine. Furthermore, for professionals like them, one flop more or less was just part of the game. All the people who did look at the footage proved not to be very helpful; they all agreed that the African sequences could not be used with the convent and palace scenes, but nobody seemed to have a workable idea for making a satisfactory picture out of just the convent and palace scenes.

Soon all of Hollywood was buzzing about the great disaster. Everywhere I went, people asked me in sepulchral tones how things were going, or what I was up to, in the voice people usually employ to ask, How long do they give her? One day, for an agreeable change, someone stopped this brave commiseration long enough to introduce me to the English director Edmund Goulding, who I had been told was amusing and intelligent, a sort of minor wizard, and we hit it off very well. After a few moments of conversation, without any diminution of conviviality, he said in his nice British accent, "I hear you're in trouble."

His frankness was so refreshing that I hurried to match it. "Only about six hundred thousand dollars' worth. Do you have any suggestions? I've already asked everyone else."

"As a matter of fact I do," he replied without hesitation. "Shelve it. I hear it's old-fashioned." Then he added, in a whisper, "And make a talking picture!"

He said he had made a thorough study of sound in pictures for Adolph Zukor the year before, and he was convinced that within two years no film would be made without it. Furthermore, he knew that Joseph Kennedy had somehow merged his set of companies with the Radio Corporation of America;

therefore, he should hasten to be among the avant-garde of sound producers, particularly since he also owned a string of RKO theaters to install the sound systems in at low cost. The RCA sound system was called Photophone, Mr. Goulding explained to me, as opposed to Vitaphone, which belonged to Warners, and Movietone, which belonged to Fox.

"But those things sound awful," I said.

"The technique of sound pictures has to be improved, or realized, I should say," Edmund Goulding countered, "but the idea is inevitable and right. Believe me, Chaplin, Garbo, and you . . . are going to have to talk. I've studied all this and I know."

Everyone I spoke to after that said Eddie Goulding was one of the brightest idea men in pictures. In fact, he was brimming over with ideas. The trouble with him, people said, was that it was difficult to keep him in one place long enough to complete an idea or to keep him from fiddling with it and changing it once he got it. For all of that, I thought, he was likable and unusual, and it sounded as if he knew a bit about Joseph Kennedy's empire to boot; things it might be very useful for Joe himself to know. So I called him up soon after we met and asked him if he would like to direct me in a talking picture.

"Yes," he said. "In fact, I hoped you might take my hint."

"When?" I asked.

"The sooner the better," he replied.

"I'll call you in a day or two," I said.

The next night at dinner Joe was in a jovial, tender mood for the first time in days, so I dared to broach the subject.

"Joseph, I have a favor to ask."

"What is it?"

"An English director named Edmund Goulding wants to make a picture with me. Just a light, easy picture. It wouldn't take long. I told him I'd let him know, because I wouldn't do anything without asking you. But as long as we're stumped on Kelly for the moment, I think I should work with this man while I have the chance." I was making it sound like a cupcake I could turn out in an afternoon, being careful not to mention the word "talking."

"Don't get impatient," Joe said with a smile. "Maybe we're not stumped on Kelly, after all."

"What do you mean?"

"People tell me this Pole Richard Boleslavsky is an important director. I showed him what there is and asked him if
he'd be willing to work on it with us."

"What did he say?" I asked.

"He said he would. He wants a month to work with it on his
own first. And . . ."

"And?" I prodded, certain that he was about to say he
didn't want me to work on anything, ever, that he wasn't
involved in.

"And now I come to the part you're not going to like. This
Boleslavsky and I agree that we can save the film *if* we add
sound to it. Now, Gloria, you may not think much of sound as
it's been up to the present. But I think it's the coming thing.
So does everyone else. And for that reason I've merged RKO
with—"

"Stop!" I shouted, with a little yelp of delight. "You're
going to say, RCA, and I know all about it. Joseph, I'm ten
minutes ahead of you for once. Darling, the picture *I* want to
make is a talking picture, and I think I can be done with it
before Boleslavsky is ready to go to work."

When he understood what I was saying, he went off into
peals of laughter and whacked his thigh—sounds I hadn't
heard from him in over a month. I ran around behind his
chair, circled his neck with my arms, and rested my chin on
his head. The curse of *Queen Kelly* was removed, and we
struck a bargain. If I could produce a script with Edmund
Goulding in the month Joe had to be in New York, then Joe
and I would produce it as my first talking picture, and use the
best of the technique we learned from making it to finish
Queen Kelly with style and elegance.

That same evening I called Edmund Goulding. "We start
on Monday morning," I said, "at my house."

A few days before Joe left to go east, I walked in on him in
the middle of a phone call. Since he seemed very agitated
with the person on the other end of the line, I asked with
gestures whether he wanted me to wait in the next room, but
he gestured back no, so I sat down opposite him.

He kept saying "your hospital" and "that hospital," and he
spoke frequently of a special ambulance he had offered to
donate, but the gift appeared to be contingent on a guarantee
from the person on the other end of the line that his daughter
Rosemary could be cured. His voice went up and down with

impatience and annoyance, until he finally snapped that he would call and talk to somebody else the next day. Then he slammed down the receiver.

My education with Dr. Bieler had left me with an insatiable curiosity about other people's symptoms and illnesses. I was forever urging people to go to him, and I never tired of telling them what he had done for me. I innocently asked Joseph, therefore, "What's the matter with Rosemary?"

He hesitated, and in order to get him to talk I said that no matter what it was, I thought he ought to bring the child to California to see Dr. Bieler.

I had seen him angry with other people, but now, for the first time, he directed his anger against me. It was frightening. His blue eyes turned to ice and then to steel. He said they had taken Rosemary to the best specialists in the East. He didn't want to hear about some three-dollar doctor in Pasadena who recommended zucchini and string beans for everything. Furthermore, he snarled, he didn't want me touting that quack to people with serious problems, or to anyone he knew, for that matter. People must think I was unhinged, suggesting that grave illnesses could be treated with squash.

"But, Joseph," I explained quietly, "it's not only what you eat that helps your body heal itself. It's what you *stop* eating."

"I don't want to hear about it!" he roared. "Do you understand me? *Do you understand me?*"

He quickly calmed down, touched my hand very gently, and motioned for me to wait for him outside.

Once on the other side of the door, I contemplated leaving, but I sensed a need in him that disallowed any display of anger or hurt feelings on my part.

When he emerged moments later he was himself again, and he couldn't have been more charming and considerate for the rest of the evening. In fact, he thanked me over and over again for seeing him through the Von Stroheim nightmare, as he put it. But neither of us mentioned medicine or Rosemary again.

After he left for New York I asked Eddie Moore, the sweetest of the horsemen, what was wrong with Rosemary, who was two years older than my Gloria. Eddie looked unhappy that I had asked, and cautioned me that this was a very sore subject with the boss. Then he tapped the side of his head with the tip of his index finger several times and said softly, "She's . . . not quite right."

Poor Joe, I thought sadly. He was already, in my eyes,

extremely complex. Did this mean I had seen only the tip of the iceberg?

At thirty-eight Eddie Goulding was more than just the triple-threat actor, director, and script writer of which there were many in Hollywood; he had, additionally, a vast knowledge of the technology of both the camera and the microphone, and he promised to do extremely well in talking pictures because he and half of his friends were trained in the diction of the British stage.

People always remembered him first as the man who had scripted and directed *Sally, Irene and Mary* at Metro-Goldwyn-Mayer in 1925, shortly after he arrived from England. In that film of backstage rivalry, romance, and glory, he had cast three young actresses and made instant successes of them—Joan Crawford, Constance Bennett, and Sally O'Neil. Now, four years later, Joan Crawford was almost a star, grinding out an average of five pictures a year at MGM. Eddie had directed her once more, and she had also made several films with Jack Conway, my old flame from Triangle days, who worked now mainly at Metro. At the start of 1929 she was the talk of Hollywood for dating Doug Fairbanks, Jr., much to Doug Senior's chagrin. There were bets that the twenty-one-year-old actress could never catch Doug Junior, who was not yet twenty, and step up to the Pickfair set on his arm while Doug Senior breathed, but before many months were out, she had. Constance Bennett, the Sally of Eddie Goulding's film, was the daughter of actor Richard Bennett. A beautiful slim blonde, she showed up everywhere with Hollywood's fast set. I knew both of these young women to speak to, but not well, and I was amazed when Eddie Goulding told me that I was Joan Crawford's idol, the woman she wanted to be like. I could not quite imagine a person feeling that way about another person.

Eddie said we should write an original script for our picture, and I agreed, although I warned him that we had only a month to do it in. We worked in the big breakfast room overlooking my garden, where Raoul and I had scripted *Sadie Thompson,* and after one day I hired a court stenographer to take down virtually every word we said because I realized that Eddie had a tendency to drop a pearl, then pursue a totally different subject, and then not be able to retrieve the pearl. Eddie, in turn, said he would like Laura Hope Crews, a friend of his, to collaborate with us because he knew of no one in the world with a better ear for the spoken word, and if we were both about to launch ourselves into sound, he thought we had better have a script with plenty of rich, convincing dialogue. Laura Hope Crews, then, joined us in our sanctuary, and also took over my guest room, for the duration of the writing, which turned into a day-and-night marathon.

One minute the three of us praised each other, the next we fought like savages, and the demure stenographer took it all down—script dialogue, gossip, arguments, and sandwich orders.

We started with a character named Marion, a legal secretary from Chicago, my hometown. Marion meets and marries a young man from a wealthy upper-class family on Lake Shore Drive and has a baby boy. The groom's family try to break up the marriage and gain custody of the child, so in order to keep her baby, Marion has to accept favors from her former boss, which puts her respectability in question, but in the end everything is concluded happily. Whenever the characters started acting or speaking like English people, I had to bring Eddie back to America. For instance, when he said Marion would accept favors from her boss in order that her child could have a pony and go to public school, I had to explain that that wouldn't convince anyone, that in America a child could get a pony ride for a dime and that good public schools—as opposed to private schools, which were what he was talking about—were free. We disagreed, then made up, then quickly managed to disagree again, but we kept inching forward. After one particularly dreadful row, which occurred at the end of our first ten days of confinement and anxiety, Miss Crews burst into tears, said she could take no more, and left; but that same evening she called to ask if we had solved the problem that had caused her misery, and when we said yes she moved right back in the next morning, raring to go again.

Somehow we met our deadline. In three weeks we had a tight script. When Joe Kennedy returned from New York, I was able to invite him to Crescent Drive for a reading. He said he would be there at ten in the morning with the horsemen.

When ten o'clock came, the horsemen arrived but not Joe. Eddie Moore said he was detained, and that we should go ahead without him. I read my part, Laura read the other women's parts, and Eddie read the men's parts and the camera angles. When we finished they all said they loved it, and Eddie Moore called Joe, who invited us all to Rodeo Drive for lunch. When we got there I saw still another side of Joe Kennedy hidden to me until then. He hadn't been detained at all. He confessed to me privately that he had had such a case of nerves at nine-thirty, fearing that I would fail and that we were jinxed, that he couldn't leave the house. Only when Eddie called to say everything was hunky-dory had he become himself again. Now, suddenly, he was laughing and playful, calling for champagne for the creative artists and the boys, and demanding that we read the whole thing over again right then and there before soup was served.

He thought it was marvelous, and decided that Eddie Goulding could do no wrong. He was astonished, therefore, when Eddie, in typical fashion, announced sometime before coffee that the script had a terrible hole in it. There was a bridge missing between the first and second parts, he felt, and he looked accusingly at Laura Hope Crews and me as if to say, How could you have let this happen? "The audience can't just see Marion, out of the blue, dressed in gorgeous clothes in a deluxe apartment with her former boss. It happens much too fast. The mood's not right. In fact, it's awful." Then as the silence of defeat resulting from a victory called too early began to settle on the luncheon party, Eddie went blithely ahead and solved the problem himself—brilliantly, from Joe Kennedy's point of view. "So we have to establish the new mood and let the audience figure it out," Eddie thought aloud. "And since it's a sound picture, we should—yes, do it with music. Marion could sing him a love song. Gloria, do you sing?"

"She sings beautifully!" Joe Kennedy called out like a proud parent. "Of course she can sing. And she should sing in *Queen Kelly* when we remake it. Why, Gloria wanted to be an opera singer when she was young. She's told me so many times."

Before I could be embarrassed that he had, as it were, compromised me in front of strangers, I read easily in the eyes of both Eddie Goulding and Laura Hope Crews that our secret was no secret to begin with. I realized that Hollywood saw us as a modified version of William Randolph Hearst and Marion Davies, only unimpeachable because we were both solidly married with children; beyond whispers, therefore, and entirely free of the possibility of louder accusations. So be it, I thought; at least I don't have to spend the next two months or two years or two decades playing games. "It's true," I said aloud; "I can sing."

The very next day, while we were all debating about whom to hire as a composer, Eddie Goulding broke his own record for inventiveness and wrote a song himself. The only trouble was, he didn't know musical notation, so he couldn't write it down. "Keep whistling it," I told him. "Laura, hum it with him. I'll find someone to write it out in notes." I called a friend, who called a friend, who sent a dear old violinist to the house, and he wrote it down. Then Eddie spoke to Elsie Janis and got her to write lyrics. They called the song "Love, Your Magic Spell is Everywhere." Eddie also came up with the title for the picture: *The Trespasser*. That was it. We had done it all in a month.

From then on, nothing was too good for us. Before Joe returned to New York, he left orders at Pathé that we were to have anything we wanted, and he got George Barnes on loan from San Goldwyn again for me, this time without any out clause. Then Eddie said one cameraman was not enough, the way he wanted to shoot the picture, so we got Greg Toland too. Except for the man to play opposite me, we had cast most of the characters as we made them up. Once we had hired them, we had only to pick a leading man. The Pathé casting director urged me to test a tall, dark, handsome newcomer called Clark Gable, and he tested very well. Moreover, Eddie and I both would have liked to introduce someone new; but in a white tie and tails, the young actor was just not at home. Marion's swain had to look and act very North Shore—someone like Craney Gartz. In addition to having huge ears, Mr. Gable looked like a truck driver and spoke like a private eye—an attribute that wouldn't have mattered six months earlier. With Eddie in agreement, therefore, I chose Robert Ames.

From the first moment on the set I was consumed with curiosity about the technical side of shooting a sound picture, but acting in one, as far as I was concerned, was no different from acting in any other picture. In quality films we had always had scripts, and we had memorized them, and we had said the lines as we played the scenes. We hadn't mouthed them or pronounced them in an exaggerated fashion. Therefore, the fuss that actors soon began making about the difficulty of "shifting" to sound struck me as perfectly foolish. The only adjustment was in knowing where the microphones were and playing to them as well as to the camera, and that was merely an exciting extension of regular acting in pictures.

We took rolls of tape and blocked out the studio stage into imaginary rooms. We rehearsed on this area with the technicians, the set designers, and the crew so that they could figure out the lighting, sets, and camera and microphone positions. The cutter sat in the rehearsals and the shooting with a stopwatch, timing everything. Sound film could not be cut without leaving bleeps on the track, so we had to do close-ups, medium shots, and dolly shots in one go. A reel of film lasted nine minutes; therefore, we planned our sequences to fit within reel lengths. In one sequence where I moved from room to room, we had twelve cameras filming simultaneously. We had been told that if we shut one camera off, it might change the level of electrical current and affect the other cameras, so we kept them all going and wasted film in order to save costly time. The crew moved walls of the set aside or raised them as I moved from room to room, but the cameras and mikes were stationary.

We made the picture in twenty-one shooting days, and we had planned it all so carefully that the editing took no time at all. The whole process, from day one in my breakfast room, when Eddie and Laura and I began on the script, until the picture was edited, scored, and ready for shipment to United Artists, took a little over three months. Moreover, *The Trespasser* was the least expensive picture I had made since becoming a star.

When the UA sales force in New York screened the picture, they were sure it would be a winner at the box office. They wanted, therefore, to get it into theaters as soon as possible. The Rialto in New York, the flagship of the UA theater chain, was booked until November, so they asked for my permission to have the world premiere in London in September. I said I would let them know the next day.

Before I could call Joe Kennedy and ask him what he thought, he called me. He had heard about the London proposal from E.B. and he was thrilled.

"But if I go away in September, won't that interfere with *Queen Kelly?*" I asked.

"No," Joe replied. "Sam Wood and Delmar Daves came up with a terrific new treatment that Boleslavsky likes, and

I've got Laura Hope Crews to collaborate on the revised script. Kitty is the rightful heir to the throne all along in this new version, and there's a happy ending. If we just add songs and not dialogue, according to Boleslavsky, it will require very little reshooting. The script, however, will take some time. So we can be back from London before he's ready to go."

"Who's we?"

"Well, me, for one. Nobody's going to keep me from attending my first big London premiere. And Henri. You can go to Paris first and pick him up."

"Joe, before you go any further," I said firmly, "you and I cannot travel on the same boat going over even if we're going to meet my husband."

"We won't be alone." He lowered his voice then and began speaking in even tones, as if he were addressing a nervous patient. "Rose is coming. She's never been to Europe, and I've promised her this trip. Please, Gloria, she wants to meet you."

"Joe Kennedy, do you think I would travel with you and your wife to—"

"And my sister. You and Rose will never have to be alone together."

"Now, Joe—"

"Gloria, listen to me. You two are going to have to meet sometime, and this is the perfect time—Europe, lots of people, lots of activity, lots of fuss. Please, Gloria."

When his mind was made up, there was not a big enough lever in the world to move him. I might argue all day, but I knew he would only out-argue me. By now he was busily naming dates and suggesting side trips to Paris and a few cathedrals. He said E.B. would arrange for all the tickets. He said I was making him very happy. He said everything would be fine.

"Have E.B. get an extra ticket" was all I said.

"Why?" Joe Kennedy asked suspiciously.

"As an excuse for some privacy, if nothing else," I said tartly. "I can't spend five solid days on a boat with you and your wife and sister."

"Oh! Oh, I see. Fine," he said. "Anything you say."

Anything you say. As I put down the receiver I had to smile. He had just asked me to throw a shawl over my scarlet letter and have tea with his wife and my husband and the vicar, doubtless, not to mention the press, and he was saying, "Anything you say," as if he were indulging me.

I had not heard from my old friend Virginia Bowker for ages, so that night I called her in Chicago and, to her surprise, invited her to London to the premiere of my first talking picture.

Virginia grasped the curious situation in which she was taking part the first day on the ship, but whether Mrs. Kennedy did or not I couldn't tell. Only a few years older than me, Rose Kennedy was sweet and motherly in every respect. Most of the time she and her female relative treated Virginia and me like a pair of debutantes it was their bounden duty to chaperon. They always commented enthusiastically on our pretty dresses and on the way we had our hair fixed, and they worried aloud every time I ordered food from the waiter: "Gloria, are you *still* dieting?" But the main concerns of Mrs. Kennedy's life, she made plain from the start, she had reluctantly left at home in order to see a bit of Europe with Joe. She talked endlessly about her children; there were eight now, she exclaimed happily, the youngest just a year, the next-to-youngest almost three, and so on up to Joe Junior, who was fourteen. She asked how my Joseph and Gloria were, and told me how marvelously behaved they'd been when they visited that once in Bronxville. Her innumerable references to church activities indicated beyond a doubt what her second great source of comfort was.

If she suspected me of having relations not quite proper with her husband, or resented me for it, she never once gave any indication of it. In fact, at those times during the voyage when Joe Kennedy behaved in an alarmingly possessive or oversolicitous fashion toward me, Rose joined right in and supported him. In the salon after dinner one evening, he openly and without apology talked and joked confidentially with me and left the other three women to converse among themselves; but when a man at the next table turned his chair around to look at me, Joe became white as chalk, leaped to his feet, and loudly ordered the other man to mind his own business and stop staring at me. Before I could think of how to conceal my mortification, I heard Rose emphatically agreeing with Joe's action, saying she didn't understand how I stood being on constant public display, unable to travel two teps without my husband or somebody else to protect me. She thought it was shocking. Was she a fool, I asked myself as I listened with disbelief, or a saint? Or just a better actress than I was?

Mrs. Kennedy's husband got off in Southampton to arrange for the premiere of my film, and my husband met us in Le Havre to assist the American visitors to Paris and through the museums and churches and couturiers' salons there.

Henri treated Rose like a duchess. He had booked rooms and arranged tours and planned dinner parties, and I made sure that the smartest Paris dressmakers broke their necks outfitting Rose and her sister in custom-made clothes at off-the-rack speed. Then Henri packed his own bags, saw to the shipment of everyone else's, and accompanied us to England. Rose told me over and over what an absolutely "mah-velous" husband I had, employing the same strange sound to pronounce the first part of the word that Joe used to say "Hah-vad," but without any innuendo that I could detect.

The English press treated the world premiere of my first talking picture as a major event, something akin to the tribute I had paid France by making *Sans-Gêne* there, and gave extensive coverage to every detail of it. Reporters tailed us from the dock to the train to the lobby of Claridge's. They began by asking all the usual stuff: where the clothes I was wearing came from ("All British wool, the suit and cape both, made by an English tailor in New York"); my children's ages; my shoe size; my plans for a next picture. A few asked why *Queen Kelly* had been shelved ("Oh, it hasn't been shelved. We're still working on it. It's going to be a very important picture. With sound, did you know that?"). But in the main they wanted me to talk about talking pictures—the adjustments required to make them, the psychological disturbances involved in hearing one's own voice and trying to match it with one's picture, the future possibilities of sound. They seemed astonished when I informed them I found talking pictures no more difficult to make than—I recoiled as I heard myself using their phrase—silent pictures. I said that, after all, I hadn't been a deaf-mute since 1915; what, then, should be so surprising about the fact that a microphone was now picking up what I said? I had not changed; technology had. Deep down, what I probably meant was that *The Trespasser* had been child's play after *Queen Kelly,* but I couldn't say it because at every interview, just out of the photographers'

range but ready to chime in at every opportunity, was Joe, so
proud and happy that his mouth was perpetually half open in
an ecstatic smile.

The premiere was at the New Gallery Theatre, and a file of
policemen had to thread our group of six from the cars
through a crowd of thousands in the street to our seats in the
mezzanine. The audience applauded when we arrived, applauded again when the picture came on, so loudly they
almost drowned out the sound, and stood and applauded
when the picture was over. Joe Kennedy had arranged to
have a mike on the stage so that I could speak to the audience
right after they heard me recorded on the screen; therefore,
while they stood and cheered, he grabbed my hand and led
me downstairs and to the stage. When they heard my voice
and could see me forming the words I said live in front of
them, they roared so loudly I could literally not hear myself
speak. At a party afterward, the press announced to me that
The Trespasser was certain to be my most successful picture.

The following day a crisis arose when several newspapers
questioned whether my singing voice was real. I had spoken
from the stage of the New Gallery after the picture but I had
not sung—they wanted to know why. Joe Kennedy went into
elated action at the first mention of doubt. He got on the
phone and arranged to have me sing a song in the middle of
someone else's concert at Queens Hall several nights later.
Since the orchestra didn't have music for "Love, Your Magic
Spell Is Everywhere," we picked a simple lullaby they could
play, and again Joe led me proudly to the stage. I was so
nervous for once that I didn't even know what key I was
singing in, but the audience loved it and music critics said the
next day that not only did I sing well but I sang without a trace
of an American accent.

With the arrival of talking pictures, everyone in the world
was suddenly conscious of accents. The funny part was that
most of the men with all the money in Hollywood, from Joe
Kennedy to Adolph Zukor, had heavy accents themselves,
and many of them could neither detect a phony accent nor
verify an authentic one. Aileen Pringle had the prize story
along these lines. An actress of real style and charm, Aileen
had acted with George Arliss and other celebrated stage
performers before she came to Hollywood. She had a marvelous voice, yet right in front of her, as she sat across the desk
from him, Harry Cohn called someone in New York to ask if
she spoke English properly. Like many Hollywood moguls,

Harry didn't dare trust his own ears, but at least he was honest about it.

Joe Kennedy's constant fervent attention to me in London escaped the press' mention and his own family's notice, presumably, but it pained me because I saw that Henri was hurt by it. Several times when we were alone he alluded to it and seemed on the verge of saying what he really felt, and I almost wanted him to, because in spite of the fact that we had spent less and less time together since he started with Pathé in Paris, we still loved each other deeply and I wanted always to be honest with him. If Henri had ordered me then and there to leave pictures and live with him on the farm he owned in France, I would have obeyed him. But he didn't. He couldn't. Joe Kennedy had compromised us both with his promises of enduring security, which Henri wanted at least as much as I did. But until security came, Henri was in Joe's employ and I was literally owned by him. My whole life was in his hands. Never before had I ever trusted another person to the extent I had Joe. In addition, I was genuinely fond of him. The man fascinated me. I honestly didn't know what to do. I had to trust that Joe would either salvage *Queen Kelly* or find some other way to make us all successful, because he had the clear ability to do so, and I prayed that Henri would have the patience and love to wait until I could simplify my life again. For the moment, however, our three lives were tied in a complicated knot, and there was no way I could untie it. I, too, had to wait and hope.

Only once did Henri say he felt we were growing apart, and I answered by saying that that wasn't true, really, that he had to trust me.

But after the London premiere, Joe was more enamored of me than ever. In addition to his great infatuation, he now saw me as the only person he trusted in pictures who could instruct him, mainly because *Queen Kelly*, his important film, in which he had not wanted me to do anything but act, was foundering, and *The Trespasser*, my off-the-cuff effort of a few months, was a great success.

Before we left London, he asked me to help him make some decisions concerning Pathé. One of these involved the acquisition of stars and potential stars. He asked me to look over a list of actresses he had and tell him whom I thought he should test or sign. I told him to hang on to, among others, Ann Harding and Carole Lombard, and I suggested he track down Constance Bennett, who wasn't on the list.

We were with Henri, who asked, "Who's Constance Bennett?"

"A blonde," I said jokingly, as if to denegrate the whole class of girls born fair. "In fact, you've met her."

A bit sadly, I reminded him of happier days for the two of us, in particular a lunch at the Colony with René Hubert and Forrest Halsey just after we landed in New York in 1925. The maître d' had secreted some illegal champagne under the table for us, and in surreptitiously removing the cork, Henri had squirted some on a girl at the next table. As he jumped up and apologized and attempted to sponge off her shoulder with his napkin, she turned and said, "Think nothing of it, Marquis. I never complain about bathing in champagne." That, I explained to him, as I had at the time, was Connie Bennett.

"Is she ever in Paris?" Joe asked.

"I'm sure she is," I said. "She's everywhere."

"Henri, see if you can locate her and put her in touch with me," Joe said in a combination of friend and employer.

Two days later we sailed for home and Henri returned to Paris.

Between the September premiere of *The Trespasser* in London and the New York premiere in November, the Roaring Twenties came to an awful end for many people. On Black Tuesday, October 29, the stock market crashed, and in the following weeks bankers and brokers all over America, unable to face financial ruin, jumped out of windows. Some of the richest people in the country lost everything. William Fox, for example, a charter member of the pinochle club, the man who built the Fox studios and headed the list of moguls trying to stop me from making *Sadie Thompson,* was worth over $3 million in September. He had just bought the Roxy Theatre in New York for more than $1 million. In November he was finished.

Not Joseph Kennedy. On the contrary, he was whacking his thigh with glee in the opening weeks of November. He told me he had sold all his Wall Street holdings well before the bottom dropped out of everything. Now he and his horsemen were playing a waiting game with the people who hadn't been so smart—waiting to pick up the pieces, for pennies.

In view of the nation's economic situation, UA asked me to be at both the New York and Chicago openings of *The Trespasser*. The New York premiere made the London one look like a failure. The crowds in the street were such that there was a real fear of my being trampled to death. Joe Kennedy ordered two of his Irish horsemen to grab me under the arms while the other two elbowed their way through the mob. As I felt my feet leave the ground, I could tell that someone behind me was standing on my train, so I screamed for one of the horsemen to pick it up. Ted O'Leary moved so fast to obey me that he yanked my feet up in the air right along with the train of the dress. I was now completely horizontal, headfirst, face down, like a battering ram, and that is the way they carried me through the crowd and into the theater lobby. If the two men holding my arms had let go, my face would have smashed on the sidewalk. As they set me down, people standing up on the mezzanine level applauded rapturously. It was quite an entrance, worthy at least of Mack Sennett.

Inside the theater, as soon as the lights dimmed and the audience started clapping, police came and led us out through a side door and back to the hotel. The next day the UA publicity department sent Lance Heath the following summary of the critical reception:

TIMES QUOTE SWANSON GIVES BETTER PERFORMANCE THAN SADIE THOMPSON UNQUOTE WORLD QUOTE SWANSON TRIUMPH BRILLIANT PERFORMANCE UNQUOTE MIRROR QUOTE SUPREME TRIUMPH GREAT PICTURE STOP   SHE TRANSCENDS PERFECTION STOP GLORIOUS GLORIA AS SHE NEVER WAS BEFORE UNQUOTE NEWS QUOTE HELD PREMIERE AUDIENCE AT RIALTO BREATHLESSLY FASCINATED STOP   UNDISGUISED TEARS TRICKLED DOWN CHEEKS OF FIRST NIGHTERS STOP   SWANSON AMAZING PERSON WITH ADDED CHARM OF SOFT TONES AND EFFECTIVE SOPRANO SINGING VOICE UNQUOTE SUN QUOTE EXCEPTIONALLY ENTERTAINING STOP   FASHIONED BY EXPERT DIRECTOR STOP   TRESPASSER IS SUCCESS UNQUOTE TRIBUNE QUOTE SHE IS IMPROVED BY ARRIVAL OF MICROPHONE STOP   AUDIENCES WILL DELIGHT IN IT AND BRING IT ENORMOUS POPULAR SUCCESS UNQUOTE EVENING WORLD QUOTE FINEST THING SHE HAS EVER DONE STOP TRESPASSER WILL AMASS MILLIONS FOR ITS PRODUCERS STOP HER SPEAKING VOICE IS REVELATION ONE OF BEST STOP   IT HAS VIBRANCE AND FEELING STOP   HERE IS THE VOICE WITH IT

UNQUOTE AMERICAN QUOTE GLORIA SUPERB REMAINS SUPREME
SHE IS AS EVER THE QUEEN UNQUOTE TELEGRAM QUOTE TRI-
UMPH STOP   HER PERFORMANCE SUPERB PICTURE SPLENDIDLY
PRODUCED EXCELLENTLY ACTED FILM WHICH SHOULD PROVE
TREMENDOUS SUCCESS UNQUOTE JOURNAL QUOTE SWANSON
GIVES EXCELLENT PERFORMANCE STOP   MUCH CREDIT GOES TO
EDMUND GOULDING FOR SWIFT PACE AND SUSTAINED TEMPO OF
DIRECTING UNQUOTE GRAPHIC QUOTE TRESPASSER BOX OFFICE
PLUS TO LAST FADEOUT STOP   SHE FLAUNTS STUNNING WARD-
ROBE AND WEARS CLOTHES AS ONLY GLORIA CAN UNQUOTE
STOP   UNDERSTAND SWANSON REMAINING IN CHICAGO TO OPEN
PICTURE UNITED ARTISTS THEATRE THURSDAY NIGHT   REGARDS

While the success of the New York opening of *The Trespasser* pleased Joe Kennedy, it did not make him happy. And
although *Queen Kelly* could easily have been construed as the
minor disaster of an ambitious producer who was about to
recoup his losses nicely on his first talking picture, that was
not good enough for Joe. He had to prove himself to me and
to himself. He saw *The Trespasser* as my baby and *Kelly* as
his. He could have ended 1929 with his name up on the screen
in every theater in America: Joseph P. Kennedy presents
Gloria Swanson in *The Trespasser*. But he hadn't considered
the picture important enough to care about that at first, and
by the time critics all over the country said it was, it was too
late. By then his pride wouldn't let him take any credit or
claim any billing. All he could think of was presenting me in
something that was his. Something important.

Before I left New York for the Chicago premiere, Ted
O'Leary called to say an important person wanted to see me.
Joe Kennedy had already left the city on business, so I didn't
ask questions; I just said, "Fine." Whenever one of the
horsemen called me, which was rarely, I never asked questions, and they had orders never to mention names and places
on the telephone. Such a call usually meant that Joe had
arranged to have me meet someone he wanted to impress or
do business with, and that might be anyone from the president of a bank to the prime minister of Great Britain.

Ted O'Leary picked me up at the hotel in the late afternoon. On the drive through Manhattan to another hotel he
mentioned, I casually asked him if he knew who the person
was I was going to see. "Yes," he said, "his name is
O'Connell." He was answering without answering, and when

..e saw that that annoyed me, he added, "A friend of the Kennedys'." The name meant nothing to me.

The door of the hotel suite was opened by a young man in a clerical collar. "Thank you for coming," he said, without registering any surprise at seeing me. "His Eminence will be with you in a moment." Then he disappeared.

His Eminence! I shot a look at Ted O'Leary, who carefully avoided it. Before I could say anything, there was a rustle of taffeta or silk, and an old man, probably in his seventies, appeared, all in red except for his shoes. Ted O'Leary stepped forward and introduced the stranger to me as Cardinal O'Connell of Boston. The old man smiled cordially. He was a pleasant-looking person in a rather sickly sort of way. There seemed to be no eyes behind his glasses, nothing but smoky circles. He had beautiful manicured hands, and his robes smelled of incense.

He thanked me for coming and asked me to sit down, in a strong, orator's voice, which, nevertheless, he gave the impression of holding in check in normal conversation. I sat down stiffly, apprehensively, on the edge of the chair he indicated, and he sat opposite me. Then he excused Ted O'Leary and we were alone.

The cardinal began by complimenting me on having achieved such success at such a young age, but the tone in which he said it told me all too clearly that we were not about to discuss my pictures, none of which he had probably ever heard of, except for *Sadie Thompson*.

"Thank you," I said in a cool, pert voice, a voice that did not oblige him, that said only, Let's get to the point.

He studied me carefully before he spoke again. Then he said he would like to talk to me about my association with Joseph Kennedy. I told him my association with Mr. Kennedy was a business association, the details of which were all handled by Mr. E. B. Derr, a colleague of Mr. Kennedy's, who held power of attorney for me and acted in my name. I suggested that His Eminence contact Mr. Derr.

Straightening himself in his chair, the cardinal said with some bluntness that it was rather my personal association with Mr. Kennedy that he wished to speak about.

"There is nothing to discuss," I said, rising and making a movement in the direction of the door.

The cardinal stepped in front of me, blocking my way, and fixed me with his filmy eyes. "You are not a Catholic, my child," he said. "Therefore, I fear that you do not grasp the gravity of Mr. Kennedy's predicament as regards his faith."

"That is true," I said. "But Mr. Kennedy *is* Catholic. Therefore, shouldn't you be talking to him?"

Cardinal O'Connell now unleashed his orator's voice. "I am here to ask you to stop seeing Joseph Kennedy. Each time you see him, you become an occasion of sin for him."

I did not know enough about the church to argue properly, but I was getting angry. "If Mr. Kennedy had told you in confession that I am an occasion of sin for him, Your Eminence, then you have no right to discuss it. Isn't that correct? And if he didn't, then you have nothing to discuss."

"Please listen to me," the cardinal said in firm tones. He told me that Joe had spoken about our relationship with some of the highest representatives of the Catholic Church. Since there was no possibility of dissolving his marriage under church law, he had sought official permission to live apart from his wife and maintain a second household with me. That was impossible, the cardinal explained. Furthermore, he went on, as one of the most prominent Catholic laymen in America, Mr. Kennedy was exposing himself to scandal every time he so much as appeared in public with me.

"Then tell him so," I said, furious but still stunned by what the cardinal had just said.

"Have you no feeling for his family?" he asked.

"Of course I do," I replied, "just as I have for my own."

His voice was calm again when he said slowly, for emphasis, "As a Catholic, there is no way Joseph Kennedy can be at peace with his faith and continue his relationship with you. Please consider that very carefully."

"I shall," I said, putting on my gloves. "But I repeat, it's Mr. Kennedy you should be talking to." The audience was over. I waited silently until the cardinal stepped aside. When he did, I let myself out, leaving the door open behind me.

To regain my calm and clear my head, I walked down the stairs to the lobby, asking myself over and over the question I had not been able or willing to put to the cardinal: Who had asked him to see me? Rose Kennedy? Joe himself? Their families? Friends? I was simply baffled, particularly after the trip to Europe two months before.

Ted O'Leary was waiting downstairs.

"Why didn't you warn me?" I asked him.

"I knew if I did, you wouldn't come. I'm sorry," he added. "Orders."

"Whose?" I asked. "Joe's?"

"Oh, no, Joe knew nothing about it. All I can tell you," he said, "is that it was Cardinal O'Connell who contacted me."

I took Virginia Bowker with me to the Chicago opening, which proved no less triumphant than the one in New York. Along with *The Trespasser,* the management there showed *Elvira, Farina, and the Meal Ticket,* which I had made at Essanay during my first year in pictures. It brought the house down. Virginia and I laughed until we cried, and spent the rest of the evening reminiscing about the days of two-reelers and dill pickles and Francis X. Bushman and the Sweedie comedies.

After both premieres, thousands of fans wrote to the newspapers and to UA and Pathé asking whether the singing voice in the picture was really mine. In the end Lance Heath had to make up a press release and send it to major newspapers in cities where *The Trespasser* played. The following headline, for instance, appeared over a column-long article in the Dallas *News* a few days after the Chicago premiere.

SWANSON STUDIOS SEND PROOF
THAT ACTRESS CAN SING

AFFIDAVITS, TESTIMONY, ASSERTIONS
SENT TO "NEWS'" REVIEWER

I did not mention my meeting with Cardinal O'Connell to Joe Kennedy when he called me in Chicago, but it continued to worry me slightly; and I became aware that in speaking to Joe I was listening intently for some nuance, some sign of guilt or remorse in his voice that hadn't been there a month or a year ago. There was none. On the contrary, he was all revved up to start on *Queen Kelly* again and told me to hurry back to the Coast. I said I was bringing Virginia with me for a visit, and Joe was pleased because he liked her.

"Have them write in one extra talking nun, will you?" I asked him. "I'd like Virginia to be in the picture."

"Fine!" Joe said. "So would I!"

In addition to wanting a close friend on hand so that I could avoid being in public alone with Joe, I wanted someone at the house with the children and me for Christmas. Henri had

written me to say that he felt it would be easier if he stayed iⁱ
Paris this year. That was a terrible blow to me, signifying a
crisis I couldn't bear to face, at least alone. I confided in
Virginia on the subject of my marital difficulties, but inasmuch as Henri was in Joe's employ, and Joe was the subject of
our estrangement, I tried never to speak with Joe about
Henri.

I was all too aware, as Virginia and I boarded the train to
California, of how complicated and fragile my life had
become all of a sudden; and I thought how ironic it was that
this should happen just at the moment when I had regained
my place among the brightest stars in the hearts of all
America.

When we got to California, Richard Boleslavsky was
almost ready to start shooting. Laura Hope Crews and
Lawrence Eyre had collaborated on new dialogue and a
different ending, and all new sets had been built on the Pathé
lot. Seena Owen and Walter Byron were back to shoot the
added scenes with dialogue and music, and Joe Kennedy had
brought Vincent Youmans from New York to write several
songs for me to sing. On December 9, we began filming. As
soon as we saw the first rushes, however, all the accumulated
excitement evaporated. The new scenes didn't look like Von
Stroheim's work or have the same mood or texture. The
actors, too, were responding differently to Boleslavsky; they
seemed like different people. Even the sets clashed. Two days
later Joe Kennedy, without consulting anyone, as far as I
knew, sent the actors home and suspended production. Total
costs had now risen to $800,000.

This time he was not in despair. He was resigned. He said
there was no sense in throwing more good money after bad on
a project that now seemed in every way behind the times.
After the holidays, he said, he would have editors piece *Kelly*
together as best they could, and we would release it. At the
same time, though, we would begin a new picture.

In mid-December he left for the East, and Virginia and I
started pulling a lavish Christmas together. A week before
Christmas, to my surprise, presents for the children arrived
from the Kennedys. Now I was really baffled. If Rose
Kennedy had set me up with Cardinal O'Connell, would she
also have sent gifts to my children? I had decided to lie low
regarding the Kennedys for Christmas, but now I couldn't do
that. I called Miss Crossman at my office in New York and
told her to shop for the Kennedy children immediately. Eddie

Goulding had mentioned a marvelous miniature billiard table that was on the market, so I told Miss Crossman that if she could get one of those delivered in time, she should send it from the children and me to the whole family. The next day she phoned back to say they were out of stock everywhere. She had, therefore, followed my alternate instructions and sent individual gifts to all the Kennedy children. These she started to rattle off: "An army ambulance for Bobbie, an unbreakable doll for Jean, a—"

"Fine, Miss Crossman, fine. Thank you," I said. "And Merry Christmas."

"Merry Christmas, Miss Swanson," she said.

Miss Swanson is right, I thought sadly.

Much as I cared for Joseph Kennedy, he was a classic example of that person in the arts with lots of brains and drive but little taste or talent. I knew that he wanted more than anything in the world to produce a successful picture and have his name on it; therefore, I made up my mind to try to make that dream come true in 1930. Before I could exert a single effort, however, he came back from the holidays to announce proudly that he had commissioned John and Josephine Robertson to write a comedy for me, and Vincent Youmans to compose songs for it. Six weeks later he kissed me at dinner and presented me with a bound copy of the script. It looked beautiful, but when Virginia and I read it that night, we were aghast. It was absolutely terrible.

I didn't have the heart to tell Joe, so I asked him if I could let Allan Dwan read it, and he said to go right ahead. Allan, of course, agreed with Virginia and me and said he had no qualms whatsoever about expressing his opinion to Joe Kennedy. The next day, therefore, he came to my bungalow at Pathé and told Joe calmly and deliberately that the script stunk. I watched the blood drain from Joe's face at the same time I heard Allan say, "Don't buy it."

"It's already bought," Joe said. "I commissioned it."

I could see that Joe was utterly crestfallen. Since I was determined not to let another *Queen Kelly* creep up on him, I signaled Allan frantically and implored him to take it home, read it again, and see if he couldn't come up with some ideas to liven it up. Allan looked daggers at me and said he couldn't promise anything, but he would try. That night he called me and said it was hopeless.

"Please, Allan," I said. "Remember, we started with nothing a couple of times when we worked for Paramount."

"Nothing would be preferable," Allan Dwan said.

"Look, it means everything to Joe Kennedy to succeed with an idea that started out as his. Even if nothing's left of the idea by the time the picture's finished, let's try to give him that. Try, Allan."

The next day we had another meeting in my bungalow. In a voice not much more cheerful than a raven's croak, Allan advanced a couple of ideas for saving the script and a couple of suggestions for lightening the tone of the dialogue. Soon he had Joe chuckling agreeably and congratulating him on his efforts.

"You see, Gloria," Joe said, "just a few changes and it will be fine."

"You'll need a different title, too," Allan was saying.

"Don't you like the title?" Joe asked in a disappointed voice.

"I hate it."

"All right," Joe said. "But what shall we call it?"

"Let's make it first and then name it," Allan said. "It'll be less confining to work that way."

"Oh, I think we should name it now," Joe said, and my heart sank. We were back to *The Swamp.*

"Well, I don't," Allan said, and Joe yielded.

It takes another Irishman, I was thinking.

Then Joe started talking money, but Allan said it was too soon for that. He proposed instead working up a few scenes with actors, and if Joe liked them, they could then sit down and write up an agreement. Joe was all for the idea.

Allan and I then rounded up some actors and improvised several scenes until they satisfied us. The situations were funny, and the dialogue was bright, and when we performed them for Joe and the horsemen they all laughed until they said their sides ached. Joe said we had done wonders, and told Allan to go ahead and start the film. He would give orders at Pathé to give him anything he wanted.

"Just one thing," Joe said. "I'd feel much better if we had a title. Now."

Allan eyed him suspiciously, but he didn't remind him that they had agreed to wait and name the picture when it was finished. Instead we invited some writers to dinner a few nights later and said we wanted suggestions for a title. We started telling the story and reading bits of dialogue until omeone shouted out, "What a Widow," and Allan Dwan said to Joe Kennedy, "There's your title."

"Find out who said that and give him a Cadillac," Joe said, laughing and banging his thigh. "I mean it."

The winner of the Cadillac turned out to be Sidney Howard, the Pulitzer Prize-winning playwright.

In the pause between this preliminary activity and the actual filming of the picture, I received the following letter from Henri:

Gloria darling. We have come to it . . . that which should never, never have happened . . . has come to be! How it happened? Why it happened? Who started it? Let's pretend we don't know. The past is the past.

The fire has burnt the beautiful temple that was our love. We thought it was built of marble, and we wake up to find it has crumbled like the dust of clay. Little can be saved out of the burning ashes. But let's try and preserve our sweet friendship, our regard for each other, our decency!

It is very hard for me to write all this, darling—and forgive me if I call you darling—but that is the only way I feel and always will feel about you. But it is necessary that I should write you, as something has to be done about the present situation.

We have come to a point when a decision has to be taken. We know we have to take it—we are not fooling ourselves or anybody else—and the more we delay things now, the more awkward they are going to become.

The bridges are broken between us—nothing ever can mend them—we both know it. And though my feelings towards you are sad and very very sweet and loving—I have had to come to the realization that we can never again hope to live together as man and wife.

So, darling, let's face it. I ask you please to make it public that we are separated. Later on in a very quiet way a divorce should come but only when and the way you will want it. Please let me hear from you so I can give out the exact same statement. And we should both refuse to talk about any other issues.

If you will be sweet enough to do that, darling, it will

make things much easier for both of us, in case I would
have to go to the States. It would avoid a lot of nasty and
very unnecessary publicity.

There is lots, lots more I could say to you, Gloria, and
would like to say—but what's the use? If you have kept
some of my old letters, you may read them. Their only
fault is that they did not, could not, express half of what I
felt for you. That kind of feeling never dies, Gloria, but
sometimes it is better to pretend to forget about it.

I am going to seal this letter without rereading it,
because if I did I wouldn't send it—and I must.

Good-bye, darling—it's all, all over now.

                                                        Henri

How like him not to so much as mention Joe. I knew as I
read the letter ten, twenty times that I would always love this
handsome marquis; indeed, loved him more even then, at
that moment, than I could ever love the man on whose
account we were separating. That was the sad part of it.

Allan Dwan pulled out all the stops to make *What a Widow* a
sophisticated dress-up comedy. I played a rich young widow
who takes a trip to France, where she becomes the darling of
society and the prey of every dashing playboy on the Continent. Allan cast Owen Moore and Lew Cody in major roles
and sent out word that he wanted six gorgeous young men to
play a group of lovesick swells who trail me everywhere I go.
Sam Wood sent over one stunner whom we did the favor not
to cast in such a trivial part. His name was Joel McCrea, and
he was simply too handsome and too gifted to be wasted on
anything but stardom. I told him so. We also created a small
part for Virginia Bowker inasmuch as she had not got to be in
Queen Kelly. The real hero and star of the picture from the
beginning was René Hubert. He designed a whole wardrobe
for me, including all my jewelry except for a jeweled fan that
held lipstick in the handle, which I designed myself. When
Allan saw it, he opened a scene with a marvelous close-up of
me reflected in it. The ultramodern interiors were gorgeous,
the work of the Chicago architect Paul Nelson.

One evening when I arrived at the house on Rodeo Drive
for dinner with Joe and Vincent Youmans, I all but tripped
over Constance Bennett, leaning on an umbrella stand in the
foyer smoking a cigarette. We said hello and I asked her if she

d been in Paris recently. She said yes. I asked her if she was staying for dinner. No, she said. Since she was not known for her shyness, I assumed these laconic answers meant either that she was embarrassed to be seen there or that I had put her off by being so much at home. She reminded me of Frances Marion's great line about typical Hollywood females: "I don't know why she doesn't like me. I never did anything for her." In order not to prolong her discomfort, I said good night and moved on into the library. When Joe came downstairs, I asked him what Connie Bennett was doing there. "Going out with one of the boys," he said with a wink. He was in a chipper mood, as he always was since work had begun on *What a Widow*, so he added, to tease me, "She couldn't hook the boss, so she settled for one of the boys." He laughed loudly and winked again as we went into the living room to join Vincent Youmans.

As the shooting progressed, the mood of the initial improvisations proved hard to preserve. Polishing silly, spontaneous madness is difficult going at best, and Allan had a number of handicaps to cope with. Owen Moore was not well at the time, and Lew Cody could not remember his lines, so we had to reshoot many of the scenes, and each time we did, we lost some of the original bounce. In addition, while it was no small coup to have Vincent Youmans as our songwriter, the songs he came up with were never going to make anyone forget "Tea for Two." Lastly, Joe Kennedy had insisted on unique titles at the start of the picture, principally so that no one would miss the one that said, "Joseph P. Kennedy Presents"; therefore, I got Dudley Murphy to create something extra special—tricky animated titles, which required considerable time, money, and effort.

When the movie was almost finished, Joe Kennedy told me one evening he had a surprise for me. He led me downstairs and unveiled a portrait of him by Geza Kende, for whom he had been posing secretly for weeks. Earlier that year Kende had painted a portrait of me and separate ones of the children. The painting depicted Joe the way he must have told the artist he wanted to look—severe and elegant, very much the chairman of the board, perhaps even a touch of royal family. I had to smile to see Joe's face glow with pleasure as he studied this other self from a seat on the couch. He also had sepia reproductions of the painting mounted on heavy paper, waiting only for the final touch of his autograph. That night was the first time I truly believed that Joe's dream of

power extended far beyond being president of some h[...]
corporation. He lingered before the painting and said he wa[...]
planning to open an office in Washington and probably build
a house there, near the real figures of power in this country.

In spite of all Allan Dwan's creativity and hard work, *What
a Widow* was simply not the picture to fulfill the hopes or
satisfy the ambitions of a man like Joe Kennedy—never mind
that Joe himself had commissioned it and set the tone for it.
Even if it had satisfied him, however, it did not, at the end of
1930, please the American public, whose attention was
focused on the Great Depression and the rise of organized
crime. The public of 1930 demanded brash musicals to cheer
them up or, better still, gangster pictures to thrill them;
otherwise they were not willing to part with their hard-earned
quarters. Therefore they rejected *What a Widow* and sent Joe
Kennedy back into the angry, miserable state he had experienced at the failure of *Queen Kelly*. In fact, his defeat was
more acute this time around because his name was attached
prominently to this failure, in elaborate animated titles.
Although he never spoke of *The Trespasser* unkindly, it irked
him that *my* picture, between his two willful disasters, was
successful in the public's eyes, and that everybody, by late
that fall, said I would surely receive another Oscar nomination for it.

I had been with Joe the day Sidney Howard personally
thanked him for the car he'd given him for dreaming up the
title *What a Widow*. In fact, everyone at Pathé and half the
people in Hollywood knew the whole story. I was surprised,
therefore, when my accountant, Irving Waykoff, called and
asked me why Sidney Howard's automobile had been charged
to my personal account.

"It should be charged to the budget of the picture,
shouldn't it?" Irving asked.

"Of course it should," I said. "I'll ask."

I understood very little about the books. When Gloria
Productions paid me my weekly salary, it was just a transac-
tion on paper. Pat Sullivan wrote a check on the corporation
account and it was deposited in my personal account. All my
bills were forwarded to him, and he signed checks on my
personal account to pay them. Irving Waykoff went over
my accounts to catch errors and did the preliminary work on
my taxes, but the final tax returns were also prepared by
the Kennedy office.

In the middle of dinner on Rodeo Drive one night in

...ovember one of the horsemen happened to mention Sidney Howard's name. That reminded me that I'd forgotten to mention the accounting error. I remarked quite innocently, "By the way, Joe, Irving Waykoff tells me I paid for Sidney Howard's Cadillac out of my personal account. How come? You give Sidney Howard the car; I didn't. He thanked you for it, not me. So I think it's only fair that you pay for it."

I was joking, assuming the whole thing was a bookkeeping error. But Joe Kennedy became so agitated that he choked on his food. He looked at me the way he had looked the day I suggested he take his daughter Rosemary to Dr. Bieler. When he regained his composure, he stood up without a word and left the room.

He did not come back, and at the end of thirty minutes or so Eddie Moore offered to drive me home. In the car I asked him what the matter was, but he was nervous and guarded in his replies.

I waited then for the call or note of apology I was sure would come. I imagined Joe crushed and ashamed at having behaved so childishly, and I was quite ready to forgive him, of course, because I cared for him deeply. How could I not care for the man for whom I had given up a marriage and a title, the man I still trusted to effect important changes in the motion picture business, the man who always managed to intrigue me, even when we disagreed, with his courage and energy and scope of vision and daring? But no message arrived from Rodeo Drive.

Some days later I heard Joe Kennedy had left for the East. He had not so much as called to say good-bye.

Next my accountant was told that Mr. Derr would no longer handle my books for me, and on December 31, 1930, E.B. sent me the following letter on a plain piece of paper with no letterhead, no salutation, no complimentary close:

Gloria Productions, Inc., and
Gloria Swanson,
Los Angeles, California.

This is to state that if Power-of-Attorney was ever given to me by the Gloria Swanson Productions, Inc., or Gloria Swanson, that it is now revoked and no longer effective.

I further state that I have never used such Power-of-Attorney, if such Power was ever in existence, for

anything other than what Miss Swanson, or the Gloria
Swanson Productions, Inc., authorized me to do, or with
their full knowledge.

And if such Power-of-Attorney was ever in effect and
ever used by me, I hereby guarantee that I never used
such Power during the entire calendar year of 1930.

Edward B. Derr

By then Henri and I had begun divorce proceedings. The
news from André Daven in Paris was that Henri was seriously
involved with Constance Bennett. The news from New York
and the trade papers was that Joe Kennedy planned to
disengage himself from picture production and devote himself
more and more to politics, after having acquired a fortune of
$5 million in a few short years in the movie industry. It was as
if the two men—my ex-husband and my ex-paramour—had in
some mysterious way, through me, canceled each other out
and moved on.

I was completely on my own again, without love and
without security.

CHAPTER 17

When Joseph Kennedy left California, he claimed to have cleared millions in motion pictures and to have made me financially independent. Irving Waykoff, however, soon made it clear that the second part of the claim, the part about me, was not true. Irving had been paying my bills as they were submitted to him without asking questions, but now he informed me that I was anything but rich, or even financially independent. I had been living a life of royalty, but I had been paying for it out of my own earnings. When we went through my books, we found such interesting items as Sidney Howard's car and a fur coat Joe Kennedy had given me as a present, not to mention more substantial items like the private bungalow Joe had built for me on the Pathé lot. As the auditing proceeded, the figures began to tell the oldest story in the world. Moreover, the accounts were in an impossible tangle. It would take a year to sort them out, and it soon became clear that the Kennedy offices would provide no help in the matter.

I hired lawyers and accountants, and they all confirmed what Irving had told me to begin with: I had some property and lots of possessions, but I also had two children and a career that had been badly tarnished of late. It was imperative that I go back to work immediately and start recouping some of my recent losses.

Work? I could hardly summon the strength to do anything but sit and stare dumbly in front of me. Once again I had misjudged people and had been deceived by someone I had totally trusted, and I was stunned and in pain. In spite of my reputation for will and stamina and pluck and durability, all I wanted was to call for my mother or to hold my babies in my arms and sob for a month, or a year for that matter, and claim for once my natural right as a woman to feel nothing but vulnerable. But although I could feel anguish and despair as well as the next woman, I couldn't succumb to them, or wouldn't, I didn't know which. I just wasn't built that way. I was an Aries. I was a survivor. For me endings would always be inseparable from the beginnings of what followed, and so I got up like a spaniel coming out of a lake and shook off my tears.

As soon as I was certain that I was being nominated for an Academy Award for *The Trespasser,* I went into action to take advantage of the fact. If I was ever going to be able to demand star's terms again, it would be on the strength of *The Trespasser,* not *Queen Kelly* in any of its pasted-together versions, or *What a Widow.*

I called up Louis B. Mayer at MGM and arranged to see him. A Russian immigrant living in Boston, Mr. Mayer at thirty had bought the New England distribution rights to *The Birth of a Nation.* Now, at forty-five, he was head of a large studio. The only other thing I knew about him was that he disliked Joe Kennedy. He had even turned down Joe's invitation to speak at the famous Harvard symposium. He mentioned this on the phone and again when we were seated in his office.

I put my cards squarely on the table: my personal affairs were in a shambles; I didn't have the time or energy to resume independent production; I therefore wanted to make a deal with him to produce my pictures for United Artists release. Mr. Mayer had tried several times to merge MGM with UA, but largely because of Charlie Chaplin's opposition, he had never succeeded. Therefore, he was naturally interested in signing an agreement with me. I asked for $250,000 per picture and he asked for four pictures. We shook hands on it and he said he would draw up a contract. Just as the contract was ready for signing, however, he called and said he thought it would be a good idea if I talked to Joe Schenck before committing myself. I knew perfectly well what that meant: there had been a meeting of the pinochle club.

I had felt resentful about Joe Schenck ever since our troubles over *Sadie Thompson,* but when I went to see him, e treated me like a long-lost child. He raved about *The Trespasser* and spoke often in terms of the United Artists family. He said he didn't want me to leave. He would match whatever L.B. had offered me. He said he could think of lots of properties that were absolutely right for me; he would also see that I stayed right on top. At heart Joe Schenck was a very sentimental man. "Let's let bygones be bygones, Gloria," he said. "Rudy's gone. And Norma's retired. Griffith's . . . well. We should stick together."

"Very well, Mr. Schenck," I said, with a certain degree of real warmth.

A week later we signed a million-dollar contract for four pictures. I later learned that I was much better off in every way at UA than I would have been at MGM. For one thing, Pat Sullivan and E. B. Derr were now Metro employees. They had broken with Joe Kennedy on very unfriendly terms before he left Hollywood, and Joe had let L. B. Mayer know through the grapevine that he was furious he had hired them. I got all this from Mr. Mayer's trusted assistant Eddie Mannix, who came up to me after one of my meetings with his boss and said, "Your friend is sure carrying a torch for you." By my "friend," Eddie meant Joe Kennedy. He told me Joe had tried to put pressure on Mr. Mayer to keep him from hiring me.

After that I heard many other stories about Joe's long arm reaching out to control me. I also began to realize how many people disliked him intensely. But there had been no communication between us personally since that evening at dinner when I asked him why I should pay for Sidney Howard's car.

Early in February, Sport Ward wrote that he had seen him. Sport had taken a golfing vacation in Havana and Palm Beach in late January. In Palm Beach, he said, he had met Joe Kennedy and Eddie Moore, in the company of a woman who had been on Sport's boat going down and who people told Sport—to his vast amusement—was Gloria Swanson. At the end of his long letter, with his tongue coming right through his cheek, Sport recounted the situation in Palm Beach, humorously so as not to hurt me, but in enough pointed detail so that I could not mistake that he felt I was well rid of Joe.

It was not until some two weeks later when I was in Palm Beach, where I ran into Joe Kennedy, that I discovered my mistake. . . . I saw Joe and Eddie Moore several times and you were not with them. I saw nothing unusual in that, as I had been led to believe that you two had had some words.

Finally, however, Joe gave a big house warming in a new apartment he had taken, and there you were. I was glad to find that a reconciliation had come about, and was very disappointed when you left, all dolled up in your little flowered chiffon dress and big drooping hat, to go to the dog races at Miami Beach with Joe. When you two finally returned, I had decided that I would have a good chat with you, and find out how this big change had come about. I no more than got seated when a stranger came in, and Joe bringing the stranger up, introduced you to him as Nancy Carroll. Of course this was a terrible blow to me, and it took all the wind out of my what-you-may-call-it, leaving me flat.

I then realized for the first time that there were two people who answered the description which had been given me—you and Nancy Carroll. Of course Joe and I had a good laugh over it afterwards, and that was the best excuse I could think of for having a lot of drinks.

Nancy Carroll was an actress in pictures, but I didn't know her. Yet within the month, ironically, we appeared together on another list besides Joe Kennedy's: that of those nominees for the best-actress Oscar in the 1929–1930 season who lost out to Norma Shearer. The other two unsuccessful nominees were Ruth Chatterton and Greta Garbo, the greatest star to arrive in Hollywood in ten years. That season too, Wallace Beery, Maurice Chevalier, Lawrence Tibbett, and Ronald Colman lost out in the best-actor category to George Arliss. If there was ever an example of oranges and apples in the short history of the Academy, that group of five was it.

Indiscreet, my first picture with Joe Schenck, was about a girl who falls in love with the author of a book called *Obey That Impulse.* In order to show her love, she tries living up to the book's precepts, and in doing so she almost loses the author and breaks up her sister's romance to boot. However, in the course of some light dialogue and a few songs, difficulties vanish and happiness comes back into view for everybody. In synopsis the story didn't seem too bad, but the finished script was dismal; and although the songs were by Tin Pan Alley's ious trio of De Sylva, Brown, and Henderson, they were undistinguished as well as quite wrong for my kind of voice. In order to keep me from backing out on the whole miserable project, Joe Schenck and Sam Goldwyn signed up Ben Lyon as my leading man and a wonderful young director named Leo McCarey. Barbara Kent and Arthur Lake played the other couple. We all tried our best, but the final product was so weak that Joe Schenck thought it might be smart to follow up my success formula with *The Trespasser* by having the premiere in London.

To cheer me up, he also told me that my next picture would be altogether different. He and Sam Goldwyn had acquired the rights to David Belasco's latest Broadway production for me, *Tonight or Never* by Lily Hatrany. Helen Gahagan, who was in the play in New York, had married her leading man in it, a handsome blond version of John Boles named Melvyn Douglas, and Goldwyn was bringing him to Hollywood to re-create his original role. Furthermore, Sam Goldwyn and Joe Schenck had commissioned Coco Chanel to do all my clothes for the picture. Therefore, Joe outlined coaxingly, while I was in Europe for the premiere of *Indiscreet* I could spend a month or two in Paris being fitted for a fabulous wardrobe. Then in September we would begin shooting *Tonight or Never*, which Joe guaranteed he would make a major picture.

After *What a Widow* and *Indiscreet*, I was only too happy to get away from Hollywood for a few months. In the early spring of 1931 I took Virginia Bowker and the children and enough staff to keep us all dressed and fed and left for New York. For the first time in years I was a free person—no husband, no jealous lover, no secret trysts to keep. I decided to have a good time.

We stopped in New York long enough to visit with Sport and a few friends and see some theater. June Walker was playing in *Waterloo Bridge*, but the biggest dramatic productions were Vicki Baum's *Grand Hotel* and Marc Connelly's *Green Pastures*. The only musical I was dying to see was *Three's a Crowd*, which starred Libby Holman, Fred Allen, and my outrageous darling Clifton Webb. In New York I met, through Sport, lots of new people, including a man named Jeff Cohen, who was a bit affected and a wastrel to boot, everybody said. He promptly begged me to marry him, which I declined, and to make use of his beautiful, empty house in Paris, which I accepted, but on the condition that I pay rent.

Since I was traveling with children and maids, life would b[ ]
much easier in a house than in a hotel.

Once I had installed the children and staff in Jeff Cohen's
house, which was all he'd promised and more, I headed for
London with Virginia. Noël Coward met us at the station. On
the way to my hotel Noël rattled off the guest list for a gala
dinner United Artists was throwing before the premiere:
Lady Mountbatten, Lady Ashley, Harold Lloyd and his wife,
Doug Fairbanks, Eddie Goulding . . . "And, my dear, King
Alfonso of Spain."

"Really?"

"Really," Noël said. "He's just arrived in exile here. It
couldn't be more convenient."

The dinner was very grand, and the premiere turned out to
be quite successful. I said a few words from the stage before
the picture came on, and the audience cheered wildly. Then
we took the dinner party back to Claridge's and danced until
dawn. Noël played the score of his new show, Cavalcade, for
us, and we laughed and sang the songs with him. The great
find of the evening for me was not King Alfonso, but Sylvia
Ashley. We hit it off perfectly and in the course of a few hours
we were behaving like old friends. The next day the London
reviews of Indiscreet were either enthusiastic or so polite they
seemed enthusiastic, I couldn't tell which; but in view of what
I was expecting, they made me very happy indeed. I left
immediately for Paris, and Eddie Goulding and Noël Coward
promised to join me in a day or two to celebrate.

For the next week I had fittings at Coco Chanel's every day
and went out dining and dancing with Eddie, Noël, and
Virginia every evening. Eddie and Noël were two of the most
amusing men in the world, and after several years of dinners
mostly with Joe Kennedy and the horsemen and a few
discreet friends, I felt in their company as if I had suddenly
run away and joined the circus.

On our second or third night out, we were sitting at a table
in a little night club off the Champs Elysées when Noël waved
to someone across the room.

"Am I seeing things, or does that man you just waved at
have two dogs with him?" Virginia asked.

"He does," Noël said. "In fact, he always does whatever he
pleases." He added to Eddie Goulding, "You know Michael
Farmer, don't you?"

"Yes, of course," Eddie said, and turned and waved too.

"Who's Michael Farmer?" I asked.

The man with two dogs," Noël said with mock impatience, as if I hadn't been paying attention. "You can't turn
around and gawk, darling. Come on, let's dance so you can
get a look at him. He's very good to look at."

From the dance floor, I casually observed a dark-haired
man of about thirty sitting alone on a banquette against the
wall, with two small dogs at his feet, a black one and a white
one. Noël described him as a moody Irish playboy who spent
his time fishing and hunting and sailing whenever things were
in season, wherever the international set happened to be
enjoying themselves. He was the "adopted son" of a rich
American woman named Mrs. Hubbard. "I can't believe
you've never heard of him," Noël said, and at the same time
he waved to the Irishman to join us.

That sort of brusque, good-looking man people refer to as
the strong, silent type, Michael Farmer with his dogs soon
crossed the floor to our table. A dedicated sportsman who
dressed like an English earl in the evening, he had a physique
like Henri's and the chiseled facial features of a Craney
Gartz. He ordered a round of drinks and downed his own in a
matter of minutes, the way people drink when they feel ill at
ease. Then he asked Virginia to dance and kept her on the
floor for three consecutive numbers. At two I said I had a
fitting the next morning, and we called it a night. When we
got back to the house, I explained to Virginia who her
admirer was and told her she had made a lucky catch.

"Lucky catch, my foot," she said; "all he did was ask a
thousand questions about you. I was never so angry in my
life. If you hadn't said it was time to go home, I would have."

A few days later Noël returned to London and Jeff Cohen
arrived in Paris, weeks ahead of schedule. He checked in at
the Ritz, where Eddie Goulding was staying, and immediately began telephoning me for lunch and dinner dates,
"alone," as he always said suggestively. When I put him off,
he found excuses to come to the house for things he said he
needed. I felt very awkward telling a friend of Sport's he
couldn't drop by his own house, but every time he came he
begged me to spend time with him. I resented being compromised, so I finally called Eddie Goulding to say that when my
first set of fittings with Coco was over in two days' time, I
thought I would move into the Ritz and give Jeff Cohen back
his house.

"He doesn't want the house; he wants you," Eddie told
me.

"I realize that. But I don't want him," I said. "Nor do want to play hide-and-seek for a month."

"I have an idea," Eddie said. "Michael Farmer has invited me to join him on his sailboat for a few weeks, and he asked if you'd like to go along—you and Virginia. He's very sweet, Gloria. Why don't you leave the children and come with us? You need the vacation, and furthermore, Jeff Cohen can't reach you on a boat."

"Where can I leave the children?"

"Right where they are, in Cohen's house. I told you, Gloria, it's not the house he wants. By the time we get back from the Riviera, he'll probably be gone."

Three days later we boarded Michael Farmer's comfortable boat in Cannes and sailed to Monte Carlo. The weather was perfect, Mr. Farmer turned out to be a generous host and an excellent sailor, and I had not felt so relaxed in years. We vacationed for a month, alternating between the boat and hotels along the coast, and because it was the height of the season we saw dozens of people we knew at a string of parties in Nice and Cannes and at Eden Roc. Michael was on everybody's guest list, and hostesses made a great fuss over him, but no matter where we went, he devoted more and more of his attention to me.

One night he arranged cars and boats and errands and hostesses in such a way that Virginia and Eddie would be late getting back to the boat and he and I would be alone for a few hours. Subtlety was not his long suit, so I could see perfectly well what he was doing, but he did it so sweetly and sympathetically that I didn't struggle—on the contrary. Late that night, on the beautiful deck under a host of shining stars, he put down his cognac, announced very earnestly that he loved me, and kissed me. I kissed him back and enjoyed every minute of it, but I told him to find someone else to love; after all, he was two years younger than me, and I was not yet legally divorced. The last thing he could ever cope with, I told him, was a divorced screen star with two children.

"You're the only woman I'll ever marry," Michael Farmer said with deep solemnity, but I didn't take him seriously.

He followed us back to Paris a few weeks later and called me every day. So did Jeff Cohen keep calling, and to make matters worse, they found out about each other and both became violently jealous. In order to finish my fittings and have some time with the children, I moved out of Jeff Cohen's

se to a suite at the Ritz and told Eddie Goulding to tell
everyone that my vacation was over, and that I would be busy
until I left for America in mid-August.

During the first days of August I discovered a hard lump the
size of a pigeon's egg on my right breast. After agonizing in
solitude for a few hours, too frightened and despondent even
to mention it to Virginia, I called Dr. Vodéscal, the man who
had saved my life in 1925. He told me to come to his office in
an hour.

After examining me, Dr. Vodéscal explained that he would
remove the little tumor right there in his office and send the
tissue to be analyzed by two or three pathologists, just to be
certain there was no error. He strapped me onto his examining table and gave me ether. When I came to, I had a small
bandage on my breast, and Dr. Vodéscal told me not to
worry; he would have news in twenty-four hours. No one can
convince a woman not to worry in such a situation, however.
I brooded every waking moment until I returned to him the
next afternoon.

"*Rien de grave*," he said, and he was smiling fondly. The
lump, as he had suspected, was a milk cyst, a common
occurrence which in my case was probably caused by my
interrupted pregnancy in 1925. "These little cysts frequently
show up years later," he continued, and then repeated, "*Rien
de grave.*" He said the other symptoms we had discussed were
quite ordinary also. "But this time, my dear Marquise, you
must not interrupt the pregnancy. You may be risking your
life if you do."

I had to sit down. "Dr. Vodéscal, do you mean . . . ?"

"Yes," he replied, "you and the Marquis are going to have
your little baby at last."

I began to cry, from sadness and frustration, but in spite of
everything, mostly from joy. "I am divorced," I told the
doctor at last, to his embarrassment, "but I will certainly have
the baby anyway. *Merci, Docteur.*" As I wept softly and he
patted my hand, I repeated with growing assurance, "*Je vous
assure, je suis heureuse. Très heureuse. Très, très heureuse.*"

I had some good reasons to be happy. I didn't have cancer,
and I was going to have a baby. All to the good. But I also
had to make a movie. And I hadn't had a husband in
residence for over a year. In fact, my divorce would be final in

two months. And another thing: Joe Schenck and Sa
Goldwyn would raise the roof when they found out. The
happiness I anticipated, then, was going to take some doing.

As soon as I left Dr. Vodéscal I started to scheme, and by
dinner-time I thought I had everything worked out. In the
Ritz dining room I cautiously outlined my plan to Virginia
and Eddie, in whom I confided everything. I would finish up
with Coco Chanel in another week and then hurry back to
Hollywood and make *Tonight or Never* before I started to
show. Then I would find some excuse to go on an extended
vacation, probably in New England. "And here's where you
two might come in," I said timidly, with a beseeching look.

"Well?" Virginia said when I paused.

"Well . . . ," I replied, "inasmuch as I've already adopted
one baby, nobody would be surprised if I were crazy enough
to do it again as soon as I became single. They already think
I'm peculiar, so that's not the problem. The problem for me is
having it. In the middle of a four-picture contract I can tell
Joe Schenck just about anything—that I'm ill, that I'm having
a nervous breakdown, that I'm going on a religious retreat—
just about anything, *except* that I'm having an illegitimate
child. Therefore, I was wondering if you two would consider
getting married just long enough to be able to pretend to have
a baby, and then I would pretend to adopt it."

"What!" Eddie Goulding cried.

"You're joking!" Virginia exclaimed.

"Don't say no just yet," I pleaded.

"I've already said it," Virginia declared.

"Who's the father?" Eddie asked.

"Michael Farmer," I told him. "We were together on the
boat one night. I can still scarcely believe it happened. I
mean, it's an absolute fluke. For years I desperately wanted a
baby with Henri and I couldn't get pregnant. Then for years I
was constantly terrified I would get pregnant with Joe
Kennedy—which *he* wanted in the worst way—but I didn't.
Now, out of the blue, some black-Irish playboy tips his
yachting cap to me once in the moonlight, and bingo!—I'm
pregnant. Believe me, if I weren't so happy, I'd be furious."

"How about marrying him?" Eddie asked.

"I don't even know him," I said. "All I know is that if
Henri couldn't adjust to my life style, Michael Farmer
certainly couldn't."

"Amen," Virginia Bowker said solemnly.

The following day Coco Chanel, tiny and fierce, approachıg fifty, wearing a hat, as she always did at work, glared furiously at me when I had trouble squeezing into one of the gowns she had measured me for six weeks earlier. It was black satin to the floor, cut on the bias, a great work of art in the eyes of both of us. I said I would try it with a girdle, but when I stepped before her again, she snorted with contempt and said anyone a block away could see the line where the girdle ended halfway down my thigh.

"Take off the girdle and lose five pounds," she snapped briskly. "You have no right to fluctuate in the middle of fittings. Come back tomorrow and we'll finish the evening coat with the sable collar. Five pounds!" she cried again, unable to restrain herself. "No less!"

That night Michael got me on the line and begged me to see him. I said I wasn't feeling well, but that I'd be sure to call him before I left for America in a week. Later on, Eddie called me to say Michael had come up to him soused in the Ritz bar and sobbed for an hour.

"I've never known him like this, Gloria," he said. "The poor chap is madly in love with you, do you realize that?"

"You're just saying that because you don't want to marry Virginia Bowker," I said, but Eddie wouldn't let me laugh the matter off.

"Just talk to him once," he said. "Please."

"You're right, I should. Tell him I'll have dinner with him on Thursday," I said.

My immediate concern was my weight. At night, trying to go to sleep, I thought of the elastic straps on Dr. Vodéscal's examining table. Why, I wondered, couldn't the great house of Chanel sew surgical elastic into underpants for me? It would eliminate the corset line and keep me slim enough for two months to shoot the picture, before I looked once again like a fat little Billikin doll, as I had before Gloria's birth. When I went to Coco's the next day I took a large roll of the elastic material with me and explained what I wanted: a rubberized undergarment to the knees, or rather, two or three dozen of them.

"Impossible!" her corset maker shrieked.

"Try it!" I said.

"No! Lose five pounds!" Coco yelled.

"Maybe I can't!" I screamed.

"Why not?"

"Reasons of health, maybe. Look, *just try it*," I pleaded. "And if it doesn't work, I'll lose five pounds."

George de Bothezat would have been pleased to see 𝗂
staking my life on my invention.

With evident displeasure, the corset maker ran up the
panty girdle in muslin first. It worked. Then she made it in
snug elastic. It worked even better, although it took three
people to get me into it. With the lavish confidence of Harry
Houdini hearing twenty padlocks snap shut, I then raised my
arms to receive the black satin cut on the bias over my head.
It fit like a glove.

On Thursday, as I dressed for dinner, I decided to be
honest with Michael Farmer. He was in a state over me,
according to Eddie, so I presumably owed him some explanation if I was deciding never to see him again.

"Don't drink so much," I told him early in the meal,
expecting him to take umbrage and make my eventual exit the
easier. But he didn't resent the remark. If anything, he took it
as a sign that I cared. He pushed his glass aside and smiled
apologetically.

"I love you; you have to know that," he said. "I want to
marry you."

"Michael, listen to me. I've had three unsuccessful marriages. My last husband said it was impossible to be married
to me because I was a businesswoman first and a wife second.
Perhaps he was right. In any event, I don't really want to be
married again. I'm not even sure I believe in marriage
anymore."

"Don't you think that's a bit selfish?" he asked. "To live on
my boat till I fall in love with you and then walk away
scot-free?"

I smiled ruefully and said with utter calm, "I'm anything
but away scot-free, Michael, believe me. I'm pregnant. By
you."

He was struck dumb. When he recovered himself, he said,
"Then marry me."

"I can't," I said. "First of all, I know I would only make
you unhappy."

"I'm unhappy now," he said. "What's the difference? And
I'll do everything I can to make you happy. You're the only
woman in the world I *could* marry now."

"No."

"Please."

"No. Now don't let's talk about it anymore."

"Will you see me again?"

"All right."

next day he called to say he had booked passage on the *Aquitania* in the name of Mr. and Mrs. Martin Foster. We would sail the next week, he said, arrive in New York August 14, and be married the next day.

"No."

"Then I will notify the press that you are pregnant with my child. I mean it."

"How dare you!"

"Because I love you. How many times do I have to tell you that? And you love me too, if for no other reason than because you're pregnant by me. Please, Gloria. Please."

Maybe it was his due, I thought. Maybe I had no right to have the baby alone when its indisputable father was begging to marry me. A father's established existence would certainly make all the difference to the studio moguls—of that there could be no doubt.

He was waiting.

"All right, Michael," I said.

"You will?"

"I will."

When Virginia returned to the suite an hour later and I told her I was marrying Michael, she sat down stunned. "Then you really must love him, after all," she finally said.

"Why do you say that?" I asked.

"Because if it's just a question of getting married, you could pick any name out of the telephone book or *Who's Who,* and you know it. With you it'll never be a question of having to get married, pregnant or not. If you're getting married, it's because you want to."

"Maybe you're right, Virginia. I honestly don't know."

After that, everything worked like magic. I introduced Michael to the children. Then Virginia took them on a separate boat and promised they'd be in California when we got there. Michael and I slipped quietly aboard the *Aquitania* as Mr. and Mrs. Foster and sailed on the eighth. In my luggage I had a whole wardrobe designed for me by Chanel, including a stack of sturdy elastic panties. I had cabled a friend in New York State, Dudley Field Malone, to see if he could speed up my divorce so that we could be married on arrival. I don't know how he arranged it, but we drove to Elmsford, gave him our passports, and were married by the mayor there in Dudley Malone's parlor on August 16, 1931.

Then we raced back to Manhattan and booked reservations on the first train to California. Less than an hour out of New

York, Michael went to find a porter and order ice and glasses for some champagne we had smuggled in with us. Before he returned, a man passing in the corridor recognized me and called out my name: "Gloria!" It was Clifton Webb, heading out to California after his Broadway run. He was in the very next compartment, he informed me. "In fact, it's incredible, my dear," he said, "but for the first time ever on this damn interminable train ride, I know not just one, but *two* other passengers."

"Who's the other?" I asked.

"An Irish friend named Michael Farmer," Clifton said. "I'll introduce you, and we'll all take an oath to keep each other from being bored to death for once on this run. Why are you laughing? Don't tell me you know him!"

"Not very well," I said, laughing harder. "But I'm married to him. And it's a secret."

"But, darling, you told me in New York your divorce wasn't final!"

"I'm not sure it is," I said; "that's why this marriage is a secret," and by now I was laughing so hard that tears were coursing down my cheeks. "Sit down, Clifton, and have some champagne."

Behind him, Michael had just appeared with a porter carrying a tray with a bucket of ice and glasses on it.

When we arrived in California, Michael checked into the Beverly Hills Hotel across the road from the house, and I reported for work.

Tonight or Never told the tender, romantic story of a young concert singer engaged to an aging nobleman but enamored of a mysterious stranger who is in reality an impresario intent on signing her to an opera contract. Mervyn Le Roy, the director, a relative of Jesse Lasky's, had had a juvenile crush on me when he was allowed to play a newsboy in *Prodigal Daughters* in 1922, so we had a good time recalling those days when Sam Wood sat in the director's chair. Ferdinand Gottschalk was cast as the aging aristocrat, and Melvyn Douglas played the handsome young impresario. If Melvyn ever guessed that the woman in the love scenes with him was three months pregnant and bound into elastic underwear under all the Chanel finery, he never gave the slightest indication, and naturally, I couldn't enlighten him. I did rutinize the rushes with thin lips and a nervous eye, but I continued to look all right up there on the screen as the weeks passed. Every one of Coco's seams held.

Throughout the filming, Michael spent his days with Clifton Webb and the debonair society set and his evenings in the house with the children and me, and no one else in Hollywood had an inkling that we were anything but the most casual acquaintances. As soon as my final divorce papers arrived, however, in order to avoid any possible ugly scandal, we eloped to Yuma, Arizona, and were remarried there. I promptly informed Sam Goldwyn and Joe Schenck that I had taken a fourth husband, and to show my good faith I even allowed our first wedding pictures to be taken on the set with Mervyn Le Roy and Melvyn Douglas. The studio reveled in all the ensuing free publicity, particularly since Michael was just the sort of fascinating European figure Hollywood could never resist, until the mayor of Elmsford, New York, announced that he had married us in August. The resultant controversy over whether or not I had been committing bigamy in the interim kept the columnists busy for a week or so, but after that, most mentions of the subject occurred in mere conjunction with the coverage of another social event— the wedding of Constance Bennett and the Marquis de la Falaise de la Coudraye. If Connie's happy groom felt neither wronged nor concerned, the gossip weavers reasoned, why should *they* be?

Once Michael and I could honorably appear in public together, people deluged us with invitations, and soon Michael was in his element in Hollywood. He golfed, lunched, and weekended with the smartest people in pictures until I had finished shooting. Then, before Louella Parsons and all the other columnists could begin counting months on their fingers, we took the children and sailed the long way to Europe via the Panama Canal.

I knew if I spoke to Joe Schenck before we left, he would cause a terrible row and demand, if possible, an abortion. It was too late for that, of course, and I was the wrong woman to threaten with disgrace or ruin. After sixteen years in pictures I could not be intimidated easily, because I knew where all the skeletons were buried. Moreover, I had married Michael Farmer precisely in order to have my baby in peace, not in order to fail to have it. So I opted for discretion and I trusted to Joe Schenck's sentimental streak. I wrote him from

Europe saying I needed a rest period of a year before I co
make another picture. He did not reply, but his lawyer did, by
invoking several conditions in my contract in order to cancel
it. That meant I had no producer to lean on, just friends.
Since the preservation of my reputation and career was now
up to me alone, I did what many of my friends had done
before—went into seclusion and adopted a secret code for
communicating.

Most celebrities operated as if it were a fact of life that half
the people who worked for the two major telegraph companies, Western Union and Postal Telegraph, especially in
Hollywood, were in the pay of the newspapers. Therefore,
during periods of enforced secrecy, they worked out codes for
sending messages. That is what I did in the fall of 1931 with
my secretary and key employees. Frequently we used the
device of combining two cables into one message. For example, I might send the odd-numbered words of a message (1, 3,
5, 7, etc.) in a Western Union telegram, and the even-
numbered words of the message in a Postal Telegraph telegram. My secretary, Miss Crossman, would then combine the
two sets of words before deciphering the message. The words
we used were not words, either, but meaningless combina-
tions of letters. Below is the Swanson-Farmer cable code for
the fall of 1931 and the winter of 1932, when my private
secretary, press secretary, lawyer, banker, and accountant
were in California and Michael and I were in Europe, living in
a goldfish bowl as usual, awaiting the baby that had already
cost me half of a million-dollar contract.

NAMES

Abien	G.S.
Abifo	M.F.
Abiku	Baby
Abioy	Wright
Abira	Waykoff
Absoh	Heath
Abspi	Crossman

CHANGE OF ADDRESS

Absum	We are leaving for _____
Abtau	Will arrive in _____
Abtey	Address us at _____

cfry   We are traveling incognito as _____

NEWSPAPER INFORMATION

Acfub	Louella Parsons prints story that _____
Adaad	Louella Parsons asks _____
Adabe	Los Angeles newspapers print story that _____
Adafi	New York newspapers print story that _____
Afcel	Los Angeles newspapers ask _____
Afcip	New York newspapers ask _____
Afcow	Florabel Muir prints story that _____
Afcry	Florabel Muir asks _____
Afcub	Associated Press prints story that _____
Agcem	United Press prints story that _____
Agcir	Universal Service (Hearst) prints story that _____
Agcox	I am advising papers here that _____
Agden	I am advising papers in New York that _____
Agdis	Suggest you tell reporters there that _____
Atafy	Do Paris or London papers say anything about _____
Atale	Do New York or Los Angeles papers say anything about _____
Atbun	Photographers
Atdok	Reporters here act very favorably
Atdup	Reporters here very troublesome
Ateax	They want to know about _____
Atfay	Newspapers give as source of story _____

ARRIVAL

Atfec	Prospective arrival
Atfig	Event expected about _(date)_
Atfom	Boy
Dubcu	Girl
Dubew	Pounds
Dubme	Ounces
Dubog	Birth certificate recorded at _____
Dubri	Birth certificate will be recorded at _(date)_
Elata	Impossible to hold up certificate
Elaxe	Doctor announcing that _____
Elbem	Doctor announcing event expected _____
Elbir	Doctor announcing eight months arrival
Elbox	Principal's condition is _____

| Esdiz | Principal feeling very good |
| Esdof | Principal feeling poorly |

MISCELLANEOUS

Evboy	Instruct Crossman to _____
Evbew	Instruct Waykoff to _____
Evcat	Instruct Heath to _____
Evcex	Instruct Wright to _____
Evcib	Please send by mail _____
Kiflo	Please send by cable _____
Kifos	Deposit with Bankers Trust New York _____
Kigim	Have deposited with Bankers Trust New York _____

We spent Christmas in the Hotel Princesse in Paris. Gloria was eleven now, Joseph nine, and the baby inside me was visibly growing almost by the minute. Before leaving for St. Moritz, where we planned to spend the winter and enter the children in private schools, I went to the Ritz Hotel to see Sylvia Ashley. I had heard she was about to undergo surgery, and I wanted to recommend that she consult Dr. Vodéscal before she let anyone operate.

To my amazement, her suite was a veritable gallery of photographs of Doug Fairbanks. When I asked her about it, she said, "But I thought you knew. After all, you introduced us, remember, at that dinner with King Alfonso. It's frightfully complicated. He's on his way here now from America."

As we began to talk, she revealed that she and Doug had a much more intricate code for telegrams than the one Michael and I had worked out. They had to: Sylvia was known to everyone, and Doug had Mary. They *really* lived in a goldfish bowl. I wished her luck, gave her Dr. Vodéscal's name, and said I would see her in London in the spring, when I arrived to have the baby. When I told her I refused to have it in a hospital, she said she would try to arrange to have the midwife to the royal family be with me during my confinement.

In St. Moritz we needed an entire floor of the Suvretta House for all of us plus a governess, maid, and secretary. The children loved the idea of living above the clouds, and the weather was magnificent; even at twenty below the sun shone. Michael was in his element; he skied and climbed, and led the social whirl when the sun went down. Adolphe

Menjou and his wife were the only other refugees from California over New Year's and we became very close.

During this period in the Alps, so tranquil in every other way, Michael underwent a strange transformation: he began to create occasional jealous scenes. If I so much as asked a waiter for more water, he would grow suspicious, then furious, then resentful. In the furious stages, he was likely to grab me roughly or shake me as he was to threaten me with words. One evening he jabbed me forcefully in the ribs in an effort to push me away from him, and I realized I was physically frightened of him during these tantrums. When I announced the next morning that I was leaving him, he churlishly replied that as long as he had all the passports, I was not free to go anywhere. I then locked myself in my room, and he stood outside in the corridor and sobbed and begged me to forgive him. He was as sincere in his repentance as he was in anger, so I forgave him, and for a week he was totally kind and considerate. But I never knew when the volcano might erupt. Therefore, I soon told him I would feel safer in London than in St. Moritz, in the event that the baby should arrive early, and we set off, leaving the children in Switzerland with the governess.

In London I called a few friends and told them I was looking for a house to live in temporarily. Lady Thelma Furness, Gloria Vanderbilt's twin sister, had a charming house on Farm Street, near Berkeley Square—the house, in fact, where Thelma's friend Wallis Simpson had kept the Prince of Wales company recently while Thelma was away in the States. The house was empty for the moment, so we settled in to wait for the baby, and see old friends.

One of the first people I called on in London was Elinor Glyn, whom I hadn't seen for about five years. She seemed unchanged.

"You amaze me," I told her. "What on earth do you do to keep from having wrinkles?"

"I exercise my face, my dear," she said. "It's not enough to play tennis and swim and exercise your body. That sort of thing will do nothing for your face. You have to exercise it."

She demonstrated by jerking the muscles of her face in one direction, then in the other, and contorting her jaw, her ears, and her scalp in the strangest fashion. She told me she had helped more than one big star get rid of the lines in their face. Even Clara Bow did the exercises, she said.

Then we had tea and she told me I looked beautiful

pregnant. She had not changed one bit. I passed her tip on to friends, and all that spring in London, it was not unusual to catch someone in the act of doing Elinor Glyn's facial exercises. I certainly did them myself, for I had never, ever, doubted Elinor's voodoo.

In March, Sylvia and Doug came to the house on Farm Street and brought with them Major Norton, one of the heads of United Artists in London. When we got around to talking movies, Doug asked me why I didn't make a picture in England, where costs were unbelievably low compared with costs in America. Since I was married to Michael, Doug continued, I was a British citizen by marriage and therefore able legally to form a British company and produce films.

"What about Michael?" I asked, for I was very frank with Sylvia and Doug on the subject of my on-and-off difficulties with this young husband.

"Involve him," Sylvia said without hesitation. "He has his boat. Get the writer to put a boat in the story, and let Michael be in the picture. It might be just what he needs."

"Sylvia's right," Doug said, and sure enough, when I suggested the idea to Michael that evening, it filled him with boyish enthusiasm. He loved the thought of working with me.

While I swelled to bursting, therefore, in the following weeks, I also made plans to make a picture in the fall. Major Norton and Doug helped me raise money through United Artists investors, and I found a writer to collaborate on a story with me. When we got bogged down, I wired to ask Eddie Goulding if he would write and direct for me again. He said he was committed to MGM, but he recommended the editor of *The Trespasser,* Cyril Gardner, who was anxious to start directing. Then I asked Noël Coward to suggest someone to play opposite me in a story of marital misunderstandings set in the upper reaches of society, and he said I couldn't do better than Laurence Olivier, a young man he had taken to New York with him to play the second lead in *Private Lives.* Mr. Olivier was in Hollywood, but when I contacted him he said he would return to London to make the picture in September. By the time I got my first labor pain, everything was set.

That same day Sylvia arrived with the royal midwife and two obstetricians. It was April 5, 1932, and when I opened my eyes in the early afternoon, Sylvia was standing at the foot of the bed with my baby in her arms. It was another girl. She was beautiful. She was perfect. Before I could get her in position or her first feeding, she went from a smile to a scream in a split second. She was Michael's child, all right. I called her Michelle, for him.

Her first days on earth were some of the sweetest and tenderest I had ever experienced. It had been twelve years since I nursed a baby, but I had not lost the sense of that total union with another creature that had been inside you, part of you, just days before and now was a separate person, but one still doing you the supreme honor of taking all its love and nourishment from you.

That week I instructed the governess in Switzerland to bring Gloria and Joseph to London. They were both fascinated by their tiny sister when they saw her.

For some reason, pleased as Michael was to be a father, the baby's birth seemed to give rise to several more serious bouts of jealousy in him. The first of these occurred over the telegrams I received. "Who's Francis Lederer?" Michael asked, glancing through them.

"He's a very nice Czech actor. I met him once or twice in Paris. That's terribly sweet of him to send a telegram."

"Yes, isn't it?" Michael said sarcastically. "Don't ever mention his name in front of our child again!" His lips were trembling with rage.

"I didn't mention his name," I said firmly. "You did."

"Did you hear me?" he demanded loudly, as if I had not spoken.

I started to say, "Michael, don't be absurd," but before I could get the phrase out, he had charged out of the room, banging the door behind him.

A week later, when we were out driving the baby through Hyde Park one afternoon, he said, apropos nothing, "I don't want you to lunch alone with Major Norton anymore."

"What are you talking about?" I said with annoyance. "He's helping me raise money for the picture."

"Oh, is that so?" he said. "I know what he's up to, and I never want you to be alone with him again. Tell him so! If I catch you together—ever—I'll kill him! I'm not joking."

With that he grabbed my hand and forced it into his jacket pocket, which contained a small revolver. I shuddered. The whole scene was so bizarre it couldn't get into a bad movie script: Gloria Swanson riding through lawns of daffodils with one hand holding her new baby and the other pressed by her husband against a gun, with which he was threatening to kill a harmless business associate he claimed to be her lover.

In an instant I took total control—the lioness with her cub.
I didn't even raise my voice. "Michael, stop this nonsense or
I'll call the police. It's ridiculous playacting and you know it.
You're a father now, not a rich brat with a boat and a hunting
lodge, and unless you behave like one, I'll divorce you. Like
that! Is that clear?"

His eyes filled with tears, and he kissed my hand. "I'm
sorry," he repeated again and again. By the time we reached
home, he was completely himself, and by evening he was
utterly charming.

More and more I was the playactor after that, always
anticipating difficulties in order to avoid scenes. I had to be,
because I had four children, not three, and the grown-up one
was like the little girl with the curl. When he was bad, I
almost couldn't bear him.

The phone was ringing. I fumbled for it in the dark and at the
same time switched on a light. It was four in the morning.
When the operator said it was a transatlantic call from
Chicago, I could only imagine Mother was ill.

"Gloria?" a little, staticky voice said. "This is Virginia."

The connection was terrible.

"Louder, Virginia!" I yelled. "Is it Mother?"

"No!" Virginia was yelling now too. "There's someone
here who wants to talk to you!"

"Who?"

After a pause a man's voice shouted, "Hello, Gloria, this is
Joe." In spite of the detectable Boston accent, I couldn't
believe my ears until he said, "Joe Kennedy, Gloria."

It had been a year and a half since I heard that voice, and
the sound of it infuriated me.

"It's four o'clock in London, Mr. Kennedy, and I'm
nursing a new baby. What do you want?"

"I read about your baby," he shouted. "We just had one
too. We named him after Eddie Moore. That isn't why I
called."

"I should hope not!" I yelled. "Why did you call?"

"Do you know who's here with me, Gloria? The next
President of the United States, Gloria! He just won the
Democratic nomination. I want you to say hello to him."

It was so blatantly opportunistic that I was stunned.

"How dare you?" I shouted.

"Seriously, Gloria. He wants to say hello to you. Wait a second while I—"

"Don't bother! I don't want to talk to him and I don't want to talk to you!" I slammed down the phone.

By then Michael was wide awake and so was the baby.

"Who was that?" Michael demanded suspiciously.

"The next President of the United States, presumably. But I hung up on him."

That morning I had a long, apologetic cable from Virginia. She said she was sorry to have wakened me, but Joe had called her down to the convention center and begged her to call. She said he wanted me to know that if I needed help financing the new picture, he stood ready. She also said Joe had told her to tell me he had been promised a Cabinet post, probably Secretary of the Treasury, if Roosevelt went on to be elected in November.

We called the finished script *A Perfect Understanding*, and I thought it would be an easy and straightforward film to make. We had lots of good English actors on hand, and wonderful facilities were available at the Pinewood studios outside London. Major Norton got United Artists in Britain to advance the money for preproduction costs and a group of South African investors came forward to lend me the rest of the money, but I had to put up my UA stock as collateral.

I knew that Michael would probably be stiff and amateurish in the small role he had to play, but I was prepared to work with him and I counted on the fact that fans would be curious to see my husband in a film with me. Moreover, once I met the leading man I knew that Michael's inadequacies would probably slip by unnoticed for the most part. Females in the audience were certain to keep their sights on Mr. Olivier every second. I had told Noël Coward I wanted a Ronald Colman type. Laurence Olivier was much better than that. His good looks were positively blinding. He was twenty-five but looked twenty-one, and that worried me until he grew the mustache I suggested for him; it aged him to the point where we became a perfectly believable couple. As for his acting, everyone from Ellen Terry to Sybil Thorndike had declared him England's greatest young talent. He could almost not make a wrong move, his instincts and technique were so finely coordinated.

Nevertheless, problems began to accrue with the arrival of the director, Cyril Gardner. A bit inexperienced but keenly intelligent, he certainly had the necessary talent to direct a romantic comedy of manners, had he not had the misfortune to visit a fortuneteller before reporting on the set. The woman had told this morosely superstitious man that both his parents were soon to die and that he himself would perish on his return voyage to the United States. Before I could give him a stiff drink and say stuff and nonsense, his father was taken to the hospital, where he died a few days later. From that time on, Cyril was a total wreck, but it was too late to replace him.

Subsequently, in London and on location in Cannes, one costly accident followed another. First Larry Olivier was in an auto collision, and although he was not injured, had to spend days in court. Then half the cast came down with a virulent form of flu. Then Cyril Gardner's mother took ill and died, as per the gypsy's prophecy. Nothing seemed to go right. One day when I was in the projection room looking at rushes, a lab technician ran up to me in alarm. Before he could speak, I said jokingly, "Please don't tell me the lab's on fire."

He gulped with relief and said, "How did you know?"

It was true. The lab where the film was being developed had caught fire. Although the technicians threw a third of the negative out the window to save it, most of it had to be shipped to America for reprocessing, all at enormous cost.

At that point I ran out of money. Joe Schenck's company refused to lend me any. Joe Kennedy, who had originally written to say he would provide any additional money I needed, had never followed up on his offer, and I was too proud to call him, even though the bank was ready to shut me down. In the end United Artists called a special meeting of the board and bought my UA stock back from me for $200,000. With that I completed the film.

When we finished shooting and began editing in the fall, I hoped and prayed that the picture would be a great success. If I had ever needed one, it was now.

When I was through nursing Michelle, I sent all three children to Maidenhead on the Thames with Miss Simonson, their governess. In view of the pressures on me, not to mention the never-ending scenes with Michael, I sensed that the best thing

... them was to live apart from me for a month or two until I had solved my problems. When schooltime came and things were no better, I sent them all to Gstaad in Switzerland with Miss Simonson. I knew there was a marvelous school there for Gloria and Joseph. Whenever I had a few days in a row, I traveled to Switzerland to see them. Michael frequently went with me and he showed real affection for the children, but his moods were so unpredictable when we were alone that I was reluctant to expose the children to them, so I kept them in Gstaad.

Once the picture was edited and set for a London premiere in February of 1933, I sailed with Michael for the States to prepare the publicity for American distribution of the film. All the way over, we quarreled constantly, usually over nothing.

Bit by bit, the whole world seemed to be falling apart. In Hollywood, Louella Parsons called me off the record to say Mary Pickford was miserable over the fact that I had introduced Sylvia Ashley to Doug; Mary felt it was the direct cause of her breakup with Doug, and according to Louella she had started drinking over it. I had to call Mary and tell her very frankly, first, that Sylvia was a marvelous friend, and second, that most marriages break up not because of a third party, but because they are ready to break up. "I'm in a marital mess myself, Mary," I said, "but I've got no one to blame but myself, and I tell myself so every day. What's more, we can't stop being friends. We've been friends too long." She agreed, or said she did, but she sounded awful.

Then I discovered another lump on my breast. Dr. Bieler was away at the time, and the doctor I saw frightened the life out of me by insisting on immediate surgery. I flatly refused and made plans to sail to France. If anyone was going to cut me, I vowed, it would be Dr. Vodéscal or some other trustworthy doctor.

Before we left for Paris and Switzerland to see the children, Carole Lombard phoned and asked us to have dinner with Bill Powell and her. I adored them both, and I needed an amusing evening more than I needed medicine, so I accepted with pleasure. Over dinner, however, Bill Powell shyly confessed that he needed cheering up. He had developed a lump in an unmentionable place, he said, and the doctors were rushing him into surgery in a day or two. Then I confessed that I had a lump too, and Bill told me to have a drink, not a ridiculous little glass of wine but a real drink. One led to more, and before the night was over I had had so many that I gave way to my feelings of doom and dived from the high dive into their swimming pool fully dressed. Michael, feeling no pain and also fully dressed, jumped right in after me and fished me out.

In Paris, Michael swore by a doctor named Dermartel, who removed the second lump and told me the following day it was benign, but I was almost too emotionally exhausted to rejoice.

Then we spent ten days in Gstaad with the children, and as always it tore me apart to leave them.

After the London premiere of *A Perfect Understanding,* the critics were friendly but not enthusiastic. After the New York premiere a few weeks later, the critics were indifferent. Franklin Roosevelt, the new President, had closed the national banks and inaugurated the New Deal; Americans were consequently in no mood to see a group of high-born Britishers engage in well-spoken domestic 'squabbles in the courts and on the French Riviera.

A Perfect Understanding, which had started out so smoothly, was a disaster. To make things worse, at a time of national economic crisis, it was the only picture I had ever financed largely with my own money. The only happy economic aspect of the endeavor was that Great Britain exempted me from paying normal taxes in view of the costs I had sustained, which were beyond my control.

After that I seemed to be floundering, traveling back and forth to Europe without purpose. Months passed, until I realized one day to my horror that we were already into 1934. For the first time in my life I felt that time was slipping away unproductively. Although I had discussed numerous projects, I had not made a picture in two years. More important, I couldn't remember when I'd last been happy. The people I knew were ill, many of them, and growing older, getting gray. I was so insecure I couldn't make firm decisions.

In January of 1934 my attorney, Lloyd Wright, called to say that Herbert Somborn wanted to see me. Since Gloria's infancy Herbert had always been a devoted father, punctual in picking her up at the house for visits with him, generous with gifts. Whatever our personal differences, I couldn't fault Herbert in his love for his child. I assumed the message meant that he wanted to know when Gloria was coming home next, but even that would have been rather odd, for we generally did not communicate directly even over Gloria, and I knew perfectly well, besides, that the two of them corresponded on their own all the time. Perhaps she was not writing to him as regularly as he wished, I thought, and perhaps he was alarmed enough to ask me personally if she was all right.

"Give me the number," I said to Lloyd. "I'll call him."

"Let me give you the number of his doctor, Gloria," Lloyd said. "Herbert's in Cedars of Lebanon Hospital. I think it's serious."

I called the doctor, who told me Herbert was dying of cancer. "He seems most anxious to see you," the doctor said. "He hasn't much time, Miss Swanson."

The next day I went to the hospital. Herbert looked awful, but his mind was clear. We talked about Gloria, of course. He said how much he loved her, and I could feel tears filling my eyes, but I fussed in my purse for a cigarette to conceal the fact. Then he said he was sorry about the way he had handled our divorce, and I said that was all long ago and forgotten. He slowly studied my face, as if testing it for the truth of my reply.

"You're the only woman I ever loved, Gloria," he said. "You're still the only one I totally trust. They say I don't have cancer. Is it true? Can I get well?"

I had called him Daddy fifteen years ago. It didn't seem possible—I hardly knew the man. Out of lingering bitterness, I had usually been absent on purpose when he came to pick up little Gloria. We had probably not exchanged two dozen words in a decade.

I patted his arm. "They told me I *did* have it a year ago, Herbert, but I didn't. It doesn't matter what they say. You'll get well. Believe me. I'm going to call Gloria and tell her we saw each other today."

Our good-byes a minute later were final, but I could tell by Herbert's face that I had convinced him to the contrary.

After two and a half years of being married to Michael— where had the time gone?—I had stopped trying. I didn't know which way to turn. Finally my lawyer advised me confidentially to file for a California divorce without delay.

"But, Lloyd," I said, "I can't have another divorce. What about my career?"

Lloyd was severe. "Your career couldn't be in more jeopardy than it is. You have no idea what a wreck you are. You're not thinking straight. Believe me, Gloria, you're heading right into a nervous breakdown. For your children's sake, you have to take drastic measures before it's too late."

The time was approaching when Michael, as a British citizen, would have to leave the country to renew his visa. When Lloyd Wright, with my permission, refused to ask the immigration authorities for an extension, Michael exploded, because he knew what the gesture meant.

"You want me away because you intend to get a divorce. Isn't that it? *Isn't it?*"

I nodded, and he stormed out of the house without another word.

The nightmare could end now. Once he was in Europe, in March, I sent him the following letter:

Dear Michael:
    The inevitable divorce which we have often discussed, I want to get now. The unpleasant things which happened leading up to your departure were to me the climax. You might wonder why I let you go without telling you how I really felt, but I thought it easier for you and truly I wanted to save myself the little energy I had left for something more than another discussion; also and most important, I thought with you away, I could think clearly for the future and in the future what we might mean to each other. I find it impossible to put together all the little pieces that have been so badly torn—and even if I could, for what, to be torn again?
    Not the things I want, but the things I need to make me happy, I know and so do you Michael, if you really can be honest with yourself, you cannot possibly give me. You will never know tolerance, understanding, or little kindnesses toward me.
    I have great responsibilities and I want very much to be able to meet them; this I can only do providing the unpleasant side of my home life is removed. Surely you have not been any too happy yourself, and since that is true, why should you or I cling to this marriage?

The sweetness in our lives is that we have a beautiful baby. I wanted her so much and you wanted a child before you were thirty-one. Our marriage has served that purpose. Why continue it now, when it has little else to offer and our lives are so terribly far apart?

Our quarrels now are only a reflection of the ugliness of the past which has never been allowed to die, and which definitely should, if not for our sake for Michelle's.

Certainly our divorce will not be a surprise to the world. I intend to get it as quickly as possible on the grounds of incompatibility. There need be no unpleasantness about it.

I am not in any particular hurry to get my divorce, but I thought there would be less publicity if it were filed in California while I am in the East.

I am aware of the problem of the children, but it seems difficult to discuss this with you until . . . I know exactly where I am going to be for the next six months or so, and whether and when I get a chance to go to Europe to see them during that time.

When we meet I hope we can be friends—something we unhappily never have been.

This letter will probably be waiting for you when you return from Norway. I am sure you have had a nice time. And, Michael dear, it is my sincere wish that you will always have a nice time.

Do let me know how Michelle and Miss Simonson are enjoying Paris.

I shall cable you when I leave for New York and my address there.

> Affectionately,
> Gloria

He didn't reply directly. Two weeks later, though, Sylvia Ashley sent me the following notice from an English paper.

MR. MICHAEL FARMER

Mr. Michael Farmer, husband of Miss Gloria Swanson, has arrived in Paris from Norway, where he has been fishing and denies that he is seeking a divorce.

"A divorce suit could only come from my wife's side," he said.

He added that after a brief stay in Paris he planned to go on a round-the-world yachting tour.

Michael was right back where he was when I first met him in 1931.

. I was the one who had changed. Greatly.

CHAPTER 18

When I first came to Hollywood, I gawked, like any
other fan, at celebrities. I remember going to the South-
west Tennis Tournament on a September afternoon and
seeing Gloria Swanson and Herbert Marshall there, and
thinking what a perfect couple they looked, how elegant,
how entirely like movie stars.

—ROSALIND RUSSELL,
Life Is a Banquet

The day I initiated divorce proceedings against Michael
Farmer, I was ready to retire to a desert cave and rethink my
life. My first instinct was to gather the children to me for
comfort, but Gloria and Brother were in the middle of a
school year in Gstaad and Michael threatened to dispute
custody of Michelle, so I hesitated. Everyone I knew, from
Lois Wilson to Allan Dwan, urged me to go right back to
work, as if that were the easiest thing in the world after
breaking a contract with Joe Schenck and ending a partnership in United Artists; I stoutly told them all I intended to do
just that, but I dreaded making the first call.

I was spared the embarrassment. Irving Thalberg phoned
me to inquire if I would like to sign with MGM, and I almost

died of gratitude. Then, before we had even discussed terms, Erich Pommer, a producer at Fox, called and offered me the starring role in a screen version of *Music in the Air*, the Broadway hit of 1932 with music by Jerome Kern and book and lyrics by Oscar Hammerstein II. This was Christmas in March to someone whose own lawyer said she was on the verge of a breakdown, but I managed to restrain myself from telling Mr. Pommer that. Instead I said I was nominally committed to Mr. Thalberg at MGM.

"Well, in that case," Mr. Pommer said, "we can announce that you are on loan to Fox from MGM for this one picture. It's done all the time."

I had the inspiration and courage to pause.

"There's a terrific screenplay," Mr. Pommer was saying enthusiastically, "by Howard Young and Billy Wilder. It's perfectly suited to you or I wouldn't be calling."

Better and better, I thought. O Aries! I thought. In my calmest voice I said, "Perhaps we should meet and talk. I'm free tomorrow, if that's convenient for you."

The next day Mr. Pommer agreed to all of my conditions, and we signed a contract. Only then could I uncross my fingers and take over a sumptuous star bungalow on the Fox lot for the duration of the picture.

Music in the Air tells the story of two temperamental opera stars in Munich who are looking for a new opera to stage. They love each other but they fight constantly. When a handsome young schoolmaster and his fiancée from the Bavarian Alps arrive in the city to try to sell the fiancée's father's songs, the diva woos the schoolmaster to make her lover jealous, while the lover in turn plays the same game with the schoolmaster's beautiful girl friend. In the final scenes the two couples are correctly reunited, the girl's father's songs form the basis for the stars' new opera, and everyone ends up happy and successful and rich.

As my co-star, director Joe May wanted John Boles, whom I had cast in his first picture, *The Love of Sunya*, and who was now a big name in the movies. Mr. May chose June Lang and Douglass Montgomery as the young lovers, and for the character parts picked Reginald Owen, Marjorie Main, and Al Shean, of Gallagher and Shean. With this cast and a lovely score, which included such songs as "I've Told Every Little Star," "The Song Is You," and "We Belong Together," Fox felt they could afford not to stint. They built a whole Bavarian lage as well as reproductions of the Munich zoological garden and opera house on the lot; they commissioned René Hubert to design fabulous clothes for me; and they engaged Dr. Marifiotti, Caruso's voice coach, who had helped me on and off since *The Trespasser,* to work with me on my songs.

We all felt fairly certain of success during the shooting, but the picture flopped. Hollywood producers learned once again that the taste of New York and Broadway, during the darkest days of the Depression, was no barometer for the taste of the nation at large. The nation at large ignored *Music in the Air* and rushed instead to see *Stand Up and Cheer,* a musical starring a six-year-old Shirley Temple.

After that, Irving Thalberg went back to looking for the "right" property for me, and Dr. Marifiotti tried to persuade me to become a concert and opera singer. When I mentioned a concert tour to Irving he encouraged me, saying it would be the best publicity in the world for me just then. Therefore, I told agents in the East they could go ahead and arrange a limited series of personal appearances in New York, and Dr. Marifiotti and I went to work preparing a program.

Several weeks before I left for New York, Eddie Goulding took me to dinner at the home of Richard and Jessica Barthelmess. The entire British colony in California seemed to be there, and Eddie took me through the whole house and garden introducing me to everyone I didn't know. In the bar he led me up to a handsome man in his early forties with a gentle face and soft brown eyes.

"Gloria Swanson. Bart Marshall."

Mr. Marshall looked at me and smiled and said, in one of the most perfect musical voices I had ever heard, "How do you do? I'm very pleased to meet you. May I get you a drink?"

"Yes, please," I said, utterly charmed by the man, "I'll have some champagne."

"Anything for you, Eddie?" he asked as he turned toward the barman, but Eddie was waving at people in the next room. "Darling, I'll be right back," Eddie said. "You'll be all right with Bart, won't you? He's very nice." Then he was gone.

"Here you are," the beautiful voice was saying, and as I turned to take the glass from him, he smiled the most devastating of smiles and said, "Cheers."

"Cheers."

Lots of people came up to speak to one or the other of us as we stood there together. Herbert Marshall was obviously very well liked. Once, feeling I might be impinging on his privacy, I readied myself to walk away and find Eddie, but with perfect timing he anticipated that and said, "May I get you some supper?"

"That's very nice of you. Yes, please."

I realized I was as awkward as a fourteen-year-old girl shoved into the presence of—whom? I couldn't imagine, for surely no one was more attractive than the man getting me some supper. I had not been so instantaneously drawn to anyone since the night Mickey Neilan said hello and led me out to dance and told me he planned to marry me, all before I knew his name.

We sat at a table with Eddie and a group of his friends. They all seemed charming and bright, but I didn't hear a word anyone said but Mr. Marshall, and I finally felt like such an idiot for listening so attentively to him that I told Eddie I had to get up early for a voice lesson.

When he took our farewells Bart Marshall shook my hand without undue pressure, which disappointed me, but as I drew it away, he said softly, "May I call you?"

I wanted to say, "Yes, Yes! The sooner the better. I'll be in agony until you do!" but I managed to edit my inner hurricane down to: "Of course. I'd be delighted."

No one had heard a word of our exchange.

Driving back to my house, I asked Eddie Goulding if Bart Marshall was married.

"Yes, to Edna Best, the actress. But they live apart most of the time. Should I ask why you want to know?"

"No."

"I thought not," Eddie said.

Within a week Bart Marshall and I were madly in love. I could no more have prevented it from happening than I could have blown out a klieg light in one small breath or run barefoot up the Matterhorn. Beside him all the other cultivated men I had ever known seemed just a bit coarse.

Norma Shearer once described her reaction the first time she saw Herbert Marshall play a love scene on the screen: "I thought I had never seen a lady so thoroughly and convincingly loved. He is both manly and wistful. He wins the sympathy of women because his face expresses tenderness

and silent suffering." In those few words Norma caught
perfectly the essence of Bart Marshall.

Born into a British theatrical family, Bart was just starting
out on the stage when the war began. He was seriously
wounded in battle in France, and his right leg had to be
amputated, but he determinedly mastered walking on an
artificial leg without limping and soon became a favorite
leading man in London's West End. For a few years after his
marriage to Edna Best, the couple were a popular acting team
on both sides of the Atlantic. Bart was in a few silent pictures
and with Miss Best in a couple of talkies, but not until he
played Jeanne Eagels' lover in *The Letter,* made in Astoria in
1928, did Paramount invite him to Hollywood. Since then he
had made pictures with Claudette Colbert, Norma Shearer,
Marlene Dietrich, Miriam Hopkins, and Kay Francis. He was
a favorite of Ernst Lubitsch's, and when I met him he told me
Mr. De Mille was looking for a film for him.

I soon learned that I was not the first woman to be involved
with him since his arrival in Hollywood. Everyone seemed to
know, for example, that he had had affairs with Kay Francis
and Miriam Hopkins. His past didn't interest me, however.
After all, I had one of my own. His married life was none of
my business either, really, but the time came when we had to
talk about it—when Edna's friends began pointedly to cut
Bart if we appeared in public together.

"What about her?" I asked him one night.

"Edna doesn't want to live in California," he told me, "and
my work is here. We've talked of divorce many times—long
before I met you—but I'll talk to her in earnest now, because
I want to marry you."

That was enough for me. I didn't need or want any further
details. Bart rented a house across the street and half a block
away from mine, and we went everywhere together, taking no
trouble whatsoever to avoid being seen. In the eyes of the
press, by keeping separate houses we were obeying the rules
and earning our right to privacy. Hollywood had come a long
way since the days of Fatty Arbuckle. Prohibition was over.
Marion Davies was just another fashionable hostess. Even
Mary Pickford was headed for the divorce courts for a second
time. In fact, everybody, it seemed, had been divorced at least
once or twice, and the public loved to keep count of all
ex-wives and ex-husbands of celebrities. The major gossip
columnists were now more concerned with protecting the
industry and serving as publicity agents for the big moguls

than with gunning down sinners, and the public had more important concerns in 1934 than to know or care whether Herbert Marshall and Gloria Swanson dined out together without being married.

The only requirement was to humor the press, usually by way of being charming but noncommittal. Bart resented intrusion, however, particularly after a few drinks, and he always had at least a few. When I went east for the tour he followed me to New York, and there one evening he caused a commotion that made its way into the gossip columns. We were at El Morocco late one evening with Sport Ward and another friend, Lily Havemeyer, when a photographer closed in on us and began taking flash photos. This was standard procedure at El Morocco, whose owner got pictures of as many famous people as he could against the zebra-striped upholstery and supplied them to newspapers and magazines, but Bart Marshall didn't know that; therefore, as soon as he saw me look the least bit annoyed, he told the photographer his behavior was an outrage and ordered him from the table. The next morning in all the papers, and from that day forward, we were an "item," in the sense of being unmarried lovers. Bart's career was not affected; he was a man, and British to boot. But my career, already in partial eclipse, caused grave concern to those friends who were determined to make me a star again. Although they all said they were not worried in the least, they were worried. Nevertheless, the best and dearest of them refused to give up because they could tell that for the first time in five years, since the exciting success of *The Trespasser,* I was happy.

When I returned to California, Irving Thalberg said it was time to start preparing an MGM picture for me. He asked my friend Frances Marion, one of the biggest writers in Hollywood, to go to work on a story. Frances' husband, George Hill, with whom she had collaborated on a long string of successful pictures, would direct it. And for my leading man, Irving said with rugged determination, he had two people in mind—Clark Gable and Herbert Marshall.

Late that summer Bart said Edna Best was coming to Hollywood with their little girl for a visit, and I cringed at the thought that the two of us might bump into each other by accident and be forced into an unpleasant confrontation. The day after she arrived, however, Bart called to say he had told her about us and had asked her for a divorce. I was so relieved I almost didn't hear the next thing he said: she wanted to meet me. They were invited that afternoon to the home of Ernest Torrence, one of the pillars of the British colony; would I come too and speak briefly with Edna?

This was the stuff movies were made of, the sort of scene actresses were willing to break contracts and change studios for, but the notion that someone would elect to experience it in real life temporarily cut my breath off. Surely it had to be either unendurably civilized and polite, I imagined, or charged with anguish and disdain, for how could it possibly, given the circumstances, be reasonable or honest or beneficial? If it became overwrought, Edna Best and I both had all the long, necessary training to play it to the hilt, and for that very reason I chose at first to avoid it. Then curiosity and simple decency made me have second thoughts. To refuse the opportunity to meet the woman who could suggest it in the first place, and who had given the man I loved his only child, and who therefore, perhaps, had the right to request it, seemed cowardly, insincere, unworthy.

On the other end of the line Bart was waiting to persuade me, in the event I refused, which I could tell he was expecting me to do. Therefore, I surprised us both when I controlled an unseasonable shiver that was shaking me from head to toe and said, "All right. What time?"

"Six?"

"I'll be there. But by seven, Bart Marshall, I'm hoping to be back here for dinner. With you."

"I promise, my darling. And don't worry. She's very nice."

Ten times on the way to Ernest Torrence's house I wanted to order the driver to turn around, and fifty or a hundred times I wondered if I looked all right, by which I meant: something more than just "the other woman," poised and brittle and clotheshorsey and a trifle hard. Mr. Torrence opened the door for me and led me to the living room, where Bart introduced me to his wife. She was fair and slim, with pretty English features and marcelled hair, and moments later the two of us were seated alone in a small upstairs sitting room.

Despite our flawless deportment and businesslike efficiency, the interview strained both of us, I could tell. We didn't call each other by first name or last name, we merely raised issues; our conversation was a series of delicate exchanges, as if we were passing a valuable paper-thin goblet back and forth, precisely and carefully, for fear of breaking it.

She knew Bart loved me, she said. Did I love him? Yes.

That did not altogether shock her, did it? Surely she had been aware of previous infidelities on his part, hadn't she? She had.

There was a child to consider. I could understand that, couldn't I? Of course. I had children of my own.

Did I realize that he drank too much? Yes. Could anything be done about it? No need. He was essentially a social drinker, but a heavy one.

It would take some time to work out a divorce. In the meantime, they were talking about a trial separation. Was that clear? It was now.

When we walked back downstairs, we were as calm as two people who had exchanged a secret or a recipe. A moment later I made a movement to leave, and Bart took his place at my side.

At the front door I said, "If you cross this line now, bring all of yourself with you, Bart."

He took my hand, waved to my chauffeur to go on alone, and led me to his car.

From then on we were off limits, quarantined, in the minds of most socially prominent celebrities. The ostracism was never declared; we just didn't receive many invitations in the ensuing months, separately or together. We saw only a very few friends, including Carole Lombard, Grace Moore, and Vilma Banky and Rod La Rocque, who were married now and dead to the elite since Rod had punched a producer in the nose for insulting Vilma, and Aileen Pringle, who was always in disfavor with one studio executive or another. But Bart and I didn't mind. We were so happy together, even alone, that a little company seemed a lot.

Bart's career didn't suffer in the least. He was a uniquely sensitive type, and the public couldn't get enough of him. He was making on the average of five or six pictures a year, and the studios were careful to keep the papers from soiling his image. Our ostracism, therefore, was purely social.

People always referred to my house as "904," for its number on Crescent Drive. One day I called Bart at the studio and told him to dress for dinner because, I told him, some brave people had finally risked the wrath of proper

Beverly Hills and accepted an invitation to dinner at 904. When he arrived, looking marvelous, we had a drink alone in the library. I explained that our guests were having drinks elsewhere and would arrive at the dinner hour. He asked who they were, and I said it was a surprise. At eight the butler came and announced dinner, and Bart and I walked down the long hall together arm in arm. In the candlelit dining room a second butler was pouring wine for twelve guests, already seated at the table. I told Bart we were sitting across from each other at the middle of the table—French style, not British. By then Bart realized that all the dinner guests, the men in white ties and the bejeweled ladies, were mannequins, which I had rented—dressed—for the evening. He laughed his gorgeous laugh for minutes, literally, and then we swung ebulliently into the mood of a typical California party, carrying on crazy conversations with the guests to the right and left and discussing all the people who had sent us into exile. The two butlers and the maid could hardly keep straight faces. After dinner we begged our guests to be excused so that we could watch a picture in the projection room.

Hours later, when we came back upstairs, I froze in my tracks as we passed the dining room, where the candles were out and the electric lights were glaring. All the chairs with the dummies on them were pulled back from the table now, and I noticed for the first time that the dummies were legless, so as to rest on upright chairs. Bart couldn't conceal the terrible shock that spread over his face. It was awful. I started to cry. Then I heard him laughing, roaring rather, both at the sight of the dummies and the perplexity they caused in me. He put his arms around me, kissed me, and said, "My most only. Stop your crying. This is the best time I've had in years."

He was sweet beyond belief. One day a friend called me in hysterics because her doctor had told her she had to have a breast removed; she had cancer. She was in despair over the fact that the man she loved would surely leave her—even if she survived—because she would be incomplete. I calmed her down and insisted on driving her to Pasadena to get Dr. Bieler's opinion. Bart sat between us in the back seat and we both tried to soothe her, but she was out of control in her grief and fear. At last I reached over, grabbed her hand, and slammed it down on Bart's artificial leg.

"Feel that," I said, "and listen to me. Love has nothing to do with missing parts. Does it, Bart?"

"No, indeed," Bart said, so gently that she stopped crying. Then he put one arm around her and the other around me for the remainder of the drive.

Dr. Bieler said he doubted the lump she had was malignant and sent her to a surgeon he knew, who removed the tumor the way Dr. Dermartel had removed mine. It was benign, and my friend told the original doctor so in all the rage of perfect health. But by then, even if she had lost a breast, she could believe after an hour with Bart Marshall that such a thing did not mean an end to living. Or loving.

That summer we saw Irving Thalberg and Norma Shearer privately, but it was difficult for a time for Irving, as a studio head, to appear with us in public. However, one day in September we got an invitation from Norma and Irving to a huge party they were giving. The message was very clear: Irving had decided it was time to declare us socially acceptable again. When we arrived together, everyone rushed up to greet us warmly as if to say, Where have you been? I wanted to say, Home with the plague, but instead I just smiled and said we'd been *so busy*. I couldn't care less what any of them thought. Bart and I were back on shore, that was the important thing, and I would always be grateful to Irving for it.

Shortly after that, Bart said, "Why don't *you* have a party now?"

"All right," I said. "Whom shall we invite?"

"Gloria and Brother and Michelle," he said, and I burst into tears. "You know it's all you want in the world, darling. Why don't you bring them back and put them in school here?"

"It's high time, isn't it?" I said. "But it won't be easy."

Getting the children back from Europe involved luck, a complicated timetable, and a certain amount of derring-do. Michael had moved Michelle and Miss Simonson into his adopted mother's house in Paris, and in order to obtain a California divorce expeditiously, I had not dared to defy his wishes. Even when the divorce was final, however, I knew it could be contested in courts in England and France and Ireland, which might involve months of delay, and I did not want to provoke a legal hassle or an international scandal that would affect Michelle. Therefore I contacted my friend Arlette Marchal in Paris and told her to alert Miss Simonson to have Michelle ready to leave for the States in a month. I felt certain that Michael would not fight for custody once the baby was back with me. The trick was getting her back without upsetting him.

Arlette Marchal was my contact with Michelle during periods when Michael demanded custody. Arlette had played the Queen of Naples in *Madame Sans-Gêne,* and I had helped her get a Hollywood contract. After playing a series of unsuitable roles, she had returned to Paris, but we had always remained close friends. When I contacted her in September, she replied that Michael was not in Paris and that the governess was willing to travel to America with all three children. It was time to act.

I sent Ethel, my maid, to Switzerland to get Gloria and Joseph out of the schools they were attending and take them to Paris. There Arlette moved Michelle and Miss Simonson out of Mrs. Hubbard's house and booked passage for the two women and the children on the first boat leaving for New York.

When they arrived, we had a marvelous reunion. Gloria was fourteen now, Joseph was nearly twelve—much too old to be called Brother—and the baby was two and a half. The two older children were so happy to be back on Crescent Drive and so fed up with private schools that the greatest gift I could give them was permission to go to public school with all their old friends.

They had dinner their first night back with Uncle Bart, who charmed them immediately. Furthermore, Michael caused no rumpus whatsoever over the hasty removal of Michelle. In fact, I imagined he was probably relieved. He could never have raised a child alone, and I had removed from him the onus of ever having to admit it. Therefore I had a peaceful, if slightly unusual, family life going again, and I rejoiced in it. Carole Lombard called me "the clucking hen," and I loved the name because it was accurate. I was content. And if I didn't have a busy career, for a while at least, so much the better, I thought. I had two years of catching up to do with my babies, who resented more than anything in the world being thought of as babies. Two of them were quite grown-up. They all spoke fluent French.

All through what was left of 1934 and 1935, the Hollywood press spoke often of my next picture, and spoke of it

enthusiastically as a big comeback. Irving Thalberg and
Frances Marion had settled on a remake of Elinor Glyn's
story *Three Weeks*. Frances said she thought it would be just
right. Irving said there would be no mistake this time.

Comeback . . . just right . . . this time—ominous phrases
all for someone just turning thirty-six, but then, if you live a
star's life and are not a fool, you live it from day to day, and
think about your appointment with the manicurist and your
son's teeth and your daughter's dancing lessons and the leaky
faucet in the hall bathroom and your mother's birthday, just
like everyone else; whereas if you look at a star's life from the
outside you assume she doesn't worry about any of those
things but exists only in a career, just blazes in a remote
firmament, turning this way and that before her mirror,
having temper tantrums, going mad unless she has constant
contracts to sign and can make a picture with someone like
Ronald Colman every other month.

For the first time, the real image and the created image
seemed to be at war. On the one hand, I was a lucky
American girl, picked at random out of millions, who had
succeeded admirably and could therefore take it easy for a
while. On the other, I was a legend—a sacred monster, in
Jean Cocteau's phrase—a fading star the public had worshiped long enough, who was in search of a new type of role
to fit.

In reality, I was happily in love with a nice man, lived in a
big house in a small town, had three beautiful children and
lots of friends, and for the first time in twenty years was not
working.

Meanwhile, Irving Thalberg's plans for *Three Weeks* went
steadily forward. For several months we had conferences and
even talked about schedules and casting. Then a terrible
reversal occurred. George Hill, the director, died in an
accident, and there were rumors that his death was a suicide.
This so shattered Frances Marion that she couldn't continue
work on the project for months. I understood perfectly. They
were both great friends of mine, and my heart went out to
Frances. She promised me she would get back to the script
again as soon as possible, and I told her not even to think
about it until she felt able. By the time she began to mend,
however, all Hollywood was whispering about Irving Thalberg's health, saying he was mortally ill. When he called me
to apologize for his slowness later that year, I told him not to

give it a thought, that I was busy at the moment as a producer and he was doing me a favor giving me a breather.

This was only partially true. What work I had as a producer was slight indeed. In September, Eddie Goulding told me he had interested Warners in remaking *The Trespasser* with Bette Davis and he was sure they would pay good money. Would I sell them the rights? I said of course I would, and called my accountant, who informed me that the rights were legally controlled by Joseph Kennedy.

"Are you sure?" I asked, perturbed as always to discover any further extension of the irksome old entanglement.

"Positive," he said.

"Then have my secretary find out where he is," I snapped, "and I'll contact him myself."

Joe Kennedy still stayed in touch with me, always through Virginia Bowker, and he was always so bouncy and good-natured when he phoned that I had ceased to carry a grudge. Nevertheless, I always refused to see him and I never initiated any contact. His calls were invariably to report a new honor or position bestowed on him, and I could tell that he was thereby compensating for the great failure of his life, as an artistic producer, and seeking from me, his partner in that failure, as he saw it, approval and recognition. He had last phoned the year before, to tell me President Roosevelt had appointed him to head the new Securities and Exchange Commission. We hadn't, however, been close or mentioned business in over five years.

My secretary found out from his office in Washington that he was sailing for Europe on the *Normandie*, so I sent him a telegram.

DEAR JOE WILL YOU PLEASE GIVE ME THE STORY RIGHTS TO THE TRESPASSER BECAUSE I WISH TO REMAKE IT CABLE ADDRESS GLORISWAN BEVERLYHILLS BON VOYAGE YOU LUCKY DOG

The following day he cabled back a typical message, as if a whole disastrous partnership had never been formed, as if bountiful were his middle name, as if I were a silly child who would forget to tie her shoes unless he left me specific instructions.

DELIGHTED GIVE YOU ALL ASSETS CORPORATION INCLUDING STORY HAVE YOUR LAWYER ACCOUNTANT TO WHOM WE SENT FIGURES

ADVISE YOU THEN CORPORATION COULD BE DISSOLVED DONT
RELINQUISH STORY GRATIS SEVERAL WANT IT GOOD LUCK
    JOE

I actually had to smile. That pair of telegrams signaled the
end of the artistic collaboration that had been destined to
change the history of the cinema and make us both millions.

In our first year together, Bart and I often discussed marriage, but I always told him, quite sincerely, I was in no rush
to take husband number five, just for the sake of being
married. As long as I had my three children, and him right
across the street, and the press would let it go at that, I was in
fact probably better off without an extra notch in my belt. The
truth of the matter was, I wanted Bart to take all the
initiative, if and when we were married.

Dear as he was, he had serious weaknesses, the greatest of
which was his overly docile disposition. He couldn't bear to
hurt anyone, or disappoint anyone, or shock anyone. He let
relationships ride, often when they most needed attention,
and as soon as he sensed guilt or pressure for not dealing with
people directly and forcefully, he would always turn to
alcohol rather than face a painful scene. I soon understood
why Edna Best had asked to talk to me. She obviously knew
that although Bart could present our situation to her in all its
romantic power and ask her to forgive him for an emotion
beyond his control, he would never be able to see or discuss it
in any practical light.

By the end of 1935 Bart was drinking heavily. I finally
decided the situation couldn't continue as it was, and I knew
by then that Bart was incapable of taking the initiative to
change it. There was a ghost between us—the ghost of Edna
and their unresolved separation and the child he had given
up. I was sure it was torturing him and as a result was making
life unbearable for me, and the longer things continued as
they were, the more difficult the situation was sure to
become. I therefore urged Bart to go to London and
straighten things out once and for all, and I asked his agents
to back me up. When he delayed, we continued to prod him
until at last he postponed a picture and booked passage.

I had never seen him so nervous as when I put him on the
train in Pasadena. As he was boarding, I slipped a letter in his
pocket explaining exactly how I felt. I told him to be

absolutely honest. If he couldn't live with his conscience, once he saw his child, then he must tell me so and we must end our life together. If there was no way to kill the ghost between us, then it was time he knew it and was brave enough to tell me so, and I would be brave and generous enough to understand. Just before the train pulled out, I motioned to him that there was something in his pocket.

He called me from Arizona the first time the train stopped and told me not to worry; he would be back free in a month. Two weeks after that he called from London. On the advice of agents and friends, he said, he and Edna had let the press announce a reconciliation.

"Everyone thinks it's the best thing to do just now. For everybody," he said.

I was silent.

"In terms of career," he said, getting more and more anxious. "Don't be upset, my most only; it doesn't mean anything. I'll explain when I get back. I'm coming back next week."

"Why, Bart?" I said, struggling to control my voice. "So that I can go through the pain of being that other woman who broke up a happy home all over again? No, thank you. I think you should stay there until you're reconciled completely. Oh, Bart!"

"Please, darling. It was a very difficult situation—"

"Good-bye, Bart."

I hung up and began sobbing. Facing what I now knew about Bart was almost unbearable because I loved him, but I made myself face it. I might go on loving him, but I would never respect him again or feel happy with him again. Therefore, it was better not to see him again until I was in complete control of myself.

I left for New York in a week's time, thinking we would pass each other en route, but he took a later boat than the one he had wired he was taking and somehow managed to track me down in New York.

He asked if he could come to my hotel, and I refused. Then he asked if I would go to his hotel. Knowing a scene was sooner or later inevitable, I decided to have it then and there, three thousand miles away from my children and in his hotel, so that I could terminate it when I had to. I asked him for the room number and said I'd be there in a half-hour.

When I arrived, the door to his suite was open. The room smelled of stale smoke and liquor. He stood at the window, looking out over Central Park, but he soon felt my presence and turned to face me. He was shaking, his face was bloated, his brown eyes were dull with pain. He had a glass of whiskey in his hand.

"Oh, my darling, I'm sorry," he said. Then he bit his lip to keep from crying.

"I am too," I replied in a little, trembling voice.

He set down the glass and took a step toward me, but I stopped him with a cry that was half command, half plea: "No!"

I turned to start out the door, but his quiet sobbing froze me in place.

I turned back, wanting to see him once more, wanting even to talk, but knowing I couldn't control myself for more than a few words.

"Bart, you're not being very nice to yourself."

"My most only," he began and took another step toward me.

If he reached me, I knew I would yield, so I turned and walked as quickly as I could to the elevator.

After that, I knew that only work could make Hollywood endurable, so I began sending out discreet but urgent signals.

When Mr. De Mille took over the Lux Radio Theatre, he hired me to star in one of the early broadcasts, and it was very successful, with mobs of fans outside the studio, but it didn't get me back in pictures.

Irving Thalberg told me to be patient. As soon as he finished *Romeo and Juliet* with Norma Shearer, he said, we would get back to work on *Three Weeks*. But in 1936 poor Irving died, and *Three Weeks* died with him.

Then MGM talked with me about a contract and told Frances Marion to tailor a script called *Maisie Kenyon* for me. Before the screenplay was finished, however, Frances had a row with MGM and made a deal with Harry Cohn to become a producer at Columbia. She told me not to feel bad; *Maisie Kenyon* was a lousy script. She told Harry Cohn that the first thing she wanted to produce at Columbia was an important picture for me. Harry said that was a terrific idea, but for months they couldn't agree on a property, so I finally accepted a friend's invitation and went to London for the coronation of George VI.

I had been in London only a few days when an urgent cable arrived from Harry Cohn. Frances had found the perfect story: *The Second Mrs. Draper* by Noel Pierce. Harry said he was ready to buy it if I would come right back to Hollywood and sign a contract. Then Frances called to say it was all true. So I cut my trip short and rushed back to California, but by the time I got there, Harry had decided the role in the story wasn't right for me. He had bought the story, he said, but he was shelving it. "I don't want you to play a stepmother," he said, "an older woman involved with a young guy. I want you in a very sympathetic role."

Harry then put me on salary at Columbia and told his story department to come up with something for me fast. Finally somebody suggested a treatment of a play Tallulah Bankhead had starred in on Broadway. It had a marvelous death scene and it was very sympathetic, so I called Harry and said I would like to read it to him. I was taking no chances. On his own Harry Cohn was not likely to read anything heavier than a racing sheet, and I wanted him to take in every word of this story. He said fine and we arranged to meet at his home. I worked carefully on the treatment and read all twenty-five pages of it to him, giving it everything I had because I knew it would make a marvelous picture. I was in tears when I finished and Harry said that was wonderful; he would think about it and phone me the next day.

I stayed in all morning waiting for his call. Finally the phone rang.

"It's Harry Cohn, Gloria," he said. "The answer is no."

I wanted to scream, but I said very calmly instead, "But why, Harry?"

"Because if David Selznick wants to sell it, that means it can't be any good."

In one sentence Harry Cohn had epitomized Hollywood, and deep inside me a dam burst. I flew into the greatest rage of my life. I told him exactly what I thought of him and all the other vulgar boors in the studios who wouldn't know a good story if it bit them. I said Columbia was the Tin Pan Alley of Hollywood and he was the fitting president for it. I screamed and swore and called him everything I could think of. I only stopped, exhausted, when I realized that I had pulled the thirty-foot telephone cord out of the wall.

The next month I canceled my contract, put the house on the market, and moved to New York. I had stayed too long at the fair. It was 1938. In another year I would be forty. I didn't want to be insane as well, and there was a very good chance I would be if I didn't get out of Hollywood immediately.

The very next year *Dark Victory,* the story Harry Cohn turned down, became a great success on the screen. It starred Bette Davis.

CHAPTER 19

Gloria Swanson is on her way to being the wealthiest woman in the nation . . . Her new business is financing refugee inventors, who arrive here with not much coin, but full of ideas—the one thing the Nazis cannot rob— She bankrolls them for a percentage of the earnings . . . Everything is on the up-and-up . . . Her recent trip to South America was not a pleasure jaunt, as she told the gazettes, but a business trip to interest mine owners there in her new alloy . . . It is supposed to be much lighter than the stuff now used in planes—and much stronger. Her big backer is an American ambassador.

—WALTER WINCHELL,
Daily Mirror (1942)

When I moved to New York early in 1938, my accountants told me I was worth about a quarter of a million dollars, my asking price per picture for a decade, a fifth of the amount I had made on *The Trespasser* alone. The days of royal suites and dinner parties for two hundred and fleets of foreign cars suddenly seemed as unreal as the plots of my worst films, but since the recollection of them was painfully vivid, I had no need to ask where the money had gone. Rather, I had to ask myself what to do next, now that I could no longer support myself in pictures. I found a large apartment, enrolled the children in school, and racked my brains for a new line of work.

In many ways I had not been fortunate in my choice of men, particularly in the area of money. In all four marriages I had footed all the bills, and now most of the money I had made was gone. During this period Gustave Schirmer, heir to the international music-publishing firm and a dear friend, asked me many times to solve the problem of what I should do by marrying him, all because once when he asked me, "What do you want most, Gloria?" I replied without a second thought, "A sense of security." However, even though Gustave was the dearest, most generous man in the world and utterly devoted to me, I didn't love him and I felt I never could, and I told him so quite honestly. But it didn't discourage him. He went right on asking.

One night I entertained a small group of friends in my apartment, including Gustave. When the last guest had left, I went to my dressing room and got ready for bed. My bathroom separated the dressing room from my bedroom, which was furnished like a sitting room. When I opened the door to my bedroom, all the lights were on, and there at the desk sat Gustave. I was startled, then shocked, then angry.

"How did you get in here?" I demanded.

"I fixed the front lock when I went out," he said sheepishly. "Don't be angry. It's a surprise. Look."

He pointed to the bed, on which was the biggest rag doll I had ever seen. At Gustave's prodding, I opened a note in the doll's hand and saw it was the first clue in a sort of treasure hunt. One clue led to another in the room, most amusingly and most ingeniously, and after about twenty minutes a final clue directed me to a large plant on a table near my bed. There was a shovel in the plant and a poem about roots attached to it, so to Gustave's great delight I dug down into the dirt until I unearthed a metal box.

"Now, what's this, Gustave?"

"Open it," he said modestly.

The box was full of papers—Gustave's shares in Schirmer's. I gasped.

"You wanted security," he said. "There it is."

"But, Gustave, I can't . . . I can't."

"Please."

"Gustave, you must understand. I meant what I said. I can give you friendship, but I don't love you."

The joke had become serious. He was wiping away tears. So was I.

"I know that," he said, "but you could marry me in name only."

"Never, Gustave, you dear, marvelous man. I wouldn't do that. Please take these now and go."

He protested, but I put the box in his hand and saw him out. In the foyer it fell open and all the shares spilled out on the floor. As I picked up the last one, he refused to take it. Instead he ran to the elevator and left.

I put it in safekeeping with his name on it and was happy to give it back to him sometime later when, to his surprise, he had need of it.

It was a most unusual experience, just as Gustave was a most unusual man, and it proved something remarkable to me: however important security was to me, I couldn't be dishonest when it came to love.

Whenever I went over all my old associates for clues to interesting work, invariably the most exciting was still George de Bothezat and his help with my wireless communications system. Nothing seemed more mysterious and wonderful to me than the area of scientific invention, and I began more and more concentratedly trying to think of a way to work in that area. I started to buy *Popular Science Monthly* and all the other technical magazines I could get my hands on, and I talked to everyone knowledgeable I knew in New York about patents. One person after another said that scores of European scientists were trying to get out of Hitler's Germany, so I finally decided to set up a company in America to employ such scientists abroad and share in the profits of their inventions, which I would market and publicize. At first I hoped to include George de Bothezat in my scheme, but I learned that he was unwell, so I didn't bother him.

I rented office space in Rockefeller Center and called my company Multiprises, Incorporated. Gustave Schirmer, faithful and adoring as always, helped me round up a board of directors involved in industry, and I began making up a list of ideas to be explored if I ever got some scientists to work for me. I had all the innocence of the brash amateur, so I didn't know enough to put any limits on my catalog of utopian products-to-be-invented or products-to-be-obtained.

For example, I jotted down "luminous paint" because I

knew from my own experience that I could sell carloads of it in Los Angeles alone. Hollywood dinner invitations routinely included road maps, but still guests often ended up sitting in a car on a dark street while the chauffeur ran up and down the road with a flashlight looking for a number on a mailbox or a curbstone. Luminous paint was in fact available here, I found out, but not in any long-lasting variety. That existed only in Germany. Then couldn't we have it shipped to this country and get a license to sell it in North America? I asked. Yes, but it would take time, my consultants said, and probably voluminous correspondence, given German bureaucracy.

"Then we'll send someone to Germany to cut through the red tape," I said, and with that remark, which startled my listeners, I made my first contribution to the field of experimental technology, i.e., that you use money to save time, not the other way around. When I asked Gustave Schirmer if he knew of anyone who could go to Germany and get things done in a hurry, over and around the proper channels, he said, "Yes. Iffi Engel."

Iphigenia Engel, a tiny tornado with blond hair worn in a boyish bob, dressed in tailored suits and talked like Marlene Dietrich. She traveled everywhere in the music world, of which Germany was still the center, because her brother was president of Gustave's company and he relied on Iffi's efficiency. When I explained that I wanted her to seek out the inventor of long-lasting luminous paint or the firm that manufactured it and tell them I wanted to arrange to sell it in America, she didn't bat an eye. She said she could leave in a week. Before she sailed, she asked me to autograph a dozen photos of myself for her to take with her, in case, as she said, scientists went to movies. I told her if she should ever need help in Paris, to call Henri, and I gave her the name and address of his club: the Travellers, 25 Champs Elysées. "He was my third husband," I explained, "and since he divorced Constance Bennett we're very good friends again."

Iffi cabled from Berlin in May that she had found the inventor and was headed for Vienna, "to scout around." When she returned, she began her report to me with a question: "Did you make a movie where you swung out over an audience on a rose-covered trapeze and threw your shoe into the lap of a married man?"

"Yes, I did," I replied. "*Zaza,* in 1923."

"There!" Iffi Engel cried in triumph. "I found an engineer

in Vienna who remembered every scene. He saw it in a tiny
theater in the basement of his apartment house when he was
fifteen. He couldn't believe G. Swanson of Multiprises was
Gloria Swanson. I gave him an autographed picture and a
letter asking him to take charge of the Paris office of
Multiprises. I signed it with your name, which I traced off the
photo. He's in danger, you see."

"But we don't have a Paris office," I said.

"I know that," said Miss Engel haughtily, "but the Gestapo
doesn't. I used your husband's address: 25 Champs Elysées. I
explained everything to your husband when I stopped off in
Paris. He will send telegrams to Vienna and Berlin from time
to time renewing the offer, urging Kobler and the others to
come to Paris."

"Wait a minute," I interrupted. "Who's Kobler?"

"The engineer I gave your picture to," she said with
repeated emphasis, as if she were coaching a very slow
learner. "He heads a small syndicate of inventors which
includes the man who invented luminous paint. Since Hitler
moved into Austria in March they are not safe. Especially
Kobler, whose father refused to experiment with poison gas
in the Great War and escaped to Switzerland. The name is
therefore well known, and Herr Kobler has already been
apprehended twice by the Gestapo. He's a Jew. So are
Karniol and Neumann. Kratky is a gentile, but they're all in
danger, really."

"Miss Engel," I said, halting her firmly, "how many men
are you talking about?"

"Five, including the paint man. They are all brilliant young
scientists. I have had a friend go over their credentials."

"And they are willing to work for me?"

"Of course, but you have to get them out of Germany and
Austria first, or they'll be imprisoned. Your husband will try
to get them to Paris. After that, you must bring them to
America," Iffi said. "Their lives are in terrible danger. All
Jews under Hitler are in danger now."

"But how do I get them to America?" I asked.

"On temporary visas, probably, at first," she said. "Your
husband will let you know. He's very nice," Iffi added, as if
she had been discourteous not to say so sooner.

In December 1938 I had a letter from Henri saying he
thought it would be wonderful if I could come to Paris soon.
That meant he either had the Germans in Paris or had

arranged for us to go to Berlin and get them. I cabled him
back in mid-January:

DEAR HENRI ARRIVING PARIS TWENTY FIFTH STOPPING CRILLON
IMPORTANT YOU IN TOWN WHEN I ARRIVE BECAUSE OF BUSINESS
   GLORIA

As I stepped off the boat train in the Gare St. Lazare, four
young men ran up to me. One of them handed me a little
bunch of violets; one of them said, "Hello, hello," in a heavy
German accent; a third said, "Gloria Swanson," very loudly
and sang a few bars of "Love, Your Magic Spell Is Everywhere."

"Richard Kobler?" I asked.

"Richard Kobler, here," said the one with glasses.

"Leopold Karniol," said the second.

"Anton Kratky," said the third, who was also the oldest.

"Leopold Neumann," announced the fourth, who laughed
a good deal of the time.

"You got here from Berlin?" I asked very slowly.

"Ja," one of them said, and another said, "Zürich," and
turned himself into an airplane and made an engine sound.

They stood back politely, looking at me with adoring eyes,
and I was so moved that I embraced them one by one. Then I
said, "Marquis de la Falaise," and the short one pulled
several much-folded telegrams out of his pocket and smiled.

"He sent for us," he said with a heavy accent, and added,
"He will be Hotel Crillon at four o'clock."

"Then let's go," I said, and they picked up all of my
luggage and we went in two taxis to the Crillon.

They were willing but hobbled in English, and I spoke no
German at all, so we conversed in well-spaced syllables and
sign language and had coffee and croissants in my suite until
Henri arrived. The minute he entered the room they all
leaped to their feet, shook his hand, and signaled to me their
immense pride in being associated with this brave and
generous man, who, blissfully for us all, spoke French and
German and English. To please them, Henri told me in front
of them how they had got to Paris, and as he related their
adventures, they would from time to time correct him with
the utmost courtesy on the minutest details, in order, I
gathered, that the story afford me its maximum effect.

Kratky and Karniol and Neumann had saved us a trip to
Berlin, Henri said, by making it on their own via Zurich.

Kobler had had to bluff and play a role. After being arrested several times by the Gestapo, and aware that he couldn't take all his Austrian Kronen out of the country without arousing suspicion, he packed his best clothes and his file of letters from Multiprises in New York and the Marquis de la Falaise in Paris and checked into the Grand Hotel in Vienna. There he sipped coffee in the hotel lounge and sent a steady stream of telegrams to New York and Paris right under the nose of the Gestapo until his temporary visa was cleared and he could depart for Paris. They all smiled happily through to the end, when Henri stood and shook their hands and told them he would contact them the following day. Then they all shook my hand and left.

As soon as we were alone, Henri and I embraced warmly. He looked absolutely marvelous. I told him Baby Gloria was now a college girl at Stanford and Michelle was just starting school. Joseph was at boarding school in Rhode Island, I said, going through a religious period. He talked of becoming a Catholic, which probably had something to do with the fact that Joe Kennedy was his godfather.

"Are you still in touch with him?" Henri asked, with just a hint of embarrassment.

"No, not really. He calls to tell me when he's appointed to something. The last time was a little over a year ago, when Roosevelt appointed him ambassador to Great Britain. Joe was in Los Angeles for something and called me from the Beverly Hills Hotel right across the road. The same old Joe. He said he wanted to come over, can you imagine? I told him I was having a dinner party and couldn't see him. But because he could see the house from the hotel, I promptly had to call up six people and tell them to get right over. I told them to arrive in as many cars as possible so that the driveway would look totally full. They did, and as a result I didn't see Joe."

Henri laughed. "How about marriage, Gloria? Do you think you'll remarry?"

"Oh, I don't think so," I said. "Four's enough. And you?"

"Yes, I hope so," he said. "I want you to meet her while you're here. Constance Bennett was never the Marquise de la Falaise, you know, because you and I were never properly divorced according to French law, but I would like Emmita to be. You will like her."

I felt wistfully sad for a moment, so I changed the subject. "What about our German inventors? What do we do now?"

"It is very difficult," Henri said. "They have only visitor's visas, so they cannot leave France except to go back to Germany, and they will go into hiding before they do that. It's terrible for Jews under Hitler, Gloria."

He told me I might even be saving their lives by sponsoring them to America. Until their visas to the States were obtained, he added, it would be very useful if they had freedom to travel so that in case they had to leave France for any reason, they could get back in, but there were strict laws forbidding that. He said I would also have to pull strings in America to extend their visas once they got there.

As we were talking, the phone rang. An American woman was calling to say she had heard I was in Paris and would like to invite me to a party in two days' time. I declined politely, saying I was in Paris only briefly and on business. She then dangled as bait names of people who were going to be at the party, and in each case I said I didn't know So-and-so. She coaxed for a minute more, but I was firm. When I hung up, Henri asked me why I had mentioned a certain name in my conversation.

"Those were all guests this American woman said were coming to her party. I told her I was busy."

"But that man you mentioned is the official who can get the visas I told you about. Kobler wants to go to Brussels to see a motor he's heard about. If you could persuade that man at the party to give you a traveling visa for Kobler—and the others—it would be a tremendous help. You might even get to buy your first invention for Multiprises."

"Oh, Henri," I groaned, but I quickly swallowed all pride, called the woman back, and told her excitedly that I *was* free *after* all and would be *delighted* to come to her party.

On the appointed evening I was almost the first guest to arrive. The blond hostess said we knew each other from Palm Beach, but I had no recollection of her. I made a point of talking to every one of the nearly thirty guests at her party, including the official, who arrived alone. He chatted agreeably when we met, but I could tell he was just being polite, for he devoted almost the same number of minutes to each guest. About an hour later I saw him shaking hands with the hostess a second time and knew that he was leaving. It's now or never, I told myself, and walked over to say my own thanks and make clear that I was leaving too.

He smiled pleasantly and said, "May I assist you to your hotel?"

"Are you sure it's no trouble?"

"No, of course not," he said and walked me to the car.

Knowing exactly how far away the Crillon was, I started up practically before the engine did. "Isn't it strange? Yesterday I was told you were the only person in France who could help me, and tonight we have the opportunity to meet."

"In what way were you told I could help you?"

"It's actually official business, I believe. Could I see you at the ministry tomorrow or the next day? I don't think it would take more than ten minutes . . ."

"But of course." He gave me his card and told me to call his secretary. "This is my private line," he added, pointing to a spot at the bottom of the card.

"Oh, thank you," I said. "This has been such a lucky coincidence."

"A bientôt," he said, with a smile that belied my ridiculous false innocence, as he saw me to the door of the Crillon.

The next morning I telephoned for an appointment and went to the ministry. There I said I would like a traveling visa to Belgium for a young refugee I was sponsoring to America. The dignified official fixed me with his eyes and listened carefully. After a pause he said, "You are asking me to break a law that I made."

My heart sank. We stared at each other. He frowned. I expected him to shake my hand and see me out. Instead he walked to the high windows that overlooked the courtyard, twiddling his thumbs behind his back. Then he turned quickly and marched back to his desk. "There must be some way to accommodate such a beautiful lady," he said. "May I have your permission to give this my consideration for, let us say, twenty-four hours? Perhaps you could return tomorrow and bring your protégé with you."

The next day I took Richard Kobler with me to the ministry. He had all his papers with him, and those of his three colleagues as well. I vouched that they formed the entire staff of my office in Paris, and mentioned my husband, the marquis, numerous times. There was nothing to do after that but wait.

Two days later a uniformed courier arrived at the Crillon with an envelope for me. I phoned Henri and we opened it together. When Henri walked to the phone and called Kobler and told him to come over immediately, I knew it was great news.

"I can hardly believe it," Henri said. "They can travel like Frenchmen and apply immediately for visas."

In the end Richard Kobler and I did not go to Brussels, after all, but my remaining days in Paris were exciting ones. We talked about inventions and ideas for Multiprises by the hour. Before I left Paris, we all had dinner together, and Henri brought Emmita. She was South American, very lovely, warm, elegant, intelligent, a perfect match for my dear marquis, whom I promised I would relinquish my title through lawyers in America so that Emmita could become the second Marquise de la Falaise de la Coudraye.

At the end of March I had a letter from Leopold Neumann.

My dear Big Chief,

It is now about 2 weeks that you left Paris, *aber* the remember of your presence is so strong, that my pity will not go away from me.

I find, every day more, that it was my greatest fortune in my life, to find your friendship. I see the circumstances on which the other refuges are forced to live and you will understand my gratitude against you and my will, to do all, so that you will never regret to have me distinguished with your friendship.

In the time since your departure nothing is happened. The days come and go and it is no reason to leave my hotel, because I have nothing to do in the Hotel Crillon. Therefore I remain allways at home, working in my atelier.

. . .

I thank you very much for your cable, informing us, that you are well arrived in New York. *Aber* I must protest against the signature of this cable. I can't aknoledge your title "Little Chief." I am the inventor of your name "The Big Chief" and I never give the permission to make from our Big Chief a little Chief. Napoleon was also a small man, *aber* was he not in spite of his small body the Big Chief of his company? You see, there is no reason to change your rank.

. . .

I am now hoping that my wife will come to Paris on the next Sunday. She is still sick, but it will better for us if she is living in Paris, where I can do myself the best for her recovering.

I understand, that you are not long enough far from Paris to have forgotten the refuge "slang," wich you learned from us. Therefore, I suppose that you will understand the tenor of this letter. *Aberrr,* to avoid every misunderstanding, I declare, that this letter is written not in pidgin english, but in refuges slang, a new kind of the english language wich is discovered from Mr. Richard Kobler in collaboration with me and wich is understood only by the founders of this language and the single pupil, the Big Chief.

Now, my dearest Big Chief, I will be very glad to hear soon from you and I remain yous thankfully

L. Neumann

Richard Kobler was the first to get his U.S. visa, valid for six months. When he got to Ellis Island, however, he said in his bad English that Miss Swanson wanted him to stay all summer, and since it was then June 20, 1939, the official on duty wrote in two and a half months. I was sure I could get the visa extended, but just before that was necessary, Hitler attacked Poland, and France and England declared war. When Kobler inquired about his status at the French consulate, downstairs from our Multiprises office in Rockefeller Center, the official who looked at his papers said, "You are now an enemy alien. You cannot return to France. You would be interned." So Kobler was saved, and we were able to get all the others out of Europe to America: plastics expert Leopold Karniol, metallurgist Anton Kratky, and acoustical engineer Leopold Neumann. Karniol had the most trouble; he had to spend nine months in Cuba waiting for a proper U.S. visa. At last, however, all four of them were at work in a small factory I acquired in Queens, refining their ideas into salable products. We tried everything we could think of to get the last member of Kobler's syndicate—the man who invented luminous paint—out of Germany, but it was not possible. All we could find out was that he was in a concentration camp.

In the summer of 1939 I bought a new hat and went to California to cry at my daughter's wedding. She was no longer little Gloria, I reluctantly told myself, but Mrs. Robert Anderson, so beautiful, confident, and happy that I couldn't even in honesty resort to the argument that she was too young. She was just right, and certainly several years older than I had been that day I tore to Santa Barbara and then to Pasadena with Wally and Mother. But I cried anyway, long and sweetly.

Back in New York, I threw myself into publicizing Multiprises and working for Wendell Willkie in the 1940 presidential election. Although I had voted for FDR earlier, I didn't believe in three terms for one man, particularly a sick man, and I feared that Roosevelt's sympathies might steer us directly into war. As a mother of an eighteen-year-old son, that was the last thing I wanted, much as I hated Hitler and condemned his policies. Moreover, inasmuch as the country was barely out of a serious recession following a critical depression, I felt it was time for new leadership. Millions of Americans felt the way I did, including Joe Kennedy, who was extremely unpopular in Great Britain, where he was still ambassador, for his opposition to America's possible involvement in the European war.

I rented an old boarded-up theater on Fourteenth Street, where Mr. Griffith had had his first studio, and organized free shows at two o'clock every day. We showed movies, and in between we invited speakers to address the audience. I made my first political speeches there that fall, for Wendell Willkie, and I started out so excruciatingly nervous that I trembled, but I forced myself to speak without notes and I watched the political pros, and after a while I got so carried away that I often wound up banging on the podium and demanding a change for the country. Audiences loved watching me as a political activist and poured into the Fourteenth Street theater. Of all the guest speakers who came to talk there and share the podium with me, the most memorable by far was Ayn Rand, who had a fascinating mind and held audiences hypnotized.

In spite of our efforts Willkie lost, but by only five million popular votes, in a large and close election. Roosevelt's re-election forced Joe Kennedy to resign his ambassadorship in London, but before he did, he saw Henri there. Henri was fighting in the war by then and had been among the 350,000 troops evacuated to England from Dunkirk in June.

Henri corresponded with me in irregular bursts all through 1940. He won his second Croix de Guerre for bravery in Flanders, but after that he made every effort to get out of

France with Emmita, who refused to leave without him. I helped as much as I could, through my lawyers, to obtain his final divorce decree from Constance Bennett, and later Joe Kennedy and I together, but separately, pulled every string we could to get the two of them safely to America. Henri's frantic letters were all the goad I needed. They brought the awful war home to me as the newspapers never could. On October 21, 1940, for instance, he wrote:

Gloria dear,

I have written several times, but I don't think you received my letters, so I am taking the opportunity of a reliable channel to try once more. I received your wire addressed to the club and answered it twice; did you receive one of my cables? Probably not. You see, it is impossible to cable from Paris so one has to try all sorts of tricks to get a cable off and usually the tricks fail. Anyway, the penalty is so great if one does get caught that I can't blame people for not doing what they have promised and received money for!

The only hope for me now is to try and get to America, and that is getting more difficult every day. First, we French have passports which are no more valid and the only way to get them renewed is to go and apply in Vichy in the free zone. This is not easy as it is forbidden for all men who have served in the war and who are in the occupied zone to leave it. A German permit is required and has to be applied for, in order to cross the border. Of course, if you have received my letters, you will understand that that is particularly difficult for me. If I did succeed anyhow in getting to Vichy and I might risk a few shots at night (they'll miss me), in order to get there, I will have to prove to the French government that I have to go to the U.S. and be useful there, as the only visa they give is a diplomatic one. I would have to prove either that I have a contract awaiting me there or some other urgent matter which requires my presence overseas. If I don't get the diplomatic visa, I can't leave, because Spain would not let me go through its territory, and in order to get to Lisbon I have to go through Spain! This must seem very complicated to you, darling, and you are right, it is! I am also trying to get someone in Washington to get my reentry permit renewed and a cable to that effect, sent to the consulate in Paris. This someone is J.P.K., who was very kind to me in London when I landed half naked from Dunkirk and who promised me then that he would get me away when the time came. Well, the time has come! Another difficulty is that once I leave for Vichy, I must leave with my belongings, because if they do grant me a passport, I will have to leave for Spain from there. But if they turn me down, I will be stuck, because I won't be able to return to Paris! So you see how simple it all is.

All this, however, does not deter my will to leave at all costs. I succeeded in getting away unhurt from Dunkirk, I succeeded twenty days later in getting away from a prisoners' camp in Brittany (with Emmita's help), and I will succeed again (I hope) with your help and that of J.P.K. Your help I need in the form of a contract. A fake one, of course. Multiprises would be fine, if your name is not on the stationery, because otherwise they might smell a rat! If Pierre Merillon is in N.Y., you might try and persuade him to lend his support in Vichy; he has been made an envoy extraordinary to the U.S. by Marshal Pétain and is very powerful in the new government circles. If you do get in touch with him, you can tell him that I have been awarded the Croix de Guerre for my conduct in Flanders and that having received this distinction twice, in two wars, I cannot be suspected of trying to "funk it." I was also cited for distinguished conduct by the British army in June. All this is of course going to help me in Vichy, but it may be necessary for Merillon to help with a cable. If it is, when I do get to Vichy I will send you a cable saying "Ask Pierre." There is also another very important reason why I must get to N.Y. and that is my divorce with Miss B. It is essential that I be in America when she divorces me, because if I am not, the divorce will be invalid in France and I can never get it validated, meaning of course that I can never marry again. I have had the advice of the best American and French lawyers here and they all are of the same opinion. Furthermore, there is going to be a law very soon forbidding divorces in France! so I better hurry in order to get in under the line. Please, dear, as soon as you receive this letter send me a cable to the Travellers saying: "Bailly well." Excuse the style of this letter, please, but I have so much to say that all sorts of disconnected thoughts come bubbling to the tips of my fingers, which does not help my style or my typing!

If you could send me some kind of contract, a big juicy one, the juicier the better! It would help to get the French authorities in a pleasant mood towards my going abroad. If nothing works, however, and I have to remain here, God only knows when and if we shall ever see each other again, especially if America gets into the war too! By the time we shall be rescued from the powers of evil, as Mr. Churchill says, we shall all be dead of starvation, disease, and boredom, and the rescuing party will only find two skeletons, one tiny one, Emmita, and one larger, me!

I know now what a rat caught in a trap must feel like! Claustrophobia is too mild a word to explain this desperate feeling. That's why I will try anything in order to escape. As for Emmita, she could leave if she wanted to, but she says she will stay with me whatever happens. God bless her.

I am occupying my time by writing the account of my twenty days of battle in May in a British armored car. I kept a diary practically hour by hour of what was going on. We covered in that period over fifteen hundred miles fighting continuously against German armored cars, tanks, and motorised infantry. We went on, with practically no sleep and no warm food, for twenty-one days, and sixty percent of my squadron lost their lives in the bravest and most hopeless fight that ever was put up against overwhelming forces. One by one, all our cars were put out of action and we drove the two remaining ones which had been shot so full of holes that they looked like sieves, and were caked with the blood of the dead, into the sea on the beach near Dunkirk.

. . .

I hate to finish this letter because there is so much I want to say and I don't know when I will have the opportunity of writing another one, but I think that by what I have written so far you realize what is to be done and how in order to help me get out of here, I need (a) an American renewal of reentry permit, or (b) a contract of some kind to help get a French visa or passport and Spanish visa. For the renewal of my American reentry permit I have written to J.P.K. and addressed the letter to Rockefeller Center; I think he has an office there. I heard that he was leaving for America in a week and I hope to God my letter will get to N.Y. in time to reach him. My letter to him is leaving the same way and same day as this one. So, if you hear that he has returned to England before this letter reaches you, you will know that my hopes in that direction are flustered! Of course there will still be the chance that his secretary in N.Y. might forward my letter to London.

I am sending you through someone who will reach N.Y. at the end of November a picture of me taken a few days before the big battle started, so that if you don't see me for a long long time . . . it will remind you anyway of my funny face!

I send you a big kiss and lots of love, darling. God bless you, and may we meet soon again.

Yours ever,
Henry

As soon as I received this letter, six weeks after Henri wrote it, I sent him a telegram saying "Bailly well," as he had requested, and went into action, calling everyone I knew and having an elaborate, official-sounding contract drawn up.

The solution to Henri's problem was just and right. Two years earlier, in order to get my inventors out of Germany, he had made himself the head of the imaginary Paris office of Multiprises. Now, when I prepared the fake contract with Multiprises for him to show to the French puppets at Vichy, Richard Kobler and Leopold Neumann signed it. The lifebelt Henri had helped create for them, they now threw back to him. Emmita escaped with him, and they arrived in New York in April 1941. They camped out in my Fifth Avenue apartment long enough to catch their breath and have a reunion with Emmita's mother. Then they went to Santa Barbara, where they were married. Again our efforts succeeded, for in spite of Constance Bennett's struggles to the contrary, Emmita, upon her marriage, became the second, not third, marquise, wife of Henri de la Falaise de la Coudraye.

In the summer of 1941, to my great surprise, RKO offered me the lead in a picture entitled *Father Takes a Wife*, co-starring Adolphe Menjou, and they promised to make a great fuss about its being a major comeback if I was interested. I was more apprehensive than interested, if the truth be told, but I was very fond of Adolphe Menjou, whom I'd known well for years, so I asked them to send me a script. The story was a light comedy about a famous actress who marries a shipping tycoon. Their marital squabbles are intensified by the magnate's family and are resolved through the agency of a young Latin American singer. Fluffy, I thought after a quick reading, but suitable. I asked how much they were willing to pay, and the producer, Lee Marcus, said $35,000. A comedown as well as a comeback, I said to myself, but I accepted the offer, which was exactly $35,000 more than any other studio had offered in seven years. It would also give me a chance to see all my friends, Gloria and her husband, and Henri and Emmita.

The director, Jack Hively, treated me like returning royalty; so did the cast; so did the Hollywood press. I enjoyed the shooting because Adolphe was in top form and the young Latin, Desi Arnaz, was very good too. In addition, RKO got René Hubert, who still did most of my personal wardrobe, to design my costumes, and the company launched a large publicity campaign, filling the ads and posters with such flattering headlines as THERE'S GLAMOUR ON THE SCREEN AGAIN BECAUSE GLORIA'S BACK! and YOU'LL SWOON OVER HER TRUNK-FULS OF STUNNING FASHIONS!

By the time *Father Takes a Wife* came to the nation's movie houses, however, Americans were not thinking much about glamour or stunning fashions. After the Japanese attack on Pearl Harbor on December 7, they were thinking rather about war and uniforms. Even if the picture had been out-and-out marvelous, given its trivial subject it was not likely to find an audience in a country at war, and it was not quite in the marvelous category, by anyone's standards. Therefore, I pocketed my $35,000 and returned to cinematic oblivion.

In the meantime, Multiprises was showing its first signs of returning my investment. Leopold Karniol devised a process for making buttons out of plastic, which suited the war economy admirably, and Anton Kratky came up with a carbide-steel-alloy cutting tool that promised to be revolutionary. I began making a few exploratory trips to interest customers in South America in these and other inventions-in-progress in Queens and was met with an enthusiastic response. The war effort, however, soon overtook such private interests, and Anton Kratky and Leopold Neumann asked permission to work for the U.S. government developing industrial diamonds for the duration. We kept our office, but as long as the war lasted, it was obvious that Multiprises was going to be a small concern.

In April 1932, three months before Florenz Ziegfeld died, he had asked me to appear on the New York stage in a revival of *Show Boat*, and I had refused because I had an absolute terror of the stage. June Walker had told me I was crazy, that if I could act in pictures, I could act in plays and musicals, but I didn't believe her for a minute, and through the years I continued to turn down all comers who tried to lure me to Broadway. Even when I had no movie career left to jeopardize, I refused to go on the stage.

In 1941, however, a writer-producer named Harold Kennedy was clever enough to offer a challenge rather than make an offer. First he wrote me an interesting letter and I invited him to tea, in the middle of which he asked if it was true that some European play was being translated for me.

"It seems so," I said, "but I'm not anxious to begin a stage career unless I'm satisfied the material is just right." I had said all this many times before, but this time the person I said it to didn't respond in the usual way. Instead he said, "Don't you think, Miss Swanson, it would be wiser to begin in a play that had already weathered the critical storms, and to start in summer stock rather than on Broadway? In other words, try out *yourself* instead of the play? After all, maybe you won't be able to adapt to the stage. Not everyone who can act in pictures, you know, can act in plays."

I sat amazed. This nattily dressed stranger with his unprepossessing manner had called my long-standing bluff, in my own living room. He knew I was petrified at the thought of acting on a stage, and he was saying: Relax, I'll teach you, where you won't make a fool of yourself if you're awful.

"What play?" I asked, with defensive alarm. "And where? And you don't mean this coming summer, do you? I doubt if I'll be free."

He told me he would give it some thought, knowing full well that I would be as free as air, just too terrified to admit it. He phoned in a few days and suggested a George Kelly play called *Reflected Glory*, which Tallulah Bankhead had done on

Broadway in 1936. "It's right for you," he said, "and it's worth reviving."

"Where?" I asked, as if he were an enemy I could defeat if I found the right question.

"How about Poughkeepsie?" he asked. "It's close to New York, but the big critics don't go up there." You'll be safe there, was what he was saying, and I had a burning desire to snatch at my opportunity and say grandly, coolly that in that case I wasn't interested. But I didn't, and I was quite aware that he knew I wouldn't. Get it over with, he was signaling, and if you're lousy, at least you won't have to go on making feeble, dishonest demurs for the next decade or so; but if you're not, we can both make some money and you can begin a whole new career.

"All right, Mr. Kennedy," I said, "make the arrangements," and I knew as I said it that if he ever got me through an opening night anywhere, he would have earned his victory.

Harold Kennedy selected a cast and put me to work early learning lines because he sensed without my telling him what I feared most about the stage: retaining all those thousands of words. For weeks I drove my secretary crazy prompting and cueing me, and still I went into rehearsal with the book in my hand. The last week we rehearsed in Poughkeepsie, I was an utter wreck. When it came time for the dress rehearsal, I still clung to the book like a security blanket. To my mortification, I had to insist that the fireplace on the set be big enough so that Harold Kennedy could sit in it with the book and prompt me. By then I was a tigress to be pitied and Harold was a thin-lipped saint. Everyone in the cast dreaded opening night, and when it came, I was beyond terror. I didn't know a word, I swore. Nobody backstage dared speak to me for fear the spring would snap and I would think I was Napoleon. Trembling like a leaf, I gave Harold his final warning that if he left the fireplace, I would leave the stage. Then I heard my cue, and as I walked onstage, my heart was pumping so outrageously that I was sure it was visibly lifting me up and down off the ground. There was a thunderclap of applause that lasted a minute, and I blessed all the people of Poughkeepsie. Then I opened my mouth, and the words came out, all of them, in the right order, by the thousands. By the time the curtain came down and I kissed Harold Kennedy, I had had the thrill of my life, a bit like my first airplane ride in

1919. From then on, I began in earnest to look for a play that I could bring to Broadway.

Once my panic had left me, I became fascinated by the differences between screen acting and stage acting. For one thing, people were always saying that a bad actor can fool you on the screen but not in a real theater. I quickly felt the reverse. In a theater you can fool everyone past the tenth row if you're good, but on the screen you can't really fool anyone for a second. The great thrill of the theater for me was in that intimate interaction between the audience and you that goes on every minute, every night, until the curtain comes down and you all go home.

The following year Harold put together a package of three one-act plays for me: *Man of Destiny* by George Bernard Shaw, *The Old Lady Shows Her Medals* by J. M. Barrie, and *The Playgoers* by Arthur Wing Pinero. Francis Lederer, the European actor and matinée idol, appeared opposite me in all three plays, and we called the package *Three Curtains*. In the first play I was a spy, in the second an old charwoman, and in the third an English aristocrat.

When I told Clifton Webb that I was acting with Francis Lederer, whom I had met years before but didn't know well, Clifton rolled his eyes dolefully toward the ceiling and said, "Be careful, darling. Believe me, Francis Lederer has a terrible reputation for being temperamental and difficult."

"I don't care, if he's good," I said.

Rehearsals were no longer a trial for me, and when we opened in Baltimore I got the best notices of my life. I arranged for Michelle, who was then in boarding school, to come and see me, and when I entered as the charwoman she didn't recognize me. She left her seat and ran backstage in a panic to see what was wrong, and was incredulous when I came offstage. She stayed in town for several days and watched the show each night from the first or second row. The last night she asked how I could cry real tears every night at the exact same spot in the play, when a whistle sounded offstage.

"I don't cry, darling," I told her. "The old lady does."

Her eyes almost popped out of her dear little face when I said it, and from then on, she talked frequently about becoming an actress when she grew up.

We played Washington next, and the critics raved. At that point it was decided that we would move the show to

Broadway after Boston. But on opening night in Boston, the worst thing that can happen to an actress on stage happened to me. The moment I entered, Francis Lederer, responding to some deep-seated resentment or frustration or anger—I couldn't tell which—came out of character and began to parrot my lines after I said them. The audience, realizing something was very wrong, began to mutter uncomfortably and laugh nervously. Under my breath I ordered Mr. Lederer to stop what he was doing, and he did, and we got through the evening somehow, but the show was a shambles. The next morning the Boston *Post* carried a large headline: BACKSTAGE ROW THREATENS TO CLOSE PLAY.

We spent a week trying to recast the show, but it was no use. It would have required a whole new rehearsal schedule, and there was no time for that, so *Three Curtains* closed in Boston at the end of the week.

I was shattered, for I had painfully discovered another difference between pictures and the stage: a picture lasts for years and years, even if you're terrible in it, whereas a stage performance is over each night. Only a few critics can suggest to people who didn't see it how good or bad it was.

"Never mind," said Harold Kennedy, "you're going to shine on Broadway yet."

"None too soon," I said. "I've been a grandmother for over a year now." It was true. Gloria had started building a family in California.

In my son Joseph's second year at Antioch College in Yellow Springs, Ohio, his draft number came up and he had to go into the army. During his basic training in 1944, he wrote from Camp Breckenridge in Kentucky and asked me if I would ask former Ambassador Kennedy to see if he could get him a transfer into a different company, which Joe did. Joseph admired Joe Kennedy enormously and thanked him in a long letter, which pleased Joe greatly. Despite his shaky sense of spelling, Joseph's letters from the army gave every evidence of a sweet, rapidly maturing person:

You have no idea how much I miss your domestic instincts. Here I am with a lovely stripe to sew on my sleeve and no one to sew it on for me. I will probably sew it on so crooked that I will be busted from my exhaulted rank of P.F.C. before I even have a chance to get used to it.

My Lieutenant, D—— W——, has very subtilly suggested that he would very much appreciate an autographed picture of you. And since I am such a good soldier these days, anything he appreciates I too would appreciate.

I am so glad that the play is such a success because I know how hard you must have been working on it. Congratulations. I am looking forward to seeing you on the stage for the first time.

What has become of that invention for putting color photography on black and white film? I am interested because I think that I have a pretty good idea on the subject unless they are using it already.

I have just finished a letter to Mr. Kennedy. It is hard to try and thank a man for so many things in one letter without making it sound repetitous, but I did the best I could. I was in the midst of writing to find his address when I got your second letter.

When his basic training was over, Joseph came to New York on a three-day pass before he entrained for the West Coast. I took him out for a fancy evening at the Stork Club, and I was tremendously proud of him. In certain ways Joseph had been a slow starter, but I could tell that he had suddenly turned into a man, curious about himself and the rest of the world. Before he left, he asked, "Mother, would you mind if I tried to find my real mother while I'm on the Coast?"

"I think it would be wonderful if you did, Joseph," I said. "I'll give you the name of the orphanage. Go and ask. Your real mother should see what a fine person you are."

"You never met her?" he asked.

"No, Joseph, I never asked to meet her."

In August, Joe Kennedy, Jr., was killed in the war in Europe, and Joseph and I both wrote to Joe to tell him how sorry we were. Death was close suddenly. Many people I knew were being killed. When my Joseph was shipped to Europe later that year, I had trouble being brave because we were closer than we had ever been and I couldn't bear the thought that he might be a war casualty. I couldn't refrain from returning to the subject he had brought up months before.

"Did you find your real mother in California?" I asked, trying to sound fair and interested.

"No," he said. "I never tried."

Since divorcing Michael Farmer, I had had a couple proposals of marriage, but I turned them all down, including Gustave Schirmer's, and believed quite firmly that I would never marry again. In 1945, however, when an affable, well-groomed, rich, presumably unimpeachable man named William Davey proposed to me on very short acquaintance, I accepted, both because he was wealthy and independent and because Michelle was after me constantly to remarry. She wanted a home and two parents in it like all the other girls at her boarding school, she said, and she took an immediate shine to William Davey when she met him.

I was touring at the time with Conrad Nagel in a play called *A Goose for the Gander,* which Harold Kennedy had written for me and which was headed for Broadway. William Davey and I had a quiet, private wedding. While I was still on tour I had my apartment completely redecorated and William moved in, but he continued to maintain his beautiful Park Avenue apartment as well.

The play got very bad reviews in New York, but it had a modest run anyway, mainly because old friends and old fans felt obliged or curious to see me on a big Broadway stage.

One night early in the run, when I came offstage and went to my dressing room, I found my new husband there in a belligerently drunken stupor, hanging on the shoulder of his valet. I had known a number of drunkards in my life, even loved a few, but this was my first experience with an alcoholic who drank secretly and underwent complete character change in the process. I questioned the valet, who reluctantly confided that William had tried frequently and desperately to control his habit, but without success.

That weekend Michelle and I went to Alcoholics Anonymous, got all of the organization's literature, and put it on every imaginable surface in the apartment. But our efforts only frightened or annoyed William; we never knew which. Without a word he packed his bags and moved back to his Park Avenue apartment. The marriage had lasted not much more than a month—scarcely long enough to order new towels and stationery; but in spite of the fact that it was an embarrassment to explain the impetuousness of the whole process to friends and family, I considered myself well out of it.

In 1947, after the war, after my marriage, after Joseph's safe return to college, when I was dividing my time between Multiprises, which was a going concern again, and summer stock, I felt not quite right while I was on tour, so I consulted a doctor. He diagnosed a tumor in my uterus and recommended surgery. Panicked, I consulted a second doctor, who confirmed the diagnosis of the first. A third doctor, a famous gynecologist, not only agreed with the other two but advised a complete hysterectomy.

"When?" I asked.

"I wouldn't wait longer than three months," he said with concern. "The sooner the better."

As soon as I finished the run of the play I went to see Dr. Bieler in California.

He said, "Gloria, what is the function of a protein?"

"It's a cell builder."

"Are you fully grown?" he asked me.

"Dr. Bieler, don't pull my leg. You know I'm forty-seven."

"Well, but maybe you're a ditchdigger. Or are you a tennis pro? A football player?"

I said, "What are you trying to tell me?"

He said, "Well, you just think now."

Reasoning with my common sense, I asked, "Are you saying maybe I could try to starve this thing?"

"I have a sneaking hunch," he said. "You had a child in 1920. This is 1947. You told me you had a hard time with the first birth. You were torn inside and out. This has been going on all this time—because you don't get cancer overnight, you don't get tumors overnight; they sometimes take twenty years to grow. Now, this is a possibility. Have you been eating a lot of protein?"

"Well, I guess I have," I said.

"All right," he said, "what are you going to do about that, if it's a cell builder?"

"Do you really think I can starve this to death?" I asked again.

He smiled in a strange way and said, "You get enough protein; you don't need all that animal protein."

"All right," I said. "As of this moment I shall not eat any more animal protein. How long do you think it will take?"

He said, "I don't know. A year, two years, maybe three."

By that time, I whispered to myself, I'll be fifty. But I'll also be intact, I thought with pleasure.

Jimmy Jemail, the well-known inquiring reporter of the New York *Daily News,* took pictures of passers-by in the street and questioned them on current events. His photos and interviews ran as a regular feature in the *News* opposite the editorial page. In the spring of 1948 he called me frantically one day to say the paper was launching a television station, WPIX, and was planning to transfer his column to the new medium, with live interviews. He asked me if I would please hurry down to the *News* building and let him interview me on the street. It was urgent.

I was on my way out the door to buy drapes, but I said I'd stop by the *News* building and talk to him first. I'd be right down. When I got there, Jimmy Jemail and I walked along the street and talked and joked pleasantly while a television crew followed us with a camera and a crowd stood and watched. Then Jimmy Jemail thanked me and I left to find my drapes.

About a month later a WPIX executive phoned and asked if he could come and see me. Almost as soon as he arrived in the apartment, he asked me if I would like to do a weekly television show—The Gloria Swanson Hour or something like that. We talked for a while, and then several times more, and although I had no interest in television up to then, I finally consented to do a weekly interview program and we signed a six-month contract.

Instantly my life became chaos. The phones never stopped ringing. For weeks the *News* gave me advance publicity. We weren't anywhere near ready for the first show on time, but we had to go ahead and shoot it anyway, with me screaming and threatening and vowing that I would never do another. I called Lois Wilson to be a stand-in guest star, and the *News* took our picture together in front of the old portrait of me by Geza Kende. The picture appeared on the cover of the first issue of *TV Guide,* a little magazine that sold for ten cents and listed all television programs being shown that week. There were not many, that week or in the weeks to come. The other new program listed in the first issue was a variety show introduced by another news columnist, Ed Sullivan. But everyone told me that television was the future, that the number of sets in New York alone had suddenly risen in a year from 17,000 to 300,000.

We shot the show live at the WPIX studio each Thursday. The set was supposed to be my apartment, and at first the script called for a secretary and a maid, but later the show was aired at night instead of in the daytime and we changed my maid to a butler—played by the brilliant stage comedian Eric Rhodes. Together Eric and I did everything, from writing the script to programming all the interviews. There were usually between eight and twelve guests on each program, and between the interviews Eric and I invented an endless number of topical routines to enliven the proceedings. We worked like a charm together.

We decided to break the show into four quarter-hour sections. "Glamour on a Budget" was usually a session with my secretary and me. The secretary might buy a raincoat or a purse or a blouse, and the two of us would talk about it in detail and about the store where she'd got it or about the manufacturer. "Chef's Holiday" consisted of interviews with chefs from a whole range of New York restaurants, from the Colony to Schrafft's. Usually these chefs would describe a dish or actually cook it in the kitchen on the set. In "Design for Living," the third section on each show, I would talk with manufacturers or experts on new, interesting objects for the home—everything from new kinds of bookcases to distinguishing marks on silver to Castro convertible sofas. "Trend," the final section, brought to the public's attention the fashionable goings-on in New York that week, from charity balls to horse shows. The guests in this section were asked to wear designer clothes, and we would discuss the clothes and the designers as well. It was a balanced, useful, domestic show, which looked as if it were really happening in an apartment. However, we were always ready to break the pattern for the sake of a funny routine. For instance, during the "Chef's Hour" that Thanksgiving, Eric and I worked up a hilarious sketch in which we ourselves cooked the turkey. All in all, it was exhausting, but it was also challenging and often fun.

WPIX was thrilled with the program and audience response was wonderful. As the term of my first contract drew to a close, the studio wrote up a new one, this time for three years. I didn't sign it immediately, however, because there was no mention of paid vacation time. Shortly before Christmas I bent over a banister on the set one day—we were demonstrating how to decorate your apartment for the holidays—and proceeded to have sharp pains in my abdomen. As they carried me out of my apartment to the hospital, the unsigned contract was still on a table in the foyer.

In the hospital three doctors announced it was my appendix and prepared to operate immediately.

"I know it's not my appendix," I said.

"How do you know?" one doctor asked imperiously.

"Because it's my body, and I know it very well. I can tell what's wrong. It's a twisted intestine, I think."

When the pain persisted, they implored me to let them operate, and friends also urged me, and since I would recover in a week and therefore have to miss only one show, I finally consented, but with sincere ill will. After the operation they declared their work a total success and proudly showed me the tiny scar. The following day, however, I still had the exact same pain. They tried to give me painkillers, but I refused to take them. After five days I called a small conference. "You had your way with the appendix," I told them. "Now do me the favor to open me up again and see if I don't have an ulcer or an abscess from a twisted intestine."

They did what I asked and found that I was right; an abscess had formed. It was a costly mistake, and I resented it. I had lost an appendix, certainly needlessly, and undergone surgery twice just to prove to three doctors that they didn't know everything; and in the meantime three weeks, instead of the promised one, had gone by.

One of the networks had sent me a TV set to watch while I was recuperating, and in that short time I saw more than enough to convince me that I didn't care for the medium. For six months I'd been so busy appearing on it that I'd never sat down and watched it. Now that I did, it depressed me. "That's awful," I said about one program after another. It looked cheap and thrown-together, most of it, too black-and-white, too crude. And I realized as I watched how much energy that medium had sapped me of in six months, how close I'd come to ulcers.

Finally, at the end of three weeks, I made up my mind to stop. I called my secretary, Miss Griffith, and dictated a letter of resignation to WPIX from my hospital bed.

Once again, I didn't know what my life from there out would be, but I was certain it wasn't going to be television.

An hour and a half exactly after that letter of resignation was delivered, the phone rang. It was the casting director from Paramount in Hollywood. He said they wanted me to go out there and have a screen test.

"I've made two dozen pictures for Paramount," I said. "Why would they need to test me?" I didn't want to say I dreaded screen tests, that if I had ever had to depend for work on screen tests or auditions, I would have wound up selling ribbons, not acting. Instead I added, "In any case, I'd have to ask the doctor."

"Doctor!" the casting director exclaimed. "What's wrong?"

"Look," I said, "you called me, I didn't call you. This is a hospital number you've reached. I'm recovering from surgery."

"Oh, no!" he said. "How bad is it?"

"Not serious," I said, softening. "It was my appendix. I should be home in a few days."

"All right, we'll get back to you, Miss Swanson," he said apologetically.

That was that. I didn't think much more about it. There had been similar calls in the past. After *Father Takes a Wife* I was no longer optimistic about comebacks.

The calls from Paramount continued, however. Once I was back in my apartment, it was the producer, Charles Brackett, who called. He asked me if I was well enough to travel and I said yes, I thought so. Then he assured me we were talking about a major role in a major picture.

"Who's directing it?" I asked.

"Billy Wilder," Mr. Brackett said.

"I know Mr. Wilder," I said. "That is, he was a writer on one of my films, *Music in the Air*."

"I know," Mr. Brackett said. "Now, can you come out for the test? We're very anxious to talk to you."

He offered a suite at the Beverly Hills Hotel. He also mentioned a salary of $50,000 if the screen test satisfied everyone.

Much as I hated the idea of a screen test, at that point $50,000 was music to the ears of someone who had been creating a whole TV show for $350 a week.

"I'll arrange it," I said, "and call you back."

When I hung up, I turned to Mother, who was sitting in the apartment with me. She was Mrs. Woodruff now and lived right across the street from me.

"Mother, we've had a dreadful Christmas," I said. "How would you like to make up for it and go to Beverly Hills with me for a few weeks? We can spend time with Gloria and her children," I coaxed her. "Wouldn't you like that?"

CHAPTER 20

When Mother and I arrived in Hollywood in January of 1949, I called my friend George Cukor before I phoned the studio and asked him if he thought it would be unreasonable of me to refuse to do a screen test. I told him I was terrible in them.

"Who's the director?" George asked.

"Billy Wilder, and the producer is someone named Charles Brackett."

"In that case, yes, it would be unreasonable. They're the brightest things at Paramount. They made *Lost Weekend* together, and *A Foreign Affair*. If they ask you to do ten screen tests, do them, or I'll personally shoot you."

Another dear friend, Alexander Tiers, gave me the same advice. So did William Powell. So did Clifton Webb. So did Allan Dwan. So did Mickey Neilan.

I was thoroughly subdued, therefore, prepared to submit to anything, when I met with Billy Wilder and Mr. Brackett the next day. Mr. Wilder and I chatted pleasantly but not at length about *Music in the Air,* our last picture together. I had had one other Hollywood failure in the fifteen intervening years, while he had become a leading writer-director who at forty-four was elfish, witty, confident, and a bit overactive. Mr. Brackett, quieter, more refined, the New York, Eastern type, was in his mid-fifties. They immediately said that I should think of the screen test as a formality, done mainly for the young man they had in mind for the lead.

"Who is that?" I asked.

"Montgomery Clift," Mr. Brackett said. "A promising new star. Excellent. Have you seen him?"

"No," I said. Then, changing the subject, I asked if I could see a script. They informed me that they had only a few pages. They were still working on the rest, they said, and hadn't even decided definitely how it would end.

"Well, what's it about?" I asked.

Mr. Brackett said it was based on a story he and Billy had written together, in which an ex-movie queen attempts to dominate a younger man, a writer, and return to pictures. There was a murder in it.

"Who murders whom?" I asked.

"We honestly aren't sure yet," Billy Wilder said. "Look over this short scene to get a feel of it," he added, handing me three typewritten sheets. "That'll be plenty for the test. We just want to have a look at you."

Several days later I ran the test with a blond young man, and Billy Wilder and Charlie Brackett registered total approval. In fact, they raved. We signed a contract a few days later. Then I rented a house on Mulholland Drive and settled in with Mother for a stay of three or four months.

Paramount soon asked me to report for some publicity pictures, and when I got there, they had me pose with Mr. Balaban, president of Paramount, and with Adolph Zukor, who was now chairman emeritus of the board. Mr. Zukor and I embraced and talked about the old days, and he said everyone was very excited about this new picture, which they were calling *Sunset Boulevard*. I asked Mr. Brackett if the script was finished, and he said not yet; in fact, they had decided to keep it very loose and compose it as they went along, adding and subtracting and changing as they saw fit.

"How about Mr. Clift?" I asked. "Is he here?"

They told me then that Montgomery Clift had objected, through his agent, to playing scenes of romantic involvement with an older woman. Therefore, they shyly asked, would I mind doing another screen test, since now their fear was that I looked too young for the man they had chosen to replace Montgomery Clift.

"And who's that?" I asked.

"William Holden," Mr. Brackett said. "Joe Gillis, the writer in the script, is supposed to be twenty-five and you're supposed to play fifty. But Bill Holden is thirty-one and nervous that you'll look too young. We may have to age you with make-up. Not too much. Just a little."

"But women of fifty who take care of themselves today don't look old," I said. "That's the point. Can't you use make-up on Mr. Holden instead, to make him look more youthful?"

They consented to try, if only out of tact, and after they looked at the test, they decided I was right. They changed Bill Holden's hair and adjusted his make-up and left me a spruced-up fifty, which was exactly my age.

By then they had more of the script for us. The story was narrated by the corpse of Joe Gillis, after it is fished out of a swimming pool on Sunset Boulevard. The script described my character, Norma Desmond, very sketchily: "She is a little woman. There is a curious style, a great sense of high voltage about her." The tone of the piece was a mixture of gothic eeriness and nostalgia for the old Hollywood of the twenties. For Norma Desmond's butler and ex-husband, they had signed Erich von Stroheim. For a group of old friends— referred to as "the waxworks" by Joe Gillis—who arrive to play bridge with Norma, they had signed Anna Q. Nilsson, H. B. Warner, and Buster Keaton.

"There's also a scene with Cecil B. De Mille," Mr. Brackett said, "and he's agreed to play himself. We're really going to mix up Hollywood then and now, real and imaginary. What do you think?"

"I don't know," I said, speaking the unveiled truth.

For Norma's house they had rented a marvelous twenties palace in the Renaissance style from Jean Paul Getty; and they were going to shoot the scenes of Mr. De Mille right on the set of the picture he was currently making, *Samson and Delilah*. Mr. De Mille's secretary told me he was having her cue him daily on his lines and that he was very nervous about appearing in front of a camera.

I told him, "Mr. De Mille, if you're just yourself, you'll be wonderful," and with that I grasped with fearful apprehension, for the first time, that the same certainly applied to me to a great extent, that I would have to use all my past experience for props, and that this picture should be a very revealing one to make, something akin to analysis.

Billy Wilder deliberately left us on our own, made us dig into ourselves, knowing full well that such a script, about Hollywood's excesses and neuroses, was bound to give the Hollywood people acting in it healthy doubts, about the material or about themselves, depending on their individual security. The more you thought about the film, the more it seemed to be a modern extension of Pirandello, or some sort of living exercise in science fiction. Early in the shooting, Bill Holden said that he needed to know more about Gillis in order to fill out the character, that the script was incomplete and unclear and therefore frustrating for him as an actor. "How much do you know about Holden?" was all Billy Wilder would say.

Edith Head and I together created perfect clothes for my character—a trifle exotic, a trifle exaggerated, a trifle out of date. For my scene with Mr. De Mille, I designed a hat with a single white peacock feather, remembering the peacock-feather headdress everyone was so superstitious about when Mr. De Mille and I made the scenes with the lions in *Male and Female*. When Billy Wilder and the set designer asked me for personal props from my own life, I thought twice but I supplied them: scores of stills in old frames; the Geza Kende portrait; an idea for a large plaid bow on my head in one scene, a bit like those Mother had me wear as a child, a bit like the ones Sennett bathing beauties wore; the fact that Mr. De Mille had usually referred to me as "young fellow."

In April, Erich von Stroheim arrived from France. We had long since reconciled our differences over *Queen Kelly*, but I hadn't seen him in eight or nine years, not since I had gone backstage in Chicago when he was in the touring company of *Arsenic and Old Lace*. He looked grand, and we reminisced for hours when Billy Wilder showed us a print of *Queen Kelly* and asked me if he could use a scene from it for a scene in *Sunset Boulevard*, where Norma and Joe are watching one of her old pictures. Of course I didn't mind, I said; it was a brilliant idea because almost no one had ever seen *Kelly*. Erich and I even decided it had weathered the years very well, glowed like a classic, and might actually be rereleased, in a version better than the one that had been tacked together in the early thirties for release principally outside the United States.

Mr. De Mille took direction like a pro. Erich von Stroheim, on the other hand, kept adding things and suggesting things and asking if scenes might not be reshot—very much in his grand old manner of perfectionism regardless of schedule or cost. Billy Wilder always listened patiently to his suggestions, and took some, but more often he would say that he really didn't see how this or that change would improve the scene or further the story, and therefore he thought we should leave it alone. In one scene Erich, as Max, Norma's butler and

chauffeur, drives her and Joe to Paramount in her old Isotta
Fraschini with leopard upholstery. Erich didn't know how to
drive, which humiliated him, but he acted the scene, and the
action of driving, so completely that he was exhausted after
each take, even though the car was being towed by ropes the
whole while.

The scene where Norma plays bridge with a few old friends
came closest to giving us all the creeps, but it reminded us
too, once again, of exactly who we were. Anna Q. Nilsson
and H. B. Warner had made several important pictures
together, *One Hour before Dawn* in 1920 and *Sorrell and Son*
in 1927, before Anna's career had been cut short by a riding
accident. H. B. Warner had also been my leading man in
Zaza and had played Christ in Mr. De Mille's great early
biblical epic *King of Kings* in 1927. Anna had recently
returned to the screen as a character actress and looked
splendid, but H.B. appeared brittle, almost transparent,
when he showed up. Buster Keaton, the fourth member of
the bridge party, looked ravaged, as indeed he had been, by
alcohol. The last time we had spent any time together, he was
still married to Natalie Talmadge and I was the Marquise de la
Falaise.

"Waxworks is right," Buster muttered in his unmatchable
deadpan, as the four of us assembled for the scene, and we all
howled with laughter.

In their brilliant script, which they unrolled for us day by
day, Billy Wilder and Charlie Brackett had cleverly kept this
ghostly world of oldies separate from the young Hollywood
aspirants who form the other half of Joe Gillis' life; therefore,
I had no scenes with Nancy Olson or Jack Webb. I only saw
the rushes, and even that, in this Pirandello framework, was
somehow perfectly appropriate. As for Bill Holden, he could
not have been better. His craft and honesty impressed me
more each day we worked together.

The atmosphere of the picture was a bit ghoulish, but Billy
Wilder arranged for some marvelous light moments during
the shooting. In one scene I did a Chaplin imitation, a bit like
the one I did in *Manhandled* in 1924, and the wardrobe
department brought in fifty derbies for me to choose from. As
if that weren't funny enough, the next day when I walked on
the set wearing the one I had picked, Billy Wilder and the
whole crew were wearing the forty-nine that were left over.
And two days later, when we shot a scene of Norma and Max
burying Norma's pet chimpanzee, Mr. Wilder directed me to

remove the Spanish shawl covering the chimp in the white coffin, and when I did so, the stuffed monkey was also wearing a derby.

As the weeks went by, I hated to have the picture end. None had ever challenged or engrossed me more. The final mad scene raised problems. I had to descend a grand staircase crowded with extras and a few real people like Hedda Hopper, in a state of derangement, and Billy Wilder wanted me to come down on the inside of the stairway where the steps were narrowest. On high heels I would have tripped for sure, so I played the scene barefoot. I imagined a steel ramrod in me from head to toe holding me together and descended as if in a trance. When Mr. Wilder called "Print it!" I burst into tears. I had a party planned for this last day, but then and there the cast and crew gave me one instead, right on the set. Everyone was in a great state of emotion, and Mother and Michelle and I said that night in our rented house on Mulholland Drive that there were only three of us in it now, meaning that Norma Desmond had taken her leave.

Not quite, it turned out. Preview audiences complained so strongly about the film's long opening—in which the corpse of Joe Gillis is taken to the morgue, where it converses by means of voice-overs with the other corpses and starts to tell the story—that Billy Wilder cut ninety percent of it, much as he liked the black humor of the material, and got some of us back to shoot a few replacement scenes.

That time we really did finish, and agreed unanimously that Billy Wilder had provided us all with the time of our lives. He had also brought in a blockbuster.

The evening of the first big screening in Hollywood, Louis B. Mayer had a dinner party for about twenty people. From there we went to the Paramount screening room, where the audience of three hundred people seemed to include everyone in motion pictures. I caught a glimpse of Mickey Neilan as we walked to our seats, and someone told me Mary Pickford was there. These affairs are known for being morbidly restrained, devoid of the slightest overt reaction, but that night the whole audience stood up and cheered. People clustered around me, and I had trouble moving up the aisle. Barbara Stanwyck fell on her knees and kissed the hem of my skirt. I could read in all their eyes a single message of elation: If she can do it, why should we be terrified? She's shown us that it can be done!

"Where's Mary?" I asked.

"She can't show herself, Gloria," someone said. "She's overcome. We all are."

The Paramount executives were so pleased with *Sunset Boulevard* that they asked me, long before the picture was ready for release, to do a publicity tour, ostensibly to promote one of the studio's new films, *The Heiress*, starring Olivia de Havilland, Ralph Richardson, and, ironically, Montgomery Clift. In fact, however, Paramount and all the other studios were pouring money and effort at a great rate into counteracting the bad publicity caused by the eruptions of scandal in the early months of 1950. The first of these was the nationwide uproar created by Oscar-winning Ingrid Bergman's giving birth to an illegitimate child, whose father was Roberto Rossellini, the Italian film director. Americans everywhere went purple at the thought that the good girl, the saint, the nun of pictures, should flaunt her adultery in their faces, and the studios were once again spending millions to prove that all Hollywood wasn't bad. The second source of fearful scandal was Senator Joseph McCarthy, who announced in Washington that he had lists of Communists all over America bent on the overthrow of our government. Hollywood was trembling. I personally admired Ingrid Bergman enormously for having gone ahead and had her baby, not to mention the fact that I considered her the finest actress to grace Hollywood since Greta Garbo—another Swede—had arrived in 1926. I also doubted that there were Communists hiding behind every corporation desk and director's chair. But while I spoke what I felt to my friends, I managed briefly to be a good-will ambassador for the industry, now that I had so recently, like the prodigal, returned to it, as if from the dead.

I took Michelle with me and toured America for Paramount, a bit as I had done with Henri in 1925. I shook hands and visited hospitals and spoke on radio and television and made appearances in movie theaters and hosted cocktail parties and posed for pictures. In Chicago I saw Virginia Bowker and talked to the media about our days at Essanay. In Dallas I received the Neiman-Marcus Award for my contribution over the years to the world of fashion.

In Boston I had a private visit to make. I went to the gynecologist who had recommended a hysterectomy for me three years earlier. I asked him to examine me, and I studied his face intently as he did so.

"The tumor isn't there, is it?" I asked.

"No," he said uneasily.

"Don't you want to know how I got rid of it?"

"Yes," he said, "I do. How?"

"I went on a diet."

He threw back his head and laughed loudly.

"Obviously you don't understand," I said, without a trace of humor. "I stopped eating animal protein for three years and starved that tumor. If I'd listened to you, I'd be minus most of my female parts today and probably growing a beard. Therefore, I'm the one who should be laughing, Doctor, not you. Good-bye. And please, don't send me a bill."

By the time I finished the tour, I was famous all over America again. Then *Sunset Boulevard* ope ed at Radio City Music Hall a d i theaters across the cou try i August 1950, and it was pronounced the best movie ever made about Hollywood. Instantly I had requests to make personal appearances everywhere, and I began to receive stacks of scripts to consider. In November I was asked to a Command Performance of *Sunset Boulevard* in London, and I took Michelle along. She was so impressed that she asked to stay on by herself and study drama, and I told her she could. In the meantime I returned to New York to begin a radio show, after signing a contract to make a film in London the following year.

I could hardly keep up with myself.

A few days after I got back to New York, José Ferrer called from California and asked me if I would like to be in a play with him on Broadway.

"I'd love it, of course," I said playfully. "When?"

"Next month."

"Are you joking?"

"No," he said. "It will be a short run, three weeks only, to raise money for the American National Theatre and Academy."

"I'm afraid it's not enough time for me," I said, wheedling out but trying to sound like a good sport.

"Of course it is," he fired back. "All you have to do is play the lead."

"Is that all?" I said. "What are you doing?"

"Producing, directing, and playing the other lead," he said, as if to embarrass me with the puniness of the demand he was making on me.

"What's the play?"

"*Twentieth Century* by Ben Hecht and Charles MacArthur. Do you know it?"

"I saw Eugenie Leontovich and Moffat Johnston in the original production," I replied, "and Carole Lombard and John Barrymore in the film. Why do you want to do that?"

"Because it's still one hell of a play!" he exclaimed.

He was getting too excited, I thought, so I said, "I really don't think I can consider it on such short notice. I'm doing a regular radio program, you see. But thank you for thinking of me."

"For God's sake, don't say no until we've talked," he said. "I'm flying to New York tomorrow. Can I see you then?"

"All right."

I had to smile. He was my kind of person.

Born in Puerto Rico, José Ferrer at thirty-eight had risen to be one of America's few esteemed classical actors. Within recent memory on Broadway, he had played Iago in *Othello* with Paul Robeson, Uta Hagen, and Margaret Webster; the lead in a revival of *Charley's Aunt;* and Cyrano de Bergerac—all with resounding critical success. He was then making his first major picture in California, the film version of *Cyrano*.

The following day he appeared in my apartment and performed the whole Hecht-MacArthur play, taking all the parts, including mine. The man was a tornado. He rode over every objection I raised; said it would be a fantastic romp for both of us, as if he didn't know I had been on Broadway just once and had been roasted; said I was marvelous in *Sunset Boulevard*—in short, kept talking until I agreed to a first-rehearsal date, which was in a week.

He directed as well as he talked, with passion and punch and sensitivity, and made everything work—even the old gags. *Twentieth Century* is an exhausting farce to play. Set on the train running between New York and Chicago, it involves a broke producer's attempt to get his former girl friend, a temperamental star, to sign a new contract with him before the train arrives at the terminal while a host of strange characters parade through the car confusing the issue.

We opened on December 24 at the ANTA Theatre, and the

critics did handsprings. Before we had played two days, arrangements were under way to move the production to the Fulton Theatre on January 15.

I had finally made it to Broadway, in utter triumph, at fifty-one, opposite one of the best actors in America, who was twelve years my junior and seemed to delight in throwing me around the ANTA stage and then the Fulton stage like a bean bag every evening. When nominations for Academy Awards were made in February, Joe was nominated for best actor in *Cyrano* and I was nominated for best actress in *Sunset Boulevard*. After that, audiences whistled and shouted at each performance during a scene when I had to wave an Oscar in the air and Joe had to ask me sarcastically what I had won *that* for.

As the time for the awarding of the Oscars approached, the audiences at *Twentieth Century* got more and more excited, because word was out that it would be a very close contest between Bette Davis, star of *All About Eve,* and me, and one critic after another announced that I was the favorite in the race. Joe was also a favorite until, all of a sudden, shortly before the awards, his name appeared on a list before the House Un-American Activities Committee in the McCarthy witch hunts. Then everyone who knew Hollywood's long-standing cowardice in the face of scandal and bad press assumed he didn't stand a chance.

Nevertheless, when he found that my birthday was March 27 and the awards broadcast was March 29, he announced that we would combine the two and listen to the Academy Awards on the radio. I thanked him, and before I knew it, the small dinner had grown into a large party at a night club with reporters and photographers and a direct hookup to the Coast. Joe invited all the nominees who happened to be in New York, and that turned out to be almost as many as there were in Hollywood.

On March 29, at the party at La Zambra, Joe surprised everyone by winning an Oscar and I surprised everyone, except Bette Davis, probably, and Judy Holliday, who was sitting next to me, by losing. I honestly didn't care, but I could see in the faces of everyone at La Zambra, and everywhere else I went in the weeks after that, that people wanted me to care. In fact they seemed to want more than

that. They expected scenes from me, wild sarcastic tantrums.
They wanted Norma Desmond, as if I had hooked up
sympathetically, disastrously, with the role by playing it.

I began to have a problem. If I said I didn't care, people
would pity me and say I had a bad case of sour grapes. If I
told them I was an Aries, that it was not in my nature to be
dejected, they would think I was mad, and the Gloria-Norma
identification would be made forever in the eyes of the press.
It was easier to say nothing. And meanwhile, more and more
scripts arrived at my door that were awful imitations of *Sunset
Boulevard*, all featuring a deranged superstar crashing toward
tragedy.

Finally I made a decision—the millionth, it seemed, to an
aging grandmother who had been there and back many times:
I didn't want to spend the rest of my life, until I couldn't
remember lines any longer or read cue cards, playing Norma
Desmond over and over again. And if serious producers and
directors were foolish enough to think that was the only role I
could play and get box-office returns, then it was time to look
around this highly diversified world and find some other
things to do before I died.

Where was I? The daily radio show was exhausting, but I
would discontinue it when I went to Hollywood in August to
make the one picture I had been offered that wasn't another
Sunset Boulevard. After that, I had a number of offers for
another Broadway play.

Was that all? Was that the rest of my life, with minor
variations?

No! There was painting, wasn't there? I had always wanted
to paint seriously.

And sculpture.

And journalism, maybe.

Or fashion.

O Aries!

Part
Three

CHAPTER 21

DATELINE: The New York *Post*, February 22, 1980
BY-LINE: Eugenia Sheppard

On March 6 Gloria Swanson, slim, chic and probably carrying a single red carnation—her favorite touch—will be ensconced at a booth at the New York Coliseum. She will be selling the first-day covers, prized by collectors, of the new stamp she has designed.

In the eight decades of her spectacular life, Gloria has accomplished whatever she has tried and has never limited herself to one career.

Besides being the first movie star to make a million, she has appeared on the stage, has written a column, and designed dresses. A one-time student at the Chicago Art Institute, she had a one-woman show of her paintings and sculpture, including a bronze head of herself, in London two years ago.

The invitation to design the stamp puts her in an exalted group that includes Miró, Chagall and Dali, who have all shared the same honor.

The painting, which will be reproduced on both 15- and 28-cent stamps which will be made available to the public the very next day, is intended as a tribute to the '80's as the United Nations Decade of Women.

On a black background, it shows the earth in a blinding light, just as the astronauts have described it. Inside the earth is a vague, roughly formed foetus.

Asked if she thought Women's Lib would appreciate

being represented by motherhood, she gave the questioner her usual, cool, factual answer, "How else do they think they got here?"

Married six times, Swanson has two daughters, six grandchildren and two great-grandchildren.

Right now her Fifth Avenue home is a chaotic place of notes and old files while she writes her autobiography with the help of her husband, William Dufty. It will be called "Swanson on Swanson" and is scheduled for publication by Random House next fall. It is said to be as frank and straightforward as the lady herself.

Although I had gone to bed late the night before, I was up very early. I had never liked to lie in bed in the morning, and now, it seems, the older I get, the less sleep I need. I had the apartment all to myself because Bill, my husband, who was helping me research and prepare my autobiography out of the endless files of correspondence and scrapbooks I have saved through the long years, was away on a writing assignment of his own.

On the table in the library were neat stacks of 8½-by-11-inch serigraphs of my first-day cover design, beautifully printed on fine rag paper and published by the United Nations for sale to collectors. It was to accompany the UN Stamp Issue of March 7, honoring the UN Decade for Women, 1976–1985. I had signed all 1,250 copies the day before. A messenger was supposed to pick them up later in the day, after I got back from opening the philatelic exhibition at the Coliseum.

I opened the windows and found it was a fine, warm morning for early March, so I chose a white linen suit with a black velvet collar and waistcoat and a black beret—very springy. At ten-fifteen my daughter Gloria and her husband, Wilfrid Daley, arrived at the apartment to accompany me to the Coliseum, and at ten-thirty the doorman buzzed to say a limousine was waiting downstairs.

A pleasant young woman emerged from the back seat of the UN limousine and presented me with one red carnation. I smiled to think how carefully her office had done its homework on me, thanked her, and introduced her to Gloria and Wil. Then we got in the car—Wil in the front with the chauffeur and we three ladies in back—and drove through Central Park to Columbus Circle.

A crowd of several hundred people in front of the Coliseum followed us into the building and jammed the large entrance hall, where a small speakers' platform had been erected. Mr. Shull, president of the American Stamp Dealers Association, introduced me, and I made a short speech expressing my gratitude and my best wishes for the success of the exhibition. Then I cut the ribbon that officially opened the show, and Gisela Grünewald, head of the UN Postal Administration's marketing section, awarded me the UN Decade for Women silver medal. After that, several UN representatives led me the length of the vast open space filled with dealers' booths to the stand set up by WFUNA (the World Federation of United Nations Associations), where cachets, or envelopes printed with the painting I had made the previous spring, were on sale. Other cachets in the WFUNA series, by such outstanding artists as Marc Chagall, Alexander Calder, Norman Rockwell, Andy Warhol, and Joan Miró, were also on display.

My painting on the cachet showed the earth in a trail of light streaking across the black infinity of space toward the viewer. I had painted the continents and oceans to suggest an embryo, and in the lower right-hand corner I had written: "Woman, Like Mother Earth, Has an Eternal Rendezvous with Spring." If ever there was a statement obviously made by a female Aries, that was it, and I was pleased with it because I believe it.

As people bought the first-day covers, they closed in on me to get my signature on them, but I told them I could not start signing autographs; if I did, I would be there all day. Instead, I told them to mail the covers to WFUNA and I would autograph them and have them sent back within a few weeks. Then I shook hands with the UN officials, beckoned to Gloria and Wil that it was time to go, and headed for the main exit.

"What shall we do now?" I asked Gloria when we reached the street.

"Do you want to have lunch? It's such a beautiful day," she replied, and I said that sounded wonderful. First the chauffeur dropped Wil off at his office, and then he drove Gloria and me to Le Cirque, a nicely appointed restaurant with an excellent staff, one of the few I trust and enjoy in all of New York. I had what I always have there, bottled water and a small portion of Spaghetti Primavera, made with a light cream sauce and blended with slightly crunchy vegetables. Gloria and I talked mostly about family, as we usually do when we're together, especially about her daughter's two children, my two great-grandchildren, a girl and boy. I told her I had heard from Michelle, my other daughter, and her husband in Paris, and that I was going to visit them for a few weeks, probably in the late spring or fall. Then I said, "I also heard from Richard Kobler yesterday. He and his wife are coming from Switzerland next month and passing through New York."

"Who's Richard Kobler?" Gloria asked.

"Don't you remember?" I exclaimed. "He was one of those inventors I got over from Europe to form Multiprises in 1939, the year you married Robert." Robert W. Anderson, Gloria's first husband, died in 1966.

"I guess so, vaguely," Gloria said.

"He and another man have invented a whole system for teaching retarded children, slow learners," I said. "He's totally keyed up. I can't wait to hear about it."

It was then a little after one, and I said I had to work.

"On your book? Still?"

"Yes, but it's nearly finished, and I had more years to write about than most."

We live only a few blocks apart on upper Fifth Avenue, so we walked uptown together. On our way home I recalled Multiprises for her, how it had started, how the war had pretty much ended it, how through the years I had lost touch with all my inventors except for Kobler. Before we parted I asked her if she and Wil could come to the UN reception that evening. She said they had a dinner engagement but they would try.

In the apartment I went over a long list of queries and suggestions from Jason Epstein, my editor at Random House, who was anxious for me to finish the memoirs in a few weeks' time so that the book could come out in the fall and I could make a cross-country publicity tour before Christmas. He wanted me to describe the car Wallace Beery drove in California and the undergarment we used to call a teddy bare—lots of particular things like that. I wrote out answers to the easy questions and made notes to myself about the rest.

In spite of the soaring phone bills, it was usually easiest to call friends and check out facts with them. I had long since learned not to trust what was in other people's memoirs and biographies.

As soon as it was past noon California time, I phoned Allan Dwan. At ninety-four, the dear genius still has a phenomenal memory, and I needed to clear up a few facts about *What a Widow*. The phone rang and rang. They were out. I made a note to call him the next day. Then I phoned King Vidor.

"Hello, Mr. Vidor," I said. "This is Gloria Swanson."

"Hello!" he said, in his quiet, refined voice, a bit surprised to hear from me.

"I'm writing my memoirs," I said, "and I wonder if you can answer a question that's been troubling me."

"What is that?" Mr. Vidor asked.

"Do you remember Cyril Gardner?" I asked.

"Yes."

"Well, when he came to England to direct me in *A Perfect Understanding* in 1932, a psychic told him that his parents would both die soon and that he himself would die on the boat to America."

"Who would die? Gardner?" King Vidor asked.

"Yes. Now, the upshot was that his parents both *did* die, and that made him so frightened that he wouldn't sail for America. Finally an American movie director over there got him totally drunk and practically shoveled him onto the next boat that was sailing, before he even knew where he was. Was that you?"

"No," King Vidor said after a slight pause.

"Well, it was an American director. Who could it have been?"

King Vidor thought for a moment and then suggested a lesser name from the past.

"That may be it," I said. "Do you have his number? I'll call him."

"I'm afraid it's too late for that," Mr. Vidor said in his reserved, distinguished manner, and when I realized what he meant, I started to laugh and so did he.

"I'll just have to leave it out," I said. "But it was such a nice story."

We were both still laughing when I hung up.

I worked until five, when I stopped to get ready for the reception for me at the United Nations. It was scheduled for six-thirty, too early for a long evening dress, I reasoned, so I had planned to wear a short dress. When I considered, however, how many people from different countries were going to be there, I guessed that a number of women would wear long dresses and I didn't want to embarrass them. Therefore, I decided to please everyone, offend no one, be a diplomat. I chose a calf-length silk crepe dress, black all down the right side, white on the left, and a white hat with an eye veil. I knew they would ask me to make a brief speech, but I hadn't thought about it and I wasn't about to start at half past five. My best speeches were always spontaneous ones. I trusted once again, therefore, that when the time came, the words would come too.

At six the doorman buzzed and announced another limousine. My escort greeted me charmingly with another red carnation and a card on which were printed the names of the other people who would speak at the reception: Yoshio Tagaya, director of the UN Office of General Services; Sidney Willner, chairman of the WFUNA Executive Committee; and Annabelle Wiener, director of WFUNA. Mrs. Wiener was the person who had proposed my doing the painting for the cachet in the first place; we had since become fast friends.

The reception took place in the spacious UN Delegates' Dining Room, overlooking the East River, just as darkness was falling. I stood in the receiving line and shook hands with five hundred guests—UN ambassadors, postal officials, philatelists, dealers, and the press. A man in formal attire stood at the door and loudly announced all the guests as they entered the room. Ambassadors from twenty-two nations, some with names that hadn't existed when I was young— Kampuchia, Lesotho, Sri Lanka—appeared to shake my hand. The Costa Rican ambassador was a woman, and that pleased me. At one point I had to stifle a laugh—when I was ceremoniously introduced to my own daughter and her husband, who had, after all, managed to stop by briefly.

At seven-thirty Mrs. Wiener introduced Mr. Tagaya and Mr. Willner, who gave me glowing praise as an artist and as a woman. Then I stepped to the microphone and said, "My cup runneth over," and received a second long ovation. I told them I had spent most of my artistic life as a member of a team, along with a director, a producer, a costumer, a set designer, a crew, and a supporting cast. As a painter, however, I had had to act alone, take full responsibility, conceive and execute and assume any blame, if there was blame; and I thanked the United Nations, during their Decade for Women, for trusting me to do that. I said that the United Nations still had great work to do, and that we should all be eager and proud to take part in it.

It was a gentle speech, not at all a fighting one like those I had made during the fifties in Washington and elsewhere in my efforts to help get the Delaney Amendment passed and change the world, and at the end of it everyone applauded again. Then they led me downstairs for a fifteen-minute interview on UN radio, to be broadcast in part or in translation all over the globe.

By then Gloria and Wil had left, and I had the UN driver deliver me home.

It had been a nice day. The weather had held, and I was happy with the fuss over the cachet. For years I had dabbled as a painter and sculptor, and suddenly, within fifteen months, I had had a one-woman show in London and done this painting for the United Nations.

It was eleven o'clock, but I wasn't tired. Eleven o'clock— that was eight o'clock California time. Time for one more call before I went to bed. I direct-dialed Raoul Walsh's house, and he answered the phone.

"Handsome!" I cried, in the tough voice of Sadie Thompson, as I had so many times with Raoul through the years.

"Sadie!" he yelled back.

"How are you all?"

"Fine, just fine! And you?"

"Fine." I told him about the reception at the UN, and he thought it was terrific. Then I said, "Listen, I want to straighten one thing out in these memoirs of mine. The day we met in my garden . . . the first day . . . Henri was there . . . do you remember?—who first suggested making a film of *Rain?* Did you? Or did I?"

"We both did," Raoul said. "We were thinking like one person that day, don't you remember? You couldn't separate it."

"That's what I thought," I said, "but I wanted to check with you."

"When are you coming back out here? We're dying to see you."

"Soon," I said. "As soon as this book is finished. Good night, Handsome."

"Hey, wait a minute! Let's hear you say it."

"All right," I said. Then I gave it to him, the way I had given it to Lionel Barrymore when Raoul was directing me in 1927: "'You'd yank the wings off butterflies and claim you were saving their souls, you psalm-singing son of a bitch!'"

"Ha, *ha!*" Raoul shouted. "That's it! Good night, Sadie."

CHAPTER 22

Never say never, for if you live long enough, chances are you will not be able to abide by the simplest of such injunctions. In 1919, for example, I promised my father I would never fly in an airplane again. Although I waited until Daddy died to go back on my word, I have flown hundreds of thousands of miles since then, in propeller planes, in giant jets, and in one of the early successful helicopters, over Niagara Falls, when I felt like a hummingbird. As a guest of the National Aeronautics and Space Administration, I was even invited, by Wernher von Braun himself, to sit in one of the first space capsules, before astronauts ever flew in it. In 1921, after two unsuccessful marriages, I told myself and millions of fans that I would never marry again. I have had four more husbands since then. In 1925 I said I would complete my contract at Paramount and never make another picture, and in 1951, after a successful comeback that threatened me with typecasting for the rest of my life, I vowed I would never play another aging movie queen. As recently as 1974 I made a feature picture in Hollywood and played in it an aging movie queen—myself, Gloria Swanson. So it's no use saying never. Never is a long, undependable time, and life is too full of rich possibilities to have restrictions placed on it. Since I decided in the early fifties to make an effort to diversify my creative life, I have been a happier person, more relaxed, more open to new experiences, less apt to be trapped in any single area for long. Movies have been just one part of my life since then. The other parts have been just as fascinating and equally rewarding. But I'll start with movies, for they've been with me longest.

In the summer of 1951, after Joe Ferrer and I gave a party at Sardi's for our replacements in *Twentieth Century*, Robert Preston and Binnie Barnes, I went to Hollywood to make a picture called *Three for Bedroom C*. Based on a Goddard Lieberson novel, the picture was a light, romantic farce about a famous Hollywood star and her young daughter traveling on a train from Chicago to Los Angeles in a compartment that is also booked by a shy, handsome professor of biochemistry. It was my first film shot entirely in color. I designed my own costumes and by chance discovered the leading man, tall, attractive James Warren, whom I found selling his pottery and paintings in Los Angeles. I called Milton Bren, the director, who gave him a screen test and cast him the very next day. Margaret Dumont and Hans Conried were in the cast, as well as Fred Clark, who had just acted with me in *Twentieth Century*, and we all had great fun making the film, but the critics seemed disappointed not to find Norma Desmond aboard. The picture was not a success, and for the next few years I turned down movie scripts about actresses and devoted myself instead to radio and television and designing.

I was never out of Hollywood for long, however, and in the spring of 1953, when the Academy Awards were televised for the first time, Joe Schenck asked if I would accept a special award on his behalf which he was being given for long and devoted service to the industry. Joe, who had served a brief jail sentence for the sins of Hollywood bookkeeping, was doubtless shy to appear on TV on that account, as well as on account of his failing health, but I was proud to accept the award for him. In some strange way, Joe Schenck was one of the few honorable bandits of early Hollywood. In going to jail quietly, he had, I felt sure, also taken the blame for a number of less scrupulous colleagues. Mr. De Mille, too, received a special award, the Irving Thalberg Award. I was appalled that he had never won an Oscar for directing, although, thank heaven, his circus picture, *The Greatest Show on Earth*, was voted best picture for 1953. Mary Pickford and Janet Gaynor and many other early stars also took part in the ceremonies. Hollywood was pulling out all stops to look like a great old tradition, but those of us who had been there from the beginning were too wise and weary to be impressed. All the young stars backstage were dressed to the nines, in gorgeous gowns to the floor, dripping with bangles and jewels. I wore a short sable-brown silk dress and a little sable bolero, and when I came off stage with Joe Schenck's Oscar and was passing Greer Garson, I heard her say good-naturedly, "You bitch. Here we've all been getting gussied up for this for weeks, and you waltz in in your little brown wren number and make us feel like a bunch of tarts."

My next picture, called *Nero's Mistress,* had a stellar international cast, including Brigitte Bardot, Vittorio De Sica, and Alberto Sordi, but it was so bad that six years elapsed between the shooting in Italy in 1956 and the picture's release in a dubbed version in the United States in 1962. Nevertheless, it gave me an opportunity to be near Michelle, who had a brief acting career of her own in pictures in Europe until she gave it up to marry and settle down in Paris. In fact, it seemed so good to be in Europe again that I stayed for several years, in Spain, in France, and in Italy. During most of that time, when I wasn't playing Agrippina in *Nero's Mistress,* I worked as a roving journalist for United Press. I covered everything from bullfights in Spain to the wedding of Grace Kelly and Prince Rainier in Monaco. UP told me they wanted my frank reactions on anything I cared to write about as long as it was of interest to Americans at home and abroad. Therefore I wrote hundreds of short pieces on everything from the old European custom of kissing ladies' hands . . .

In this pseudo-handkissing group you will find the Novice, you can be sure. He will always unmask himself by committing the one unpardonable sin in handkissing circles—bringing your hand up to his face rather than bending down to your hand. . . . In all the various styles of handkissing, I still miss the click of the heel. I must remember, when I get to Paris, to ask Erich von Stroheim whatever became of it.

. . . to the shows at the Folies Bergère:

Ah! Quelle Folie, the title of the present production, has thirteen letters in it, like the titles of all the past productions, and like those, it will probably run for three or four years. That is why a fortune can be spent on the sets and "costumes," consisting mostly of fantastic headdresses. . . . What the French mind doesn't understand is that if there were less nudity, the show would be more shocking, or more beautiful, depending on your point of view. As it is, the nudity gets tiresome. . . . Of course, I spent a good part of the time seeing if I could detect paraffin on their bodies, for I had been told they dunked themselves in it to give their skin a desired firmness. My top frustration of the evening, because I'm a detective at heart and just love to debunk magic, was in trying to figure out how the 1955 model of a fig leaf could possibly stay in place without any visible means! Next time I go to the Folies Bergère, I am taking binoculars.

My last feature picture was *Airport 1975*. When Universal Studios sent me the original script in the spring of 1974 and I realized they wanted me to play the aging alcoholic actress in it, I turned it down flat. Immediately, however, producer William Frye, director Jack Smight, and Edith Head all turned up at my New York apartment and said they would make any changes in the role I wanted if I would just play it. After lengthy discussion, someone suggested I simply play myself, Gloria Swanson—not an alcoholic but a health-food freak, not a gin-soaked philosopher but a normal human being dictating her memoirs into a tape recorder. That proved an irresistible challenge. In my favorite scene in the picture, all the passengers have to prepare for a crash landing. Quick as a flash, I dump my jewels out of my portable, crashproof, fireproof safe and lock up the tapes of my memoirs instead. We shot location scenes at Dulles Airport in Washington, D.C., and in Salt Lake City. During the shooting of the studio scenes at Universal in Hollywood, Bill Frye gave me a star bungalow, and there I became a star attraction, pointed out by the guides over a loudspeaker to thousands of tourists on buses who passed by every day. It was marvelous.

Before his death Erich von Stroheim released a short version of *Queen Kelly*, and many modern critics who had never seen the film, or any part of it, soon proclaimed it a masterpiece. Since then, many of my early pictures have been shown at film festivals around the world. Each time this happens, the same sad questions are always asked: Does anyone know of a print anywhere of *Beyond the Rocks*, the film Rudy Valentino made with me in 1921? Can anyone locate a print of *Madame Sans-Gêne*? Does anyone have a complete copy, including the last reel, of *Sadie Thompson*? I would love to see them again and know they're not lost forever. That, after all, was supposed to be the great virtue of pictures—that they would last forever. Alas, thousands upon thousands of early films, in the years when they were not being shown because they were not considered fashionable, or old enough to be museum pieces, crumbled in their cans. The celluloid disintegrated with age.

If I was already a vintage actress in pictures in the early fifties, I was still a glamorous pioneer as far as television was concerned, thanks to my WPIX series of programs in 1948. When I returned to New York after making *Three for Bedroom C*, therefore, I hosted many radio and television shows similar to the old WPIX ones.

Then Bing Crosby became a television entrepreneur, and in 1951 and 1952 his company produced two low-budget series, *Royal Playhouse* and *Rebound*. These succeeded so well in the ratings that the company began planning a fancier series of drama shows for 1953. They called the series *Crown Theater* and asked me to introduce all twenty-six shows and star in four of them. They bought stories for the scripts from such fine writers as Louis Bromfield and Richard Llewellyn, and they hired the finest of Broadway and Hollywood talent to act in them, stars such as George Brent, Claude Dauphin, and Charles Winninger. *Crown Theater* launched me as a national television personality, and I have never been far from a television studio since then. I have watched this medium, this form of entertainment, grow from nothing to become the national pastime, and although I am as critical of it at times as I am enthusiastic about it at other times, I am always intrigued by the potential of it as a universal, around-the-clock, in-the-home tool of instruction.

Over the years I have often appeared on talk shows, from Merv Griffin's to Mike Douglas' to Johnny Carson's, probably because I always frankly discuss those things that either interest or annoy me, from high fashion to the education of children, from film festivals to governmental intervention to prevent the food we eat from being contaminated by pesticides, and I suspect that is where I have acquired the large live audience I have whenever I walk two blocks in New York or California. "Hey, Gloria!" a workman in a hard hat will call out of a construction ditch. "Hello, Miss Swanson!" a group of eight-year-olds waiting with their teacher for a bus will carol. I love it, and I always stop and talk with them, now that I often have the time. I ask the workman if he wants some vitamins to counteract the bad air in the ditch where he's working. I tell the children not to eat junk food.

I've played a wide variety of roles on many of the big TV drama and comedy series—*Straightaway, Dr. Kildare, Burke's Law,* and *The Beverly Hillbillies,* to mention a few. On November 22, 1963, I was filming a play on the *Kraft Suspense Theatre* with Dan Duryea when the producer, Luther Davis, walked on the set and announced that we would have a one-minute silence; the President had been shot in Dallas. My first reaction was one of shock and horror. I had talked with Joe and Rose about this boy when he was a child, and now he had been meaninglessly, violently shot. Poor Joe, I thought; the dream of his life, first for himself and then for his sons, to become President—and then to have it end in tragedy. I sent a telegram of condolence the next day. I sent another when Joe had his stroke, and signed it "Kelly."

My greatest television experience was appearing with Carol Burnett. I have seen all the great comediennes, including Mabel Normand and Fanny Brice and Bea Lillie, and I consider myself and a few others very good mimics, but as far as I'm concerned no one touches Carol in either field. I watched her show for eleven years, and I still collapse with laughter every time I see a rerun of her Norma Desmond takeoff. It's even better than her Mildred Pierce takeoff. When I wrote to tell her so, in 1972, she wrote back and asked if I would be her guest star on a show during the coming season. I said I would be thrilled, and soon she called back to ask if I could tango and if I would do a Charlie Chaplin impersonation and sing a song. I said I could and would. We rehearsed and taped the whole show in five days. I danced a tango with six gorgeous young Valentinos, I sang a song, and Carol and I, as a charwoman and Charlie Chaplin, did a Sennett-type skit complete with a Keystone chase. It all came out predictably wonderful. There has never been any performer in any medium better at what she does than Carol Burnett.

In the early seventies I starred in a full-length horror film called *Killer Bees,* made specially for television, and although I read the script with trepidation, I ended up thinking it was terrific and said yes. I played a German woman, the mother of Craig Stevens. We shot the film in Hollywood and on location in the beautiful Napa Valley above San Francisco. We saved the scenes with the bees for last, as Mr. De Mille had saved the lion for last in *Male and Female*. The picture turned out to be a classic in the genre, I think, and it is rerun frequently in America and abroad. People always ask me, "Weren't you terrified to do those scenes with the bees?" I always want to say, Not as terrified as I was to have a lion put his paw on my back in 1919, but instead I explain that I was really worried only about my ears, so I put cotton in them, and that anyway the bees were sluggish at the start, when they put them all over me, and only came alive as the lights warmed them up. Furthermore, we were told that they had all their stingers removed, but that is the kind of information it is always hard to believe.

In November 1951 I opened on Broadway in *Nina* by the French playwright André Roussin. Directed by Gregory Ratoff and co-starring David Niven and Alan Webb, the comedy was a failure, although I have always felt it shouldn't have been, and I didn't act on Broadway again for twenty years. In between, of course, I acted in summer stock and on the West Coast.

Then suddenly, in 1969, when I was seventy, I was offered two Broadway roles in one year. The first was a replacement for Katharine Hepburn in *Coco*, the musical based on the life of my old friend Coco Chanel, and I actually began preparing for the part, but at the last minute negotiations broke down with the producers and Danielle Darrieux replaced Katie. Before I even had time to register disappointment, however, producer Arthur Whitelaw phoned and asked me to take over the Eileen Heckart role in a comedy called *Butterflies Are Free*. The role was that of a Westchester widow whose son is blind and living alone in a hippie pad in Greenwich Village. When the woman learns that her boy is having an affair with the girl in the next apartment, she comes to town to break up the affair, and in the course of her attempt she learns instead to let her baby go. That week I went and saw the play and loved it and the role, which I persuaded Arthur Whitelaw to let me play outside New York, for a while at least. Eve Arden had played the role in California briefly, but there had been no other productions around the country.

I opened in Chicago in the fall of 1970 and I hated the way I looked because it affected my performance, so before I opened in Cleveland I threw away the wig I was supposed to wear, tinted my pewter-colored hair light-brown, and changed the dress and coat I had been wearing for a pantsuit. The transformation worked like a charm; I felt right as Mrs. Baker at last and settled in for a run of nine months in twenty major cities across America.

Back in New York, Arthur Whitelaw asked me to play *Butterflies Are Free* on Broadway for a limited run of six weeks. I agreed and opened in September 1971 with David Huffman, who had been playing my blind son on tour, and Pamela Bellwood, who had been playing the young girl in the play on Broadway. The critics all reviewed the show again, the box office picked up immediately, and our limited run ultimately stretched to Christmas and beyond.

One of the great things about the Broadway run was driving to work and back. Since I didn't come onstage until the end of the first act, I didn't have to be at the Booth Theatre until the curtain-time rush was over, so I bought a yellow Toyota and drove from my apartment to the theater every night. At that hour it took only about eight minutes at my rate.

Henri, my third husband, in attempting to explain the dissolution of our marriage to the press, at one point said kindly and honestly, "I married a businesswoman." In fact, he was wrong. At the time he was describing me, I was only a woman learning to become a businesswoman, an actress struggling to master the thousand difficulties involved in producing. Whatever, business fascinated me then as it has fascinated me ever since.

In 1939, with the four young inventors I brought to America from Germany and Austria, I set up Multiprises in New York, with a factory in the borough of Queens to manufacture the fruits of their invention, particularly cutting tools made from a special alloy concocted by Anton Kratky. At forty, therefore, I was a factory owner, something I had always wanted to be, surrounded by brilliant engineers, the sort of men whose minds had always excited me, and I might have made a considerable fortune had not the war come along. Two of the inventors asked to work for the U.S. government for the duration, and shortly after that one became a consultant for the Edison laboratories. Meanwhile, another company won the wartime contracts that might have made Multiprises a large concern, and although my firm survived the war, it did so without any great prospects. I lost many thousands of dollars in it before I finally shut down the plant and the office, but Multiprises was nevertheless one of the most inspiring, challenging ventures of my life. As for my inventors, Leopold Karniol died, Leopold Neumann I lost track of, and Anton Kratky, I believe, returned to Europe. Richard Kobler I hear from at least once a year still. Knowing him alone would have made Multiprises worthwhile for me.

My next business venture—in fashion design and sales—proved to be much more commercially successful than Multiprises and lasted much longer. It started in September 1950 when I was invited to Dallas for five days to be a recipient of the Neiman-Marcus Award for Distinguished Service in the Field of Fashion, the most coveted award in the world of fashion. The other awardees, they told me, would be Pauline Trigère, Bonnie Cashin, and Gardner and Fleur Cowles. I assumed the honor was being extended to me for my long years as the established clotheshorse of the movies and for my frequent appearance on lists of the world's best-dressed women. I had certainly never publicized the fact that for years I had designed most of my own clothes or at least worked hand in glove with the recognized designers I trusted in the business, such as Edith Head and René Hubert.

Before I went to Dallas, I designed a complete wardrobe for my five-day stay and had the designs executed by dressmakers in Los Angeles. One of the Marcus brothers, Edward, met me at the train, and on the way to the hotel asked me where I'd got the hat I was wearing, which consisted of three cloches of the finest French felt in different colors, pulled on one over the other, with a string of felt tied through two holes in the top to keep the stack of cloches in place.

"I designed it," I said. "I call it the Tri-traveleur, because you can roll it up and carry it in a suitcase or purse. You can wear any of the cloches alone or stack them in any order, with just the bottommost brim of the lower two showing, as I'm wearing them now."

"It's stunning," Mr. Marcus said. "Would you mind if we borrowed it to copy for a display?"

"Not at all," I said. "On the contrary, I'd be extremely flattered."

The store showed designer collections and had parties for

three days, and on the last two evenings put on a glamorous
fashion show, the second night being a repeat of the first. I
phoned the show's coordinator to find out what the other
recipients were wearing, because I didn't want to wear the
same color. She came to my hotel room the day before the
show and I mentioned three evening gowns I had brought
with me—a red, a black, and a white. Which should I wear? I
asked.

"Did you design them?" the young woman asked.

When I told her I had, she asked if she could see them, and
I modeled all three for her. I was actually very proud of them.
The red was iridescent silk, black on one side and red on the
other, with a cord gathering the material around the knees
and a pleated skirt below, with a large French rose of the
same fabric at the left knee, and with a black net cape worn in
full swirls over the bare shoulders. The black was a light wool
with black fox trim around the knees and on a long black
shawl worn over the bare shoulders. The third gown was
chalk-white faille, with a tunic of the same fabric worn over
the long tight skirt and a chocolate-brown poncho worn over
that.

"They're all nice," the coordinator said. "Why don't you
wear the black Monday evening and the red Tuesday evening?"

"All right," I said.

On Monday night the huge salon was beautifully decorated, and everyone in the fashion world was there. It was the
most elegant show of its kind I had ever seen. It started with
morning clothes and progressed to afternoon dresses and
evening gowns. I was thrilled to see my Tri-traveleur worn
with one of the daytime outfits. Then, down the long, raised,
carpeted ramp paraded models in the most heavenly collection of gowns imaginable, by Balenciaga, Givenchy, Balmain,
Fath, Schiaparelli, Dior, and—I gasped when I heard the
familiar syllables—Gloria Swanson. Neiman-Marcus had
raided my hotel room and was showing my white evening
dress! The whole room burst into applause, and I burst into
joyous, uncontrollable tears. I think that was almost the
proudest moment of my life, except for waking up twice to
find babies I'd produced by my labor. I know for sure that five
Oscars couldn't have made me half as happy. They showed
the dress both evenings and awarded me their beautiful
plaque. I felt blessed.

Before I left Dallas on Wednesday, Stanley Marcus asked me to visit him in his office. He sat there, distinguished beyond belief, the aristocrat of aristocrats, and after I had thanked him for the award and the thrill of having my dress shown, he said, "You know, our whole family has been studying you every single day for five days. Everything you've worn here is your own design, isn't it?"

When I answered yes, he said, "Well, you're a fool if you don't get into the fashion business. I'm going to give you the number of Herbert Sondheim. He has one of the best fashion houses in New York. Call him, and he'll suggest people for you to contact."

In New York I called Mr. Sondheim, who called a Mr. Green, who had lost his designing partner. Before Mr. Green and I could reach an agreement on a contract, word got around Seventh Avenue that I was up for grabs, and a man named Carl Rosen phoned me and asked if I would at least talk to him before I signed with anyone else. I said fine, and the dapper young man arrived at my apartment the next day with a lawyer and a stenographer. His company, Puritan Fashions, was not a house of *haute couture*—on the contrary, they were strictly concerned with volume business and dealt largely in half sizes, dresses cut amply for bosomy women— but Mr. Rosen talked so well and so convincingly that I told him to draw up a contract. I would see what I could do in a year to improve rack dresses designed mostly for stout women.

Puritan had a line called Forever Young, which I took over. For a decade and more I went to department stores across America with it, and every year I traveled to Paris and Florence to get ideas from the big designers' shows. I talked by the hour to salesgirls and fitters because they're the people who know both dresses and customers, and then I would suggest changes and improvements to Carl and Mr. Rosen, Sr. I talked them into making dresses with generous hems and seams, for example, so that women could feel good buying the smallest possible size and then let it out if necessary. I showed them that a waistline is not horizontal; on the human body it dips in back, and so it should on dresses if they are to fit properly. I told them as a general rule to shorten sleeves so that dresses in the line didn't look like old ladies' dresses. I taught them that the first feminine feature that goes, with advancing age, is the neck; therefore, cut your dresses low, I said, not high, in the neck, so that the neck will appear long, not short and thick. And so on. And all the while, the loving image I kept in mind was that of my own dear stout mother.

The company soon went from making less than $10 million a year to making over $100 million. Our association lasted for nearly twenty years, and when I left Puritan, it was with a contract for yearly payments for the rest of my life. I like to think that during my tenure I made the average stoutish woman in America look a little more glamorous in clothes off the rack than she had before 1951.

Briefly, for a few years in the mid-fifties, I also entered the cosmetics industry, mainly because I wanted more women to use cosmetics made exclusively with safe, heathful ingredients, like pure olive oil and pure sesame oil, as opposed to mineral oil, which takes vitamin B out of your system, or corn oil, which comes from a plant customarily sprayed with insecticides. A New Jersey manufacturer concerned, as I was, with the pure-food movement approached me, and we issued for a time a line of cosmetics called Essence of Nature. I designed the bottles and boxes and made sure that the line consisted of only a few basic, natural items which I could honestly and proudly advertise. In interviews I always said that I could eat or rub on my body any ingredient in our products, they were so pure. In a short time, however, the manufacturer changed chemists without my approval, so I soon withdrew from the cosmetics industry altogether. To this day, whenever a big store tracks down the source of one of the pure cosmetics I use—and which I almost always buy from health-food stores—a store representative invariably approaches me to see if I will sponsor the product on a large scale. I always say no, because I know full well that as soon as a small producer or manufacturer in Mexico, say, hurries out of a motive of greed to increase his output, the quality of the product will suffer, and I would no longer be able to sponsor or use it.

In conclusion, if I wasn't a businesswoman when Henri and I divorced, I became one—a good one, I hope, and a scrupulous one—soon after.

For years people I didn't know considered me an obsessive crank about food and diet. I didn't care. I still don't, and the longer I live, the more people join me in the certainty that your body is the direct result of what you eat as well as what you don't eat. Dr. Bieler taught me that in 1927, and every day I live merely reinforces his lessons. I know my body. I like it and I trust it. I don't stuff it full of bad food, and I don't let surgeons start cutting into it the minute I have a pain somewhere, because pain, as Hal Bieler told me in 1927, is a divine signal, telling you to take care of yourself with proper diet, not necessarily telling you or a doctor who hardly knows you that some part of you has to be cut out or numbed with drugs. Health is just everyday sensible care of your body. I can't understand why people can't get that through their skulls.

This brings me to a confession, or another confession, I'm not sure which, for confession seems to be the ever-present hazard and temptation of a person writing memoirs. Because I take care of my body, it doesn't look like the body of a woman of my years. Therefore, interviewers and acquaintances, as soon as they feel they dare to ask, inevitably pussyfoot up to the irresistible question: Have you ever had your face lifted? No, I always reply, and it's true, but I did have my eyes fixed, right after I made *Nero's Mistress* in Italy, while I was still living in Europe. When my beau of the moment—one in a long line of beaux, suitors, and escorts during the many years I was single—came to visit me there, he registered shock because fatty little whiteheads had developed under my left eye since he last saw me. When he told me I was silly not to undergo simple cosmetic surgery, I told him about Richard Barthelmess, who had been pressured into having bags removed from under his eyes as soon as they appeared. The doctors made such a mess of poor Dick's eyes that he had to wear dark glasses for the rest of his life and his career was ruined. Yes, but, my beau said, cosmetic surgery had improved greatly since the days when Richard Barthelmess had his eyes fixed, and he implored me to see a doctor. At last I gave in, reluctantly, and the surgeon I went to said it would be a simple matter to remove the tiny bumps. He could not, however, repair just the one eye. He would have to do both. I consented, and the operation was successful, but I have always had a twinge of guilt about it.

I became a fanatic about healthy food in 1944, when it became common practice in the United States to spray crops with insecticides, and as soon as I learned in 1951 that one U.S. Congressman, Representative James J. Delaney from New York, was devoting himself to having laws passed to stop the food we eat from being sprayed and manured with harmful chemicals, I threw myself into supporting him in every way I could. In 1952 I was the guest speaker at the Congressional Wives Club in Washington, on a day when Bess Truman was the guest of honor, and instead of telling the six or seven hundred women at the luncheon "all about Hollywood," as I'm sure they expected me to do, I made them listen to a hundred horrifying facts about female hormones being injected into chickens, and the poisoned condition of crops and soil all over our country, and I begged them to go right home and force their husbands, by whatever means they could bring to bear, to vote for the Delaney Amendment.

After that I spoke whenever and wherever I could get a platform, the last time at the Advertising Club in Washington in 1957, when Drew Pearson asked me to talk to the Big Brothers Organization, made up of prominent businessmen. A lot of other people who sensed the dangers in the increasing use of pesticides also spoke out, and still it took years, from the time Mr. Delaney started agitating until 1958, to get the amendment passed into law. Even then, ever since, powerful lobbies keep the Food and Drug Administration and the Department of Agriculture from properly enforcing the law. Therefore, I still appear every time I have the chance to persuade purchasers to shop in health-food stores and demand nothing but chemical-free foods. It is insanity for citizens of the richest nation in the world to be slowly poisoned to death in order to satisfy the greed of the big food and chemical cartels.

My proudest possession is the following citation from Jim Delaney, which hangs framed in my library.

August 15, 1958

Dear Miss Swanson:

I am sure you will be interested to know that chemical additive legislation was passed by the House on Wednesday. The enclosed pages from the *Congressional Record* will give you the details.

While the committee bill which was passed was not all that I wanted, it is a definite step forward and will afford the public appreciably improved protection. I insisted upon, and succeeded in getting the committee to accept, an amendment prohibiting the use in food of any cancer-inducing chemical—one of the strong features of my bill.

Your own personal campaign for additive legislation was of great help. After you addressed the congressional wives here in Washington, many Members spoke to me about the deep impression you had made. Your many radio and television appearances and your speeches around the country did much to alert the public to the hazards of insufficiently tested chemical additives and the need for regulatory legislation. I know that the thousands of letters which poured into congressional offices here had their effect in helping bring about Wednesday's action.

A bill now goes to the Senate, and though adjournment seems near, I believe there will be time to push it through.

I am most grateful to you for the valuable contribution you have made to this cause.

With kindest regards, I am

Sincerely,
James J. Delaney, M.C.

Giants excluded, I consider anybody who weighs over two hundred pounds fat, and time was when I could not refrain from telling such people so. I have since learned that talking usually does no good; that you can teach only by example; but before I came to that conclusion, I had met the man who was to become my sixth husband and I had told him he was killing himself. We sat next to each other at a conference in New York relating to the work of Dr. Andrew Ivy, the proponent of the anti-cancer agent known as Krebiozen, and when lunch was brought in from the nearest delicatessen, I watched him unwrap one cube of sugar after another and drop them into his mug of coffee. Finally I could stand it no longer and said, "That's poison, you know. I wouldn't have refined sugar in my house, much less in my stomach." He smiled, stirred his coffee and drank it, and if I even knew his name was William Dufty, I forgot it until a number of years later.

In 1965 he sent me a copy of a book he had translated from the Japanese called *You Are All Sanpaku*, about the efficacy of brown rice. I called to thank him and tell him I liked the book, and in the course of our talk I invited him to tea. When he arrived at my apartment, he in no way resembled the man I had spoken to at the conference. He had lost eighty pounds, he told me, was down to a hundred and thirty-five, and had become a complete convert to proper, wholesome, natural food. We had arrived at nutrition consciousness by different routes, but we had many corresponding views. He told me he had rid himself of all his maladies by means of careful diet, and in doing so, had become a very good cook of grain dishes, steamed vegetables, and surprise desserts in which raisins, dates, and other natural sweeteners took the place of sugar. In fact, after tea he stayed and cooked dinner. That's how it started.

After that we saw each other often and became good friends. He was still married legally, to a woman he described as his future ex-wife, but that didn't bother me in the least. We took a number of trips together, in this country and abroad. In 1968, for example, we traveled to Russia in winter, a fantastic experience, and in the midst of being tourists with a guide, spent two extraordinary afternoons in the company of Professor Alexei Pokrovsky, head of the Soviet Bureau of Nutrition. The professor was fascinated by my size and condition, for a woman of my age, and therefore by my diet, which agreed in theory with his own, so I described Dr. Bieler to him and listed the things I ate and didn't eat, and he made voluminous notes. That was the sort of experience that Bill and I enjoyed enormously together.

In 1975 Bill finished his book *Sugar Blues,* on the evils of sugar in the average American's diet, and I went on a tour of about thirty cities all over America to publicize the book with him. Before a second tour began, to publicize the paperback edition, Bill asked me to marry him. I was speechless. Our relationship seemed just fine as it was. All I could say was "You know how I'd hate to have you become just a number—number six. Do you really want to marry me?"

"Yes," he said.

"Why?"

"Because I want to take care of you."

The words traveled through me like lightning, warming me as they went. No one had ever said them to me before, and yet I knew in my blood they were what I had always wanted to hear from a man. With very moist eyes I said, "But, Bill, I care too much for you to give you a number."

"Then don't," he said. "You can always say instead that I'm your first organic husband."

That did it. I laughed so hard that I cried, and we were married quickly, quietly, in 1976, just after he turned sixty, just before I turned seventy-seven. Our life together, that of two mature people with mutual interests and individual projects, is perfectly described by Kahlil Gibran in *The Prophet:*

> Give your hearts, but not into each other's keeping.
> For only the hand of Life can contain your hearts.
> And stand together yet not too near together:
> For the pillars of the temple stand apart,
> And the oak tree and the cypress grow not in each
> other's shadow.

I have painted and sculptured ever since my mother took me to Saturday classes at the Art Institute in Chicago when I was a child. My paintings are realistic, usually oils, and my favorite subject is probably flowers, although I paint occasional landscapes and a few studies of people. I prefer to do still lifes because they're available all the time, and I often paint at night.

My sculpture is very personal; in fact, for years my subjects were family and close, close friends. Molding them in clay, with great care for accuracy, was a way of loving them and touching them and becoming intimate with them. My fondest early recollection is of sculpturing Gloria in 1923, when she was three and we were living in New York. I would rush back from filming *Zaza* in Astoria in the early evening and spend an hour or so with my baby, sculpturing her beautiful little head. I had to work fast, often without even bothering to take off my hat, because she hated to sit still, and as soon as she did, the animation would go right out of her face. I had the head cast in bronze when I finished it, because I was so happy with it, and it is in my library to this day, along with one of Michelle, which I did when she was twelve.

Only once until recently was my work shown publicly, when I was living in Rome in the mid-fifties. I had some of my paintings I wanted framed for Mother in the apartment I rented, and one fine day my landlady announced that she had arranged with a friend of hers to show them in a gallery.

"Absolutely not!" I protested, and three days later the paintings were hanging in the gallery. It is impossible to say no to an Italian landlady, particularly if she is a bit grand, as anyone who has lived in Italy any length of time knows. When she told me with confident enjoyment that there were offers to buy all of the paintings, I said again, "Absolutely not. They belong to my mother. I only brought them with me for framing."

"Not all of them belong to your mother." She wasn't asking, she was announcing; and before she could defeat me entirely again, I said, "All but the small vase of carnations do." Two days later she declared that she had sold the small vase of carnations, and so I became, unwittingly, protestingly, on the most modest scale, a commercial, or professional rather, artist.

Years later the chairpersons for a gala auction to benefit the Actors Fund of America asked me to model a shawl that had been Eleonora Duse's, which someone had donated, and asked further if I would like to contribute something of my own. A friend suggested that I auction my talent and my time—in other words, do a head of whoever would bid highest for a Swanson original. To give people some idea of what they were bidding for, I lent for exhibit at the auction two heads I had done, one of Bill Dufty and one of myself. A gallant young Greek stockbroker was the highest bidder, and his confidence and generosity gave me the chance to sculpture someone purely professionally, someone I didn't know, for a sort of a commission. I enjoyed the experience immensely, but I held my breath right up to the finish, at the same time I thanked heaven someone hadn't bid to have me do a baby. Babies are the hardest subjects.

In the spring of 1978 I got a call from a young man named Brian Degas in California. Through Claire Trevor, the wife of Milton Bren, who had produced and directed *Three for Bedroom C,* Mr. Degas had heard that I sculptured in my spare time. If I took my work seriously, he was saying, I should show it and have critics look at it. He asked if he could see my work, with an eye to arranging a one-woman show in a new gallery in London in the fall, and once he had come to New York and seen the pieces in my apartment, he said he thought we could go ahead.

"What do you mean, go ahead?" I sputtered, trying for all I was worth to sound calm. "I don't have enough pieces for a show, or time enough to make more."

"If we planned the show for November, you'd have six months," Mr. Degas said, in his light voice and British accent. "Couldn't you do four or five pieces in that time?" His tone implied that any halfway dedicated person could do forty or fifty pieces in that time.

I studied him studying me and squirmed. He was a handsome Argentinean, a writer and producer by profession, and he read me like a book, just as he recognized panic trying to pass for aloof control. He applied gentle pressure of another sort, then, by saying that he thought we could include some of my paintings in the exhibit as well, if there seemed to be not enough sculpture. Here was another Italian landlady, bursting with life force and Latin determination, and I wisely yielded to his charming, relentless pressure, knowing that to do otherwise would be absurd and time-consuming.

I frantically did three or four more pieces, and then several more with renewed confidence, and the show opened to the enthusiastic reviews of the London critics in November of 1978, just as Brian Degas had so calmly predicted.

I showed the heads of my children and my husband and all the new pieces. One bronze of crossed arms, life-size, with a relaxed right hand and a grasping left one, poised just above some gold coins, I called "The Right Hand Doesn't Know What the Left Hand Is Doing." A headless madonna figure with an exposed left breast, holding a baby whose tiny hand is reaching for the breast, I called "And There Shall Be—Life." The most popular piece in the show was a mask and a man's hand and a letter. I called the piece "The Letter" and had a real letter in my handwriting in the bronze hand. I meant to convey by the expression on the mask that the letter was one of farewell and to suggest that every ending is also a beginning. Very ambitious, but that is what I meant. The first day of the show, and then each succeeding day thereafter, the letter was stolen, and each day, therefore, I made up a new letter, wrote it out, and placed it in the hand. Thus I made a long string of endings and beginnings in a few weeks' time, and invented a sort of living but unreal mailbox, and amused and delighted the London press. An added bonus to the stir caused by the show in England led to my commission from the United Nations the following spring to paint a first-day cover for their Decade of Women series. In trying to create a piece containing the themes of birth and hope and peace and fertility in the age of space, I instinctively began to paint the earth as a bright ball in the black sky, with an embryo easily detectable in the outline of the pink and blue continents. The title: "Woman, Like Mother Earth, Has an Eternal Rendezvous with Spring."

In the course of a year Brian had forced me to present hitherto concealed parts of myself to the public for testing, and my success made me feel twenty years younger. Not unnaturally, therefore, I asked him while I was working on the UN painting, "Where do I go from here? What next?"

"How about writing your memoirs?" he asked, as if that could be done in a few months also, and Bill, my husband, gave an enthusiastic nod at the suggestion.

I was trapped again, but happily, for writing about myself would certainly be a bit like playing myself in *Airport 1975*—frightening at first, then amusing, then exciting, and finally revealing, if I was lucky.

Let me go over my checklist of essentials once more.

Love.

Work.

Health.

Art.

I've talked about those.

Family.

I've talked about that too, but I have a few words left to say. I am blessed at eighty-one with two daughters, six grandchildren, and two great-grandchildren. They are the joys of my life. In 1975 my son, Joseph, died, much too soon, much too young. In 1979 one of my four granddaughters died, much, much too soon, much, much too young. They have been my greatest sorrows.

Life and death.

They are somehow sweetly and beautifully mixed, but I don't know how. I have only had intimations. In 1966 my dear, sweet mother died. She was her own woman, had married three times, had had one child, me, and had fulfilled herself. Every week on Sunday, I had called her when we lived apart, and every year on my birthday I sent her flowers. I nursed her for the last weeks of her life as if she were my baby. Finally, as she lay in a hospital bed in California, dying of a stroke from a transfusion I hadn't wanted her to have, I kept whispering in her ear, "Let go, my little mother, let go." It was as simple as that. The moment was there. I knew it. So, I'm sure, did she.

There have to be patterns and reasons, but we can never seem to figure them out logically or completely. If we wait and search, however, we stumble from time to time onto partial answers.

For example, the greatest regret of my life has always been

that I didn't have my baby, Henri's child, in 1925. Nothing in the whole world is worth a baby, I realized as soon as it was too late, and I never stopped blaming myself. Then in 1979 Bill and I traveled to Japan, and at a Buddhist temple at a place called Kyo San, or Honorable Mountain, our guide and a Buddhist monk led us up through the most timeless, peaceful landscape I have ever seen, asleep or awake: a mountain forest of giant cedars, with a network of pathways lacing the area, and ancient graves everywhere. At one point I noticed a tiny stone figure near the massive roots of one of the cedars. Then another. Then I realized that there were hundreds. With little cloth bibs around them.

"What are these?" I asked.

"Babies," the guide said. He crouched down for a closer look at one stone. "Fifteen hundred twenty-five. This baby's life was ended before he was born."

Then he and the monk must have seen how deeply moved I was, for they showed me how to pay respect in that place. They gave me a dipper of water and indicated that I should pour it over the tiny stone figure. Then I burned the incense the monk gave me and left some grains of rice.

As we stood up, I was crying fresh tears out of a guilt I had carried for fifty-four years. The guide and the monk exchanged some words, and then the guide said to me, "We all choose our parents. We choose everything. No blame."

I believed him. The message came to me too directly for me to disbelieve it. I believe it to this day. In fact, I tried to convey a bit of that message on the first-day cover I designed for the United Nations. And since that day on the Honorable Mountain I look at my children and their children and their children with respect and awe as well as love.

Things are not clear yet, not by a long shot, but they are getting clearer than they were that day in the summer of 1898 when I picked Joseph Swanson and his wife, Adelaide, to be my parents.

PHOTOGRAPH CREDITS

Index

539

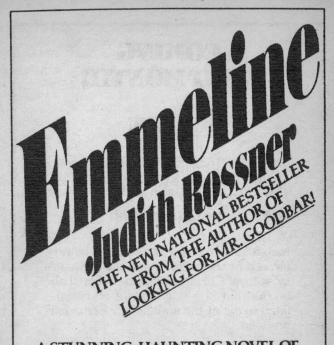